ISLAM
Continuity and Change
in the Modern World

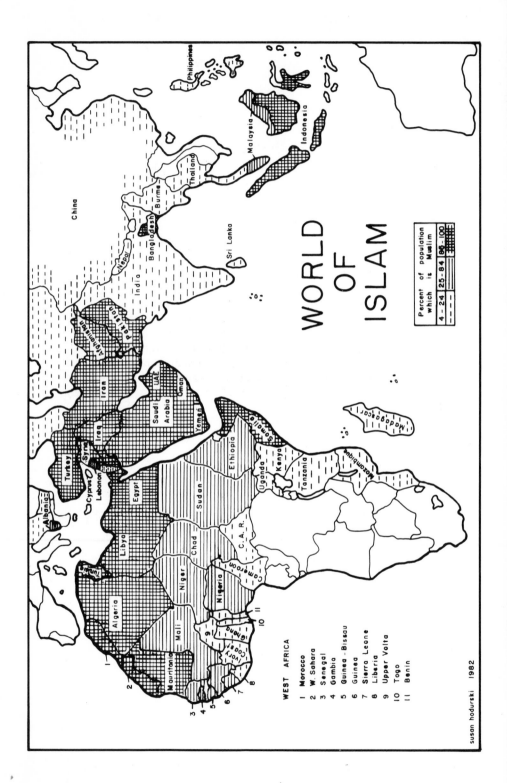

WORLD OF ISLAM

Percent of population which is Muslim

| 4-24 | 25-84 | 85-100 |

China
Philippines
Malaysia
Indonesia
Thailand
Burma
Bangladesh
Nepal
India
Sri Lanka
Afghanistan
Pakistan
Iran
UAE
Oman
Saudi Arabia
Yemen
Iraq
Syria
Turkey
Cyprus
Lebanon
Egypt
Libya
Albania
Tunisia
Algeria
Mauritania
Mali
Niger
Chad
C.A.R.
Sudan
Cameroon
Nigeria
Ethiopia
Somalia
Uganda
Kenya
Tanzania
Mozambique
Madagascar

WEST AFRICA

1 Morocco
2 W. Sahara
3 Senegal
4 Gambia
5 Guinea - Bissau
6 Guinea
7 Sierra Leone
8 Liberia
9 Upper Volta
10 Togo
11 Benin

Ghana
Ivory Coast

susan hodurski 1982

About the Book and Author

Islam: Continuity and Change
in the Modern World
John Obert Voll

This book goes beyond the headlines to explore the broad dimensions of Islam, looking at the vitality of the main elements of the faith across the centuries and finding the basis of today's Islamic resurgence in the continuing interaction of varying styles of Islam—fundamentalist, conservative, adaptationist, and individualist—and in the way each of these styles meets the challenges of the modern era. Dr. Voll's discussion encompasses the full range of Islamic experience and communities, including areas where Muslims are minorities. He carefully presents a balanced view that recognizes modern Islam as dynamic and complex, deeply rooted in the past, yet profoundly conditioned by recent events.

John Obert Voll is associate professor of history at the University of New Hampshire, specializing in the culture and history of the Middle East. He is the author of *Historical Dictionary of the Sudan* and the forthcoming *The Sudan: A Profile* (Westview). Dr. Voll has also conducted research in Cairo, Beirut, and in the Sudan.

ISLAM
Continuity and Change in the Modern World

John Obert Voll

Westview Press • Boulder, Colorado
Longman • Essex, England

Copyright © 1982 by Westview Press, Inc.

Published in 1982 in the United States of America by
  Westview Press, Inc.
  5500 Central Avenue
  Boulder, Colorado 80301
  Frederick A. Praeger, Publisher

Published in 1982 in Great Britain by
  Longman Group
  Longman House
  Burnt Mill
  Harlow
  Essex CM20 2JE England

Library of Congress Card Catalogue Number: 82-2829
ISBN (U.S.) 0-89158-9317
ISBN (U.S.) 0-89158-983X (pbk.)
ISBN (U.K.) 0-582-78343-7

Printed and bound in the United States of America

Dedicated to Sarah, Layla, and Michael,
whose support makes research possible

Contents

Preface

Much has been written recently about the contemporary Islamic experience. However, I believe that there is still a need for a discussion of the modern history of Islam that goes beyond the current headlines, and I have tried in this book to present such a study. The world of Islam is vast and diverse, but it is important to attempt to see the full extent of that world, both in time and space. The current resurgence of Islam is not something that suddenly appeared on the world scene. It is part of a long evolution of the modern Islamic experience that has its foundations in the eighteenth century and earlier. As a result, I have tried to show both the significant elements of continuity and the significant factors of diversity.

Any book that discusses the modern development of Islam in Africa, the Middle East, Asia, and elsewhere must cover a tremendous range of subjects. There are some advantages to having such a book written by a group of scholars, each with a particular regional expertise. However, such collections frequently lack clarity and cohesiveness. The advantage of having one person write such a book is that the whole picture can be presented within a single analytic framework. It is for this reason that I have written this book by myself, and I hope that the reader will find that the advantages outweigh the problems of my attempt to cover such a broad subject.

Clearly, I owe a great debt to the many people who have aided me, either through their personal encouragement or through their scholarship. Among this large group I especially want to thank Richard P. Mitchell and Leon Carl Brown. Their scholarship, instruction, and friendship are important in whatever virtues this book may have, although they have no part in its faults. I also want to express my deep gratitude to my wife, Sarah, and my children, Layla and Michael. Their cooperation and encouragement made it possible for this book to be written—that is why it is dedicated to them.

John Obert Voll

Note on Spelling

The problem of spelling names and terms originally written in other alphabets has never been satisfactorily solved. In order to work for some uniformity of usage without adopting the cumbersome transliteration systems of formal scholarship, I have chosen to follow the spellings used in a book that people reading this one might also have read: Arthur Goldschmidt, Jr., *A Concise History of the Middle East* (Boulder, Colo.: Westview Press, 1979). For names and terms that do not appear in that book, I have attempted to use spellings that appear in commonly used sources of information for the general reader.

ISLAM
Continuity and Change
in the Modern World

1
Introduction

Islam is a dynamic force in the contemporary world, and in the 1980s, at the beginning of the fifteenth Islamic century, movements of Muslim revival have increasing visibility and influence. From the Islamic revolution in Iran to Southeast Asia and West Africa, the entire world of Islam is in active motion. Previously unnoticed currents of religious conviction have come to the surface and appear to be major elements in determining the course of events.

This situation comes as a surprise to many people, and it raises great issues about the future nature of society in the modern world and creates crises for policymakers. Until recently, the decline in the influence of religion was being described, and the eventual demise of the effectiveness of the historical religions seemed to be predicted. The decline was taking place in all of the major world religions, and it can be clearly noted in the discussions of Islam. In general terms, it was felt that the processes of modernization have undermined the basic foundations of traditional religion. In particular, it was felt that secularization, the separation of religion from politics and social institutions other than specifically religious ones, was an inherent part of the modernization process. As a result, it was believed that religion would play an increasingly limited societal role in the future.

The resurgence of Islam in the final third of the twentieth century creates a need for a reexamination of the modern history of the Islamic world. Perhaps, in the long run, the predictions of the demise of religion will be accurate. However, the assumptions and conclusions of such theories can no longer be accepted as readily as they once were. In a world in which a growing number of states are reexamining their legal structures in the light of the Quran and the requirements of traditional Islamic law, Islamic law cannot be described simply as an anachronism whose jurisdiction is being progressively limited. In a world in which radical Islamic social programs are being defined, it is no longer possible to state without significant qualifications that "the secularization of the polity is in many respects a prerequisite for significant social change."[1] In a world of militant Islamic activism, one cannot say quite so confidently that "in recent years Islam has so declined in authority and vitality that it has become a mere instrument for state policy, although it is still active as a folk religion."[2]

This book is based on the assumption that the currently visible resurgence of Islam is not simply the last gasp of a dying religious tradition. The general basis for this assumption results from an examination of the experience of the Islamic community in modern history, which broadly concludes that the Islamic world, like other societies in the contemporary world, is in the process of a major transformation. However, the result of that process will not be identically modernized, secularized societies. The shape of global, "postmodern" society is only beginning to emerge, but it seems clear that the special identities provided by the major religious traditions of the world will have an important role to play in that unfolding social order.

A fundamental issue is the nature of the religious traditions in the postmodern world. It is possible that fundamentally new ideas and institutions have been given a traditional appearance by the established religions. Using that point of view, one might see the current revival of Islam as a desire to provide familiar forms for basically non-Islamic ideas and institutions. Many commentators follow that line and believe that present Islamic activism is primarily nationalist or socialist or economically motivated movements dressed in the garb of religion. That viewpoint seems, at heart, to deny the possibility of a truly Islamic-inspired anti-imperialism or an Islamic-oriented desire for social transformation.

Another alternative, suggested by the analysis in this book, is that the Islamic community is entering a new phase, not the end, of its history. It is possible to see the current resurgence as a continuation of basic themes, even though those themes may be assuming new forms. To ignore religious desires and to concentrate only on the economic drives or secularized political motives is to limit unnecessarily the scope of our understanding. In the broader perspective of Islamic history, the dynamic vitality of the faith has assumed a variety of forms as historical conditions have changed. Any examination of Islam in the modern world must take that past experience into account if the present is to be adequately understood. It may be possible that part of the Islamic resurgence is putting modern sentiments into Islamic garb, but it may also be possible to discern new and modern forms of the continuing Islamic vitality.

Three-Dimensional Approach

If those new and modern forms are to be discerned, three dimensions of the Islamic experience in the modern world must be examined. Clearly, important individuals and groups must be identified. In the Islamic world, local conditions vary, and each movement is in some ways unique. It is therefore important to keep in mind the specific circumstances of each area and movement. One dimension of the study, then, must be to describe those separate groups and the local conditions in which they developed.

In discussing the causes of revivalist and fundamentalist movements, analysts often see those movements as emerging from a particular set of circumstances. Discussions of the Mahdist movement in the Sudan in the late nineteenth century, for example, focus on the sociopolitical conditions in the Sudan following the Egyptian conquest of that territory. More recently, the rise of the Ayatollah Khomeini in Iran has been seen in terms of the policies of Mohammad Reza Shah Pahlavi during the preceding decade, and the Islamic fundamentalist policies of General Zia al-Haqq of Pakistan have been examined in terms of the current political alignments in that country. Such interpretations are important for seeing events and movements in the context of the specific conditions in which they occur. However, since movements continue over time and expand, an understanding of their dynamics requires more than an examination of the policies of one ruler or the tensions within one society at a given moment.

When one seeks to define the basic nature of such movements and when one searches for the basic issues involved, the need for an additional analytical dimension becomes clear. Islamic activist movements have not occurred in isolation from the rest of the world; instead, they have been involved in the broader interactions of modern global history. Therefore, the second dimension to be examined is the relationship of the various Islamic movements to the basic dynamics of modern history. How that relationship is interpreted varies with the perspective of the analyst. The Islamic resurgence may be described as a part of the changing relationships among various regions in the world system of capitalism created by the emergence of an industrial society in the West. Other analysts may see the resurgence in the context of the changing natures of political legitimacy and social authority in the conditions created by modernization. Still others may see it as a theological and social reaction to the implications that modern ideas and institutions have for traditional societies. The common factor in all those approaches is the interaction of the Islamic tradition with the ideas and institutions of modern society. In this dimension, the major theme is the response of Islam to modernization and development.

That is the modern dimension of Islam in the modern world, and it provides a perspective that is broader than the one that is achieved by concentrating on the details of specific movements. However, even that broad dimension may miss key elements that are involved in the contemporary Islamic experience. In concentrating on the issue of the impact of modernization, analysts sometimes attempt to fit the Islamic experience into a model that is based on the experience of Western society rather than Islamic society. For example, it is often noted that Islam has not experienced a huge change similar to the Protestant Reformation in Europe, and some feel that such a change is needed if Islam is to adapt successfully to the challenge of modernity. Such a viewpoint is thought provoking, but it often ignores the fundamental differences between the structures of Western and Islamic societies. The separation of church and state may be a crucial aspect of secularization and modernization in Western society, but it is hard to translate the meaning of that issue to Islamic society, in which religious institutionalization has not involved the formal structure of a "church."

The necessary third dimension to be examined, therefore, is Islam itself. Islamic revival is not unique to the modern era, and throughout its history, the Islamic community has faced the challenge of changing conditions. For instance, militant activism has been one feature of the Islamic experience. Activist Islamic groups in the twentieth century can be seen as having underlying similarities because they are involved in modernization, but they also can be seen as part of a continuing tradition, and they must be viewed in their Islamic as well as their modern context. The forms the Islamic experience has taken maintain a continuity that spans the gap between premodern and modern so by recognizing the Islamic dimension, one stands a better chance of avoiding the pitfalls of using only an analytical model, which imposes alien categories upon the modern Islamic experience.

All three of these dimensions are important, and they form the basic framework of the analysis in this book. Islam in the modern era is seen as the interaction of the specific aims and goals of individuals and groups, which are affected by particular local conditions, with the factors of the dynamics of modern development and the continuity of the Islamic tradition.

Overview

The history of even modern Islam begins with the life of the Prophet Muhammad in the seventh century. The community (*ummah*) established by the Prophet at that time provided the actual historical foundation for the later Islamic empires and social institutions and also is the ideal against which later Islamic societies have been judged. At that time, the basic patterns were set. Chief among them is that the Islamic experience is one in which all aspects of life are seen as directly affected by and subject to the message of the faith. Muhammad was a religious guide, military commander, social organizer, and political leader. Through his leadership and that of his successors, this unity of roles and the comprehensive nature of the faith were firmly established. To use modern terminology, Islam is not just a religion, it is a total way of life.

The main outlines of the development of the Islamic community are the basis of the Islamic dimension of this study of modern Islam, and the evolution of the Islamic experience and the main themes that have emerged are examined in Chapter 2. A key element in this historical experience is the way (or ways) in which the Islamic community has met the challenges of social and historical change, and certain themes provide the foundation for a real continuity within the Islamic world. These themes have been presented in different ways, and the challenges of change have been met by the different styles of the Islamic experience.

The history of Islam in the past two and a half centuries shows the interaction of the different forms of the Muslim experience in the context of modern world history. The beginnings of the modern Islamic experience are in the eighteenth century, and those foundations are discussed in Chapter 3. A significant factor, and one that emphasizes the importance of the Islamic dimension, is that the eighteenth and early nineteenth centuries were times of active Muslim revival movements, whose emergence was affected only to a limited degree by the rise of modern society in the West. Many of the great movements of the time, like the Wahhabi movement in the Arabian Peninsula, were inspired by motivations that arose within Islam itself. The tired maturity of the great Islamic imperial systems of the day and the large number of departures from strict adherence to the Quran and the Traditions of the Prophet gave rise to an Islamic revivalist spirit that was already visible before the threat posed by the West was apparent to many Muslims.

That factor is significant because it created a momentum on which later revivalists could build. The tradition of an indigenous religious activism has been at times obscured by the more dramatic events of Western domination and Westernizing reforms. However, that tradition provides an illuminating backdrop for an understanding of the resurgence of Islamic activism in the last third of the twentieth century. By the beginning of the nineteenth century, the indigenous reformism began to be overshadowed by the modernizing reform programs instituted by leaders in the major Islamic states, especially Mehmet Ali in Egypt and Mahmud II in Istanbul. The more purely Islamic revivalist movements became increasingly confined to peripheral areas that were not yet significantly affected by Western expansion.

In Chapter 4, the increasing dominance of Islam by the Western powers will be traced. By the end of the nineteenth century, virtually no part of the Islamic world had avoided significant contact with Western economic and imperial power, and fundamental issues were raised by the visibly dominant power of the non-Muslim West. In addition to trying to create effective military institutions, Muslims began to deal with ideological questions in defending and redefining Islam in the new circumstances. A desire for independence from Western control grew, and a basic issue became how best to gain that independence. By the early part of the twentieth century, the last of the major nonmodernist religious activist movements had been defeated, and the best option seemed to be some form of Western-influenced nationalism and secular reformism.

The Islamic experience in the first two-thirds of the twentieth century is discussed in Chapters 5 and 6. In the first half of the century, there was a variety of programs, the major ones being the secular-reformist nationalism of people like Mustafa Kemal Ataturk in Turkey, liberal Islamic modernism as seen in the works of Muhammad Iqbal in India and some Arab writers, and neofundamentalism in a variety of formats, like the Saudi monarchy or the Muslim Brotherhood in Egypt.

After World War II, the political system of most Muslim countries was dramatically changed as the old European empires broke up, and most Muslim peoples gained their independence. One of the major themes of the period was the apparent subordination of Islam to other causes. Islam served as an important component of nationalism and helped to mobilize people in the cause of political independence. Islam also came in conflict with the modernist ideologies, especially the new forms of socialism advocated after independence.

Many people viewed fundamentalist Islam as a reactionary force, and militant fundamentalism was often in conflict with the leading socialist reforming movements. At the same time, there were also signs of fundamentalist activism as an underground opposition to established modernizing regimes. Although outlawed, the Muslim Brotherhood formed a basis for opposition to Nasser's regime in Egypt, for example, and religious leaders in Iran began to provide a focus for opposition to the shah.

By the end of the 1960s, militant Islam became more visible. The reemergence of activist fundamentalism is examined in Chapter 7, along with other developments in the 1970s. The more radical socialist states had failed to solve the major problems of development and political organization, and the new revolutionary movements illustrated that a fundamentalist Islamic government is not necessarily reactionary. The experiment in new forms of government initiated by the Libyan revolutionary regime is an example. The further possibilities of an Islamic radicalism have been explored by Ali Shariati, an Iranian sociologist, and those ideas have influenced the development of new militant groups. By the end of the 1970s, there were clear signs of a militant Islamic resurgence, which is taking many forms.

The final chapter explores the reasons for that resurgence in terms of the broader dimensions of the book. In the continuing interaction of Islam with modern ideas, new strengths have been discovered by the Muslims. The pluralist and morally confused world of the 1980s has major problems that perhaps cannot be solved by the old, standard modernist ideas, and it is not at all clear that the secular and rational solutions have worked even in Europe or the United States. The present and future pose both challenges and opportunities for Islam. The old lines of continuity have not been destroyed, and they may provide a basis for future Islamic societies.

2

The Islamic Dimension: Community and History

The history of the Islamic community is a dynamic part of the Islamic experience. The early and continuing success of Islam provided a confirmation for Muslims of the message of the revelation, and the starting point for an understanding of Islam in the modern world must be the historical experience of the *ummah* (the Muslim "community"). The long interaction between changing conditions and the permanently established Quranic message has set patterns and ideals, and the continuing impact of that interaction provides the basis for the Islamic dimension of an analysis of modern Islam. The foundation for the Islamic awareness of historical experience is set in the Quran itself, as it "lays great emphasis on the fact that the process of history is not neutral in respect of nations and communities for it says clearly, 'God is on the side of those who fear Him and do good.'"[1]

In the broader dimension of the Islamic heritage, there are many significant elements, which can be divided into two general themes: the common elements of the continuity of the Islamic experience and the basic elements of diversity within the Islamic community. Each of those themes influences the manner in which Muslims meet the challenges presented by changing conditions in the world and in the various Muslim societies.

The Islamic Community in History

The Basic Concept

The heart of the Islamic faith is the belief in one God who is directly involved in the affairs of humanity. God is seen as requiring submission to His will and as having made that will known to mankind through revelations to a series of prophets. For Muslims, the final and complete form of those revelations was given to the Prophet Muhammad in the seventh century. It was carefully recorded in the Quran and is the foundation of Islam.

7

Muslims, then, are those people who accept the unique oneness of God and recognize that Muhammad was the messenger of God.

That simple foundation for faith and experience has significance for all aspects of life. The revelation did not just define a creed or a set of beliefs; it set forth the basic blueprint by which humanity should live. In this way, the Quran is the foundation for an ideal society, which Muslims believe will result from submission to God and His will. To be a Muslim is not simply a matter of individual belief; it means participating in the effort to implement God's will on earth. As one modern Muslim explains it, "Islam teaches not only that the realization of the good is possible in this world but that to bring it about here and now is precisely the duty of every man and woman."[2] In the broadest sense, the Islamic community is that community which works to implement God's will as defined in the Quran here on earth in the contexts of history and society.

The experience of the Muslim community is a key part of the Islamic message, and joining in the effort to create God's society on earth is an important vocation for all Muslims. The success or failure of the actual community is a major concern. Political structures, economic practices, and social customs are all relevant to the concerns of faithful Muslims. However, throughout Islamic history, there has been disagreement over the ways God's will is to be implemented. These disagreements form the basis for a variety of styles and modes of Islamic experience, and they provide a starting point for understanding the dynamics of Islamic history.

Muhammad and His Community

The Muslim community began during the lifetime of the Prophet Muhammad, and by the time of his death in 632, the basic principles had been established. "The Muslim Community as a fabric of society, with its principles of internal solidarity, was brought into being under his own hands even though it underwent further important developments later."[3] The Muslim community as it emerged during the life of the Prophet became a model for later Muslims as they attempted to live up to the commands of God and to create society in accord with the revelation.

The early community was not simply an utopian creation of later imagination; it was a functioning, real community, however much subsequent generations may have idealized it. In its actual experience, the community set the patterns that have guided the habits and customs of later Muslims. Those patterns have provided an important element of continuity over the centuries of Islamic experience.

The keystone of the new community in the seventh century was the Prophet. Underlying similarities in leadership styles within the Muslim world, down to the present, "can be traced to the days of the Prophet Muhammad—himself the model par excellence of political leadership."[4] In Muhammad, there was the distinctive unification of political, social, and religious concerns that characterizes the Islamic tradition.

Muhammad was born in Mecca, a commercial and religious center in the western Arabian Peninsula. When he was about forty, he began to have religious experiences, which took the form of visions and revelations from God for the guidance of humanity. On the basis of those revelations, he began to preach to his fellow citizens in Mecca. He gained a small following, but most of the influential leaders in the city opposed him.

The message preached by Muhammad was not abstract but had a direct bearing on the personal and social conditions of his time. That fact was the cause of the opposition to him as well as the reason why some people followed him. At the heart of the revelation was the declaration that there are no gods other than the one God. In a town that was a religious sanctuary for polytheistic tribal cults, that declaration was a direct attack on the prestige and position of the local leaders. The revelation also called for a sense of social responsibility toward the poor and underprivileged and warned of the coming Day of Judgment. That call for social responsibility also aroused opposition in Mecca since social obligations were being neglected by the wealthy merchants there.

After a period of persecution, Muhammad accepted an invitation to move to Yathrib, an oasis community north of Mecca. The tribal groups there were involved in self-destructive feuds, and they had asked that Muhammad become the arbitrator and judge for them. In 622, Muhammad and his fellow believers made the move from Mecca to the town that was later to be known as Medina ("the city" of the Prophet). The importance of this move for Islam is emphasized by the fact that Muslims date the beginning of the Islamic calendar from 622, the year of the migration (*hijrah*).

In Medina, the role of the Muslim group changed from being a persecuted religious minority to that of a self-governing community. This new community came in conflict with Mecca and developed relations with many of the tribes of the Arabian Peninsula. Ultimately, even Mecca submitted to Muhammad, and at the time of his death in 632, the community included most of the Arabian Peninsula.

Muhammad personally played a key role in the emergence of the community. He continued to be a religious leader, but, in addition, he was the major coordinator of political and administrative affairs and the military commander. All aspects of the life of the community were subject to the message of the revelation. Muhammad showed a tenacious adherence to the revelation of God but, at the same time, was flexible in dealing with new conditions. His ability to compromise at the right time was an important unifying factor in the community. His personal ties and personalized style of rule were reflected in an emphasis on individual obligations. His conservatism is exemplified by his willingness to accept existing symbols and customs when they could be reinterpreted in the framework of the new revelation. For example, the special place of the pilgrimage to Mecca was retained, but it was shown to have a monotheistic, Islamic significance.

During the lifetime of the Prophet, new revelations provided guidelines for coping with changing conditions. However, the process became more complex after Muhammad's death. Then direct guidance through revelation ceased, since it was generally accepted that the revelations to Muhammad were complete and perfect. In the years immediately following Muhammad's death, the records of the revelations were collected and put in a standardized form. That collection, the Quran, became the fundamental core of the Islamic faith and community.

Muslims also look to the sayings and deeds of the Prophet for guidance. A much less formalized source of information, *hadiths* (accounts of the Prophet's sayings and actions) were only gradually brought together into widely accepted collections. There was later disagreement over the validity of particular *hadiths*, but, in the long run, the body of Traditions was accepted as providing an accurate picture of the customary practices of the Prophet. This general behavior pattern, called the Sunnah of the Prophet, came to be accepted, with some diversity of interpretation, as a guide for believers that is second in authority only to the Quran.

Early Definitions of Community

The first great issue faced by the Muslims after Muhammad's death was the nature of the leadership for the community. Apparently, most Muslims did not feel that the Prophet had designated a successor. After some tension, the crisis of succession was solved when the leading members of the community accepted Abu Bakr, a respected early believer and the father-in-law of the Prophet, as his *khalifah* ("successor"; the term is usually rendered as "caliph" in English usage). Although Abu Bakr was not a prophet, he and the subsequent caliphs combined political and military leadership with religious prestige and thus continued the pattern set by Muhammad.

When some tribal groups revolted following Muhammad's death, Abu Bakr was able to reassert Muslim control, and under Abu Bakr's successor, Umar, the armies of the community began the vast conquests that were to create a great empire. The Muslims had to contend with the two great empires of the Middle East in the seventh century—the Sasanid Empire, heir to the great Persian imperial tradition, and the Byzantine Empire, successor to the Roman Empire in the eastern Mediterranean. Muslim armies captured the Byzantine provinces of Syria and North Africa and conquered all the lands of the Sasanid Empire from Iraq to Central Asia. In the process, the Muslim community itself became a major empire.

The rapid transformation from a small city-state to a vast empire required great adjustments, and the Muslim leadership was basically pragmatic in adapting to the changing conditions. Many problems of administration were solved by utilizing the methods, and sometimes the personnel, of the earlier empires. Practical arrangements were made to solve specific problems, and only later were those arrangements systematized. Despite this flexibility, the caliphs never lost sight of the fact that they were the leaders of an Islamic community that was bound by the message of the Quran and the actions of the Prophet.

The early unity of the community centered on the caliph. He coordinated the conquests and was the final authority in setting policy. Naturally, disputes within the community were reflected in disputes concerning the proper role of the caliph. The dynamic personalities and prestige of the first two caliphs minimized tensions. However, the third caliph, Uthman, was not as strong, and during his rule, from 644 to 656, the divisions within the community became apparent.

Uthman faced resentment from a number of groups. Although Uthman has been an early believer, he was from the Umayyad clan, which dominated Meccan politics and had led the initial opposition to Muhammad, and many pious Muslims objected when Uthman relied heavily on his Umayyad kinsmen in governing the new empire. Tribal soldiers, who had been daunted by the dynamism of Abu Bakr and Umar, began to express their resentment at being controlled by a central government. The wealth created by the conquests led to a materialism that many Muslims objected to, and they blamed Uthman for it. In 656, troops visiting Medina from one of the provincial garrisons mutinied and killed Uthman.

The murder of Uthman began the first civil war within Islam, and during the conflict, basic divisions within the Islamic community began to be defined. The groups that emerged became the bases for the long-lasting separate elements within Islam. Indeed, divisions that are still visible in the twentieth century have their origins in that early conflict.

Uthman's successor was Ali, a cousin and son-in-law of Muhammad. Ali's position in the community was distinctive. He had been an early believer, and he had a special reputation for bravery and piety. In addition, since Muhammad had had no surviving sons, Ali had the distinction of being the father of the only male descendants of the Prophet—Muhammad's grandsons, Hasan and Husayn. Although the majority of the community had accepted the caliphates of Abu Bakr, Umar, and Uthman, there were some who felt that Ali should have been chosen. As a result, there were many who were willing to accept Ali as the caliph in 656. This group has become known as the "Party of Ali," or the Shiʿat Ali, and the interpretations and historical experience of the group became the foundation for Shiʿism, the distinctive Islamic tradition that is currently the official religion of Iran.

The great rivals in this first civil war were Ali and Muʿawiyah, the leader of the Umayyads. It has been said that "the fateful struggle between Ali and Muʿawiya still agitates the minds of Muslims, scholars and non-scholars alike."[5] There were specific issues that guided the actions of those two men in their struggle, but, in the minds of later interpreters, their conflict came to be seen as being between differing views of the nature of the Islamic community. Ali represented the ideal of a community led by a divinely guided leader, drawn from the direct descendants of the Prophet. Muʿawiyah was the epitome of the practical realist. The state, under his direction, was an Arab empire guided by the principles of realpolitik. Muʿawiyah came to be seen as a "Caesar of the Arabs," and Ali's reputation reflects the ideal of rule by a pious, divinely informed figure.

When Ali assumed the position of caliph, he faced opposition from other

groups as well, and they also represented important principles in the definition of the nature of the community. His first opponents were some of the
major surviving companions of the Prophet, including the Prophet's wife,
Aishah. These opponents were probably motivated by personal reasons,
but their proclaimed goal was to insist on the application of the existing
customs and rules of the community in the punishment of the murderers of
Uthman and the election of a caliph. In a broader sense, they represented a
conservative principle as they hoped to maintain the old religious communal oligarchy.

The other major opponents of Ali were the Kharijites. After Ali defeated
the challenge of the conservatives, he had to face the troops of Muᶜawiyah.
In the course of a major battle, Ali showed signs of a willingness to
negotiate with the Umayyad leader, an idea that was opposed by a group of
militants within Ali's camp who then withdrew. They have come to be
called "those who went out," or the Kharijites. As the Kharijite opposition
has been explained, that group relied on a rigorous adherence to the implications of the revelation: There can be no rule other than the rule of God.
The egalitarianism implicit in that position led the Kharijites to say that
anyone could be caliph if he were a strict follower of the rules of God. That
concept challenged the legitimism of the Shiᶜism, the oligarchy of the old
companions, and the pragmatism of the Umayyads. For centuries,
Kharijism provided an inspiration and a rationale for revolt.

Ultimately the Umayyads emerged as the victors, and they created an effective imperial organization. In that first conflict, one can see the beginnings of the basic styles or forms of Islam: the pragmatic adapters, the conservatives, the fundamentalists, and those who emphasize personal
charisma. The interaction of those styles was a basic theme in subsequent
Islamic history.

Imperial Islam

The victory of the Umayyads began the great age of imperial Islam.
Although there were additional major conflicts within the community, the
ummah was dominated by the ideal and institutions of imperial unity for
the next three centuries. Muᶜawiyah and his successors created a large-scale
bureaucratic institution, which utilized techniques and customs that had
been firmly established in the Middle East by the pre-Islamic empires. In
organizational terms, it is possible to view the Islamic empire as a successor
state to the previous imperial systems.

At the core of the Islamic state was the caliph. He assumed many of the
functions of the pre-Islamic emperors and had the prestige that was involved in being the "successor to the messenger of God." Supporting this
leader were the administrative institutions of an expanding bureaucracy,
the military organizations of the Islamic community, and the sense of practical legitimacy provided by the desire to preserve the Islamic message in the
form of a unified Muslim community. This religious sense was given some
urgency during the early centuries of Islam by the fact that until approx-

imately the tenth century, the majority of the people in most areas of the empire had not yet been converted to Islam.

The heart of the Umayyad power was the Arab-Muslim armies that were the instruments of the early conquests. The Umayyad empire was built around an Arab elite, and as non-Arabs began to convert to Islam in increasing numbers, the Arab exclusivism of that elite began to clash with the religious ideal that gave the leaders their legitimacy. Opposition to the Umayyads grew. There were continuing Kharijite revolts, and Shiᶜite underground groups organized to support the claims of various descendants of the Prophet. In addition, many of the religious teachers and pious believers, even though they did not support Kharijism or Shiᶜism, came to have doubts about the validity of the imperial system as it had developed. These people were part of a growing group within the community, the learned men or *ulama.* Initially the only "Islamic" institution had been the caliphate, but by the eighth century, the ulama were becoming the real spokesmen for the Islamic message. In the process of defining more clearly the social implications of the revelation, those men began to question the pragmatic compromises of the Umayyads.

Internal divisions within the Umayyad elite itself and growing anti-Umayyad sentiment throughout the empire opened the way for the successful overthrow of the Umayyads by 750. The caliphate was taken over by the Abbasids, descendants of an uncle of the Prophet by the name of Abbas. This group was originally part of a Shiᶜite revolutionary movement and came to power on a wave of millenarian enthusiasm. Once in power, the Abbasids quickly divorced themselves from their Shiᶜite and radical origins. They rebuilt the imperial system along the lines of the Umayyad organization, with the crucial difference that the ruling group was now no longer an exclusive Arab elite. The Abbasids made use of non-Arab Muslims, especially Persians, and the imperial system changed from an "Arab kingdom" to an Islamic empire.

The early Abbasid period was the time of the great flowering of medieval Islamic civilization. The ideal of political unity under the caliph was maintained and closely approximated historical reality, although some parts of the world of Islam, like Spain, never came under Abbasid control. The processes of defining the Islamic tradition and absorbing many cultural elements created a dynamic sociocultural synthesis. This era saw the formalization of the great structure of Islamic law, the development of the Islamic philosophical tradition, and the general agreement on the content of the Traditions of the Prophet.

The ideals and structures of the majority of the Muslim community became more clearly defined and became what is called Sunni Islam. For this majority, the experience of the Muslim community itself had special significance. The ideal was the community formed by the Prophet and his companions, and the caliphates of the Prophet's first four successors came to be called the era of the "rightly guided leaders," or the Rashidun. For Sunni Muslims, the community that was led by those companions of the

Prophet was the model. In addition, although later Muslims may not have lived up to that ideal in every way, the actual historical experience of the community and the consensus of the believers provided a set of customary patterns (*sunnah*) for the majority of Muslims. Although Sunni Islam was very flexible, it never fully absorbed the distinctive Shiʿite and Kharijite traditions. Those remained separate forms of Islam, continuing traditions that had begun in the first great civil war.

The political unity of the Abbasid empire began to crumble in the face of a series of challenges. The empire may have been too large to maintain for long with the available technology. As the majority of the population in various areas became Muslim, the sense of urgency to maintain loyalty to a single imperial institution may have declined.[6] In addition, the contradiction between a hierarchically organized imperial structure and the more egalitarian message of the Islamic revelation may have become a factor as that message was more fully studied. The caliphate was no longer the single focus for Islamic loyalty. There was now the whole emerging vision of an Islamically oriented social order with a system of law, philosophy, and personal piety that could function without the direct intervention of an imperial leader.

Whatever the causes, by the middle of the tenth century, the Abbasid caliphs had lost effective control over virtually all of the old empire. They remained, fulfilling a generally symbolic role, until the Mongol destruction of their capital, Baghdad, in 1258, but the effective leadership in politics and military affairs was taken over by military commanders, called sultans, and the caliphate was gradually transformed into the sultanate.

The heritage of imperial Islam has had great significance as the identification of the faith and message of Islam as being directly involved in all of human affairs was firmly established during that period. Even though there were tensions between individual caliphs and various learned men, there was no question of a separation of church and state. Although the political unity of the Abbasid empire crumbled, the imperial experience reinforced the enduring feeling of the essential unity of the Islamic community. The great success of the early imperial community helped to confirm that "God is on the side of those who fear Him and do good."

Sultans and the Islamic Social Order

The end of the imperial era of Islamic history was accompanied by the emergence of a new social order with a broad range of distinctive Islamic institutions. Two major themes are visible: the militarization of the state and the development of a non-state-oriented, cosmopolitan society.

As the effective organizing power of the caliphs declined, military commanders played an increasingly important role. The army began to be recruited from a variety of sources, and by the tenth century, it was no longer dependent on the old Muslim tribal troops that had been the mainstay of the early state. A major source for the new soldiery was the Turkish peoples of Central Asia. Some of the soldiers were free-agent mercenaries, but a growing proportion were obtained through the slave markets. These slave soldiers (*mamluks*) soon became the major element in provincial garrisons, and their commanders gained a growing degree of independence from central control, although they maintained a nominal allegiance to the caliphate.

By the end of the tenth century, effective politico-military control of most of the old empire had passed into the hands of those provincial commanders. In many cases, the soldiers were not native to the areas they controlled, and their primary link to the population was a common adherence to Islam. They made no pretense of being Islamic teachers and accepted the obligations of the faith as defined by the ulama and the other religious leaders. The ulama, in turn, recognized the need for the stability that could be provided by an effective military force in a period when the old imperial order had crumbled. "Their unyielding doctrine held that any state was better than the natural state of war."[7]

For all practical purposes, the state passed into the hands of the strongest military commanders. Between the tenth and the fifteenth centuries, a bewildering array of military states emerged. Some were extensive conquest empires, and others were little more than small, garrisoned city-states. Early in the period, a number of the conquest empires were built around adherence to Shi'ite Islam and the claims of various descendants of the Prophet to leadership. The largest of that type of empire was the Fatimid, which became established in North Africa in the tenth century and controlled a large empire centered in Egypt until 1171. However, the new military, under the banner of Sunni Islam, came to dominate most of the Islamic world. The largest of those sultanates was the Seljuk, which controlled much of Southwest Asia in the eleventh and twelfth centuries.

Parallel to the militarization of the state was the creation of a cosmopolitan social order that was not state oriented. In any given area, the leading Muslim teachers submitted to and legitimized the rule of the local commanders, but their own positions were not directly dependent upon the patronage or recognition of the state. New types of social institutions emerged that were capable of functioning in the context of an alien military rule with its ever-changing politico-military elite.

Three types of social organization in that new society deserve mention. First, there was the increasing position of the ulama as a professional class within the community. There is no specially ordained clergy in Islam, but the learned men have a distinctive position on the basis of their knowledge. The formalization of Islamic law standardized the Islamic learning that identified the ulama, but the structure of the law was not monolithic. In the Sunni tradition, four systems of legal thought (*madhhabs*) were recognized as valid. Those four systems—Hanafi, Maliki, Shafi'i, and Hanbali—provided a basis for social identification as well as the content for instruction. The education of the ulama also became more carefully organized. Islamic education is characterized by a high degree of informality and personalization, but during the period of the sultanates, special educational institutions (*madrasah*s) became focal points for the ulama class. Although no special church or clergy emerged, the ulama became a distinctive social group, one that was important for the preservation of the Islamic community.

The second style of social organization was related to the piety and religious practices of the masses. In the early days of Islam, there had been mystics who had lived reclusive lives of piety and asceticism. However, the tradition of a personalized, mystic piety, which is called Sufism, gradually developed a theological-philosophical structure of thought. At first, this type of thought was opposed by the more legalistic ulama, but the two approaches were successfully reconciled by the teachings of Abu Hamid al-Ghazali (d. 1111). Intellectually, the culmination of this tradition came with the work of Muhyi al-Din Ibn al-Arabi (d. 1240), who developed a full-scale elaboration of Sufi theology along monistic or pantheistic lines.

The social organization of this tradition appeared in the Sufi associations. These organizations, called *tariqah*s, began as informal groups of disciples gathered around particularly famous Sufi instructors. By the twelfth century, the organization of those groups had become more formalized, and *tariqah*s became large-scale, popular associations based on pious devotional traditions. They served a wide range of functions that increased social integration and cohesion. There was no central organization for all the *tariqah*s, but many individual orders, like the Qadiriyyah, spread throughout the Islamic world. The *tariqah*s, like the *madhhab*s, provided a means of integration that transcended the boundaries of the separate, militarized states and helped give a cosmopolitan, unifying structure to the transcontinental social order of Islam.

The third type of organization that linked various sections of the Islamic world together was a commercial one. The conquests and regional stability of imperial Islam had built up a momentum of trade and commerce, which survived the collapse of the imperial system. Interregional trade continued and often flourished, despite the political fragmentation of the Islamic world. There was no central organization to coordinate economic enterprises, but merchants in the various parts of the Muslim world were directly, if informally, connected.

The new social order was clearly linked to the basic ideals of the Islamic revelation. It was more egalitarian in mood than the hierarchical imperial order had been, and the people appear to have made a more conscious effort to be aware of and conform to the requirements of the faith. In this effort, the ulama fulfilled the critical roles of clearly defining the legal structure and then of aiding in the implementation of the message. They were the teachers, judges, and intellectual guides, and they provided a sense of order and legitimacy at a time when the political and military aspects of society were in relative disorder. One might say that the ulama gave a sense of political identity and order to society, and the Sufi leaders provided a similar sense of legitimacy and order on the individual level. Within the *tariqah*s, the individual Muslim could find his place in the social order. He found spiritual support and psychological comfort, which firmly made him part of Islamic society.

The new Islamic society extended beyond the confines of politico-military borders. Even though the imperial structure had disintegrated, the era of the sultanates was one of dynamic Islamic expansion. In some cases, the expansion was military, as new sultans created empires for themselves. Turkish warriors, for example, brought an end to the Byzantine Empire when they conquered Constantinople in 1453. Other warriors brought a growing proportion of the Indian subcontinent under Islamic control. However, wandering Sufi teachers, ulama, and Muslim merchants also expanded the borders of the Islamic world, converting individuals and then whole societies to Islam.

In the process of this expansion, the different styles of Islam interacted. There was a great spirit of adaptation and flexibility in the face of new circumstances, not just on the part of pragmatic military commanders but also on the part of many Sufi teachers. However, the willingness to compromise was checked by the conservative feelings of most of the ulama, who were unwilling to accept change at too rapid a pace. When that check was not sufficient, a more vigorous opposition to compromise often arose in the form of a fundamentalist movement that demanded a more strict adherence to the specific regulations of the Quran and the Sunnah of the Prophet.

The period of the sultanates left a significant heritage. The tradition developed of state structures' being firmly in the control of the pragmatic military commanders. The state was not, however, a secular institution; it was subordinate to the ideals of the Islamic faith and part of a broader sense of Islamic community. In the absence of a formal, institutionalized church, the state continued to be the political manifestation of the Islamic community.

The evolution of the Islamic social structures emphasized the ideal of a community that is integrated as a whole through personalized associations. Although there were rich and poor, leaders and followers, elites and masses, the social groupings did not create entities (like class or church) that stood "between the individual and the community of the faithful" as a whole.[8] In this way, the sense of belonging to the *ummah* became a central feeling, and for the Sunni majority, that sense had a higher claim than loyalty to a particular state. That tradition of social order has helped to shape modern sociopolitical development in the Islamic world.

Sultanate "Gunpowder Empires"

The dynamic expansiveness of the Islamic community led to a brilliant political and cultural florescence in the sixteenth and seventeenth centuries, the most visible aspect of which was the emergence of a broad band of militarily strong, wealthy, and expansive imperial systems. These states have been called the "gunpowder empires" because they were the product of the harnessing of gunpowder technology for military and political goals.

That technology involved a transformation of government that "aided the rise of centralized governments at the expense of feudal lords. . . . The states that successfully made the transition to the age of gunpowder were those that strengthened their administrative and commercial classes at the expense of the landowning aristocracy."[9]

The special characteristics of the sultanate system and the Islamic social order initially aided that transition. The landowning aristocracy was not as strong or as well organized as it was in other parts of the world, and there was no institutional church to impede development. When the transition could be tied to the welfare of the Islamic community as a whole or to some general sense of Islamic mission, it was initiated with relative speed. The cosmopolitan, interregional connections facilitated the spread of the new organizations as well.

The largest and best known of the gunpowder sultanates were the Ottoman Empire in the Mediterranean region, the Safavid state in Iran, and the Moghul Empire of India. However, the network of Islamic states spread far beyond those core areas. In the east, expanding sultanates had been established in the Philippine Islands and throughout the East Indies by the beginning of the sixteenth century. Among the most important of those were the sultanates of Sulu, Malacca, and Atchin. During this time, Islam became the major religion in the islands and peninsular areas of Southeast Asia. The momentum created by this period of flourishing meant that even the long centuries of Dutch imperial control could not stem the tide of Islam.

The world of Islam extended north and south of the three core empires as well. In Central Asia, a series of Muslim sultanates succeeded the Mongol states and established Islam as the faith of the majority of the population. To the south, along the East African coast, a line of commercially oriented city-states provided a firm base for the development of Islam. West of the Ottoman Empire, Islam was expanding vigorously into West and Central Africa. By the beginning of the sixteenth century, Islam had become the religion of the rulers of a series of large states, including the Songhai Empire. This experience of the Islamic community needs to be remembered, but "the extraordinary scope and force of this Islamic expansion . . . often escapes attention. Yet an intelligent and informed observer of the fifteenth century could hardly have avoided the conclusion that Islam, rather than the remote and still comparatively crude society of the European Far West, was destined to dominate the world in the following centuries."[10]

The problem of coping with the tremendous diversity of peoples and cultures that had been brought into the world of Islam helped set the tone for this era. Each region developed its own particular methods for dealing with the sociocultural pluralism, although the overall sense of the Islamic community provided a common conceptual framework. Two alternative methods were a tolerant openness and a more strict exclusivism. During the sixteenth and seventeenth centuries, both methods were utilized. There was, however, a gradual shift of emphasis. The expansion and early consolidation of the great states were associated with a more tolerant acceptance of diversity and, in some cases, even a formal institutionalization of that diversity. By the end of the seventeenth century, there was a reaction to the compromises that were involved, and the dominant mode began to shift in the direction of greater exclusivism.

In concrete terms, this shift can be seen in the development of the diverse imperial systems. Following the Ottoman conquest of Constantinople in 1453, Sultan Mehmet II gave special recognition to the patriarch of the Greek Orthodox Church, giving him civil as well as religious authority over the Orthodox Christian subjects of the empire. In this way, the *millet*s or religious communities began to be organized in a "system of autonomous self-government under religious leaders" that eventually was extended to all major non-Muslim groups in the empire.[11] This tolerant system remained one of the foundations of the Ottoman imperial structure until the nineteenth-century reforms.

There was a similar general openness among the Muslims of the empire. The popular Sufi orders allowed practices that were not strictly Islamic but those orders were usually suppressed only when they became associated with directly antigovernment activities. Within the schools of the empire, a wide range of intellectual subjects was covered, thus following "the most broadminded traditions of sunni Islam."[12] The situation was similar in Islamic law, as the Ottomans adopted as the official school of the empire the Hanafi *madhhab*, which is generally considered to be the most flexible of the four.

During the sixteenth century, there was a withdrawal from some of the most flexible aspects of the tradition of openness. As the empire became more stable and established, an effort was made to organize the system on a more formal basis. Suleyman I, the great sultan of the century, worked "to centralize, unify, and codify the administration of a state that had been molded out of many peoples, traditions, and civilizations."[13] Government practices and executive orders were brought together into a code of law in an effort to bring them into closer conformity to Islamic law. The ulama, fearing a dilution of the Islamic message, began to limit intellectual experimentation in the *madrasah*s. On the popular level, religious organizations that deviated significantly from the teachings of Sunni Islam were more tightly controlled. This greater degree of control was related not only to the desire to purify popular practice but also to the desire to defend the empire from the threat of internal subversion, since many of the heterodox groups had Shiʿite sympathies, which gave them apparent ties to the growing Shiʿite power of the Safavids in Iran.

The adaptations were kept clearly within the bounds that had been defined by Sunni Islamic tradition. The Ottoman Empire was a Sunni state even though it maintained some of the early spirit of flexibility. In the Ottoman experience, one can see the continuing interaction of the different styles of Islam. The adaptationist style opened new ways of action, the conservatives maintained gains that had been made, and the fundamentalists kept the changes within the bounds of what was clearly Islamic.

The same general dynamic operated elsewhere in the Islamic world. The sixteenth century was a time of great Islamic expansion in India under the Moghul sultans. Sultanates had been created in northern India in the preceding era, when a Central Asian military adventurer by the name of Babur had defeated the major sultanate in that area, partly by using the new gunpowder technology. The effective creation of the Moghul imperial system was the work of his grandson, Akbar, who became emperor in 1556. Akbar built an administrative structure and worked to combine the diverse elements within his empire in a tolerant and open state system. The majority of the population in the new empire was non-Muslim, and Akbar's state was built on a tolerant acceptance of religious diversity.

In religious terms, Akbar attempted to create a broader theological foundation for the faith of his court by developing an eclectic religion, which combined the teachings of the major religious traditions of his subjects. This effort paralleled a popular religious trend that, under the umbrella of local devotional practices and Sufi pantheism, led to the emergence of new religious groups. In those new groups, there was an attempt to combine Hindu and Muslim ideas and practices.

From the perspective of the more traditional Muslims, these developments threatened to undermine the basic message of Islam and the ability to create a truly Islamic community. As a result, some of the major figures among the ulama set about to restore the balance. Although their efforts took many forms, one of the most visible was the activism of the leaders of a noncompromising *tariqah*, the Naqshbandiyyah. A key figure in that *tariqah*'s revivalism was Ahmad Sirhindi (1564–1624), who lived at the end of the tenth century of Islamic history and became known as the Renewer (Mujaddid) of the second thousand years. From its base in India, the Naqshbandiyyah revivalist spirit spread throughout much of the eastern Islamic world, and it may have played a role in inspiring revivalist feelings in Ottoman areas.

The reaction against the eclecticism of Akbar and the syncretism of the popular devotional movements spread to the highest levels of government. Sultan Aurangzeb (1618–1707) made the exclusivist spirit the basis for Moghul imperial policy. During his reign, the transition from a dominant spirit of accommodation to a fundamentalist spirit reached a climax.

This transition took different forms in various Islamic areas. There were the relatively open, cosmopolitan court of the Moroccan sultan Ahmad al-Mansur (r. 1578–1603) and the more fundamentalist attitudes of Moroccan rulers like Muhammad ibn Abdallah (r. 1757–1790) and Mawlay Suleyman (r. 1792–1822). At the other end of the Islamic world, in the East Indies, the relatively syncretist mood of Indonesian Sufism was challenged by more strict teachers like Abd al-Raᶜuf al-Sinkili (d. after 1693).

The nature of the great flourishing of Islam during the sixteenth and seventeenth centuries was not radical innovation, nor were the old traditions ultimately questioned. Marshall G. S. Hodgson suggests that "it was a florescence within established lines of tradition, rather perfecting than launching them. . . . Perhaps we may say that this florescence was not one of *origination* . . . but rather one of *culmination* in a culture already long mature."[14] In the context of the continuing visible success of the Islamic community, there was little need to question the basic traditions. It was still clear that "God is on the side of those who fear Him and do good."

Common Themes and Diverse Interpretations

The most visible aspect of the Islamic dimension is the experience of the Sunni-dominated community. The evolution of the *ummah* from the time of Muhammad, through the time of imperial Islam, and down to the great age of the sultanate empires is the manifestation of the majority interpretation of the Islamic message as it has been defined by the ruling political and cultural elites. Although this history is a crucial element in the unfolding of the Islamic experience, it is not the totality of that experience. Concentration on this line of development can obscure the luxuriant diversity within the broad framework of the basic Islamic message. Islam is a distinctively identifiable part of world history, but it is not monolithic. Part of the dynamics of Islam has been the continuous interaction between common themes and diverse interpretations.

Common Themes

All Muslims, regardless of their particular interpretations, accept certain common elements of faith. The first of those is symbolized in the acceptance of the statement that "There is no god but the one God." However it may be defined, Islam means a submission to the divine, and that principle is expressed in a clear monotheism.

The submission is not simply an abstract statement of creedal belief; it means also a common acceptance of a particular revelation from the one God. The full statement of Islamic belief that is accepted by all Muslims adds to the affirmation of monotheism the statement, "and Muhammad is the messenger of the one God." This addition has two important corollaries. It means that God's revelation through Muhammad is the real word of God and that Muhammad was in some way a significant person in the history of the world.

The revelation in its exact words is believed to be recorded in the Quran. The acceptance of the Quran is another common element, one that provides a universal base for the Islamic experience. Although there are diverse interpretations, there are no disagreements over the wording of the Quran, no conflicts over the correct translation. The Quran is the crucial sign of the revelation. In the revelation, Muhammad was instructed to say, "Even if humanity and the spiritual forces joined together, aiding each other, in order to produce something like this recitation [the Quran], they would not produce anything like it."[15]

The experience of the Quran surrounds all Muslims in a variety of ways. Its recitation is a common sound in the Islamic world; it is visually present in the decoration of buildings; and its phrases are a part of a long literary tradition, indeed, its very syntax and grammar are the basis for linguistic study and usage. The Quran overrides sectarian and geographic divergences and is a vital element in the continuity of Islamic history.

The second corollary involves the definition of Muhammad's role, and this aspect helps introduce a distinctive aspect of Islam. The revelation is in the word, not specifically in the person of the Prophet. Although some later interpretations blur the distinction, there is a resistance within the Islamic message to applying any doctrine of divine incarnation to Muhammad. The tone is set in the Quran by the statement: "And what is Muhammad, except simply a messenger? Before him there have been other messengers who have passed away."[16]

The role of messenger is, however, important when the message is from God, and his role implies certain things about the character of Muhammad. As a modern Arab writer has pointed out, "recourse to testimony is one, if not the only, foundation of the Muslim religion; for the word of God is transmitted by a witness, the veracious Prophet."[17] Without a full acceptance of the integrity of Muhammad, the validity of the Quran would be suspect. In this context, information about Muhammad's life and works provides Muslims with an additional source of guidance. Although there is disagreement over the validity of specific traditions, the idea of using the Traditions of the Prophet as a source of authority is widely accepted among Muslims.

Another common theme is the idea of unity (*tawhid*), which, on the most general level, is the principle of the unitary nature or oneness of God. It is a basic principle that is believed to have implications for the integration of all of the universe and all of human life. In specific terms, there is disagreement over the meaning of *tawhid*, but it is clear that all Muslims see the principle as a key one in terms of human life. This agreement can be illustrated by citing two interpreters of Islam who otherwise differ. A modern Shiʿi philosopher says: "To the Muslim, the idea of unity does not just mean the assertion that there is only one God sitting in heaven instead of two or three. . . . Unity is, in addition to a metaphysical assertion about the nature of the Absolute, a method of integration. . . . On the social plane Unity expresses itself in the integration of human society."[18] A modern Sunni fundamentalist, discussing the effects of *tawhid* on human life, says that "the most important effect" is "that it makes man obey and observe God's Law."[19]

All of these beliefs emphasize the Islamic awareness of the moral and ethical dimensions of the revelation. The concrete result of the revelation experience is to be the creation of a moral, divinely guided community, and the *ummah* (the Islamic "community") is an important focus for the faith of Muslims. Belief, for a Muslim, does not simply result in accepting a creed or creating a "proper" theology. Belief is intimately tied to the moral imperatives of the command and will of God. Although the emphasis varies among the various Muslim groups, this moral dimension of the faith and the critical importance of the rightly guided community are common themes within the Islamic tradition.

The oneness of God, the Quran, the significance of Muhammad, and the *ummah* are basic elements in the continuity and unity of the Islamic dimension. They are the starting points for the diverse interpretations that give variety to the Islamic experience. Different perceptions of these elements and the varying historical experiences create varying manifestations of Islam. However, this diversity is more often expressed in local variations and overlapping interpretations than in formal schisms and sectarian distinctions.

Diversity Within the Sunni Tradition

The belief of the majority of the Muslims lies within the broad boundaries of Sunni Islam as it is expressed through the ideas and teachings of the literate teachers. Although often influenced by tribal and rural elements, the process of a formal formulation of Sunni Islam has largely been an urban phenomenon. The possibility of diversity of interpretation can be seen when one asks the basic question, What is the meaning of the oneness of God within the Sunni tradition? Although all Sunni Muslims accept the basic premise, differing aspects of the divine are emphasized by different groups. The two poles of the interpretive spectrum are emphasis on the immanence of God and emphasis on the transcendence of God. Although no Muslim loses all sense of either aspect of God, there is a tendency to focus on one or the other. The Sufi tradition concentrates on the closeness of God to the individual believer, and the legalistic ulama place greater weight on divine transcendence. Within the Sunni community, when Sufism has moved in the direction of a more overt pantheism, there has been resistance, just as extreme legalism has aroused a more mystical response.

Some of the same divergence can be seen in Quranic interpretation. The Sufi commentators tend to stress the mystical or hidden meanings of the Quranic statements, and the standard scholarly commentaries tend to give greater attention to the clear and visible meaning of the revelation. Although both styles are common among Sunnis, the general tendency is away from esotericism.

The life of Muhammad has received great attention in the Sunni tradition. There were major efforts to collect and then organize the *hadiths* or Traditions, and those efforts reached a climax in the ninth century when six great collections of *hadiths* were compiled and became accepted as the standard body of the Traditions. The Traditions became, for the Sunnis, "the authoritative second source of the content of Islam besides the Qur'an."[20] These great collections are not, however, canonical. No institution has ever officially accepted them, and the verifying authority has been the general consensus of the community, which is flexible. The six collections contain contradictory material, and Muslims, from time to time, go outside of the body of *hadiths* contained in these collections for authoritative opinion.

The information provided by the *hadiths* and the records of the early community became the basis for the Sunni definition of the just society. The early community is accepted by Sunni Muslims as being a special example of the way the *ummah* should be, and later Sunni revivalists and reformers have modeled their actions on those of the *salaf* ("pious ancestors") —Muhammad and his companions. The nature of this early-model *ummah* is clearly but flexibly defined in Sunni historical literature. A wide diversity of interpretation is possible, but a relatively specific ideal is maintained.

The characteristic blend of diversity within a broad ideal is most clearly manifested in definitions of the social implications of the revelation. Sunni Muslims are in full agreement that the message of unity provides the foundation for social integration and that this fact means that the legal basis of society is Islam. However, as the Islamic legal system evolved, a single authoritative interpretation of Islamic law did not emerge; instead, a number of schools of legal thought developed. At first, there were simply local and regional applications of the Quran and the Traditions of the Prophet to specific cases. However, by the time of the Abbasids, more formal schools of legal thought (*madhhabs*) had begun to appear. By the time of the sultanates, four Sunni *madhhabs* had come to be accepted as equally authoritative, despite the disagreements among them.

The differences among the Sunni schools of legal thought do not imply that they are separate "sects" or "denominations." Rather, they emphasize different moods or techniques of law. At times, the ulama of differing schools have become involved in conflict, but usually the boundaries between the schools are easily crossed, both for purposes of intellectual identification and for legal interpretation. By the time of the great sultanate empires, geographic regional patterns of adherence to the *madhhabs* had developed, and the distinctive tone of each had been set.

Each of the schools started from the bases of the Quran and the Traditions. The Hanafi *madhhab* traces its history back to an early legal scholar, Abu Hanifa (d. 767). This school grew out of an older Iraqi legal tradition, and it gives some emphasis to personal reasoning and free judgment in legal interpretation. Because of its relative flexibility, it became the school of many major states and received official recognition from the Ottoman and Moghul sultans. It is thus widespread in the central and eastern parts of the Muslim world. The Maliki school, which traces back to Malik ibn Anas (d. 795), places greater stress on using the *hadiths* as a basis for legal interpretation, and it is more conservative in its orientation than the Hanafi school. The Maliki school became dominant in much of Africa. Muhammad al-Shafiʿi (d. 820), the founder of the Shafiʿi school, developed a more formal science of jurisprudence, which characterizes his school, by combining a strict adherence to the *hadiths* with a formal methodology of analogical deduction. The Shafiʿi *madhhab* became important in the Arabic-speaking areas of the eastern Mediterranean. The fourth *madhhab* is the Hanbali. It is the most strict in its insistence upon a rigorous adherence to the specific terms of the Quran and the *hadiths*, and it allows very little scope for individual reasoning or analogy. This school has often been associated with fundamentalism and is currently dominant in Saudi Arabia.

Within Sunni Islam there are many diverse elements. The law schools, the differing attitudes toward mystic religious experience, and other features mean that Sunni Islam is not a homogeneous religious tradition. Sunnism is the result of diversity developing within the framework of common themes in a particular set of ways.

The Special Case of Shiʿism

The major division within Islam is between Sunni Islam and Shiʿi Islam. At the heart of the split is a divergence of views over the nature of the *ummah* and the full meaning of the revelation. The Sunni majority tradition has the prestige of being confirmed by the historical experience of the community. The Shiʿi Islamic tradition, whose roots are in the supporters of Ali, has often been at odds with the concrete historical reality of the Islamic world. Ali and his supporters lost in the early conflicts, and subsequent Shiʿi leaders were only infrequently successful in the sociopolitical conflicts of the following generations.

The Shiʿi tradition developed an alternative philosophy that arose from that divergent experience. In the days of imperial Islam, Shiʿism presented a basis for opposition to the emerging establishment, and revolutionary movements, like the Abbasid, often had a Shiʿi garb. Shiʿism was a strong option as the imperial system began to crumble by the tenth century, and that century saw the creation of a successful Shiʿi movement that built the Fatimid empire and other smaller states. However, the firm establishment of the sultanate system was accompanied by a reassertion of Sunni dominance within the world of Islam.

The Shiʿi viewpoint is significantly different from that of the Sunni on many basic issues. In the framework of the common themes, the Shiʿites tend to emphasize the immanent aspects of the divine, and this emphasis manifests itself particularly in terms of the question of leadership for the *ummah*. The Shiʿi position stresses the idea of the imamate, which has implications for the positions on the nature of God, the Quran, Muhammad's role, and the true nature of the *ummah* itself.

After Ali's death, his "party" looked to his sons, Hasan and Husayn, for leadership. Husayn was killed in a conflict with Umayyad forces and became a symbol for martyrdom in the cause of Islam. Descendants of Husayn and Hasan were involved in a number of unsuccessful revolts during imperial Islam. Gradually a more formal doctrinal base was developed, and a stable, more politically passive Shiʿi community emerged, although there have always been more revolutionary groups within the Shiʿi minority. By the time of Jaʿfar al-Sadiq (d. 765), the sixth in a continuous line of leaders going back to Ali, the basic Shiʿi doctrines of the imamate had been formulated.

In this Shiʿi view, Muhammad *did* designate a successor, and that person was Ali. The validity of the succession of the first three caliphs was thus denied, and the community was believed to have been in error. The necessity of Ali's succession was related to an interpretation of the nature of the revelation in the Quran. It is said to have two levels, the openly manifest one, whose meaning is clear to all believers, and an internal meaning, known only to the divinely designated leader or imam. The imam is thus needed if the community is to have a full understanding of the word of God.

God is believed to have designated an imam in every period, but there can be only one imam at any given time. This leader must be a descendant of Ali and the Prophet's daughter, Fatimah, and he has a number of characteristics, including sinlessness. Diversity within the Shiʿi communities comes over the identification of specific imams, although the majority have come to accept a line of twelve, which ended in 940. At that time, the Twelver or Imami Shiʿism believes that the current imam was taken into divinely sheltered seclusion and will return to visible leadership of mankind at some future date as a Mahdi or messianic guide.

Other major Shiʿi groups focus their attention on different imams. One group associates itself with the tradition of Zayd ibn Ali, who led a revolt in 740. According to this interpretation, the imam is any member of the house of the Prophet who rises against the illegitimate rulers of an age. This Zaydi tradition came to be established in Yemen. Another group takes a dispute over the succession of the seventh imam as its starting point and supports the imamate of a man called Ismaʿil. As the Imami-Twelver tradition became politically passive, the Ismaʿilis maintained a more revolutionary mood. In medieval times, they were of great importance, and the Fatimids were the most successful Ismaʿili group. By the time of the great sultanate empires, Ismaʿili movements were confined to small communities in scattered areas.

Imami or Twelver Shiʿism is the most widespread of the Shiʿi groups in modern times. There are substantial groups in Syria, Lebanon, and Iraq, and in Iran, it is the religion of the dominant majority. That dominance is the result of the creation of the Safavid state in Iran during the sixteenth century. The Safavids began as a militant religious brotherhood, and, when they came to power in Iran, they established Imami Shiʿism as the religion of the state.

By the time of the Safavids, the basic positions of Imami ideology had been carefully articulated. In addition to the Traditions of the Prophet, the sayings of the imams had also been collected and were accepted as a source of authentic guidance. After the occultation or divine seclusion of the twelfth imam, the Shiʿi scholars developed a broad formulation of law and theology. The Jaʿfari school of legal thought, whose origins have been identified with Jaʿfar al-Sadiq, the sixth imam, provides the basic structure for jurisprudence. On matters other than the issue of the imamate and the choice of authentic traditions, this *madhhab* does not differ greatly from the Sunni schools of legal thought. In theology, the Shiʿi teachers share features with Sufism, especially as it was defined by Ibn al-Arabi.

In the area of political theory and community guidance, the doctrine of the imamate is distinctly different. Since the only true and legitimate ruler is the imam, any other government is at best a temporary expedient until the return of the imam. There is thus a dynamic tension between the politico-military rulers and the religious leaders. Imami Shiʿism has accepted the idea that the representatives of the secluded imam are those religious teachers whose knowledge and piety render them capable of independent interpretive judgment in matters of the faith. These people are called *mujtahids*, that is, people who can exercise *ijtihad* ("independent judgment"). It has come to be accepted that in the absence of the imam, every person should follow a living *mujtahid*, who will act as a guide and an interpreter of the faith.

The Shiʿi experience shows the interaction of the different forms or styles of Islam, although Shiʿi Islam differs from Sunni Islam on specific issues. On the broadest level, Shiʿi Islam tends to institutionalize a more personal and charismatic style. The emphasis on the continuing guidance provided by divinely instructed individuals, first the imams and then the *mujtahids*, gives a special tone to Shiʿism. In addition, one can see a flexible adaptationism in the actions of the political rulers and in the decisions of those *mujtahids* who apply the general principles of the faith to changing conditions. The emergence of a less revolutionary form of Shiʿism by the tenth century shows the existence of a conservative Muslim style, and from time to time, a more rigorist fundamentalist spirit is manifested.

Religiopolitical developments in the Safavid state illustrate this interaction and reflect the broader trends, already noted in the Sunni world, of a shift in emphasis from a more tolerant openness to a more strict exclusivism. Early Safavid rulers claimed to be spokesmen for the hidden imam, and they utilized their influence to create a relatively flexible state system. This trend reached a climax in the reign of Shah Abbas (r. 1587–1629). However, by the mid-seventeenth century, the Shiʿi ulama were asserting their own special position as interpreters and guides for the community. By the end of the century, one of the major *mujtahids*, Muhammad Baqir al-Majlisi, compiled a comprehensive exposition of Imami Shiʿism in strict and uncompromising terms. In the years following, the religious scene was dominated by a tension between two schools of thought; the Usuli, which utilized a more flexible methodology that relied on reasoned opinion and analogy, and the Akhbari, which was more fundamentalist in tone.

Diversity Through Popular Practice

The vibrant diversity of the Islamic experience is not confined to the realms of the ulama and the political rulers. Underlying the great movements of thought and social structure is the general faith of the masses.

Here, also, the common themes provide the framework for belief and action, but the application of the revelation to the issues of daily life is influenced by communal customs and local social conditions. There is a lively interaction in Islamic history between the cosmopolitan literate tradition and the "popular" religion of the people. In this interaction, two themes are of great importance: respect for the saints within a loosely defined Sufi experience and popular messianic expectations.

Popular Islam is often defined in negative terms as a type of religious experience that has been "diluted" by many non-Islamic practices. The more rigorous ulama as well as some modern intellectuals tend to condemn it as being filled with magical practices and superstitions. However, throughout Islamic history, there has been a fruitful interaction as well as a conflict between the two types of Islamic expression, as is illustrated by the role of the popularly respected local holy men.

In all of the areas that have come within the world of Islam, there were local customs built around the local religious leader of a community, and the functions performed by those figures were taken over by Muslim guides as the communities converted to Islam. Just as there were distinctive differences between the tribal shamans of Central Asia and the village spiritual leaders in the East Indies and Africa, local Muslim leadership also presents a picture of diversity. However, in general terms, those local figures were explained in Islamic terms as being individuals who were specially close to God and thus worthy of respect. In this way, a variety of "saint cults" developed.

Those saints, often called *walis*, helped to provide a focus for the emotional dimension of religion in a faith that was sometimes most vigorously defined in legal terms. In the popular faith, the immanent aspects of God tend to be stressed rather than the transcendent, so the explanations of the popular faith tended to take a Sufi form. As *tariqah* structures developed, this trend was reinforced, and there was a melding of the Sufi literate tradition with the practices of the local saints. This combination resulted in a flexibility that permitted accommodation to local conditions and was important in Islamic expansion.

The interaction of the Islamic styles has extended to the development of popular practice. Flexible adaptation was manifestly a mode of Islamic interaction on the popular level. Once Islamic symbols and themes were firmly established, even the ulama came to accept local practices as a part of the broader Islamic picture. The resulting social structures became a part of the community, and conservative Muslims sought to preserve them. However, since some local practices were clearly compromises, fundamentalist movements would sometimes arise to "purify" the religious life of a community. Because of this, the fundamentalist style often found itself in opposition to the practices of the *tariqah*s as well as to the theology of the Sufi teachers.

The second major theme in popular religion that has continuing validity is the messianic expectations. Although the achievements of the Islamic community have been great, life for the average peasant or tribesman continues to be difficult. As a result, the revelation is seen as a promise for a better future, for a world of justice without oppression. Islam was and is a vehicle for the expression of those hopes. It is widely accepted that at the end of the current era of history, God will send a special leader, the Mahdi, "who will fill the world with justice, as it had been filled with injustice."[21]

The doctrine of the coming of the Mahdi is most fully developed in Shiʿi teachings. However, despite reservations on the part of the literate, learned teachers of Sunni Islam, the expectation of the Mahdi has also become a solid part of popularly accepted Sunni Islam. "It was, then, in the hearts of the Muslim multitude that the faith in the Mahdi found its resting place and support. . . . The more, too, the Muslim masses have felt themselves oppressed . . . the more fervent has been their longing for this ultimate restorer of the true Islam and the conqueror of the whole world for Islam. And as the need for a Mahdi has been felt, the Mahdis have always appeared."[22] Militant Islamic activism, whether Sunni or Shiʿi, has often taken the form of a Mahdist movement.

Within Sunni Islam, there has also developed a less apocalyptic vision of revival. The fact that the community could and would need effective renewal came to be widely recognized, and a less messianic idea of continuing revitalization has become widely accepted. It is felt that at the beginning of each century, this process of renewal will be reawakened by a *mujaddid* ("renewer"). Although the *mujaddid* is not as militant a figure as the Mahdi, this concept has also found much popular support over the centuries.

Popular Islam presents further elements of diversity through a variety of local practices, special holy men and their associated cults, and the various movements of a revivalist and messianic nature. The faith of the masses has been shaped by the broader common themes of Islam, but, at the same time, it has also helped to develop and maintain ideals that have influenced the thinking and the practices of the intellectual and political elites.

Basic Styles of Action

Throughout this discussion, four styles of action have been noted, and they provide the network for the interaction of continuity and diversity within the Islamic experience. These four styles are the framework of social action in the Islamic dimension of this study.

The first of these styles is the adaptationist, which represents a willingness to make adjustments to changing conditions in a pragmatic manner. This style is clearly visible in the political realism of the early rulers of the community, who adopted many ideas and techniques in creating the early empires and the later sultanates. It is also manifested in the intellectual tradition by those thinkers who have adapted the Greek philosophical traditions in explaining Islamic positions. The religious syncretism of Akbar in Moghul India and the open flexibility of the popular Sufi teachers are other examples of this style.

This style of action in the Islamic tradition opened the way for the great syntheses that have given a great deal of dynamism to the development of the Islamic community. It has made it possible for the Muslims to cope with a wide variety of challenges, such as the tensions resulting from the first conquests, the problems associated with the collapse of the early imperial unity, and the intellectual problems of integrating new ideas into the basic framework of the Islamic faith.

The success of Islam brought achievements that are worth preserving, which is the motivation behind the second style, the conservative. As a great synthesis emerged, much of the learned community hoped to preserve the gains that had been made. From the very beginning, the perfection of the revelation has been seen by Muslims as requiring a reserved attitude about change that is too rapid. The opposition of the early companions to Ali may have been an attempt to preserve the type of community that had been created in Medina by the Prophet. Later ulama undertook to preserve the system of Islamic law once it had been defined. In this style, a mistrust of innovation tends to be the keynote.

The efforts of the conservatives have served the Islamic community well in times of turmoil, and they have helped to keep the compromises of the adaptationists within the bounds of what has become accepted as Islamic. In the long run, the conservative style of action has avoided supporting stagnation of the community by gradually accepting new circumstances as they have become established. It has provided a basis for the tolerant acceptance of diversity on both the doctrinal and the popular levels.

The third style is the fundamentalist. The scriptures of religions that accept the concept of the recording of divine revelations provide a basis for a common, permanent standard to use in judging existing conditions. In Islam, the Quran represents such an unchangeable standard, and the fundamentals of the faith as presented in the Quran have a universally accepted validity within the Islamic community. The fundamentalist style of action insists upon a rigorous adherence to the specific and the general rules of the faith as presented in that generally accepted record of revelation. When additional elements are also accepted as authoritative, they may also be included among the fundamentals. Thus, within Sunni Islam, the Sunnah or path of the Prophet, as defined by the *hadith* literature, is also used as a basis for evaluating Islamic practices, as are the collections of the traditions of Ali and the imams within Shiʿi Islam.

From early times, there have been Muslims who have insisted on an uncompromising adherence to the rules of the faith, such as the Kharijites. By Abbasid times, this rigorism was being espoused by some of the Sunni ulama, and a careful study of the life of the Prophet and *hadith* scholarship became the focus of attention for those who demanded that the Islamic community act strictly in accord with the Quran and the Sunnah. A leading figure in this style of action was Ahmad ibn Hanbal (780–855), whose rigorism set the tone for the strict Hanbali *madhhab* and for later Sunni fundamentalists, including Ahmad ibn Taymiyyah (d. 1328) and the eighteenth-century revivalist, Muhammad ibn Abd al-Wahhab.

The distinction between the fundamentalist and the conservative styles is important. Fundamentalists are unwilling to accept compromises and are more often critics than defenders of existing conditions. They utilize a literal and rigorous interpretation of the Quran and the Sunnah as a basis for judging existing practices. They frequently are political activitists, and they often are disturbing elements and upset social stability.

The fundamentalist style serves as a corrective adjustment mechanism. In the context of change and adaptation, fundamentalists work to keep the basic Islamic message in full view of the community. When adjustments to local conditions or the adoption of new ideas and techniques threaten to obliterate the unique and authentically Islamic elements, fundamentalist pressure begins to build. In one sense, the mission of Islamic fundamentalism is to keep adjustments to change within the range of those options that are clearly Islamic. Such efforts can be seen in the work of the Naqshbandiyyah during Moghul times in India.

The fourth Islamic style places emphasis on the more personal and individual aspects of Islam. Although all Muslims recognize the communal implications of the revelation, there is a style that tends to subordinate legal structures and communal institutions to the personal aspects of piety and the leadership of charismatic, divinely guided individuals. The Shiʿi conception of the imamate and the popular belief in the Mahdi are broad, political manifestations of this style. It is also seen in the Sufi tradition of personal piety and the importance of the local spiritual guide. This style of action permeates the whole Islamic experience, and in a general sense, the resistance of the Islamic tradition to the creation of a formal church structure and an ordained clergy is a product of this individualized spirit.

These styles are not formal, separate movements within the Islamic community but represent orientations for action within the broader Islamic experience as a whole. In any specific group or individual, the styles are combined with varying degrees of emphasis, and they can be used as an analytical framework for understanding the dynamics of Islamic history.

The Islamic dimension of this study includes the historical experience of the community. In that history, there is a dynamic interaction among the elements of continuity and diversity, including the interplay between the challenge of changing conditions and the steady adherence to the fundamentals of the faith. The way these elements interact is described by observing the various styles of Islam. The heritage of the Islamic community is the foundation of the modern history of Islam.

3

The Foundations of the Modern Experience: Revival and Reform in the Eighteenth Century

The eighteenth century is often viewed as a "dark age" of Islamic history, and descriptions focus on the disintegration of the great sultanate empires and a general sense of decline. This perception is influenced by a knowledge of the subsequent Islamic experience as the nineteenth century was a period of loss of control to Western imperial powers, and the perspective is defined by a series of assumptions that have been developed as a result of knowing the later history. It has been assumed that the Islamic viewpoint represented a "traditional" world view that inevitably clashed with modern ideas and was, also inevitably, defeated by them. The implicit question in many of these discussions is, Why was Islam unable to cope with the basic dynamics of modern history?

The final quarter of the twentieth century is a time when this historical interpretation needs to be reexamined. Clearly, in view of its continuing vitality, Islam has been able to achieve at least some significant success in coping with modern conditions. The old-fashioned Western imperialist could complacently state that Islam's "gradual decay cannot be arrested by any modern palliatives however skillfully they may be applied."[1] But that statement was made when there appeared to be no way to stop European expansion. In the days when modern Islamic thought could be relatively accurately described in terms of "the intellectual confusions and the paralyzing romanticism which cloud the minds of the modernists,"[2] the decline of Muslim vitality could be emphasized. However, the resurgence of Islam at the beginning of its fifteenth century requires not just different answers to the old questions, but a reformulation of the questions.

In the process of this reexamination, the history of Islam in the eighteenth century assumes a new significance. With the current status of Islam in mind, it is clear that the elements of continuity are stronger in the modern context than has been thought. The struggles related to Western politico-military control and to the influence of Western ideas have obscured but have not eliminated the basic dynamics of Islamic continuity. It is now possible to speak of the emergence of a "posttraditional" Islamic society, a society that is not simply a transplanted version of modern Western society. In that emergence, the underlying Islamic experience has been shaped in some important ways by the history of Islam in the eighteenth century. The basic question is not, Why did Islam fail? because it has not "failed." Rather, the question is a more complex one: What are the elements of the Islamic experience that continue to have vitality and how have they developed in the context of the modern global experience?

General Eighteenth-Century Themes

Local conditions, modern issues, and the Islamic continuity provide the three dimensions of the history of the Muslim world in the eighteenth century. Within this framework, it is possible to identify the general themes of the Islamic experience. Primarily, those general themes have been defined by the interaction of Islamic and modern elements, and the specific forms have been shaped by particular local conditions. Three such themes are the decentralization of political control with a realignment of the major politico-economic elements, a reorientation of the Sufi tradition, and the emergence of revivalist movements that aimed at the socio-moral reconstruction of society.

Political and Economic Realignments

The sixteenth-century florescence produced the great sultanate empires, which had a relatively high degree of political centralization. By the eighteenth century, those large states were crumbling under a variety of pressures. Although local conditions differed, some common features in that decentralization process can be identified.

One factor is that the premodern, agrarian-based imperial systems tended to alternate between periods of strong centralized power and times of greater decentralization. This cycle was described in the Islamic context by a great Muslim writer, Ibn Khaldun (d. 1406). He noted that the vigor of the victorious conquerors and the social cohesion of their supporters tend, over time, to weaken as the fruits of their success come to be enjoyed. In each of the great sultanate empires, emerging vested-interest groups came into conflict over the control of the wealth and power of the state. As powerful groups consolidated their positions, they developed a resistance to change and reform, even when the state itself was clearly being weakened. In this way, influential sections of the elite became manifestly conservative, and the states were less able to cope with change. Effective power then shifted away from the centralized control of the sultans. Ibn Khaldun's analysis was in the minds of Ottoman observers and was used by them to interpret the Ottoman troubles at the beginning of the eighteenth century.

The economic aspects of the situation are now being studied more systematically. The Western challenge to Islamic society was only beginning and was not widely felt. Growing European power resulted in some defeats of Muslim forces, but it had not yet reached the stage of open domination and clear military superiority. However, the less immediately visible impact of the emerging European economic system was already beginning to have an influence. The economic structures associated with the sultanate empires were based on state control of the flow of capital within the society, and the ability of the merchant and commercial groups to accumulate large amounts of capital was limited by the state's imposition of market controls, customs levies, and price controls. In addition, interregional trade that crossed political boundaries tended to be primarily in nonessentials and luxury goods, the major consumers of which were the political elite.

The beginnings of the transformation of the European economy provided the Middle Eastern merchants and producers with new opportunities. New markets for basic goods like foodstuffs and cotton were created, and they were beyond the control of the sultanate governments. These markets were made more appealing by the higher prices offered by European purchasers. The Islamic governments attempted to limit, if not prohibit, the export of basic goods, but they were not successful. The contraband trade with Europe grew and provided a major flow of capital that was outside the control of the Islamic governments. One result was the encouragement of commercially oriented groups that were increasingly independent in economic terms. Local notables and provincial leaders benefited from this change, and their strength increased at the expense of the central government.

The process of a diffusion of power was visible within the central institutions themselves. In the sixteenth century, the dominant figure in most states had been the sultan, but by the eighteenth century, other officials were assuming greater prerogatives. A good example is that decision-making powers in the Ottoman Empire were assumed by officials like the grand viziers, the shaykhs al-Islam, and the palace eunuchs. Such officials resisted reforms that would again centralize power in the hands of the sultan, and thus they undermined the state's ability to cope with the other problems of decentralization.

Under these circumstances, one of the most visible trends in eighteenth-century history was the emergence of regional, provincial, and local notables who had increasing degrees of independence or at least autonomy. Although in many cases, nominal allegiance to the sultan was maintained, power was being effectively decentralized, and the sultanate empires were greatly weakened—in some cases, they disappeared. The balance of effective political and economic power in many areas was shifting away from those groups that had been dominant in the early days of the sultanate empires.

Reorientation of the Sufi Tradition

The second general theme of eighteenth-century Islamic history was a reorientation of at least some elements of the Sufi tradition. This reorientation was manifested in two areas: a significant evolution in the Sufi theological and philosophical positions and a further development of the organization of the *tariqah* and its function in society.

In intellectual terms, Sufism had become widely identified with the pantheistic style of theology expressed by Ibn al-Arabi. In this formulation, God is seen as the only reality, and the Sufi path becomes a striving for absorption into that ultimate being. Other themes reflect Neoplatonic ideas of the eternal word and light manifested through the prophets. Such a definition of Islam emphasized the immanent aspects of the divine and tended to accept the validity of any religious experience. In this way, Sufism provided a theological foundation for open accommodation to other faiths and for syncretism. Although the *tariqah* leaders on the frontiers of Islam were not often sophisticated Sufi philosophers, the symbolism and formulations of this style of Sufism gave them a doctrinal basis for their own adaptable eclecticism.

During the eighteenth century, the long dialogue between representatives of this type of mystic thought and the more strict Sunni ulama gained new momentum. In many areas, scholars worked to reinterpret the Ibn al-Arabi tradition in less pantheistic terms, and commentators on his most famous works gave greater emphasis to the transcendence of God. They restated the goal of the Sufi path in terms of the individual being in harmony with the spirit of the Prophet rather than losing individual identity by absorption into the absolute being. It is possible to see a shift toward the more moderate mysticism that had been defined by al-Ghazali in the twelfth century, which was reflected by a revived interest in the writings of that teacher.

Although much of this intellectual activity still used themes found in Ibn al-Arabi's writings, some teachers explicitly rejected his work. This rejection was not new in the Islamic world as the more rigorous fundamentalists had usually been quite explicit in attacking positions held by Ibn al-Arabi. The great Hanbali scholar Ahmad ibn Taymiyyah had vigorously condemned that style of Sufism in Syria, and the Naqshbandiyyah revivalism in Moghul India had included a similar attack. During the eighteenth century, the most visible example of the rejection of Ibn al-Arabi was the Wahhabi teachings in the Arabian Peninsula, and the continuing strength of that rejection is reflected in the attempt by Egyptian fundamentalists in 1978–1979 to remove the books of Ibn al-Arabi from libraries and university curricula.

The eighteenth-century developments in the *tariqah* organization were complex. Affiliation with a *tariqah* means many different things. Literally, the term *tariqah* means "path" and refers to the devotional "path" of special exercises and litanies developed by a great Sufi teacher. Becoming a member of a Sufi order involves learning this devotional path from the teacher himself or from one of his disciples. As an organization, what is called a *tariqah* may be an informal group of individuals who share a respect for some particular teacher's devotional exercises, or it may be a more formally organized association with specially appointed leaders and administrators. Some *tariqah*s are identified with important families of religious teachers, and others are tied to particular social or economic groups.

Since the twelfth century, *tariqah*s have, from time to time, provided the organizational framework for a variety of social movements. By the time of the great sultanate empires, *tariqah* affiliation had become a mass phenomenon and most people had some type of tie to a Sufi brotherhood. Groupings of soldiers, artisans, and others were integrated into the broader Islamic community through *tariqah*-style affiliations. As those structures provide the potential for mobilizing large numbers of people, *tariqah*s were at times the basis for movements of revolt. The origins of the Safavids lie in a militant *tariqah*, and the foundations of the Murabitun and Muwahhidun movements, which established medieval states in North Africa, were organizations built around the leadership of holy teachers. The ulama reaction to Akbar's religious policy was organized through the Naqshbandiyyah Tariqah.

The Naqshbandiyyah in India may have been an influential prototype for the *tariqah* development in the eighteenth century. Most activist *tariqah*s had been relatively heterodox in terms of theology, but the Naqshbandiyyah Tariqah aimed at combating compromises of the faith. Increasingly, in a wide range of areas during the eighteenth century, better organized and more activist *tariqah*s along the lines of the Naqshbandiyyah Tariqah emerged. These new groups were vehicles for purification and revival rather than for adaptation and synthesis. These organizations thus reflected, in their activism, the reorientation of Sufi thought that was taking place. The more world-negating pantheism of medieval Sufism was being replaced by organizations in which "the *emphasis* had shifted more towards the positive issues of society, whether in political, moral or spiritual terms."[3]

In the eighteenth century, intellectual and organizational trends brought forth what has been called Neo-Sufism.[4] Building on the traditions of the earlier leaders like Ibn Taymiyyah and Ahmad Sirhindi, some *tariqah*s provided the framework for movements of purification and adherence to a rigorous interpretation of the Islamic tradition. Older syncretistic and possibly heterodox styles of Sufism did not disappear, but Neo-Sufism had become an important element in the Islamic world by the end of the eighteenth century.

Spirit of Socio-moral Reconstruction

During the florescence associated with the sultanate empires, the emphasis was on the adaptationist style of Islam, but, gradually, the other styles of action set limits on the compromises formulated by the adaptationist rulers and intellectuals. The changing historical circumstances of the seventeenth and eighteenth centuries provided opportunities for more conservative and more fundamentalist elements. Local conditions meant that the process was diverse, but there was a relatively widespread spirit of socio-moral reconstruction based on a more strict adherence to the Quran and the Sunnah of the Prophet.

The general conditions within the Islamic world helped to inspire this mood. The imperial sultanates had become less effectively organized, and military defeats, the growing ineffectiveness of administration, and economic difficulties presented a picture of degeneration that inspired some people to engage in reforming action. The general tolerance of a wide diversity of local customs and their apparent acceptance, even by the ulama, aroused indignation over what was seen as a dilution of Islam. The targets for criticism were the adaptationist practices of the rulers and Sufi groups.

On the positive side, the reforming spirit called for a moral reconstruction of society. The ideal was the early Islamic community, and the program offered was, with varying details, a return to Islam as it is defined by a literal interpretation of the Quran and the Sunnah of the Prophet. Some aspects of the Islamic tradition were emphasized and others rejected. The development of Neo-Sufism is one aspect of this picture. Similarly, the concentration on the life of the Prophet and the early community meant that the study of *hadith* literature was important. In the movements that emerged in the eighteenth century, there was an apparent coming together of *hadith* scholarship and Neo-Sufism, and the prominent teachers were both *muhaddiths* ("*hadith* scholars") and participants in the new style of Sufi thought—one of the best examples being the major eighteenth-century Indian teacher, Shah Wali Allah. There was also a tendency to rely less on the authority of the great medieval teachers and to claim the right of independent judgment (*ijtihad*) in interpreting the fundamentals of the faith.

The eighteenth century was thus a time when there was a major revivalist effort within Islam, and the lines of that effort were similar to efforts in preceding periods. Although there was already some impact from the modernizing West, that was not the primary or most visible challenge that aroused the reforming spirit. Just before the time of European dominance, a reformist-revivalist tradition had been established in the mold of the fundamentalist style of Islamic experience, and that tradition created an underlying theme for the modern Islamic experience. Social groups and associations had been created to meet the issues raised by the adaptationists within the Islamic community, and those groups had a fundamentalist mood, which has always been close to the surface in the past two centuries. Thus, the style of the eighteenth-century spirit of socio-moral reconstruction has provided the counterpoint to the adaptationists' secularizing reforms. When the latter weaken or appear to have failed, as was frequently the case by the 1970s, the more fundamentalist style emerges into full view.

During the eighteenth century, the leadership for the revivalist movements came from the scholars of Islam. The scholars were often able to inspire political figures to support them, and, when that happened, the result was the creation of new states based on their teachings. However, the eighteenth-century fundamentalist spirit was not tied to the changing political boundaries of the time. Ulama traveled widely, often disregarding politico-military rivalries, and were part of a broad, cosmopolitan network. As a result, even though the specific history of a revivalist movement in any given area might be distinctive, there were direct lines of interaction among the revivalist ulama. One such line was the gradual expansion of the Naqshbandiyyah from South Asia into the eastern Mediterranean areas; another was the influence of North African teachers in central Islamic lands. The central position within the Islamic world of the cities of Mecca and Medina and the annual pilgrimages to those holy cities made them important points of interchange. There, groups of scholars from throughout the Islamic world provided one focus for the interacting cosmopolitan network. Other important centers were the great schools in Cairo, Damascus, and the imperial capitals.

Although the pragmatic mode of adaptation did not disappear, there was a new emphasis on the fundamentalist style of action, and the eighteenth century was a time of vital interaction in the continuing definition of the nature of the Islamic community. The Islamic dimension provides the framework for the variety of experiences in the Islamic world; an examination of the "local dimension" gives substance to the generalizations about eighteenth-century Islamic themes.

Local Dimension: The Ottoman Experience

The Ottoman Empire in the eighteenth century brought together a tremendous variety of peoples. To examine the history of Islam in the context of this complex structure, it is helpful to distinguish between the experience of the imperial state itself and the Islamic movements that were not directly part of the state structure. These two aspects were interconnected in many ways, as when non-state religious teachers led revolutionary movements or when important political leaders became the patrons of "unofficial" religious leaders. However, if it is remembered that the state and the non-state experiences are simply two facets of the broader history of the empire, it is possible, for purposes of analysis, to deal with them separately.

Islam and the Ottoman Empire

The general political history of the Ottoman Empire in the eighteenth century is filled with wars, revolutions, and periods of instability. In terms of the major themes, one can consider that the eighteenth century began, in political terms, with the failure of the Ottoman armies to capture Vienna in 1683. That failure exposed the Ottoman weakness to the view of the Europeans, and in subsequent campaigns the Ottoman army collapsed. Continuing defeats in the field and military mutinies in Istanbul finally produced a reaction in the form of powerful reformist efforts. In the face of imperial disaster, conservative groups and corrupt vested interests were willing to accept some reorganization efforts that were aimed at increasing the effectiveness of the army and the efficiency of the administration. However, as soon as the immediate threat had passed, the reformers were forced out of office and were replaced by leaders who would tolerate the old inefficiencies once again. In effect, a pattern emerged that "epitomized all the glories and disasters of the Ottoman Empire in its age of disintegration. The pattern was a quick recovery from disaster followed shortly by a stalemate and subsequent collapses."[5]

There was a line of reforming administrators who attempted to revitalize the imperial structures. Some of the most famous of those reformers came from the Koprulu family, the first Koprulu to become grand vizier, the chief Ottoman administrator, having been Mehmet Pasha, who assumed that post in 1656. The eighteenth-century reforming viziers increasingly came to accept the idea that the adoption of specific European techniques might aid the empire. Such an approach can be seen in the policies of grand viziers like Husayn Koprulu (1644–1702), Damad Ibrahim (in office, 1718–1730), and Mehmet Ragib in mid-century. The culmination of this trend was the reform program of Sultan Selim III (r. 1789–1807), who made a major effort to create a "new order" (*nizam-i-jedid*).

A variety of forces worked against the success of those efforts, but mostly it was the conservative elements that worked to preserve conditions as they were. Despite the problems of the empire, its inefficiencies benefited a number of groups. Ineffective central control provided opportunities for local and provincial notables to increase their own personal power, and any reform of the central administration that was too successful would limit their control. As a result, they opposed such reforms, and the eighteenth-century political history of the empire is marked by the increasing power of those local dignitaries. Despite the reforming viziers, the process of decentralization continued throughout the century.

In addition to the local notables, there were strongly conservative elements within the central imperial organization. The bureaucrats participated in a system of buying and selling offices that profited them personally but undermined the efficiency of the administration, and efforts to reform the administrative structure met with the resistance of those officials. A similar situation was presented by the military. The heart of the Ottoman military was the Janissary Corps, and by the eighteenth century, the janissaries had become directly involved in many nonmilitary activities. They had maintained the privileges of their military elite status even though they had become an ineffective military force, and they were unwilling to accept new techniques or training that would require them to abandon their lucrative nonmilitary activities. As a result, they were also a conservative force.

The official religious leadership also fit into the same pattern. The Ottoman state had created a large hierarchy of religious offices to administer the religious aspects of the empire. In the sixteenth century, a well-organized curriculum and a careful structure of official positions had been established, and that system had created a mechanism for fruitful cooperation between the rulers and the ulama. With advancement based on long education and merit, the hierarchy had helped to strengthen the sultanate in its religious legitimacy and had provided well-trained scholars to fill a variety of positions. However, the creation of this organization "carried with it the seeds of considerable trouble for the state" since it intensified the natural conservatism of the ulama and opened the door for the corrupt practices of nepotism and the sale of offices.[6]

By the eighteenth century, these problems had become a major factor in the religious establishment. The higher, and more lucrative, offices were dominated by a few great families, and it became common for untrained men to hold major teaching positions through nepotism. The highest official in the hierarchy was the shaykh al-Islam. As the leading religious official in the empire, the shaykh al-Islam was a powerful political figure, and during the eighteenth century, the holders of that post were important conservative figures. "Ironically it was the very cohesiveness created by the hierarchical structure, which had yielded great benefits to the state in the sixteenth century . . . which from at least the eighteenth century on lent such power to the efforts of the ulema to block often necessary reforms and innovations."[7]

It should be noted that the conservatism of the establishment ulama was not based on the nature of Islam itself. In the sixteenth century, the leading figures of the emerging hierarchy had been important in the adaptations that were made by the sultans of the time. It was the structural context in which the later hierarchy found itself that was the basis for the ulama conservatism. Other Muslim leaders, those not in the upper levels of the state organization, did not maintain as conservative a style as the "high ulama" of the state did in the eighteenth century. Opposition to the practices of the official ulama sometimes came from people in the lower levels of the hierarchy and at other times from popular religious leaders outside of the state organization.

A series of events in the eighteenth century illustrate the interaction of these forces, and they give an insight into the history of Islam as it related to the development of the Ottoman state. The first of these was the "Edirne incident" of 1703, which has been called "a high water mark in the influence of the ulema in the affairs of state."[8] The major opponent of the reforming grand vizier Husayn Koprulu was the shaykh al-Islam Feyzullah. Feyzullah had been the tutor of the sultan, Mustafa II, and was appointed shaykh al-Islam when his former student came to the throne in 1695. Through Feyzullah's personal influence over the sultan and his ability to manipulate the state patronage system, Feyzullah came to dominate the government. He succeeded in driving Husayn Koprulu from office and controlled the subsequent grand viziers. He persuaded the sultan to name Feyzullah's son as his future successor in the position of shaykh al-Islam, and there were some who felt that he aspired to hold the combined posts of shaykh al-Islam and grand vizier.

Through his domination, Feyzullah roused opposition in many quarters. His rejection of the Koprulu reforms created financial problems, and a revolt was sparked in 1703 by the mutiny of janissaries who were demanding back pay. They were joined by large numbers of religious students and low-level official ulama and others who had been antagonized by Feyzullah. The rebels gained control of Istanbul and soon marched on the sultan's palace in Edirne. In the end, Feyzullah and many of his associates were caught and killed, and the sultan himself was deposed by the dissidents.

The career of Feyzullah illustrates the potential power of the establishment ulama group. However, his personal characteristics and ambitions alienated many within the religious establishment itself, and as a result, the ulama conservatives rejected what might have been a drastic change in the role of the ulama leaders. Feyzullah was motivated by personal greed, did not present a broad program based on some organizing principle, and was unable to mobilize support beyond those who benefited directly from his patronage. He was a corrupt pragmatist rather than a conservative or a fundamentalist. The Edirne incident shows that it was possible for one of the ulama to assume a major political role. However, within the upper levels of the Ottoman official ulama, there were few after Feyzullah who seized the opportunity. "There are no ulema of political distinction in the eighteenth century who could match the influence of Feyzullah Efendi. With the Empire's frontiers contracting, and with opportunities for significant employment declining as a result, the ulema appear to have given up their political pretensions in return for security for themselves and their children."[9]

A second illustration of the forces in operation during the eighteenth century is the cycle of events associated with the Tulip Period, which ended with the Patrona Khalil revolt in 1730. The sultan who came to the throne after the Edirne incident was Ahmed III, and he ruled until 1730. After a careful manipulation of the divisions among the groups that had placed him on the throne, Ahmed III was able to revive imperial reform efforts. The leading figure in this effort was Damad Ibrahim, Ahmed's grand vizier from 1718 until 1730. Ibrahim made great efforts to become well informed of developments in Europe, and some of the new techniques were utilized. In the palace itself, some Western European fashions came into vogue, and one of the fads was the cultivation of tulips in the gardens of newly built pleasure pavilions. On the more serious side, Ibrahim's reform effort aimed at strengthening the powers of the central government, this time making use of European techniques rather than simply using the golden age of Ottoman power as a model for reform.

The policies of the Tulip Period were, however, unable to solve the basic difficulties of the empire. Revenues were increasingly lost through contraband trade, and the diversion of tax revenues by powerful local notables and provincial governors increased. Popular unrest was encouraged by inflation, rural banditry, and oppressive taxation, and the reforms attacked the interests of important conservative groups. The period was brought to an end when all the elements of opposition came together in Istanbul and overthrew both the sultan and his grand vizier in the course of the Patrona Khalil revolt of 1730.

That revolt involved a realignment of forces within the ruling elite. Prior to this period, the major support for the centralized sultanate had come from the military elite and the ulama. However, the centralizing reforms became more closely associated with European ideas and were colored by a French-influenced secularist trend. As a result, the antireform movement assumed a more clearly religious tone, and "Thus a religiously oriented anti-western movement became the second strand running across the whole history of the Turkish transformation, in contrast to the Westernist strand."[10] The ulama played an important role in defining the religious basis for the opposition and in giving it legitimacy.

In the decades that followed, there were continuing efforts to introduce Western techniques into the Ottoman system. The tradition of the reforming viziers was maintained by a series of capable administrators, and their reform efforts created a small body of men within the ruling elite who were committed to strengthening the central power. They were aided by European advisers, particularly in the military, but their efforts were constantly interrupted by the activities of the conservative forces. The experience of Claude-Alexandre Comte de Bonneval (1675–1747) is a good example. After a career of military service in European armies, he began serving the Ottoman Empire in 1729 and worked to train new-style military groups. His fortunes rose and fell with the reformist political leaders, and his military engineering school only survived him by three years, being closed because of janissary opposition in 1750.

Many factors complicated the dialogue between reformers and conservatives. Throughout the century, the empire was engaged in wars with neighboring states, and although there were a few victories, the overall results were military defeats and expensive treaties. The conflicts with the European powers played an ambiguous role in the fortunes of the reformers. On the one hand, clearly visible weakness and defeat provided a rationale for reforms that even the conservatives accepted in times of impending collapse. On the other hand, the wars provided an emotional context that allowed the conservatives to arouse significant opposition to the adoption of Western ideas and techniques, which were the tools of the enemy and therefore subversive.

The reformers were unable to diminish the power of the local notables, and the international wars gave provincial leaders an opportunity to use the government's need for their military assistance as a way of gaining concessions from the state. Increasingly, the most productive areas of the empire came under the control of men only nominally loyal, if that, to the sultan. This situation deprived the central government of needed revenues and further strengthened the forces that opposed effective centralizing reform programs.

The culmination of the eighteenth-century reform efforts and the evolution of the relationship of Islam to the Ottoman state came with the programs of Sultan Selim III, who ruled from 1789 to 1807. The Ottoman reforms arrived at a major turning point with Selim's attempts to create a "new order" (*nizam-i-jedid*). "In most ways Selim was a failure. His reforms were limited and eventually dissipated. . . . He went little beyond strictly military and technical innovations to the more fundamental political, social, economic, and judicial developments which had provided the necessary context for their successful operation in Europe. Yet in his efforts, and in the factors which defeated him, lay the seeds of modern Turkish reform."[11]

Faced with external challenges and internal disintegration, Selim III attempted to create a more effective imperial structure. The focus of his reform efforts was the military, and he worked to reform the Janissary Corps and then to create a new, modern-style military force. There were also efforts to improve the administrative structure and financial organization, but those efforts were less well organized. In the long run, the most important part of Selim's program was that under his leadership, knowledge of the West spread to a broader range of people within the empire. Also, the reformist tradition gained strength and became firmly identified with the idea of introducing Western techniques.

Selim III set a basic pattern for the modern Islamic experience. In the face of the changing conditions, the adaptationist style of the Muslim leaders became associated with a particular type of reform program, a program that involved adopting European methods. From the time of Selim to the present, political adaptationism has meant Westernizing reform.

With adaptationism in the political arena being co-opted by the Westernizers, the possibility of a more rigorously Islamic adaptationism was submerged and is reemerging only in the last quarter of the twentieth century. The identification of adaptationism with Westernization may have been inevitable, given the military strength of European states, the penetrating power of the Western economic system, and the seductive appeal of modern ideas as defined by the West.

The manifestly Islamic reactions to the changing conditions tended to be conservative, fundamentalist, or individualist in style, and the ending of Selim's program shows the continuing strength of those forces in the Ottoman Empire at the end of the eighteenth century. Selim was overthrown in 1807 by a combination of antireform forces. Local notables joined with janissaries to provide the military force for the rebellion, and the movement was given legitimacy by the ulama, who felt that the reforms ran counter to Islam. Even though Selim agreed to accept the demands of the revolutionaries and to dismantle the *nizam-i-jedid*, he was deposed. The conservative shaykh al-Islam issued a ruling that authorized his deposition on the grounds that Selim's reforms had been contrary to religion and tradition.

"Unofficial" Islam in the Ottoman Empire

Most of the religious teachers and leaders living within the Ottoman Empire were not part of the official hierachy. Learned scholars taught in a wide variety of schools that spread far beyond the official institutions for training the state ulama. There were also the Sufi leaders, whose *tariqah*s had an important impact on the political life of the empire but were largely outside of the formal Ottoman religious establishment.

The Islam of the community and the Islam of the state overlapped in some areas and competed in others, forming complementary parts of the picture of Ottoman Islamic life. Two important parts of that picture were the developing roles of the non-state ulama and the continuing evolution of the *tariqah*s. One of the heritages of Islamic society was the generally autonomous operation of Islamic structures and groups outside of state structures. Ulama and *tariqah*s in the Ottoman provinces had some lines of direct contact with the state hierachy, but they pursued their own lines of operation in the general life of the community.

The non-state ulama were the main definers of the sociolegal implications of Islam for most people. In the provinces, it was the local scholars rather than the state-appointed judges who were the most influential ulama, and they were supported by a complex network of pious endowments and other gifts. In Damascus, for example, a large number of endowed instructorships and supported religious positions had been created as early as the twelfth and thirteenth centuries.[12] Although some of them had been funded by sultans and other politico-military leaders, they had not become a part of the state system when it was formalized by the Ottomans. In the eighteenth century, the central government had some role in determining who would hold certain positions, but most of the major posts were not filled by people from the official hierarchy. That was clearly true for the muftis in each of the four schools and was also true for the lucrative instructorships in the Umayyad Mosque.

The reformist-conservative struggle that highlighted the eighteenth-century history of the official religious establishment was not as important among the non-state ulama, for whom the emphasis was more on the study of the traditional intellectual disciplines and issues raised by the internal development of Islamic society. Egypt and the Arabian Peninsula are special cases and will be examined separately, but in the rest of the "Arab provinces" of the empire, the different styles of the Islamic experience interacted in usually rather undramatic ways.

The ulama in those provinces were quite cosmopolitan in their orientation. Scholars from areas as widely separated as India and North Africa came and studied, and often settled and became well-known teachers, and similarly, the native ulama frequently traveled as a part of their education. The learned community was not parochial in its attitudes and experiences in terms of the larger Islamic world, although there was little familiarity with anything outside of the world of Islam. There was a sense of Islamic community that transcended political boundaries.

The traveling scholar was a part of a broad network of interregional ties. Two important lines of contact were through the study of the *hadith*s and the learning or "taking" of the *tariqah*s. Among the academic disciplines, the study of the Traditions of the Prophet was one that most encouraged travel. The custom was firmly established that the study of the *hadith*s was most validly accomplished by wandering from teacher to teacher, listening to their verbal transmissions of the Traditions and their comments on the great medieval collections. In the early development of *hadith* study, the focus of attention was on the *isnad*, or chain of authorities transmitting the account. This emphasis continued in later study, and scholars sought out the old traditionists, or *muhaddith*, as a way of shortening the length of their own chain of authorities. The "certification" of a scholar came not through a diploma granted by an institution, but by a permission document from his various teachers authenticating the instruction given. A scholar's credentials were general lists of his teachers and their *isnad*s. Although the study of Islamic law and other disciplines followed a similar pattern, there was less emphasis on the need for travel in order to gain prestige or a major reputation. As a result, *hadith* studies played an important role in the cosmopolitanism of the eighteenth-century ulama.

Initiation into a *tariqah* was another element of interregional contact. During the eighteenth century in the Arab provinces of the Ottoman Empire, the development and expansion of the *tariqah*s was the area of most visible change. Among the ulama there was a growing sense of the desirability of a redefinition of the Sufi tradition. Although few of the ulama rejected Sufism, there were many who were active in an effort to bring it more in line with a stricter interpretation of Islam. One manifestation of this effort was the growth or expansion of certain *tariqah*s among the ulama. The two most important were the Naqshbandiyyah and the Khalwatiyyah.

The Naqshbandiyyah spread from India to the eastern Mediterranean world in the seventeenth and eighteenth centuries, and it carried with it some of the fundamentalist tone associated with the Indian Naqshbandiyyah revival. The leaders of the order insisted upon a careful adherence to Islamic law and clearly disassociated themselves from the heterodox tendencies and latitudinarianism of the older, popular Turkish brotherhoods. As a clearly Sunni order that was relatively free from the excesses of the orders of the masses, the Naqshbandiyyah Tariqah had a strong appeal among the ulama, both within and outside of the religious establishment.

That *tariqah* spread to the Ottoman territories through a number of channels. Earlier groups had been associated with the Turks in Central Asia, but two main lines entered in the seventeenth and eighteenth centuries, both arising out of the activist Indian tradition. The most prominent line was associated with Ahmad Sirhindi, who was active in opposing syncretism in Akbar's time. The chief propagator of this *silsilah*, or line of transmission, was Murad al-Bukhari (1640–1720), a student of the son of Ahmad Sirhindi. Murad al-Bukhari traveled widely in the eastern Mediterranean areas and gained a reputation for piety and learning. He initiated many ulama in a number of areas, and Sultan Mustafa II gave him special grants of land and other sources of income. He settled in Damascus, and his wealth and reputation laid the foundation for a prominent place for his descendants among the ulama of that city. By the end of the century, his family had provided many of the Hanafi muftis in the city, and some members were important teachers. The Muradi family had close associations with Abd al-Ghani al-Nablusi (1641–1731), a leading Sufi writer and a member of the Naqshbandiyyah.

The other major Naqshbandiyyah line spread through Mecca. Its propagator was Taj al-Din ibn Zakariya (d. 1640), a contemporary of Ahmad Sirhindi and a fellow student with him of Muhammad Baqi billah. Taj al-Din settled in Mecca, and his students established the Naqshbandiyyah in Yemen and elsewhere. Through this line, the Naqshbandiyyah spread to Egypt.

The Khalwatiyyah Tariqah has a longer history in Arab lands. Its origins are obscure, but it arose in the general area of western Iran and eastern Turkey. It was distinguished by its emphasis on individual asceticism and withdrawal for meditation. In its early days, it appears to have had strong links with the Shiʿi tradition and to have placed little emphasis on conforming to the rules of Islamic law. It may also have been related to movements of popular unrest and local religious practice. Because of its encouragement of individual actions of piety, it did not maintain a single line of organization but, rather, split into a number of suborders that shared little more than a common tradition of devotional practices and litanies.

A variety of suborders of this *tariqah* spread through the Ottoman lands, and it gradually moved away from its Shiʿi connections and antinomian tendencies. As a part of this evolution, it became increasingly popular among the ulama and propertied classes. By the eighteenth century, the order was one of the most widely accepted among the ulama, and during that century, it became an important vehicle for the emerging Neo-Sufism. A key figure in this development was Mustafa ibn Kamal al-Din al-Bakri, who died in 1748. Mustafa al-Bakri was a student of both Abd al-Ghani al-Nablusi, the famous Sufi teacher and Naqshbandi in Damascus, and Abd al-Latif al-Halabi, a leading Khalwatiyyah shaykh in Aleppo. Al-Bakri thus combined the *tariqah* of Ottoman ulama respectability with the reinterpretation of the Sufi theology of Ibn al-Arabi and the more activist mood of the Naqshbandiyyah. He was a tireless traveler in the eastern Mediterranean regions, and he had many students in Syria, Jerusalem, Egypt, and the Arabian Peninsula. His own special branch of the Khalwatiyyah, the Bakriyyah, became the parent of activist *tariqah*s throughout the Islamic world. By the end of the eighteenth century, the revivalist Khalwatiyyah had inspired orders throughout the Ottoman territories and beyond into Islamic Africa.

In the central parts of the Ottoman Empire, the development of the *tariqah*s and the activities of the non-state ulama did not produce many openly political movements, and the representatives of the fundamentalist style of Islam tended to be more moderate and less activist than in other areas. The Hanbali scholars of Damascus, for example, were important teachers of tradition and carried on the distinctive strictness of their school. At the same time, in contrast to the Hanbalis in the Arabian Peninsula, they tended not to be militant revivalists. In these areas, the Neo-Sufism of the ulama created a tone that consolidated fundamentalist tendencies among the non-state religious leadership. Although there was a strong conservative spirit among these teachers, the general style for coping with changing conditions, when major challenges arose, was to opt for a more fundamentalist than adaptationist style of Islam, even though the latter was increasingly the dominant style of the politico-military leadership.

The culmination of these tendencies in the Ottoman areas outside of Egypt and the Arabian Peninsula can be seen in the career of Khalid al-Naqshbandi, who died in Damascus in 1827.[13] He was born in the Kurdish area of northern Iraq and combined many of the tendencies of his day. His education was the result of wide travels and he had a cosmopolitan awareness of the Islamic world of his time. He studied not only in the major cities of the eastern Mediterranean, but also in India, where he was initiated into Ahmad Sirhindi's line of the Naqshbandiyyah Tariqah. He returned to Iraq and Syria where he had a long and successful career as a teacher and *tariqah* leader.

His life was characterized by support for rigorous fundamentalism. He had close ties to ulama who were sympathetic to this style of Islam, like the Muradi family in Damascus, but he frequently aroused the hostility of the conservative ulama by accusing them of laxness and of diluting Islamic purity. In so doing, Khalid helped to confirm the fundamentalist tone of specifically Islamic solutions to the challenges of change at the beginning of the nineteenth century. It has been suggested that the Khalidi branch of the Naqshbandiyyah helped to establish the Sufi shaykhs as key figures in the movements of popular opposition that occurred later.[14] The revivalist orientation and sociopolitical concerns for the purity of the community made the great shaykhs a natural focus for such movements. Naqshbandis in the line of Khalid were important in leading the Kurdish nationalist movements and in organizing Islamic opposition to the nineteenth-century Russian expansion into Islamic areas.

The main themes of eighteenth-century Islamic history are visible in the Ottoman experience. Political and economic realignments saw the forces of decentralization become stronger, and the official ulama played an important role in that decentralization as a conservative force. The reorientation of the Sufi tradition was especially noticeable among the non-state ulama, although it did have some impact within the official state religious hierarchy. An important feature of the reorientation was the expansion of the two major Neo-Sufi orders, the Naqshbandiyyah and the Khalwatiyyah/Bakriyyah as study of the *hadiths* helped to provide a basis for a spirit of socio-moral reconstruction. Among the religious leaders in the government, that mood took the form of opposition to Westernizing tendencies and reformism. Although much of the opposition to reform can be traced to individual and group interests, the Islamic spirit of revival was also present. In the interaction of these styles, important foundations were laid for future attitudes. In coping with the changing conditions, adaptationism came to be identified with adopting Western techniques and the secularizing of the reformers. As a result, more specifically Islamic reactions tended to assume a conservative or fundamentalist style. It was to be a long time before this eighteenth-century pattern would be broken and a more effectively Islamic adaptationism would emerge.

Egypt: A Special Ottoman Case

The Ulama and Egyptian Society

The history of Islam in Egypt during the eighteenth century presents a picture that diverges somewhat from the main lines of the Ottoman experience centered in Istanbul. Egypt was a province of the Ottoman Empire, but the increasing forces of decentralization provided opportunities for virtually autonomous rule by the politico-military elite. Control of Egypt was mainly in the hands of the Mamluks, the political heirs of the old slave-soldier aristocracy that had ruled Egypt before the Ottoman conquest in 1517. In this system, the "rulers and ruled formed different ethnic and linguistic units."[15] The Mamluks were a faction-ridden ruling elite that engaged in a great deal of internal conflict, and their struggles for power in the eighteenth century increasingly created general conditions of instability, which was reflected by a number of popular revolts among the urban and rural Egyptian masses. There was an Ottoman governor, but his position was weak because he lacked an effective military force and had to rely upon his personal ability for political manipulation.

Those factors provided the framework for the major political and economic realignments that took place. The expansion of the European system of trade and exchange brought changing patterns of economic enterprise to Egypt during the eighteenth century, and the accompanying commercial revival helped to provide resources for a variety of groups. In the process, the "Mamluk *beys* emerged as the political elite in alliance with a number of rich merchants who formed the economic elite after a series of internecine struggles between their rivals, the Janissaries and other feudal military groups."[16]

The ulama emerged during the century as a distinctive sociopolitical force. As Mamluk factional strife increased, the ulama were called upon more frequently to act as mediators. They not only arbitrated among the Mamluk factions, but they also acted as a link between the ruling elite and the general population. Frequently, the ulama were called upon by the people to intervene with the rulers in order to correct some injustice or to reduce oppressive measures.

The actual power of the ulama was defined by certain special conditions.

They did not control any military forces themselves, and their ability to influence the direction of affairs depended upon their personal persuasive powers. They were not, in other words, an organized political faction with military power, and their influence rested upon their ability to direct public opinion and to persuade the rulers. By making use of the Friday sermons and their own individual followings, they could mobilize popular demonstrations in support of or in opposition to government policies. In terms of the ulama self-image, they believed that "it was not their duty to act directly to maintain law and order, that is to take the initiative, for they were not the governors. . . . Their function was to assist the governors by offering advice and good offices."[17]

During this time of significant change, that role of mediation was of growing importance. The Mamluk leaders came to rely more and more on the ulama, and the religious leaders showed a growing willingness to participate in politics. When the French occupied Egypt in 1798, they needed the aid of the ulama to an even greater extent than the Mamluks had. Napoleon created a special council composed entirely of ulama, "who were to help him legislate, maintain order, and act as an intermediary between the French authorities and the people."[18] The defeat of the French by British and Ottoman forces by 1801 provided further opportunities for the ulama to function in the political arena, and one of the leading ulama, Umar Makram, became the major spokesman for local opinion. He was able to mobilize the ulama and other local leaders to reject the Mamluk leadership, secure the deposition of the Ottoman governor, and gain the appointment of Mehmet Ali as the new governor.

The actions of Umar Makram and the successful nomination of Mehmet Ali by the Egyptian ulama represent a climax in the political development of the religious leaders, as after the appointment of the man they had supported, the ulama withdrew from such an active political role. In line with long-standing habits, the ulama were unwilling to take a direct role in the government except in crises. When there was strong leadership, as there was under Mehmet Ali, the political activity of the ulama declined.

The sociopolitical role of the Egyptian ulama has a particular tone, and the eighteenth-century pattern is important in terms of its implications for later history. The ulama were not organized into a unified institution, although there were some influential organizations such as the great Islamic university of al-Azhar. It was as molders of public opinion and as an informal force in society that they had their real power. The ulama kept that style of informal organization, even when they may have had an opportunity to assume more direct political power. In this way, they made it possible for a strong, nonulama leader to gain control and begin the process of reconstructing the institutions of a strong central government. Mehmet Ali's leadership soon became identified with modernizing reform, and the tensions already seen during the rule of the Ottomans were to build in Egypt between Westernizing adaptationism and more conservative religious leadership. However, in Egypt, the ulama had tentatively withdrawn from the political arena, and thus they had weakened their ability to resume a more active political role.

That style of operation has been an important feature of the modern development of Islam in Egypt. The religious leadership had, and sometimes still has, the ability to influence the mood of public opinion, but there is still no formal organization for direct political action or for a direct governmental role for the ulama. Religious sentiment operates in the context of a religiously "unincorporated" society.

Al-Azhar: Egypt's Religious Establishment

Cairo has long been a great center for Islamic education. During the era of the early sultanates, the Mongol conquests and other turbulent events had undermined, if not destroyed, the effective influence of many of the great medieval educational institutions in the eastern part of the Middle East, but the Mamluk sultans had provided patronage for many schools in Egypt. Following the Ottoman conquest in 1517, many of those schools lost control of their endowments, but the great school of al-Azhar, centrally located in Cairo, was able to win support from the new rulers. Gradually, al-Azhar came to dominate the educational scene, and by the eighteenth century, it had developed a great reputation throughout the Islamic world and attracted students from many lands.

The teachers and other ulama associated with al-Azhar formed a religious establishment within Egyptian Islam, and those ulama who held official posts in Egypt could not match the reputation and popular influence of the shaykhs of al-Azhar. During the eighteenth century, the university was a focal point for much of the political activity of the Egyptian ulama, and the shaykh al-Azhar, or leader of the university, was a major figure in both religious and political life.

The role of al-Azhar as a community of scholars is illustrative of the distinctive character of Egyptian Islamic life. Because the university attracted scholars from so many different areas, it became an important center of Islamic cosmopolitanism. Students who returned from Cairo to their homelands were an important factor in the diffusion of ideas within the Islamic world. In that way, for instance, Neo-Sufism spread into Africa as disciples of Mustafa al-Bakri and the revitalized Khalwatiyyah Tariqah introduced those ideas to the founders of influential orders in North and West Africa.

At the same time, the university itself was curiously parochial. The principal teachers were local shaykhs who had themselves been trained in the university, and the cosmopolitanism was largely a feature of the ulama who came to the university to learn rather than a result of the travels of many of the Azhari teachers. The teachers tended to draw back from activist fundamentalism or social radicalism, and during the upheavals of the eighteenth century, the university stood for stability rather than for revolution. Although it acted to oppose excessive oppression on the part of the ruling class, it also helped to control the more activist popular opposition to the status quo. Militant Islamic activism of either a fundamentalist or a messianic character tended to arise outside of either the Egyptian or the official Ottoman religious establishment.

Nonestablishment Religious Life

Spreading beyond the core of the ulama of al-Azhar was a broad spectrum of religious life, but it is difficult to draw sharp lines of definition because the various parts of the Islamic community were in constant interaction. The local religious establishment itself was not a closed corporation. "The social background of the Egyptian ulama differed from that of the ulama of the rest of the Ottoman Empire, for there was no aristocratic hereditary caste of high as against lesser ulama. . . . Most of the prominent ulama were of fallah, peasant, origins."[19] The educational system provided by al-Azhar was a means of genuine social mobility and helped to keep the religious leaders aware of the needs and views of the masses. However, the more prominent ulama tended not to be spokesmen for positions that would challenge the politico-social system as a whole.

From time to time, individuals and groups that expressed a more radical position emerged to represent the views of the general population. The great nineteenth-century Egyptian historian, Abd al-Rahman al-Jabarti, describes an incident early in the eighteenth century that illustrates the complex interaction of the various Islamic groups in Egypt.[20] A man began preaching to the people in one of the mosques, and he vigorously condemned the practices of some of the *tariqah*s in venerating Sufi "saints." His message was basically that of a vigorous fundamentalist, and it soon attracted a number of followers. As a group armed with clubs moved through the streets, some people went to al-Azhar to seek the opinion of the ulama there, and two major shaykhs at the university said that the preacher was in error. The preacher then demanded a debate in the court of the *qadi*, the official Ottoman Islamic judge in Egypt. When the *qadi* saw the size of the crowd, he went to the military authorities, and after much discussion, the preacher was suppressed by the armed forces. In this incident, the conservatism of the Azhar shaykhs is evident. One also can see the complex lines of interaction among the different groups and the care that was taken in dealing with a popular street preacher.

Popular religious views were more frequently presented through the *tariqah*s. There, too, it was not simply a matter of the ulama on one side and the lower classes on the other. A prototype of the popular *tariqah* in this era was the Bayyumiyyah, which was established by Ali al-Bayyumi (1696–1769), a *hadith* scholar and, initially, a follower of one of the branches of the revivalist Khalwatiyyah. The Bayyumiyyah Tariqah made significant departures from the Khalwatiyyah spirit and appealed more directly to the lower classes. Bayyumi's ecstatic form of Sufism was condemned by many of the more conservative ulama, but, at the same time, the shaykh al-Azhar thwarted attempts by those ulama to ban the weekly *tariqah* meetings. In his writings, Bayyumi maintained "the legitimacy of the developing religious counterculture," and they reflect the fact that the popular orders sometimes defended the lower classes.[21]

For most Egyptians, religious life was centered around the activities of daily life. Local teachers and festivals were focal points of attention, and customs were shaped by indigenous traditions as well as by Islamic teachings. The practices of popular Islam were a combination of elements that were believed to be Islamic by the people and usually tolerated by the ulama, even when they appeared to contradict a strict interpretation of the Quran and the Sunnah of the Prophet. It was only in times of crisis or special political oppression that the official institutions attempted to influence the religious life of the masses.

Religious life in Egypt was thus a series of overlapping elements. The ulama establishments, the *tariqah*s, and the local practices all interacted in various ways. In general terms, the Azhar-oriented establishment was conservative, and the *tariqah*s might have supported fundamentalist activism or continuation of the daily routines. Rigorous activism tended to be related to but outside of the religious establishment itself. This pattern of activist, nonestablishment organizations continues throughout the modern history of Islam in Egypt and can be seen in the rise of the Muslim Brotherhood in the twentieth century.

Egypt and the Larger Islamic World

Cairo was a major religious and intellectual crossroads during the eighteenth century, and the cosmopolitan community of visiting scholars and local teachers played an important role in the development and spread of ideas. That role was particularly important in the two key areas of the emergence of Neo-Sufism and the continuing trends in *hadith* scholarship.

Scholars went to Cairo from many parts of the Islamic world, both as students and as pilgrims on their way to Mecca and Medina, and that cosmopolitan group interacted with the local establishment in a variety of ways. Some of the scholars came into conflict with the local conservatives, and others were accepted as a part of the establishment.

The Egyptian scholars played a significant role in the eighteenth-century interest in *hadith* studies. There was a long tradition of *hadith* scholarship in Cairo, and many of the major reference works in *hadith* studies had been compiled by great Egyptian teachers in the late Middle Ages. The work of Ahmad Ibn Hajar al-Asqalani (d. 1449), for example, has been described as "the final summation of the science of *hadith*,"[22] and his commentaries on the major collections of the Traditions were known throughout the Islamic world. Later scholars of the Traditions in Egypt also had international reputations. The name of Zakariya al-Ansari (d. 1520) appears in the chain of transmission of many of the *muhaddith*s of the eighteenth century, and a key figure leading up to the eighteenth-century interest in *hadith* study was Muhammad al-Babili (d. 1666). Al-Babili attracted many students, including some who became the major figures in the emerging fundamentalist mood of the eighteenth century. Those students included the great Hanbali mufti of Damascus, Abu al-Muwahib ibn Abd al-Baqi, and the important Neo-Sufi shaykh in Medina, Ibrahim al-Kurani. Thus, the foundations for *hadith* studies were well laid in Cairo.

During the eighteenth century, the changing economic conditions gave added impetus to Cairene *hadith* scholarship as the revival of commercial activity increased the importance of the merchant classes who patronized the *hadith* scholars. Informal discussion groups provided a place where local scholars could gather together with people outside the religious establishment and with itinerant scholars, and there was a general rise in the standards of religious scholarship and in the methods of critical analysis.[23]

A high point was reached with the work of Muhammad Murtada al-Zabidi (d. 1791), one of the major scholars of his day. He was born in India and studied in many major centers of learning. He studied *hadith* in India with one of the great scholars of the time, Shah Wali Allah al-Dihlawi, and then continued his studies in Yemen, especially in the city of Zabid. After further travel, he settled in Cairo and became one of that city's leading intellectuals. His massive works in many fields brought him widespread fame, and his scholarship in disciplines related to *hadith* study were of great importance in providing a climax to the developments of the period.

Al-Zabidi was not simply a traditionist as he was also active in the redefinition of Sufism. One of his best-known works was a commentary on al-Ghazali's work, which gave added impetus to the movement away from the Ibn al-Arabi tradition within Sufi thought in the direction of formulations more in accord with a stricter style of Islam. Just as al-Zabidi combined Indian and Egyptian traditions of *hadith* scholarship, he also joined together the Neo-Sufism of Shah Wali Allah in India, the Naqshbandiyyah ideas that had developed in both India and the Arabian Peninsula, and the Khalwatiyyah-inspired Neo-Sufism of the eastern Mediterranean.

Egyptian Neo-Sufism in the eighteenth century was the product of many forces, but the most visible element was the Khalwatiyyah tradition as defined by Mustafa al-Bakri. The Khalwatiyyah/Bakriyyah tradition was rigorist in tone and aimed at a strict adherence to the rules of the Quran and the Sunnah. The order's leaders, at least, were involved in a careful study of the *hadith*s, and, in this way, the growth of the order paralleled the intellectual trends of the time. Al-Bakri's students included men who became some of the major *hadith* teachers later in the century. His leading deputy, or *khalifah*, in Egypt was Muhammad ibn Salim al-Hifnawi (d. 1767). Al-Hifnawi taught *hadith* and other subjects in al-Azhar and eventually became shaykh al-Azhar. In addition, he initiated many people into the Khalwatiyyah *Tariqah*. Al-Hifnawi and his fellow students of al-Bakri met students from all over the Islamic world and brought them into the Bakriyyah tradition. However, the relative individualism of the Khalwatiyyah style meant that what emerged was a large cluster of related suborders rather than a single, centrally organized *tariqah*. Included in the list of suborders were the Rahmaniyyah, found in Algeria and Tunisia, and the Tijaniyyah, founded by a student of one of al-Hifnawi's *khalifah*s.

The circle of *hadith* scholars and *tariqah* shaykhs around al-Hifnawi was one that was sought out by many visiting ulama, and it appears to have been influential in shaping their thought. One of the early intellectual leaders of Islamic revivalism in West Africa, Jibril ibn Umar, found his way into the Hifnawi circle while he was in Cairo. This was also true of a major scholar from India, Abd al-Rahman al-Aydarus.

The Bakriyyah was thus an important part of Egyptian Neo-Sufism in the eighteenth century. It was not, however, the only element. Muhammad Murtada al-Zabidi was only one of a long line of scholars that had gone to Cairo from the eastern parts of the Islamic world. Many of those scholars were associated with the revivalist Naqshbandiyyah tradition, which helped to reinforce the reformist currents set in motion by the Khalwatiyyah activity. The Yemeni line of the Naqshbandiyyah was introduced into Egypt by Ahmad al-Banna al-Dimyati (d. 1715). He had studied *hadith* in Mecca and had been initiated into the Naqshbandiyyah order there. Other scholars associated with the Naqshbandiyyah, like al-Zabidi, also helped to present its revivalist ideas to the Egyptian cosmopolitan circles.

A third element in Egyptian Neo-Sufism was the influence of the North African teachers. The most apparent role of the North African ulama in Cairo was as students and visitors who traveled through the city and carried ideas back to their homelands. However, those North Africans may also have made a significant contribution to the nature of Neo-Sufism as it emerged by the end of the century. In North Africa in the fifteenth and sixteenth centuries, Sufism had become effectively organized as popular associations as the veneration of holy men provided a focus for the mobilization of large numbers of people. There was less emphasis on the need for a disciple to follow a long and arduous path and more on the personal attachment to an individual holy man. The great shaykhs and their organizations became an important factor in North African society.

It is possible to say that in the eastern Mediterranean, Sufism tended to be a more individual pursuit while in North Africa it became "collectivized."[24] In the new-style organizations, the validating principle was the special sanctity of the teacher rather than the legitimacy of his *silsilah*, or chain of authorities. Rather than seeking a metaphysical union with a pantheistically defined God, North African Sufis concentrated more intensely on the Prophet. By the eighteenth century, some North African *tariqah* leaders stressed that the purpose of the Sufi devotions was union with the spirit of the Prophet rather than union with God. They claimed validity for their *tariqah* on the basis of permission given to them directly by the Prophet.

North African scholars traveling through Cairo were familiar with those ideas. Although the excesses of "saint worship" were rejected by the Neo-Sufis, the ideas of more effective mass *tariqah* organizations and a less pantheistic orientation for the Sufi path were appealing to the new spirit. By the end of the eighteenth century, Neo-Sufism in Cairo appeared to be combining the more fundamentalist content of the Khalwatiyyah and Naqshbandiyyah traditions with the forms of North African Sufism. This combination was appealing to many and helped to provide the foundations for the activist revivalist orders that emerged early in the nineteenth century.

The Islamic Center: Mecca and Medina

The center of the cosmopolitan world of Muslim scholars and believers is the homeland of Islam, the two cities of Mecca and Medina. Even though the Haramayn (literally, "the two sanctuaries") are on the fringes of the great political units, their centrality is emphasized by the practice of facing Mecca while praying and the requirement of making a pilgrimage to Mecca. During the hajj or pilgrimage, Muslims from all parts of the Islamic world gather. Scholars often stay for relatively long periods, teaching and studying, and some settle permanently. As a result, the Haramayn is a key point in the international exchange of Islamic ideas and inspiration.

The history of the Haramayn in the eighteenth century can be traced on two interacting levels of action. On the one hand, there is the political history of the two cities, which were dominated by local power establishments, and their relations with the Ottoman Empire, of which they were a peripheral part. On the other hand, there is the history of the cosmopolitan scholarly community, which was more directly involved with the broader evolution of Islamic thought and society. At times, the two levels seem to have been separate, and at other times, they have directly influenced each other.

Islam and Local Politics

Because of the distinctive position of the holy cities in the minds of Muslims, their rulers had to have some religious prestige. At the same time, since the days of the Umayyad caliphate, western Arabia had been unable to mobilize sufficient military power to be fully independent for long periods of time. The cities were usually under at least the nominal control of a sovereign from outside the Hijaz, the western section of the Arabian Peninsula. The title of protector or servant of the sanctuaries was taken by those outside rulers, and it was felt that the title added to their prestige. Since the sixteenth century, that role had been filled by Ottoman sultans.

The influence and prestige of the local leaders in the Hijaz set limits to the effectiveness of the control by the outside rulers, and the Ottomans never fully displaced the religious leaders as political controllers in the area. By the eighteenth century, as a part of the trend of decentralization within the empire, the Ottoman position was quite weak, and the situations in Mecca and Medina were different.

Mecca had had a long tradition of virtual political independence within the framework of loose outside control. As early as the tenth century, descendants of the Prophet, called sharifs, had been the controllers of Mecca, and for nearly a thousand years, the leading political figure in the city had been the grand sharif. The family of the early grand sharifs grew over the centuries, and the rival clans that developed within it became a firmly established aristocracy. Although the clans fought among themselves, they were able to keep the office of grand sharif within their local aristocracy. By the eighteenth century, the three major groups competing for power were the Abdallah, Zayd, and Barakat clans.

The Sharifian clans had great religious prestige, but they were primarily political interest groups. Although they were patrons of scholars and writers, they were not often directly involved in scholarly activity, and they opposed ideas and policies that would introduce significant changes in the management of the pilgrimage and in the sociopolitical context of Mecca. As a result, they were usually vigorously conservative in their style of Islam.

The situation in Medina was different as no great dynasty or single family dominated the political scene. There was a sense of city pride and a number of great families, some of whom traced their lineage back to the early Medinese supporters of the Prophet. In political terms, the great families had less power to withstand the control of the outside rulers than did the sharifs of Mecca, so the provincial governor and his garrison played a correspondingly greater role. The major Medinese families were supported by a wide variety of endowments, and they tended to monopolize the administrative positions within the mosques and other sites of religious importance. Although less independent than Mecca, Medina maintained a high degree of local autonomy, and both cities prospered from imperial subsidies and gifts from pious Muslims throughout the world of Islam.

The "establishment" in Medina was not as closed as that in Mecca. Immigrant scholars could settle, and over time, their families would be able to join the dominant oligarchy. As a result, the general style of the Medinese was not as conservative as was the case in Mecca. There was a greater sense of adapting to the changing political framework of the outside rulers and a greater willingness to incorporate newcomers into the structure of local power. The cosmopolitan scholarly community in Medina was often more lively and more directly involved in local affairs. There was also a tendency for scholars to settle in Medina rather than in Mecca.

The Scholarly Community

Mecca and Medina were major centers for study in the eighteenth century. The subjects studied were almost exclusively the basic religious disciplines, but in those, the teachers of the Haramayn had great importance for the whole world of Islam. There, as elsewhere in the Muslim world, scholars of *hadith* and teachers involved in the reorientation of the Sufi tradition had a special prominence, and the interregional communication taking place among the scholars in the Hijaz may have been an important catalyst in the evolution of those ideas. It is clear that study in Mecca and Medina had an impact on the scholars who went for instruction and then returned to their homelands.

At the heart of the cosmopolitan community of scholars in the holy cities was a core group of resident teachers, and they formed a continuing tradition of learning throughout the century. The key figures in that group were connected by close student-teacher ties or were fellow students together. They shared common academic interests and were initiated into the same *tariqah*s. They were not, however, a formally structured organization.

Twelve of the most prominent teachers in the Haramayn from the middle of the seventeenth century to the second half of the eighteenth were major figures in that informal scholarly grouping, and they came from many different backgrounds. Two were born in India, two in Morocco, three came from Kurdish areas in northern Iraq, and five were born in either Mecca or Medina, but only one of those came from a long-established family. However, all were involved in *hadith* scholarship, and all had *tariqah* affiliations with orders that were involved in the development of Neo-Sufism. Each of them was either a student or a teacher of at least three of the rest of the group.

Within the group there was a tendency to go beyond a simple acceptance of the medieval commentaries in *hadith* studies, and the members appear to have encouraged an examination of the earliest sources. As a result, they often rejected the idea that it was necessary to engage in *taqlid* (accepting the conclusions of previous scholars) and instead used their own critical efforts in an analysis of the sources (that is called using *ijtihad*). One example of that emphasis is the stress that at least some of them gave to the study of compilations of *hadith*s that were earlier than the standard collections, which dated from the ninth century and were usually the basis for *hadith* study.

The careful study of the Traditions of the Prophet was a part of a concern that those teachers had for the purifying of society by eliminating practices that were not approved by the Quran or the Sunnah. Students of these men described them with terms like "the Mujaddid [Renewer] of the Haramayn" and the "bearer of the banner of the Sunnah in Medina." Although these men were not militant activists, they were generally more fundamentalist than conservative or adaptationist in style.

That fundamentalist tone is reflected in the type of Sufism these men believed in. Although none of them totally rejected Sufism, they were not involved in the more popular or pantheistic styles of mysticism. The emerging nature of Neo-Sufism is reflected in the changing positions of this group between the mid-seventeenth century and the end of the eighteenth. The great seventeenth-century teacher, Ahmad al-Qushashi (d. 1661), had accepted some of the major theological formulations of Ibn al-Arabi, although he had opposed *tariqah* syncretism—al-Qushashi and his students were primarily associated with *tariqah*s as devotional practices and litanies rather than as social associations. Three generations of students later, scholars within the prominent group of twelve were emphasizing the study of al-Ghazali rather than Ibn al-Arabi, and they were beginning to establish *tariqah*s that were large-scale organizations as well as traditions of devotional practice.

Within the core of the cosmopolitan group of scholars, the main lines of Neo-Sufism were being defined. The Naqshbandiyyah perspective was combined with the North African style of organization to produce the reforming orders of the late eighteenth and early nineteenth centuries. Mustafa al-Bakri, the chief figure in the revivalist Khalwatiyyah, studied *hadith* and other subjects with at least three of those leading Haramayn teachers. In turn, he initiated into the Khalwatiyyah one of the group's Medinese scholars and students, Muhammad ibn Abd al-Karim al-Samman, who later established the Sammaniyyah Tariqah, an order of the activist, Neo-Sufi type.

A similar interaction can be seen in terms of the Indian ulama. A number of the members of the Haramayn group were affiliated with the Naqshbandiyyah through a chain of authorities going back to Ahmad Sirhindi. The major teacher of that line in India during the eighteenth century was Shah Wali Allah al-Dihlawi. Wali Allah studied *hadith* with the Haramayn group and later became one of the most significant teachers in India. One of his students was Muhammad Murtada al-Zabidi, who studied in Arabia with members of the group himself and went on to become one of the leading scholars of *hadith* in the eastern Mediterranean region. Many people in the cosmopolitan Haramayn group later became his students.

The Haramayn cosmopolitan scholarly tradition may not have been the cause of eighteenth-century Islamic revivalism, but it had connections with most such movements in addition to the ties with al-Bakri, Wali Allah, and al-Zabidi. Abd al-Ra'uf al-Sinkili (d. after 1693), an opponent of Sufi excesses in the East Indies, studied with early teachers in the group. Late in the century, the founders of activist Neo-Sufi *tariqah*s like the Tijaniyyah, the Sammaniyyah, the Sanusiyyah, and the Khatmiyyah were associated with the group. Teachers who laid the foundations for the holy war in West Africa and the jihad movement of Ahmad Brelwi in India also had some contacts with this Haramayn tradition. The best known of the movements established by students of those teachers was the rigorously fundamentalist one that was led by Muhammad ibn Abd al-Wahhab, whose followers came to be called the "Wahhabis."

In the eighteenth century, Mecca and Medina were clearly more than places of pilgrimage. They were important centers for the cosmopolitan world of Islamic scholarship, and movements associated with the scholars of the Haramayn were crucial to the development of Neo-Sufism and the revivalism of the time.

Wahhabis: Rigorous Fundamentalism at the Center

The spirit of socio-moral reconstruction reached a peak in the eighteenth century with the fundamentalist movement established by Muhammad ibn Abd al-Wahhab (1703–1792). The followers of this teacher call themselves the Muwahhidun, that is, believers in *tawhid*, but they are more commonly known as the Wahhabis. Because of the movement's general fame and its location at the center of Islam, the Wahhabi movement has come to represent the prototype of rigorous fundamentalism in the modern Islamic experience.

Since the eighteenth century, the term *Wahhabism* has become "a kind of umbrella term—the 'Wahhabi idea'— . . . summed up as a reassertion of monotheism and equality of men combined with varying degrees of reinterpretation of the actual positive legacy of the Islamic tradition for the reconstruction of Muslim society."[25] That "idea" has its clear foundations in the eighteenth-century Islamic experience. Wahhabism built on the existing currents of thought and carried them to their culmination in militant fundamentalism. In this sense, the Muwahhidun were not typical of the eighteenth-century revivalists or the later movements that grew out of their work, but represented the polar end of the spectrum that runs from fundamentalism to open adaptationism and syncretism.

The career of Muhammad ibn Abd al-Wahhab and his works combine the major themes of the fundamentalist style of eighteenth-century Islam. He was born in central Arabia to a family of teachers attached to the Hanbali school. He was trained in the most strict of the Sunni schools of law and then went to Mecca and Medina for more education. In the Haramayn, his major teachers included Muhammad Hayat al-Sindi, one of the key figures in the cosmopolitan revivalist group. He received rigorous training in the study of *hadith* and was frequently reminded of the gap between the ideal community that was described by the traditions and the society that he saw around him.

After further travels, he returned to his homeland, the Najd region in central Arabia. There he began to preach, calling upon the people to abandon the practices of popular religion and adhere strictly to the Quran and the Sunnah. For some time he met with opposition, but eventually one of the local chieftains, Muhammad ibn Saud of Dariyah, accepted his call. The alliance that was formed between the fundamentalist teacher and the warrior chief produced a militant Islamic state, and it expanded rapidly in the Arabian Peninsula. The momentum created by the combination of religious enthusiasm and military skill was maintained after the deaths of the original leaders. The Saudi-Wahhabi forces raided the Shiʿi holy cities in southern Iraq in 1802 and captured Mecca in 1803, and the first decade of the nineteenth century was the high point of the first Saudi state. The Ottoman leaders became concerned about the new challenge to their authority and sent the newly created Egyptian army against the Saudis. In the war that ensued, there was a direct conflict between forces created by the new Westernizing adaptations of rulers, which were characteristic of the nineteenth century, and forces created by the dynamism of eighteenth-century Islamic revivalism. The Saudi-Wahhabi forces were defeated, and by 1818, the first Saudi state had been brought to an end. However, the foundations had been laid for the twentieth-century emergence of a successor fundamentalist state.

Basic Positions

The teachings of Muhammad ibn Abd al-Wahhab reflect both the general traditional themes of the Muslim fundamentalists and the more specific concerns arising out of the eighteenth-century experience. He carried the reinterpretation of the Sufi tradition to a logical fundamentalist conclusion and vigorously rejected the whole structure of the Sufi devotional practices as being unwholesome innovations. He proclaimed that veneration for any human, however saintly, constituted *shirk* or polytheism. Anyone who participated in such practices was declared an unbeliever and subject to the death penalty for leaving Islam. In the absoluteness of his rejection of Sufism, he went beyond virtually all other Muslim fundamentalists—both those who had preceded him and those who succeeded him in later generations. However, the example of the Wahhabi movement gave an added impetus to the element of eighteenth-century socio-moral reconstructionism that objected to the syncretistic tone of later medieval Sufism.

Muhammad ibn Abd al-Wahhab replaced the pantheistic style of Sufi theology with a renewed emphasis on the interpretation of *tawhid*, the oneness of God, that stressed God's transcendence. In that interpretation, there was emphasis on strict obedience to the word of God and on the full responsibility of the individual believer. The "Sufi path" was to be accepted only if it meant a striving to purify the heart from vices and sin in order to obey more fully the commands of God.[26]

In that context, it was the obligation of the believer to think for himself, rather than accept blindly the words of others. Muhammad ibn Abd al-Wahhab wrote that men should examine their condition and the condition of the people of the age who simply took their faith from their fathers and borrowed prevailing local customs. He reminded his readers that it would do them no good if, after death, they told the questioning angels, "I heard the people saying something, so I said it, too."[27]

Implicit in that position is a rejection of the unquestioning acceptance of the medieval scholarly authorities, and blind *taqlid* or imitation was rejected in examining the importance of the Quran and the Sunnah. The position of the shaykh and his followers was that it was not obligatory for any Muslim to follow any persons in their faith except the Prophet himself. The Quran and the Sunnah were the two fundamental and binding sources for Islamic faith and law, and anything beyond those two sources was binding only insofar as it reflected the clear meaning of the revelation.

The followers of Muhammad ibn Abd al-Wahhab denied that that position meant a rejection of the works of the earlier teachers, but they did object to placing such works on the same level as the Quran and the Sunnah in being required guides for the believer. In this way, the Wahhabi position insisted on the right of an informed independent analysis of the fundamental sources of the faith (*ijtihad*). Although they did not feel that total *ijtihad* was necessary, they believed that it was of continuing importance in special cases. In this recognition of *ijtihad,* the movement reflected concerns that were a part of traditional fundamentalism and eighteenth-century socio-moral reconstructionism, and that recognition was one of the features that distinguished the movement from the conservative style of Islam.

Impact of Wahhabism

In addition to laying the foundations for the twentieth-century Kingdom of Saudi Arabia, the eighteenth-century Wahhabi movement had a broad impact. It provided a striking example at the center of the Islamic world of rigorous fundamentalism in practice, and by its success, the movement was able to show Muslims from other areas that militant purification was possible. In this way, it gave added emphasis to the eighteenth-century mood of socio-moral reconstruction along strictly Islamic lines.

Some caution must be exercised, however, in assessing the direct impact of Wahhabism. It has been common at times to assert that any teacher who happened to go to Arabia in the eighteenth century and who returned to his home full of fundamentalist enthusiasm was somehow influenced by the Wahhabis. That assertion is clearly an underestimation of the role of the scholars of the Haramayn, and it ignores the broader Islamic trends of the century. It is worth noting, for example, that many of the revivalist movements that had emerged by the end of the century did so in the framework of Neo-Sufi thought and organization rather than by following the Wahhabi attitude.

It is clear, even with those reservations, that Wahhabism was a significant element in the Islamic world, and its example was important at the time. The movement's ideas were viewed favorably by a reformist Moroccan sultan, Mawlay Suleyman, and they helped him define the bases for his opposition to Sufi practices. Other contemporaries were also directly affected. In the long run, the teachings and writings of Muhammad ibn Abd al-Wahhab and his followers provided an inspiration for twentieth-century Muslim thinkers, particularly in the movement that came to be called the Salafiyyah. In those later movements, the ideal of a comprehensive program of social and political fundamentalism and a rigorous opposition to Sufism were fully developed and the debt to the Wahhabis acknowledged. In this way, the Wahhabi movement can be seen as a prototype of the rigorous fundamentalism that is a part of the twentieth-century Islamic experience.

Islam in the Indian Ocean Region

Modern scholarship often makes distinctions between arbitrarily defined regions and calls them the Middle East, South Asia, and Southeast Asia. Although such distinctions are a convenience for some kinds of analysis, they create boundaries that did not exist within the eighteenth-century Islamic world. The whole Indian Ocean region was, especially in terms of the cosmopolitan ulama groups, a loosely integrated unit. Trade, political contacts, and wandering scholars provided the means for a significant interaction among the various parts of the region. Thus, although there were special local conditions that shaped the Islamic experience, it is important to keep the broader regional networks in mind.

The largest single unit within the region was the Moghul Empire, but since it was a land-based imperial system, it did not dominate the region in political terms. Groupings of small sultanates and city-states provided the political context for much of the region, and important clusters of them were in the islands and peninsulas of Southeast Asia, the southern Arabian Peninsula, and along the East African coast. Those groups interacted along the sea-lanes, and by the eighteenth century, there was a new element of growing importance that also tended to be based on the oceanic lines of communication. That new element was the development of the great European trading companies, which had the military support of the emerging Western imperial systems. European powers had become a factor in the Indian Ocean region when the Portuguese intruded during the fifteenth and sixteenth centuries, but that Portuguese challenge had been successfully contained. During the eighteenth century, it was the British, French, and Dutch who were the growing European commercial and military forces in the region.

Within the Islamic community, the major lines of communication were outside of the state systems themselves. There was a constant movement of scholars throughout the region, following the lines of trade. One factor was the travel to and from Mecca and Medina, which brought Muslims from South and Southeast Asia to the central Islamic lands. In the opposite direction, there was a movement of scholar-missionaries from Arabia and India to the more removed sections of the region. Within this framework, there were great ulama and merchant families that maintained a network of contacts throughout the region.

One of the underlying dynamics of eighteenth-century history was the gradual fragmentation of the region. Significant regional interaction continued long after the end of the century, but it was more restricted than it had been earlier. An important factor in this change was the gradual consolidation of influence and then control by the European powers. As the European economic "world system" became more important, the lines of local trade were disrupted, and the older economic networks that had supported the Islamic interaction were replaced by networks that were Europe oriented.

These broad changes produced a climate in which the conservative style of Islam was weakened. In reaction to the changing circumstances, the other Islamic styles assumed an increasing importance. Fundamentalist and adaptationist styles interacted, and in some cases, there was also a tendency for withdrawal into a more individualized, passive Islam. That latter trend was sometimes encouraged by the adaptationists, who began to accept some of the secularizing implications of the Western ideas.

Moghul India and Shah Wali Allah

During the eighteenth century, the Moghul Empire collapsed as an effective system of political control in India. The last years of the reign of Aurangzeb were filled with revolts, and following his death in 1707, wars of succession and the rise of local and provincial powers brought an end to the politico-military unity that had been created by Moghul rule. Hindu and Sikh princes competed with local Muslim commanders and Afghan and Persian invaders for dominance within the subcontinent, but no single local power was able to establish a long-lasting position of strength. In the long run, a foreign power, Great Britain, assumed control over much of India, but during the eighteenth century, the British were simply one of a large number of competitors. Their ultimate victory would not have been clear to many, if any, informed observers of the time.

The Muslim response to the changing situation was dominated by the career and works of Shah Wali Allah al-Dihlawi (1702–1762), in whom one can see the interaction of the broader themes of eighteenth-century Islamic history with the special local conditions in India. Wali Allah represents an important climax point for Indian Islam. On the one hand, his career was a high point in the evolution of Islam that had been set in motion by the rise of the Moghuls and the emergence of Naqshbandiyyah revivalism, and on the other hand, his work provided the foundation for virtually every major Muslim movement in India since that time.

Like other eighteenth-century Islamic revivalists, Wali Allah was not primarily concerned with the challenge of the modernizing West, and his reformism arose out of the interaction between the changing local conditions and the Islamic dimension. In that way, the starting point for Islamic thought in modern India was inspired more by "indigenous" factors than by "foreign" ones. This quality of having arisen from within the Islamic tradition rather than simply being a reaction to the modern West gives a special character to Islamic revivalism in the context of modern history.

Two great issues set the framework for Wali Allah's work: the decline of the Muslim community as a whole in India and the disunity and conflict within that community. In dealing with the first issue, Wali Allah was a vigorous fundamentalist and reaffirmed the authenticity of the Islamic revelation. However, in dealing with disputes among Muslims, his goal appears to have been one of reconciliation, and his major formulations attempted to create positions that could unify Muslims holding diverse views.

Wali Allah mistrusted syncretistic trends, and, in that, he continued the Naqshbandiyyah opposition to tolerant religious universalism. He was in a direct line from Ahmad Sirhindi in his opposition to compromises with non-Islamic practices, and he attacked the rulers for not imposing punishments in accord with Islamic law and accused the local Sufi teachers of encouraging idolatry. In addressing all classes of Muslims he said, "O children of Adam, you have wrecked your morals, made your living miserable and drifted into the care of Satan. . . . You have adopted such vicious customs as have corrupted true faith. . . . You behave and indulge in frivolous acts like the ignorant communities."[28]

Wali Allah did not organize a formal movement or create a special association. The structures that he developed were schools for instruction, through which he hoped to provide the basis for a revitalization of Islamic thought and, by this means, restore the Islamic position within India. He himself looked to various Muslim commanders to lead the military struggle. When those failed, his successors began to create more directly politico-military organizations. Thus, the militant activism of the fundamentalists in the early nineteenth century followed Wali Allah's ideas but went beyond his own type of organizational activity.

In dealing with the problem of Muslim disunity, Wali Allah utilized many of the major eighteenth-century themes. His style, in terms of interpretation, was fundamentalist, but his goal was reconciliation, not condemnation. Wali Allah was active in the development of Neo-Sufi ideas. The Naqshbandiyyah teachings of Ahmad Sirhindi had created a school of thought that opposed the ideas of Ibn al-Arabi, and the main disagreement centered on the meaning of the oneness of God. Ibn al-Arabi's relatively pantheistic idea of the unity of being (wahdat al-wujud) had been opposed by Sirhindi, who had proposed the idea of unity in the manifestations of God (wahdat al-shuhud). That idea emphasized God's transcendence rather than the mystic unity of God and the material universe. In the seventeenth century, those positions had become identified with political factions and had been the slogans for two different concepts of the empire. A war of succession to the Moghul throne that began in 1657 had pitted two brothers against each other, with one representing the syncretistic spirit of the earlier sultan, Akbar, and the other, the fundamentalist reaction of Ahmad Sirhindi. Aurangzeb, the latter, had won, and the tone of Moghul policy had become more fundamentalist.

In the context of the collapse of Muslim political unity, it was important to reconcile the two positions. Wali Allah argued persuasively that the two concepts were basically different metaphors describing the same underlying reality. Through this line of thought, the broader range of Sufi thought in India was reintegrated into a single intellectual structure, and the extremes of pantheistic speculation were reduced. At the same time, Wali Allah worked to have tariqah practices conform more closely to the prescriptions of the Quran and the Sunnah. "To check the spiritual decadence of Islam in his age, he completed the work begun by Shaykh Ahmad Sirhindi, the channelling of the streams of Sufi spiritual heritage into traditional Islam. This also involved a composition of Sufism's internal differences of practice, and a synthetic merging together of the various Sufi disciplines of India into one."[29]

That merging was an important part of the development of Neo-Sufism in the eighteenth century. Wali Allah carried forward the reinterpretation of the teachings of Ibn al-Arabi and made it possible to reject pantheistic extremes without fully rejecting Sufism. In his preaching on moral rectitude, he laid the foundation for the more militant Neo-Sufi groups, and his role was similar to that of Mustafa al-Bakri. It is, in fact, worth noting that Wali Allah and Mustafa al-Bakri shared at least one teacher; they both studied with Abdallah ibn Salim al-Basri, one of the members of the revivalist scholarly group in the Haramayn.

The eighteenth-century emphasis on the study of *hadith* is also reflected in the work of Wali Allah. His *hadith* studies, like his interpretations of Sufism, show his dual concern with reconciling divisions within the Muslim community and bringing Islamic practice more into line with the Islamic ideal.

One of the lines of division was the separation of the Sunni Muslims into the different schools of law. Although there was mutual recognition among the scholars in the different schools, the differing interpretations sometimes led to vigorous disputes. In his work, Wali Allah subordinated the study of law to the discipline of *hadith* studies. Like Muhammad ibn Abd al-Wahhab, Wali Allah rejected the practice of *taqlid* if it meant blind adherence to the teachers within the law schools' traditions. Instead, he believed that *ijtihad* was necessary, and the only two unquestioned sources for Islamic law, according to that position, are the Quran and the Sunnah. Thus, the study of the traditions takes precedence over imitation of the earlier jurists' writings. That belief was made clear when Wali Allah was once asked what was his *madhhab* or legal school. He replied, "I try my best to combine all the points of agreement in all the schools, and in matters of variance I adhere to what is proved by the genuine *hadith*—which, thank God, I can do."[30]

Wali Allah is an important figure in the development of the attitude toward the study of the *hadiths*. One aspect of the Naqshbandiyyah revival was the development of a rigorist tradition in the study of *hadith* that was associated with Abd al-Haqq al-Dihlawi (1551–1642), who had introduced new methods of *hadith* transmission and popularized *hadith* study. Wali Allah developed ties with that tradition and then studied with some of the major revivalist *muhaddith*s in Mecca and Medina. Like other scholars in those groups, Wali Allah did not accept the standard ninth-century *hadith* collections as infallible or not open to question and analysis.

Wali Allah's position is shown not only in his general acceptance of the idea of the continuing validity of *ijtihad* but also in the *hadith* material that he studied. Like some of his teachers and fellow students in Mecca and Medina, he gave preference in his *hadith* analysis to the *hadith* collections that were earlier than the standard ninth-century compilations. In doing so, they gave special precedence to the *Muwatta* of Malik ibn Anas, the founder of the Maliki law school. Wali Allah's position that Malik's work was the foundation of the science of *hadith* is similar to the statement of a West African who studied and taught *hadith* in Medina a little later. That scholar called the *Muwatta* the "first source" and the most widely used of the ninth-century collections the "second source."[31]

The line of interaction between the *hadith* studies led by Wali Allah in India and those conducted by the scholars in Mecca and Medina continued throughout the century. Muhammad Murtada el-Zabidi, one of the leading *hadith* scholars in the later part of the century, was a student of Wali Allah before settling in Egypt. Wali Allah also had an important impact on the later development of Islam in India. His work in reformulating Islam on a basis broader than that of the traditional schools of thought made possible a wider range of adaptation than the more strict fundamentalism of the Wahhabis. His influence may have been an important factor in the relatively early development in India of a modernist adaptationism that was Islamic in its orientation. He thus inspired both fundamentalism and adaptation within later Indian Islam.

The Transformation of Southeast Asia

The islands and peninsulas of Southeast Asia are at the eastern periphery of the Indian Ocean region within the Islamic world, and the Islamic experience in the area is distinctive and clearly influenced by local conditions. However, despite the distance to the central Islamic lands, the major trends of eighteenth-century Islam had an impact on the Southeast Asian Muslim communities.

From the perspective of modern history, a key element in the eighteenth-century experience was the development of European imperialism. However, it is possible to miss significant aspects of the Islamic experience in the area if one concentrates on the activities of the Dutch East India Company and the other European groups. The ultimate domination of the area by the Dutch, British, and French was not yet evident during the eighteenth century. Modern Western historians sometimes find it convenient to think of non-Western societies in the eighteenth century as stagnant, crumbling structures, falling almost without effective resistance in the face of the European expansion. But even in Southeast Asia, where the local states were quite small compared with the Ottoman or Moghul imperial systems, that assumption is not a very accurate one.

The general picture is probably more correctly presented by a Dutch historian, J. C. van Leur, who has noted that the eighteenth century "did not know any superior Occident, nor any self-isolating Orient no longer progressing with it. It knew a mighty East, a rich fabric of a strong, broad weave with a more fragile Western warp thread inserted in it at broad intervals."[32] There were a number of important factors that interacted. Clearly, there was a "Western thread," but there were also local elements whose evolution was not governed simply by the European encroachment. This discussion of the Islamic history of Southeast Asia in the eighteenth century will focus on the experience of the territories within modern Indonesia.

At the beginning of the eighteenth century, there were a large number of smaller states competing for power as the coming of Islam in the preceding centuries had provided the foundations for sultanates that were scattered throughout the islands. In addition, European forts and trading centers had been established. The Portuguese had been a factor since the sixteenth century, when they had conquered Malacca, a key commercial and military center. However, by the eighteenth century, the major European power was the Dutch East India Company, which had built a number of settlements, especially on the island of Java. Dutch naval power and commercial activity were an important part of the shifting scene.

Islam was firmly established in the islands although it was not universal, and Indonesian Islam exhibited distinctive characteristics. During the long centuries of the introduction and spread of Islam throughout the islands, its propagators had made significant adaptations to the local conditions. It had been introduced by merchants and itinerant teachers who had been willing to take on at least some of the coloring of the local religious customs. The pre-Islamic culture had been strongly influenced by Hinduism and Buddhism, which meant that the more pantheistic styles of Islam had the greatest success. As the older monarchies had begun to convert to Islam, they, too, had maintained forms and moods that reflected the Hindu past. Therefore, Indonesian Islam was distinctively adaptationist.

That Islamic experience was challenged in the seventeenth and eighteenth centuries on two fronts. One was the growing power of the Dutch, and the other was the development of a fundamentalist style of Islam. Those factors operating together helped to shape the form taken by Indonesian Islam in the nineteenth and twentieth centuries.

The expansion of Dutch control in Indonesia was gradual. Although there was some increase in the amount of land that was under the direct control of the Dutch, the primary method of expansion was to exert influence on and then to dominate the existing states. In this way, the Dutch controlled most of the sultans and other local rulers by the end of the eighteenth century. Although some local rulers fought the Dutch expansion, at times successfully, the traditionally political institutions were increasingly unable to resist effectively. Dutch commercial and military power was gradually replacing adaptationist Islam as the basis for the ability of the old-style monarchies to remain in existence.

The form and context of the local Indonesian states were very different from those of the Ottoman Empire. There was, however, a general similarity in that the adaptationism of the rulers became identified with the expansion of Western ideas. Opposition to this identification often took the form of fundamentalist Islam, and it was the nonadaptationist style that assumed the duty of preserving an authentic identity. "If colonialism created the conditions in which an oppositional, identity-preserving, willed Islam could and did flourish, scripturalism [i.e., fundamentalism] . . . provided the content of such an Islam."[33]

The emergence of fundamentalism was not simply the product of Dutch expansion as it also evolved within the context of Indonesian Islam as the area interacted with the broader Islamic world. Themes and interactions similar to, and sometimes influenced by, those found elsewhere can be seen in the experience of Indonesia at this time.

The theological foundations for the adaptationist mysticism of Indonesian Islam were the ideas of Ibn al-Arabi and similar Sufi writers. By the mid-seventeenth century, some Indonesian ulama had become convinced that the pantheism of that Sufism was not in accord with the Quran and the Sunnah, and the attack on that style of mysticism had received a strong impetus when a scholar from India arrived in the sultanate of Atjeh in Sumatra. That teacher, Nur al-Din al-Raniri (who stayed in Atjeh from 1637 to 1644) had strongly opposed the implications of the idea of *wahdat al-wujud* ("unity of being") as presented by Ibn al-Arabi. In his fundamentalist attack, he had been supported by the sultan, and he had an impact on later Indonesian Islam.

Al-Raniri's theme had been carried on by an Indonesian scholar named Abd al-Ra'uf al-Sinkili (d. sometime after 1693). That scholar had studied for nineteen years in Arabia, where he had been a student of Ahmad al-Qushashi and Ibrahim al-Kurani, two figures in the Haramayn revivalist group. Although he had not been as extreme in his polemics as al-Raniri, he had worked diligently to eliminate the extremes of pantheistic mysticism. He had returned to Indonesia with the permission of his Medinese teachers to propagate the Shattariyyah Tariqah with devotional practices that were more in accord with a fundamentalist style of Islam. His studies and translations became major works in the literature of the more strict Muslims in Indonesia.

The positions of al-Raniri and al-Sinkili represent a withdrawal from the kind of Sufism that had developed as a result of the adaptationism on the local level. That withdrawal was also a movement away from the theological positions of Ibn al-Arabi and often entailed a direct attack on his ideas, which reflects the general development of Neo-Sufism in the general Islamic world.

In the eighteenth century, others among the best-known ulama continued that position, reflecting the later stages of Neo-Sufism in the central Islamic lands. In Sumatra, that continuation is visible in the works of Shihab al-Din ibn Abdallah Muhammad and his son, Muhammad. "Shihabuddin's aim was to criticize current excesses in the practice of mysticism,"[34] and one vehicle he used was to attack the ideas of *wahdat al-wujud* and to reemphasize the transcendence-oriented meaning of the doctrine of *tawhid*. His son was affiliated with a Neo-Sufi *tariqah* that found its way to Indonesia in the second half of the eighteenth century, the Sammaniyyah, which had been established by Muhammad ibn Abd al-Karim al-Samman, the student of Mustafa al-Bakri. Muhammad ibn Shihab al-Din prepared a Malay translation of a life of al-Samman and aided in the spread of this new type of *tariqah*.

The major propagator of the Sammaniyyah Tariqah was Abd al-Samad al-Palimbani, who lived for a long time as a student and teacher in Mecca. His best-known work was a translation of the writings of al-Ghazali, which reflects the interest in the Sufi theologian's work in Neo-Sufism. Al-Palimbani also wrote a summary of some lectures that were given in Mecca in 1763 by Ahmad al-Damanhuri, an Egyptian scholar who claimed, like Shah Wali Allah, to be proficient in all the law schools, judging on the basis of tradition rather than on simple imitation of earlier scholars. Another work dealt with holy war and urged believers to combat infidels. This last treatise inspired writings that circulated during holy wars against the Dutch in the nineteenth and twentieth centuries.

Through the works of these teachers and others like them, the foundations of the modern Islamic experience in Indonesia were built. As European powers came increasingly to dominate the area, this more fundamentalist style of Islam often provided the rationale for resistance. Opposition was not usually organized in the traditional courts of the old rulers as they tended to adapt to the changing circumstances and became client-states and part of the colonial ruling system. As a result, activist Islam tended to take the form of non-state associations, and through this type of organization, large numbers of people could be mobilized. Large-scale resistance also did not arise out of the popular religious practices of the villagers. Only when the population was inspired by a more fundamentalist rationale could they be aroused to action. The potential division between state-oriented, Western-influenced leadership and fundamentalist Islam that began to emerge in the eighteenth century is a continuing feature in the Islamic history of Southeast Asia.

South Arabia: A Linking Area

The small states and communities of the southern and eastern shores of the Arabian Peninsula were an important focal point in the linking together of the Islamic regions of the Indian Ocean basin as Muslim scholars and merchants from this area moved throughout the region and provided an important means for tying the scattered parts of the Indian Ocean basin together. Those scholars and merchants also connected those Muslim communities to the broader Islamic world.

The cities and towns of Yemen and the Hadramaut were natural stopping points for pilgrims coming from the east and south, and students often stopped and studied with the local ulama on their way to or from Mecca and Medina. The ports were also convenient focal points in the pattern of trade, and merchants and ulama from these areas traveled widely, taking with them their goods and ideas. These itinerants from the southern part of Arabia were a common part of Islamic life throughout the Indian Ocean basin. They helped to spread Islam, and they also established branches of their families in many areas.

During the eighteenth century, there were opportunities for local political forces and economic groups to expand their influence. In the sixteenth century, Portuguese naval power had disrupted the old political and economic networks by controlling the key harbor locations and being a major force. However, by the eighteenth century, the Muslim rulers had been able to defeat the Portuguese and to reassert local control. Although other European powers were beginning to enter the area, they were still not a dominant force, and the British and the French appeared often as potential allies as well as enemies. The British, for example, cooperated with Persian forces in driving the Portuguese out of Hormuz at the mouth of the Persian Gulf.

Local rulers were able to maintain a high degree of independence, and in some cases, they expanded the areas under their control. In southern Arabia there were two states with distinctive Islamic traditions. In Yemen, the Zaydi form of Shi'i Islam had been established in medieval times. A line of Zaydi imams led the community, sometimes as an independent state and sometimes under the overlordship of an outside power. There was a long history of Ottoman attempts to establish power over the imams of Yemen, which continued throughout the eighteenth century. However, in the context of Ottoman decentralization, the imams were largely in control.

The Zaydis were primarily the mountain and highland peoples, and the majority of the population in the coastal plains and lowland areas was Sunni and affiliated with the Shafi'i law school. The two groups both competed and cooperated. In the cities of the plains, a tradition of respected scholarship developed, which was especially centered in the mosques of Zabid and the surrounding areas. During the eighteenth century, there was a general fluctuation in the areas under the control of the imam and the areas that were on the fringes of the control of the Ottoman governors and the Meccan sharifs.

The other distinctive political context was in Oman. The Ibadi branch of the Kharijite movement had been firmly established in Oman early in Islamic history, and like the Zaydis in Yemen, the Ibadis had alternated through the centuries between independence and some type of external control. The Ibadi community was traditionally led by an elected imam. During the sixteenth century, the Portuguese established forts along the Omani coast and were a dominant force, but the Ibadi imams of the seventeenth century drove the Portuguese out and began a significant military and commercial expansion along the East African coast. In the middle of the eighteenth century, Oman was threatened by invasion from Iran but overcame that threat under the leadership of Imam Ahmad ibn Said, who turned the scattered Omani-influenced territories into a flourishing sea-based empire. He founded the Bu Said dynasty, which has ruled Oman since that time. After the death of his son and successor, the Bu Said rulers ceased using the title of imam and generally were known as sayyids or sultans.

The Bu Said dynastic state had religious prestige because of its ties to the Ibadi tradition, but it was not an elective imamate of the style most in accord with Ibadi beliefs. As a result, from time to time, Ibadi groups would elect an imam, and the more fundamentalist groups would challenge the dynastic state. During the eighteenth century, the sultanate faced a growing challenge from Wahhabi expansion, and there were problems in dealing with the increasing power of the European states in the Indian Ocean. The Omani sultans solved these difficulties by adapting to the changing conditions. In 1798, the sultan signed a treaty with Great Britain, which granted the British an exclusive role in Omani foreign relations in exchange for British protection and support for the dynasty. This arrangement preserved the sultanate and is the basis for the modern history of Oman.

Along the rest of the Arabian coast, from Yemen in the southwest to Kuwait in the northeast, the eighteenth century was the time when the modern states emerged as distinct political entities. Between Yemen and

Oman, a cluster of small princedoms and city-states led by people who were considered saints emerged. In 1732, the territory around Aden and Lahej became independent from the control of the imam of Yemen. This feat was accomplished by the founder of the long-lasting Abdali dynasty of Lahej. Similarly, in the Persian/Arab Gulf coasts of the peninsula, leaders of migrating tribal groups established a long chain of city-states, which were dominated by aristocratic clans. The current ruling families of Kuwait, Qatar, Bahrain, and many of the constituent parts of the United Arab Emirates emerged at that time. Like Oman, most of these states established special relations with Great Britain, which helped to ensure dynastic continuity and, through the local autonomy allowed by the arrangements, to insulate the areas from many of the developments of modern Middle Eastern history. As a result, these states entered the era of their independence in the last third of the twentieth century with social and political institutions that were still fundamentally similar to those that were created in the eighteenth century.

The relatively parochial political developments should not obscure the important role of the cosmopolitan community of scholars of southern Arabia. In some ways, the high degree of local autonomy made it possible for ulama and merchants to roam freely while maintaining ties with their homelands, and the great religious families of Yemen and the Hadramaut in particular established branches in many areas. A good example is the experience of the Aydarus family, one of a number of families that developed a reputation for both piety and scholarship. The family was Sufi but avoided identification with the more ecstatic and pantheistic styles—the founder of the family in the fifteenth century, for example, had studied the teachings of al-Ghazali. The family was supported by pious endowments in their original home of Tarim. Abu Bakr al-Aydarus (d. 1508) had moved to Aden, where he had established a branch of the family and had become the "patron saint" of the city. During the sixteenth century, a number of family members had settled in India, where they became wealthy scholars and influential religious teachers in the palaces and courts. By the eighteenth century, there were prominent branches of the family all the way from the cities of East Africa to the islands of Southeast Asia, and children in the family moved freely from one area to another in search of education and employment.

The Aydarus family provided one of the more remarkable itinerant scholars of the eighteenth century, Abd al-Rahman ibn Mustafa al-Aydarus (1723–1778). He was born in South Arabia and studied and traveled widely in India, living there for ten years. He traveled extensively in the eastern Mediterranean regions and settled in Egypt, and he studied with many of the major teachers in the revivalist group in Mecca and Medina and was an active scholar in the Naqshbandiyyah. His students included some of the leading figures in late-eighteenth-century Neo-Sufism, and he may well have been an important link among those scholars. Through him, for example, one can see a connection between the great Naqshbandiyyah family in

Syria, the Muradis, and the Khalwatiyyah students of Mustafa al-Bakri in Egypt such as Muhammad al-Hifnawi.

In the career of Abd al-Rahman al-Aydarus, one has a microcosm of the role of the southern Arabian scholars in the eighteenth century. They were links that brought together scholars and ideas from many parts of the Islamic world. The schools of Zabid flourished during this period, and education there had an impact. Muhammad Murtada al-Zabidi, for example, felt that his instruction in Zabid was of such importance that he often referred to himself as "al-Zabidi" (i.e., a person from Zabid) even though he was born in India. The history of South Arabia in the eighteenth century thus emphasizes the importance of that era as a foundation for modern history and shows the interconnected and cosmopolitan nature of the eighteenth-century Islamic world.

Islamic Africa in the Eighteenth Century

Another great region of interaction within the eighteenth-century Islamic world was Muslim Africa. Like the Indian Ocean basin, this was a vast area with distinctive local conditions, and it was involved in a broad, regional network of exchange. The East African coast was part of the Indian Ocean network, and it was tied to the rest of the Islamic world through southern Arabia. The rest of Muslim Africa had a different orientation. The major lines of interaction spread in a great oval. There was the line across the North African coast and the north-south lines to the sub-Saharan Sudanic areas. There was also by the eighteenth century the beginnings of significant east-west travel along the pilgrim routes stretching through the savanna areas just south of the desert. A focal point in this network was Egypt, through which most African Muslim scholars passed on pilgrimage and to which many went for study. The movement of scholars and ideas within this large oval made the area a special, interconnected region with diverse local conditions.

Within the area, there were many major developments that were conditioned by local circumstances. Along the Mediterranean coast, the Muslim communities had a long tradition of adherence to the faith, and in that area, the eighteenth century was a time of further evolution of long-standing institutions and customs. In the southern half of the oval, Islam had not been as firmly established, and the expansion and consolidation of Islam were important factors. However, despite these differences, there was much mutual interaction, and the developments in the older Islamic areas influenced and inspired trends in the newer Islamic areas.

Ottoman North Africa

During the sixteenth century, Ottoman control had extended to the coastal regions of North Africa in the areas of modern Libya, Tunisia, and Algeria, but by the eighteenth century, the provincial garrisons had assumed a significant degree of autonomous control. However, the sultan in

Istanbul continued to have some influence. "Even on the distant borders of the Maghreb the sultan exercised sufficient political control throughout most of the eighteenth century to maintain the integrity of the Empire in this tumultuous zone. What disorganized the eighteenth century politics of the Ottoman frontier in the western Mediterranean was the rise of the modern western nation state and not the actions of the Maghreb corsair communities."[35]

The European challenge to the Islamic communities of North Africa was not, in the eighteenth century, a threat in ideological terms. It was, rather, a continuation of the long politico-military struggle for control in the western Mediterranean, and the main lines of that conflict had long been in terms of military power. In this context, the role of Islam had been and remained one of helping to mobilize the local forces to oppose European military expansion. In the eighteenth century, the new element was the growing economic involvement of Europe, which helped to alter the structure of local power but was not yet a major challenge to Islam as a faith.

Operating within the context of both victories and defeats, the main lines of the Islamic development were primarily inspired locally. The most important feature of Islamic life was the development of the Sufi *tariqahs* and their role in society. There was no dramatic break with the past, but orders with a more Neo-Sufi orientation were emerging by the end of the eighteenth century.

These general movements were part of an assertion of local identity in Islamic terms, not only against European forces but also against the ruling military elite, which was primarily recruited outside of the area. The movement took different forms in Libya, Tunisia, and Algeria. The basic social framework included the foreign military elite, local ulama and Sufi saints, and the great tribal organizations. In each of the three areas, the interaction took a different form.

In Libya, the Karamanli family created a dynasty within the military elite that lasted from 1711 until 1835. Its center was in Tripoli where the local religious establishment was small and relatively weak. There were resident teachers that traveling ulama would meet and mention in their accounts, but the strongest local forces were the tribes. Ottoman control beyond the coastal cities was limited, and the Karamanli leaders faced frequent resistance from the various tribes. Religion did not provide a significant force for local mobilization or organization until the nineteenth century, when the Sanusiyyah Tariqah was established in the country.

The situation was significantly different in Tunisia. There, an ulama elite dominated the religious scene, and there were important Islamic institutions under their control. The city of al-Qayrawan had been a center of Islamic learning from the days of the first Muslim conquests, and although its prestige and prosperity had declined by the eighteenth century, it was still in many ways the leading Islamic center in the country and a place scholars went to from many parts of the Muslim world. There were also judgeships and other religious posts, many of which were centered in Tunis, the largest city.

In political terms, Tunis and the surrounding areas came under the control of a dynasty of Ottoman commanders established in 1705 by Husayn ibn Ali (d. 1740). In contrast to other military elites in the area, the Husaynid dynasty aided in the gradual assimilation of the Turkish troops, and "by the beginning of the nineteenth century the process was complete and the Husainid dynasty had become a Tunisian dynasty."[36] An important part of this process was the interaction of the local Tunisian religious establishment with the foreign military class.

The Tunisian ulama were the most prominent spokesmen for the general population, and the affiliation that was of greatest importance was not membership in a Sufi order but adherence to the Maliki law school. The official school of the Ottoman Empire was the Hanafi, and there was a history of tension between the local Maliki establishment and non-Tunisian Hanafi appointees to religious posts. By the eighteenth century, support for the Maliki institutions had become a symbol of the assertion of a special local identity. The Husaynids were able to win the support of the Maliki establishment by patronage and gradually reduced the antagonism between the adherents of the two schools in Tunisia.[37]

The characteristics of the Tunisian ulama and their relationship with the dynasty were shaped by the nature of the religious organization in Islam. The law schools were not formal associations but schools of thought and traditions of learning. As a result, adherence to the Maliki school did not mean that there was a formal churchlike structure to provide institutional support for or place constraints upon individual scholars in their dealings with the rulers. In Tunisia, the major organized religious institutions were the various educational institutions and local mosques. The mainstays of the Maliki establishment were the Zaytuna University Mosque in Tunis, and the various mosques in the religious center of al-Qayrawan. By endowing new instructorships and refurbishing the buildings, the political leadership was able to win support from the religious establishment without creating an independent, nationally organized religious association.

The success of the political elite in their religious policy helped to create a relatively conservative mood within the religious establishment in Tunisia, and it reinforced the unincorporated nature of the ulama groupings and reduced the susceptibility of the Tunisian Muslim community to more fundamentalist organizations and ideas. That situation was to provide the foundation for a distinctive tone for modern Islam in Tunisia.

The Algerian experience during the eighteenth century was also different. There, the military ruling elite tended to remain apart from the local population, and the local Islamic leadership was also of a different character. Although the Maliki school was the dominant *madhhab* in Algeria as well as Tunisia, it did not provide the major focus for Islamic affiliation in Algeria. The major Muslim leaders in Algeria were associated with Sufi *tariqah*s, and centers built up around local saints, their families, and their tombs. These centers were quite well organized, and their involvement in the life of the people was comprehensive. In contrast to the ulama of Tunisia, the Algerian religious leaders belonged to formal associations that had the capacity to mobilize large segments of the population for political and military as well as religious purposes.

The eighteenth century was a time of major religious organizational activity in Algeria. New religious orders were created, older ones were revitalized, and increasingly by the end of the century, these orders came to assume a Neo-Sufi tone. As the military rulers became more oppressive in their demands upon the population, "these fraternities catalysed the discontent of the population and gave a formidable religious interpretation to its anti-Turkish sentiments."[38]

Some of the leading orders illustrate the ties of Algeria to the broader world of Neo-Sufism. In the first half of the century, orders with virtual political independence controlled a number of areas. As in the case of the Tayyibiyyah in the northwest, the creation of the order did not involve much in the way of a fundamentalist style. A more revivalist and militant tradition was created by Ahmad al-Darqawi (1760–1823), an ascetic teacher who preached against the exploitation of piety by the established orders. His followers became involved in a wide range of politico-religious activity. Although his own establishment was in Morocco, his influence soon spread to western Algeria where, in 1805, one of his local deputies led an attack on the Turkish rulers. He himself did not organize a formal brotherhood, but all across North Africa, Darqawiyyah derivatives had emerged by the end of the eighteenth century, and many of his followers had established close ties with Neo-Sufi teachers in the eastern Mediterranean area.

By the end of the century, Algeria was prepared for the vigorous activism of the Islamic revivalist style that emerged in the following century. The older orders were involved in a wide range of popular practices that could arouse fundamentalist opposition. However, most of the organized revivalism used the forms of the older orders, and Neo-Sufi ideas provided the inspiration.

Morocco

Morocco never came under direct Ottoman control, and Islamic institutions there also had a distinctive character. Political leadership was in the hands of groups with strong ties to the local population rather than being an alien military elite. During the sixteenth and seventeenth centuries, the older medieval institutions of central control had crumbled, and in the anarchic conditions, a number of small states had arisen. Many of those states had been formed by local religious leaders, and respect for local saints, or marabouts, had become a major factor in North African religious life. In times of political disorganization, these marabouts became major political figures.

There is a long tradition in the region of political activism related to religion. Two great medieval empires had their origins in religious orders, and the militance of those two groups, the Murabitun and the Muwahhidun, was tied to a spirit of religious revivalism combined with political activism. In the fifteenth and sixteenth centuries, local saint veneration had become firmly integrated into the formulations of Sufism and *tariqah* structures.

One aspect of this "maraboutism" was a common belief that the spiritual power of the holy man could be inherited by his descendants, so the dynastic principle came to be accepted. It was natural for special reverence to be paid to the descendants of the Prophet Muhammad, and sharifs had played an important role in the religiopolitical life of the country. These trends had culminated in the Sharifian empire of the Saᶜdian dynasty, which united most of Morocco in the sixteenth century.

It was the collapse of Saᶜdian power that opened the way in the seventeenth century for the resurgence of small, marabout-led states. By the end of that century, one of the states, led by a Sharifian family, had reestablished relatively strong central control and established the Alawite dynasty, which is still on the Moroccan throne.

The eighteenth-century Moroccan political system thus had rulers with special religious prestige and close ties to the structures of the local Islamic community. The sultans were important religious figures and could utilize Islamic sentiments to mobilize the population. At the same time, the Moroccan sultans recognized the potential political power of the other religious groups and worked to co-opt or limit the influence of the marabouts.

In the context of eighteenth-century Islam, the sultans tended to support the more fundamentalist positions, as they were being developed by the Neo-Sufists, as a way of curtailing the influence of the local *tariqah*s, which could be accomplished by campaigns against the "non-Islamic" practices of the local saints. During the century, the sultans were often associated with this revivalist viewpoint, but there were some problems with this association since, by the end of the century, the idea of establishing Neo-Sufi *tariqah*s as vehicles for fundamentalist reform resulted in new orders in Morocco that could sometimes challenge the authority of the sultan. This problem arose during the reign of Sultan Suleyman. "Himself a strictly orthodox Muslim, Mawlay Sulayman was influenced after 1810 by Wahhabism, which led him to take a firm stand against maraboutism, at the very time when both the recently-founded order of the Darqawa and the earlier order of the Wazzaniyya [the Tayyibiyyah] were undergoing a great expansion in Morocco."[39]

The general development of Sufi organization and Islamic studies in North Africa had an impact on the broader Islamic world. Scholars from North Africa not only went to the eastern Mediterranean to study, but some remained and became prominent teachers. Those scholars from North Africa, or the Maghrib, made contributions in the two important areas of *hadith* studies and Neo-Sufism.

Scholars of *hadith* from the Maghrib were an important part of the cosmopolitan community of scholars in Mecca and Medina, and they were also often associated with revivalist ideas. An early scholar in this group was Muhammad ibn Muhammad ibn Suleyman (1626–1683). Born in Morocco, he received an education in the *hadith*s from the major scholars of his day in the Maghrib and was also initiated into local Sufi orders. After further studies in Cairo and the holy cities, he traveled widely and became an associate of the Ottoman grand vizier, Ahmad Koprulu. In Mecca he soon became a major political force, dominated the grand sharif for a time, and instituted a number of "radical reforms designed to improve the lot of the foreign elements and the poorer classes in Mecca at the expense of the old aristocracy."[40] With the fall of his patron, the grand vizier, he went to Damascus where he continued to teach and attract students from many areas.

Most of the major teachers of *hadith* in Mecca, Medina, and Damascus in the early eighteenth century studied *hadith* under Muhammad Ibn Suleyman. In his works on *hadith*, he combined study of the ninth-century collections with a study of Malik's *Muwatta* and may have been an important influence in that orientation of eighteenth-century *hadith* studies.

A later North African scholar of similar importance was Muhammad Ibn al-Tayyib (1698–1757), who was born in Morocco and taught most of his life in Medina. In order to advance the study of the *hadiths*, he studied lexicography extensively. As a result of that emphasis, he inspired his best-known student, Muhammad Murtada al-Zabidi, and through him had a substantial impact on the intellectual developments of the day.

Late in the eighteenth century teachers from North Africa were also important in creating activist *tariqahs* that utilized the ideas of Neo-Sufism. The *tariqah* tradition of being well-organized, popular associations that had developed in the Maghrib was an influence in the organizational form that Neo-Sufism took and in the process, a Moroccan scholar named Ahmad ibn Idris (d. 1837) was an important figure. Initiated into activist *tariqahs* in North Africa, he taught for many years in Mecca. "His biographer says that he based his Sufi practice solidly on the Qur'an and Sunna, accepting only these as *usul* (foundations) and rejecting *ijma* (consensus) except that of the Companions upon which the Prophet's Sunna is based."[41] That statement reflects both the more fundamentalist style of Sufism and the emphasis on a knowledge of *hadith*. His expertise in the Traditions of the Prophet was widely known. When Ahmad's reformism brought him into conflict with the conservative establishment in Mecca, it was as a *muhaddith* that he was examined publicly by a panel of ulama. (A favorable account of his disciple-biographer notes that he was able to confound his critics and emerged with an enhanced reputation.)[42]

Ahmad ibn Idris was eventually forced out of Mecca and moved to Asir, between Mecca and Yemen. There he established a community that in many ways was similar to the marabout-led communities of North Africa, and his descendants remained virtually independent rulers of the area until after World War I. In that community, one can see a combination of fundamentalist concepts and the more politically activist organizational ideas of North African maraboutism. The followers of Ahmad ibn Idris were to establish a number of *tariqahs* that became significant elements in nineteenth-century Islamic revivalism, including the Sanusiyyah in Libya, the Khatmiyyah in the Sudan, and the *tariqah* line that produced the Salihiyyah in Somalia.

Ottoman North Africa and Morocco were important contributors to the general history of eighteenth-century Islam, and that century also saw the creation of local Islamic institutions that would distinguish those countries in the modern era. Those local institutions ranged from the confirmation of a conservative style of religious leadership in Tunisia to the emergence of activist religious brotherhoods in Algeria and Morocco.

Islam in Sudanic Africa

In the vast belt of territories that stretch from the Atlantic to the Indian Ocean basin, between the Sahara and the heavily forested areas, Islam played a dynamic role in the eighteenth century. This savanna region is often called "the sudan" or Sudanic Africa, using the traditional Arabic name of *bilad al-Sudan* ("land of the blacks"). In Sudanic Africa, Islam was introduced at different times in different sections, but it was generally a clearly present element by late medieval times. It was spread by wandering merchants and teachers as well as by soldiers, and Islam in Sudanic Africa shares many of the features of Islam in Southeast Asia.

When Islam came into the area, there were already established political structures and social institutions. As a result, the main themes of Islamic history in Sudanic Africa deal with the interaction between Islam and the existing basic elements. In this interaction there were two main phases.

The first phase was while Islam was gradually spreading southward from the established Muslim communities on the Mediterranean coast. Special impetus was given to that expansion in the western areas by the Murabitun and Muwahhidun activist Muslim movements, which had been established in Morocco in the eleventh and twelfth centuries. Islam had a distinctive role in Sudanic societies during this phase, which lasted until the eighteenth century in most areas. It was, in many ways, a special class cult. It was the religion of the commercial and clerical classes who traveled widely within the region, and Islam was the faith of the interregional cosmopolitan elements. In addition, Islam became a special religion of dynasties or imperial structures in many parts of Sudanic Africa. Rulers combined the cosmopolitan advantages of Islam and the Muslim groups with particular local, non-Islamic customs and rituals and so gave their rule legitimacy among the majority of their non-Muslim or barely Islamized subjects.

The basic Islamic style, on the part of the converting rulers and the Muslim teachers and traders, was adaptationism. "Religious life was characterized by accommodation or, more correctly, by a dualism or a parallelism of the old and the new—the African idea of harmony of society maintained itself over against any idea of Islamic exclusiveness. Consequently, Islam's challenge to traditional life was largely neutralized."[43] This was the period of the "mixers," who combined pagan and Islamic practices. Although there were a few protesters, like Muhammad ibn Abd al-Karim al-Maghili (d. 1504), the general tone, even of the ulama, was either adaptationist or, once the compromise had been set, conservative.

By the eighteenth century, dynamic new themes were emerging in Sudanic Islam. As Islamic consciousness spread beyond the limited class base of the first phase, it was possible to organize movements that called for a more rigorous adherence to Islam, with fewer compromises in all areas, especially the political realm. The century was "the birth time of the theocracies, which in a series of revolutions engulfed almost the whole Sudan before European control was imposed."[44] The leaders in this new consciousness were drawn from the ulama and were teachers who were inspired by a vision of a more clearly Islamic society. During the eighteenth century, those scholars created a tradition of a militant, more fundamentalist Islam in the Sudanic belt. Although not always victorious themselves, they paved the way for the holy wars that characterized Islam in the Sudanic areas during the nineteenth century.

In West Africa, there was at least some memory of the medieval theocratic traditions of the Murabitun and the Muwahhidun. In Futa Jallon, a highland area in modern Guinea, some of the earliest efforts in the Islamic transformation took place. There, a scholar named Ibrahim Musa (sometimes called Karamoko Alifa, d. 1751) proclaimed a holy war against the local rulers and took the title of *almami*, meaning "the imam" or leader. He and a revivalist warrior, Ibrahim Sori, who became the almami in 1776, created a revivalist state with active schools as well as militant armies. However, the almamis in Futa Jallon did not succeed in creating an effectively cohesive state, and the "theocratic republic" was always troubled by internal division as well as by external attack. The revivalism of Futa Jallon did succeed in spreading to other areas, inspiring similar movements.

In Futa Toro, in the Senegal area, a similar state was created. After studying in Futa Jallon, Suleyman Bal preached against the local rulers in Futa Toro and announced that an almami should rule there too. He himself refused the post, but another scholar, Abd al-Qadir, was named almami in 1776. Although he was killed in 1806, the imamate continued until the French occupation. In other areas, similar movements led toward holy wars and the creation of theocratic states.

During this time, another feature of Sudanic Islam was being consolidated as the traditions of scholarship and respected local holy men were being combined with the introduction and expansion of some of the great Sufi *tariqah*s. The oldest of the major brotherhoods in West Africa is the Qadiriyyah, and its introduction and spread there was associated with a prominent religious family, the Kunta. Ahmad al-Bakka'i al-Kunti (d. 1504) was the first major figure in that family, and his influence extended from Timbuctoo to the Atlantic. Ahmad's son Umar is reported by Kunti historians to have had close ties with a famous scholar with strict views, Muhammad al-Maghili, and a major teacher in Cairo, Abd al-Rahman al-Suyuti. Whether or not those three scholars actually had close personal connections, the Kunta clearly identified themselves with the rigorous fundamentalist style of Islamic scholarship represented by al-Maghili. They combined that scholarly activity with an affiliation with the Qadiriyyah.

The real spread of that combination of scholarship and Sufism through the Kunti family occurred in the eighteenth century under the leadership of al-Mukhtar al-Kunti (1729–1811). He was "widely renowned for his sanctity and scholarship throughout West and North Africa, and to him is attributed the revival of the Qadiriyya and the Maliki *madhhab* (school of jurisprudence) in much of West Africa."[45] Al-Mukhtar created a vast confederation of tribal groups and supporters with real influence in political, economic, and religious affairs. Through his work and that of his followers and associates in the order, the Qadiriyyah was active in many parts of West Africa and was tied to the forces of revival. There were Qadiriyyah centers with at least some ties to the Kunti leaders in Futa Jallon, Futa Toro, and later militant revivalists like Uthman dan Fodio.

Tariqah leaders in West Africa were not isolated from the development of Neo-Sufism in the central parts of the Islamic world. Scholars on pilgrimage had contacts with Neo-Sufi leaders and brought back with them their ideas and affiliations. Jabril ibn Umar, the major teacher of Uthman dan Fodio, for example, studied in Cairo with Muhammad Murtada al-Zabidi and Yusuf al-Hifnawi, the brother of the Khalwatiyyah leader in Egypt, Muhammad al-Hifnawi. Early in the nineteenth century, the Tijaniyyah began to spread in the area, and it brought with it its style of Neo-Sufism.

In this way, the eighteenth-century mood of socio-moral reconstruction was clearly visible in western Sudanic Africa. The combination of traditions of scholarly study and Sufi organization played an important role in the development of the Islamic community there and created the activist foundations for the militancy that was a major feature of Islam in the following century.

In the eastern sections of Sudanic Africa, there was less militant activism, even though some of the same basic issues were present. In some states, the rulers were Islamic, but they still maintained pre-Islamic practices in an adaptationist mixture that was accepted by the local Muslim teachers. As in West Africa, Islam in this area tended to be most closely identified with particular classes. As a result, the issue of the relationship between local practices and the Islamic message was important in the east as well as in the west. However, the major sources of Islamic influence were Egypt and the Arabian Peninsula, and the spirit of militant revivalism and the marabout political institutions were not a significant part of the messages coming from the centers in Egypt and the Haramayn. The more conservative spirit of al-Azhar was reflected in some of eastern Sudanic Islam.

An Islamic state, the Funj sultanate, had been established in the Nile valley during the sixteenth century, but although officially Islamic, many older practices of political ritual and organization had been continued there. Gradually, the Nilotic Sudan came under increasing Islamic influence. Scholars who had studied in the Haramayn or in Egypt established school communities and introduced a more accurate study of the fundamentals of the faith. Early in the seventeenth century, for example, Ibrahim al-Bulad Ibn Jabir was the first to teach the standard textbooks of Maliki law in Funj territory. Around the same time, some of the major *tariqah*s, like the Qadiriyyah, had been introduced. However, the product of this growing Islamization was still a relatively tolerant style of Islam, open to substantial adaptation to local customs and practices. Local scholar-saint dynasties emerged and were the major focuses for both Islamic learning and popular religious practices.

By the end of the eighteenth century, the development of Neo-Sufi ideas had begun to penetrate into the Funj territories, first through Sudanic pilgrims who had studied under Neo-Sufi figures in the Haramayn. The Khalwatiyyah of Mustafa al-Bakri was introduced into the Sudan through the Sammaniyyah, which had been established in the Haramayn by al-Bakri's disciple, Muhammad ibn Abd al-Karim al-Samman. Ahmad al-Tayyib ibn Bashir, a pilgrim from the Sudan, was initiated into that *tariqah* in Medina and carried the order back to the Sudan in 1800. There he had success in winning the allegiance of some of the major established families, and the *tariqah* expanded rapidly. This Sammaniyyah branch in the Sudan included the late nineteenth-century militant fundamentalist, Muhammad Ahmad, the Sudanese Mahdi.

Other significant Neo-Sufi groups to enter the Sudan at this time were associated with Ahmad ibn Idris, the popular Neo-Sufi teacher in the Haramayn from North Africa. One of his students was Muhammad al-Majdhub al-Sughayyir (1796–1833). That man was a member of one of the major Sudanese holy families, and on his return to the Sudan, he reorganized the family *tariqah* along more activist lines. The other major Sudanese order to follow the tradition of Ahmad ibn Idris is the Khatmiyyah, which was introduced into the Sudan early in the nineteenth century by Muhammad Uthman al-Mirghani.

Sudanese Islam was thus entering a new phase by the end of the eighteenth century. The new style of teachers was more firmly committed to a more rigorous adherence to Islam than the earlier religious leaders had been. However, the preaching of those new scholars did not result at that time in a militant holy war, as happened in West Africa. Instead, the indigenous development of Islam was stopped by the Egyptian conquest of the Sudan around 1820, which introduced a totally new element since the conquering Egyptian army was the product of the modernizing reforms of Mehmet Ali. The more standard pattern of Sudanic Islamic evolution was thus abruptly replaced by the problems of dealing with modernization as well as Islamizing trends.

Emergence of Modern Shiʿi Patterns in Iran

Political Context

Safavid power was crumbling in Iran by the beginning of the eighteenth century, and in the context of the resulting political struggle and military attacks, important developments were taking place within Shiʿism. Those developments created the basis for the role of religion and religious leadership in modern Iranian history.

The political and military history of Iran during the century began with the increasingly ineffective Safavid state's facing a series of revolts. Those revolts culminated in an invasion by Afghans, who captured the Safavid capital of Isfahan in 1722 and ruled for seven years. In reaction, a great leader of the Afshar tribe, Nader Khan, organized the support that was still loyal to the Safavid house. He succeeded in defeating the Afghans and restored the Safavid shah to the throne. However, Nader was the real power in the state, and he finally assumed the throne himself as Nader Shah in 1736. He built a large conquest empire that controlled all of Iran, brought a stop to the Ottoman advances, and successfully invaded northern India. However, his abilities were military rather than administrative, and he did not create a stable imperial system. His harsh measures of control soon created opposition, and he was killed in 1747. Following his death, various tribal and military groups competed for control in the chaotic situation. After half a century, in which there was virtually no central control in Iran, one of those groups, the Qajars, emerged victorious. In 1795, Aga Muhammad, the Qajar leader, was proclaimed shah and centralized control was reestablished in Iran.

Shi'ism and the Iranian Identity

Until the time of the Safavids, Shi'ism had not been explicitly identified with the Persian cultural tradition, although it had been one aspect of the Islamic experience in Iran. The proclamation of Twelver Shi'ism as the religion of the Safavid state and the subsequent conversion of the majority of the population to Shi'ism during the Safavid era were major turning points in the history of Islam in Iran. The Safavids "presided over the fusion of Shi'ism with the Iranian national consciousness."[46]

The Safavid form of this fusion placed great importance on the state and the role of the monarch, and during the Safavid era, Shi'i Islam was both state supported and state supporting. The shah assumed a special role as an agent of the hidden imam and thus had a religiously based authority. In establishing an "official" religion, the Safavids created a government-related group of ulama. Before the Safavid period, there had been relatively few Shi'i ulama in Iran, so the emerging ulama class of "imported" scholars and new local teachers was, initially, tied quite closely to state patronage.

By the end of the eighteenth century, an independent group of Shi'i ulama had emerged. The leading figures were scholars whose independent interpretations had been accepted by the majority of the population. These *mujtahids*, as they were called, stood outside of the organization of the state, and the foundation of their authority was independent from the patronage of the state. The non-state ulama became a major religious force, which competed with the government religious establishment and the shah himself. As the state structure weakened, the *mujtahids* played a more prominent role until, under the last Safavid shahs, great *mujtahids* like Muhammad Baqir al-Majlisi came to dominate the political system itself.

With the collapse of the Safavid monarchy, the Shi'i ulama essentially liberated themselves from the monarchical institution. In the absence of effective central control, Shiʿism was able to become the basic Islamic expression of the Iranian identity without reference to a particular monarchical structure. "The eighteenth century was, then, a period in which Shiʿism, its learning and institutions, defied political and social decay to maintain its dominance in Iran."[47] The stage was thus set for the modern dual elements of monarch and *mujtahid*, sometimes cooperating but more often in conflict.

Conflict over Definition

The most visible challenge in the eighteenth century to the special Shiʿi tradition in Iran came from some of the political leadership. Nader Shah made a major effort to redefine the place of Shiʿi Islam within the Islamic world by working to gain recognition from the major Sunni powers. There are many possible reasons why he made that effort. It could have been because he wanted to unify the Islamic world under his leadership, or it could have been a justification for his suppression of the Shiʿi ulama, both state and non-state, as a part of his efforts to strengthen the monarchy. He may also have been inspired by his own religious convictions and background, in which there were at least some Sunni elements.

Whatever his reasons, Nader Shah attempted to integrate a redefined Shiʿism into the Sunni tradition. He rejected the Shiʿi condemnation of the first three caliphs and enforced that position within his realm. In addition, he tried to secure Ottoman recognition of Twelver Shiʿism as a fifth Sunni school of law, to be called the Jaʿfari school after the sixth imam, Jaʿfar al-Sadiq. The whole pattern of Shiʿism as built on the idea of the imamate was to be replaced. Neither the Sunni Ottomans nor the major Shiʿi teachers of the time accepted Nader's redefinition, although he was able, through military force, to "persuade" a few teachers to agree with his ideas. Clearly, the monarchy was not accepted as a vehicle for interpreting the faith, and in the long run, Nader's efforts only deepened the gap between the ulama and the monarchy.

The results of Nader's attempt reaffirmed the Shiʿi emphasis on the Islamic style that concentrated on the role of individualistic leadership, and the role of the imamate in the Shiʿi tradition was a continuing affirmation of that distinctive style. The adaptationist efforts of Nader Shah failed to change this orientation.

Among the Shiʿi ulama themselves, that orientation was also reaffirmed in a series of doctrinal conflicts that had long-term significance. By the beginning of the eighteenth century, two major schools of Shiʿi thought had emerged, the Akhbari and the Usuli, and many of the leading teachers settled in the Shiʿi holy cities in Iraq in order to avoid the growing political and military disorders in Iran. Those cities, Najaf and Karbala, are the sites of the tombs of Ali and Husayn and are major centers of Shiʿi devotion and study.

The heart of the controversy between the Akhbaris and the Usulis was the role of the ulama in guiding the people. The Akhbari position emerged as a type of Shi'i fundamentalism as that school held that the Quran and the Traditions from the Prophet and the imams were sufficient guidance for the community. The function of the ulama should be simply searching through the sources for solutions to problems. The Akhbaris felt that there was no need for scholars to use independent judgment (*ijtihad*) and that, in fact, *ijtihad* was an unsound innovation. This doctrinal position cut at the very heart of the evolving role of the Shi'i *mujtahid*s as guides for the community. In its fundamentalism, the Akhbari school was a move away from the charismatic, individualized style of leadership in Shi'ism.

The Akhbari group dominated the intellectual studies in the Shi'i holy cities for a good part of the eighteenth century. By the end of the century, however, the Usuli position had emerged as victorious, largely as a result of the efforts of Aga Muhammad Baqir Bihbihani (1705–1803). The Usuli position reaffirmed the importance of the role of the *mujtahid* as the guide for the community. In the absence of the imam, the community needed some guidance in coping with changing conditions, and the Usulis asserted that the learned scholar was capable of authentic independent judgment and that such a scholar was a necessary agent of the hidden imam. As such, every person should accept the direction of a *mujtahid*.

The Usulis recognized that there might be a variety of interpretations among the *mujtahid*s as a result of changing conditions or different viewpoints. Thus, although the judgment of the *mujtahid* must be followed by his supporters, "it established no precedent and believers are forbidden to follow the rulings of a deceased mujtahid in place of a living one."[48] The victory of the Usuli position by the end of the eighteenth century affirmed the importance of the living *mujtahid*s as the necessary guides for all believers.

The political implications of that position form a major part of the modern history of Iran. Since the Islamic message is valid in all areas of life, the political guidance of the *mujtahid* is, at least in theory, as binding as his social and doctrinal guidance. "The monarch was theoretically bound, no less than his subjects, to submit to the authoritative guidance of a *mujtahid* and in effect to make the state the executive branch of ulama authority."[49] Although it is possible for the ulama and the monarchy to cooperate, when there is an assertion of a strong monarchical role in society, it is possible that *mujtahid* and monarch will come into conflict. In many ways, it is possible to say that the Usuli triumph in the eighteenth century created the necessary foundation for the triumph of the Ayatollah Khomeini in this century.

There was a third school of Shi'i thought at the time that went beyond the Usuli in terms of the role of the charismatic leader. This school was established by Ahmad al-Ahsa'i (1741–1826), and his followers came to be called the Shaykhis. He may have come from an Akhbari background, rejecting the idea that legal reasoning limits the direct charismatic authority of the imams. Stressing the continuing metaphysical position of the imam as a guide for humanity, a doctrine of human access to the imam through a particular intermediary was developed. Thus, the Shi'i style of charismatic individualism was maintained, but the general validity of the *ijtahid* of the ulama was denied. In the early nineteenth century, al-Ahsa'i and his followers clashed with the major ulama leaders and the Shaykhi teachings were declared heretical. However, the Shaykhis had established the basis for a continuing charismatic messianism and played a role in the later messianic revolts.

The messianic strand in Iranian Islamic history helped to reinforce the significance of the Usuli victory. The main popular spokesmen for the faith were not within the political structure but outside of it, in a position to mobilize large-scale support for opposition movements. Islamic leadership became, in this way, a major check on the power of the monarch in Iran.

Conclusion

Throughout the Islamic world, the eighteenth century was a significant formative period, and developments during the century helped to determine the shape that Islamic movements would take in the following centuries. One significant feature that emerges from a study of the eighteenth-century Islamic experience is that Islam became a basis for the assertion of an authentically indigenous identity, which was often in opposition to the emerging political structures. That situation occurred from Southeast Asia through Iran and the Ottoman Empire to the states of West Africa. In some cases, there was a relatively conservative resistance to reforms instituted by political leaders; in other cases, fundamentalist movements, which aimed at a socio-moral reconstruction, were created.

In contrast, many governments in the Islamic areas emerged as the leading forces for adaptationism, and increasingly, adaptationism meant coming to an accommodation with the new forces, both economic and military, of the modernizing West. This trend only strengthened the nonestablishment character of many of the activist Islamic movements.

A look at the eighteenth-century Islamic experience helps to emphasize the importance of the Islamic dimension of modern Muslim history. That Islamic world was not simply a stagnant, inert mass on which the West imposed its control and ideas, and the reformism and revivalism that are visible in the modern Islamic world are not simply the result of contact with the West. Authentically Islamic movements of self-criticism and revivalism were already emerging in the eighteenth century, and the special characteristics of those movements are an important part of the interaction between Islam and the challenges of modern history. Although the role of the modernizing West is important, the role of the forces that have arisen out of the Islamic dimension of the modern Muslim experience cannot be ignored.

4

European Domination
and Islamic Response

The Islamic world faced a major challenge during the nineteenth century. Expanding Western European states and economies played an increasing role in determining events, both on a global scale and within Islamic societies. By the end of the century, many Muslim territories were under direct European control, and much of the rest of the Muslim world was dominated by the West. The basis for this European capacity for domination was the transformation of Western society through the processes of modernization. In the past, world civilizations had competed, with advances and defeats usually being determined by local quantitative differences in power, but the bases of power were fundamentally the same. However, the emerging modern society in the West had a qualitatively different type of power, enabling physically small states like England to dominate large parts of the globe.

The interaction of this new basic life-style with the older life-styles and world views is a fundamental theme of modern world history, and it provides the second major dimension that is required for understanding the history of Islam in the modern world. The Islamic dimension and the modern dimension represent the framework within which local Islamic histories develop.

At times, the Islamic-Western interaction has resulted in fruitful cooperation, but the prevailing tone in the nineteenth century was one of conflict. Rather than partnerships emerging, the primary arrangement was domination-subordination. The context for the Islamic experience was thus often one of struggle, and the new Western ideas and techniques were seen as being in competition with the Islamic ideals. From a strict Islamic standpoint, adaptation in this context gave the appearance of surrender. It was not until the end of the nineteenth century that significant efforts were made to create an Islamically oriented adaptationism.

Part of the problem for Muslims was a growing awareness of Western power and the feeling that the strength of the modern ideas and institutions was in fact qualitatively different from the Islamic sources of power. For a community whose historical experience tended to reinforce the idea that "God is on the side of those who fear Him and do good," the visible strength of the modernizing West posed grave problems, and at times, it created a sense of unease. It has been said that "the fundamental spiritual crisis of Islam in the twentieth century stems from an awareness that something is awry between the religion which God has appointed and the historical development of the world which He controls."[1] This crisis arose out of the nineteenth-century history of the Islamic world.

Conflict and spiritual crisis are only part of the story. In addition, building on the eighteenth-century foundations, there is a theme of socio-moral reconstruction, and that effort utilizes lessons learned from the interaction with the West but remains authentically Islamic. Although the nineteenth and early twentieth centuries were dominated by the mood of spiritual crisis, this other theme has continued to build. By the final third of the twentieth century, it has assumed many forms, but it is no longer clearly subordinate—as it seemed to be in the nineteenth century—to the theme of crisis.

In the diversity of the Islamic experiences during the nineteenth century, some general trends can be discerned. There was a continuing momentum of the eighteenth-century developments that gave inspiration to Islamic activist movements in many areas. There were also substantial efforts to introduce Western techniques in the creation of more effective state structures. The success of both of those efforts was limited in the nineteenth century in the face of growing European dominance, and as that fact became clear, efforts were made to redefine Islam in order to meet the challenges. Along with that redefinition, other activities developed, sometimes in conjunction with and sometimes in competition with Islamic sentiments. These activities involved more clearly secularist attitudes, ideas of radical reform, and nationalism.

Three general types of evolution can be seen within that framework. One centered around the efforts of adaptationist Westernizers; the second began with an eighteenth-century style of militant reaction to the Western expansion and then, after defeat, there were efforts at reorientation. In the third type of evolution, there was a continuation of an eighteenth-century type of activity, which was not dominated by the West for some time but was finally affected by European imperial control. In addition to these experiences with the imperialist West, there were a few areas, particularly in Africa and China, where Islamic revivalism emerged outside of the context of interaction with European imperialism.

Adaptationist Westernizers and Nineteenth-Century Islam

The nineteenth century was a time of dramatic reform programs. Those were frequently undertaken by colorful, strong personalities, some of the

best known of whom were Mehmet Ali in Egypt and Mahmud II, the reforming Ottoman sultan. Those men were not the only ones in the Islamic
world who tried to create modern-style armies and administrative structures, but they are the most visible of a major type of Muslim leader that
was emerging during the century. The reform programs took place in a still
functioning political system, which was bureaucratically organized and accepted as legitimate by a majority of the population. The personnel within
that apparatus was a distinct official class whose fortunes were tied to the
continued effective existence of the state.

The leaders worked under a variety of challenges to restructure a government and to increase its role in society in order to cope with new problems.
The techniques and methods used by the rulers were not determined by past
tradition alone; they were willing to adapt and adopt whatever appeared to
have the potential for strengthening their government and meeting their
goals. In the nineteenth century, the source of most of the ideas for this type
of reform was the West. Although there had been a long history of interaction with Western states, there had not been a period of fundamental intellectual preparation for political change. Rather, in those established,
bureaucratically organized governments, "selected members of the existing
political class experimented in a piecemeal, pragmatic fashion with Western-inspired reforms."[2]

The ideas and techniques were relatively new to both the reformers and
the society, but the role of the political elite was basically a continuation of
the adaptationist style of Islam. None of the reformers renounced Islam, but
they were not primarily concerned with doctrinal issues or with creating
religiously oriented roles for themselves. Like the early caliphs and the
Umayyads, they made use of the available techniques in a pragmatic way in
order to strengthen the state. Similarly, like the Umayyads, they were
sometimes criticized by the more conservative and fundamentalist Muslims
for the compromises that were implicit in their adaptations.

In his analysis of one of those early Westernizing reformers, L. Carl
Brown proposes a useful general framework for viewing the adaptationist
style of reformers who operated within the context of bureaucratic governments.[3] He suggests that in the bureaucratic states, the first, pragmatic stage
is similar in countries like Egypt, the central Ottoman Empire, Tunisia,
Morocco, and Iran. It is only after the first reformist efforts have been initiated by members of the political elite that a "reformist ideology" can
develop. After the first phase, the experience varies. The existing political
elites may break down in the process, creating major crisis situations. A second possibility is that reform continues to be imposed from the top by a
small dominant group. In that case, "an expanded state is left to dominate a
people now stripped of traditional political patterns and left only to
demonstrate the violent swings of political activity associated with 'mass
society.'"[4] In a third pattern, the reforms create a gradually expanding circle
of participants, and, through evolutionary processes, a modernizing society
emerges with a minimum of violence. Some aspects of each of these types of

experience can be seen in the developing Islamic experience of the nineteenth century.

If one focuses on the modern Islamic experience, the details of the reform programs and the political history are not as important as the developing interaction of the Islamic styles. In the larger bureaucratic states, the adaptationist reformers were clearly the dominant group. After early clashes, the more conservative Muslims tended to be cowed into submission. They could at times influence the pace of reform, but even that strength declined as the reforms undermined the old bases of conservative power. In the long run, as reformism became established, the conservatives began to assume the role of preservers of the early reforms. An interesting example of that phenomenon is the history of the fez, the headgear of North African origin. There was conservative opposition to its adoption as a part of the army uniform during the period of the early Ottoman military reforms, but, a century later, the prohibition of the fez aroused conservative opposition.

Effective, organized opposition to reform, in Islamic terms, was largely the product of a fundamentalist style of activity. In addition, by the end of the nineteenth century, the currents set in motion by the early reforms had begun to produce "ideologies of reform" that sometimes went beyond the positions of the later rulers. Intellectual adaptationism created a theme of Islamic modernism that sometimes supported and sometimes opposed government policies, and nationalism and socialism also began to appear as alternative orientations. A final element that limited the power of the reformist rulers was the European powers, as European political interference and economic activity had a major impact on the outcome of the indigenous reform programs. In some cases, as in Egypt, European military occupation or political dominance meant that the ability to initiate government policy effectively passed into foreign hands.

The Central Ottoman Empire

The reform programs of the nineteenth century in the central Ottoman Empire had some foundations on which to build. The more traditional reforms of the preceding century had opened the way for at least a small portion of the ruling elite to accept Western techniques, and the work of Sultan Selim III had helped to create a small core of able men who had some experience with Westernizing reforms. At the same time, the abrupt end of Selim's *nizam-i-jedid* showed the continuing power of the conservative forces within the state.

Mahmud II emerged from the conflicts at the end of Selim's reign as the new sultan. He was interested in pursuing a reform program but had to work very cautiously in order to avoid the same fate as Selim. Mahmud managed to survive by balancing a variety of forces and by gradually infiltrating men who shared his goals into the upper levels of the religious establishment and the Janissary Corps. In addition, he was able to avoid serious defeat at the hands of the Europeans and the various semi-independent provincial notables. Having organized his support, Mahmud began a more dramatic reform effort in 1826, and the first target of this program was the Janissary Corps, which revolted and was crushed. By 1826, Mahmud had substantial support for the abolition of the janissaries, since even the conservative religious leaders saw their ineffectiveness as a threat to the empire.

For the conservative ulama, the destruction of the janissaries was a serious blow, even though they had supported it, because their destruction meant that there was no longer a military force that could act to support the ulama's interests. As a result, Mahmud was able to undermine the sources of the ulama strength with greater effectiveness than his predecessors. The religious establishment gradually lost its administrative autonomy, and control over the pious endowments increasingly passed out of the hands of the conservative ulama. The establishment of new schools meant that the government elite was increasingly drawn from people whose education was significantly different from that of the ulama.

The role of Islam in the Ottoman state was changing, and, with that change, the ulama increasingly lost effective influence. The reforming leadership did not reject Islam, and it was usually careful never to go beyond what would be tolerated by the majority of the Muslims. Islam was, after all, the ultimate basis for the legitimacy of the Ottoman sultanate. The ulama generally had two options. Most remained basically conservative, trying to slow the pace of change and to keep it within clearly Islamic bounds. Unfortunately, "the majority of the ulema shut themselves off from the contemporary world in their medieval medreses [*madrasahs*] and courts of Holy Law."[5] The other option was to accept the inevitability of change and to make an active effort to reconcile tradition with reform through an active involvement in the political realm.

In the period following the death of Mahmud II in 1839, there were some important examples of ulama participation in the reform efforts. Although their participation was limited in scope, these men helped to open the door for attempts to adapt Islam to the new conditions, and the period is often called the era of the Tanzimat or "reorganizations." In general terms, the reorganizations were efforts to restructure Ottoman public life and to create a more effectively centralized empire. The Tanzimat took place in the context of a growing European involvement in Ottoman affairs and the continuing relative weakness of the empire. It was, however, a significant effort in reformist programs of modernization, and it created a modern-educated class and effectively restructured the imperial system in more modern terms.

The Tanzimat resulted in some changes in the specifically Islamic institutions, and the imperial religious establishment was brought under greater bureaucratic control. The office of the shaykh al-Islam continued to have importance, but during the Tanzimat, the position was held by men drawn from the lower levels of the ulama rather than from a few great religious families, as had been the case earlier.[6]

A few ulama made a direct and important contribution to the Tanzimat.

The most famous of those was Ahmad Cevdet Pasha (1822–1895), who was trained in the traditional religious curriculum but had also studied modern subjects. He was respected by both the reformers and the leading ulama, and as a result, he was a logical choice when the reforming grand vizier, Mustafa Rashid Pasha, requested the shaykh al-Islam to name a religious scholar to assist in the drafting of the legal codes. Cevdet was the major figure in the creation of the Majalla, a vast formulation of a civil code that combined Islamic legal principles with new legal ideas. In this effort and in other ways, Cevdet was an influential figure in the Tanzimat, and his attitude reflects the best of constructive conservatism in Ottoman Islam. "Cevdet was essentially conservative. . . . This conservatism did not blind him to reality. . . . He recognized the need for bringing the Ottoman legal and judicial system into step with the times, but he advocated the modification and adaptation of the indigenous Muslim law instead of the importation of alien law wherever that was possible."[7] The narrow vision of most of the Ottoman ulama, however, is reflected in the fact that Cevdet was forced to leave the ulama establishment and become a part of the administrative structure in order to accomplish his goals.

The period of the Tanzimat saw the end of the first phase of reformism, and the simple pragmatic adoption of techniques was placed in a broader framework of emerging intellectual formulations. In this intellectual activity at the end of the nineteenth century, there was a vibrant diversity, but three main themes can be seen, and Islam provided some of the framework for each of them.

The first theme was a criticism of the Tanzimat for not going far enough, and it was expressed in the writings of a diffuse group, sometimes called the Young Ottomans. Those men were strongly influenced by European liberal thinking and feared that the Tanzimat represented political maneuvers to create the foundations for an absolutist government. Namik Kemal, one of the leading figures in this movement, wrote of one of the imperial decrees establishing the basis for the Tanzimat that on the surface, "one would think it to have been made as a surety for the life, property, and honour of every individual. But the truth of the matter is that it was proclaimed for the purpose of securing the life of the state."[8]

This liberal critique of the reform program had its Islamic dimension. The Young Ottomans appealed to the egalitarian principles in the Islamic tradition and justified liberalizing reforms in Islamic terms. Their goal was a constitutional and parliamentary system with the restoration of Islamic law. "This would not, however, mean a simple rejection of Westernization and a return to the immediately preceding past; what was needed was a return to the true spirit of early Islam, which recognized the sovereignty of the people and the principle of government by consultation."[9] The Young Ottomans were early representatives of a style of Islam that is common in the modern era—a style that is essentially adaptationist but appeals to a fundamentalist style of reasoning.

The second theme was more directly Islamic in nature. As it became obvious that the reform programs were unable to stem the tide of the growing European dominance, some thinkers advocated a more rigorous reliance upon Islamic principles as the first line of defense. With the death of some of the major Tanzimat leaders, growing financial problems, and a difficult international situation by the 1870s, there was a tendency to place greater stress on the Islamic basis of the state and the need for effective Muslim unity. News of defeats of Muslims elsewhere and their mistreatment by non-Muslim governments aroused a greater sensitivity to the need for greater Muslim cooperation throughout the world of Islam.

The Islamic reaction to these conditions took two forms in the Ottoman Empire. One was to emphasize the role of the Ottoman ruler as the leading Muslim figure in the world. It was felt that he was not just the sultan and head of the empire but also the caliph and spokesman for Muslims throughout the world. Sultan Abdulhamid II, who came to the throne in 1876, actively pursued a policy based on this Pan-Islamic ideal, established ties with Muslims in many areas, and attracted leading figures to Istanbul. In areas far beyond the borders of the empire, there were Muslims who looked to the sultan-caliph for help. In the long run, the concrete results of the Pan-Islamic policies were limited, but a broader sense of Islamic unity was fostered. The second type of Islamic reaction was a growing willingness to defend Islam intellectually. European scholars denigrated Islam, Muslims began to debate with them, and in the process of those discussions, Muslim intellectuals began to create an intellectual framework for Islamic modernism.

A leading figure in both the intellectual defense of Islam and the development of Pan-Islamic ideas was Jamal al-Din al-Afghani (1839–1897), whose influence was not limited to the central Ottoman lands. He traveled and taught in Iran and Egypt and spent some years in Europe. He preached the necessity of Islamic revival and unity and vigorously affirmed that Islam was fully compatible with reason and modern science. For a time, he was among the intellectuals who were supported by Abdulhamid II in Istanbul, but his political ideas were ultimately too revolutionary for the regime of Abdulhamid.

The third theme in the emerging intellectual framework in the later part of the nineteenth century was the increasing absolutism of the Ottoman ruler, which is especially associated with the policies of Abdulhamid II. In many ways, that sultan was a culmination of the Tanzimat even though he represented a repudiation of its liberal constitutional ideals. He was faced with many crises and took dramatic, authoritarian measures. "He developed a structure of personal control that, with the centralized system of administration created by the Tanzimat, made possible a far more extensive and complete autocracy than anything ever achieved previously by the greatest of the sultans."[10] Modernizing reform, as the rule of Abdulhamid illustrates, gives added power to the instruments of state control. It can create the conditions for autocracy as well as for democracy.

Islam's role in Abdulhamid's autocracy was to provide legitimacy. Abdulhamid consciously identified himself with the emerging Pan-Islamic themes, and he received support from a wide variety of people who were persuaded that the secularism inherent in many of the Westernizing reforms was a growing threat to Islam. This support came not only from the conservative and fundamentalist elements; even someone with real commitment to reform, such as Ahmad Cevdet, gave support in many ways to Abdulhamid's autocratic policies.

The culmination of nineteenth-century Ottoman history came with the rise of the Young Turk movement, which ultimately captured control of the state by revolution in 1908. Resistance to Abdulhamid developed among the new generation of modern-educated people that had been created by the continuing reforms and development. There was real diversity within the movement that overthrew Abdulhamid. The basic themes of the nineteenth century manifested themselves in terms of plans for the future of the empire. Liberal constitutionalism was the most widely accepted platform, but there was disagreement over whether the empire should be strongly centralized—thus continuing in a different form the trends toward autocracy—or whether it should become a more decentralized federation. Because Pan-Islamic policies were associated with the sultan, they were not as visible in the Young Turks' programs, but there was still a strong element of looking to Islam to provide the basic identity of the state.

That issue of basic identity was complicated by the emergence of nationalist feelings even within the Ottoman educated elite. For some of them, ethnic and linguistic heritages were becoming more important than religious communal ties. That nationalist sentiment had long been an important aspect of the attitudes of the non-Muslim subject peoples who opposed the Ottoman imperial centralization, but now the two major Muslim elements within the empire also began to experience nationalist stirrings. The Arabic-speaking Ottomans began to speak of the Arab fatherland, and among the Turkish educated people, there was an emphasis on the Turkish nature of the ruling elite within the empire. For a time, Turks with that sentiment hoped to unify the larger world of the Turkish-speaking peoples, which stretched from the Balkans to Central Asia. The most realistic focus for this nationalist feeling was to focus on the Turkish-speaking heartland of the empire in Anatolia. Within the Young Turk movement, one can thus see the beginnings of the complex issue of the relationship between nationalist sentiments and Muslim religious loyalties.

The Ottoman Empire at the end of the nineteenth century exemplifies the major issues of Islam at the time. Reform involved adapting to Western techniques and ideas, and believing Muslims had to decide what impact this had on their faith. The possibilities of both liberalism and autocracy that were inherent in the Westernizing reforms were reflected in the Islamic responses. The first phase of a relatively simple, pragmatic reformism was replaced by efforts to redefine Islam in terms of the rapidly changing conditions. The reassertion of Islamic authenticity, the restatement of Islam in terms of modern rationalism, and the subordination of Islam to other approaches were common themes in the Islamic experience at the time, and they were manifested in the movements within the Ottoman Empire.

In terms of Islamic styles, adaptationism was a major force, in both political and intellectual terms. The majority of the Muslims within the empire may have been basically conservative in style, but conservatism was forced to accept a continually changing reality. Within the Ottoman Empire itself, there were few major movements that were explicitly fundamentalist, although a fundamentalist tone was present in a number of ways. The Quran and the Sunnah were often cited as validation for positions that were progressive or reactionary. The traditional modes of the individualistic style of Islam were not a prominent aspect of the changing Ottoman experience, but personalized faith might have aided acceptance of the secularist implications of the reforms, and emphasis on charismatic leadership might have given messianic dimensions to nationalism and the various opposition movements.

Islam and Nineteenth-Century Egypt

Egypt in the nineteenth century was still officially a part of the Ottoman Empire, but it was virtually independent of direct Ottoman control. Following the French invasion of Egypt in 1798, a strong ruler, Mehmet Ali, emerged as the ruler. He was a military adventurer who had gone to Egypt with the Ottoman army and used the strength of his character and the chaotic local conditions to soon become the Ottoman governor and ruler. He instituted a vigorous program of reform that aimed at creating a modern state capable of withstanding foreign control. The period of his rule (1805–1849) was an era of pragmatic reforms in Egypt, and those reforms transformed the basic political and economic structures along Westernizing reformist lines.

Under his successors, the reform programs continued but in a more flamboyant, less austere manner. His son, Said (r. 1854–1863), and grandson, Isma'il (r. 1863–1879), rebuilt cities, extended transportation systems, expanded educational facilities, and generally pursued active reformist policies. However, their extravagance created grave financial problems, which led to a European control of Egyptian finances. When Isma'il encouraged local discontent, he was deposed, and Egyptian opposition developed under the influence of students of Jamal al-Din al-Afghani and dissatisfied military officers. The resulting revolt, under the leadership of Ahmad Urabi, led to the British occupation of Egypt in 1882. For the rest of the century, Egypt was still nominally a part of the Ottoman Empire and ruled by autonomous governors, but those governors were under the firm, if technically indirect, control of the British. For all practical purposes, the ruler of Egypt after 1882 was Lord Cromer, the British agent and consul general in Cairo until 1907. Cromer continued programs of economic and administrative reform but was distinctly autocratic in style. In a sense he became the Abdulhamid of the Nile without Islamic regalia.

Within this general political framework, the Islamic experience developed in ways that were roughly parallel to the developments in the central Ottoman Empire. The ulama establishment maintained a basically conservative style, neither mobilizing effective resistance to the reforms nor fully accepting them. By the second half of the century, there were significant efforts toward "ideologies of reform," and the two key themes were the emergence of Egyptian nationalism and the formulation of Islamic modernism. Individual religious leaders played important roles in those activities even though the majority of the ulama were less active.

The ulama had helped to bring Mehmet Ali to power, but they soon became dependent upon him as his reforms reduced their financial and administrative independence. The modernizing programs of Mehmet Ali and his successors "dealt a heavy blow to the ulama. Politically and economically they were rapidly displaced by the new bureaucracy, and the new foreign merchant class. Intellectually they were outdistanced by the new westernized intelligentsia."[11] The ulama remained an important factor in influencing public opinion, but they basically used their position to encourage obedience to those in power. They did not attempt to assume direct political control but used their position to preserve tradition as best they could under the rapidly changing conditions of the time.

The ulama did, however, produce a number of men that were crucial in the formulation of modern Egyptian thought. Rifaʿa al-Tahtawi (1801–1873) had a sound traditional education in the Islamic disciplines, and at al-Azhar, he had been influenced by Shaykh Hasan al-Attar, a religious teacher who had had a relatively cosmopolitan experience and was sympathetic to the reform program of Mehmet Ali. Al-Tahtawi went to Paris with a major diplomatic mission as its religious teacher and gained a familiarity with French life and thought. In Egypt, al-Tahtawi was an important figure in the development of a new educational system and made a great contribution by encouraging translations and language instruction. Through his own translations he became, for many Egyptians, an instructor in European ideas, but he was not simply a transmitter of ideas. He also worked to provide a basic intellectual framework in which Islamic and European ideas could be integrated. He supported reform but, at the same time, encouraged continued adherence to the basic teachings of Islam. In this way, he helped to lay the foundations for Islamic modernist thought. He was also enthusiastic about the historic glories of Egyptian civilization and wrote that within the universal Islamic community, there were special national communities that were deserving of loyalty. Thus, he also helped to build the foundations for Egyptian nationalism. It is significant that this important formulation came from someone drawn from the ulama class, but it is also significant that like Ahmad Cevdet in Istanbul, the positions al-Tahtawi held were outside of the ulama establishment.

In Egypt itself, Islamic developments tended to avoid militant activism, and the great Muslim leaders of the nineteenth century, like al-Tahtawi, accepted the existing political framework. There was, however, a point when that acceptance might have changed as the potential for a militant religious activism appeared in conjunction with the Urabi movement of 1879–1882. Jamal al-Din al-Afghani, the itinerant advocate of Islamic revival and unity, went to Egypt in 1871 and taught there for eight years. He soon attracted a circle of followers, many of whom were students at al-Azhar, and the inherent political activism of his message led many of them to take an active part in political events during the last years of Isma'il's reign and after his deposition. However, following Urabi's defeat and the British occupation, the leading religious activists went into exile and soon reverted to more politically passive roles.

The leading Egyptian follower of Al-Afghani was Muhammad Abduh (1849–1905), another Egyptian with basic ulama training who became a leading intellectual. He was inspired by al-Afghani and took part in the upheaval associated with the Urabi movement. In exile, he worked with al-Afghani in publishing and plotting, but by 1888, he was back in Cairo and basically accepted the politico-military realities of the British occupation. His goal became the reformulation of Islamic thought and the revitalization of Islamic society through integrating modern and Islamic ideas and techniques.

Abduh soon was able to put many of his ideas into practice through a series of public positions that he held. He was made a judge and in 1899 became the mufti of Egypt, the head of the religious court system. In that position, he worked to reform the religious courts, and his legal rulings reinterpreted Islamic law in terms of modern conditions. In addition, he helped to reform the structure and curriculum of al-Azhar University. In his scholarly work, he provided a reinterpretation of Islam, explaining how Islam could provide a moral basis for a modern society. In that analysis, he used themes that had already been developed in the eighteenth century but put them in a contemporary context. He felt that a basic purpose in his life was "to liberate thought from the shackles of *taqlid*, and understand religion as it was understood by the elders of the community before dissension appeared; to return, in the acquisition of religious knowledge, to its first sources, and to weigh them in the scales of human reason . . . and to prove that, seen in this light, religion must be accounted a friend of science."[12] In that statement of purpose, one can see the call for independent judgment (*ijtihad*) and the fundamentalist desire to return to the basic sources of the faith, as well as a vindication of modernist rational thought and science.

Muhammad Abduh was the leading Muslim thinker of his day, and his work had an influence on Islamic thought far beyond the boundaries of Egypt. His heritage was, however, a mixed one. On the one hand, his reaffirmation of the truth of Islam helped to inspire intellectual fundamentalist movements in the twentieth century. On the other hand, his acceptance of reason provided justification for a rationalism by some thinkers that went beyond what he himself might have accepted as legitimate. Clearly, with Muhammad Abduh, modernist thought had become firmly established in the Islamic experience.

At the same time that Islamic modernist thought was developing, the modern form of Egyptian nationalism was emerging. During the nineteenth century, there was a growing awareness of the special heritage of Egyptian civilization as archaeological discoveries opened the world of ancient Egypt to modern eyes. Men like al-Tahtawi and Muhammad Abduh had a special feeling for the Egyptian homeland, but their views were tempered by a special loyalty to the Islamic tradition. However, in the second half of the century, there were intellectuals who placed less emphasis on the Islamic heritage in Egypt and were concerned with freeing Egypt from foreign control.

That new sense of nationalism was a part of the Urabi movement, but at the time the potential nationalists were divided. There were Egyptian military officers, like Ahmad Urabi himself, who resented the privileges of the Turkish military officers who dominated the Egyptian army. There were also the Islamically oriented reformers, who followed al-Afghani's ideas, and the supporters of the idea of a constitutional parliamentary regime. Following the defeat of the Urabi movement and the British occupation, overt nationalism was less visible, but in the last decade of the century, there was a revival of nationalist activity. That revival was led by a French-educated Egyptian lawyer, Mustafa Kamil (1874–1908), an effective orator and a skilled political propagandist. His primary goal was to rid Egypt of the British occupation forces, and he thus appealed more to sentiments of national pride than to religious loyalties.

Mustafa Kamil identified nationalism with modernization. In 1906 he wrote: "We have realized for over a century now that nations cannot lead an honorable life unless they follow the path of Western civilization. We were the first oriental people to shake hands with Europe, and we shall certainly continue along the path we have taken."[13] Kamil did not ignore Islam, but he viewed it in the light of modern nationalistic sentiments. He gave some support to Pan-Islamic causes, but as a way of removing foreign control from Egypt. He was not a well-organized political theorist, but he appears to have thought of Islam largely in individualistic terms, implicitly accepting the secularism of much of modern thought. For him, religion was an individual matter of personal faith and morals, so he was an early believer in one type of individualistic Islam that evolved in the modern context. That type allowed a personalizing of religion and a separation of it from the realm of economics and politics. In that belief, Kamil was in sharp contrast to the emerging Islamic modernist thought.

Kamil led the Hizb al-Watani (National party) until his death. Before World War I, that group was largely an organization of the modern-educated elite rather than a mass party. However, the nationalist movement did help to awaken Egyptians to more political issues and paved the way for a mass nationalist party following the war.

In Egypt, the first phase of reform was followed by a period in which great efforts were made to respond intellectually and actively to the changing conditions. Militant revolt was not, however, a viable possibility following the British occupation, so significant militant opposition did not occur until after World War I. Under the leadership of Muhammad Abduh and Mustafa Kamil, Islamic modernism and Egyptian nationalism emerged as influential intellectual forces. In Islamic terms, the styles of Islam most visible at the end of the century were intellectual adaptationism with a fundamentalist shading in Muhammad Abduh and an individualist shading in Mustafa Kamil.

Islam and Reform in Tunisia

During the nineteenth century, Tunisia went from a relatively autonomous province of the Ottoman Empire to the status of a French protectorate, but it remained a monarchy and reflected the trends that were taking place in Egypt and the central Ottoman Empire. A first phase of pragmatic, if somewhat haphazard, reforms was undertaken by Ahmad Bey, who ruled from 1837 until 1855. New schools were established, military modernization was undertaken, and there was a general attempt to expand the role of government while maintaining the traditional structures. Under pressure from modern-educated Tunisians and European powers, a constitutional regime had been established by 1860. However, financial mismanagement led to increasing problems, and tax increases and economic problems created the conditions for a major tribal revolt in 1864, which spread to urban areas. Ulama participated in that revolt in an effort to regain some of their financial privileges, which had been lost through the reform program. The revolt was put down, but the financial problems were not solved, so in 1869, a European commission took control of Tunisian finances.

The need for more effective reform programs was clearly visible when one of the leading nineteenth-century Muslim reformist thinkers, Khayr al-Din Pasha, became the Tunisian prime minister in 1873. Although he was forced to resign in 1877, he succeeded in creating a coherent reformist framework for later Tunisians. Despite the reforms, however, Tunisia was unable to avoid increasing European domination, and in 1881, French military forces occupied the country and established a protectorate. Although the monarchy was formally preserved, real political control was in French hands. The first phase of pragmatic reform had been followed by the emergence of a reforming ideology, but the end result, in political terms, was foreign control.

The role of Islam in this history is similar to its role in Egypt and Istanbul. The ulama establishment was basically conservative in its style, but it gradually accepted reforms and seldom participated directly in the opposition movement. Instead, the ulama relied on their political skills to limit the changes and to remove reformers from positions of power, but in the long run, the ulama accepted a reorganization of religious finances and Zaytuna University. Major reform leaders had ties with the ulama, but no major figure emerged from the Tunisian ulama to shape the ideologies of reform in the manner of Ahmad Cevdet in Istanbul or Muhammad Abduh in Egypt.

The leading figure in nineteenth-century Tunisian reformism was Khayr al-Din Pasha, a Mamluk of Circassian origin who went to Tunis in 1840. He was active in the reforms of Ahmad Bey and had substantial experience in dealing with Europeans. He reached the peak of his power in 1873–1877, when he was the Tunisian prime minister. Both as a political leader and as a writer he was a key figure in the development of reformist ideology. His influence spread beyond Tunisia, as is reflected in the fact that after his resignation as prime minister in 1877, he went to Istanbul where he became grand vizier of the Ottoman Empire for a short time in the early days of Abdulhamid II's reign. However, his favorable attitude toward a constitutional regime soon clashed with the emerging autocracy there, and he retired.

Khayr al-Din was knowledgeable in both European affairs and Islamic learning. His basic goal was to reform Islamic society in a way that would profit from European experience but remain true to the Islamic heritage. He believed that "there is no reason to reject or ignore something which is correct or demonstrable simply because it comes from others."[14] One of the key parts of his reform program was an emphasis on education that combined traditional Islamic learning with a knowledge of the West, and while he was prime minister, he established Sadiki College, which attempted to do just that. That college and his own influence shaped the next generation of Tunisian leaders. Khayr al-Din was clearly an Islamic adaptationist who worked to create a modern but still Islamic society.

Following the establishment of French control, there was a period of quiet adjustment for the Tunisian educated elite. However, like Muhammad Abduh in Egypt, most of that Tunisian elite felt that direct resistance to the French was useless and worked to reform society within the framework of French control. Followers of Khayr al-Din and graduates of Sadiki College found their way into minor administrative posts, and a group known as the Young Tunisians emerged. With the Young Tunisians, there was an effort to move from passivity to self-assertion.

Unlike the contemporary Young Turks or the Egyptian nationalists, the Young Tunisians tended to avoid revolutionary activity and militant opposition to European control. They assumed more of a linking role, trying to explain the French to the Tunisians and represent Tunisian interests to the French. An example of this effort was the establishment of the Khalduniyyah school in 1896, which attempted to instruct people with a more traditional religious education in the modern ideas. Although Sadiki College emphasized European language instruction, the Khalduniyyah school gave greater emphasis to instruction in Arabic.

In the Young Tunisian movement, there was a relatively broad spectrum of religious views. The predominant mood was one that saw Islam in primarily personal terms with the broader issues of social structure and communal identity being governed by modern ideas. The group moved in the direction of an individualized style of Islam within the framework of a modern, secularist orientation.

A more rigorously Islamic position also developed under the influence of the Pan-Islamic politics of Abdulhamid and the teachings of Muhammad Abduh. A leading figure in that trend was Abd al-Aziz al-Thaᶜalibi, a person with a thorough religious training but with a fundamentalist rather than a conservative style. For al-Thaᶜalibi, modernism was a tool for strengthening Islam rather than an end in itself. He aroused ulama opposition in Tunisia by his attacks on the existing religious practices, and his emphasis on the Islamic identity of Tunisians ran counter to the assimilationism of most of the Young Tunisians. He was thus an adaptationist with strong fundamentalist leanings. When the Young Tunisians were suppressed by the French in 1912, following a series of relatively minor frictions between the government and the intellectuals, it was al-Thaᶜalibi's more militant nationalist tone that survived.

Within all the Ottoman-related areas there was a general pattern that was repeated with local variations, as can be seen in the experiences of the central Ottoman Empire, Egypt, and Tunisia. The main impetus for reform came from the dominant political elite, and it was adaptationist in style and oriented toward Western ideas. At first, that impetus took the form of pragmatic reform programs initiated by rulers like Mahmud II, Mehmet Ali, and Ahmad Bey. Such reforms were accelerated and took a more organized form by the middle of the century in the hands of leaders like Ahmad Cevdet, Ismaᶜil, and Khayr al-Din Pasha. In religious terms, the efforts did not constitute a rejection of Islam but, rather, were an attempt to integrate Islamic ideas and Western techniques.

By the end of the century, the process had gone further, and a variety of ideologies of reform had emerged. Two main types can be identified. One was more secular in orientation and emphasized the Westernizing dimensions of reform. This type provided a foundation for nationalist feelings and, in religious terms, adopted a more individualized style of Islam. Islam was seen as a primarily personal matter, and the Western secularizing assumptions of a separation of religion and politics were accepted. The other ideology of reform was Islamic modernism. Because of the Pan-Islamic policies of Abdulhamid, it was an important political factor, and in the case of thinkers like Muhammad Abduh, the emphasis was placed on social reform and a reorientation of religious attitudes. The two types of reform ideology were adaptationist with an individualist tone and adaptationist with a more fundamentalist tone. However, in those Ottoman states, fundamentalism did not emerge as the organizing principle for militant activist movements.

Morocco: Traditional Monarchy

Outside of the Ottoman Empire, there were two states that maintained their independence within the Islamic world, Morocco and Iran. In these cases, the governments were less effectively organized in bureaucratic terms but maintained monarchical institutions that were closely tied to the local conditions. In both of these states, the reform efforts were less well organized, and the non-state structures were much stronger.

The sultans of Morocco ruled over a loosely controlled area. Government structures were less comprehensive, a great deal of political power was in the hands of the great tribal chiefs and local religious notables, and the extent of the sultan's control depended upon his ability to secure the cooperation of those local magnates. In doing so, the sultan relied upon the military forces at his personal disposal, and those made available to him by his allies. The armed forces of the central government were never as clearly dominant in Morocco as they were in the Ottoman areas in the eastern Mediterranean. The Moroccan monarch, however, had an additional source of strength in his religious prestige among the general population. As a sharif, he benefited from the respect given to holy men and the tradition of special respect accorded to the monarchical sharif.

During the nineteenth century, there was constant tension in Morocco created by internal struggles for power and the growing expansion of European political and economic influence. Because the sultan was unable, in the long run, to prevent the European expansion, he faced religiously inspired opposition. In this context, it was difficult for any nineteenth-century Moroccan monarch to initiate effective Western-inspired reform programs. No figure similar to Mahmud II emerged, and those reforms that were attempted tended to be haphazard and halfhearted. The most vigorous effort was made by Sultan Hasan, who ruled from 1873 to 1894. He hoped to check European expansion through the adoption of Western techniques, especially in the military, but the general structure of society could not adjust rapidly enough. The result was the way was opened for a further expansion of European influence. Following Sultan Hasan's death, weak leadership, internal revolts, and a vigorous French expansionism created the conditions for the loss of Moroccan independence. In 1911, the French intervened in a revolt, and they established a protectorate in 1912.

The Islamic dimension of that history is complex. The dominant religious institutions were the monarchy itself and the great religious orders and marabout centers. The formal ulama class had some influence in the urban areas, as teachers and scholars, but they were not important as a focus for religious identity and loyalty. As a result, they tended to follow the lead at various times of either the *tariqah* leaders or the sultan.

In contrast to the political passivism of the ulama establishments in the Ottoman areas, the marabouts and the *tariqah*s had a tradition of political activism in Morocco, and they were frequently rivals of the sultans for control of various areas within the country. This context provides an important framework for the Islamic experience of Morocco during the nineteenth century.

Sultans in the late eighteenth century had taken a number of important religious initiatives. Sultan Muhammad ibn Abdallah (r. 1757–1790) had encouraged a revival of religious scholarship and had worked to reform the curriculum of the major Islamic university of Qarawiyin. In scholarship, he had emphasized the study of *hadith*s and had supported a fundamentalist tone. His son, Mawlay Suleyman (r. 1792–1822) attacked the popular religious practices of the marabouts and the *tariqah*s, and he sent a delegation to Mecca in 1812 for discussions with the Wahhabis and accepted many of their interpretations. The sultans were thus directly involved in the development of revivalist ideas in the evolution of Moroccan Islam. This was one way of asserting their control over the marabout forces.

During the nineteenth century, the major form of action taken by the sultans against the religious orders was military efforts to limit their control. From time to time, local saints were important figures in supporting revolts against the ruling sultans. There were also cases in which the sultans recognized the local autonomy of the religious leaders and thus secured them as allies. That situation was true in the case of the leaders of the Tayyibiyyah who dominated the hinterlands of Tangiers. At the end of the century, the sultans gave some encouragement to scholars who had been influenced by the teachings of Muhammad Abduh that criticized some of the Sufi practices. However, that encouragement did not place significant restraints on the influence of the *tariqah*s.

The basic position of the sultans was a conservative one as they attempted to maintain their leadership role within Morocco. To accomplish that goal, they sometimes utilized adaptationist styles, but in a haphazard manner, just as they sometimes supported fundamentalist ideas. However, too rigorous a fundamentalist position might undermine their own prestige based on their position as sharifs, and they were either unwilling or unable to become vigorous reforming adaptationists in the manner of Mahmud II or Mehmet Ali.

The other major set of Moroccan Islamic institutions, the *tariqah*s and the marabouts, maintained a similarly ambiguous conservative style. At the end of the eighteenth century, Neo-Sufi ideas had been brought to Morocco, and Moroccans had played an important role in the development of Neo-Sufism in the central Islamic lands. However, the basic patterns of mass organization were already in opposition to at least some of the patterns of the popular religious practices associated with Moroccan Sufism. As a result, Neo-Sufi revivalism had a greater impact on the ulama of Morocco than on its marabouts.

The Tijaniyyah Tariqah was the major Neo-Sufi order in Morocco. It was established by Ahmad al-Tijani (1737–1815), a scholar born in southern Algeria. He had studied *hadith* in Fez and joined major Moroccan orders before going on a pilgrimage to Mecca in 1772. While on pilgrimage, he had studied with Mahmud al-Kurdi, a leading member of the revivalist Khalwatiyyah in Cairo, and then with Muhammad ibn Abd al-Karim al-Samman in Medina. When al-Tijani returned to North Africa, he announced that he had received special authorization from the Prophet to establish a new *tariqah*, which reflected the Neo-Sufi emphasis on a mystical relationship with the Prophet rather than on union with God. In Fez, al-Tijani was welcomed by the reform-minded Sultan Suleyman, possibly as a result of the sultan's opposition to the older Sufi brotherhoods. Many government officials became affiliated with the Tijaniyyah. Although the order was influential, it did not become the basis for a large-scale, transtribal movement of Islamic revivalism in Morocco, although it did in other parts of Africa.

Al-Tijani taught that the Tijaniyyah was the culmination of the *tariqah*s, and he required initiates to give up their membership in other orders. He also said that it was forbidden for Tijanis to visit living saints or the tombs of dead ones, reflecting a fundamentalist theme.[15] The rigorous exclusivism of the order meant that although there were branches of the brotherhood in many areas, the Tijaniyyah did not spawn a host of distinctive suborders in a manner similar to Mustafa al-Bakri's Khalwatiyyah. The cohesiveness of the Tijaniyyah tradition was characteristic of a number of Neo-Sufi orders that emerged early in the nineteenth century.

During the nineteenth century, the Tijaniyyah in Morocco remained quite closely tied to the monarchy. The major centers of the order developed in Algeria around the family of the founder. In Algeria, the Tijaniyyah came to cooperate quite closely with the French, but the Moroccan branch was less willing to aid the French after the establishment of the protectorate. The Tijaniyyah was thus an order within the developing Neo-Sufi tradition, but it was not particularly involved in instigating activist movements with a countrywide political significance.

Most of the other major *tariqah*s in Morocco continued in the marabout tradition, and they had a significant but localized influence. Because of the nature of the spiritual authority of both the sultans and the marabouts, there was always either potential or open competition. The marabouts succeeded in maintaining their local positions, and the sultans were able to keep the influence of any given Sufi teacher localized. As a result, the *tariqah*s were not able to organize any large-scale resistance movements as *tariqah*s elsewhere did. Rather than resisting the expanding influence of the French, the major Moroccan orders tended to cooperate with the Europeans as a way of resisting the power of the sultans. Such cooperation was true, from time to time, of the Tayyibiyyah and the Darqawiyyah, and after the protectorate was established, the old-style orders were a major source of Moroccan collaboration with the French.

By the end of the nineteenth century, the impetus for Islamic reformism had passed from the people who were influenced by Neo-Sufism to those who were influenced by the emerging ideas of Islamic modernism as expressed by Jamal al-Din al-Afghani and Muhammad Abduh. This school of thought came to be called the Salafiyyah, meaning those who follow the pious ancestors (*salaf*).

One of the earliest people to introduce Salafiyyah ideas into Morocco was a scholar, Abdallah ibn Idris al-Sanusi (d. 1931). He came into contact with those ideas during a pilgrimage in 1870 and, on his return to Morocco, was named by the reformist sultan, Hasan, to a royal council of prominent scholars. Al-Sanusi advocated a literal interpretation of the Quran and a strict adherence to the Sunnah, and he opposed local Sufi practices. A second, more active figure in promoting Salafiyyah ideas was Abu Shuʿayb al-

Dukkali (1878–1937). He studied in Egypt and taught for a time in Mecca, and after his return to Morocco, under the French protectorate, he was active as a judge and a legal scholar. Abu Shuᶜayb helped to reform the curriculum at the major Moroccan Islamic university and to spread Salafiyyah opposition to popular Sufism. He and his student, Mawlay al-Arabi al-Alawi, were major forces in educating the emerging nationalist Moroccans, and they provided the intellectual foundations for the more politically active Salafiyyah type of movement that emerged following World War I.

The Moroccan Salafiyyah provides a contrast, then, to the more conservative style of the major Islamic institutions in that country. Neither the *tariqah*s nor the sultans were able to create an effective adaptationist reformism, and they were not significant sources for ideologies of reform. That role was thus left to the ulama and the educated groups, who laid the foundations for a modernizing ideology within the framework of fundamentalist modernism.

The Qajar Dynasty: Monarchy in Shiᶜi Society

In Iran during the nineteenth century, the monarchy operated within the framework of a Shiᶜi society and had much less direct religious legitimation than the sultanate in Morocco. By the time of the Qajar unification of Iran at the end of the eighteenth century, Shiᶜi political thought had quite clearly defined all government other than that led by the imam as illegitimate. Believers were to accept the existing regime as necessary for public order and stability, but religious guidance in all matters, including political ones, was to come from the *mujtahid*s and ulama in general rather than from the political rulers.

There were inherent tensions in a sociopolitical order of that type. One basic line of tension was between the political rulers and the religious leadership. Even though the Iranian ulama generally accepted the monarchy, they worked to limit its powers and to restrain the arbitrary rule of the Qajar shahs. In this effort, they had strong allies in other major segments of the population. The leaders of the great tribes and the major ethnic minority groups also resisted a strengthening of the powers of the central government and frequently cooperated with the ulama. In some cases, *mujtahid*s were among the leading spokesmen for those ethnic groups whose religion was Shiᶜi Islam. Some of the minority groups were Sunni Muslims, but even they would at times cooperate with the *mujtahid*s to limit the shah's control. Another social group with similar goals was the merchants of the bazaars or city markets. Control of the traditional economy was in their hands, and any expansion of the power of the central government often meant increased state supervision in the bazaars. The bazaar merchants were one of the leading groups of lay supporters of the ulama, tied to them by common background and a firm adherence to Iranian Shiᶜi Islam. The ulama, tribal and ethnic groups, and bazaar merchants represented an informal alliance of forces to act as a check upon the monarchy and to limit its ability to initiate and implement policies that would significantly alter the structure of Iranian society.

The strength of those forces and the general weakness of the Qajar shahs meant that nineteenth-century reform efforts in Iran were not very effective. No clearly dominant reformer emerged, and most of the reform efforts were considered by the general population to be foreign interference in Iranian affairs. Opposition to efforts to create a more effective central government could be either the traditional Shiʿi opposition to monarchical "tyranny" or the opposition to foreign ideas that would undermine the Islamic foundations of society. By the end of the nineteenth century, those sentiments had succeeded in keeping the monarchy weak but had been unable to stop European military and economic expansion.

The problems faced by the modernizing reformers in Iran are illustrated by the fate of the major reform efforts during the century. In the early years, Abbas Mirza, the crown prince, worked to introduce military reforms, although without parallel administrative and financial reorganization. He had some success, but military defeats at the hands of the Russians destroyed much of his work. He died in 1833, before his father's death, and never came to the throne. Although he had tried to win ulama support, their call for a jihad during the Russian wars had limited his ability to negotiate, and their opposition to foreign techniques had laid him open to the charge of departing from the Islamic faith.

In the middle of the century, a grand vizier under Nasiruddin Shah, Mirza Taqi Khan, called Amir Kabir (in office, 1848–1851), attempted major administrative and legal reforms. The ulama considered those reforms to be attempts to limit their role in society, and they were able to arouse popular opposition to them and to support the court intrigues of the grand vizier's enemies. The result was that Amir Kabir was dismissed and then murdered in 1851. "After his fall, only Mirza Husayn Khan Sipahsalar among Qajar ministers contemplated any serious reform, and the demand for reform was to be associated with that for a form of government consultative at least in appearance."[16] Attempts to expand the power of the monarchy were increasingly associated with concessions to the Europeans, and "reform" came to have a religious and an antimonarchical tone.

The Shiʿi ulama in Iran emerged as the spokesmen for the nation instead of the interests of the state, which helped to set a conservative and religious foundation for Iranian nationalism as it emerged in the modern era. In addition, the ulama became the allies of the proponents of liberal reform because of the shared aim of wishing to limit the power of the monarch, but this alliance did not result in the creation of a modernist Islamic ideology. The interpretive freedom given to the *mujtahid*s by the traditional Shiʿi theology, as it had developed in the eighteenth century, made adjustments and alliances possible without intellectual adaptationism of a modernist type.

That fact had an impact on the development of modernizing reformist thought. By the end of the century, a group of Iranians who had received a modern education and experience began to play a more important role in Iranian history. Through journalism and their political activism, they had an impact on the formulation of the antimonarchical positions. However, the integration of modern and Islamic ideas was always tentative, reflecting the ulama-liberal interaction that produced an alliance but no synthesis.

An extreme case of the loose integration is that of Mirza Malkum Khan (1833–1908). Malkum Khan was from an Armenian Christian background but was himself a Muslim, although the depth and nature of his commitment to Islam was sometimes suspect. He was involved in organizing secret societies, was active in the political plotting of the second half of the nineteenth century, and was a strong supporter of the Westernizing reforms in Iran. He called the ulama ignoramuses but recognized the need for their cooperation if the reform programs were to be implemented successfully. Thus, whatever cooperation existed was in the form of an alliance rather than a successful integration of ideas. In 1889–1890 he published a newspaper, *Qanun*, which, along with his other writings, helped to introduce Iranians to the modern concepts of government. Although the ulama might not have agreed with him, they utilized concepts such as a constitutionally elected assembly in their cooperation with the Westernizing reformers against the power of the monarchy.

The relationship between Malkum Khan and the ulama emphasizes a basic aspect of the development of Islamic thought in Iran. The ulama and the Westernized intellectuals were able to avoid, for a critical period, dealing with the problems of the ideological implications of modernization in an Islamic society. The possibility of an antimonarchical alliance based on the common political interest of limiting the power of the shah allowed the ulama to be a key focus for nationalist sentiments, and even political reformism, without having to develop an Islamic modernism or a fundamentalist Islam in modern garb. For example, in the days of the constitutional movement in 1906 and later, it was possible for scholars like Muhammad Husayn Na'ini (1860–1936) to defend the constitutional cause in terms that basically reaffirmed traditional Shi'i political theory with little reference to that cause's modern ideological context or implications.

Similarly, the Westernized intellectuals were able to treat the alliance with the ulama as a "marriage of convenience and necessity." Modernizers like Malkum Khan recognized that their views were counter to those of the ulama and opposed by most of them. However, the intellectuals' response was generally to conceal or at least understate their "real" positions rather than to attempt to develop an effective bridge in intellectual terms between the Islamic and the Westernizing positions.

Although Jamal al-Din al-Afghani inspired efforts to integrate Islamic and Western ideas elsewhere, he did not have significant success in Iran, where his role was more that of a political agitator. His followers had some impact in the political intrigues at the end of the century—one of them murdering Nasiruddin Shah in 1896—but the main thrust of Islamic thought remained dominated by the *mujtahids* rather than by the new Muslim modernists.

The central theme in the development of religious activism was the relationship between the ulama and the state. However, another line of eighteenth-century religious development was also important for a time during the nineteenth century. The charismatic messianism of the Shaykhi movement provided the impetus for a movement of religious revolt in the middle of the century, and the Shaykhi teachers encouraged a popular expectation of the coming of the Mahdi. In 1844, Ali Muhammad, a student of a major Shaykhi teacher, declared himself to be the Bab (Gateway) to the Truth and the initiator of a new prophetic age. The Bab soon clashed with the ulama because of his criticism of their practices and then his followers began to revolt, coming into conflict with the state as well as with the religious leadership in Iran. The Bab gained a relatively large following in a short time, which illustrates the potential religious activism of large segments of the population. However, the government suppressed the movement and executed the Bab and other leaders. In exile, the remnants of the movement continued the tradition in a more politically passive form, and the major surviving element followed Baha'Allah in the establishment of the Baha'i religious tradition. Within Iran, the followers of the Bab, the majority of whom became part of the Baha'i group, remained a persecuted religious minority but had little direct role in Iranian affairs after the suppression of the original movement.

The more significant evolution of Iranian religious activism and nationalism took place through the activities of the ulama and other groups in their interaction with the monarchy. The character of this development is illustrated by two major events. One was the successful opposition to a tobacco concession granted by the shah to a British firm in 1890, and the other was the constitutional movement of 1905–1906. In both of these cases, the shah was seen as the tool of growing foreign control in Iran and the supporter of corrupt and tyrannical governmental practices. Large-scale opposition emerged, and the alliance of the ulama, the bazaar merchants, and the new educated class was able to force the shah to accept the popular demands. The common goals of the three major elements in the alliance were a limitation of the powers of the monarchy and an elimination of foreign influence in Iran. Characteristically, however, the success of the opposition movements was based on an alliance of diverse forces rather than on a common ideology of reform.

In 1906, the alliance succeeded in forcing the shah to accept a constitution with an elected parliament. The haphazard Westernizing reform efforts of the nineteenth century had created a group of Iranians with a modern education who, through their writings, were able to provide the conceptual terminology for the constitutional movement. However, the reforms had not built a structure of modernized institutions to support those ideas. The monarchy itself was weak, and the state, in contrast to the states in other Muslim areas, could not provide an effective focus for the modernizing efforts.

With the success of the constitutional movement, the divisions within the alliance came to the fore. In addition to the continuing threat of Russian and British imperial ambitions, the new regime had to cope with significantly different perceptions of what the nature of the government should be. Three competing viewpoints had emerged. The modern-educated group worked to create a basically secularized, democratic regime, although at least some in this group realized the need to give some recognition to Islam in order to maintain the support of the majority of the population. The second group was drawn from the ulama. Although they resisted many of the secularizing tendencies of the modernizers, they continued to support the constitutional cause. They felt that a constitutional government would be a way of limiting the tyranny of the rulers and, through the assembly or parliament, would provide a vehicle for the defense of Islamic ideals. In this way, the basic themes of Shiᶜi political theory could be reconciled with the existing reality. A clear statement of this constitutionalist viewpoint was presented in a significant book by Muhammad Husayn Naᶜini (1860–1936), and that work had a long-term impact on the political thought of the majority of the Iranian ulama. Significantly, the book was not an exposition of a new, modernist Shiᶜism but, rather, a reaffirmation of traditional Shiᶜi political theory in a different context.[17]

The modernist tendency in the constitutionalist movement was clearly adaptationist and, in its religious aspect, accepted the individualized nature of religion in a secularized context. The constitutionalist ulama were more conservative, but there was some willingness to accept adaptationism in terminology. The third group was more clearly fundamentalist in style. Shaykh Fadl Allah al-Nuri led those people who felt that there could be no dilution of Islamic law, and he and his supporters joined forces in an attempt by the shah to overthrow the constitutional regime, which triumphed briefly in 1908. Shaykh Fadl Allah allowed the execution of well-known religious laymen, and when the constitutionalists returned to power, Shaykh Fadl Allah was executed. This fundamentalist effort represents an additional theme in the development of Iranian Islam in the modern era. Shaykh Fadl Allah was one of a series of militant ulama who opposed secularist compromises and were willing to become political activists in support of their position.

Summary

The Islamic state systems that survived in the nineteenth century had a variety of experiences. In each of them, there were attempts at modernizing reform programs, but those attempts were more coherent in the central Ottoman Empire, Egypt, and Tunisia than in Morocco and Iran. In all cases, the expanding European power played a role that both encouraged and ultimately thwarted the reform efforts. By the end of the century, a more Islamic reaction had developed. Some of the reformers maintained a semblance of Islamic loyalty, but increasingly, in their view, Islam was to be a personal matter. This viewpoint recognized the implicit secularism of the Westernizing reforms and gave rise to a new form of the individualistic style of Islam, which is well illustrated by the Egyptian nationalism of Mustafa Kamil.

A more specific Islamic orientation developed through the work of scholars like Muhammad Abduh in Egypt and the Salafiyyah movement, which grew out of that trend of Islamic modernism, and an adaptationist style with an Islamic emphasis developed. That style provided a vehicle for integrating Western and Muslim ideas. In Iran, the integration was more in terms of a political alliance than an intellectual synthesis. As a result, the constitutionalist ulama there were more conservative in style, and that situation created an opening for a more explicitly fundamentalist position. This potential for a nationalism with a more fundamentalist tone was realized later in the twentieth century in Iran and had its counterparts in the Moroccan Salafiyyah and al-Tha'alibi in Tunisia. This more militant Islam provides a link between the eighteenth-century activism and the resurgence of Islamic sentiments in the last quarter of the twentieth century.

Militant Reaction and Reorientation

In those areas of the Islamic world where the governments were less effective, nineteenth-century events followed a different pattern. The resistance to Western expansion and internal decline produced vigorous Islamic reactions that followed the eighteenth-century patterns, and there was less effort to introduce modernizing reforms of institutions because of the weakness of the local rulers. By the end of the century, the more traditional Islamic reactions had clashed with the European imperial expansion directly and had been defeated. In the aftermath of that defeat, significant efforts were made to adjust to the new circumstances, and Islamic reformism, modernist adaptationism, and nationalism emerged as the major ideological styles.

Islam in Nineteenth-Century India

At the beginning of the nineteenth century, India was in turmoil. After a century of revolt and warfare, the Moghul Empire was no longer an effective governing structure, the Indian subcontinent was divided into warring states, and the British were gradually expanding their influence and control. Within the Muslim community, the most important intellectual force was the tradition of the great eighteenth-century thinker, Shah Wali Allah. His followers and descendants were, at the beginning of the nineteenth century, the source of most of the dynamic developments taking place within Indian Islam.

In the face of this disintegrating situation, Muslims began to react with a vigor that was characterized by a fundamentalist militancy. During the first half of the century, a number of activist groups raised the banner of holy war, and others supported programs of Islamic revivalism. In tone and in general intellectual content, these movements were direct continuations of the eighteenth-century trends. However, by mid-century, the ability of these groups to win their battles had declined, and a great rebellion that spread throughout much of India in 1857 became a major watershed. After the British had crushed the revolt, British domination of all of India was clear, and few militant groups arose. Instead, major efforts were made in the direction of adapting to the new reality. Those efforts took the forms of an Indian Islamic modernism, a conservative revivalism, and the beginnings of Muslim nationalism in India.

The political dimension of Shah Wali Allah's ideas took concrete form in the movement established by Ahmad Brelwi (1786–1831). Ahmad had been a student of Wali Allah's oldest son, and his reformist ideas rested on the foundations of that major tradition of scholarship. Ahmad Brelwi was upset by the deepening decline of Muslim fortunes, believed that the decline was due to a departure from the faith, and opposed the popular religious practices and compromises with local Hindu customs. He gained widespread respect and followers through active preaching tours, and after a pilgrimage to Mecca in 1821, he organized a special religio-political state and initiated a holy war to restore Muslim rule in India. He was killed in battle in 1831, and much of his army was scattered, although his followers were able to continue a limited preaching of fundamentalist reform.

The movement of Ahmad Brelwi is often called a Wahhabi movement, but he probably received no direct inspiration from the teachings of Muhammad ibn Abd al-Wahhab. However, Ahmad Brelwi clearly was within the tradition of eighteenth-century socio-moral reconstructionism. Through Shah Wali Allah's teachings, he had direct ties to the broader movements of eighteenth-century Islam, and in his opposition to popular Sufi practices and syncretism, he was part of the developing Neo-Sufi tradition. That fact is possibly reflected in some of his specific teachings. Like his near contemporary, Ahmad al-Tijani, he claimed direct inspiration from the Prophet Muhammad, which provided the foundation for uniting the major *tariqah*s into the Muhammadiyyah Tariqah. That Neo-Sufi theme of using a *tariqah* based on direct contact with Muhammad and calling itself the Muhammadiyyah Tariqah was a part of a number of contemporary movements, including the orders established by students of Ahmad ibn Idris. In addition, Ahmad Brelwi also placed emphasis on the importance of the *hadith*s and opposed the authority of the four medieval schools of law if that authority required *taqlid*.

Eighteenth-century themes provided the basic foundations for this movement of Islamic revival in India. Ahmad Brelwi attempted to meet the challenges of the early nineteenth century with tools that had been created in the previous century, and his defeat helped to show that those tools were not sufficient in the changing circumstances.

Ahmad Brelwi's movement was largely influential in central and northwest India, and there were similar movements in other parts of India at the same time. One of Ahmad Brelwi's students, Mir Nithar Ali, commonly called Titu Mir (1782–1831), established his own movement in Bengal. He organized Muslim peasants in opposition to the Hindu landlords and British commercial interests and attempted to reform the popular religious customs. He soon clashed with British forces and was killed in 1831.

Another militant movement at the time was the Fara'idiyyah, which was established by Hajji Shariat Allah (1764–1840), a teacher who had studied in Mecca for almost twenty years. There he may have come into direct contact with Wahhabi ideas, and he was clearly influenced by the more general socio-moral reconstructionism of the time. He initiated a vigorous reform movement in Bengal, and many of his key themes were common contemporary ones: an emphasis on the oneness of God and a rejection of those popular religious customs that ran counter to a strict interpretation of the Quran and the Sunnah. He also supported the cause of Muslim peasants against the landlords and British commercial interests. His son, Dudu Miyan (1819–1862), succeeded him as leader of the movement and gave it a careful organizational structure. Dudu Miyan created what was essentially a separate government for members of the Fara'idiyyah and soon clashed with the authorities. After he was arrested in 1847, the movement weakened without his leadership, and it gradually became just one of many religious movements in the area.

The era of large-scale militant Muslim movements reached a climax in the general Indian uprising against the British in 1857. What began as a mutiny among both Muslim and Hindu troops in the British army soon became a widespread series of revolts against the British. Many different groups participated, and the character of the opposition depended upon local conditions. Although Muslim religious leaders participated, the uprisings did not represent a unified Islamic opposition to imperial rule. The ulama in Delhi were persuaded to declare the revolt a holy war, and some scholars established a religious state in Thana Bhawan. The leader of that latter group was Imdad Allah (1815–1899), a noted Sufi teacher who fled after the rebellion to Mecca, where he became a popular teacher and had an influence upon the later Indian Muslim reform movements.

The British were able to crush the uncoordinated revolts, and the 1857 rebellion marks a major turning point in the history of Indian Islam. Although small-scale militant Islamic groups continued to revolt from time to time, the major Islamic movements after 1860 assumed a different form, and most Muslim leaders accepted the reality of the British military dominance. Like Muhammad Abduh in Egypt, they set out to revive and reform Islam within the context of foreign control. Militant Muslim revivalism had failed, and the need now was for ways to adjust to Western domination and modern ideas.

The leading figure in this reorientation of Indian Islam was Sayyid Ahmad Khan (1817–1898). Sayyid Ahmad had worked as a young man for the East India Company, and after 1857, he strove to reconcile the Indian Muslims and the British. In intellectual terms, he attempted to integrate Western and Islamic thought because he believed that a Muslim adjustment to the modern intellectual realities was absolutely essential. He said, "If people do not shun blind adherence, if they do not seek that Light which can be found in the Qur'an and the indisputable Hadith, and do not adjust religion and the science of today, Islam will become extinct in India."[18]

In order to carry out his program, Sayyid Ahmad worked to translate Western works into Indian languages, helped to organize special education committees, and established a modern institution of higher education for Muslims—the Muhammadan Anglo-Oriental College in Aligarh, which became a major center for Islamic modernist education in India. His general approach to integrating modern scientific thought with Islam is stated in his axiom that nature, which is the work of God, is identical with the Quran, which is the word of God. Through his writings and life work, he created the intellectual foundations for Islamic modernism in India. He also helped to revive the communal morale of Muslims, and he resisted nationalist pressures to have Muslims join the emerging Hindu-dominated Indian nationalist movement. By helping to revive Muslim pride and by encouraging Muslim separatism, he opened the way for Muslim nationalism and the creation of the state of Pakistan.

The implications of the positions taken by Sayyid Ahmad Khan led to a variety of developments, either reacting in opposition or developing the positions further. The work of an associate of Sayyid Ahmad's, Chiragh Ali (d. 1895), illustrates the radical potential of the new modernism. Chiragh Ali rejected the whole structure of medieval society as outmoded. He engaged in a vigorous defense of Islam against the criticism of Christian missionaries and other Europeans, but he did so on the basis of an analysis and interpretation of the Quran rather than by defending existing Muslim practices. In the defense, he presented arguments through the vehicle of a rational historical analysis, saying that "Islam exists as a religion distinct from a social system, though Muslims in various phases of their history confused the individual or cumulative experience of their social systems with the Quran."[19]

That development produced what has been called "speculative fundamentalism."[20] In that style, a modernist adaptationism is combined with a rejection of all classical sources of Islamic law and thought except the Quran itself. Positions are supported by a rigorous, if speculative, analysis of the Quran, and everything else in the Islamic tradition is viewed in its historical context. It was possible for Chiragh Ali, and others like him, to argue that Muhammad did not set up a formal legal system and did not require his followers to do so; thus, Muslims are free to develop legal systems that are in accord with the specific conditions of their own times and are not bound by systems developed by Muslims in other times or places. This speculative fundamentalism opened the way for a radically modernist form of Islam.

The position of Sayyid Ahmad Khan was not accepted by all of the major Muslim teachers and the richness of Indian Muslim thought at the end of the nineteenth century and the breadth of the foundations provided by Shah Wali Allah are clearly visible in the variety of the more conservative positions that had emerged by the end of the century. New educational institutions were a leading part of the more traditional revival. In 1867, an Islamic school was established at Deoband by scholars in the tradition of Wali Allah. Although some of the scholars had participated in the ulama militancy led by Imdad Allah in 1857, their goal now was to revive a rigorous study of the traditional Islamic disciplines and to provide a link between the Muslim community and its traditional identity. The Deoband school was relatively conservative in accepting the validity of the law schools and fundamentalist in rejecting compromises with Hindu customs and also in rejecting the adaptationism of Sayyid Ahmad Khan. The Deoband theological school established an international reputation and had ties with the ulama of al-Azhar in Egypt.

The more conservative style was also manifested in other important schools. The oldest and most conservative of the major schools was the Faranji Mahal in Lucknow, which maintained a traditional curriculum and was relatively aloof from the arguments of the modernists and active traditionalists. A less conservative school was the Nadwat al-Ulama, which was established in Lucknow in 1894. Its leaders attempted to find a middle path between the modernism of Sayyid Ahmad Khan and the conservativism of Deoband and hoped to provide the training necessary for the ulama to be able to reassert their role as the moral leaders of the Muslim community in India.

A more rigorous fundamentalism of a traditional rather than a "speculative" type also emerged in the late nineteenth century in the form of a group known as the Ahl al-Hadith (People of Hadith), who built on the tradition of *hadith* study that had been firmly established in India by Shah Wali Allah. The movement emphasized a reliance on the Quran and the Sunnah, and its members were unwilling to accept the teachings of the medieval scholars as binding unless they were directly based on the fundamental sources of the faith. In this belief, they were continuing the eighteenth-century trends in *hadith* scholarship and were an important link between modern and premodern developments.

In addition to adaptationists, conservatives, and fundamentalists, the nineteenth-century Indian Islamic experience produced a major movement that can be seen as an assertion of the individualist emphasis on charismatic leadership. This was the Ahmadiyyah movement, which was founded by Mirza Ghulam Ahmad of Qadiyan (1839–1908). He claimed special revelation from God and regarded himself as a prophet and the promised messiah. Although in many ways the Ahmadiyyah remained within the bounds of the Islamic tradition, other Muslims rejected the Ahmadiyyah as heretical. By the early twentieth century, the movement had become a separate religious community and had become active in missionary work outside of India.

The vigorous activity within the Indian Muslim community during the nineteenth century shows the dynamism of Islam in the early modern era. Movements both built on the Islamic foundations of the past and reacted to the changing modern conditions, and the community was not isolated within the Islamic world. Sayyid Ahmad Khan was aware of the works of Khayr al-Din Pasha in Tunisia, and Chiragh Ali read the works of al-Tahtawi in Egypt as well as the writings of Khayr al-Din. The Ahl al-Hadith were influenced by nineteenth-century Yemeni scholarship, and virtually all educated Muslims were aware of developments in Egypt and the Ottoman Empire. The second half of the nineteenth century was a time of real Islamic resurgence in India in intellectual and religious terms, although it took place in the context of foreign politico-military control. In this resurgence, all of the traditional styles of Islamic action were visible in varying forms as the Muslim community worked to meet the challenges of modern history.

Muslim Activism in Southeast Asia

During the nineteenth century, a number of dynamic tensions provided the framework for the development of Islam in Southeast Asia. The old tension between a localized, syncretic Islam and a more rigorous, cosmopolitan faith continued. The main lines of that interaction had already been set in the eighteenth century and were manifested in the reforming crusades that were led by ulama who had been on pilgrimage and the work of others who had been influenced by the cosmopolitan trends in the Indian Ocean basin. This old tension often involved conflict between the religious leaders and the established rulers. The second conflict involved the expansion of Dutch control and the local resistance to developing Western imperialism. Since the Dutch attempted to work through the local rulers and the courts, the two conflicts often merged, and the holy wars were both attempts to reform religious practice and expressions of opposition to expanding foreign control.

The general pattern of development was similar to what was taking place in India. The old local state systems were crumbling and were not able to provide effective leadership for the reformist efforts. Resistance and reform followed eighteenth-century lines rather than adopting reform programs of a Westernizing type. The more traditionally structured Islamic reactions produced militant movements, which ultimately were defeated by the forces of European imperialism. However, this phase of militant resistance was spread throughout the century, in contrast to the Indian experience, because Dutch control expanded only gradually throughout the islands of the East Indies. As the Dutch consolidated their position in an area, local militant resistance would arise and, usually after a long struggle, would be defeated. It was not until the end of the century that the Muslim communities in Southeast Asia reached the stage where most religious leaders accepted the inevitability of foreign control and initiated significant nonmilitary efforts of reform.

For the Muslims in Southeast Asia, the nineteenth century was a time of a long series of bitter and hard-fought holy wars, which had the dual purpose of reforming local religious practice and resisting the Dutch. The character of these conflicts shows that Southeast Asian Islam was not isolated from the rest of the Muslim world. As changes took place elsewhere, they were reflected in the developing attitudes in Southeast Asia.

The early holy wars still followed eighteenth-century patterns. In 1803, three scholars returned from a pilgrimage to Mecca and began a vigorous preaching mission to reform the local religious practices in Sumatra. Their active preaching upset the existing balance between the local chiefs and the religious teachers. The movement the scholars started was called the Padri movement by the Europeans and *kaum puteh* ("white ones") locally because of the requirement that men wear white, Arab-style robes, and it expanded by persuasion and force from village to village. By 1820, the Dutch became involved as they hoped to expand their power by aiding local rulers who were opposed to the *kaum puteh*. After sixteen years of fighting, the *kaum puteh* were subdued, but, during that time, the movement gradually evolved into a relatively unified Muslim front, led by the *kaum puteh*, that opposed the infidel foreigners. In the process, the ulama emerged with great prestige as the spokesmen for indigenous interests. Descendants of the *kaum puteh* leaders later became respected religious teachers who continued to support a more rigorous adherence to Islam and played an important role in the emergence of Islamic modernism in Indonesia.

A second major war in the first half of the century illustrates many of the same trends. Dutch control during the first two decades of the nineteenth century had an unsettling effect and opened the way for a growing exploitation of the local population. The Java War from 1825 to 1830 was led by a local sultan's son, Dipa Negara, who had retired from court life to engage in religious meditation. He had gained a reputation for visions and was persuaded that his mission was to purify Islam. Rebellion broke out when he was insulted by a Dutch official, and he was soon supported by many of the ulama. Some of the Javanese nobility remained loyal to the Dutch, but gradually, as in the case of the *kaum puteh*, the ulama-led movement of opposition to the compromises of court life became a holy war against the infidel foreigners. Militant revivalist Islam again provided the ideology of revolt against foreign rule, and the fundamentalist ulama gained strength among the general population as the old court nobility became identified with the Dutch.

The third great war of the nineteenth century was the result of Dutch control expanding into the area of the old, and now ineffective, sultanate of Atjeh in Sumatra. Atjeh had remained independent—although that status depended primarily on the Anglo-Dutch Treaty of 1824, which defined spheres of influence and guaranteed the independence of Atjeh—but in the second half of the century, it became clear that the Dutch intended to extend their control into the area. In an interesting illustration of the cosmopolitan, if naive, view of the Achinese sultan, he appealed to the Ottoman sultan for aid against the growing Dutch interference, and some people from the court contacted the U.S. and Italian consuls in Singapore. After a new Anglo-Dutch Treaty, the Dutch invaded Atjeh in 1873, and a long war began.

The old court and the local notables were ineffective in the resistance. The real leaders were the ulama, and the war rapidly became a holy war against Dutch aggression. Gradually, the sultan and then the local governors accepted Dutch rule, and the ulama became identified, as they had in the other conflicts, as the true representatives of local opposition to alien rule.

Although the Atjeh resistance was similar in many ways to the fundamentalist style of militant Islam visible elsewhere in the early part of the century, it also reflects late-nineteenth-century movements as well, as there was a sense of Pan-Islam as it was promoted by Abdulhamid II in Istanbul. Local enthusiasm was aroused when a Turkish warship passed through Singapore on its way to Japan, and Southeast Asian Muslims were aware of events like the Russo-Turkish War of 1877–1878 and the Mahdist uprising in the Sudan in the 1880s. All of those events helped to keep alive the hope of a general Islamic movement that would defeat the European imperialists.

Ironically, the international ties of the Muslim community were aided by the consolidation of Dutch control, and less militant but still strongly revivalist movements had emerged by the beginning of the twentieth century. On the negative side, the identification of the old ruling class with the colonial administration removed the major rival of the ulama as the leaders of the majority of the population. However, on the positive side, the Dutch improved the communications system and thus opened up previously isolated communities to Muslim influence. In addition, the expansion of the Dutch administration meant that Muslims were given subordinate clerical positions and sent to many areas where they acted as conscious or unconscious missionaries.

One major impact of a more modern communications system was a significant rise in the number of Southeast Asian Muslims going on pilgrimage. Despite restrictions imposed by the Dutch, the pilgrimage was a significant part of Muslim life in Indonesia, and in the second half of the century, the increase and improvement in steamship services made the holy cities more readily accessible. The experience of being in Mecca and Medina inspired a desire to bring local Muslim life more into accord with a strict interpretation of the Quran and the Sunnah. In this way, the popularity of the pilgrimage helped to support a fundamentalist style of reformism. In addition, a large community of Southeast Asian scholars became established in Mecca and Medina, and they participated in the major currents of Islamic thought and were an effective channel for their transmission back to their homeland.

International contacts and ties were a part of the inspiration for the militant holy war movements during the nineteenth century. These contacts were also important in the emergence of a less militant but still reformist Islam as it emerged by the end of the century. An early leader in this shift, who also provided a more modernist tone, was Shaykh Ahmad Khatib (1855–1916). He was a descendant of a Padri teacher in Sumatra and went to Mecca in 1876 where he remained and became a well-known teacher of Shafiᶜi law. Although he did not return to Indonesia, his students became major figures of Sumatran and Malayan reform. He was relatively traditional in his approach to legal studies and did not accept some of the ideas of Muhammad Abduh, although he was familiar with them.

Another Sumatran descendant of a Padri teacher, Shaykh Muhammad Tahir ibn Jalal al-Din (1867–1957), was more directly involved in spreading the ideas of Muhammad Abduh's Salafiyyah to Southeast Asia. He also taught in Mecca for a time after studying at al-Azhar as well as in the holy cities. Early in the twentieth century, he began publishing a newspaper called *al-Imam* in Singapore, and it circulated widely in the area. He supported and spread Abduh's ideas and opposed local popular religious practices. In legal opinions, he based his conclusions on the Quran and the Sunnah rather than utilizing traditional opinions from the law schools. He and his associates established a school with a modernist curriculum, which became a model for other schools. Muhammad Tahir was representative of a new generation of Muslim leaders who accepted the political realities of the time but continued the reformist spirit. The activities of this generation soon led to the creation of relatively large-scale organizations that were active in religiocultural affairs, education, and politics. In this way, the foundations were laid for the twentieth-century experience of Southeast Asian Islam.

During the nineteenth century, adaptationism in Southeast Asia largely took the form of collaboration with the growing Dutch power on the part of the local rulers. There was little effort at modernizing reforms, if for no other reason than the rulers did not have the power to implement them. Conservative-style Muslims were those who worked to preserve the old cultural compromises that were manifested in the local popular religious practices. Throughout the century, the conservatives were on the defensive, not so much facing the attacks of modernizing reformers as facing those of the revivalist fundamentalists.

In Southeast Asia, it was the fundamentalist style of Islam that flourished during the nineteenth century. Rigorous reformism became identified with opposition to alien rule, and in many rural areas that reformism provided the leadership that replaced the older-style religious conservatives. The holy wars led by the fundamentalists could not stem the tide of Dutch expansion, but neither could the Dutch eliminate the influence of the activist ulama. By the end of the century, though, a significant number of ulama had begun to exercise their reformist zeal against social practices and traditional ideas in a less politically militant manner. In that change, the influence of emerging Islamic modernism in the Middle East and India played a role.

The Algerian Experience

In Algeria, the domination of the French was more complete than that of the Dutch in Indonesia or the British in India. The weak Ottoman governors were replaced by French rule in the years following the French invasion in 1830, and there was no opportunity for local governments to adopt reformist programs. Opposition to European imperialism was almost entirely the work of the local religious and tribal leaders. Because the French policies undermined the very nature of Islamic society in Algeria, there was little incentive to create a reformist movement similar to Abduh's, which accepted the political realities. The Algerian religious leaders who cooperated with the French did so as political allies, preserving their own interests, rather than in an effort to create an effective synthesis of Western and Islamic ideas. It was not until the twentieth century that effective Islamic modernist or Algerian assimilationist movements developed.

The foundations for a nineteenth-century religiopolitical activism were being laid early in the century, before the French invasion. As the Turkish governors in Algiers became more ineffective and oppressive, local political leadership was assumed by marabouts and *tariqah* leaders. There were revolts by the Darqawiyyah and Tijaniyyah orders against Turkish rule, and popular support for the *tariqah* leaders made it possible for the orders to create states in the existing political vacuum. This conflict with the Turks also made it possible for some of the *tariqah* leaders to see the French as allies in the struggle. In this way, some of the major brotherhoods established alliances with the French, and that cooperation continued throughout the century. In particular, despite its Neo-Sufi origins, the Tijaniyyah in Algeria became closely associated with the European rulers. The early Tijaniyyah attempts to establish a state of their own had been thwarted, first by the Turks and then by other militant orders who opposed the French. The Tijaniyyah thus allied themselves with "the enemies of their enemies" and accepted French rule.

The most famous militant Muslim leader in nineteenth-century Algeria was the Amir Abd al-Qadir (1808–1883). Through his family and education he had direct ties to the major trends of the eighteenth-century Islamic world, and between 1830 and 1847, he led a major movement of resistance to French control. The ancestors of Abd al-Qadir had been local teachers in Algeria, and they had maintained a family devotional tradition of adherence to the Qadiriyyah Tariqah. His grandfather, Mustafa ibn Muhammad al-Hasani (1747–1798), had reorganized the family order along Neo-Sufi lines after studying in the eastern Mediterranean, in particular with Muhammad Murtada al-Zabidi in Cairo. On his return to Algeria, Mustafa had enlarged the activity of his family's branch of the Qadiriyyah, and the family center became a well-known place of learning. Mustafa's son, Muhyi al-Din (1776–1834), had continued this revival and had gained a large following among many of the major tribes.

Abd al-Qadir, Muhyi al-Din's son, grew up in the context of this revived *tariqah*. He went with his father to the eastern Mediterranean where he studied *hadith* in Damascus and is said to have been initiated into the Naqshbandiyyah Tariqah by the revivalist-reformer, Khalid al-Naqshbandi. On his return to Algeria, Abd al-Qadir began to assume a position of leadership in his family's order.

Following the French invasion, tribesmen in western and central Algeria turned to Muhyi al-Din for resistance leadership. He finally agreed to guide the jihad and soon turned over its direct leadership to Abd al-Qadir, who was both an able military commander and an effective political organizer. Abd al-Qadir soon established a militant movement that was both an army and a state. He showed himself to be a fundamentalist in spirit but willing to accept new techniques if they would make his army and administration more effective. He consciously modeled his creation on the community of the Prophet and the early caliphs, but he did not encourage messianist enthusiasm. Through a long series of campaigns and negotiations, he fought the French for almost two decades. Finally, internal divisions within Algeria and the military power of the French defeated him.

Abd al-Qadir was not the only religious teacher to oppose the French as a number of local preachers also organized resistance movements. However, some of the most important of those were men who proclaimed themselves to be the Mahdi and refused to cooperate with Abd al-Qadir. Their opposition diluted Abd al-Qadir's strength, since he had to subdue them as well as fight the French. In addition, Tijaniyyah rivalry with Abd al-Qadir's family brought that order into conflict with the amir's forces. Thus, internal divisions were one factor that weakened the Algerians' ability to stop the French expansion.

After the final defeat of Abd al-Qadir in 1847, there were other resistance movements, but none had the large-scale support or the effectiveness of the earlier movement. Most of the revolts were led by religious figures, and Islam became clearly identified as a major source of opposition to imperialism. However, the collaboration with the French by some of the major *tariqah*s did not make the relationship between Islam and opposition to foreign rule as clear as it was in some other parts of the Islamic world.

There were clearly socioeconomic political reasons for revolt, but French power made revolution on those pragmatic grounds impractical. After the defeat of Abd al-Qadir, most revolts had to be based on an ideology that could transcend the material realities. Politically passive Sufism and even traditional revivalism, if it was based on prudent fundamentalism, could not provide the inspiration for revolt. Building on the teachings of Abd al-Qadir, prudent fundamentalism advocated emigration from the infidel-controlled areas if a successful holy war were not possible. Adaptationism, conservatism, and fundamentalism did not provide the basic Islamic style for continued opposition to the French. It was the individualistic style of Islam, which emphasized charismatic and messianic leadership, that provided the vision necessary for revolt in the face of French power.

For almost half a century after Abd al-Qadir's defeat, what has been called a "general apocalyptic awareness"[21] provided the basis for some religious activism. That sentiment accepted the possibility of establishing a realm of just rule through charismatically led revolutionary movements aided by divine intervention. A number of revolts of this type took place, but by the end of the century, the spirit had begun to fade. The apocalyptic vision had been kept alive in a number of local religious centers, but gradually, the French succeeded in destroying this institutional base. "Once this network was disrupted apocalyptic action disintegrated into banditry, civil disorder, passive resistance or resignation."[22]

In Algeria, the Muslims faced not only the overwhelming military power of European imperialism, but also a growing community of European settlers who came to dominate local politics and the economy. That domination severely limited the options that were open to Muslims who were willing to undertake even intellectual adaptationism. Islamic society in Algeria was disrupted, and it was not until much later that Algerian Muslims began to develop effective "ideologies of reform." In contrast to the rich diversity seen in Muslim India and Indonesia, there was little beyond efforts at simple survival within the Algerian Muslim community. With adaptationism apparently blocked and other styles of Islamic action stymied, Algerian Islam acted with passive resistance or resignation, waiting for new opportunities, which would be provided by the changing conditions created by World War I and the events of the interwar era.

Russian Expansion and Islam

Muslim communities in the Eurasian steppes faced the expanding Russian Empire. In a process that began in the sixteenth century and was essentially completed by the end of the nineteenth, a variety of Muslim groups came under Russian control. These groups can be divided into four general types, within which there was substantial diversity.

In the Volga River area and the Crimea Peninsula, Muslims had long been in contact with Russia, and they were the earliest to be conquered. By the nineteenth century, overt military resistance had virtually ceased, and large-scale Russian immigration was rapidly changing the demographic character of those areas. The major themes of the Islamic experience there were related to adapting to clearly permanent incorporation into the Russian Empire. In addition, the relative success of the Russian efforts to convert Tatar Muslims to Christianity provided an added challenge. In this context, Tatar Muslims of all classes were open to efforts of Islamic revival in the framework of a modernist style of Islam.

At the beginning of the nineteenth century, a second group of Muslim communities were coming under Russian control in the Caucasus region between the Black and Caspian seas. There, Russian expansion met militant Muslim opposition, and the local groups retained special ethnic and linguistic identities that would become the foundation for later nationalist sentiments.

The third and fourth groups were in Central Asia, in the general area called Turkestan. In the northern part of that area, the Kazakhs had only recently converted to Islam and had remained a largely nomadic society. The Russians were able to win the cooperation of a substantial proportion of the old tribal nobility, and Russo-Kazakh cooperation was an important theme. However, great tensions had arisen by the end of the nineteenth century as a result of a growing number of Russian settlers taking over the pasturelands of the nomads.

In the southern part of Turkestan, Islam was a long-established feature of the urban culture, and great cities like Bukhara and Samarkand had been centers of Islamic learning since the days of the Abbasid empire. Some of their commercial wealth and cultural life had crumbled as a result of a long series of invasions during the later medieval period, but in the early years of the nineteenth century, there were still relatively well-organized states led by the khans of Bukhara, Khiva, and Khokand. During the century, Russia established diplomatic ties with those states, and then, as control of the Kazakh areas was established, the khanates were drawn into the Russian Empire as relatively autonomous regions. In the khanates, the Russians felt that the older, conservative style of Islam could keep the Muslim communities backward, and the Russians supported the old institutions. Because of this induced isolation, reformism and nationalism were delayed.

In all of these areas, Muslim political institutions were either ineffective in the long run or nonexistent. As a result, there could be no reforms of the style instituted by Mahmud II or Mehmet Ali. In this way, the Russian Muslim experience was closer to that of Algeria or India. Governmental reform programs were guided by European rulers and were intended to increase Western control rather than to create modern Islamic states. Islamic developments in the nineteenth century thus took place outside of the government structures.

As was the case in other areas, initial Islamic activism took relatively traditional forms. One of the most dramatic movements of this type was in the Caucasus region of Dagestan, where, during the seventeenth and eighteenth centuries, there had been a flowering of Islamic thought. Scholars from Dagestan had traveled widely and had participated in the major trends of eighteenth-century Muslim thought. They were part of the cosmopolitan community of scholars in Mecca and Medina and were noted teachers in Damascus, Aleppo, and elsewhere. During this time, the Naqshbandiyyah was introduced into Dagestan, and under a series of activist leaders, it provided an organizational vehicle for uniting the local peoples against the Russians. This Naqshbandiyyah movement reached a climax under the leadership of Imam Shamil, who was able to maintain a holy war against the Russians for twenty-five years. His final defeat came in 1859.

Opposition to Russian control in the other areas conquered during the nineteenth century was less well organized and less successful. The groups in Turkestan were poorly armed and localized in attitude. Only the tribal and traditional khans had large potential organizations, but after some initial resistance, which was quickly brought to an end by the overwhelming Russian military force, the old political elites tended to accept the military realities. When revolts did occur, they were usually led by local religious preachers, who would collect a small band of followers and be quickly subdued. Typical of those was an uprising in Andizhan, in eastern Turkestan, in 1898. There, a local Sufi leader, Muhammad Ali (known as Ishan Madali), gained a special reputation for piety and organized an effort to overthrow the Russians in the whole region. His men, armed with charms and cudgels, were stopped in two days.

The last great uprising under the czarist regime, which occurred in 1916, continued to have the same weaknesses of the nineteenth-century movements. The Russian government issued a decree conscripting non-Russian workers for war labor. Coming in the midst of the unsettled conditions of World War I, this measure became the catalyst for widespread revolts throughout all of Russian Turkestan. There was, however, virtually no coordination in the uprisings, although in some areas the opposition assumed the form of a holy war against the infidels. The military weakness of the Muslim populations was again clearly shown. Despite the facts that Russia was in the midst of its World War I efforts and the uprisings took place in many areas in a vast region, the rebellion was totally suppressed in a few months.

By 1916, other less militant movements were emerging within the Muslim communities under Russian control. The traditional means of protest were being replaced by activities of revival and reform that were better suited to the modern conditions. By the end of the nineteenth century, a vigorous Islamic intellectual revival had begun to take place, and it took a number of religious and cultural forms. Islamic thought and education had been strongly conservative, but some intellectuals began to break away from the old conservatism, which avoided any change in order to preserve Islamic traditions in the face of the challenges posed by Russian rule. In these developments, Muslims in the Volga region and the Crimea provided much leadership.

Even in the different context of Russian control, participants in the revivalist movement developed positions and ideas that were similar to those found elsewhere in the Islamic world. One of the early leaders in this break with the traditional conservatism was Shihab al-Din Marjani (1818–1889), a teacher and writer in Kazan in the Volga basin. He rejected *taqlid* and advocated direct study of the Quran and the Sunnah, and he worked to reform the educational curriculum. Although he hoped to return to a pure form of Islam, he believed that that was compatible with modern scientific ideas. Through his work, he provided a basis for Islamic modernism in Russian and inspired a wide range of Muslim intellectuals.

An important part of this religiocultural revival was the modernization of the national languages. Some scholars were convinced that important factors in the backwardness of the Muslim peoples of Russia were their ignorance of their own languages and the absence of a literature in those languages that could bring Islamic culture and new ideas to the general population. Abd al-Qayyum Nasiri (1824–1904) helped develop and popularize a Tatar literary language based on local dialects. Elsewhere efforts to modernize Azeri Turkish and Kazakh resulted in the publication of books and newspapers and stimulated a literary florescence.

These developments were joined together in the work of Ismaʿil Gasprinski (1851–1914), a Crimean Turk who had had a modern education and traveled widely in Europe and the Islamic world. He was an active journalist, working in Paris and Istanbul, and he began publication, in Russia, of a Turkish-language newspaper called *Tarjuman* in 1883. He hoped to provide a vehicle for bringing modern ideas to Russian Muslims and also for unifying those Muslims. Influenced by the ideas of Pan-Slavism, he was an early advocate, if not the initiator, of Pan-Turkish ideas, and he used his writings as a means of developing a common Turkish language, which he hoped would replace the variety of Turkish languages and dialects. Although he did not succeed in this endeavor, his Pan-Turkish ideas were influential not just in Russia but also among the emerging Young Turks in the Ottoman Empire. His goals of providing a sense of general Turkish identity and creating a common literary language became the basis for the curriculum of the schools he established. In those schools, the aim was also to introduce the Russian Muslim communities to modern ideas. This broad combination of themes was to be the "new foundation" (*usul jadid*). Gasprinski's model schools were imitated throughout Russia and inspired educational efforts in Turkey and Iran. On the basis of this inspiration, the advocates of the whole general movement of Muslim religiocultural reform came to be called Jadids.

Gradually, Jadidism took more political forms, especially after the Russian Revolution of 1905. Muslim political parties were organized, and some secret revolutionary groups were established. Inspired by the Young Turks, Young Bukharan and Young Khivan associations were created. In this activism, there was great diversity, ranging from those people who advocated cooperation with liberal Russian groups to those who supported radical revolutionary goals or regional nationalist programs.

By World War I, the Muslim communities under Russian control were exhibiting a real vitality. The major style was modernist adaptationism, and the conservatism of the old ulama and political elites was on the defensive and tied to czarist autocracy. There was, however, little overt secularism, and the intellectual vitality was tied to the religiocultural revival of the late nineteenth century. Islam was a key part of the identity being asserted by the various movements, and this Islamic sentiment was influenced by and adapted to modern ideas. In Jadidism, there was less of a fundamentalist tone than was found in the Salafiyyah or similar movements elsewhere in the Islamic world. However, the Islamic dimension was a crucial component in the emerging nationalist identities of the Muslim peoples of Russia.

Summary

In large parts of the Islamic world during the nineteenth century, direct European control was established, and in those areas, the politically oriented reformist pattern was not possible. In India, Southeast Asia, Algeria, and Russia, special patterns of Islamic development emerged. The first phase was not, as it had been in the states that maintained at least a formal independence, an attempt at pragmatic, modernizing reform. The first phase was, rather, a more religious and traditional resistance to the advancing European power. With varying degrees of speed, these militant movements were crushed. Muslims were then forced to face directly the challenge of European control, in intellectual as well as in political terms. The result was an Islamic revival with varying degrees of strength, weakest in Algeria and probably strongest in India. Efforts to create an Islamic modernism provided new intellectual foundations for religious thought in the modern context. This work often combined with the emerging nationalist sentiments, which often were influenced by and had some influence upon the development of Islamic modernist and nationalist movements elsewhere. In this way, although local experiences were distinctive, there was still some sense of the broader cosmopolitan unity of the Islamic world.

Imperialism and Revivalism Without Modernism

Direct European invasion and control were not the only types of imperialism that affected Muslim communities in the nineteenth century. Non-European states, some Muslim and some non-Muslim, also expanded or reestablished their rule over Muslim groups. This activity produced Islamic responses that were more traditional in nature and did not lead directly to the development of Islamic modernist ideas. In addition, there were some areas into which European powers were expanding in which the traditional structures of society remained relatively intact. In those areas as well, the Islamic response followed the older patterns rather than producing a modernist adaptationism.

In these areas, like Somalia or the Nilotic Sudan, the activist movements frequently had direct ties with eighteenth-century developments or followed long-standing patterns of sociopolitical action. In the late nineteenth century, Islamic activism in those areas assumed a form that from the perspective of the twentieth century, might be seen as proto-nationalism. However, taken in their own terms, those movements were assertions of local identity and autonomy that used traditional bonds of religion and tribe or ethnic group as a basis for unity of action. If, at times, they became a component of an emerging nationalist movement, they did so without passing through a stage of significant ideological redefinition.

Mecca and Medina

One of the first areas of the Islamic world to face expansion by modernized Islamic armies was the Arabian Peninsula. At the beginning of the nineteenth century, the Wahhabi movement reached a peak of its power with the conquest of Mecca and Medina. This culmination of eighteenth-century fundamentalism led to the invasion of Arabia by the armed forces of Mehmet Ali as the Ottoman sultan asked Mehmet Ali to bring an end to the Wahhabi expansion and threats to Ottoman prestige and security. In 1812, the Egyptian army reconquered the two holy cities, and by 1818, the Wahhabi state had been crushed. After a vicious series of punitive measures, the Egyptians withdrew to the western areas of the peninsula, where they maintained control until almost mid-century, when direct Ottoman control was restored.

The Egyptian occupation and the restoration of Ottoman control did not mean the creation of a new political system. The old arrangement of a formal imperial control with the sharifs of Mecca and the notables of Medina handling local affairs was reconstituted. The Egyptian commanders and the later Ottoman governors were, however, in a position to ensure that the grand sharif was a relatively cooperative person. In view of the threat that Wahhabism had posed, any sharif or local notable who showed tendencies toward fundamentalist reformism was viewed as a potential enemy.

The situation reinforced the normal conservatism of the local religious establishments, and it also gave them added support in dealing with those ulama in the cosmopolitan scholarly community who became too popular or were visibly active in calling for reforms. The local religious notables were able to get Egyptian and then Ottoman support when they wanted to limit the activities of Neo-Sufi teachers like Ahmad ibn Idris. That scholar faced a series of public examinations and finally felt it necessary to leave the holy cities. He settled in Asir, between Mecca and Yemen, where his descendents established a virtually independent religiopolitical regime.

Despite the limitations, the international community of scholars continued to be an influential intellectual center. Through traveling students and pilgrims, the Haramayn continued to act as a distribution point for ideas. However, that international scholarly group was no longer in the forefront of Islamic thought. Its teachers continued to work and rework the themes that had been developed in the eighteenth century, and although those ideas could still inspire Islamic revival efforts, the efforts were now more traditional in style. Shaykh Ahmad Khatib, the Sumatran scholar who taught Shafiʿi law in Mecca after 1876, is a good example of the change in the Haramayn. His approach to legal studies was very traditional, and he had strong reservations about modernist ideas, but his students who returned to Southeast Asia became major figures in the Islamic reform movements there. In a way, the Haramayn became a refuge for the more conservative thinkers who sought to escape the emerging modernism of Cairo or India—for example, for some prominent Egyptians who taught in Mecca, such as Muhammad Basyuni and Mustafa Afifi.

In the second half of the nineteenth century, Meccan religious leaders did become directly involved in movements that were more modern in style, but they did so without a significant redefinition of their Islamic intellectual framework. They were active in the emerging Pan-Islamic movements and eventually were involved in nationalist activities, often giving them an Islamic dimension.

Throughout the nineteenth century, the Haramayn continued its role as an incubator for activist Neo-Sufi movements. Early in the century, Haramayn scholars played a role in the development of the Sammaniyyah Tariqah, which spread in Africa; the development of the Tijaniyyah; and the education of leaders of the Padri movement in Indonesia. The scholars had at least some impact on Ahmad Brelwi, the Indian Muslim activist, and on leaders of holy wars in West Africa. The followers of Ahmad ibn Idris, the

North African Neo-Sufi teacher in Mecca, produced a group of orders that were influential in the African Islamic revivals, including the Sanusiyyah in North and Central Africa, the Khatmiyyah in the Nilotic Sudan, and the Ahmadiyyah in South Arabia and East Africa. In the second half of the century, a second generation of scholars in the tradition of Ahmad ibn Idris provided education and inspiration for people who were active in the Pan-Islamic movement as well as the leader of the holy war in Somalia at the beginning of the twentieth century. Thus, although the intellectual community in the Haramayn was no longer in the forefront of the new style of thought in the Islamic world, it remained an active and influential part of the cosmopolitan world of Islamic activism.

Mecca provided an environment that could arouse Pan-Islamic feelings, especially among the pilgrim scholars, and it remained one of the few places that seemed beyond the control of the Europeans. One European who lived in Mecca late in the nineteenth century wrote, "The fact of students from all regions living together keeps the consciousness of the wide diffusion of their religion, and puts away the idea that is brought by many youths from Frankruled lands that the Moslems are condemned for an indefinite time to servitude."[23] In this manner, Mecca inspired the emerging Islamic reform efforts, even though it did not participate directly in them.

The holy cities were not untouched by the effects of modernization in the Middle East. The introduction of printed texts of the great ninth-century collection of *hadith*s by Muhammad ibn Isma⁶il al-Bukhari, for example, had an effect on the manner of instruction in the Traditions of the Prophet. The improvement of transportation systems brought larger numbers of pilgrims, and on the political level, the increasing centralization of the administration of the Ottoman Empire, especially in the autocratic days of Abdulhamid II, meant that Istanbul was able to exert more control in the area. The building of the Hijaz Railroad from Damascus to Medina in the first years of the twentieth century was a concrete manifestation of both of those factors, since it not only facilitated the flow of pilgrims, but also made the dispatch of imperial troops easier.

The major new mood in Mecca came from the ruling sharifs rather than from the scholarly community. Members of the leading Sharifian families traveled widely and became familiar with Ottoman politics. Some received a modern type of education in the schools in Istanbul, and most were aware of the major political currents of the time. In this context, the leading sharifs began to operate in the new political style and participated in Ottoman parliaments and societies; some even had contacts with secret revolutionary groups.

The leading figures in this development were members of the Awn clan of sharifs, led by Husayn ibn Ali (1852–1931), a grandson of the grand sharif who had been appointed by the Egyptian occupation forces in 1827. Husayn ibn Ali was born in Istanbul and circulated freely in the official and court circles. Following the Young Turk Revolution in 1908, he secured the appointment of grand sharif of Mecca, and he worked to establish autonomous, if not independent, power. His growing mistrust of Ottoman intentions led him finally in 1916 to revolt against the sultan with the aid of the British. He attempted to assume the title of king of the Arab countries, and after World War I, he claimed the title of caliph. In his actions, one can see the foundations for Arab nationalism, but his goals were probably more clearly religious and personal than nationalistic. He provides a good example of the transition to the more modern forms of action without a stage of intellectual modernism.

In Mecca and Medina during the nineteenth century, the currents of the previous century clearly continued to flow with vigor. In the cosmopolitan scholarly community, a fundamentalist style of Islam was gradually becoming more conservative. At the same time, the conservative establishment found itself faced with new political realities, and it gradually assumed a vigorous political adaptationism that was conservative in intellectual content but modernizing in the form that its political activism took.

Localized Revivalism in the Western Indian Ocean Basin and the Arabian Peninsula

In a number of areas in the western Indian Ocean basin and the Arabian Peninsula, special local conditions produced a variety of Muslim activist movements during the nineteenth century. Those movements tended to lack the cosmopolitan flavor of the Meccan experience, but some of the elements of the Meccan pattern can be seen in them. The economic and political conditions of the region were being changed by the growing European imperial involvement, and new and more modernized regional powers played a role. However, the interaction between modernized and local forces did not result in significant intellectual reorientations. Islamic activism followed lines that had been set in the eighteenth century rather than moving in the direction of an Islamic modernism. By the end of the century, this activism had created religiously based movements of "national" unity, or Islamically based political forms, that provided the foundations for local states in the twentieth century.

Wahhabis. The first Wahhabi state had been crushed by the Egyptian invasion of the Arabian Peninsula and the outside imperialist force that these fundamentalists faced was Middle Eastern rather than European. The Egyptian occupation of the central parts of the peninsula was not long lasting, and the interaction was primarily military. This conflict did not pose an intellectual or a religious challenge to Wahhabi fundamentalism.

The Wahhabi forces, led by the Saud family, were soon able to reestablish control in the Najd, the central region of the peninsula. Led by Turki ibn Abdallah, who ruled from 1823 to 1834, a vigorous fundamentalist state was recreated. Under Turki and his son, Faysal (d. 1865), the "second" Saudi state was a major local power, but it did not have the international significance of the earlier state. Turki and Faysal were guided by a firm adherence to the religious traditions of their family and movement, but they were also relatively pragmatic in setting their political goals. They did not insist on a vigorous expansionism as one description of Faysal emphasizes. "Farsighted enough to realise that he could not convert the whole world to Wahhabism, and that if he tried he would again bring ruin on his people and himself, the Imam Faisal played a lower bid. He was a devout Wahhabi, but, instead of attacking Karbala, he received a British diplomat in his capital."[24]

The period of rule by Turki and Faysal was important in the development of Wahhabism. Following the defeat at the hands of Mehmet Ali's armies, the movement could have faded and become simply part of the historical record. However, those two leaders were able to rekindle and confirm the adherence of many of the tribes to their movement, and that adherence survived the subsequent disintegration of the state at the end of the century.

Another important aspect of this era is that the basic Wahhabi ideas were more fully defined and applied in the administration of the state. Major teachers, including Turki and Faysal, wrote letters defining the Wahhabi position on a wide range of specific issues. Those letters and a number of legal decisions and opinions, which were carefully collected, provided the fundamentalist state with a more clearly defined ideological basis. In this definition, there was a realistic application of fundamentalist ideas to existing conditions, but there was no adaptationist attempt to combine fundamentalism with modern ideas. There was little need for such a combination because of the limited nature of the involvement of modernized forces in the area.

During the period, there was significant intellectual activity that was associated with the movement but was not directly religious. There were a number of sound historians who focused on the history of Wahhabism, and an active group of poets emerged. A description of the work of those poets by a major Egyptian intellectual and scholar of the twentieth century, Taha Husayn, provides conclusions that can be applied to the movement as a whole at the time.

> It cannot be said that they brought about a renaissance of poetry or that they created what had not existed before, but at least they returned in their poetry to the ancient style and gave us in the twelfth and thirteenth [Islamic] century that sweet Arab song, which had not been heard in the memory of living men. This song, whose authors did not imitate the city folk nor force themselves to search for new and strange expressions, was conceived in liberty and borne along by all the greatness, the yearning for the highest ideal, and the strong longing for the revival of ancient glory, which filled its soul.[25]

After Faysal's death in 1865, the Saudi state began to crumble in the face of rivalry among members of the ruling family and attacks from enemies. By the end of the century, the state had been defeated, and the Saudi princes were living as political refugees. A grandson of Faysal, Abd al-Aziz (1880–1953), created a third state in this fundamentalist tradition, the twentieth-century Kingdom of Saudi Arabia. He began the process in 1902 when he led a small band of soldiers and recaptured the old Saudi capital of Riyadh.

There was thus another revival of the Wahhabi movement at the beginning of the twentieth century. Like the second revival, it did not involve a departure from the fundamentalist ideals of the movement. There was little intellectual or doctrinal adaptationism, but there was a real element of pragmatic adaptationism in the political realm. This fundamentalist revival was little influenced by the emerging Islamic modernism, but it came to have an impact on that modernism by encouraging a fundamentalist tone in the Salafiyyah, who were impressed by the success of Abd al-Aziz.

The Wahhabi experience in the nineteenth century built the foundation for an active and influential twentieth-century state. In an area where contact with the forces of the modernized Middle Eastern states and European imperialism was comparatively limited, a rigorous fundamentalist style was maintained, although it came to be tempered by a political adaptationism. By maintaining this style through the difficulties of the nineteenth century, the Wahhabi movement was able to emerge early in the twentieth century as the leading example and exponent of fundamentalist activism in the Islamic world.

Oman. In Oman, there was a similar continuation of a fundamentalist Muslim style but with a significant variation from the Wahhabi experience as pragmatism in the political realm became separated from the fundamentalist tradition in institutional terms. The tradition of the special Ibadi imamate continued as the major focus of the fundamentalist loyalties, but the imamate came to be a rival of the ruling sayyids of the Bu Said dynasty. In the Saudi state, the religious teachers supported the ruler, and the rulers were able to maintain a combination of roles of leading the religious movement and the state; in Oman, a significant tension developed between the two roles.

During the first half of the nineteenth century, the rulers of Oman were successful in expanding Omani power. Under Said ibn Sultan, who ruled from 1804 until 1856, a vast, sea-based empire was created. Omani control extended well down the East African coast, and a major center was firmly established in Zanzibar. The port of Muscat, in Oman, was an important trading center in the western Indian Ocean basin. However, Said faced the growing involvement of Britain in the area, and because of its naval power, that country soon assumed the role of permanent supervisor of much of the region. Said became a firm ally of Britain and, through pragmatic measures, maintained Omani independence and commercial prosperity. He tended, however, to be a merchant prince and political realist rather than claiming a religious basis for his authority. The more conservative Ibadi teachers opposed this style of rule and attempted to take control of the state following Said's death.

Between 1856 and 1868, the fundamentalist opposition gained strength while Said's successors proved to be weak leaders. In 1868, the fundamentalists, led by a major teacher, Said ibn Khalfan al-Khalili, and Azzan ibn Qays, a member of a branch of the ruling family, revolted and gained control of the government. They attempted to create an imamate that would control both religion and the state, and the tone of government policy was strictly fundamentalist. For a brief period, the coastal commercial centers and the inland areas were effectively ruled by the same person. However, the new regime was not able to cope with the problems of declining trade and did not secure British recognition. Tribes in the interior came under attack by Wahhabi warriors, and general unrest began to increase. By 1871, Turki, a son of Said, was able to organize forces sufficient to overthrow the imamate and reestablish a more pragmatic regime.

In the restored state, the rulers continued to follow more pragmatic policies, but Oman was no longer a major regional power. It was closely tied to British imperial power, although independent in terms of internal policy, and the monarchs faced regular tribal revolt and continuing fundamentalist resistance. At the end of the century, Sultan Faysal ibn Turki attempted to be more independent of British guidance but was forced to submit in 1899. That sultan's efforts were diplomatic, and he did not attempt to declare his independence through modernizing reforms.

The fundamentalist elements continued within the framework that had been firmly established during the century. Some of their leaders were relatively effective political organizers, but virtually none of them made any attempts at a further development of Ibadi ideas. The fundamentalism became a conservative fundamentalism, committed to the establishment of a traditionally defined imamate. The fundamentalists' response to British influence and the political adaptationism of the sultans was to elect a new imam, and the twentieth century began with this type of action. In 1913, Salim ibn Rashid al-Kharusi was elected imam, and he gained control of much of the inland territory. The dynamics of the nineteenth century had set the stage for twentieth-century Omani history.

South Arabia. During the nineteenth century, the centers of Muslim learning in southern Arabia lost some of the prominence they had had in the preceding era. It was a time of turmoil, with military adventurers and British imperialism playing important roles. The British took control of the port of Aden in 1839 and gradually built up a network of alliances with the local rulers to protect their position in the port, which imposed an anarchic stability on the region, and no local ruler could merge as a dominant force. A major complicating factor was the ties of the local communities throughout the Indian Ocean basin. South Arabians prospered as military leaders and as scholars in regional states, especially in India, and those mercenary soldiers often brought their wealth, expertise, and sometimes their troops back to South Arabia, where they added an element of instability.

The great scholarly and religious families continued to be influential in local affairs, but their schools did not attract as wide a range of students as in previous centuries. Sound conservative scholarship, sometimes with a Sufi tone and sometimes with a more fundamentalist style, characterized the work of the South Arabian ulama. There was, however, little intellectual adaptationism and not much participation in the intellectual movements of the time.

By the end of the century, South Arabia was divided into the city of

Aden, which was an active commercial center dominated by the British, and the rural areas, which were led by local chieftains who were tied by treaties to the British. The old traditions of Islamic scholarship were preserved, but in both the political and the intellectual realms, the style was increasingly conservative. The only exception to that trend was in Aden itself, where modern commercial life was creating a whole new way of life, but British control suppressed any potential tendencies of independent political or intellectual life there. Essentially, in South Arabia, there was direct and indirect imperialism with little revivalism of either a fundamentalist or an adaptationist style.

Yemen and Asir. In the regions of Yemen and Asir, the principal imperialist forces in the nineteenth century were the Ottoman Empire and Egypt. At the beginning of the century, neither area was under direct outside control, but the reformist and centralizing policies in Istanbul soon led the Ottoman leaders to attempt to reestablish control in western and southern Arabia. After a long series of campaigns, that goal was largely achieved. The Zaydi imam in Yemen was forced to accept Ottoman troops and recognize Ottoman suzerainty, and the various groups in Asir submitted.

At the beginning of the twentieth century, especially after the Young Turk Revolution in 1908, the Ottoman control crumbled in the face of revived political activism in both regions. In Yemen, the Zaydi imamate had never been destroyed, and in 1891, highland tribesmen had followed an imam who had not accepted the Ottoman control. That man, Muhammad ibn Yahya of the Hamid al-Din family, provided a focus for the antiforeign sentiments and opposition to Ottoman rule. Although the Ottomans were able to maintain control in some of the urban areas, Yemeni resistance continued. In 1904, there was a resurgence of opposition under Muhammad's son, Yahya, who was able to force the Ottomans to grant him recognition. A treaty establishing the Imam Yahya's control in the highlands, but leaving the coastal areas in Ottoman hands, was signed in 1911. The state established by Yahya was committed to a rigorous application of Islamic law. In his public positions, the imam was clearly fundamentalist in his style, so the Yemeni "national" resurgence was closely tied to Zaydi fundamentalism. With the collapse of the Ottoman Empire during World War I, Imam Yahya extended his control to the coastal areas with a Sunni majority, but he maintained his own fundamentalist style in setting policy.

The attempt to establish a fundamentalist Islamic state without political or intellectual adaptationism was not possible in many parts of the Islamic world by the end of the nineteenth century as such states were usually destroyed by the expansion of more modernized Islamic states or by European powers. However, Imam Yahya succeeded because of a combination of factors. The relative isolation of his domain and the difficulty of military operations in Yemen gave him some protection. The collapse of the Ottoman Empire eliminated the major regional enemy, and the reviving Wahhabi state was unable to expand its control into Yemen.

The experience of Asir was in contrast to that of Yemen. A local dynasty of religious leaders was led by descendants of the Neo-Sufi teacher, Ahmad ibn Idris. Until the end of the nineteenth century, the Idrisi family had a primarily religious role, but the local political leadership was discredited by the successful reestablishment of Ottoman control and the Idrisis gradually assumed a more active political role. The key figure in that increased role was Muhammad ibn Ali al-Idrisi (1876–1923), a great grandson of Ahmad. He had wide experience, having been educated at al-Azhar and the Sanusiyyah center in Libya and having lived for a time in the Sudan. When he returned to the Asir, he organized an effective local administration.

Muhammad al-Idrisi was committed to a rigorous adherence to Islam, but he was also a skillful and cosmopolitan diplomat. He had ties with Italians and British and was able to balance Ottoman, Yemeni, and Meccan political forces. He led a revolt against the Ottomans in 1910 and was the first independent Arab leader to sign a treaty of alliance with the British during World War I. Following that war, he preserved his independence by cooperating with the expanding Saudi power at the expense of Grand Sharif Husayn in Mecca and Imam Yahya. After Mohammad al-Idrisi's death, his successors were not able to maintain the same independent position. Asir became first a Saudi protectorate and then, in 1934, was formally incorporated into the Saudi kingdom.

The Neo-Sufi tradition of Ahmad ibn Idris provided the foundations for a movement of resistance against Ottoman imperial control. In style, this movement maintained the fundamentalism of its origins, tempered by a pragmatic adaptationism in terms of political operation. It would not appear, however, that Muhammad ibn Ali al-Idrisi made any major efforts toward an intellectual reorientation of the tradition of his ancestor, despite his education in Egypt at the end of the nineteenth century. The political adaptationism of the Idrisi movement did not extend to creating a proto-nationalist mood among its followers. As a result, the Asir revolts did not eventually lead to an Asiri nationalism.

Among the best known of the nineteenth-century scholars in south-western Arabia was Muhammad al-Shawkani (1760–1834). He was a Yemeni teacher trained in the Zaydi tradition, but his ideas had an impact far beyond that limited circle. His works were known to and cited by Chiragh Ali in India and Hasan al-Banna, founder of the Muslim Brotherhood in Egypt, for example, and his historical studies and biographical works continue to be widely used. Al-Shawkani's impact remained that of a single scholar rather than setting in motion a more general movement. The major themes of his scholarship are fundamentalist in tone. He vigorously rejected *taqlid* and what he thought was slavish adherence to the medieval law schools and so provided a justification for *ijtihad* that was useful to Sunni as well as Zaydi scholars. In intellectual terms, his influence was greater outside of Yemen than in his homeland, and he was unable to create the foundations for an Islamic modernism in southwestern Arabia.

The East African Coast. The political situation in the Indian Ocean coastal areas of Africa was fluid during the nineteenth century. Sea-based powers established positions of control in the cities and on the islands of the coast, but the inland areas were not effectively subjugated by the coastal states. Early in the century, the sultans of Oman created their empire, which controlled many major ports in East Africa. By the end of the century, Omani rule had been replaced by the European powers, with Britain, France, Germany, Italy, and Portugal all getting at least some territory. Although the foreign rulers affected trade and economic relations, there was little modernizing restructuring of local societies, except in the sense of a growing integration into the global network of Western capitalism.

Islam's role in those changing conditions was complex. On the one hand, Islam, like the foreign imperialists, came from the outside and was centered in the ports and commercial centers. On the other hand, it made significant progress in converting the hinterland tribesmen in some areas, and by the end of the century, it was providing a unifying ideology for resistance to European rule.

Before the nineteenth century, even in areas like Somalia, where many inland tribesmen had been Muslim for a long time, Islamic life had been basically tied to tribal organizations and customs. It was an adaptationist Islam, and it had made substantial compromises with local conditions. During the nineteenth century, some of the spirit of Neo-Sufism spread in the region. The result was the establishment of a number of orders whose base of support was intertribal and whose style was more fundamentalist. These *tariqah*s were active in establishing educational and social centers and taught a reformist Islam in the Neo-Sufi pattern.

Among the most prominent of those orders were the Shadhiliyyah, the Qadiriyyah, and the Salihiyyah. The Shadhiliyyah was led by Shaykh Muhammad Ma'ruf (1853–1905), a sharif in the Comoro Islands of South Arabian origin. He was initiated into the Yashrutiyyah branch of the Shadhiliyyah, an order that had its center in Palestine and was active in the Pan-Islamic movement supported by the Ottoman sultan. Under Muhammad Ma'ruf's leadership, the Yashrutiyyah was active in establishing centers and doing missionary work in the whole eastern coastal region. Although the leaders of the brotherhood sometimes attacked the policies of the local rulers and occasionally faced European controls, the order did not become a major political force. Rather, its significance was in consolidating the position of a more rigorous Islam in the region.

The Qadiriyyah played a similar role, and its most important figure in East Africa was Shaykh Uways al-Barawi (1847–1909). The Qadiriyyah tradition was more flexible and less influenced by Neo-Sufi ideas, and the Uwaysiyyah, a suborder created by Shaykh Uways, was less reformist than the Yashrutiyyah. The Uwaysiyyah approved of the practices associated with special respect for local holy men and was less rigorous in restricting the popular religious practices. However, Shaykh Uways was an active preacher and organizer, and he was especially influential in the Somali areas, where the Uwaysiyyah provided a major vehicle for action that could transcend tribal loyalties. He was an effective revivalist but not a fundamentalist reformer. As a result, he came into conflict with a more fundamentalist group and, in 1909, was murdered by one of its members.

That rival order was the Salihiyyah, which was led by Muhammad Abdallah Hasan (1864–1921) of Somaliland. Muhammad Abdallah, called Mad Mullah by his British opponents, was the leader of the revivalist *tariqah* that led a major anti-imperialist holy war at the beginning of the twentieth century. The origins of the movement are clearly within the Neo-Sufi tradition. While on pilgrimage, Muhammad Abdallah had been initiated into the Salihiyyah by its founder, Muhammad ibn Salih (1854–1917), the religious heir of one of the major students of Ahmad ibn Idris. When Muhammad Abdallah returned to his homeland, he began to preach against the local popular religious practices and created an effective religiopolitical organization. In his reformism, he soon clashed with the Uwaysiyyah, and in his political militance, he came into conflict with the British, whose domination of Somalia was growing. For more than two decades, he led a militant resistance movement against the British and other imperialists.

Although Muhammad Abdallah was fundamentalist in style, he was willing to adapt in political terms when compromises were necessary. For one period during the holy war, for example, he signed a treaty with the Italians and was willing to accept their nominal protection as a way of forestalling the British advances. In this way, he was a political pragmatist although he was not willing to assume an adaptationist style in ideology. Because of his ability to organize a movement that transcended tribal differences, he is seen by many as a proto-nationalist, laying the foundations for a later Somali nationalism.

In East Africa, the nineteenth century was a time of considerable Islamic activism, much of it inspired by eighteenth-century Neo-Sufi traditions. Although the mood was often revivalist and reformist, little effort was expended in creating Islamic modernist positions. When late-nineteenth-century Islamic developments influenced East African affairs, that influence was more in the form of an activist Pan-Islam than of an Islamic modernism. In some areas, that activism helped create the basis for later nationalist movements.

The Sanusiyyah Tariqah

One of the most vigorous and widespread movements inspired by the Neo-Sufi tradition was the Sanusiyyah Tariqah, which was established by Muhammad ibn Ali al-Sanusi (1787–1859), a North African scholar who was a student of Ahmad ibn Idris and a major thinker in his own right. In his work, al-Sanusi combined the major themes and movements of late-eighteenth-century Islam. As a student in North Africa, he had studied with the founders of the Darqawiyyah and Tijaniyyah Tariqahs and was already a well-known teacher before he went on a pilgrimage to Mecca. He was an expert in Islamic law and *hadith* and often clashed with the conservative religious establishments because of his fundamentalism. In Egypt, he clashed with the ulama of al-Azhar, especially over his advocacy of the right of *ijtihad*. Similarly, as a leading follower of Ahmad ibn Idris, he came into conflict with the conservatives in Mecca.

After the death of his teacher, al-Sanusi moved to the area of modern-day Libya, leaving a well-organized group of followers in the holy cities and the surrounding tribes. In Libya, he created a growing network of educational and social centers, which provided a basis for unity among the scattered and often conflicting tribes of the region. He was committed not only to the reform of local religious practice but also to the missionary expansion of Islam. As a result, members of the Sanusiyyah were sent into a number of areas in Central and West Africa. The result of al-Sanusi's work was the creation of a vast, loosely structured community that was based on a fundamentalist style of ideology. In terms of sociopolitical dynamics, al-Sanusi and his successors were brilliant adaptationists, creating a structure that could integrate tribal communities without destroying the underlying foundations of the social order. In intellectual terms, however, al-Sanusi must be viewed as a culmination of Neo-Sufism rather than a precursor of Islamic modernism.

The Sanusi leaders were fully aware of the threat by the European expansion in the Islamic community. Although they were not as fanatically anti-Christian as the late-nineteenth-century French propagandists suggested, they were not willing to accept European expansionism without a struggle. At first, the major areas of the Sanusiyyah were relatively isolated, but by the end of the century, a series of clashes with French forces had limited and then reduced the areas under Sanusi influence in Central Africa. Finally, in 1911, the Italian invasion of Libya brought European imperialism directly into the Sanusi homeland. At first, the Sanusiyyah joined forces with the remaining Ottoman troops in opposing the Italians, but the sultan soon withdrew his troops, and the order was left as the only organized opposition to the Italian invasion. In this way, the Sanusiyyah became a focus for modern Libyan nationalism.

The anti-imperialist struggle gave the Sanusiyyah a modern function, despite the fact that its ideology remained largely free of Islamic modernist ideas. Like revivalist movements elsewhere, political pragmatism and the struggle against imperialism led to political adaptationism, but intellectual fundamentalism continued.

Mahdism and Revivalism in the Sudan

The Islamic experience in the Nilotic Sudan was a special case in the interaction between imperialism and local Islamic communities, and in some ways, it was similar to the experiences in India, Algeria, and Southeast Asia. A previously strong Islamic state was already in the process of disintegration by the end of the eighteenth century as the Funj sultanate was wracked by civil wars and had lost effective control in much of the area. As in those other states, it was at this point of political disintegration that outside forces invaded and gained control of the region.

But in contrast to the cases of India, Algeria, and Southeast Asia, the conquering force was an Islamic state, Egypt, rather than a European one. In this way, the Sudanic situation was similar to those of the states and groups in the Arabian Peninsula that faced Egyptian and Ottoman expansionism. However, unlike the grand sharifate of Mecca and the imamate in Yemen, the Funj sultanate tradition was not strong enough to maintain itself in the face of outside control. Egyptian rule created a new political system in the Sudan, and the old political order disappeared. The new structures were influenced by the reformist experience of Egypt, and Westernizing reformism thus came to the Sudan through Muslim but non-Sudanese hands.

The impact of this distinctive experience upon the development of Islam in the Sudan was profound. Neo-Sufi revivalism had begun to enter the Sudan during the last years of the Funj rule, particularly through the Sammaniyyah and the Khatmiyyah Tariqahs. After the Egyptian invasion in 1820, the traditional Muslim revivalists did not face a crumbling regime that had accepted local popular religious practices but, rather, a government that itself seemed to encourage Islamic reformism. Whatever the religious position of Mehmet Ali may have been in Egypt, the Egyptian government in the Sudan assumed an overtly Islamic role. During the conquests, the commanders had proclaimed themselves to be representatives of the caliph-sultan. After consolidation of Egyptian control, the government worked to create an ulama establishment that could counter the influence of the local religious teachers whose influence was tied to popular religious customs.

Neo-Sufi teachers faced a choice: They could support this new, apparently Islamic government and, in that way, combat popular religious practices, or they could oppose the "foreign" rulers but, in that way, support the local teachers whom they might otherwise oppose. The latter course was chosen by at least two major groups. The Sammaniyyah held aloof from the new rulers and often criticized their policies, and in the process, the order became rather thoroughly "sudanized"—i.e., it adopted local customs and practices. The Majdhubiyyah, the order of Muhammad al-Majdhub al-Sughayyir, a student of Ahmad ibn Idris, took part in the early revolts against the Egyptians and remained a potential source of militant opposition.

The major religious group to cooperate with the Egyptian regime was the Khatmiyyah Tariqah. The founder of this order was Muhammad Uthman al-Mirghani (1793–1853), a member of a scholarly Meccan family who had been a major student of Ahmad ibn Idris. He had traveled widely in the Sudan during the last days of the Funj, and his son, Hasan, became the head of the *tariqah* there in the early days of Egyptian rule. In contrast to most of the orders in the Sudan, the Khatmiyyah was effectively centralized in its activities throughout the Sudan rather than being confined to a specific locality. This "nationwide" organization was aided by the establishment of the more centralized political regime with which the order cooperated.

By the final quarter of the century, substantial dissatisfaction with Egyptian rule had developed in the Sudan. Although there were many reasons for the dissatisfaction, it was the leaders who articulated the unrest most effectively, and the opposition Neo-Sufis played a crucial role. Although most of the Sammaniyyah shaykhs had adapted themselves to local practices, the fundamentalist message continued as a part of their tradition. A Sammaniyyah teacher, Muhammad Ahmad (1848–1885), began to preach against the corruption of the faith that he saw around him, and in 1881, he declared himself to be the expected Mahdi. He led a holy war against the Egyptian regime and its local allies, and among his early strong supporters were not only people from his own *tariqah*, but also the leaders of the Majdhubiyyah. By the time of his death in 1885, the Mahdist movement, or Mahdiyyah, had gained control of much of the Sudan, and a fundamentalist regime had been established. His successor, the Khalifah Abdallahi (1846–1899), maintained the independent Mahdist state until the British and Egyptian armies conquered the Sudan in 1899.

The Mahdist state in the Sudan was a factor in Islamic activism throughout the Islamic world. Although the writings of the Mahdi were not widely circulated and few Muslims had direct contact with the regime, knowledge of the success of the Mahdists helped to inspire activism elsewhere. Muslims in Indonesia, West Africa, Mecca, and elsewhere heard of the Mahdist movement, and many felt that it marked the beginning of the Islamic revival that would defeat the infidels' imperialism.

In local terms, the Mahdist movement had great significance. Although it was militarily defeated in 1899, it provided an experience of "national" independence that many twentieth-century Sudanese nationalists could remember, and it also created a movement that transcended tribal and local loyalties and could be a basis for later nationalism. In that respect, the Mahdist movement was similar to the Khatmiyyah. The development of Islam during the nineteenth century gave the Sudan two "nationwide" organizations, and those two groups provided popular support for the two styles of nationalism that emerged in the Sudan during the twentieth century—one supporting union with Egypt, and the other supporting an independent Sudan.

In general terms, the Sudanese Islamic experience has been characterized by two extensions of the Neo-Sufi tradition. The Mahdiyyah maintained a more rigorous fundamentalism in both intellectual and political terms, and the Khatmiyyah was more adaptationist in its political activities but did not depart significantly from the intellectual formulations of its founder.

Summary

In many areas of the Islamic world, a pattern developed that was different from the pattern in areas that came under direct European control. In some areas, there was contact with a variety of imperialisms that did not fully disrupt the traditional structures of society or break the influence of an eighteenth-century type of activism. In a third pattern of Islamic development, the traditional responses continued to have validity and support, which was made possible by the type of imperialism faced.

In that third pattern, the phase of traditional resistance may have come later or was not as completely defeated. There might have been political adaptationism in the course of a struggle or in creating a functioning government, but there was little activity aimed at redefining Islam in modern terms. Instead, the phase of the development of Islamic modernism was either bypassed or postponed, and the traditional Islamic activism became a kind of proto-nationalism rather than a modernizing reformism.

Revivalism Without European Imperialism

European expansion was clearly a dominant feature of the nineteenth-century experience of the Islamic world. However, despite what seems to be the almost universal character of that imperialism, there were areas in the Islamic world where developments were only peripherally affected. In those areas, the internal dynamics of the movements worked themselves out to a significant extent before European intervention played a significant role, and the primary characteristic of Islamic activism was an assertion of Islamic identity in opposition to elements that were primarily premodern. The two major areas where this situation prevailed were in West and Central Africa and among the Muslim communities in China.

West and Central Africa

The early nineteenth century was a time of tremendous activism among the Muslim communities in West and Central Africa. Developments during the eighteenth century had prepared the way for a wide variety of movements to bring about an Islamic revolution in the region. Prior to the nineteenth century, Islam in those areas had been only one element in a complex network of relationships, and the chief characteristic was an adaptationism that accepted a mixing of Islamic and non-Islamic elements. However, by the end of the eighteenth century, the revolutions in Futa Jallon and Futa Toro and the expansion of more dynamic Sufi orders had signaled the coming of a new era.

The new dynamism may have been indirectly affected by the changing patterns of trade that were created by European activities, but it was primarily an activism that operated in circumstances that were not affected by European expansionism. The great issues were the purification of Islamic practice and the creation of more clearly Islamic political regimes, and it was the eighteenth-century mood of socio-moral reconstruction that dominated. It was not until the end of the century that expanding European control became a major factor. By then, most of the early activist movements had settled into a more conservative phase or were disintegrating because of internal divisions following the death of the early leaders whose charisma had held the movements together.

The first great wave of Islamic revolutionary movements is associated with the Islamic revivalism of Uthman dan Fodio (1754–1817) in northern Nigeria and the central Sudanic areas. Uthman had ties with the Qadiriyyah tradition in the region, and his teacher had studied under Neo-Sufi leaders like Muhammad Murtada al-Zabidi and Yusuf al-Hifnawi in Egypt. Uthman preached vigorously against the local religious practices, which had been accepted by the local ulama and rulers. He soon became convinced that this older establishment was essentially pagan and began, by 1786, to organize holy wars in opposition to its domination.

The reforming holy war of Uthman dan Fodio spread rapidly, and by 1809, a large theocratic empire had been created. Uthman himself soon withdrew from direct leadership in favor of his son, Muhammad Bello, and brother, Abdallah ibn Muhammad. The dream of a purely Islamic state was not realized, but the new political order that emerged was clearly Islamic and was based on the fundamentalist ideology of its founder. However, particularly after the death of Uthman, the founding ideology could not prevent internal rivalries, and the theocratic empire became a group of warring princes who were more interested in preserving their own interests than in continuing the effort to purify the faith. When the British and other European powers moved into the area at the end of the century, the dynasties accepted foreign control with little resistance. In Nigeria, they became a part of the British system of indirect rule, through which the princes maintained local autonomy.

The early activism was infectious and soon spread beyond the borders of Uthman's state. In Adamawa to the east, a teacher with revivalist inclinations, Modibbo Adama (d. 1847), heard of the holy war and went to Uthman. He was given the banner of jihad and returned to his homeland where he succeeded in establishing a revivalist state. Similarly, a vigorous teacher from Masina to the west, Shaykh Hamad (Ahmad Lobbo), participated in the early days of the jihad of Uthman and then returned home. As a result of a holy war in the Masina region in 1810–1818, he succeeded in establishing a vigorously Islamic, fundamentalist state. Following his death in 1844, his successors maintained a fundamentalist spirit. Although his grandson was defeated by another militant Muslim leader, al-Hajj Umar, in 1862, the Masina theocracy survived until the French conquest in 1893.

As Uthman dan Fodio's warriors moved east, they met the forces of another revivalist teacher, Muhammad Amin al-Kanemi (d. 1835). Al-Kanemi was a highly respected teacher in the state of Bornu, and the crisis created by the attacks from the west allowed him to take control of the state from the old ruling dynasty. An effective ruler, he created a state on a more fundamentalist style of Islam. Under his successors, the Islamic spirit was maintained, and the state remained independent until conquered by a Muslim military adventurer, Rabih al-Zubayr, in 1893. When the British established control in the Bornu area, the descendants of al-Kanemi were incorporated into the structure of indirect rule.

By the middle of the nineteenth century, the major theater of militant activism had shifted further to the west, and the leading figure was al-Hajj Umar Tal (1794–1864). Born in Futa Toro, he had been raised in the tradition of theocratic militancy there. He had traveled widely, and while on pilgrimage in Mecca he had been initiated into the Tijaniyyah Tariqah. On his return, he had stayed in the court of Muhammad Bello in Sokoto, where he had married Bello's daughter, and he had spent some time in Masina with Shaykh Hamad. In this way, he combined a familiarity with the Neo-Sufi tradition with the experience of the new revolutionary states in Central Africa. After his return to his homeland, he declared a jihad in 1852 and soon created a large conquest empire based on the ideals of Islamic revival. Although he clashed with the French at times, he accepted a demarcation of spheres of action and carried on his holy war against the African states to the east rather than continuing a war against the French.

Al-Hajj Umar was killed in 1864 before he could fully consolidate his regime. His conquests did, however, confirm the dominance of a more militant Islam in much of West Africa. His successors faced internal divisions, which made effective resistance to French expansion impossible, and the state was conquered in a series of campaigns that ended with the defeat of Umar's son, Ahmad al-Shaykh (Amadu Seku), in 1893. Like the other militant Islamic states of the region, the empire of Umar was drawn together by a fundamentalist vision, but after the passing of the original inspiring leader, it was unable to maintain effective unity.

The second half of the nineteenth century was a period of a high level of religious enthusiasm and activism in the Muslim communities of West and Central Africa. Many people expected the arrival of the Mahdi or a great renewer. In every area, there were local teachers who directed this enthusiasm in the direction of expanding and consolidating the position of Islam in society. This was done in a style that usually had a fundamentalist tone, although the degree of willingness to accept local customs varied widely. Although there were great leaders of holy wars, like Uthman dan Fodio and al-Hajj Umar, there were also local leaders who were less militant.

In the Senegal area, there was a remarkable array of local religious leaders. One of the best known was Ma Ba (d. 1867), a scholar born in Futa Toro whose revivalist efforts soon brought him into conflict with the French. The holy war that Ma Ba declared in 1862 was primarily against local "compromising" Muslims, and for a period of time, the French remained neutral but were eventually drawn into the conflict. It was, however, a local non-Muslim chief who defeated and killed Ma Ba in 1867. Other leaders rose and fell in the following years, and the French gradually expanded the area under their control. Internal divisions and local rivalries meant that even militant Islam was not a sufficiently integrative force to unite the area in opposition to the French.

In the end, the French victory aided rather than hindered Islam in the region. By destroying the old political structures and imposing a kind of unity, the French opened the way for Muslim preachers to spread throughout the countryside, and groups that had remained stubbornly outside of the Islamic world were converted. A forerunner of this new mode was Ahmad Bamba (d. 1927), who began in 1886 to organize a suborder of the Qadiriyyah called the Murids. In that order, there was a great deal of flexible adaptation to local customs and a willingness to cooperate with the French. The order encouraged manual labor, especially agricultural, and the Murid communities played an important role in the development of agriculture in Senegal under French rule. After the militance of the early years, a more adaptationist and less fundamentalist Islam was emerging. The success of the Murids did not, however, eliminate the more fundamentalist style of Islam, which was firmly established as a significant element in West African Islam.

In Mauritania, the Qadiriyyah was an important part of the developing Islamic experience. In an area that was a polical anarchy and dominated by tribal groups with particularist attitudes, the order came to play an important role as mediator. The leadership of the order was provided by the revivalist tradition established within the Qadiriyyah by al-Mukhtar al-Kunti in the eighteenth century. A student of al-Kunti, Shaykh Sidiyyah al-Kabir (1775–1868), established a wide network of *tariqah* centers and followers in Mauritania. Although he was not a militant leader of a holy war, his work also represents a major step in the more rigorous Islamization of the region and illustrates the ability of Islam to provide an identity that could transcend local and tribal loyalties.

Another major Qadiriyyah shaykh in Mauritania was Muhammad Mustafa Maᶜal-ᶜAynayn (1831–1910). His father had been a student of al-Mukhtar al-Kunti but had broken with that tradition of the Qadiriyyah and had established his own suborder called the Fadliyyah. Maᶜal-ᶜAynayn studied with his father and then went on the pilgrimage. During that trip, he established good relations with the Moroccan sultan, and he maintained an interest and involvement in Moroccan affairs for the rest of his life. He became increasingly disturbed by European expansion and eventually organized opposition to the French in both Morocco and Mauritania. Through his followers, he set up a virtually independent state with the help of the Moroccan sultans. With the failure of the sultans to resist the French in the first years of the twentieth century, he made an effort to claim the throne for himself, but his army was defeated by the French, and he died in 1910. "If Maᶜal-ᶜAynayn accelerated the coming of nationalism in both Morocco and Mauritania, he was unfortunately unable to cope with foreign military technology or diplomatic pressures. . . . Although both Morocco and Mauritania would like to claim him as one of their national leaders, he clearly belongs to the era before mass nationalism in the Maghrib."[26]

During the latter part of the nineteenth century, there were also a number of leaders who claimed some religious legitimacy for their movements but were primarily military adventurers. They were able to utilize at least some of the more modern style of weapons that were being introduced into the area, and their military acumen gave them brief moments of success. Two of the most famous of these were Samori Ture (1830–1900) and Rabih al-Zubayr (1845–1900). Rabih began his career as a slave raider in the Nilotic Sudan. He became a supporter of the Sudanese Mahdi but soon moved into

Central Africa, where he created a well-disciplined army and set himself up as a ruler in the region of Chad. Although he had contacts with the Mahdist movement, he was not a religious reformer; his aims were that of a military opportunist. When he was defeated by the French in 1900, his state collapsed.

Samori Ture was of greater long-term significance although he, too, appears to have been primarily a military adventurer. In the Mandinka area of West Africa, he created a short-lived conquest empire, which provided a vehicle for transcending localist loyalties among the Mandinka tribes. His religious ties were much stronger than those of Rabih. Samori Ture declared himself to be an almami and worked to encourage Islamic education and the elimination of non-Islamic practices in the areas that he conquered. His conquests broke the power of the local non-Muslim and compromising Muslim leadership, thus aiding the evolution of a more rigorous Islam. He was defeated by French forces in 1898 and died in exile. During the twentieth century, he has become a symbol of Mandinka opposition to European imperialism, but he was not himself the creator of a nationalist movement.

The nineteenth-century history of Islam in West and Central Africa shows the expansive dynamism of Islam. The major movements were fundamentalist in style, working to create societies that were in accord with the Quran and the Sunnah. Conservatism was associated with preserving the old compromises with local customs, and in virtually all areas, that style of Islam was significantly reduced in influence. By the end of the century, fundamentalism, because of its successes, had taken on a more conservative tone, and the descendants of the holy warriors had accepted imperialist protection in order to preserve the state structures created by the early jihads. The experience of contact with the West had little impact on the ideology of West and Central African Islam. Throughout the century, the general conditions were determined more by local factors than by European expansion until finally, at the end of the century, the European armies imposed control throughout the region. However, by the time of this conquest, the initial momentum of Islamic revivalism in most areas had been slowed by internal rivalries and dynastic disputes. In many ways, the imposition of European control provided an opportunity for Islam rather than a limitation. By destroying or controlling the rival local institutions, the social disunity that had hindered Islam previously was reduced. In the new context, Islam expanded rapidly through peaceful means rather than as the result of the militant holy wars that characterized much of the nineteenth-century experience.

Islamic Activism in China

The spirit of militant Islamic activism affected virtually all Muslim communities during the nineteenth century, and even the relatively isolated Muslim groups in China were aroused. In China, some of the issues involved were similar to those found elsewhere. In particular, Chinese Muslims faced the issue of how much compromise with local custom was possible. There had been Muslims in China for many centuries. Initially, they were non-Chinese groups who had come as merchants or, as in the Central Asian territories of China, as wandering nomads. As foreign groups, the problems of integration with the local cultures were not significant. However, under the Mongol and Ming dynasties, from the thirteenth to the sixteenth centuries, many of the communities had become Sinicized. Some Muslims held high positions in the imperial court, and it had become possible to speak of Chinese Muslims rather than simply Muslims living in China.

The establishment of the Manchu dynasty in the seventeenth century had brought a regime to power that was less tolerant of Muslims than previous rulers had been. At the same time, the normal internal evolution of the Chinese Muslim community had led to the question of how much compromise with Chinese traditions was possible for someone who claimed to be a Muslim. In Kansu Province, where there was a significant Muslim population, a revivalist group had emerged during the eighteenth century. This group, called the New Sect, had been led by Ma Ming-hsin and had called for a reform of local religious practices. The group had been influenced by the general Sufi developments, and its teachings had emphasized distinctive Muslim practices and had called for a rejection of many compromises with local customs. Conflict between the New Sect and the older establishment, often called the Old Sect, had led to fighting and New Sect revolts in 1781 and 1783. Although the New Sect was proscribed after 1783, its followers continued to be active in the Kansu area.

During the nineteenth century, the Chinese empire faced a variety of revolts. The efficiency of the imperial adminstration declined, and increasingly oppressive measures led to widespread popular unrest that manifested itself in further uprisings. With the imperial forces occupied in fighting revolts at the center of the empire, Muslim communities on the periphery took the opportunity to revolt as well.

There was a large Muslim community in the southern province of Yunnan, along the Burmese border. That community composed from 20 percent to 30 percent of the population and was subject to much social and political discrimination. In 1855, a rebellion broke out under the leadership of Tu Wen-hsiu, who named himself Sultan Suleyman of a new Muslim state. The central government was unable to send troops to mount an effective campaign until other more central rebellions had been crushed. The Muslims state therefore lasted until 1873, when Manchu troops finally defeated Tu.

In Kansu, the New Sect produced a dynamic leader, Ma Hua-lung, who led his followers into rebellion in 1862. Again shielded by rebellions closer to the center, the followers of Ma Hua-lung gained control of a number of cities in the province. It was only after a long and difficult campaign that the imperial armies were able to crush this rebellion, also in 1873. In both Kansu and Yunnan, the Muslim revolts were the result of many factors, but they represented movements of self-assertion on the part of the Muslim communities that had been largely adaptationist up to that time. A vigorous activism with fundamentalist overtones helped to make the revolts possible.

A third major Muslim revolt within the Chinese empire was not so directly related to issues of cultural assimilation. In the far western territories of the Manchu state, the boundary between Turkish groups in China and those beyond China's control was very vague. When the news of the Muslim revolts to the east reached the Muslims in Sinkiang, they were encouraged to revolt as well. In 1862–1863, small-scale uprisings were quickly crushed, but the unrest grew. The Chinese governors were unprepared for a large-scale uprising, and Muslim rebels soon were able to win dramatic victories. The revolt was uncoordinated in the early years, with various local commanders attempting to set up their own states. During the struggles among these Muslim leaders, one of them appealed to a Central Asian khan for aid, and in 1865, the khan of Khokand sent a force under the command of Yaqub Beg (1820–1877), who soon established himself as the ruler of much of the area. His independence was recognized by both Britain and Russia, and it was not until 1877 that Chinese imperial forces could restore Manchu control in the area.

Those three revolts and a large number of smaller outbreaks during the nineteenth century were reactions against Chinese imperial administration. Although they were affirmations of a separate identity in the face of imperialism, the empire involved was not European and, in terms of its impact on those Muslim peoples, was not an inspiration for modernizing reforms. The Muslim communities were relatively small and had few resources at their command, and with the reestablishment of imperial control, the possibility of a separate, politically independent existence was destroyed. Although the revolts were assertions of identity, they did not serve as proto-nationalist movements because of the weakness of the communities involved. Instead, most Chinese Muslims began to integrate their opposition efforts with the efforts of other Chinese who opposed the Manchu dynasty. By the beginning of the twentieth century, the Muslims had begun the process of redefining their role within China, which involved a withdrawal from separatist ideas and the adapting of Islamic modernist ideas to the Chinese context.

Conclusion: Nineteenth-Century Islam in Perspective

The nineteenth century was an era of dynamic evolution in the Islamic world. For those Western observers who see the resurgence of Islam in the later twentieth century as a new phenomenon, a study of nineteenth-century history should give a new perspective. Islamic civilization has never been stagnant or unchanging. In the face of a variety of challenges, nineteenth-century Islamic communities engaged in a wide range of activities that were aimed at both creative preservation and active adaptation. In some cases, the efforts were successful, and in others, there was failure. The most visible failure was the attempt to stop European military and economic expansion. By the end of the century, virtually all of the Islamic world was under some form of European control.

The three basic dimensions of the modern Islamic experience provided the conditions for the relative successes and failures in the nineteenth century. The Islamic dimension provided the starting point. In virtually all parts of the Islamic world, it was the ideas, emotions, and structures that had developed during the eighteenth century that were the base for the early nineteenth-century responses to historical change. In particular, Neo-Sufism and the general mood of socio-moral reconstructionism opened the way for vigorous reformism and militant fundamentalist activism.

The second dimension was provided by the expanding West. European military and economic expansion presented the prospect and then the actuality of a loss of Muslim control, and the implications of the modern Western ideas challenged the formulations of the general Islamic ideological framework. The results of the interaction of those two dimensions was determined by special local conditions, which were the necessary third dimension of modern Islamic history.

A number of patterns emerged from that interaction of elements. One pattern was dominated by the adaptationist Westernizers and developed in those areas that were able to maintain at least nominal political independence throughout the century. The first phase of this pattern was set by rigorous and pragmatic reforms that were possible only when Muslim rulers were part of an effectively functioning and politically independent regime. This phase was followed by a phase in which "ideologies of reform" emerged. Those took a variety of forms, sometimes mutually supportive and at other times competitive. In particular, Islamic modernism tried to provide an intellectual basis for integrating Muslim and modern Western ideas in all realms of activity, while Muslim secularists accepted the individualization and separation of religion that was implicit in much of Western thought. A third basic position was represented by the emergence of nationalist ideals that accepted ethnic and linguistic bases for identity rather than emphasizing the religious identity. The role of each of those positions depended upon local conditions, so that in Iran, there was an emphasis on a religiously based reformism and nationalism, with little modernist success, while in Egypt, both modernism and nationalism emerged as important intellectual orientations.

A second pattern developed in those areas where Muslim governments were already crumbling and the leaders were not in a position to institute reform programs. In such areas, European control was rapidly and firmly established. The first phase involved primarily fundamentalist rather than reformist resistance, and that was followed by military defeat and then efforts at redefinition and reorientation in the context of foreign control. That second phase was characterized by a vigorous intellectual activity in many areas, with Islamic modernism and nationalism being the two dominant forces and a variety of more fundamentalist or conservative positions also evolving. In India, Russia, and Southeast Asia, the final decades of the nineteenth century were a time of intense activity, while in Algeria, the crushing

French control meant there was less opportunity for either Islamically oriented or nationalist activity.

The interaction of imperialism and revivalism without modernism provided the basis for the third important nineteenth-century pattern. In a number of areas, the underlying social conditions and the nature of the imperialist challenge led to a revivalist activism that did not involve either Westernizing reform programs or Islamic modernism. In those areas, leaders who based their authority on nonmodern, Islamic foundations were able to create relatively successful movements of resistance, and in some cases, they created the foundations for a twentieth-century state. Although not basically nationalist themselves, those movements can be viewed as having a proto-nationalist nature. The foundations of the twentieth-century states of Saudi Arabia, Oman, and Yemen and the monarchies of Jordan and Iraq are found in such movements. In addition, at least some of the nationalist identity in the Sudan, Somalia, and Mauritania rests on similar movements. In other areas, like China and West and Central Africa, the religious revivalist movements did not face European imperialism directly until after the initial dynamism of the movements had declined, so it was the more conservative successors who faced and then accepted European control without a major reformist or modernist effort. In that pattern of experience, there was often a pragmatic adaptationism in diplomatic and political terms but a rigorous adherence to a usually fundamentalist style in ideology.

In all of the patterns, the four basic styles of Islamic experience interacted. In general, because of the dramatically changing conditions, the conservative style was weakest, struggling to halt or at least retard the process of change with little success. Adaptationism was most visible in political terms early in the century and in the great reform programs and pragmatic responses of the leaders throughout the century. Adaptationism also became a major style of intellectual activity with the emergence of Islamic modernism and nationalism. Through movements characterized by charismatic leadership and in the emergence of a Muslim "secularism," the individualist style of Islam experienced a significant evolution, and the fundamentalist style was at the heart of much of the resistance to European expansion and even gave a particular tone to many of the adaptationist policies. The reaffirmation of the fundamentals of Islam provided inspiration for modernists and nationalists as well as for those who rejected all compromise with the West. The nineteenth-century experience clearly shows continuity not only with the earlier traditions of Islam, but also with the movements and issues of the late twentieth century.

5

Twentieth-Century Islam: Dominant Majorities in the Middle East and Africa

Introduction

The widespread European imperial presence in the Islamic world did not produce Muslim stagnation. Although few areas were not dominated by the Western powers at the time of World War I, the dynamism visible in Islam throughout the nineteenth century continued in the twentieth. The era from World War I until the middle of the 1960s was a time of significant and dramatic changes within the Islamic world, in both political and ideological terms. Many independent states emerged during the period, and a variety of ideological developments occurred. Those events were accompanied by militant revolutions and gradual evolutionary changes that transformed the face of the Islamic world.

From Community to State

One of the most dramatic reorientations that accompanied the twentieth-century transformations was a redefinition of the basic operating unit. Throughout Islamic history, the transnational sense of community had been a key element of Islamic identity. The community (*ummah*) had been the major general focus of loyalty. Tribal groupings, dynastic states, and other local organizations had been of great importance, but they had not provided the framework for special ideological orientations as the local and regional groups had been viewed within the broader context of the Islamic faith and community. Even when empires had assumed a distinctive religious character, as in the case of the Safavid support of Shiʿism or the Zaydi imamate in Yemen, the transnational nature of the ideology had not been forgotten. No one had assumed that only an Iranian could be an Imami Shiʿi believer or that only a Yemeni could be Zaydi or that only an Ottoman could be Sunni.

149

During the twentieth century, two developments have worked to modify that situation. One is the evolution of nationalism in the Islamic world, and the other is the increasing importance of the structure of the state in society. These two trends often support each other, as an independent nation-state has been the goal of many intellectuals and political activists. In the process, the ideals of the cosmopolitan Islamic community have not been forgotten, but they have had to share the stage with the interests of the nation and the state. The *ummah*, the nation, and the state have become sometimes competing and sometimes complementary focuses of loyalty for Muslims.

Thinking of the state or the nation as something other than a unit subordinate to Islam emerged as a part of the interaction with the West. The process began in the nineteenth century when literary movements among Turkish- and Arabic-speaking groups gave rise to a sense of communities identified by language and culture rather than by religion. Special regional heritages and distinctive ethnic-linguistic traditions provided the basis for a new kind of group awareness. Although Islam was often a part of this awareness, the new sense of "nation" often crossed the boundaries of religious communities. In the Egyptian nationalism of Mustafa Kamil, for example, the special Egyptian Christian community, the Copts, was included in the population of the "Egyptian nation," and non-Egyptian Muslims were outside of it. Another case is the early development of Arab nationalism in Syria and Lebanon. There, Christian Arabs played an important role in defining the Arab nation's goals. In that new sense of nation, the loyalty of political activists was to the national community rather than to the transnational *ummah*. There was thus the potential for competition between the nation and the *ummah*, although there was also the possibility of one loyalty strengthening the other.

Although nationalism is a powerful force, the state has emerged as the most effective basic operating unit within the Muslim world—a vivid example of the influence of the West and of European imperialism in the Islamic world, because the boundaries of the emerging Muslim states were drawn by the imperialists. It has been observed that these boundaries had little relationship to local circumstances. Devised as balance-of-power compromises, many cut across ethnic, linguistic, and cultural units. Although the political units created were artificial, they defined the territory for the modern states in the Islamic world. A measure of the strength of the state systems created in this manner is that even after independence, virtually no state structure has gone out of existence in Muslim areas. There have been attempts to combine states, using the emotional appeal of nationalism, but few of those attempts have had significant long-term success.

The states defined by those boundaries were the major theaters for nationalist and anti-imperialist activities. As the Muslim areas became independent, it was in the form of those new states, and the new state system incorporated older institutions in some cases and created new centers of loyalty in others. Monarchies associated with more traditional religious contexts became identified with the new states and their corresponding nationalisms. In this way, for example, the sultans in Morocco became Moroccan kings, and the leader of the Sanusiyyah Tariqah became the leader of Libyan national resistance and later the first king of an independent Libya in 1952. Increasingly, the shahs in Iran, especially after the overthrow of the Qajar dynasty in 1925, appealed to explicitly Iranian rather than Islamic sentiments. In other areas, the "artificial" states gave the identity for Sudanese or Iraqi or Nigerian nationalisms, to list only a few of the many movements.

The tendency for the state to be the major political actor was reinforced by the global political context of the twentieth century, in which effective recognition was given not to religious communities or to traditional groupings but to states. The experience of being controlled by Europe and the process of gaining independence created both nations and states as alternatives to the *ummah* in providing group identity and ideological bases for social and political organizations.

A clear example of the changing nature of political symbols and organization is the resolution of the issue of the caliphate. The office of the caliph had ceased to be an effective symbol of the political unity of the *ummah* by the time of the Mongol destruction of Baghdad in 1258, but in the late eighteenth century, the Ottoman sultans began to revive the title. In areas that were lost to European control, the Ottomans negotiated, as a part of a series of peace treaties, for recognition of the Ottoman ruler as the "spiritual leader" of the Muslims in those territories. This distinction between temporal and spiritual leadership was acceptable to the Western negotiators because it was familiar to them, although it was not a significant part of the Islamic tradition. The Ottomans hoped that this concession would keep the way open for restoration of Ottoman rule when conditions changed. Abdulhamid II utilized the role of caliph in implementing his Pan-Islamic policies.

Muslims outside of the Ottoman Empire welcomed the revival of the caliphate, and their enthusiasm was heightened by the gradual elimination of most other independent Muslim rulers by the end of the nineteenth century, making the Ottoman sultan (and caliph) the single most important ruler in the Muslim world. The caliphate can be seen as a major symbol for the political hopes of the *ummah* as a transnational Islamic community. The weakness of that symbol as a basis for actually mobilizing Muslims became apparent during World War I when few Muslims answered the call to holy war issued by the Ottoman sultan-caliph.

Following World War I and the defeat of the Ottoman Empire, a nationalist regime was established in Turkey, which first abolished the office of sultan in 1922 and then abolished the caliphate in 1924. In India, a movement developed in support of the caliphate. Between 1919 and 1925, the Khilafat movement was able to mobilize substantial support in conjunction with the emerging Indian nationalist movement. However, Indian Muslim attempts to intervene in Turkish political affairs only alienated the nationalist leadership in Turkey, and soon after the abolition of the caliphate, the movement in India collapsed. Efforts elsewhere to keep the caliphate alive resulted only in a series of conferences that resulted in no agreement upon an effective course of action, and those efforts gained little popular attention or support. From time to time after 1924, other Muslim rulers attempted to assume the title of caliph, but those claims were more closely associated with personal, dynastic, or national politics than with a transnational sense of the *ummah*. The Muslim world had become a series of states, and the sense of Islamic unity, though maintaining a substantial emotional appeal, was a shared sentiment rather than an organizational basis for specific programs.

Lines of Evolution and Transformation

Because of the importance of the state structures, the general lines of political evolution in the twentieth century provide an important framework for understanding the general experience. Sociopolitical institutions developed in a variety of ways, but there were some experiences that were common to many, but not all, Muslim states.

The pattern of political evolution can be traced in three phases. The first was the struggle for independence from direct or indirect European control. Few areas had been able to escape some significant form of Western political or military intervention and domination, and in those areas that did, like Yemen, old institutions and relationships remained relatively intact but depended upon remaining isolated from global affairs. In most of the Islamic world, the more traditional means of resistance had failed to stop European expansion, and the spirit of opposition gradually assumed new forms—the most common being a growing sense of nationalism. This nationalism meant an affirmation of special local cultural identities through political movements, and Islam was an important component, especially in mobilizing popular support. During this first phase, the common goal of the elimination of foreign domination meant that Islamic activism and nationalism were mutually supportive.

The second phase came with the achievement of independence. The unit that became independent was a state rather than a religious or a national community, and the potential for tension existed among nation, state, and *ummah*. The organizers of the independence movements became the new rulers, so there was continuity between the two phases. However, the basic goals gradually changed from anti-imperialism to national unity and development. In this context, tensions often arose, and they led to political instability in some areas.

In states in which a consensus on national goals and the nature of the basic structures was not achieved, or where the institutions of the new states could not cope with the challenges posed by independence, there has been a third phase. Either through revolution or coup, the initial ruling group (and their general ideological approach) has been overthrown. The postindependence regimes introduced a reorientation of policies and ideology, and they usually initiated programs that aimed at a basic sociopolitical transformation through methods that reflected a more modern and radical style. By the middle of the 1960s, many of the major Islamic countries had experienced this third phase, while in others, like Jordan and Morocco, the independence regimes remained in power. Other states, like Yemen, which had remained independent, experienced a revolution that brought to power regimes that were inspired by the "third-phase" experience elsewhere.

Parallel to this political evolution, there was an evolution in the dominant type of ideological approach to the challenges of the modern era. The failure of the more traditional resistance movements added to the appeal of a more adaptationist approach, which was strengthened by the apparent success of a vigorous Westernizing reform program in Turkey following World War I. The leader of that effort, Mustafa Kemal Ataturk, succeeded in winning a war for national independence in 1919–1922, and his secularist modernization program provided a dramatic example for other leaders and reformers in the Islamic world.

Nationalist leaders in many areas supported programs of reformism and modernization. Elite group and class interests kept most of them from proposing a program of radical social transformation, but the general mood included an increasing popularity for Westernizing reforms. As a result, when states achieved independence, their leaders were committed to adaptationist programs, and frequently the new state structures were direct copies of Western political models. In many areas, the monarchies and parliamentary regimes created during the twentieth century were unable to solve the problems of the new states. Often the new structures became vehicles for preserving dynastic, factional, or class interests as leaders resisted ideas that involved making major changes in the socioeconomic order.

The ideology of this type of leadership went a step beyond the thinking of most of the late-nineteenth-century movements in a willingness to accept Western ideas. There was less conscious effort to integrate the Islamic heritage with modern ideas and techniques, and more attention was paid to creating modernized nation-states. When the heritage of the past was important, it was as a support for a nationalist movement or a postindependence national unity, and the development of a more specifically Islamic orientation was left in the hands of people who maintained a fundamentalist style. In the early part of the century, those fundamentalists were admired, but they increasingly came to be considered as obstacles to modernization. The dominant group, especially in the political realm, was the nationalist-Westernizers.

The nationalist-Westernizers were political activists but not often very radical in their social and economic programs. Following World War II, a younger generation emerged that felt that this approach was a failure and advocated a more radical adaptationism, one that would bring about a revolutionary transformation of society. The most frequently used label for this new ideology was "socialism," often used with a qualifying adjective, as in "Arab socialism." This ideological position was clearly committed to modernization and involved an acceptance of secularism. Religion was to be a matter for personal faith, and the old religious structures were to be clearly separated from politics. The role of religion in this context was to support radicalism: Islam as a revolutionary faith could be cited as a support for contemporary revolutionary ideology, and Islam as part of a great heritage could provide support for national unity. In many cases in the emerging radical ideology following World War II, if Islam was not openly rejected, it was subordinated to the emerging socialism.

By the 1960s, the dominant ideological position was that of modernizing reformism, and there had been a transition from the nationalist-Westernizers to modernizing nationalist-socialists in many areas. In either form, this modernizing reformism was largely secularist in approach and tended to put Islam in a subordinate position. By 1965, the more radical approach seemed to be sweeping the Islamic world. The most prominent leaders were men like Gamal Abd al-Nasir (Nasser) in Egypt, Ahmad Ben Bella in Algeria, Sékou Touré in Guinea, and Sukarno in Indonesia. They were clearly identified as spokesmen for a new radicalism rather than as representatives of Islam. Even more conservative or fundamentalist leaders were initiating programs that had the appearance of moving in a radical direction, as can be seen in the land reform programs of Mohammad Reza Shah Pahlavi in Iran. Yet, by the end of the 1960s, that surge had faltered, and the way had been paved for the new approaches that were to become characteristic of the 1970s.

In intellectual terms, there was a long evolution. Beginning with an Islamically oriented modernism, the Islamic world adopted an increasingly secularist and radical position, which reached a climax in the middle of the 1960s. This development ran parallel to the political experience of moving from nationalist resistance to independence and then, in some areas, to postindependence regimes.

The Islamic Dimension

In those transitions, Islam played a number of different roles. Adaptationism was clearly the dominant style of Islam from World War I until the mid-1960s, and three interrelated types of adaptationism were important during that period. Islamic modernism was the first type, continuing the dynamic trends of the nineteenth century. However, it became involved in apologetics and often sterile arguments, so the general tone shifted from intellectual activism and rationalism to a rather vague historical romanticism. The more vigorous thinkers within the Islamic modernist group split and moved in two directions. One line built on the adopted Western ideas and emphasis on reason and helped to create the secularist-reformist position; the other concentrated on the reaffirmation of Islam and became increasingly fundamentalist in style.

The second type of adaptationism was the secular reformism and nationalism that came to dominate most Islamic countries between the two world wars and later, and the third was the more radical reformism of the post–World War II era. In each of these three types, the Islamic element was progressively weakened or subordinated, and these types of adaptationism encouraged the emergence of a more individualist Islam. On the one hand, Islam was seen as a personal matter, to be separated from politics. On the other, the older Islamic style that looked to charismatic, individualized leadership helped to support the emergence of dramatic, reformist leaders. The old messianic expectations could find new forms, and the Mahdi could appear in the guise of the "father of the country" or its revolutionary savior.

The conservative style of Islamic experience was much less visible during the first two-thirds of the twentieth century. Clearly, in times of accelerating change in all aspects of life, the conservative position is a difficult one to define since the "radical" position rapidly becomes the conservative one, and leaders who are the heroes of change can suddenly be charged with conservative obstructionism. Thus, the nationalist-Westernizers of the interwar period often considered the Islamic modernist positions as conservative, but in the postindependence revolutions, those nationalist-Westernizers were overthrown as conservative obstacles to progress.

On a broader social level, the general conservatism of everyday life must be remembered as habits and social customs change less rapidly than government structures and constitutions. There is a gradual transformation of everyday life that is sometimes invisible to the participant. This universal kind of conservatism is, in the Muslim world, tied to Islamic values and symbols and provides an Islamic foundation for the more dramatic and visible elements of modern history. On the political level, this type of conservatism meant that as political activism changed from an elite phenomenon to mass movements, its character assumed a more religious tone and nationalist and radical slogans and symbols had a different significance on the level of the masses than among the Western-educated elite. This more religious substratum began to be more effectively mobilized by the expansion of modern means of communication. At first, the Westernizing and radical reformers were able to control this process of mobilization, but one element of the changing conditions of the 1970s was that with more effective communications, it is possible for the political elite to lose control of the general population that makes up the religious substratum. This loss of control is clearly seen in the emergence of the Islamic revolution in Iran.

In the 1970s, the style of Islam that was able to mobilize the religious substratum was the fundamentalist style. The conservative style preserved the potential for religious mobilization, but conservatives, by definition and spirit, will not take the initiative, so the fundamentalist style has continued to be an effective force during the twentieth century, although it has been obscured at times by the successes of the adaptationist reformers. Fundamentalist activism did not succeed in stopping European expansion, but a few bastions were maintained. Some people saw the success of the Wahhabi movement in reestablishing the Saudi state as a counterexample to the Turkish reform program of Ataturk. In addition, in intellectual terms, a rigorous affirmation of Islam appealed to some and was supported by anti-European sentiments, which was why a more fundamentalist student of

Muhammad Abduh, Muhammad Rashid Rida, was well known, and his works were widely read in the Islamic world.

In the years before World War II, a new format for fundamentalism began to emerge: the private, sometimes secret, association. In contrast to most previous fundamentalist movements, these associations were not always led by ulama, and they often appealed to a wide range of people who had significant experience with a more modern life-style. The most famous of this new style of group is the Muslim Brotherhood (al-Ikhwan al-Muslimun), which was established in 1928 by Hasan al-Banna in Egypt. Some of these associations, like the Salafiyyah-inspired movements in North Africa, were directly associated with, if not the core of, the emerging nationalist movements, but in other areas, they became the opponents of the nationalist political elite.

In the years following World War II, the growing influence of radical reformism undermined the influence of the fundamentalist groups, and both the fundamentalist states and the associations came to be considered reactionary. They were the "enemies" of the radical regimes, and it became popular to see such fundamentalist organizations as rearguard groups fighting a losing battle in the face of the increasing secularization of society. As the events of the 1970s show, this loss of influence did not destroy fundamentalism; it only obscured the continuing appeal of fundamentalism for a wide range of Muslims who were facing the challenges of modern history. A more fundamentalist style of Islam was a leading element in the decline of radical socialism by the end of the 1960s.

The Local Dimensions

The tremendous diversity of conditions within the Islamic world meant that the strengths and weaknesses of various types of experience and the lines of evolution varied, and many elements were involved. The eighteenth- and nineteenth-century foundations often set limits to the twentieth-century experience and provided initial motivations. Another element was the different ways the European powers dealt with the Muslim populations under their control. The Russians treated them as subordinate groups but part of the whole state system, while the British often utilized techniques of "indirect rule," thereby preserving the older forms of social and political organization. The imperial boundary lines were another important element since they defined which groups of people would have to interact with each other in anti-imperialist nationalism and in postindependence nation building.

Within the boundaries of those states, there are three types of sociopolitical environments for Muslim communities, and those environments are a crucial element in defining both the specific challenges faced and the way they are met. Slightly more than two-thirds of the world's Muslims live in political units in which Muslims are the clearly dominant majority, making up 85 percent or more of the population.[1] In those dominant majority states, Islam is closely associated with the national identity and, often, with the structure or ideology of the state. Key issues are the relationship between modern and Islamic ideas and structures, how the Islamic element of the national identity should manifest itself, and the definition of appropriate political and social institutions that will be in accord with the faith of the citizens.

A second type of political environment is that in which Muslims are either a strong minority or a weak majority of the population, between 26 percent and 84 percent of the people. Although this category only accounts for 10 percent of the world's Muslims, it is important because there frequently is instability and conflict in such states. Outside of the three distinctive states of Lebanon, Malaysia, and Albania, all of the states in this group are on the frontiers of the Islamic world in Africa. Because of the boundaries created during the time of imperial control, many of those states face major problems of national integration, and Islam is a major factor in that integration.

In the third political environment, Muslims make up 25 percent or less of the total population of the state, and almost one-quarter of the world's Muslims are in this category. There are Muslims scattered in small communities in many different countries, but these weak Muslim minorities are not necessarily numerically small as the Muslim communities in India, the Soviet Union, and China are three of the ten largest state Muslim populations in the world. These "weak minority" communities face special problems of adjustment in the modern world, and their Islamic experience has been distinctive.

Dominant Majority Areas in the Arab East

The Arabic-speaking people in the eastern Mediterranean areas, often called the Arab East, emerged during the twentieth century as an active and important element in the Islamic world. The Arabs had been the first Muslims, and the first Islamic empire, the Umayyad, had been dominated by an Arab elite. However, the emergence of the great cosmopolitan Islamic community had reduced the distinctiveness of the Arab Muslims as a separate people. Many of the newly converted people in the Middle East experienced Arabization as well as Islamization, and the old centers of the Egyptian, Mesopotamian, and Syrian civilizations became part of the Arabic-speaking world. The Arab strand became a major cultural dimension within the broader Islamic civilization rather than a special ethnic identity. Arabic was the language of religious scholarship, regardless of the ethnic background of the writers of communities involved.

A significant sense of Arab identity had emerged in the nineteenth century as a part of a literary revival in cities like Beirut and Damascus—often inspired by the works of Christian Arabs who sought a more clearly national identity not defined solely by religion—but it was not until the early twentieth century that Arab nationalist sentiments began to be clearly formulated. The pioneer areas in that formulation were modern Syria, Lebanon, Iraq, and Palestine in the Fertile Crescent. Arabic literary revival was a part of the emergence of Egyptian nationalism as well, but a sense of belonging to a larger Arab world, as opposed to membership in the Islamic community, developed only gradually in Egypt. However, the Arab East was a vigorously interacting intellectual area, and there was a great exchange of ideas among scholars in Cairo, Damascus, Jerusalem, Baghdad, and other centers.

In this area, where Muslims were and are the clearly dominant majority, the great issues were those of liberation and modernization. (The special circumstances of the Lebanese and the Palestinians are in some ways part of this experience and in other ways need to be viewed as nondominant majority communities.) There were a variety of options open to the Islamic communities of the Arab East, and local conditions shaped the choices and developments within the framework of the continuing styles of Islamic experience. The clearly dominant style was adaptationism, which took many forms, but the other styles played significant roles as well.

Adaptationist Style: Islamic Modernism and Secularism in the Arab East

Followers of Abduh. During the first two-thirds of the twentieth century, the adaptationist style took a number of forms. At the beginning of the century, the major intellectual tone was one of Islamic modernism. Gradually, however, as nationalist movements gained strength, a more secularist orientation emerged. In the Arab East, this secularism did not represent a rejection of Islam so much as a reinterpretation of Islam's role in modernizing societies. This secularism "believed that society and religion both prospered best when the civil authority was separate from the religious, and when the former acted in accordance with the needs of human welfare in this world."[2] This was an adaptationism with an individualist tone, and at times, the implicit individualist style of earlier Sufi thought helped to shape the views of these thinkers.

The Islamic modernist position was equally adaptationist but did not accept the separation of religion and polity. In this perspective, the more traditional view of Islam as being directly relevant in all aspects of life and society was maintained. However, the distinction between the two positions was seldom absolutely clear, as these two threads of Islamic thought have influenced each other and interacted throughout the twentieth century. In the Arab world, both positions arose primarily out of the developments set in motion by Jamal al-Din al-Afghani and Muhammad Abduh as most of the leading Muslim intellectuals of the early twentieth century were, in some way, students of those two men.

In the years following Abduh's death, one group built primarily upon his emphasis on the absolute truth of Islam in its essentials and moved in the direction of an increasingly fundamentalist position. The leading figure in this was Muhammad Rashid Rida (1865–1935), a Syrian who went to Cairo to study and became the leading successor to Abduh as a prominent religious teacher. He began the publication of a journal, *al-Manar*, in 1898, and it became the leading organ of Islamic reformist ideas. It was widely read in the Islamic world and was a major factor in shaping Muslim thought from North Africa to Southeast Asia. Rida emphasized the importance of basing modern Islam on the faith of Muhammad and his immediate companions, the elders or *salaf*, and from this emphasis came the name by which this school is known, the Salafiyyah.

Rida hoped to be able to create an Islamic progressive group that would provide a middle ground between what he saw as the stagnant conservatism of the old Muslim universities and the traditionalist ulama on the one hand and the excessive secularism of the Westernizers on the other. However, under his leadership, the Salafiyyah itself moved out of the "middle ground" in the direction of a more rigorous rejection of modernizing adaptationism. Following World War I, Rida gave strong support to the Wahhabi revival in Arabia, and in terms of the trends of thought in Egypt and elsewhere in the modernizing Arab East, he was losing touch with the new generations of intellectuals. Although the conservative ulama had been a major "enemy" in the early days of *al-Manar*, the opponent by the time of Rida's death was almost exclusively the emerging Islamic secularists. "So artificial and outdated to the young men who grew up following Abduh's death did Rida's thought seem that it failed to meet the new demands of life exposed to the increasing impact of Western civilization."[3]

The failure to create a dynamic middle ground in adaptationism had significant consequences, because in the interwar period, the more extreme alternatives of a more vigorous secularism, often associated with nationalism, and a militant fundamentalism became the leading movements in the Arab East. The solutions proposed by Rida and the Manar school were not realizable under the conditions of the times. Rida felt that the full application of Islamic law in society required the restoration of the caliphate at a time when the transition from *ummah* to state made such a restoration impossible, and he and his followers felt that nationalism undermined the sense of Islamic solidarity. Although they accepted nationalism as a part of the effort to gain liberation from foreign control, they did not approve of its positive ideological aspects at a time when nationalism was becoming the dominant popular sentiment.

Outside of Egypt, the Islamic modernists who followed Abduh moved in the direction of nationalist ideas rather than fundamentalist ones. Muhammad Kurd Ali (1876–1952), a Kurd from Damascus, was active in journalism and became involved in the emerging Arab nationalist movement in Syria during World War I. His primary contributions, however, were in the area of scholarship. He helped to found the Arab Academy in Damascus, and his historical studies and literary criticism were influential in reviving awareness of the Arabs' great past.

Abd al-Qadir al-Maghribi (1867–1956) was an associate of Kurd Ali and had studied with al-Afghani in Istanbul. He also emphasized a scholarly rather than a political life but was an important figure in the intellectual climate that encouraged an Arab sense of identity. In religious thought, he developed the line of rational analysis set in motion by Abduh. For example, in his Quranic commentary, he utilized a philological exegesis that rejected both the literalist and the spiritual allegorical approaches, insisting instead that interpretation should be based on an understanding of Arabic grammar and metaphor.

A more directly nationalist role was played by Amir Shakib Arslan (1869–1946), an associate of Rashid Rida from the Druze Mountain area in Syria. Arslan started from a position of rigorous loyalty to Islam but saw the Arabs as the core of Islam. He believed that "because of the special place of the Arabs in the *umma,* Arab nationalism could be reconciled with Islamic unity in a way impossible for any other—even more, that a revival of the *umma* needed a revival of the Arabs."[4] In that belief, he and Rida were in general agreement, but Arslan refused to accept the idea of European control. He was in the Ottoman parliament from 1913 to 1918 and then lived in exile, actively supporting the various movements of Arab nationalism through publications and negotiations. Although dedicated to Islam, his career shows the tendency of many of his contemporaries to ignore intellectual and social issues and to concentrate on political activities. In so doing, he was characteristic of the emerging nationalist elite that became the dominant force in Arab countries.

The Nationalist Context. Following World War I, the conditions surrounding the development of nationalism became more complex. At the beginning of the century, there had been a growing awareness of an Arab identity among the Arabic-speaking peoples within the Ottoman Empire. Although that sentiment had not been well defined in terms of its goals, there had been some sense of an Arab nation and a hope that that nation could gain political autonomy, if not independence. This feeling tended to be confined to the communities of Southwest Asia, since identity and loyalty elsewhere in the Arabic-speaking world were based on Islam or on special local institutions like the sultanate in Morocco or the emerging awareness of a special Egyptian heritage.

In Southwest Asia, the situation was abruptly changed by the World War I settlement. Separate political units were created by the European negotiators, and the boundaries of Iraq, Syria, Lebanon, Jordan, and Palestine were drawn. Until that moment, nationalist sentiments had been regional in their perspective, and nationalist movements associated with the newly created political entities had not existed. As a result, in addition to the issue of the relationship between the Islamic community and the Arab nation, there now arose the problem of defining the relationship between movements of Arab nationalism and resistance to foreign control in the newly created states (opposing the French in Syria and Lebanon and the British in Iraq, Jordan, and Palestine). A sense of Arab unity continued to be a strong emotional force, but opposition movements began to be organized within the limits of the new borders, and efforts of regional scope became less effective than more localized ones.

In the emerging nationalist movements, the emphasis on local conditions meant a withdrawal from a more rigorous attachment to Islamic unity. Although most spokesmen still saw Islam as a factor in their identity, they assumed a more secularist position in interpreting its role, and nationalist proclamations often were explicitly secularist in tone. The proclamation of the leaders of a Syrian revolt against the French in 1925, for example, was the product of both urban-educated and tribal leadership. It called upon all Syrians to fight for "the complete independence of Arabic Syria . . . and the application of the principles of the French Revolution and the rights of Man."[5]

Nationalist writers emphasized the Arab character of Islam and saw Arab unity as being necessary for any later Pan-Islamic unity. In the same vein, an Arab nationalist intellectual, Abd al-Rahman al-Bazzaz, said in 1952 at the end of a long ideological evolution: "Islam, although it is a universal religion suitable for all peoples and has in fact been disseminated among many nations and races, is undoubtedly a religion revealed first to the Arabs themselves. In this sense, it is their own special religion."[6] In another work, the same author speaks of Muhammad as the hero of Arab nationalism and of Islam "as the religion which enabled the Arab nation to assert its place in the world."[7] Those statements show the evolution of Arab-Muslim-nationalist thought from the earlier positions of men like Shakib Arslan in the direction of a more secular orientation of Islam serving the nation rather than the nation serving Islam.

In Egypt, the development of nationalism had come earlier than in Syria and Iraq, with the Urabi movement in 1879–1882 and then the National party of Mustafa Kamil. Although the Afghani-Abduh group participated in some of this activity, it was not an explicitly Islamic modernist movement, and the two lines of development were sometimes competitive. Abduh, for example, criticized some of Urabi's ideas, and later he and his associates thought of Kamil as a demagogue.

An effective mass nationalist movement did not emerge in Egypt until the end of World War I, and when it did, it was led by an associate of Abduh, Saʿd Zaghlul (1857–1927). Zaghlul had been educated at al-Azhar, studied with al-Afghani, participated in the Urabi movement, and then, like Abduh, had cooperated with the British after some initial doubts. However, at the end of the war, he became the leading spokesman for Egyptian nationalist aspirations, more in the tradition of Mustafa Kamil than of Abduh. Faced with uncompromising British officials, his attempts to present Egyptian hopes for independence were thwarted, and he won widespread support in Egypt for his proposal to send an Egyptian *wafd* ("delegation") to London to present Egypt's case either there or at the Paris Peace Conference. When the British sent Zaghlul and some associates into exile in 1919, popular demonstrations soon turned into the largest popular revolution in modern Egyptian history. Although the revolution was suppressed, Zaghlul was able to organize a large-scale nationalist party, called the Wafd, on his return from exile. As a political leader, Zaghlul concentrated on the issue of liberation rather than on reform, and his basic unit was the Egyptian nation, regardless of religious differences, rather than the *ummah*. In that sense, he was the heir to Mustafa Kamil rather than to Muhammad Abduh.

The nationalist theme within the Abduh tradition is more closely identified with Ahmad Lutfi al-Sayyid (1872–1963), a close associate of Muhammad Abduh. Lutfi al-Sayyid was part of a group of moderate nationalists who established the Ummah party in 1907, which was a rival to Kamil's party and was supported by many intellectuals. Lutfi al-Sayyid became a leading figure in the group through his position as editor of the party's newspaper, *al-Jaridah*. After World War I, many of the people from this group established the Liberal Constitutionalist party, a rival of Zaghlul's Wafd. However, Lutfi al-Sayyid and his group were distinguished from Kamil and Zaghlul more on the basis of their relative political moderation and their concern with intellectual issues than on the basis of their being less secularist in their approach. They went the opposite direction from Rashid Rida in developing Abduh's ideas, and they emphasized the importance of reason and the necessity of coming to terms with modern ideas.

Lutfi al-Sayyid and his group were aware of and felt a part of the Egyptian nation as a distinct entity. For them, Islam was a component of Egyptian society and had an important role to play, but they tended not to be concerned with the problems of defending Islam as such or with its reformation. Lutfi al-Sayyid felt that religion was a necessary foundation for social values and important in any society. Islam was to perform that role in Egypt, but other faiths were suitable in other areas. He stated: "I am not one of those who insist that a religion or a specific ethical system should be taught for its own sake. But I say that general education must have *some* principle which should guide the student from beginning to end, and this is the principle of good and evil, with all its moral implications. There is no doubt that theories of good and evil are numerous and disparate, but each nation should teach its sons its own beliefs in the matter."[8]

Following a variety of different lines, nationalism in the Arab East represented a form of adaptationism that did not oppose Islam but subordinated it. Islam played a role as a component part of the emerging national identity, whether Arab or Egyptian. Many Arab thinkers played a role in helping to define the meaning of nationalism in the context of the changing conditions of the twentieth century, and the basic positions begun by the followers of Abduh and others early in the century represent a standard orthodoxy in interpreting nationalism that was maintained until more radical forms of nationalism became dominant in the 1950s.

A person who represents a culmination of this era of nationalist thought is Sati' al-Husri (1879–1968). He was born in Aleppo, Syria, and served as an official in the Ottoman Ministry of Education. During World War I, he supported the Arab revolt against the Ottomans, and from 1921–1941, he was an educator and an official in Iraq. Following World War II, he served as the head of the cultural section of the newly formed Arab League.

Through his wide-ranging activities and many writings, he became one of the most influential definers of Arab nationalism. He felt that the basic elements of national identity were language and common historical experience, and he emphasized the importance of including Egypt within the Arab world and advocated a secular Arab nationalism. He believed that Islamic universalism could create problems for Arab nationalism if people stressed Muslim unity before Arab unity was achieved. In his view, religion could not create a political sense of community; it could only strengthen one already built on the basic ties of language and history. According to al-Husri's position, as was the case with most nationalists in this era, the prime focus was on liberation and unity, and little attention was given to issues of social reform or economic development. As a result, with the achievement of independence, this type of nationalism began to appear conservative, or at least supportive of existing socioeconomic structures. In the period following World War II, nationalism began to assume a more radical form, joining with the evolution of secularist intellectual thought in the Arab East.

Liberal Secularism. Sometimes under the influence of Muhammad Abduh and at other times emerging directly from the influence of Western thought, a wide range of more explicitly secular thinkers dealt with issues other than nationalism, although they were at times drawn into the political arena. The early part of the twentieth century was a period of intellectual experimentation, and one of the chief characteristics of intellectual secularism in the Arab East is that no well-organized, dominant movement has emerged.

One of the leading secularists was Qasim Amin (1863–1908), a friend of Abduh but whose acceptance of reason led him away from Abduh's religious emphasis. Amin's most famous works dealt with the position of women in Islamic society. He vigorously advocated the emancipation of women and supported education for them so that they could become independent and contributing members of society. He also was an advocate of individual freedom of expression, and his positions on that subject show the profound secularism of his thought: "Real freedom consists in the individual's being able to express any opinion, preach any creed, to propagate any doctrine," and "In a truly free country no one should be afraid to renounce his fatherland, to repudiate belief in God and his prophets, or to impugn the laws and customs of his people."[9]

Following World War I, that liberal secularism flourished in the Arab East, and in Egypt, it was associated with the circle of intellectuals that developed around Ahmad Lutfi al-Sayyid. They were active writers, scholars, and often were involved in politics through the activities of the Liberal Constitutionalist party. Among the many men in this group, Taha Husayn (1889–1973) gained the greatest international reputation as a leading Arab writer and intellectual. He had a traditional religious training, studied at the new Egyptian University, and received a doctorate from the Sorbonne. He taught classical literature in Egypt and was, at various times, a leading government figure in educational and cultural affairs.

In his thinking, Taha Husayn provides a good introduction to the liberal secularist ideas of the time. He was profoundly aware of his Egyptian homeland and its special heritage. In his book, *The Future of Culture in Egypt*, he argued that Egyptian civilization was essentially Western rather than "oriental" and that Islam was an element within the Egyptian identity but not its sole or primary feature. By accepting the secularist assumptions of religion as a separable aspect of society, dealing with individual emotional needs, Islam was placed on a level equal to other faiths rather than being seen as the only true faith. He applied the analytical methods of historical criticism to materials of the Islamic heritage, which created a major crisis for him. In a study of "pre-Islamic" Arabic poetry, he argued that it had in fact been written during Islamic times, and that stand aroused substantial opposition among the more conservative Muslims because it suggested that the critical method might cast doubts on the authenticity of texts that are basic to the Islamic tradition. He later wrote more inspirational religious works, which were not as rigorously critical but were aimed at reshaping religious symbols in a way that would attract modern Egyptians. He hoped that this approach would affect even the most conservative of Muslims. He wrote, for example, that al-Azhar "will fail unless the culture that it propagates throughout the Islamic world is attuned to the personality of the modern Muslim molded nowadays by secular education and modern life. There is no point in al-Azhar's waging war against the twentieth century."[10]

Much of this same spirit is reflected in the works of Taha Husayn's contemporaries, most of whom were active in both governmental and educational institutions. Muhammad Husayn Haykal (1889–1956) combined moderation in practical politics with intellectual efforts toward long-range ideological reform. In his historical studies, which included biographies of Muhammad and one of the early caliphs, he tried to present religious symbols in a way that could appeal to the more traditional Muslims while operating within the framework of modern rational analysis. For him, reason was "to be the basis of faith with the individual able to approach the Quran and God as he wished."[11] Tawfiq al-Hakim (b. 1899) has been especially active as a writer and dramatist, helping to give new forms to modern Arabic presentations, and Ahmad Amin (1886–1954) helped to redefine modern Muslim awareness of early Islamic history.

The dangers of historical analysis were illustrated by the work of another intellectual in the group, Ali Abd al-Raziq (1888–1966). He had studied at al-Azhar and Oxford and was a judge in the religious court system. In 1925, he published a book, *Islam and the Principles of Government*, which argued that Muhammad had not established a formal system of government and that no such system was defined in the Quran or the Sunnah. Therefore, the caliphate was a product of special historical circumstances and not an inherent part of the faith. Ali said: "The truth is that the Muslim religion has nothing to do with the caliphate, which the Muslims generally recognize. The caliphate is not at all a religious office; neither are the offices of *qadi* and other posts of the state. All these are simply administrative offices with which religion is not concerned."[12] This line of thought was necessary for the legitimation of a parliamentary, constitutional regime of the type supported by the liberal secularists. However, since the book was published at the time of the whole caliphate issue, it caused a great furor, and Ali Abd al-Raziq lost his job. The book provided the foundation for a long series of analyses of the relation between Islam and politics, which helped to formulate the secularist position in clearer terms.

The ideas of the liberal secularists in Egypt were reflected elsewhere in the Arab East, but the special conditions in Egypt gave them a special place there. Following World War I, Egypt had become at least nominally independent with a constitutional monarchy. Although British military forces remained in the country and British officials intervened regularly in local politics, there was a wide scope for political and intellectual activity. The rivalry between the monarch, the Wafd party, and other groups, such as the Liberal Constitutionalist party, presented the opportunity for developing a diversity of views. In this relatively flexible situation, it was possible for the moderate or "liberal" position to flourish. However, there tended to be a greater polarization in political and intellectual activities in areas like Iraq and Syria, where difficulties of national unity and integration were greater, and the choice appeared more clear-cut between collaboration with the enemy or a more radical position of opposition. Under those conditions, the liberal secularist position was not as easy to maintain, and people tended to adopt either a conservative nationalist position or a more radical secularist one.

Radical Secularism. In the years following World War II, the older styles of nationalism and liberal secularism began to be viewed by the newer generation of Arabs as being too conservative to meet the challenges of the times. Although the nationalists and liberals had gained independence, little apparent progress had been made in necessary social and economic reforms, and the political structures appeared ineffective. As a result, a new style of nationalism that was associated with a more radical approach to the problems of Arab societies gained in importance in the two decades after World War II. These emerging perspectives also have their roots in the interwar era, although at that time, they were not viewed as significant.

Some of the basic characteristics of the new viewpoints included a more clearly materialist perspective, often Marxist in approach, and a willingness to reject even an emotional role for traditional faith. There were also efforts to create organizations that would be better integrated and more effective than the personal factions and diffuse schools of thought of the old nationalists and liberals, and there was also a more conscious attempt to deal with socioeconomic problems. The emphasis of the liberal position had been on individual freedom, especially in intellectual matters, and the winning of political independence. There had also been an implicit assumption that political independence could be gained without significant social and economic reform and that those would follow naturally after independence, without direct government intervention. The new radicals rejected those assumptions.

When the new perspective became more important, it had to include a definition of the role of Islam because if it were to gain any kind of mass support, it could not simply reject the faith of the majority of the population. In this way, the Islamic context had an impact on the evolution of radical thought, and at the same time, the redefinition of the role of Islam in a radical context was an important feature of the developing Islamic experience.

In the early years of the century, the radical groups were small discussion groups, informally organized and occasionally publishing short-lived journals. In Egypt, one such group was led by Isma'il Mazhar (1891–1962), a brother-in-law of Ahmad Lutfi al-Sayyid. Mazhar accepted scientific positivism and criticized traditionalist and modernist positions alike for being unable to break away from metaphysical modes of thought. From 1927 to 1931, he published a journal called *al-Usur*, which became a vehicle for the expression of agnostic and more radically secularist ideas. In its pages, even the liberal secularists came in for vigorous attack. One writer, discussing Ali Abd al-Raziq's *Islam and the Principles of Government*, for example, said, "Why did he not say clearly and directly that the sources of authority in Islam are no longer valid and that democratic principles are superior to the Islamic?"[13] When economic problems forced Mazhar to suspend publication of the journal, he withdrew from active public life.

Associates of Mazhar in other parts of the Arab East continued their activity. In Beirut, for two years after the discontinuation of *al-Usur*, Ibrahim Haddad published *al-Duhur*, which attempted to perform the same role as Mazhar's journal but with less success. An Iraqi poet, Jamil Sidqi al-Zahawi (1863–1936), published in both of those journals. Al-Zahawi was a strong supporter of the emancipation of women and became part of a group in Iraq that had greater long-term significance than either Mazhar's or Haddad's. That group was led by Husayn al-Rahhal.

Husayn al-Rahhal has been called the Iraqi Qasim Amin and the first of the Marxists of Iraq.[14] He had traveled in Europe, witnessing the Communist Spartakusbund rebellion in Berlin in 1919, had been a student in Iraq during the 1920 revolution, and had spent some time in India. He was influenced by a variety of teachers, particularly a Marxist Armenian, and while a law student in Baghdad, he formed an informal Marxist study group in 1924. In 1924–1925, that group published *al-Sahifah*, which was primarily an intellectual journal espousing historical materialism and opposing tradition. One issue on which the group concentrated was the liberation of women, and it is worth noting that al-Rahhal's sister, Aminah al-Rahhal (b. 1919), was one of the first women in Baghdad to go unveiled, as was a member of the Central Committee of the Iraqi Communist party in 1941–1943.

The position of the al-Rahhal group regarding Islam was clear. They said that Islamic law had been "formulated for a society that existed more than a thousand years ago" and that change would take place regardless of Islamic law. They also believed that "the era when people believed in the divine guidance of natural events was gone" and that "it is not religion that moves social life but social life that moves religion."[15] When the journal was suppressed because of traditionalist opposition and political pressure, al-Rahhal formed Nadi al-Tadamun (the Solidarity Club), which for two years was active in propagating radical secularist ideas among students and in organizing student demonstrations.

One incident illustrates some of the dynamics of the developing Islamic intellectual climate. In 1927, Anis al-Nusuli, a secondary school teacher, published a history of the Umayyads for use in schools, and the book made some uncomplimentary comments about Ali, the cousin and son-in-law of the Prophet. Shi'i leaders demanded that al-Nusuli be punished, and teachers who protested were dismissed, so members of Nadi al-Tadamun helped to organize student demonstrations in support of al-Nusuli. In this incident, the extreme sensitivity on the part of the more conservative Muslims to historical reinterpretation can be seen, as it was seen in Egypt in reaction to the books by Taha Husayn and Ali Abd al-Raziq.

Following demonstrations in 1928 on another issue, the government disbanded al-Rahhal's club, and he retired from active involvement in political or intellectual affairs. However, he had introduced a generation to Marxist and radical secularist thought, and out of his circle came some of the leadership for the major radical groups that emerged in Iraq in the 1930s, especially the Communist party and the al-Ahali group.

In those two groups, radical secularism was more effectively organized. By the time of World War II, the Communist party had become a well-organized, if small, force on the Iraqi political scene, and it provided a focal point for organizing movements on a non-Islamic basis and was able to attract workers and intellectuals. It represented a viable option for people who felt that ties with traditional religion, however modified by new interpretations, would not provide an effective basis for coping with the problems of modern Iraq.

A major concern of the radical secularists was socioeconomic reform, and in 1932, a group of intellectuals and professionals began the publication of *al-Ahali*, which aimed at bringing about a socioeconomic transformation to improve the material and intellectual life of the people. The group was more populist than communist in its orientation, but it was secularist in its approach to religion. In 1936, it worked with General Bakr Sidqi in a coup that took control of the government, hoping that its members could implement their ideals. They were soon disenchanted with Sidqi's dictatorial methods, and their paper was suppressed in 1937. At that point, the group broke up, and some of its more Marxist following joined the Communist party. The non-Marxists in the al-Ahali group eventually reorganized themselves as the National Democrats in 1946, and by that time, they had taken on a more liberal position. In the course of the struggles within the National Democrat party, the noncommunist position was even more clearly affirmed by the end of the 1940s. The party thus provided a more populist and moderate option within the spectrum of Iraqi politics.

The evolution of the al-Ahali group into a more nationalist part with populist and socialist ideas represents the line of development that was necessary for radical secularism if it was to gain political power. Specifically socialist and communist organizations that did not make this kind of transition had difficulty winning mass support or political power. The early Socialist and Communist parties in the Arab East were often led by people from non-Muslim and minority groups, and such parties had to bridge the gap between themselves and the Muslims if they were to have success. This is illustrated by the experience of the Communist party in Syria. There, Khalid Bakdash, a communist of Muslim-Kurdish origin, revitalized the party, and when Soviet policy favored Arab nationalist causes, as in the mid-1930s, and again in the 1950s, Bakdash and his party prospered. However, at times, Soviet policy hindered his efforts, as was the case when Russia supported the Zionist cause in the creation of the state of Israel.

Socialist and communist thinking faced obstacles in both nationalism and Islam because they emphasized a broad sense of community as opposed to the idea of class struggle. Class warfare was seen by most Arabs as dividing the *ummah* and the nation at a time when unity was needed to eliminate foreign control. In addition, socialism and communism appeared to imply a cooperation with foreign powers, which ran counter to both nationalist and Muslim sentiments. Thus, in the years before and just following World War II, radical secularist movements performed the function of introducing new ideas of social consciousness into the Arab East at a time when liberal nationalism and Islamic modernism were not greatly concerned with socioeconomic reform. Therefore, radical secularism had an appeal and influenced subsequent nationalist and Islamic thought despite its difficulties.

Synthesis of Socialism and Nationalism. The ideology that emerged as dominant in the Arab East was neither radical secularism nor liberal nationalism but a synthesis of the two, which took a number of forms and has often been called "Arab socialism." In this development, the secularist adaptationism of the first half of the century was transformed from being basically intellectual movements into party organizations, movements with mass appeal, and groups actually in control of governments. The emergence of Arab socialists to positions of political power in the Arab East is associated with the third phase of political development, in which the ruling groups that had achieved independence were displaced by new revolutionary groups. In Syria, the revolution began in 1949 with a series of military coups and reached a climax in 1958 when a union between Syria and Egypt was created by Arab socialist leaders in both countries. The rejection of the old regime in Egypt came with the revolution in 1952. At that time, the Wafd, the monarchy, and the old liberal nationalist parties were all removed by a military coup that brought to power a group of young officers led by Gamal Abd al-Nasir (Nasser). In Iraq, the monarchy created by the British was overthrown in 1958.

The oldest of these movements is the Socialist Arab Baʿth party, organized in Syria during World War II. It grew out of informal discussion groups led by Michel Aflaq (b. 1910), the son of a Greek Orthodox merchant, and Salah al-Din Baytar (1911–1980), a Syrian Muslim. Both men were born in Damascus, received some education in France where they came into contact with the Communist party, and taught school for a time in Syria. They became disillusioned with communism, because it ignored the special needs and identity of the Arabs, and by the older nationalist leaders in their country, because they ignored the need for reform. In 1943, the two organized the Baʿth party on the basis of a socialist program of internal reform and a unity program for all Arabs. The party rejected ideas of class struggle as being divisive in the Arab nation and was vigorously anticommunist. Branches of the party were established in Jordan (1948), Lebanon (1949), and Iraq (1950), and an attempt was made to maintain a unified leadership, although the party has been plagued by factionalism throughout its history.

The Baʿth was a growing force in Syrian politics in the 1950s. The power of the old nationalist politicians, who had gained control at independence in 1945–1946, had been broken by a series of military coups in 1949, and a four-year period of more stable military rule had followed. Between 1954 and 1958, there was an era of civilian parliamentary rule in which the Baʿth and Khalid Bakdash's Communist party emerged as major forces. Fearing a communist takeover, the Baʿth persuaded Nasser, the leader of the revolutionary regime in Egypt, to join with Syria in the United Arab Republic (UAR) in 1958. The unity experiment failed, and Syria became independent again in 1961 under a coalition of conservative and radical groups. In a coup in 1963, military officers and the Baʿth took control of Syria, and, in an almost parallel coup in Baghdad, they gained control in Iraq for a few months. Internal party divisions led to another coup in Syria in 1966, which brought to power a group of younger and more radical Baʿth members, and Aflaq and Baytar went into exile. A similar group within the Baʿth gained control in Iraq in 1968. This new generation of Baʿth leadership, the Neo-Baʿth, proposed programs of state-controlled economy and land reform that were more radical than those of Aflaq and Baytar. The Neo-Baʿth continued the basic themes of the original party: emphasis on Arab unity and nationalism, the need for a social and economic transformation in Arab society, and opposition to foreign control of either the state or ideology.

With the Baʿth party, socialism emerged as an ideology that was distinctively tied to the Arab nation. Baʿth leaders insisted that theirs was not a borrowed ideology but one that arose out of the Arab tradition. The older radicalism was transformed, and all subsequent movements in this tradition had to show their independence from the domination of foreign ideas or face the charge of being "tools" of outside powers. Radicalism had become "Arabized."

In this context, the relationship between radicalism and Islam had to be more fully defined. The religious tradition of the majority of the Arabs could not simply be rejected in the name of scientific thought or historical materialism, in the manner of the earlier radical secularists. For Baʿth thinkers, Islam is part of the Arab consciousness, and the early experience of Islam is seen as the first great Arab revolution and its teachings of equality and brotherhood as the foundation for a true socialist society. Aflaq believed that "the Baʿth party, while secular in orientation, embodies a renaissance of the Arab spirit similar to that embodied in Islam," and urged Arabs to emulate the life of the Prophet because "Muhammad was the epitome of all the Arabs; so let all Arabs today be Muhammad."[16] The early Arab socialists, like the Baʿth members, thus began the process of making Islam acceptable to radicals and radicalism acceptable to Muslims.

The second major Arab socialist movement was that led by Gamal Abd al-Nasir (Nasser, 1918–1970) in Egypt. In organization and style, Nasser's movement was very different from that of the Baʿth. It originated in an informal group of military officers who took control of the Egyptian government in 1952 and was not a formal political party. The Baʿth emphasized collective leadership, and Nasserism revolved around the leadership of a strong individual. It was these differences that made the union of Egypt and Syria in 1958–1961 unworkable, despite the fact that both Nasser and the Baʿth were committed to the ideal of Arab unity. In addition, the Baʿth emphasized the importance of developing a clear and consistent ideology, and Nasserism maintained an attachment to pragmatic adaptationism, even during its more doctrinaire phase in the 1960s.

The basic principles of Nasserism gradually emerged out of the experience of the young officers after they assumed power. The great themes were the same as those of the Baʿth: Arab liberation and unity and a radical socialist transformation of society. One of the major intellectuals in the movement, Muhammad Haykal, has said that Nasserism symbolizes "the direction of liberation, social transformation, the people's control of their own resources, and the democracy of the people's working forces."[17] At first, the young officers appeared to be an extension of Egyptian nationalism opposing the ineffectiveness and corruption of the old regime. However, in 1955–1956, Nasser emerged as the most successful anti-imperialist leader in the Arab world and soon became the chief spokesman for Arab nationalism, bringing Egypt fully into the Arab nationalist orbit. Similarly, the new revolutionary regime had a vision of eliminating social and economic injustice, but a full definition of that ideal as a socialist program was not reached until the proclamation of the National Covenant in 1962. Through the nationalist successes and the general internal progress made in Egypt under Nasserite reform programs, Arab socialism became widely accepted as a popular, mass sentiment.

In Nasserism, there was a strong emphasis on the indigenous nature of the ideology and the program. Nasser himself was a devout, practicing Muslim and encouraged an analysis of the Islamic bases for socialism. The older liberal secularist and communist ideas were seen as foreign, and Islam provided a starting point for an independent socialist ideology. The Islam of

Nasserism did, however, reject those institutions and intellectual habits that were associated with traditional society. This Islamic dimension in this Arab socialism emphasized social justice and equality, sought social transformation, and was not necessarily acceptable to conservatives and fundamentalists in the Arab East. However, the great prestige of Nasser as a revolutionary nationalist and as the leading spokesman for the Arab cause helped to popularize the idea of Islam as being associated with Arab socialism. In Nasserism this association had a mutual influence because although interpretations of Islam were clearly shaped by radical attitudes, the emerging radicalism of Nasserism was influenced by the Islamic sense of community as opposed to class struggle and the Islamic sense of moral worth and values as opposed to the materialism of much of modern radicalism.

By the middle of the 1960s, Arab socialism in various forms appeared to be the most dominant ideology in the Arab East. Nasserism and the Baʿth were the two leading exponents of that view, but there were many other movements based on similar principles in other areas. Most discussion of Islam at the time saw Islam's future within the Arab socialist framework. Traditional, conservative, and fundamentalist movements were often seen as final efforts of the old styles of the Islamic experience that would eventually have to accommodate themselves to this new dynamic force or face destruction. Arab socialist regimes existed in Syria, Egypt, and Iraq. In 1962, a military group overthrew the imam in Yemen and espoused those ideals; opposition to the Saudi monarchy was couched in Arab socialist terms; there were active movements of that nature in Lebanon, Jordan, and South Arabia; and the emerging Palestinian national movement expressed itself in Arab socialist terms. However, by the end of the 1960s, the picture was clearly changing, and internal divisions and reorientations of socialist thought and practice were preparing the way for the new mood of the 1970s.

In purely Islamic terms, the rise of Arab socialism performed an important function. Adaptationist secularism, as it emerged after World War I, had been largely influenced by Western ideas, and especially in its radical form, that secularism had seemed somehow foreign to the Islamic society of the Arab East. However, in the hands of the Arab socialist intellectuals and leaders, radical secularism and the awareness of the need for social transformation became an indigenous ideology. The integration of radicalism with nationalism and Islam was an important step on the path to the "radical fundamentalism" that would emerge in the 1970s. In broader terms, that integration set the intellectual framework for the Islam of the modernizing world.

Fundamentalism in the Arab East

The most visible alternative to modernizing adaptationism was a fundamentalist style of Islam, which was the path followed by Rashid Rida after the death of Muhammad Abduh. However, during the first two-thirds of the twentieth century, Islamic fundamentalism in the Arab East was more closely associated with concrete organizations than with general intellectual schools of thought, and two movements were the clearly dominant forces: the Saudi monarchy in association with the revived Wahhabi movement and the Muslim Brotherhood. The appeal of both was built on the continuing strength of Islam in social life and on the apparent failure of the more secularist modernizing movements to solve the problems of Islamic society.

The Saudi Experience. The revival of the Saudi state and the Wahhabi movement during the twentieth century was the achievement of Abd al-Aziz (Ibn Saud, 1880–1953). In the first twenty-five years of this century, he gained control of much of the Arabian Peninsula and then succeeded in consolidating his conquests into the Kingdom of Saudi Arabia. In this revival, the dramatic leadership abilities of Abd al-Aziz gave focus to the new state, and the cement was the ideology provided by the Wahhabi tradition. As in the past, the ulama and the warrior combined in a movement that secured the allegiance of tribesmen and townspeople.

Until around 1930, the emerging state remained in a relatively traditional form. It was an enlarged patriarchal state with religious ties that transcended tribal loyalties, and the program was one of rigorous fundamentalism working to purify Islamic practice, with little awareness of any challenge from modern ideas. During this era, Abd al-Aziz created a powerful military instrument called the Ikhwan (Brothers), made up of tribal warriors who had been encouraged by their religious teachers to leave their tribes and settle in agricultural communities. There they received religious and military training and formed a well-organized core for the Saudi military. The Ikhwan were fully committed to the fundamentalist cause and were a major force in the Saudi military expansion. However, by the mid-1920s, they began to pose problems for the new state because they opposed any compromises with surrounding states. They soon clashed with British forces in the newly created state of Iraq, and they threatened Abd al-Aziz's efforts to gain diplomatic recognition. When Abd al-Aziz negotiated treaties with his neighbors, many of the more fanatical Ikhwan revolted, and the organization was defeated in 1928–1930.

Following the putting down of the Ikhwan revolt, the Saudi state entered an era of stability and consolidation. Those Ikhwan who had remained loyal to the king remained a part of the state, and Ikhwan-style zeal was an important sentiment, but Saudi expansionism ceased. The policy of Abd al-Aziz was to make whatever adjustments were necessary for political survival in the modern world but to keep the Saudi society based on the fundamentalist spirit. Thus, he was not averse to the introduction of some modern means of communication and weaponry, but the Quran and the Sunnah represented the law and the constitution of the state.

In the early days following World War I, the new Saudi state gained some prestige throughout the Islamic world. It was one of the few areas that retained political independence, and, in contrast to Turkey under Mustafa Kemal Ataturk, the Saudis remained vigorously and visibly Islamic.

However, as nationalist and secularist currents became stronger and as the Kingdom of Saudi Arabia became a stable, patrimonial state, its international popularity tended to fade. The element that brought Saudi Arabia back into international prominence was the discovery of oil in its territories.

The development of the oil industry in Saudi Arabia, especially after World War II, brought tremendous sums of money into the country, which transformed the whole context of the kingdom. As a relatively poor and puritanical state on the fringes of world affairs, Saudi Arabia had not had to face the challenges of modern history in as direct a manner as other countries, but as a wealthy oil-producing country, it could not avoid many problems. Abd al-Aziz and then his son and successor, Saud (1902–1969), tried to maintain the old spirit of the patrimonial state, but they were unable to control the corruption and inefficiency that came in the wake of too much money for the system to handle. It became clear that the troubles were of major crisis proportion by the end of the 1950s.

Pressures for reform built and resulted in Saud's younger but more experienced brother, Faysal (1905–1975), being named prime minister. Faysal had some success in reorganizing the state's finances, but tensions soon arose between him and the king, and he resigned. Saud assumed direct leadership again and appointed a cabinet that included men drawn from the small group of modern-educated Saudis who were inspired by the more radical reform programs in other parts of the Arab world. The leading members of the royal family and the Wahhabi ulama began to feel that the whole structure of the Saudi-Wahhabi monarchy was threatened, and that feeling was emphasized by the 1962 overthrow of the imam in Yemen by republican forces inspired by Arab socialism. It was clear that a government dedicated to a decisive reform of the patrimonial monarchy was necessary if the fundamentalist spirit of the state was to be preserved. In a series of actions, the leading royal and religious notables secured the abdication of Saud and the accession of Faysal to the throne in 1963. In this process, some of Faysal's major supporters were a group of his half brothers, whose mothers came from the Sudayri family.

Under King Faysal, the Saudi state entered a new era, and the keystone of the new policies might be called "pragmatic fundamentalism." The basic foundations for law and loyalty continue to be the Quran and the Sunnah, but the operating structures reflect the changing conditions in Saudi society and the Islamic world. The initial basic document of this pragmatic fundamentalism is the ten-point program announced by Faysal, at that time prime minister, in 1962. This program promised the reorganization of provincial and central governments; a restructuring of the judiciary organization; improvements in social welfare, financial, and economic development; and the abolition of all slavery. The spirit of this program is shown in the fourth point, dealing with the ulama: "Inasmuch as the texts of the Koran and Traditions are fixed and limited, while modern times and the experience of the people in worldly affairs are constantly changing rather than being limited, and in view of the fact that our youthful state is ruled according to the letter and spirit of the Koran and Traditions, it has become imperative for us to give greater attention to jurisprudence and for our jurists and Ulema to play a positive and effective part in the discussion of important matters of State."[18] This point then included a proposal for the formation of an advisory judicial council made up of jurists and ulama.

In some ways the program reflects the facts that Arab socialism was rising to prominence in much of the Arab East, and restructuring and development were recognized as being necessary. However, the foundation of Faysal's reformism remained the fundamentalist tradition. In the Saudi program, even more than in Arab socialism, there is an emphasis on the indigenous quality of the ideology. Faysal said, "We want our nation to be in the vanguard and not in the rear-guard. We do not want to be mere imitators and satellites. On the contrary, we are capable of leading, guiding and steering the helm if we hold fast to God's Book and His Prophet's Sunnah."[19] Pragmatic fundamentalism was thus emerging as an alternative to Arab socialism, and during the 1960s, there was conflict and competition between the two styles. In the heyday of Arab socialism, however, many people were willing to believe that Faysal's program was simply defensive reform and that the future lay elsewhere. Many in the Arab East considered the Saudi position to be reactionary.

By the end of the 1960s, Faysal was emerging as one of the leading figures in the Arab and Islamic world. Much of his prominence was based on the enormous wealth that the country's oil was providing, but also, as Arab socialist movements began to falter because of internal divisions and an inability to solve the pressing problems of modernizing societies, Saudi pragmatic fundamentalism was emerging as an important example. One factor was the development of nationalism, or the lack of it, in Saudi Arabia. In contrast to other areas, the political boundaries created following World War I did not come to define a unit of overriding nationalist loyalty. The Saudi identity was primarily dynastic in local terms and identified with Pan-Arab and Pan-Islamic ideals in the larger theaters of action. In this way, the Saudi monarch could emerge as a spokesman for the Arab cause and could be active in encouraging the coordination of policy among Muslim states. In this role, Faysal became a well-known and respected international figure.

The Muslim Brotherhood. In the areas more directly affected by the expansion of European imperialism and ideas, fundamentalism did not disappear as an important factor, but, given the fact that the political institutions and ruling elites were dominated by adaptationist modernizers, the fundamentalist style emerged in a new format. Traditional holy wars and the old-style organizations had little appeal, and the new fundamentalism created popular associations that were dedicated to a strict adherence to the Quran and the Sunnah. The most famous of those groups in the Arab East is the Muslim Brotherhood.

Inspired by fundamentalist ideals, the Muslim Brotherhood grew directly out of the challenge modernizing secularism posed to Islamic values. It was established in Egypt by Hasan al-Banna (1906–1949), a schoolteacher with a background of individual and family religious studies and a modern-oriented education. He became persuaded that the weakness of Islamic society could be cured only by a return to the sources of its strength, the Quran and the Sunnah. As a student and then as a teacher in Ismailia in the Suez Canal zone, he organized study and discussion groups that provided the basis for the formal organization of the Brotherhood in 1928. The organization set up schools, became active in a variety of social and cultural affairs, and soon gained a wide following throughout Egypt; in the absence of effective programs for social reform by the state and the liberal nationalists, the Brotherhood was increasingly drawn into the political arena. The cause of liberation soon engaged its attention, and it gave its support to the Palestinians. After World War II, it emerged as a revolutionary force with a program for social transformation that rivaled that of the communists and as a militant organization capable of engaging in terrorist as well as propagandistic actions. Hasan al-Banna himself was murdered in 1949 as the Brotherhood's involvement in terrorism and counterterrorism increased. The organization had ties with the young officers led by Nasser and had some influence within the new regime until rivalries led to conflict. Some members of the Brotherhood attempted to kill Nasser in 1954, and the organization was suppressed. After 1954, the Brotherhood remained active in Egypt as an underground association. In 1965, Nasser's government announced the discovery of a plot by the Brotherhood to overthrow the regime, and many arrests were made; three executions followed, including that of Sayyid Qutb, a prominent writer in the movement.

Organizations similar to the Muslim Brotherhood appeared in other countries, and they were at least inspired by, if not organizationally connected with, the Brotherhood in Egypt. The most active groups were in Syria and Jordan, and there were others in Iraq, Lebanon, and Palestine. The basic positions of all of these groups were similar.

The essential message of the Muslim Brotherhood is simple. Hasan al-Banna summarized the meaning of Islam: "First, the rules of Islam and its teachings are comprehensive, organizing the affairs of the people in this world and the next. Second, the foundation of Islamic teachings is the Book of God Almighty and the Sunnah of His Messenger, the blessings of God and His peace be upon him. Third, Islam as a general faith regulates all matters of life for every race and community, in every age and era."[20] In this vigorous affirmation of the universal validity of Islam, the Brothers viewed themselves as a part of the revivalist movements of the modern period, in line with al-Afghani, Abduh, and Rashid Rida. However, the Brotherhood sought to implement the revival rather than to engage in intellectual speculations. The Brotherhood was thus fundamentalist in its style, but it demanded adherence to the Quran and the Sunnah, not a return to the conditions of the seventh century.

The role of the organization was clearly stated in a message sent to the membership by Hasan al-Banna in 1943: "My Brothers: you are not a benevolent society, nor a political party, nor a local organization having limited purposes. Rather, you are a new soul in the heart of this nation to give it life by means of the Qurᶜan; you are a new light which shines to destroy the darkness of materialism through knowing God; and you are the strong voice which rises to recall the message of the Prophet."[21] The organization was to be the vehicle for establishing an Islamically moral society and a truly Muslim government.

In its early years in Egypt, the Muslim Brotherhood was one of the few groups that advocated a vigorous social transformation and major socioeconomic reforms. In later years, some of its leading writers began to use the terminology of the times and spoke of the Brotherhood program as being Islamic socialism. One such writer was a leader of the Brotherhood in Syria, Mustafa al-Sibaᶜi (b. 1910), who believed that Islamic socialism was "an integral part of the credo of the Muslim, who can but apply it. It constitutes a more rapid and more effectual method than any other socialism for the reform of our society."[22]

The Muslim Brotherhood appealed to more than the religiously faithful rural people and the urban lower classes. In terms of its activist members and leaders, it was a very strong movement of students, civil servants, teachers, office workers, and professionals. The appeal of the society was not to conservatives so much as to people who had already had a significant contact with Westernizing ideas and institutions. For those people, the message of the Brotherhood could provide an identity and a tie with their traditions, and the Brotherhood succeeded in creating a fundamentalism that could have an appeal in a modernizing world. Although many intellectuals and governments in the Arab East have opposed the Brotherhood as a reactionary and politically dangerous movement, it represents a successful modernization of the fundamentalist style of the Islamic experience.

The cases of Saudi Arabia and the Muslim Brotherhood in Egypt show that the fundamentalist style has continued to have some effect in the twentieth century. However, for the first two-thirds of the century, that style was overshadowed by the growing dominance of the adaptationist styles of secularism and nationalism. At the high tide of Arab socialism in the 1960s, fundamentalists were seen as an echo of the past rather than as the wave of the future.

The Changing Face of Conservatism

One of the remarkable phenomena of modern Muslim history is the flexibility exhibited by the conservative style of the Islamic experience. In a period of rapid and dramatic changes, the protectors of the existing order had to be nimble to keep up, and as new ideas and institutions became established and accepted, they soon became the objects of care and concern for the conservatives rather than the proposals of the innovators and adaptationists. Conservatism in this context is the result of a relatively rapid acceptance of any emerging consensus. In the Arab East, the most prominent conservative elements are the older Islamic institutions, the most famous of which is al-Azhar, and the various monarchies. In the latter, there are two types: those that were created following World War I and those that were based on older traditions in the Arabian Peninsula.

Al-Azhar University. The experience of al-Azhar can be taken as representative of the older Islamic institutions that survived the changes of the twentieth century. Some, like the large-scale *tariqah* organizations and independent ulama instructorships and foundations, gradually disappeared, and others, like al-Azhar, survived. The majority of the ulama associated with al-Azhar resisted the intellectual currents of change as they were taking place. At the same time, many of the leading intellectual adaptationists had some association with the institution. One link between those conservative ulama and the developing intellectual community in Egypt and the rest of the Arab world was the rector of the university. Often he played some role in the actual process of redefinition of the Islamic tradition in modern terms, meeting resistance from his conservative colleagues and, at least at times, helping to slow the pace of intellectual change among the adaptationists.

Muhammad Abduh had been active in working to reform the curriculum and teaching methods of al-Azhar, and those efforts as well as his ideas had been opposed by the majority of the teachers. Yet, in the interwar era, his teachings gained wide acceptance and later provided the basis for much of the scholarly thought of al-Azhar. The appointment of one of his followers, Mustafa al-Maraghi (1881–1945), as shaykh al-Azhar in 1928 was opposed by most of the ulama as he was in favor of major reforms. His first term in the post lasted only a year, but he then served again from 1935 to 1945 with much wider support. Al-Maraghi had previously been a grand *qadi* in the Sudan, where he was active in modernizing the Islamic legal structure and its applications.

The rector from 1929 to 1935 was Muhammad al-Ahmadi al-Zawahiri (1878–1944), whose book advocating Islamic reform had been burned by order of the shaykh al-Azhar in 1904. During al-Zawahiri's term the curriculum of al-Azhar was greatly expanded to include "modern" subjects. Similarly, after al-Maraghi's death, the next rector was Mustafa Abd al-Raziq (1885–1947), an active student of Abduh whose philosophical works had been opposed by the conservative ulama early in the century but whose ideas were a solid part of the "Azhar orthodoxy" by the second half of the twentieth century.

The conservative but flexible role of al-Azhar continued after the 1952 revolution, and the emerging dominance of Arab socialism in its Nasserite form was gradually reflected in the official position of the university. In 1958, Mahmud Shaltut (d. 1964) was named rector. During the 1930s, he had been dismissed from the faculty of al-Azhar for his modernist views, and in the 1950s he had helped to create a more conservative definition of Islamic socialism, which supported the new revolutionary position, indirectly rebutting the more fundamentalist views of the Muslim

Brotherhood writers. He emphasized the comprehensive and universal character of the Islamic message and argued that Egyptian socialism conformed to the Islamic tradition. In his view, mankind could find no "more perfect, more complete, more useful, more profound socialism than that decreed by Islam."[23] Thus, gradually, the conservatism of al-Azhar made it the protector of the newly emerging "orthodoxy"—at first, the consensus of liberal nationalism and modernism and, then, the dominant Arab socialist perspective.

"New Monarchies" and Changing Conservatism. During the first two-thirds of the twentieth century, new monarchies were created in a number of areas, and they were often the product of diplomatic negotiation rather than nationalist or fundamentalist revolutions, although they all had some roots in past institutions. These new monarchies were associated with modernist and adaptationist ideas at the time of their creation, but they soon became identified as bastions of conservatism and faced opposition from the more radical groups as they emerged. The ability of these monarchies to adapt and cope with the emerging challenges determined how long they survived, and the key element was not so much the vitality of the monarchical ideology as the ability of the individuals who occupied the thrones.

Three twentieth-century monarchies emerged out of the experience of one of the prominent sharif families in Mecca, the Hashimites, which had come to prominence through the activities of Husayn ibn Ali, who was the grand sharif of Mecca after the Young Turk Revolution in 1908. The family was active in Ottoman politics in Istanbul in the era of the Young Turks, and Husayn's sons, Abdallah (1882–1951) and Faysal (1883–1933), both served in the Ottoman parliament. During World War I, the family provided the leadership for the Arab revolt against the Ottomans and thus became the leading standard-bearers for Arab nationalism. Thus, although the prestige of the family was based on their religious position as descendants of the Prophet and leaders in the holy city, they were active in the adaptationist movements of the time.

Sharif Husayn's goal had been the creation of an Arab monarchy that would lead a united state in the Arab East, but that was not possible in the conditions following World War I. Instead, Husayn was recognized as the King of the Hijaz, and in 1921, his son Faysal was named king of the newly created state of Iraq, and Abdallah became the ruler of Transjordan. The history of each of these monarchies illustrates, in different ways, the gradual transition to conservatism in an effort to preserve the institutions that had been created.

King Husayn faced the rising Saudi power in the Hijaz and mishandled his diplomatic relations so that he became isolated and unable to call upon the support of his former allies, the British. His Arab nationalism also gave him no added support, and he attempted to return to a religiously based position of power. In 1924, the leader of the Arab revolt declared himself to be caliph of Islam, but that did not stop the Saudi advance, and they conquered the Hijaz in 1925. Husayn spent his remaining years in exile and died in 1931.

The other Hashimite monarchies fared better. Having been created by the British, they continued to have British support and gradually emerged as independent states. Faysal had been the major military commander from the family during the Arab revolt and had widespread support among the nationalists in the Arab East. He had been named king of Syria by a nationalist congress at the end of the war, but that was opposed by the French in 1920. In 1921, he became the king of Iraq. The combination of his religious prestige, his nationalist reputation, and his effective leadership skills made it possible for him to balance nationalist demands and British requirements, which gave Iraq a period of political stability that culminated in its formal independence and admission to the League of Nations in 1932.

Under Faysal's leadership, the Iraqi monarchy became the leading instrument for creating an Iraqi identity and a national integration. Just before his death, Faysal wrote, "In Iraq there is still—and I say this with a heart full of sorrow—no Iraqi people but unimaginable masses of human beings, devoid of any patriotic idea. . . . Out of these masses we want to fashion a people."[24] To do so, he encouraged a reconciliation among the disparate groups—Sunni and Shiʿi, Arab and Kurd—that composed the Iraqi population.

Following Faysal's death, the Hashimite leadership was weaker, and the army emerged as a source of antimonarchical leadership in alliance with secular groups like al-Ahali. The military coup of Bakr Sidqi in 1936 and a revolution led by Rashid Ali in 1941 had republican overtones, and the Hashimite leadership turned away from the emerging nationalist and secularist groups. During and following World War II, Prince Abdul Illah (1913–1958), the regent for the young king, Faysal II (1935–1958), increasingly turned to the tribal chieftains and the British for support. By the 1950s, the self-preservation efforts of the monarchy had transformed it from the leading liberal nationalist institution into the bastion of the older traditional elements of society and the foreign imperial power that dominated Iraq. Under these circumstances, the Iraqi monarchy was swamped by the rising tide of Arab socialism and was overthrown in 1958, and its old religious prestige, which had initially been tied to modernizing movements, was lost in the process. Leadership in religious affairs reverted to the Shiʿi ulama of Najaf and Karbala and to the more conservative urban Sunni ulama.

The most successful Hashimite monarchy was the one established in Jordan. In 1921, Abdallah ibn Husayn was named the prince of the territories east of the Jordan River in British-controlled Palestine. He had already had a career as an effective politician within the Ottoman parliament and the Arab revolt, and he had had some ties with Rashid Rida. The British created his princedom in order to lessen his opposition to the French expulsion of his brother, Faysal, from Syria. Abdallah's new state was a purely artificial unit, but he set rapidly to work to create a viable state. He never cut his ties with the British, but he was able to attract many of the old nationalists to his service, and his religious prestige helped him to win the support of the largely Sunni nomadic tribes. His social policies were conservative, but he remained dedicated to the Arab nationalist cause and emerged after World War II as one of the leading figures in the pre-Arab socialist movement for Arab unity. His army, the Arab Legion, was relatively small but one of the most effective military forces in the Arab East. It performed well during the Arab-Israeli War of 1948–1949 and enabled Abdallah to annex the West Bank territories in Palestine that had not been taken over by Israeli forces. In that action, he alienated many Arab nationalists and was murdered in 1951.

The monarchy created by Abdallah was not itself a religious institution, but part of the king's prestige rested upon his religious position and his visible devotion to the faith. He survived and strengthened the monarchy by adroit maneuvering, remaining conservative enough to win the support of the tribesmen who were the core of his military and nationalist enough to be acceptable to the modern-educated groups within his kingdom. His son, Talal, reigned only briefly, and his grandson, Husayn (b. 1935), became king in 1952. The same adept ability to balance forces proved to be Husayn's greatest strength, and the Jordanian monarchy survived a wide range of challenges and remained in power in 1980. It adopted programs of vigorous modernization but never came under the control of radical Arab socialist forces. By the mid-1960s, it was seen as a major conservative force, trying to preserve the old political structures in the midst of rapid modernization. At the same time that the Saudi monarchy was moving toward pragmatic fundamentalism, the Jordanian monarchy could be said to represent a modernizing conservatism.

In Egypt, the foundations of the monarchy went back to the time of Mehmet Ali at the beginning of the nineteenth century. Virtually independent governors within the Ottoman Empire, Mehmet Ali and his successors had been the leading exponents and implementers of Westernizing reform. Following the British occupation in 1882, the rulers had been forced into a position of accepting British domination, and the initiative for both reform and nationalism had passed into the hands of other groups. As a part of the World War I settlement, Egypt was made an independent monarchy by treaty in 1922, and a descendant of Mehmet Ali, Fuad (1868–1936), became the first king of Egypt.

The palace was now simply one of a number of competing forces in the Egyptian political scene. Leadership in the nationalist cause was in the hands of Sa'd Zaghlul and the Wafd party, and leadership in liberal and secularist thought was also outside of the palace. Fuad worked to establish the power of the monarchy firmly, but his major weapons were simply the structures of the state and British support. Neither he nor the institution had any particular religious prestige, but Islam was seen as a possible tool for increasing royal powers. As a result, Fuad attempted during the conflict over the caliphate to be named caliph, but support for that was never strong. Instead, Fuad and his successor, Faruq (1920–1965), attempted to gain religious support for their basically secular regimes by allying themselves with al-Azhar. The relatively conservative but modernist scholars who became rectors of al-Azhar preferred the monarchy to the Wafd or the more secularist intellectuals, but that support did not create religious prestige for the kings; it only gave them a way of influencing public opinion. In the long run, the inability of the monarchy to handle the growing problems of Egypt, especially under the inept and corrupt Faruq, opened the door for the 1952 revolution. The monarchy thus encouraged the conservative style of modernism in Islamic thought and had undergone a reversal in its position from being the vanguard of modernizing reform under Mehmet Ali to being one of the major obstacles to progress under Faruq.

Among the "created monarchies" in the Arab East, the one with the greatest religious identification was in Libya, which was created in 1949–1952. The first king was Idris ibn al-Mahdi (b. 1890), a grandson of Muhammad ibn Ali al-Sanusi, the founder of the Sanusiyyah Tariqah. Idris was one of the leading figures in the Sanusi order and in its conflict with Italian imperialism. During the first half of the century, the Sanusiyyah became the core of Libyan nationalism, and its heroes were the heroes of Libyan national existence. Under those conditions, Sanusi activity went in two directions simultaneously. On the one hand, it became increasingly activist in political terms, and on the other, it was more concerned with unifying resistance forces and maintaining some semblance of social life under the conditions of severe Italian repression than it was with a fundamentalist purification of Libyan society. Following World War II, the order emerged as a politically activist but ideologically conservative movement. Given the fact that there were no other "national" institutions in Libya, it was logical that the United Nations commission that "created" an independent Libya would turn to the Sanusiyyah for the leadership of the new state.

At the beginning of the century, the Sanusiyyah was involved in both nationalist activities and Islamic revivalism. The leader of the order at that time was Ahmad al-Sharif (d. 1933), a cousin of Idris who left the leadership of the order in Libya in the hands of Idris while he went to Istanbul during World War I. For a time, he cooperated with the Ottoman royal family and then aided Mustafa Kemal Ataturk in the Turkish war for independence. There was talk that he might be named caliph, and he was active in trying to reconcile Pan-Islamic ideals with the emerging Turkish nationalist reformism. However, after the abolition of the caliphate, he was asked to leave Turkey, and he spent the rest of his life in study and piety in Mecca and Medina. With his death, the Sanusiyyah order became fully involved in nationalist activities, and its underlying ideology became increasingly conservative.

After Libyan independence, the monarchy was the center of the new country's political life. Idris had great prestige as the leader of the nationalist struggle and of the major religious organization in Libya. He insisted on careful programs of economic development and worked to create national institutions, such as a parliament and an army, but he did not encourage ideological development of either an Islamic or a secularist type. As a result, the Islamic aspect of the regime became simply a justification for the existing and emerging monarchical order, and "Sanusism" became defined as the programs of social and economic development initiated by the monarchy. Those programs were often sound but did little to provide an ongoing ideological inspiration for the emerging Libyan national feeling. Ultimately, that inspiration was provided from the outside by the ideas of Arab socialism and, later, radical fundamentalism. The monarchy led the country through the hard days of its early poverty and then through the days of its growing wealth as a result of oil in the 1960s. In many ways, it survived the challenges of Arab socialism during the 1960s, and when the monarchy was overthrown in 1969, it was by a movement that was closer to the radical fundamentalism of the 1970s than to the Arab socialism of the previous decade.

The experience of the "new" monarchies emphasizes one aspect of modern conservatism in the Arab East: Conservatism does not mean trying to maintain society as it was before significant modernization but, rather, trying to slow the pace of change and preserving institutions that may have been created relatively early in the process of modernization. In general, conservatism supports an evolutionary development of society rather than revolutionary social change. Ironically, the changing face of conservatism means that it cannot be identified with a particular ideology. In Jordan, for example, it is associated with liberal nationalism, and in Egypt after the establishment of Arab socialism, it supported that ideology, defending it against opponents who desired the revolutionary overthrow of the Nasserite regime.

"Old" Monarchies. The style of conservatism that hopes to avoid any significant change can be seen in some of the monarchical systems in the Arab East. In Yemen, South Arabia, and Oman, rulers attempted by isolationism and strict controls to avoid change. In each of those areas, the prestige of the monarchy was buttressed by local Islamic traditions, but even in those isolated corners of the Arab world, change could not be stopped. As no emerging ideological alternatives of a more conservative nature were available, growing contact with the modern world produced an Arab socialist revolution in Yemen in 1962, and when South Arabia gained its independence in 1967, even the conservative hinterlands of Aden joined in supporting the new, radical secularist regime that had created the People's Republic of South Yemen. In Oman, the major problem for much of the century was the division of the country into coastal areas controlled by the sultan and inner areas under the control of an Ibadi imam. After revolts early in the century, a compromise was worked out and defined in a treaty in 1920, which established the principle of noninterference by the sultan in the affairs of the tribes of the interior. However, during the 1950s, imams led revolts against Sultan Said ibn Taymur, whose long reign lasted from 1932 until 1970. Sultan Said successfully unified the country, but even after

the discovery of oil and growing government revenues, he resisted any modernization of his country. By the late 1960s, it appeared that the only alternative to the medieval rule of Said was the rule of radical revolutionaries, who began activities in the province of Dhofar. However, Said was overthrown in 1970 by his son, Qabus, who initiated a more active program of economic development and social reform.

In the other small states of the Arabian Peninsula, a more pragmatic conservatism has emerged. In Kuwait, Bahrain, Qatar, and the small shaykhdoms that became the United Arab Emirates (UAE) in 1971, the old ruling families have worked to maintain their monarchical systems while encouraging rapid economic modernization. They have been greatly assisted in this endeavor by the tremendous revenues from the sale of oil. None of these states are explicitly religious in character, but all, in varying forms, depend upon respect for the Islamic tradition to buttress the existing political order. By a judicious financial support of Islamic and radical causes, they have managed to avoid revolutions.

The old monarchies that were explicitly religious in nature—the Zaydi imamate in Yemen and the Ibadi imamate in Oman—have been destroyed. The more flexible monarchies of tribal origin have been able to utilize the oil wealth and a pragmatic conservatism to preserve their existence.

Summary

In the tremendous variety of Islamic experience in the Arab East, a number of factors should be clear. In the first place, there is nothing inherently conservative about Islam, and conversely, conservatism may be dynastic or pragmatic, but it is not inherently Islamic except in the sense that what the conservatives were trying to preserve was premodern Islamic society. Second, although many of the pre-twentieth-century types of movements proved to be ineffective in the context of the twentieth century, the basic styles of the Islamic experience—the adaptationist, fundamentalist, conservative, and individualist—continued to provide the framework within which most people in the Arab East operated.

Finally, when Muslims were the dominant majority in a society, the basic issues were those of liberation and modernization within an Islamic framework, and the extreme secularists made little headway in their attempts to create a framework that would ignore or reject the Islamic tradition. However, when radical secularism adapted itself to the local conditions and became defined as an indigenous movement, it made significant progress. By the mid-1960s, it appeared to be dominant, eclipsing the fundamentalist and conservative movements.

Dominant Majorities in the Northern Tier

The three modern states of Turkey, Iran, and Afghanistan form the northern tier of countries in the Middle East where the Muslims are the dominant majority, and their populations represent about one-eighth of the world's Muslims. In those areas, the traditions of Islam are deeply rooted as much of the area was brought into the Muslim world in the early centuries of Islamic history. However, the local ethnic and linguistic traditions do not have the same identity with the origins of Islam as they do in the Arab East. Turkish and Persian emerged as important Muslim languages, but they represent special cultural traditions within the Muslim world. The northern tier was the homeland of great imperial traditions in both premodern and modern times, and that fact is reflected in the twentieth-century experience. As was the case in Egypt, the political units that emerged had some historical validity. In contrast to Egypt, however, these three areas maintained formal independence throughout the nineteenth century.

Adaptationism: Political Leaders as Reformers

During the first half of the twentieth century, the experience of the northern tier countries was almost unique in the Islamic world. Having maintained their political independence, their political leaders were able to initiate programs of reform and modernization that had a substantially indigenous character. The experience of those countries provides a way of seeing the potential of Islam operating in the modern world in the absence of direct European control.

At the end of World War I, important reformist leaders emerged in each of the three countries, and the contrasting results of their efforts show the importance of the foundations laid in the previous centuries and the special local conditions. Each of the three leaders was committed to the rapid modernization of his country and, because of political independence, was able to have his program become the official government policy. The success or failure of the program depended more upon local forces than outside interference.

Turkey. The most dramatic and successful of those reformers was Mustafa Kemal Ataturk (1881–1938), who created the modern Turkish republic out of the ruins of the Ottoman Empire. In many ways, he represents the culmination of the long history of Ottoman reform and modernization efforts. In Turkey at the end of World War I, there was a large group of modern-educated, experienced officials and a sound awareness of the meaning of the reform efforts. However, the experience of the autocracy of Abdulhamid II's rule and the defeat of the empire during the war had eliminated many of the possible ideological options that could be used as the basis for the twentieth-century state. Ottomanism, in either a centralizing or a federalist form, was no longer possible. The empire no longer existed, and most of it had experienced nationalist revolts or European occupation. Pan-Islam was also seen as a discredited basis for policy after the failure of the call to holy war during World War I and the lack of effective cooperation among Muslim leaders. The idea of uniting all Turkish-speaking peoples was a romantic sentiment held by a few Young Turks who continued to work among the peoples of Central Asia, but their efforts came to nothing. The remaining effective option was to build a new state based on the patriotism of the Turkish-speaking people in the Anatolian Peninsula, where foreign occupation was still limited.

At the end of World War I, even that option seemed weak, and only scattered resistance movements existed. However, the invasion of Anatolia by the Greek army and the rise of Mustafa Kemal as an inspiring mobilizer provided the impetus for the creation of a Turkish nationalist movement that defeated the Greeks and forced the European Allied powers to recognize Turkish independence. The war for independence in 1919–1922 succeeded where the Egyptian and Iraqi revolutions of 1919 and 1920 failed; Turkey was not to be a European-occupied or -dominated area. In this situation, the reformist ideals of Kemal and his associates could be put into practice. The clear victory of the Muslims of Turkey over the European states gave a special prestige and visibility to the Turkish reform effort, which was undertaken in the area of the old center of Muslim attention, the realm of the Ottoman sultan-caliph.

In terms of the modern Islamic experience, the Kemalist reform program was a vigorous application of adaptationism to the Westernizing secularist style. The old institutions of Islamic politics and society were systematically eliminated rather than being reformed. The office of the sultanate was abolished in 1922, the caliphate in 1924, and the old Islamic legal structure was eliminated in a series of reforms during the following decade. The formal organizations of *tariqah*s were outlawed, pious foundations were brought under direct government control, and religious education was taken out of the hands of the traditional ulama. The Arabic script used for writing Ottoman Turkish was replaced by an alphabet that used Latin letters, and there was a major effort to "purify" the language by eliminating words borrowed from Arabic and Persian. In this way, the language and literature of the new Turkey was cut off from the earlier Islamic literary traditions. Even reference to Islam as the religion of the state, which had been included in the first republican constitution, was eliminated in 1928.

In the place of the old political system, the Kemalist reformers worked to create a modernized parliamentary republic. The keystone of the system in terms of the legitimation of political authority was that it was to be based on the will of the people. This principle was first stated by the Grand National Assembly, the organization of the Turkish independence movement, in 1920: "The real authority is the national will. There is no power superior to the Grand National Assembly."[25] The new slogan was Sovereignty Belongs to the Nation, and the principle of republicanism was one of the six principles of Kemalism. That basis of political authority meant a transformation of the ideological foundations of the state, and the old system, in which God is the sovereign and the real authority is God's, not the people's will, was eliminated.

The other principles of Kemalism were also related to that basic transformation: Nationalism directed the focus of loyalty to the new nation-state, populism emphasized the importance of the people as opposed to the elite, revolutionism supported the willingness to accept constant transformation, and statism defined the role of the government in the economy. The remaining principle, secularism, spoke directly to the role of religion, and the Kemalist program was explicitly secularist. The secularism of the Turkish republic aimed at bringing an end to all of the old institutions of the faith, and it excluded formally religious considerations from the political arena and rejected social distinctions based on religion. However, the program did not reject Islam or oppose religion in general; rather, it aimed at making adherence to Islam a personal, individual matter in an environment where a person was not obliged to follow some externally established set of rules and doctrines. It was a secularist rather than an atheistic program of modernizing reform.

As a nationalist program, Kemalism worked to "nationalize" Islam by making it more Turkish in order that all Turks could understand their faith without having to resort to professional interpreters. In this effort, the language of the faith was an important key. Through Kemal's leadership, the call to prayer and mosque sermons came to be given in Turkish rather than in Arabic. In addition, he worked to have the Quran translated from Arabic into Turkish, something that aroused much conservative opposition. In a curious reflection of fundamentalism, Kemal said: "The Turk believes in the Book, but he does not understand what it says to him. First of all, he himself must understand directly the Book that he so seeks."[26] In this way, the secularist adaptationism of Kemal worked to create a modern, individualistic Islamic style.

In the broadest political terms, the basic question raised by the secularist policy of Turkish reform was, "Is Islam conceivable in a democratically constituted state?"[27] Turkish secularism implied that Islam was not comprehensive or directly applicable to all aspects of life, a position rejected by fundamentalists, and that continuity with past institutions and formulations was unnecessary, a position objectionable to conservatives. However, if one examines the twentieth-century Turkish experience, the answer to the question must be in the affirmative. In Turkey, Muslims live in a democratically constituted state but have remained clearly Muslim in terms of their own self-identification and by most nonextremist Islamic standards.

The Kemalist program was a liberal secularist transformation rather than a socialist revolution, and it provided the foundations for the evolution of a modernizing parliamentary democracy, with major social changes taking place without a socially destructive revolution. Although Mustafa Kemal concentrated political control in his own hands, he also created a political party, the Republican People's party (RPP), that carried on his program after his death. Following World War II, the one-party state changed to a multiparty one when the Democratic party (DP) was created in 1946.

The DP won the general elections of 1950 and took control of the government by peaceful, democratic means. In this process, Islam played some role. The narrow restrictions placed upon religion had not been fully accepted by many Turks, especially in the rural areas. Part of the DP program, which was later implemented, was to expand the programs of religious instruction and to end the use of Turkish translations of the call to prayer and the Quran. Those features were factors in the DP's electoral popularity. In 1948, the Nation party was formed, and it had a more clearly religious program that advocated Islamic revival and the substantial relaxation, if not the elimination, of the secularist aspects of Turkish policies. An indication of the continuing strength of at least a modified adherence to the Kemalist tradition of secularism is that although the DP won 53 percent of the votes, the Nation party received only 3 percent in the 1950 elections.

The Nation party was significant as it represented a continuing minority of people in Turkey who advocated a greater adherence to Islamic traditions, and it was the first manifestation of an organized fundamentalist political party within the Turkish political system. Although it was outlawed in 1954 for attempting to use religion for political purposes, it was succeeded by the Republican Nation party, which won almost 5 percent of the votes in the 1954 elections. At the same time, there was renewed activity on the part of illegal activist *tariqahs*, such as the Tijaniyyah and the Naqshbandiyyah. None of this activity, however, represented a significant challenge at the time to the dominant Kemalist secularism, even in the less rigorous form espoused by the DP.

The major challenge to the Kemalist political system came from the developing policies of the DP itself, which increasingly limited its political opposition and appeared to be moving in the direction of a one-party, dictatorial state. As a result, the leaders of the armed forces took control of the government in 1960 and brought an end to the Democratic party. The new military rulers asserted their loyalty to the Kemalist program and, in contrast to many of their contemporaries elsewhere, rapidly moved to restore civilian control of the government. A new constitution was formulated by a special constituent assembly and the second Turkish republic came into existence in 1961. One of the primary concerns of the framers of the new constitution was to create safeguards against the possible emergence of a dictatorial or one-party rule, and there were complex arrangements for proportional representation and a recognition of opposition views. However, those safeguards made it difficult for a single party to win a clear majority in the parliament, and the second republic was plagued by political fragmentation rather than by dictatorial single-party rule. Its inability to cope with political disintegration was one of the reasons why it was brought to an end by military officers in 1980.

Kemalist secularism was preserved in the 1960s, and Islam continued to function in a democratically constituted state. The progress of liberal secularism was not overtaken by radical secularism, and the initial strength of Kemalism provided sufficient momentum for survival. In contrast to the secularism in the Arab East, Kemal's secularism, from the very beginning, was closely identified with indigenous interests and did not have to undergo the process, which occurred in the Arab East, of trying to adapt secularism to local conditions. However, after the 1960 revolution, the stability of the Turkish political system was not as secure, and a variety of new ideas began to emerge. In some ways, Kemalism was becoming the established view to be preserved by "conservatives" rather than the radical ideology it had been in the days following World War I.

Governmental Reformism in Iran. The reform programs initiated by the rulers of Iran during the twentieth century never secured as broad a base of support as the those of the Kemalists in Turkey. In Iran, the organized conservative and fundamentalist religious leaders, as well as the more radical modern-educated groups, provided continuing and often effective opposition from two different perspectives. Between the two, the monarchy represented modernizing reformism that was neither Islamic enough to satisfy the ulama nor liberal enough to satisfy the educated classes. The foundations for this situation had been clearly laid during the nineteenth century, and the major themes were the efforts to create an effectively modernized Iran, to limit the potential tyranny of the shah, and to restrict, if not eliminate, foreign influence in Iranian affairs.

In the constitutional movement at the beginning of the century, the ulama, along with their allies, the traditional merchants, joined forces with the small, but articulate, group of modern-educated Iranians. This alliance succeeded in imposing some limits on the shah's power, but the constitutionalists were unable to agree on many points, including the role of Islam in the new political system. Neither they nor the shah was able to prevent foreign troops and agents from substantial interference in the country during World War I, and they also could not prevent the discovery of oil in Iran in 1908 or the exploitation of Iran's oil resources by the British-owned Anglo-Persian Oil Company (APOC).

At the end of World War I, Iran appeared to be lapsing into another era of internal anarchy and foreign domination. However, in 1921, the commander of the most effective military unit in the Iranian army, Reza Khan (1878–1944), joined forces with a modern-educated intellectual, Ziya ud-Din Tabatabai, to take control of the government. Ziya was soon forced out, and Reza became the commander of the armed forces, then war minister, prime minister, and finally, in 1925, he was crowned shah. As Reza Shah Pahlavi, he ruled Iran until 1941.

Reza initiated a program of rigorous reform and has often been compared with his contemporary, Ataturk. However, in many ways he was closer to Mehmet Ali in Egypt. He worked to create a strong, modernizing dynastic state rather than a nationalist, parliamentary regime, and to some extent, this line of development was the product of Iranian conditions at the time. When he assumed power, there was the possibility that he would declare Iran to be a republic, but the rapid mobilization of opposition to that step by the ulama made the republican option appear impossible.

In his reform program, Reza concentrated on creating a strong central government. He built a national army and used it to crush tribal and provincial forces, bringing about an effective, if militarily imposed, national unity. He expanded the modern means of transportation and communication, enlarged the government administrative structure, initiated a large number of social and legal reforms, and developed the system of modern education. Although this program hastened the process of modernization in Iran, its implementation depended more upon coercion than upon persuasion, and the program remained tied to the monarchy rather than expanding to be a national cause or ideology.

In the area of religion, Reza was not so much a secularist as a leader who attempted to bring religious institutions and leaders under the control of the state. There was little, if any, ideological dimension to this effort. The basic structure of Shiʿi theology and political theory remained based on the principles of the imamate and the importance of the *mujtahid*s, but once Reza had established himself in power, there was little that the ulama could do to utilize that religious tradition to oppose him. In the face of active suppression, they assumed a subdued political quietism while Reza progressively narrowed their legal, educational, and economic roles in Iranian society. Although he made some compromises with religious sensibilities, in general, as one religious leader recalled in 1967, Reza "did not even go through the motions of appealing to the religious."[28] Instead, he made some effort to create a structure of religious officialdom that was subservient to the state, and the ulama in that group appeared to be the major figures of the era in religious terms.

As a part of his policy of strengthening the monarchy, Reza worked to revive an awareness of the pre-Islamic Persian tradition as he hoped that an explicitly Persian nationalism would counter the influence of the religious leaders. In the long run, the only significant impact of this activity was to reinforce the Shiʿi doctrines that maintained the illegitimacy, in Islamic terms, of any monarchy other than that of the imam himself. Nevertheless, Reza strengthened the monarchy as a power in Iran. The creation of a strong military made it possible for him to have firm control of the country, and when he was overthrown, it was by Russian and British forces rather than by internal opposition.

Reza was deposed in 1941 when British and Russian troops occupied Iran, and he was succeeded by his son, Mohammad Reza Shah Pahlavi (1919–1980), who was young and inexperienced. Between 1941 and 1953, Iran passed through a period of active political development. A variety of groups, representing the full range of the Iranian political spectrum, struggled for power, and much of that political development was made possible by the development of modern education and communications during the Reza era. In the struggle, the major groups were activist ulama of a fundamentalist style, liberal and middle-class nationalists, well-organized radical secularists, and the groups associated with the monarchy and the armed forces. For a brief period in 1951–1953, the nationalists won control under the leadership of Mohammad Mosaddiq, and the government nationalized the Anglo-Iranian Oil Company (APOC had changed its name in 1935) but was unable to establish permanent political dominance. With the support of the military and others, Mohammad Reza Shah assumed full control of the government in 1953, and the monarchy reassumed its dominant position in Iran.

Mohammad Reza Shah continued the basic governmental reform efforts of his father, but in a more organized manner. Like his father, the shah's program stood between the more radical expectations of the modern-educated class and the conservative ideals of the ulama. Although he faced some opposition from both groups, including a series of major demonstrations in 1963 led by important ulama, he was able by co-option and coercion to keep the monarchy in firm control of Iran through the decade of the 1960s.

The year 1963 was an important turning point in the development of the shah's program of reforms. Up to that point, his primary concerns had been the consolidation of the power position of the monarchy, but it then became necessary to expand the base of support for the monarchy as well as to pay greater attention to programs of social and economic development. The result was the proclamation of the White Revolution in 1963, which was a cluster of specific programs that aimed at accelerating the process of the socioeconomic modernization of Iran, with the most important "principle" being the land reform that had begun in 1962. That and other "principles," like profit sharing for factory workers and the nationalization of forest resources, reflect the popularity at the time of more radical socialist ideas.

The White Revolution was proclaimed in the same year that Faysal in Saudi Arabia announced his ten-point program of pragmatic fundamentalism. However, in contrast to the Saudi program, the shah's reforms in general and the White Revolution in particular did not represent a significant reorientation of Islamic thought. In his speech from the throne delivered to the opening of a new Majlis session on 6 October 1967, in which he assessed the White Revolution, there was only the briefest mention of Islam and the high ideals of the faith were generally alluded to but not concretely related to the principles of the revolution. Shiʿi Islam remained basically as it was before Mohammad Reza Shah, who put forth no new theology of Islamic rule and no principle of secularism in an Islamic society.

The vague theology of the reformist monarchy was supplemented by Mohammad Reza Shah, however, in two ways. First, he continued and expanded his father's attempts to identify the Iranian monarchy with the traditions of the pre-Islamic Persian Empire. Two major events symbolized this effort to stress the idea of monarchical continuity and the strength of the current dynasty and, not accidentally, to show that the dynasty was Persian in a special way and not dependent upon the Islamic institutions that were controlled by the sometimes dissident ulama. Those two events were the ceremonies accompanying the coronation of the shah and Queen Farah in 1967 and the huge festival commemorating "the 2500th anniversary" of the Iranian empire in 1971.

The second way in which Mohammad Reza Shah supplemented the monarchist ideology was by claiming that he had a special divine mission to rule. He reported that he had had special visions of major Islamic figures and that his life had been miraculously saved on a number of occasions. However, neither the divine mission nor the ancient Persian tradition represented a fully articulated basis for a monarchy when the dominant majority of the people were Muslims. His reformist monarchy survived as long as he remained an adept and realistic political manipulator and leader in control of a strong military force, which was clearly the case from 1953 until at least the end of the 1960s.

The reformist monarchy of the Pahlavi dynasty was neither explicitly secularist nor essentially religious. It replaced the inept Qajar dynasty and created a strong central government in a country with many diverse elements, and through its programs of modernization, it succeeded in controlling and balancing those elements for more than half a century. That monarchy, which reached the peak of its power during the 1960s, represented an important stage in the development of an Islamic country but did not, itself, represent a significant redefinition of the Islamic experience.

Reformism and the Afghan Monarchy. Afghanistan had long been a homeland for military empires, but a more "national" monarchy did not emerge until the eighteenth century. At that time, a major tribal chieftain established the Durrani dynasty and a conquest empire, and despite internal feuds and tribal divisions, the dynasty was able to establish an Afghan kingdom. The nineteenth century was a time of great turmoil, and dynastic and tribal conflicts and the growing expansion of the British and Russian Empires encroached on Afghan territory. One branch of the dynasty established itself as the amirs of Kabul, and that family gradually expanded its power until Abd al-Rahman Khan (1844–1901) effectively unified the country. Facing a strong Russian threat, Abd al-Rahman allied himself with the British, who recognized him as the ruler of Afghanistan in return for his accepting British control of Afghan foreign affairs. During his reign, the boundaries of contemporary Afghanistan were defined in a series of treaties. His son, Habib Allah, ruled from 1901 until 1919 during a time of relative internal stability, and the position of the dynasty was firmly consolidated.

The stage was set for Afghanistan's postwar modernizing reformer, King Amanallah (1892–1960). Habib Allah was murdered in 1919 under circumstances that are still disputed, although various imperialist plots have been suspected. During Habib Allah's reign, some efforts had been made to reduce British control, and a small movement in favor of national independence and modernizing reform had developed. A key figure in that movement was Mahmud Tarzi (1865–1933), who lived in the eastern Mediterranean area where he had come into contact with Jamal al-Din al-Afghani and the Young Turks. Tarzi returned to Afghanistan during the days of Habib Allah and published a newspaper, which attacked both European imperialism and the conservative Muslim resistance to change. His daughter married Habib Allah's son, Amanallah, and through his son-in-law, many of Tarzi's ideas became government policy in the years after World War I.

Amanallah's first major act was to demand full independence for Afghanistan from the British. He declared a holy war, united general Afghan opinion behind him, and succeeded in winning British recognition of Afghan independence in both internal and foreign affairs. Afghanistan, like Turkey and Iran, was able to secure national independence early in the twentieth century, and that independence opened the way for the initiation of a government-led program of modernization. Amanallah attempted to modernize the army and to build a modern system of education. He expanded the transportation and communications system and worked to reorganize the structure of the central government. In all of those efforts, he used many foreign advisers.

Those reforms rapidly aroused opposition within Afghanistan. The modernization program directly undermined the power of both the great tribal leaders and the religious notables, and as a result, religiotribal revolts soon broke out. The resistance was primarily conservative in style, objecting to change. The dominant form of Islam in the country is Sunni, so there were not the doctrinal antimonarchical tones that there were in Iran, but the religious leaders saw Amanallah as a threat to their position and their faith. Amanallah did not develop a formal ideology of reform but, rather, was similar to the early-nineteenth-century reformers in his pragmatic approach. However, he was an enthusiast who moved more rapidly than was practical. He was unable to create a nationalist loyalty to reform as Ataturk did, nor did he create a strong army to implement his reforms by coercion as Reza did. Mahmud Tarzi observed, "Amanallah has built a beautiful monument without a foundation."[29]

In 1928, Amanallah's army was unable to stop a major tribal revolt, and rebellion soon spread. A military adventurer captured Kabul, Amanallah was forced to flee from the country, and he spent the rest of his life in exile. The anarchy soon produced a reaction, and another member of the royal family, Muhammad Nadir (d. 1933), was able to reestablish control. He set in motion a policy that was committed to Afghan independence and open to gradual modernization, but he avoided dramatic reforms that would anger the conservatives. He cooperated with the great tribal notables and worked to placate the religious leaders. He had succeeded in creating a sufficiently stable situation so that when he was murdered in 1933, the throne passed to his son, Muhammad Zahir (b. 1913), without incident. Muhammad Zahir continued to follow the restrained policies of his father and introduced reforms when they were possible without too great offense being given to the tribal and religious leaders.

This spirit of conservative reform remained the hallmark of Muhammad Zahir's policy, but it meant that a new, modern-educated class developed slowly. That class became an important force in Afghan politics as its discontentment with the slow pace of modernization grew and later led to the emergence of a more radical group. However, the dominant power for setting the tone of government policy remained with the more conservative tribal and religious leaders. Following World War II, Afghanistan followed a policy of careful neutralism in international affairs, although after the British withdrawal from India, relations with Russia became closer, and increasing Soviet aid gave an impetus to both the modernization programs and the more radical groups in Afghanistan. In 1953, General Muhammad Daoud Khan became prime minister. Under his leadership, Afghanistan attempted to reject the southern border of the country, the Durand line, which had been drawn by the British at the end of the nineteenth century, and that attempt aroused nationalist feelings that provided popular support for the government. During the decade of Daoud's leadership, the government remained paternalistic in style but accelerated the process of modernization in economic and social areas. Pressures also built for greater political modernization, and an alliance of educated groups and religious leaders helped to bring about a new constitutional regime in 1963.

In the constitution promulgated in 1964, Islam was declared the religion of Afghanistan, and the monarchy was confirmed, although members of the royal family were prohibited from participation in political parties. In defining the role of Islam, a more liberal approach emerged. In the legal system, no law was to be repugnant to the basic principles of Islam, but Islamic law was to be applied only in cases not covered by other laws. In other words, an Islamic modernism that recognized *ijtihad* provided the basic religious tone for this constitution. The new regime was intellectually satisfying to many, but in the following decade, the many divisions within Afghan society manifested themselves, which led to political instability.

The decade of the 1960s was a time of liberal experiment in Afghanstan, and there was a departure from paternalistic, "strong-man" modernization with a conservative tone. Like the White Revolution in Iran and the Saudi pragmatic fundamentalism initiated in 1963, the constitutional regime was an effort to provide a more modern structure in a society in which the majority of the Muslims were still quite conservative in their views. In Afghanistan, this modernizing effort only provided an opening for divisive forces to reduce the effectiveness of the central government and slow the pace of effective modernization.

Radical Adaptationism in the Northern Tier

The emergence of more radical thought in the northern tier was limited by the existence of reformist, independent governments. Although some modern-educated Muslims felt that their governments were not initiating sufficiently drastic reforms or moving as rapidly as they would like, the fact that the governments were clearly independent made opposition more difficult. In the nationalist mood of the time, radical criticism of government policy was easily viewed as an attack by "foreign" elements and ideas, and in addition, many of the intellectuals realized that attacking the government would aid the conservatives rather than hasten the transformation. A final element is that the reformist approaches of the government had an appeal to the more radical intellectuals, and few could fully resist the idea of an "indigenous" and activist reform effort. It was not until the government reform efforts either faltered or became more conservative, trying to protect past achievements rather than creating new ones, that significant radical groups emerged.

The relationship between the radical groups and Islam was relatively limited. As a part of their desire for social transformation, the radicals usually viewed the leaders and institutions of Islam as backward and obstacles to progress. In the northern tier countries, there was little radical effort to redefine Islam in modern terms, as the radicals were content with making vague generalizations about Islam as a socialist or revolutionary religion, if Islam was not simply rejected as a conservative social force. In this way, northern tier radicalism tended to have few direct ties with local religiocultural traditions. The closest ties came when some groups espoused the cause of communal nationalism, but, as happened in Iran with the communist group that supported Azerbaijan autonomy, the "main line" radical groups were associated with Russian communism and were often the objects of nationalist suspicion.

Radicalism and Communism in Turkey. The major factor governing the history of radicalism in Turkey was the existence of a successful, already relatively radical program that was government policy after the establishment of Ataturk's regime. Before that time, there had been small socialist groups and parties that had had only limited success in the days of the Young Turks, but the generally chaotic conditions at the end of World War I provided an opportunity for more extensive activities. Intellectuals and workers who had been in Europe and Russia returned and formed a number of small parties that made some progress, but they were soon overtaken by the emergence of the Kemalist nationalist movement. In the Anatolian Peninsula, a more active alternative to that movement emerged in the form of the Green Army, a group that brought together a number of local resistance groups fighting against the Greeks. At first the nationalist movement cooperated with those groups, but finally, when it was clear that the Green Army could not be controlled by the Grand National Assembly, it was defeated by Kemalist forces.

The Green Army combined a variety of intellectuals and military adventurers, and it proposed a radically new economic order with state ownership of the means of production. At the same time, it asserted that its program did not conflict with Islam or the national cause. "In short, the Green Army stood for an amalgam of rather radical socialism with Islamic and nationalistic overtones."[30] Other communist and socialist groups at the time did not have a military organization and made less of a point of relating their ideas to Islam. In the end, they, too, were outlawed, and formal communist and socialist organizations disappeared.

Many of the major figures in those groups were integrated into the Kemalist movement and given positions in the government. They assisted in the definition of Kemalism, and they moved to a more nationalist position. In the early 1930s, one such group was associated with a periodical called *Kadro*, which helped to define the statist economic policy of the government. Those group members who remained in some Communist party organization assisted in the process of the disintegration of their groups by engaging in a number of factional disputes.

When the radical leftist Turks again succeeded in organizing themselves on the political scene, it was during the years of party politics following World War II. At that time, at least from a radical perspective, Kemalism had become relatively conservative, and it was possible to identify a radical position that was more clearly distinguished from government policy than had been the case in the days of Ataturk. That position was emphasized during the days of Democratic party rule, and following the establishment of the second republic, the Turkish Workers' party was formed. By that time, radical parties were no longer necessarily tied to the Soviet Union, and the Workers' party appealed to some intellectuals and labor union groups. Although it never became a large party, it received around 3 percent of the votes in the general elections of 1965 and 1969, but that was only a reflection of the emergence of a reasonably well-organized and active extreme left in the Turkish political spectrum. The religious position of that new left was one of militant opposition to traditional Islamic influence in society, but because that opposition took a basically anti-Sunni form, the radical left drew some support from the Shiʿi minority groups in Turkey as well as from the more radical labor unions and intellectuals.

Radicalism, in contrast to Kemalism, did not produce a redefinition of Islam or a reorientation of its role in society. However, by the 1960s, it did begin to free itself from the stigma of association with a foreign power. It emerged at that time as a Turkish force advocating more active changes in society and became a major style of criticism of the Kemalist tradition as it was becoming more conservative. Increasingly in the 1960s, the new left engaged in militant activities and occasional terrorism, thus presenting a challenge to Turkish political stability. Although the Workers' party was outlawed in 1971, the radical position had become firmly established by that time.

Radicalism and Islam in Iran. The government's reform program in Iran was both less radical in its orientation and less successful in winning the support of the modern-educated class in Iran than the one in Turkey, which gave greater opportunity for an independent secularist radicalism in Iran. However, there were still grave problems for this position, which were posed by the strength of the independent state and the powerful appeal of nationalism and Islam as alternative bases for an ideology of reform. Radicalism faced the problems of identification with a foreign power and of an inability to mobilize mass support on the basis of its ideology.

In this context, three strands of a more secularist approach have interacted in Iran during the twentieth century. The most coherent of these, at least in organizational terms, is the development of communism and a socially radical secularism. The second is a politically oriented liberal nationalism, which is vigorously opposed to foreign influence in Iran and aware of the need for socioeconomic reform but more conservative than the communist approach in terms of actual programs. A third strand is the development of a more intellectually oriented reinterpretation of the Iranian heritage and the needs of modern Iran.

The communist movement in Iran emerged during the last years of World War I. A group called Adalat was organized among the Persian workers in Baku, in the Russian Caucasus region, and in 1918, they stormed the Iranian consulate there. The group received Russian help in becoming active within Iran, it joined forces with a local nationalist movement in the northern province of Gilan, and soon helped in establishing the "Persian Soviet Socialist Republic."

The fortunes of the Gilan movement illustrate the problems of organized communism in Iran. By associating themselves with the liberal nationalist Jangali movement in Gilan led by Kuchek Khan, the communists were able to gain a basis for support, but the communist ability to maintain that support weakened rapidly. The dependence of the local communists upon the Soviet Union raised doubts in the minds of nationalist Iranians, and the weakness of that reliance upon a foreign state was shown by the collapse of the Gilan movement when Soviet policy shifts resulted in the withdrawal of Soviet military aid. The other major communist difficulty was ideological: Opposition to religion is not popular in Iran, but communist enthusiasts frequently press the issue. In the case of the Gilan movement, the alliance with Kuchek Khan was broken soon after it was formed and one of the principle reasons was the vigorous antireligious campaign of the new communist leaders. They closed mosques, forbade religious instruction, and enacted other measures that alienated not only the conservative population but Kuchek Khan himself.

The twin obstacles of ideology and ties to a foreign power remained for communism in Iran, but the rapid growth of the more secularist, educated class and the appeal to the emerging labor groups gave organized communism a larger potential basis for support. The rigid controls of the era of Reza Shah limited the ability of the communists to take advantage of this changing situation, but the collapse of Reza's regime and the occupation of northern Iran by Russian forces provided the opportunity for the organization of the Tudeh party. The Tudeh offered a program of radical socioeconomic reform that had substantial appeal, but following World War II, a branch of the party became involved in the Azerbaijan separatist movement, and the old problems of being tied to the policy of a foreign power again weakened communism's appeal in a time of nationalist fervor. However, by careful alliance with nationalist causes and by providing a challenge to the established order, organized communism in Iran has been able to attract a wide range of adherents.

The relationship between Islam and communism in Iran is complex. Although the antireligious aspects of communist ideology, when openly espoused, created problems for groups like the Gilan leaders and the Tudeh, tactical alliances between communists and religious leaders have often been possible, and those alliances became an increasingly important aspect of Iranian politics as the monarchy became stronger. By the mid-1960s, the Tudeh had been outlawed for some time, and it was possible to conclude that "although the prospects for a renewed Communist assault on the Iranian system may be remote, Communist radicalism remains a source of ideological attraction."[31] At that time, however, it seemed clear that the major rival of communism in challenging the Iranian sociopolitical system was a nationalist and noncommunist left. As was true in many areas of the world at that time, it was indigenous secular socialism rather than religious revival that seemed to be the most important developing sociopolitical force.

The second strand of the more secularist approach in Iran is liberal nationalism, which has been a less well-organized but more popular force in Iran than communism, and its strength grew as the modern-educated class became larger. Beginning in the late nineteenth century, liberal nationalists worked to create a democratic and an independent Iran. They played a role in the constitutionalist movement at the beginning of the century but were unable to provide organized and effective leadership in the face of the strength of the conservative forces, foreign intervention, and their own internal divisions. During the era of Reza Shah, they were forced into opposition, and their liberal aims of limiting the power of an autocratic monarchy threw them into alliance again with the more conservative elements of society.

Following World War II, the liberal nationalists emerged as a major political force. Strengthened by the growth of the modern-educated classes and their identification with the nationalist cause, the liberal nationalists came to power in 1950 under the leadership of Mohammed Mosaddiq, a widely respected politician with great popular support. However, he was unable to establish a firmly coordinated political movement, and liberal nationalism remained a loose alliance of sometimes competing groups. The issue that helped bring them to power was the nationalization of the Anglo-Iranian Oil Company, but the pressures created in the subsequent dispute soon led to the collapse of the alliance and the reestablishment of the monarchy as the dominant political force.

By the 1960s, the liberal nationalists had begun to organize opposition to the shah but faced many difficulties. The shah's White Revolution included many programs they advocated, but his increasingly autocratic rule made it difficult for them to support him, and at the same time, the shah's repressive measures prevented any large-scale, effective organization of opposition. Those difficulties provided a practical reason for adopting a less secularist tone. Shi'i Islam presented a sound and fully articulated ideological basis for opposition to the expanding power of the monarchy, and a movement emerged that was a synthesis of the more liberal religious leaders with the more religiously inclined liberal nationalists. This was the Freedom movement, and its leadership included Mahdi Bazargan, an engineer who was also a writer on religious topics, and a leading *mujtahid*, Ayatollah Mahmud Taliqani. Through the thinking of such men, an ideological position developed that advocated radical socioeconomic reform in the framework of the Islamic tradition. In this way, the foundations were beginning to be laid for a fully indigenous and Islamic radicalism that was compatible with the traditions of modernizing liberal nationalism.

This ideological position was clearly less secularist than the earlier liberal nationalism, and it maintained the comprehensive validity of Islam in all areas of life. In the early 1960s, men like Bazargan and Taliqani were stressing the importance of the active involvement of the ulama in political affairs, and they were also working to reformulate the Islamic tradition in terms that would be comprehensible and acceptable to modern-educated Muslims. The old Westernizing liberalism was becoming transformed into a more Islamic movement, and in that transformation, people like Taliqani provided a link between the liberal nationalist tradition and the more fundamentalist religious leaders who were also taking a more active role, like Ayatollah Khomeini.

The third strand of the Islamic experience in twentieth-century Iran might be called secularist thought. In literature and scholarly studies, a wide variety of thinkers have worked to analyze the Persian and Islamic traditions, utilizing modern critical techniques in a lively and dynamic manner. Although communists and liberal nationalists have a strong political orientation, there is also a modernizing tradition that is not directly involved in politics, although it has political implications. Only a few such writers can be mentioned.

Ahmad Kasrawi Tabrizi (1890–1946) began his career as a religious teacher but soon became a lawyer, judge, and then history teacher. His historical studies covered political and literary history and had a major influence on the thinking of the emerging educated classes. He became a vigorous critic of social institutions and religious practices and felt that popular Shiꞌi practices hindered constructive progress, he supported representative government and a cooperative style of capitalism based on social welfare, and he believed that he was presenting an ideological path that was not a new religion but the successor to and a continuation of Islam. He was murdered by religious extremists in 1946.

A sharp contrast to Kasrawi is provided by Seyyed Hossein Nasr, who received a modern technical education at the Massachusetts Institute of Technology, studied the history of science at Harvard University, and taught for a number of years at the University of Tehran after his return to Iran in 1958. In his work, Seyyed Hossein presents a vigorous modern form of the Sufi tradition that has an appeal to many non-Muslims, and his approach to Shiꞌism is in philosophical rather than in political terms. In works like *Ideals and Realities of Islam*, he argues that the diversity of Islam is part of its strength. "Sunnism and Shiꞌism are both orthodox interpretations of the Islamic revelation contained providentially within Islam in order to enable it to integrate people of different psychological constitutions into itself."[32] Rather than writing a sociohistorical critique of Islam, Nasr's wide range of works presents a reaffirmation of Islam in mystical-philosophical terms.

The wide spectrum of positions is visible in the literary activities of the major Iranian writers, as their views range from sharp social criticism of religious conservatism to glorification of the Islamic and Persian traditions. Through the journalistic and literary activities of such authors, educated Iranians were made aware of social problems and Western ideas, and through those writings, the scope of Islamic thought in Iran was articulated and broadened.

Modernist and modernizing thought in Iran thus took many forms. Social and political radicalism and secularist thinking were often in opposition to the policies of the reformist monarchy, and in contrast to Kemalist Turkey, official reformism was unable to prevent or co-opt most intellectual movements that developed in the context of the modern conditions. Thus, liberal and secularist modernism sometimes cooperated with the more explicitly Islamic movements, and each influenced the other in many ways. However, secularist thought did not change the essential nature of the Shi'i interpretations, and by the 1960s, there was a tendency for religiously influenced syntheses to emerge.

Radicalism in Afghanistan. During the twentieth century, radical secularist movements in the northern tier were least well organized in Afghanistan, and there, the more traditional loyalties and structures remained strong. Ironically, however, it was only in Afghanistan that the radicals actually assumed power in the years before 1980, which was due as much to the special conditions in the country and its international position as it was to any strength of the radicals themselves.

Early reformism under the leadership of King Amanallah, even though relatively moderate, was more extreme than most Afghans were willing to accept, and after Amanallah's fall, the more conservative reformism of the ruling dynasty generally moved rapidly enough to keep pace with the desires of the small educated class. There was a quiet republican sentiment among some in that class that was supported by the traditional tribal reservations about strong central government. That sentiment had few visible results until the period of parliamentary politics that began with the promulgation of the 1964 constitution.

In the more open political arena of the parliamentary constitutional regime of the 1960s, a more articulate and active secularist movement emerged. The careful cooperation of the Soviet Union with the Afghan government had made a procommunist radicalism possible despite Afghan suspicions of foreign interference. Small parties and newspapers presented a variety of more secularist views, and the most important of these groups were associated with the Democratic People's party, or Khalq. That group split into two factions during the 1960s. One group centered around Nur Muhammad Taraki and the newspaper he published in 1966 called *Khalq*; the other group was more revolutionary in its pronouncements, but its major figures were active in the parliament of the time. This second faction was called Parcham after its weekly publication, and the major figures in it were Babrak Karmal and Dr. Anahita, a woman deputy from Kabul. The differences among these radicals were more over methods than ideology.

The doctrinal positions of both factions of the Khalq and the other radical secularists were pragmatic. There was little philosophical opposition to religion or presentation of theological atheism; the emphasis was on social transformation. The key parts of the radical program were land reform, changing the structure of ownership, liberation of women, and reduction of the power of religious and tribal organizations. This position appealed to many people in the emerging educated groups. Although the country continued to be dominated by the old elites, the moderate and conservative reformism of the monarchy could not inspire the students or the modern-educated classes. Already in the 1960s, although it was not clear at the time, the political and ideological spectrum was beginning to be divided into a vigorous radical minority and a relatively nonadaptationist Islamic position, with the moderate center unable to built an effective political position.

Summary. In the northern tier, radicalism developed in the context of governmental reformism within the independent states. When a government's programs were dynamic and successful, the radical position was preempted, but in those periods when governments remained conservative or became authoritarian, the radicals provided a secularist alternative. In contrast to the experience in the Arab East, however, the radical alternative in the northern tier was not successful in creating a visibly Islamic radicalism. The Tudeh and Khalq groups represented a secular and non-Islamic dimension of ideology within countries with dominant Muslim majorities.

Fundamentalism in the Northern Tier

During the twentieth century, both old and new forms of Islamic fundamentalism have been active. Some groups appear to be direct heirs of earlier traditions, and others have taken on the new form of activist associations similar to the Muslim Brotherhood. In either case, the success of the movements depends upon the ability of the reformist governments to control them. The appeal of the fundamentalists is based on the continuing vitality of the Islamic tradition, which is often preserved by the more conservative forces, and the inability of the modernizers to solve pressing problems within the northern tier societies. In this context, it must be emphasized that Islamic fundamentalism is not a conservative mood attempting to prevent change. Rather, in the context of the twentieth century, it represents an alternative program of social transformation and competes with the modernizers. When modernization programs are dynamic and provide a foundation for realistic hopes for progress, fundamentalist movements are less successful in their appeal for mass support.

Neo-Sufi Orders. Despite the programs of government reformers and their efforts to limit the strength of the older Islamic organizations, some of the Neo-Sufi orders have continued to command allegiance in northern tier countries. In Turkey, that allegiance has taken the form of secret and often terrorist activities. During the period of multiparty politics following World War II, some of the old organizations took advantage of the relaxation of Kemalist secularism to renew their public activities, and the best-known case was the revival of Tijaniyyah activity. The order had been encouraged by Abdulhamid II as a part of his Pan-Islamic policy, although it did not develop a large following in Turkey. Following the ban on Sufi orders in 1925, the Tijaniyyah, like the other orders, disappeared from public view, but in 1949, members of the order began publicly demanding a greater role for Islam in the Turkish republic. In a demonstration in the Grand National Assembly, members recited the then-illegal Arabic call to prayer, and the order gained prestige when the Arabic version was restored in the following year. At the same time, an Ankara business man, Kemal Pilavoglu, a member of the order, published books and led an attack on public monuments as being images prohibited by Islam. The destruction of statues of Ataturk and other acts of violence led to Pilavoglu's trial and conviction in 1952. Although the Tijaniyyah organized some demonstrations at the time, its importance rapidly declined after the imprisonment of its leader. The decline of the Tijaniyyah did not, however, mean the end of Turkish fundamentalist activism, only that it has taken different forms in subsequent years.

The other area where older-style organizations have continued to have influence is Afghanistan. There, great religious families associated with *tariqahs* and the old social order have been prominent in leading the opposition to modernizing reforms. One of these families was the Mujaddidi, a family associated with the Naqshbandiyyah, which had come to Afghanistan following World War I. That family had been active in Muslim revolts against communist rule in Central Asia and was a vigorous opponent of modernizing reform programs. Members of the family were involved in the dismantling of Amanallah's programs in the 1930s and were leaders in the conservative faction during the parliamentary era of 1963–1973. Another great family was the Gaylani, descendants of Abd al-Qadir al-Gaylani, the founder of the Qadiriyyah. In the period following the overthrow of Amanallah, the great religious families were more conservative than fundamentalist in style, and they were able to slow the pace of reform sufficiently so that more militant action was not necessary. However, the fundamentalist potential is clearly shown by the fact that when a radical regime came to power in the 1970s, these religious families provided much of the leadership for the emerging revolutionary groups. The transition from conservative to fundamentalist has also been a transition in organizational form from a clan- and *tariqah*-oriented structure to a more modern style of association or liberation movement.

Modern Fundamentalist Associations. One of the most dramatic aspects of fundamentalism in the northern tier is its ability to develop a variety of organizational formats to cope with changing political and social conditions. During the first two-thirds of the twentieth century, the ideological content of fundamentalism remained relatively constant but was expressed through political parties, private associations, and terrorist groups. It was not until the end of the 1960s that there were significant efforts at a redefinition of the core of the faith in fundamentalist terms.

Different groups proposed radical alterations of the existing social order, and they sometimes came into conflict with conservatives as well as with modernizing secularists. As a result, they usually drew their support from groups in society whose lives had been significantly altered by the process of modernization but who felt that they were not participating in the benefits of such development. In many cases, this element was reinforced by a sense that personal and cultural identity was being destroyed without an effective new identity being created. It is thus possible to say that fundamentalist associations in the northern tier have often been the products of modernization rather than remnants of an older social order.

Fundamentalist Groups in Turkey. The success of the Kemalist reform program and the ability of the reformist government to control, if not suppress, fundamentalist sentiments means that for many years, observers felt that Kemalist secularism had been almost completely successful. However, the attachment of the Turks to Islam remained strong, and as secularist control loosened, Islamic fundamentalism found new ways of expressing itself.

One of the oldest groups maintaining opposition to secularist trends was the group led by Said Nursi (1867–1960). Originally a member of Ittihad-i Muhammadi, an Islamically oriented group in the days of the Young Turk Revolution, he later organized the Followers of Nur (Light). He called for the reestablishment of an Islamic state that would be based on Islamic law and ruled by the ulama. Following his death in 1960, the movement lost much of its dynamism, but it was felt to be a viable threat, and successive governments took strong measures against the group.

With the development of a multiparty political system following World War II, a number of parties emerged whose programs called for a revival of Islamic values in politics and society. Although those groups have never been as large as the two major parties, they have come to represent a significant part of the Turkish political scene, showing the continuing strength of fundamentalism.

The oldest of these parties is the Nation party, which was established in 1948. It has gone through a number of organizational changes as a result of combination with other parties or, at times, of being outlawed for anti-Kemalist activities. In its form as the Republican Peasants' Nation party, formed in 1958 by the merger of the Republican Nation party and the Peasant party of Turkey, it was the only party other than the Republican People's party to survive the 1960 revolution as a separate party. In the 1961 elections, the Republican Peasants' Nation party received 14 percent of the votes, but, as other parties became established, it received only 2.2 percent in the 1965 elections. As the party's fortunes declined, it looked for new leadership, which it found in Alparslan Turkes (b. 1917), who reorganized the party as the National Action party in 1969. During the 1970s, under Turkes's leadership, the emphasis of the party's program shifted from Islamic to Turkish nationalist themes. Special militant youth squads were organized, and they attacked leftists and others, which was part of the development of political terrorism on the Turkish scene.

During the 1960s, other small parties were created, and they espoused a wide range of economically conservative programs and joined those with an emphasis on religion. Within the major parties, there were also more religiously oriented factions. During the decade, there was a tendency for those groups both to compete and to cooperate, and out of that situation there emerged a relatively strong religious party led by a former member of the Justice party, Necmettin Erbakan (b. 1926). In its first form, the National Order party, organized in 1970, it was outlawed for antisecular activities, but Erbakan soon reorganized it as the National Salvation party, which won almost 12 percent of the votes in the 1973 elections. The party gave priority to "strengthening moral values" and opposed "wild liberalism,"[33] and it received at least some support from the remnants of the Naqshbandiyyah and the followers of Nursi.

The diversity of the religiously oriented parties in Turkey is illustrated by the Turkish Unity party, which was formed in 1966. Its party emblem contains twelve stars representing the twelve Shiʿi imams, and its original appeal was to the Shiʿi minority in central Turkey. In the 1969 elections, it won almost 3 percent of the votes and gained eight seats in parliament. In contrast to the Sunni parties, whose economic programs favor free enterprise or state capitalism, the Turkish Unity party moved in the direction of more socialist platforms and eventually joined forces with the leftist groups in the Turkish Labor party.

In Turkey, the vigorous reaffirmation of Islam thus took the form of activist political parties, which was possible in the framework of a multiparty system. It was not until late in the 1960s that some of the associations began to engage in more militant and directly revolutionary actions. The dominance of Kemalist secularism limited their ability to win widespread support, so they moved outside of the regular political arena in some cases.

Religious Activism in Iran. In Iran during the twentieth century, one of the major features of the Islamic experience has been the interaction between the religious leadership and the institutions of the state. In this interaction, the ulama have played a leading role, supported by the teachings of Shiʿi Islam, and the major themes involved have been opposition to foreign interference and to monarchical absolutism. Because of Iranian independence, both the monarchy and the religious leadership were able to act with greater freedom than was the case in countries that remained under direct European control.

Ulama activism played a prominent part in three major episodes of twentieth-century Iranian history before the Islamic revolution of the 1970s. The first of these was the constitutional movement early in the century, when the religious leaders joined forces with other groups to gain a constitution. However, following World War I, the dictatorship of Reza Shah was able to suppress most of the effective political activity by the ulama. They had succeeded in demonstrating the political inadvisability of creating a republic in the 1920s and were a conservative force that set some limits upon Reza's programs.

It was only after the overthrow of Reza in 1941 that specifically religious forces began to play an overt political role, and that revival is associated with a new fundamentalist association, the Fidaᶜiyyan-i Islam, and activist religious leader, Abu al-Qasim Kashani (d. 1962). The new revivalists were not closely associated with the religious establishment and were often critical of the political quietism of the major *mujtahid*s. Although the revivalists reflected the ideological principles of Shiᶜi Islam, the movements were less traditional in format.

The Fidaᶜiyyan was formed in Tehran in 1945 as a militant group dedicated to the enforcement of the rules of the faith and to opposing secularism. The leading figure in the movement was a young religious teacher, Mujtaba Nawwab Safawi (1923–1955), who had had some technical education and had worked briefly for the Anglo-Iranian Oil Company. He was an effective orator and a charismatic leader. He was not a skilled religious scholar but used general Islamic themes as the basis for opposition to the government and foreign influence. His followers were drawn from the lower-middle-class and the lower-class urban population, and he mobilized them into an effective urban guerrilla corps dedicated to creating an Islamic state and society.

Like the Muslim Brotherhood in Egypt and fundamentalist groups elsewhere, the Fidaᶜiyyan emphasized the universal and comprehensive validity of Islam. One of its publications explained, for example, "We believe that Islam comprises and regulates all human affairs and could solve all problems which the world is facing today."[34] There was an emphasis on the unification of all Muslims and an avoidance of sectarianism by returning to the original form of Islam as practiced by the Prophet and his companions. To accomplish this, the Fidaᶜiyyan called for a holy war against those people who had departed from the faith, and the group committed a series of murders, including the killing of the secularist intellectual Kasrawi in 1946 and various government officials. The group was suppressed in 1955, and the major leaders were executed. The movement itself declined after that, but the theme of militant fundamentalism had been firmly established.

The most prominent individual in the revival of militant Islam in Iran after World War II was Abu al-Qasim Kashani. He often defended the Fidaᶜiyyan, and they worked together, but he was not the leader of the organization. He was one of the less socially prominent ulama who developed a large popular following because of his vigorous defense of Islam and his militant opposition to imperialism. He had been educated in Iraq and was involved in anti-British activity there during and following World War I. He was not politically active during the era of Reza's rule but emerged as a spokesman for militant Islam after World War II. He became the speaker of the parliament during the Mosaddiq era and helped to organize mass support for the nationalist movement. However, by 1953, he had begun to oppose the secularism of the liberal nationalists and feared that Mosaddiq was working to establish an unconstitutional dictatorship. As a result, Kashani broke with Mosaddiq and gave his support to the overthrow of the nationalist regime in 1953.

Kashani was familiar with the works of al-Afghani and Abduh as well as having studied the traditional religious disciplines. However, he was more action oriented than philosophical in his approach to Islam. He believed that Islam and modernization were compatible but that purification of the Islamic society was necessary, and he rejected secularist approaches as an imperialist method for weakening Islam. He said: "Islam warns the Muslims to resist foreign dominance and exploitation and that is why the imperialists try to confuse Muslims by advocating separation of religion from politics. According to Islamic theories of government the religious leaders are required to guide the people in social as well as political affairs."[35]

The reestablishment of monarchical power in Iran in 1953 brought an end to the second major episode of religious activism and also laid the foundations for the third. In 1963, when the shah proclaimed the White Revolution, religious leaders again became politically active. The leading *mujtahid* from the end of World War II until 1961 had been Ayatollah Burujirdi (1909–1961), a politically quietist scholar whose inclinations helped to dampen religious activism in the 1950s. However, following his death, the emerging religious leaders were more willing to assume an active political role in opposing the monarchy, and some of the leading figures in this spirit were Ayatollah Ruhollah Khomeini and Ayatollah Shariat Madari. It was Khomeini who was the most active in leading the antishah demonstrations in 1963.

The significance of the 1963 demonstrations remains subject to debate. The shah and others who favored the reform programs as outlined in the White Revolution maintained that Khomeini and others opposed the reforms because they objected to the land reforms, which would reduce their economic power. Supporters of Khomeini argue that the real reason for the opposition was to oppose the growing U.S. influence in Iran and to prevent autocratic rule and the violation of the constitution. Whatever the reasons, the 1963 demonstrations were crushed, and the shah imposed substantial restrictions on the religious leaders. However, like the opposition to the tobacco concession in the nineteenth century, the 1963 movement brought the religious leadership into the center of the opposition to the monarchy, and from that time on, the ulama were to provide most of the leading spokesmen for the opposition movement.

Although the monarchical reforms appeared to be increasingly successful in the 1960s, the forces of militant Islam were gaining organizational experience and were reemerging as a major political force after a long period of quietism. Although observers in the 1960s felt that the role of the ulama was declining in the face of the monarchical reform programs, the foundations were being laid for the Islamic revolution of the 1970s.

Summary

During the first two-thirds of the twentieth century, the dominant Islamic style in the northern tier was a modernizing adaptationism. To many people, both participants and observers, modernizing reformism was triumphant by the 1960s, and the political independence of the three countries made it possible for the governments themselves to set the tone. With varying degrees of emphasis on secularism, modern political structures were created that appeared to be increasingly divorced from traditional Islam. A new type of Islamic society was emerging, and parliaments, modern economic sectors, and religious faith had their greatest influence in terms of an individual's personal life. This trend was reinforced by the intellectual developments, as modern-educated Muslims adopted a variety of secularist positions, ranging from a radical rejection of Islam to a vague identification of Islam as a source of morality.

At the same time, however, the general conservatism of personal life among the majority preserved a respect for the Islamic tradition, and by the 1960s, there were indications that that respect could provide the basis for a more active and overt role for Islam in society. The very process of modernization itself helped to create new forms for the expression of Islamic faith through political parties, study groups, and militant associations. Islam remained a dynamic element in society, despite the apparent success of Westernizing secularism.

Dominant Majorities in the Maghrib

A third major area of dominant Muslim majorities in the Islamic world is the "Arab West" or the Maghrib, the area of modern Tunisia, Algeria, and Morocco, and many of the challenges of the modern experience are clearly visible in that area. The great issue of the meaning of modernizing adaptationism was highlighted by the experience of French rule. In the Maghrib, instead of adaptationism being a matter of what techniques might be utilized and how an indigenous modernizing reformism might be defined, it became an issue of defending a distinctive identity against the threat of assimilation into Western culture. In the nineteenth-century, Islam had played a role in defining the special identity of society in the Maghrib against outside forces, and that role is an important part of the area's twentieth-century history.

Adaptationism in the Maghrib ran the risk of losing contact with the community if it went too far in the direction of a modernizing secularism. At the same time, religiously oriented nationalists could not separate themselves too rigidly from the modern-educated intellectuals without running the risk of pushing them into an assimilationist position or weakening the nationalist cause in the face of the great pressures of French domination. Therefore, neither radical secularism nor extreme fundamentalism emerged as a significant force in the Maghrib. Other difficulties faced those religious leaders who maintained a conservative style of Islam. Those who came to accept the existing conditions of French rule and collaborated with them wrote their own obituaries as important leaders. That was especially true of the leaders of the established *tariqah*s, who were open to attack on the grounds of both fundamentalist opposition to popular religious practices and nationalist resentment toward collaborationism.

Within this framework, the Islamic experience in the Maghrib has been closely tied to the three major stages of political evolution—the struggle for independence, the new state of independence, and the "postindependence" regime. In each of these stages, Islam has played an important but sometimes different role. The key issues that have emerged are the relationship of Islam to nationalism and the role of Islam in formulating a basic sense of national unity and ideology in the independent states.

Islam and the Struggle for Independence

French control took different forms in each of the three countries. As a result, the specific path to independence varied, but at least some general aspects were shared throughout the region, with events in one country often having an impact on developments in another. In general terms, there were common key factors. The French attitude of cultural superiority in each country forced people who were willing to cooperate with them to cut all ties of identity with their own culture or to accept a clearly subordinate position or, in the case of traditional notables, to be treated as benighted but useful museum pieces. In each country, the French exhibited a clear unwillingness to adapt or compromise unless forced to do so, making violent demonstrations and conflict a necessary part of nationalism.

Islam and Tunisian Nationalism. The period following World War I was a decisive one in shaping the nature of Tunisian nationalism and Islam's role in the struggle for independence. Many of the key groups of the past were no longer significant forces in political terms. The monarchy, which had been the leading reformist institution in the nineteenth century, had become simply a puppet institution under the French system of control. The ulama continued their quietist conservatism, cooperating with the French to a degree that made them unable to assume a role of nationalist leadership, even if they had chosen to do so. The liberal intellectuals of the Young Tunisian movement had been crushed in the suppression before and during World War I. Their assimilationist attitudes had some echo following the war but were increasingly impractical in the face of French cultural arrogance and political intransigence. What remained was the Islamically oriented nationalist position of men like Abd al-Aziz al-Tha'alibi, who could appeal to the relatively conservative middle class and at least some of the increasing educated class.

At the end of the war, al-Tha'alibi organized the Destour party, which demanded independence for Tunisia. Although al-Tha'alibi and his associates were influenced by Salafiyyah ideas coming from Egypt, their party did not take a significant position in terms of Islamic reform. The party was radical in terms of its demands to the French but basically conservative in its social orientation, and it defined Tunisian nationalism in terms of Islamic and Arabic traditions. The Destour party was more of a mass movement than the Young Tunisians had been, and it laid the foundations through a nationwide organization for a mass nationalist party. However, its leadership tended to be confined to the urban Islamic middle class, which was centered in Tunis. In its approach, it relied on legalistic debate rather than on mass mobilization, and thus it did not have the strength to succeed in overcoming the restrictions imposed on the party's activities by the French.

The crucial role of Islam in mobilizing mass support for nationalism can be seen in the events that brought about the effective demise of the Destour party. The Destour presented itself as a defender of Islam, but by the late 1920s, it was the younger and more militant Tunisians who had had a modern education who were most effective in that role. Some of those younger men joined the Destour party but soon attempted to go beyond its conservative legalism. One of their major figures was Habib Bourguiba (b. 1903), a graduate of Sadiki College, which had been established by Khayr al-Din Pasha in the nineteenth century. Although Bourguiba had studied in France and was convinced of the need for major social reform in Tunisia, he vigorously defended the veil for women when that custom was attacked by a French socialist, saying that the Frenchman was trying to deprive Tunisians of their distinctive national identity. Bourguiba and his colleagues recognized the importance of modern ideas but rejected the idea of assimilation or "naturalization."

The issue of naturalization gave the younger nationalists a cause that enabled them to be united with the more religiously conservative majority of Tunisians. In 1923, the French made it possible for Tunisian Muslims to become French citizens, but few Tunisians took advantage of the opportunity because of the religious implications: It meant that a French Muslim would be tried in the French civil courts rather than in Islamic courts, which many Tunisians felt amounted to apostasy. In 1932, a mufti ruled that a naturalized Muslim could not be buried in a Muslim cemetery, which led to a series of demonstrations, and naturalized Tunisians were buried in Muslim cemeteries under armed guard only to be secretly exhumed later. Bourguiba vigorously supported the Muslim case in his newspaper, *L'Action Tunisienne*, which had begun publication in 1931. Since the leaders of the Destour party did little in this campaign and the conservative ulama remained quiet or compromised with the French on the issue, the younger nationalists could claim, as they did, that it was the modern-educated, nationalist youth and not the old conservatives who were the true defenders of Islam.

The young militants led by Bourguiba soon captured the leadership of the nationalist movement. The Destour Executive Committee censured Bourguiba when he led a demonstration on the burial issue in 1933, so he and his friends soon called their own party congress and created the Neo-Destour party in 1934. From then on, it was the Neo-Destour that led the struggle for independence, and not content with legal debates, the party created a mass organization that was able to mobilize the Tunisian people. After a long struggle, during which Bourguiba spent at least ten years in French jails, Tunisia became independent in 1956.

The thinking of the Neo-Destour leaders was clearly modern in orientation, but those men never adopted a definitely antireligious position. Bourguiba believed that a modernizing transformation of Tunisian society was necessary but that to accomplish this, a real sense of national solidarity was needed. That theory was especially true in the days of the struggle for independence. The value system common to all Tunisians was provided by Islam, and thus it had a crucial role both in obtaining independence and in providing unity in the struggle for modernization. One French administrator described these two dimensions of the Neo-Destour: "The Neo-Destour has often been reproached for its two faces: western and democratic before westerners, Islamic and xenophobic when it addresses its troops. The theorists of the party are nonetheless sincere in their love of Cartesianism. But, in a party of the people, they must speak the passionate language of the people."[36]

The key feature of Islam in Tunisia during the preindependence period was not that there was a modernist interpretation that emerged but, rather, that Islam provided the symbols and the vocabulary for a mobilization of the people in opposition to foreign rule. The instrument for that mobilization was a mass political party led by modern-educated men who were committed to the independence and modernization of Tunisia. Although accused by conservatives of atheism or hypocrisy, the extent of the identification of Neo-Destourian nationalism with Islam in the popular mind can be seen in the reported comment of an old Zaytuna shaykh in 1958, who said, "Whoever does not believe in the word of Bourguiba does not believe in the word of God or his Prophet."[37] It was not until after independence that a significant conflict between Neo-Destourian reformism and Islam arose, and even then the result was neither a radical secularism nor a vigorous fundamentalism.

Islam and Algerian Nationalism. The emergence of nationalism was a more complex process in Algeria. Although Tunisia had a relatively distinctive local identity, Algeria was not a separate area with special local characteristics before the time of the French conquest. In many ways, Algerian nationalism developed not as a movement to recover a lost national identity but as a movement to create and assert a special identity in the face of the destructive forces of French colonialism. Virtually no other area in the Islamic world faced such a concerted effort to destroy the basic social order. That effort not only took the form of a political and cultural offensive, but also utilized the establishment in the country of a large European settler population. In this context, the struggle was to define the meaning of being an Algerian, a process in which Islam played a significant role.

By the end of the World War I, there were few effective Algerian institutions around which nationalism could develop. The state was a French creation and an instrument of foreign control as well as settler domination. Tribal leaders had long been crushed into submission during almost a century of direct French rule, and most religious leaders collaborated with the

French in a conservative effort to preserve what was left of their position in society. As in Tunisia, nationalism had to come from the emerging educated class. One possible tie to the older traditions of resistance was quickly broken when the election of a grandson of the Amir Abd al-Qadir to a government council was annulled and he went into exile in 1920.

The first organized Algerian nationalist movement in the twentieth century was established in France in 1926 under the leadership of Messali al-Hajj. Many Algerians had gone to work in France and Messali's organization, Étoile Nord-Africaine, served as a combination labor union and political association for those workers. Messali demanded complete independence for Algeria, and, although the organization's program initially had a Marxist orientation, it soon came to emphasize Islamic and Arabic nationalist themes. This change was at least partly the result of Messali's contacts with Arab nationalists like Shakib Arslan while Messali was in exile in 1930. Messali was allowed to return to Algeria in 1936 when the Popular Front government came to power in France, and he began to organize a mass political movement, which became the Parti du Peuple Algérien (PPA). The PPA program denounced ideas of assimilation and demanded the recognition of Arabic as an official language as well as supporting more general themes of Islamic unity. Messali was attacked by French communists, and the man who had once been a member of the Communist party became a vigorous Muslim nationalist. Radicalism could not be combined, in French-dominated Algeria, with emerging Algerian nationalism.

The Islamic element of the expression of Algerian identity is even more visible in the career of Abd al-Hamid Ibn Badis (Ben Badis, 1889–1940). He came from a relatively wealthy, pro-French family, and in his early years, he was a quiet religious teacher. However, in 1925, he began to publish a newspaper that espoused the cause of Islamic reform. He was strongly influenced by the ideas of Muhammad Abduh and Rashid Rida, and he worked to spread the teachings of the Salafiyyah in Algeria. He and some of his friends succeeded in mobilizing a number of the Algerian ulama and, in 1931, organized the Association of Algerian Ulama. The major themes of that organization and Ben Badis's journal, *al-Shihab,* were opposition to the *tariqah* leaders and the practices of popular Islam and a condemnation of assimilationism. Ben Badis advocated a modernist interpretation of the Quran and was active in encouraging a revival of both Arabic and Islamic elements in Algerian culture, and the ulama association established schools for that purpose. These activities played a significant role in affirming the Arab and Islamic identity of Algeria. The Salafiyyah ulama were not, however, political militants until the outbreak of the Algerian revolution in 1954. Although the association was important in defining the basis for Algerian nationalism, it took no overt actions hostile to French rule.

The challenge to an Islamic and Arabic Algeria was clearly manifested by a third major Algerian movement, which spread following World War I, that accepted the principle of assimilation. As early as 1912, a party of Young Algeria had been formed by French-educated Muslims who accepted the idea of French rule and assimilation into French culture. What they worked for was full equality within a France that included Algeria. The major threat to this ideal was, ironically, the French settler community in Algeria, which opposed any measures that would reduce their privileged position. Time after time, they succeeded in forcing the French government to reject proposals that would have made assimilation possible.

After World War I, one of the leading figures in the assimilationist group was Farhat Abbas (b. 1899), whose writings express the assimilationist position clearly. He believed that the future of Algeria lay with France, and he rejected all ideas of Algerian independence. Two distinctive requests the assimilationists made were that they be able to maintain their Muslim legal status in personal matters of marriage and inheritance and that eventually, Arabic would become an officially recognized language. They were not, however, thinking in politically nationalist terms but hoped to preserve some element of their cultural identity.

The clash between the assimilationist and Islamic positions was clearly expressed in a famous and often-quoted exchange between Abbas and Ben Badis. Abbas wrote in 1936:

> If I had discovered an Algerian nation, I would be a nationalist and I would not blush for it as though it were a crime. . . . Yet I will not die for the Algerian homeland, because such a homeland does not exist. I have not found it. I have questioned history, I have asked the living and the dead, I have visited the cemeteries; no one has told me of it. . . . We have once and for all dispersed the storm clouds of fantasy in order to tie for ever our future to that of the work of France in this land.[38]

The response of Ben Badis a few months later was equally clear and stressed the importance of Islam in the definition of Algeria: "History had taught us that the Muslim people of Algeria were created like all the others. They have their history, illustrated by noble deeds; they have their religious unity and their language. . . . This Muslim population is not France; it cannot be France, it does not want to be France."[39]

French intransigence finally did what the ulama and the nationalists had been unable to do. After years of disappointment, the assimilationists finally came to the conclusion that no matter how moderate and compromising they were, they would never gain equality in a French-ruled Algeria, so Farhat Abbas gradually moved to a position of seeking first autonomy and then independence for Algeria. The elimination of the assimilationist position was dramatically illustrated when Abbas told the French Assembly in 1946, "The Algerian personality, the Algerian fatherland, which I did not find in 1936 amongst the Moslem masses, I find there today."[40] The political evolution of Algeria had effectively removed the possibility of a secularized, individualist style of Islam.

After World War II, a new configuration of nationalist movements emerged, and there was less emphasis upon reformist Islam and more on the political drive for independence. Following the death of Ben Badis, the

Association of Algerian Ulama had less political visibility, and the most prominent organizations were the Union Democratique du Manifeste Algérien (UDMA), formed as a relatively moderate and modernist political action group by Farhat Abbas in 1946, and the Mouvement pour le Triomphe des Libertés Democratiques (MTLD), the militantly nationalist organization created by Messali al-Hajj as the successor to his banned PPA. However, French repression, a continued unwillingness to compromise, and the corruption of even the few electoral rights the Algerians had combined to discredit the political methods. The UDMA's moderation had gained it nothing, and the MTLD began to split into factions, with some members unwilling to follow Messali's increasingly autocratic leadership. Some younger members with military experience opted for violent rather than political activism.

The young militants were the nucleus for what was to emerge as the major movement of Algerian nationalism, the Front de Libération Nationale (FLN). Originally formed by dissidents from the older movements and ex-soldiers with military experience, the FLN led a major armed uprising in 1954, and that led to the long Algerian war for independence. Among its early and most durable leaders was Ahmad Ben Bella (b. 1916), a young man who had had both a French and a Quranic education and had served in the French army during World War II. He had joined the MTLD after the war. Although Farhat Abbas joined the FLN during the course of the Algerian war for independence and there were other major figures in the movement, it was Ben Bella who emerged as the leader of the independent Algeria in 1962.

During the Algerian revolution, ideology was less important than the effort to defeat the French. The basic ideological themes expressed by the FLN leaders were a mixture of traditional nationalist ideals and a growing utilization of socialist and radical terminology. However, Islam played an important role as one of the identifying pillars of Algerian society, which the FLN was both creating and defending. The revolution was not a time for reflection or redefinition; it was a time for mobilization, and in that, Islam was a key factor.

French efforts to undermine the local culture were seen as attacks on Islam, which in the minds of the nationalist revolutionaries was identified with the Algerian nation. Ahmad Ben Bella, for example, recalled the moment when "deep in my heart, I felt myself becoming a rebel."[41] That was when he was fourteen; a French teacher had denounced the Prophet Muhammad as an imposter, and Ben Bella had been punished for arguing with him. Even the radical ideologue of the revolution, Frantz Fannon, saw French efforts to unveil Algerian women as a plot to destroy the Algerian nation.[42] Islam was thus a vital force in providing the symbolism and emotion of the Algerian revolution. It was complementary to, rather than competing with, nationalism.

Resistance and Islam in Morocco. The connection between Islam and the resistance to European rule in Morocco was a major aspect of the emergence of nationalism there. Following World War I, there were two major movements of a very different character, and they illustrate the potential lines of the Islamic nationalist efforts. The first and, at the time, the most visible was the active military resistance to the establishment of Spanish control in the northern part of Morocco. There, a major tribal family organized a movement that led to the establishment of an independent republic in the Rif. In many ways, this movement was a transition from a more traditional to a modern-style activist movement. A great tribal leader, Abd al-Karim al-Khattabi (d. 1920), first worked with Spanish officials in an effort to win autonomy for his people. His sons were given modern educations as well as training in traditional tribal leadership, and his son Muhammad organized effective military opposition when the Spanish refused to compromise. By 1922, he had succeeded in driving the Spanish out of much of northern Morocco, and he declared the foundation of an Islamic republic. The official policy of this regime was outlined in a state-ment in 1925, which claimed the right of self-determination and the goal of combining the basic teachings of Islam with the scientific and industrial achievements of the West. In 1926, the new republic came into conflict with the French and was defeated. However, the Rif republic emphasized the possibility that traditional leadership could create a state that would com-bine Islamic values and modernization, a pattern that was to emerge again when Morocco became independent in 1956.

The other movement that emerged following World War I had greater similarity to the beginnings of nationalist movements in the other Maghrib states. Islamic reformism of the Salafiyyah type had come to Morocco early in the century, and following the war, active study groups developed in Rabat and Fez. The Moroccan Salafiyyah was strongly opposed to the prac-tices of the *tariqah*s and eager to support Arabic and Islamic education. The leading figures in that effort were Mawlay al-Arabi al-Alawi and Abu Shuᶜayb al-Dukkali, but it was their students who gradually transformed the Salafiyyah spirit into a nationalist movement. That transformation was possibly inevitable because the "religious" positions had political implica-tions, and an attack on the leaders of the orders was an attack on the chief supporters of the French regime. It was easy to equate the doctrinal corrup-tion of the Sufis with their collaboration with infidel imperialists, and similarly, the effort to establish schools with an Arab-Islamic curriculum could provide a focus for feelings of national identity.

The leading figure in the politicization of the Salafiyyah was Allal al-Fasi, a student of Mawlay al-Arabi who was actively dedicated to the cause of Islamic reform. As his thinking developed, al-Fasi became convinced that independence was an essential first step in Islamic reform, and under his leadership, the basic theological positions of the Salafiyyah remained relatively stable while its political activism gradually grew. The issue that gave impetus to this development was the Berber Decree of 1930, by which the French removed certain Berber tribes from the jurisdiction of Islamic law and replaced it with French law and tribal custom. Religious protest and political opposition were combined in demonstrations organized by Salafiyyah groups, but the need for organization was recognized in the process, and a series of less formal groupings produced the National Action Bloc by 1932.

The intellectuals involved in the religionationalist party ranged from people with relatively conservative religious ideas and Salafiyyah supporters to modern-educated intellectuals. Although the party was initially an elite grouping, it began to develop mass support. It took a number of organizational forms, and its leaders were often jailed or exiled. One of the more modern-oriented leaders, Ahmad Balafrej, reorganized the party during World War II while al-Fasi was in exile, and the new party was called the Istiqlal (Independence) party. Al-Fasi became its leader when he returned to Morocco in 1946, and the party grew rapidly.

It was not, however, only the Istiqlal party that led the fight for independence as it developed a political consciousness among many Moroccans and helped to tie the drive for independence to the more traditional symbols and ideals of Islam. However, in contrast to the Neo-Destour party in Tunisia, the Istiqlal faced a traditional institution whose strength had not been destroyed by the experience of imperial rule: the sultanate. Although the sultan was little more than a puppet of the French, the office retained considerable religious prestige, and nationalists were willing to recognize the sultan as a symbol of the Moroccan nation. That fact became a very important element in the Moroccan struggle for independence.

The development of the sultanate as an important nationalist symbol was associated with the career of Muhammad ibn Yusif (1909–1961), or Muhammad V. He was chosen by the French to succeed his father in 1927, and they assumed that he would be quiet and docile. However, within the limits of strict French control, Muhammad gave quiet encouragement to the nationalist cause. Popular demonstrations welcoming him during a visit to Fez in 1934, and his willingness to receive visits from nationalists, as well as his support for the idea of independence during World War II, helped to cement the ties between him and the Istiqlal. Muhammad became even more active after the war, making symbolic protests against French rule, and after 1951, he began to refuse to sign decrees prepared by the French. In 1953, the French deposed him and sent him into exile, providing a clear issue around which all Moroccans could be mobilized. Serious outbreaks of violence finally persuaded the French to recall Muhammad in 1955, and he became King Muhammad V of an independent Morocco in 1956.

Thus in Morocco, the two major vehicles expressing nationalist aspirations were a religiously oriented nationalist party and a monarchy whose prestige in society rested firmly on Islamic grounds. Islam provided the symbol for mass mobilization and, even more, provided at least some of the institutional structure for an independent Morocco. It was a nationalist Islam rather than a developing modernist style or fundamentalism that was the most significant element of the Muslim experience in Morocco in the days of the struggle for independence.

Islam in the Independent Maghrib

After the winning of independence, there was a remarkable political stability in the Maghrib, despite the violence of the liberation struggle. There was, however, a significant evolution in each state from the inde-·pendence-achieving regime to the postindependence one. In this transition, the key issues relating to the Islamic experience involved the problems of modernization and nation building. In particular, once the common enemy was removed, debate arose over the appropriate ideological and pro-grammatic foundations for modernization. During the 1960s, the major development in this area was the evolution of a more secularist socialism, often of a radical style, that advocated revolutionary social transformation. This ideological approach became a powerful force by the middle of the decade but then declined in importance. Parallel to that process was a decline and then a revival of a more visibly Islamic orientation.

The most dramatic but perhaps most confusing case is the experience of Algeria. The war for independence came to an end in 1962, and the FLN began to disintegrate into its constituent parts. In the early days, before old-style politicians like Farhat Abbas joined the FLN, its program had ad-vocated a radical social transformation as well as freedom from France. In the brief conflict among FLN leaders in 1962, one of the spokesmen for the early group, Ahmad Ben Bella, emerged as the leader of independent Algeria.

Ben Bella was aware of the value of Islam as a symbol for national unity and took care to identify Algeria as an Islamic state by taking symbolic Islamic actions. For example, when he went to the United Nations in 1962, he refused to allow the serving of alcoholic beverages at a reception Algeria gave to celebrate its admission to the United Nations. He told his adviser: "Even if it is the custom, I am not going to do it. Algeria is a Moslem coun-try. She will offer hospitality according to her own traditions."[43] However, Ben Bella's actual line of policy was more clearly a secularist style of socialism, with Islam playing a subordinate role. Islam, in the emerging ideology of Ben Bella, was to be a support for socialism rather than an in-dependent force.

In that move, Ben Bella went beyond the ideas of most of the FLN members, and at the first national FLN congress in 1964, the delegates sup-ported a less revolutionary style of socialism whose guidelines would be the traditional Islamic principles. Ben Bella's increasing identification with a more "scientific socialism" was one of the factors that undermined his sup-port within the FLN and Algeria. That factor and internal rivalries within the ruling elite led to his overthrow in 1965 by a leading FLN military com-mander, Houari Boumedienne (1925–1978), and with that change of leaders, the emphasis shifted away from an internationally oriented socialist policy to a more pragmatic reformism that placed greater stress upon Arabization and Islamic values.

In contrast to many of the countries in the Arab East, the "old" socially conservative nationalist leadership in Algeria had already been eliminated by the time of independence. The independence-achieving regime was closer in tone to the postrevolutionary regimes in Iraq and Egypt than to the initial nationalist regimes. The 1965 coup was, in many ways, a pulling back from the more doctrinaire socialism that was common elsewhere in the developing world at the time. The government of Boumedienne remained committed to social transformation and anti-imperialism, but the mood reflected the fact that Boumedienne had been a student at al-Azhar and an Arabic teacher before joining the FLN.

It is in this political context that there was a continuing discussion of Islam and its nature. Even the radicals did not condemn Islam, and the Ben Bella and Boumedienne attitudes had their parallels in more intellectual works. A close associate of Ben Bella was Amer Ouzegane (b. 1920), a self-educated man who had been a member of the French Communist party but had been expelled in 1948 for nationalist deviation. He was an active ideologue in the FLN and helped to frame a number of its more radical proclamations. He was a sharp critic of the Communist party for its failure to support the Algerian revolution but blended Marxism and Islamic nationalism in his thinking. "We are seeking a symbiosis . . . between Islam and Marxist-Leninism," he said and noted that his communist friends did not understand that "the secret of progress in Arab and Moslem countries, and of the destruction of colonialism and feudalism, lay precisely in the symbiosis of Islam and of progressivist theories."[44]

A less radical orientation is seen in the works of Malek Bennabi (b. 1905), who became a prominent educator after independence. In his works, he maintained that Algeria had fallen under imperialist control because Algerian Muslims had allowed themselves to stagnate in both religious and scientific areas, and he advocated Islamic revival along with the adoption of Western science. He believed that "the common cause of error of both Modernists and Reformists . . . is that neither one nor the other has gone to the source itself of their inspiration. . . . The reformists have not really returned to the origins of Islamic thought, nor have the Modernists gone to the roots of occidental thought."[45]

In independent Tunisia, some of that same duality of approach can be seen, with the primary effort being the creation of an effectively modern Tunisia. A well-informed observer in 1962 noted that in Tunisia, "Religion is not the most important of the problems, and Islam is taken for granted since the Tunisians are Muslims."[46] The context and spirit of the role of Islam are defined in the new state's constitution, in which the principles of Islam are given as the basis for law and polity, but there is no insistence upon the letter and rule of traditional structures of Islamic law. In many ways, the independent state of Tunisia is the direct heir of Khayr al-Din Pasha and his efforts to blend modern and Islamic elements into a new synthesis.

As happened in Algeria, the old, conservative nationalists had been ousted from power before independence. In Tunisia, that happened as early as 1934 with the creation of the Neo-Destour party. The new na leadership was committed to at least the ideal of a moderniziing social transformation, and after independence, the leadership moved gradually in the direction of a more radical socialism. That trend was emphasized when the more conservative nationalist elements joined with Salah Ben Youssef (d. 1961) in his effort to overthrow Bourguiba as leader of the nationalist movement and the Neo-Destour party in the period from 1955 to 1960. Bourguiba was aided by the younger, more radical elements of the party, especially Ahmad Ben Salah, a strong labor union leader. During the 1960s, great efforts were made to establish a more centrally planned economy, and measures such as enforced creation of agricultural cooperatives and collectives were undertaken. This more radical phase was brought to an abrupt end in 1969 when Ben Salah was dismissed from his many powerful positions, and policy then assumed a less doctrinaire, socialist orientation. A major factor in the evolution was the resistance of many Tunisians to the more radical secularist spirit of the Neo-Destourian socialism.

In specifically Islamic terms, the main line of development was the growing strength of an individualized style of Islam as religion was increasingly accepted as a personal matter. It remained of importance as an element in the Tunisian identity, but in a form that was closer to the role of religion in a more secularized, modern society than in a premodern Islamic culture. The old Muslim structures and leadership groups were replaced. Religious education, for example, which had been dominated in the past by the great mosque schools of Zaytuna and al-Qayrawan, passed into the hands of the theological faculty in the University of Tunis, which was led by a committed but modernist Muslim scholar. There was no Islamically sanctioned monarchy to provide a focus for the more traditional visions, and even the powerless monarchical office of the bey was abolished soon after independence with no popular protest.

The Islamic position of Bourguiba's government was modernist and reformist. The goal was to transform Tunisians' religious attitudes as a part of the overall process of modernization without arousing popular opposition. Bourguiba attempted to present himself not as a secularizer, similar to Ataturk, but as a Muslim reformer in the tradition of Abduh. He was most successful in reforming specific structures, customs, and practices that could be considered as not being an inherent part of Islam. He reorganized the whole structure of religious endowments; transformed the laws of personal status, marriage, and the role of women; and removed independent religious control in education and the court system. However, the limits of this reform program were shown when Bourguiba attempted to change something that was an essential and basic part of Islam: the fast of Ramadan. Bourguiba attempted to persuade Tunisians that the month-long fast hindered the effort to build a strong and wealthy economy and society. In 1960, he recommended that the fast not be undertaken, but few Tunisians followed his lead, and there were many protests against his proposal. The effort was soon dropped, showing that Tunisian Muslims were willing to accept a wide range of secularist changes in Islamic practices but were unwilling to tamper with the basic fundamentals.

Even the Ramadan issue did not produce a significant fundamentalist movement. The dominant style of Islam in the era of independence has been one of secularist adaptationism, which experimented with but withdrew from a more radical position. The effort to provide a synthesis of modern and Islamic principles can be seen in the works of a number of younger Tunisians during the 1960s and is illustrated in the writings of Mohammed Taalbi. He noted, for example, that "a medieval restoration is not the desired solution" but that a vague sense of Islam simply as a factor of cohesion puts it "at the mercy of every demogogue." For Taalbi, the hope of Islam rests with Muslim scholars "trained in the disciplines of European universities" who are "concerning themselves in greater number with the history of ideas in Muslim civilization and are attempting to define the importance of the spiritual values which have modelled its humanism."[47]

In Morocco, the political scene has been dominated by the religiously prestigious monarchy as Muhammad V was the symbol of the nation and of national resistance. As a result, in contrast to the experiences in Algeria and Tunisia, the major nationalist political party, the Istiqlal, did not become the ruling group in the independent state. During the 1960s, there were active political parties, but they were under the strict control of the king—first, Muhammad V, who died in 1961, and then his son, Hasan II. In Islamic terms, the major development was the modernization of the leading institution, the monarchy. A parliamentary regime was established, but Hasan II assumed the role of the primary political leader of the country as well as being its symbol. He was able to disband parliament in 1965 and ruled directly until 1970.

The monarchy relied upon the traditional loyalty to the king, who was both the leading religious figure and the major politician of the country. In moves similar to the White Revolution in Iran and the emergence of pragmatic fundamentalism in Saudi Arabia, Hasan II made the monarchy the leading force for the economic modernization of society while attempting to avoid social revolution. In that effort, traditional Islamic themes were balanced with a reformist appeal. The two sides of the king's policy are illustrated by the various positions of women in the royal family. The king's wife remained hidden from view, acting in a very traditional manner, but the king's sister, Princess Lalla Aicha, was one of the leaders in the movement for the liberation of women, and she was appointed the Moroccan ambassador to Great Britain in 1965. That illustration is typical of the royalist policy of balancing Islamic and modern forces without creating a synthesis of the ideas involved.

The major political organizations did not fare well during the 1960s. The older Istiqlal leadership was challenged soon after independence by younger, more radical nationalists, and the result was the creation of the Union Nationale des Forces Populaires (UNFP), led by Mehdi Ben Barka, in 1959. Ben Barka was kidnapped and killed while in exile in 1965, and the leader of the old Istiqlal, Allal al-Fasi, died in 1967, which left the major potential opposition to the king without prominent leaders. The dominant theme of the opposition parties was to challenge the increasing power of the monarchy, but there was little in their programs that represented significant developments in Islamic thought during the period.

It is outside of the political arena that major intellectual issues involving Islam have been dealt with. The major themes inspired by the political context involve the debate over the preservation and the dismantling of the traditional monarchical structure. However, the broader themes seen in the rest of the Maghrib also appear in Moroccan thought: the issues relating to a reconciliation of the modern and the traditional, the Islamic and the Western. Some of the major lines in the intellectual activity can be seen in the works of Abdallah Laroui, whose views represent an intellectual nationalism influenced by a modified Marxism. He emphasizes the importance of historical awareness, but not as part of an effort to create an artificial traditionalism since a self-conscious awareness of traditional means "traditionalization at the hands of an elite that, finding itself in a position of self-defense, changes its role."[48] He thus rejects false traditionalization while recognizing the importance of the historical experience.

If one moves beyond the turmoil of politics, the major Islamic issues have not been developed in the framework of radical secularism or extremist fundamentalism. The Islamic experience has concentrated more on creating an integration of modernism and Islam, which has taken a variety of forms, as in Destourian socialism and Moroccan monarchism. What one analyst has said, comparing Ouzegane and Bennabi, describes the alternatives presented by the intellectual efforts of the Maghribi Muslims in general: "Both believe that Islam and modernism are compatible," but for one perspective, "religion is only a means to realize modernism," and for the other, "the religious is an end in itself and a basic and permanent dimension of the Moslem character."[49] The choice that is made between those two alternatives will shape the future of Islam in the Maghrib.

6

Twentieth-Century Islam: Eastern World, Nondominant Majorities, and Minorities

The Eastern Muslim World: Dominance and Struggle

Almost half of the world's Muslims live in the Indian subcontinent and Southeast Asia. The Islamic communities in the region are large but vary in their position within the broader society from being dominant majorities in Pakistan, Bangladesh, and Indonesia to being a strong minority in Malaysia to being a weak minority in the contemporary Republic of India. All of these communities have been involved in struggles for independence and have had to find some answer to the issue of the relationship between Islam and nationalism. The issue is more complex in the eastern region than it is in the Middle East and North Africa because there are "traditional" and local cultural identities that are not clearly Islamic. In addition to having to define the relationship between Islam and modernity, Muslims have also had to define their identity in relation to other nonmodern or modernizing traditions. In this way, even where Muslims are a dominant social majority, Muslim self-consciousness has operated in a pluralistic context.

The complexity of the issues gave rise to a luxuriant growth of Islamic movements and ideas covering the full spectrum of styles of Islamic experience. No single book can give an adequate introduction to the large number of groups and individuals who have been important in defining the modern Islamic experience in this region; in this work, only the main themes are identified, and an indication is given of the major types of movements.

Islam in British India

The vibrant vitality of nineteenth-century Islam continued in the twentieth century. Although the Muslims had been politically dominant in the

221

days of the Moghul Empire, they remained a minority in the Indian subcontinent. As a result, in the twentieth century, the relationship of the Muslims to the Hindu majority was an issue that was added to the problem of defining the relationship with modern ideas, and the two lines of development constantly interacted. Nationalism and modernism became the two themes that helped to define and create the variety of the Indian Muslim experiences, and each style of Islamic experience dealt with those themes in the era leading up to independence from British rule.

Adaptationist Reformism. Under British rule, adaptationism was limited to the intellectual areas and the developing definition of nationalism. Until independence was won following World War II, there was no scope for "applied adaptationism" in social or political reform programs. In both nationalism and Islamic modernism, the key adaptationist line of development can be seen as the heritage of Sayyid Ahmad Khan.

It was the emerging modern-educated Muslims who provided the leadership for the adaptationist movements in twentieth-century Muslim India. The most significant general line of evolution was the development of a modernist Islamic assertion of a Muslim identity associated with a major Muslim intellectual, Muhammad Iqbal, and the Muslim League developed as an organizational expression of that identity. Eventually, that line led to the creation of Pakistan as an independent Muslim state.

Modern nationalism had begun in India late in the nineteenth century outside of the Muslim community. The modern-educated classes had begun to work for a greater role in Indian government, and in the process of advance and disappointment, the Indian National Congress was formed in 1885 to express Indian aspirations. Leadership in the Congress was largely drawn from Hindu Indians, and two wings of Congress soon developed. A moderate, liberal group aimed at a modernized, self-governing India structured along Western parliamentary lines, and it emphasized Indian "national" unity and attempted to bridge religious communal differences. However, the other major faction within the Congress was militantly Hindu and sought independence on the basis of past Hindu glories and future Hindu leadership. In this context, the issue of nationalism as a potential rival of Islam was soon clearly raised, and modern-educated Muslims were faced with the choice of participating in the nationalist movement, which was at best secularist and non-Islamic and, at worst, militantly non-Islamic in some of its forms.

Sayyid Ahmad Khan set the tone for many of the educated Muslims by not participating in the Congress. He did not urge opposition to the new nationalist movement, but he and his followers withheld their support. They believed that in a truly democratic state, the majority would rule and this, in the Indian context, would ultimately mean the end of the Muslim community there.

It gradually became apparent that nonparticipation was not sufficient. When reforms that recognized separate Muslim electorates were being instituted, the Muslim League was organized in 1906 to present Muslim views.

For many years, the Muslim League worked to secure and maintain Muslim communal rights within the broader society. The league's solution to the problem raised by a Hindu-oriented or a majoritarian nationalism was to seek recognition for the Muslims as a special community whose representation and existence would be guaranteed within the future independent state. The league was able to cooperate with the Congress in this framework, and the two groups held joint meetings and coordinated many of their activities during World War I. The league was temporarily eclipsed by the rise of the Khilafat movement when the enthusiasm for the caliphate reached a peak. The Khilafat movement captured popular imagination, received support from the Congress, and gave its support to the noncooperation campaign of the Congress in the 1920s. However, by the end of the decade, the Khilafat movement was effectively dead as a political force in India.

As the early generation of Muslim League leaders began to pass from the scene, the new leadership expressed more militancy. The old league had been relatively conservative in approach, but during the 1930s, it became more nationalistically assertive, and the key figure in the revival of the league was Muhammad Ali Jinnah (1876–1948). He started as a member of the moderate wing of the Indian National Congress but had joined the Muslim League in 1913 and was one of the architects of Congress–Muslim League cooperation. He had remained aloof from the political turmoil of the 1920s but had become increasingly disillusioned about the prospects for special communal guarantees and separate electoral bodies for Muslims in an India dominated by the Congress. He assumed leadership of the league in 1934 and led it to a position that made it, by World War II, the generally recognized spokesman for Indian Muslims.

Jinnah gradually became persuaded that only a separate and an independent state for the Muslims would guarantee their rights, and he developed the idea of the "two nation theory." He felt that "Hinduism and Islam represent two distinct and separate civilizations and, moreover, are as distinct from one another in origin, tradition and manner of life as are nations of Europe."[1] When the Congress was unwilling to cooperate with the league in the elections of 1937 and 1939, Jinnah was convinced that separatism was necessary, so in 1940, the League formally identified its goal as an independent Muslim state in those areas where Muslims formed a majority. The name for this state had been suggested earlier by students at Cambridge University: Pakistan, formed from the names of Punjab, Afghania, Kashmir, Sind, and Baluchistan and suggesting words meaning "land of the pure."

The goal of a separate Muslim state was finally recognized by the British, and in 1947, British India was partitioned into two independent states. The partition was accompanied by large-scale communal violence and a massive exchange of population. Certain territories were claimed by both countries, and some, such as Kashmir, became the basis for long-term tension and conflict.

Pakistan was the result of the evolving nationalist efforts of Indian

Muslims, and an important aspect of that evolution is that it was the product of the modern-educated leadership within the Muslim community. The primary concern had been the protection of the community rather than a definition of what form it would take as an independent state. The modernist thinkers associated with the league were active in reformulating the philosophical foundations of Islam in the modern world, but they did little to provide a political definition of Islam for a modern state. The Pakistan movement was an assertion of an identity that everyone felt was self-explanatory, and thus, at independence, the leaders of the league had created a "state of Muslims" but had not gone very far in creating an "Islamic state."

Muhammad Iqbal (1875–1938) was the leading intellectual figure in the emerging adaptationist modernism. He was a prominent poet and scholar with a Western education, and he developed a philosophy of mystic dynamism in which Western and Islamic ideals were combined in often dramatic and poetic forms. In his most famous work, *The Reconstruction of Religious Thought in Islam*, he argued that philosophical rationality and religious intuition were complementary ways of understanding the truth, and that belief enabled him to combine a variety of perspectives. For example, in his interpretation of the problem of predestination, he developed a modern ideal of free will on the basis of doctrines similar to the idea of unity in the manifestations of God (*wahdat al-shuhud*), which had been developed by the Naqshbandiyyah teacher, Ahmad Sirhindi. Similarly, Iqbal integrated the Sufi concept of the perfect man with Henri Bergson's theory of creative evolution.[2]

Iqbal urged the exercise of *ijtihad* to bring about the necessary reconstruction of Islam in the modern world. He spoke highly of the Turkish experiment under Ataturk, but he criticized Kemalism for assimilating the idea of a separation of church and state from Europe without realizing that "it suggests a dualism which does not exist in Islam."[3] Iqbal advocated the use of *ijtihad* to help restructure Islamic law, rejecting any sense of that law as being unalterable. Iqbal combined *ijtihad* with a redefinition of *ijma* ("consensus") as a basic source of Islamic law, and he noted that traditionally the right of *ijtihad* had been limited to special individuals and that validating consensus was also restricted. However, Iqbal noted that *ijma* had not assumed the form of a permanent institution in Islamic societies because "possibly its transformation into a permanent legislative institution was contrary to the political interests of the kind of absolute monarchy that grew up in Islam."[4] Iqbal believed that the transfer of the power of *ijtihad* to a modern Muslim legislative assembly was the necessary line of evolution if life were to be restored to the Islamic legal system.

Although Iqbal was not as active in political affairs as a man like Jinnah, he was very influential and is often credited with being the founder of the idea of Pakistan. He certainly was a key figure in transforming Muslim nationalism from the struggle to win guarantees for Muslims within a larger community to the movement for an independent Islamic state. Although

Islamic separatism was implicit in the position taken by those Muslims who did not join the Congress, the first major proposal for the creation of a separate Muslim state was made in an address by Iqbal to the Muslim League in 1930. Iqbal played an important role in the conversion of league leaders, especially Jinnah, to the Pakistan idea.

Iqbal was only one of a large number of Muslim scholars and activists who were involved in the reassertion of an Islamic communal and intellectual identity. A significant aspect of this modernist-nationalist evolution was that the leaders were primarily Western educated rather than coming from traditional or conservative intellectual backgrounds, which meant that although their loyalty to Islam was strong, they were not tied to particular traditions within Islam. The Islamic identity that they worked to create was a composite one, perhaps as the result of the origins of the leaders themselves. Although Iqbal was of Sunni background, Jinnah came from a minority Shi'i community. One of the leading early modernist intellectuals, Amir Ali (1849–1928), who provided a vigorous glorification of Sunni historical Islam and whose works made possible a favorable appreciation of Islamic history among Westernized Muslims far beyond India, was a committed Twelver Shi'i believer. The nontraditionalism of modernist nationalism made it possible to ignore or overcome traditional divisions in the name of the emerging Indian Muslim communal identity.

Intellectual adaptationism was dominated by modernist Islamic nationalism, but there were other important threads as well. One critical distinction was between those Muslim leaders who were willing to cooperate with the Indian National Congress and those who opposed such cooperation. A leading figure among the modernist Muslims in India who remained closely associated with the Congress and ultimately rejected the Pakistan idea was Abu al-Kalam Azad (1888–1958). Azad's education was more traditionalist, and he had traveled in his early years in the Arab East where he had come into contact with the ideas of al-Afghani and Abduh. He published a journal and books that were widely read, in which he emphasized the importance of a thorough study of the Quran. Although his approach utilized modern methods of analysis, his emphasis and tone were more conservative. On the matter of *ijtihad*, for example, he replaced the legal concept of *ijtihad* with *ta'sis* ("reconsolidation"), "arguing that in modern times what is needed is not free or new legal speculation, but a consolidation of what he interprets as Islam's fundamental verities which would externalize the perfection inherent in it."[5]

Azad's more traditional orientation led him to support ideas of Pan-Islam, and he became actively involved in the Khilafat movement. He stressed the univeralism of Islam and, in this way, came to reject the identification of Islam as a basis for a localized nationalist movement. At first, that belief meant that he rejected the idea of cooperation with Hindu nationalists in India, but on the basis of an appeal to human fraternity and a sense of religious cooperation built on a study of comparative religion, Azad later became a vigorous supporter of integrated nationalism and was, for many years, elected president of the Indian National Congress. In addition to Islamic reservations about using Islam as a basis for local separatism, Azad found a positive basis for cooperation with the Congress in the community created by the Prophet Muhammad himself when he moved to Medina in 622. That *ummah* had contained both Muslims and non-Muslims and Azad believed that it provided a sound precedent for integrated efforts to create a community of Muslims and non-Muslims. Although Azad did not express a modernized secularism explicitly, his position implicitly laid the foundations for a position that would accept religion as a matter of personal faith and practice rather than as the basis for the political order.

In Iqbal and Azad, one sees the two lines of modernist adaptationism in British India. Both utilized modern critical analysis and, in many ways, supported similar efforts in reinterpreting and redefining Islam. It was the issue of nationalism that clearly separated them. For Iqbal, the issue of communal identity and preservation took precedence over Pan-Islamic and universalist ideas, and with Azad, a more secularist position on the issue of nationalism emerged because of an adherence to the more universalist aspects of the Islamic tradition.

Intellectual Conservatism. Azad's position on the issue of nationalism was shared by many of the more conservative ulama in India. In the context of British India, few Muslim leaders maintained a rigorously consistent, conservative political position of supporting British rule. Most social and intellectual conservatives, for example, the leading teachers at the Deoband school, adopted the more activist political position of support for the nationalist idea. However, they, like Azad, emphasized the importance of maintaining Islam as a universalist faith and not tying it to a specific local nationalism. Virtually all of the conservative ulama saw the importance of protecting the Muslim community in India but advocated doing so on the basis of practical alliances rather than on the basis of creating a nationalist Islamic ideology. A number of individuals and organizations represented the varieties of this viewpoint. One of the best known was the Jam'iyyat al-Ulama-i Hind, established in 1919 as part of the Khilafat excitement and in the tradition of opposition to Ahmad Khan's heritage. Many of its supporters, including its leader in the time of greatest nationalist ferment, Husayn Ahmad Madani, were associated with the Deoband. Madani argued that Muslims and non-Muslims could be partners in creating an independent state and that this would allow for the preservation of the Indian Muslim community without compromising the universalism of the Islamic teachings. Deoband and the Jam'iyyat opposed the league and the Pakistan movement right up to the day of partition.

The intellectual conservativism had had its roots in the late nineteenth century with movements like the Deoband school and the Ahl al-Hadith, and interpretive conservatism was preserved in the twentieth century by adopting what might be seen as a secularist position. Although many of its leaders became citizens of Pakistan, others became prominent leaders of the still large Muslim community in the Republic of India.

Fundamentalist Activism. Although the liberal nationalists often were attacked by the conservative ulama, in many ways the most important challenge to the liberal nationalist, modern-educated leadership of the Muslim community came from fundamentalist Islam. Although a number of fundamentalist groups and teachers existed, the most influential were Abu al-Ala Mawdudi (b. 1903) and the organization he established in 1941, the Jama'at-i Islami.

On the great issue of nationalism, Mawdudi presented a third option, which involved the rejection of nationalism itself. In Mawdudi's view, the programs of both the Muslim League and the Indian National Congress represented a non-Islamic emphasis on nationalism and were counter to Islam. Nationalism, whether that proposed by the league or the Congress, was a selfish principle that was prohibited by Islam, and people who espoused the nationalist cause were leading Muslims away from the legitimate goal of a truly Islamic society based on universal principles. The real revolution and true independence would come when pious men of faith in all walks of life would create a spirit of moral dedication throughout society.[6] As a result, Mawdudi attacked the ulama of the Jam'iyyat al-Ulama for a nationalism that ran counter to Islam and also, in tactical terms, risked the sociocultural absorption of Muslims into Hindu society. By 1939, the chief focus of Mawdudi's attack had shifted to the leaders of the Muslim League, whose separatist nationalism seemed to him to be tantamount to unbelief.

Mawdudi recognized that the modern-educated intellectuals in the league were not well grounded in Islamic scholarship and that their program was more a pragmatic one of survival than a step further in Islamic ideological development. The heat of the debate can be seen in Mawdudi's description of the league's leadership. "Not a single leader of the Muslim League from Jinnah himself to the rank and file has an Islamic mentality or Islamic habits of thought, or looks at political and social problems from the Islamic standpoint. . . . Their ignoble role is to safeguard merely the material interests of Indian Muslims by every possible political manoeuvre or trickery."[7]

Although Mawdudi was well known and membership in his organization grew, he was unable to counter the overwhelming appeal of the idea of an independent Islamic state. His proposals were relatively vague and idealistic, and they did not provide a means for implementing the hope that modernism and nationalism could be eliminated as major factors in Islamic society simply by faithful actions of pious men. After the creation of Pakistan, he moved there, and his movement became an important political force in the state whose creation he had opposed.

Mawdudi advocated Islamic renewal and revival. He was not opposed to modern ideas so long as the individual placed them in the proper context of the dominant sovereignty of God. For Mawdudi, the man who has chosen the right path of Islamic faith will not be misled by fantasies. In scientific investigation, he will work to "explore all avenues of knowledge and power and to harness all that exists in earth and heavens in the interests of mankind. . . . The deeper his [a Muslim scientist's] insight into the world of science, the stronger will be his faith in God."[8] However, thought and analysis were not to be pursued to the point where faith might be questioned. Mawdudi said: "You may not be able fully to grasp the wisdom and usefulness of this or that order, but the very fact that an instruction has emanated from the Prophet is sufficient guarantee for its truth and there can be no room for doubt or suspicion. Your inability to understand it is no reason for its having flaw or defect, for a common man's understanding is not flawless."[9]

Fundamentalism in Britism India took its most visible form in Mawdudi's Jamaʿat. It was not a *tariqah* or a traditional grouping of ulama; it was one of the new-style associations that manifested the fundamentalist style in a number of areas. As an organization in a relatively modern format, it was in a position to become active in the new state of Pakistan.

In general, the Islamic experience in British India was rich and varied. In dealing with the political issue of nationalism, some Muslim modernists moved toward an Islamic nationalism, and others joined forces with conservatives to support a composite nationalism, which, in the long run, had secularist implications. It was left to the fundamentalists to reject nationalism altogether. In the issue of defining the relationship of Islam to modern ideas, no one denied the importance of the effort or attempted simply to ignore the existence of the modern world. Instead, the tremendous intellectual diversity that had existed at the end of the nineteenth century continued into the twentieth, and most Indian Muslims both affirmed the validity of their faith, suitably interpreted and expressed, and worked to find a modern expression for that faith in a manner that would not compromise too strongly with secularism or undermine the continued existence of the community.

Islam in Colonial Southeast Asia

In Southeast Asia during the first half of the twentieth century, the issues of winning independence, defining national identity, and creating an ideological basis for modernization were significant. The major factor was the dominance of a European colonial power, but the experience was different from that of India. In both Indonesia and Malaya, the European dominance had been interrupted by the Japanese conquest of the area during World War II, which hastened and also altered the process of the development of nationalism.

Malayan Alternatives. In both Malaya and Indonesia, there were significant alternatives to a modernizing Islamic foundation for nationalism and independence. In Malaya, the British had preserved many of the old local sultanates, and they provided a basis for a Malay political elite that was both experienced and conservative. British policy had left religious affairs in the hands of those rulers, who soon created local religious establishments utilizing old-style religious leaders who represented traditional syncretic and Sufi Islam. The combination of traditional religious and political leadership provided a formidable obstacle to any religious reformism.

Early in the twentieth century, ideas of Islamic modernism were popular in the port cities and the Straits Settlements, which were directly ruled by the British. A lively Muslim reformist intellectual community developed in Singapore, publishing newspapers and establishing schools, which created an informal group of Muslims dedicated to reformist ideas. It came to be called the Young Group (Kaum Muda), as opposed to their conservative opponents, the Kaum Tua (Old Group). In areas of Malaya outside of the coastal cities, the Kaum Muda made little headway, but their influence spread into the islands that became Indonesia.

An important factor in the modern Malayan Islamic experience is that the Muslims there, as in India, do not compose a dominant majority of the society. By the beginning of the twentieth century, Chinese immigrants made up almost half of the population, and there was a significant Indian community. British rule tended to recognize the special position of the original population, and there was little incentive for the religiopolitical Malay elite to encourage nationalism. The Chinese and Indian communities were led by merchants and commercial notables, and they, too, had little interest in major social change. When socioeconomic radicalism emerged, it was in the form of a predominantly Chinese Communist party, which reduced the appeal of radical thought even more for the Malays.

The Muslim community in Malaya was a powerful and established bare majority or minority by the time of World War II. Its basic mood was conservative, and there was little reformist activity. The Japanese conquest destroyed British prestige and opened the door for an upsetting of the old balances. One factor in the change was that the British attempted to create a centralized, unitary government when they returned after the war. Such a government would have removed the Malays from their special position and would have given added power to the Chinese. Rapidly, the old political elite moved to create the United Malays' National Organization (UMNO) in 1946. In the face of a Chinese-dominated communist movement that soon began overt resistance, the UMNO worked to establish effective links with the older conservative leadership in the Chinese and Indian communities, which had formed the Malayan Chinese Association (MCA) and the Malayan Indian Congress (MIC). The result was the formation of the Alliance party as an intercommunal, nationalist movement, basically conservative in its orientation but carefully nonexclusivist in either racial or religious terms.

The Malayan Muslims opted for a non-Islamic nationalism as a matter of internal self-defense. In many ways, they exhibited the same conservative spirit seen in the Deoband ulama who allied themselves with the Indian National Congress in India. The issue of nationalism was resolved by avoiding any connection between it and any of the special communal identities ex-

isting in Malaya at the time. The Alliance party was the overwhelming victor in elections held in 1955, and it formed the government that gained independence in 1957. Communal tensions and conflicts were not eliminated
by this development, but the dominant style of Islamic experience was a
pragmatic conservative adaptationism. Radical secularism would have
given too much strength to a competing community, and fundamentalism
would have aroused fears and opposition among the necessary non-Muslim
partners. Those other types of Islamic experience could only develop in the
context of an independent state.

Islam in Indonesia Until Independence. The final pacification of the
Southeast Asian islands by the Dutch did not result in Islamic stagnation.
The major change was that the older forms of militant resistance were
replaced by new approaches and types of organizations; the old *tariqah-*
holy war structure was replaced by modern social and political associations.

Within the Dutch East Indies, the Muslims were, at least in theory, a
dominant majority, but non-Islamic traditions remained strong in the twentieth century. Although the line of communal demarcation was not as clear
as it was between Hindu and Muslim in India or Malay and Chinese in
Malaya, there were distinctive alternatives on which a nationalist movement could be based. The old court cultural traditions and special characteristics of local society, especially in the continuation of a Javanese
cultural identity, had only been minimally integrated into a more standard
Islamic tradition. There was a long history of tension between local syncretistic Islam and a more fundamentalist style of Islam in Indonesia, and a
potential division between the more strict Muslims and the more local, syncretistic Muslims was added to the normal modern division between the
relatively modernized and the more traditional.

In this context, conservative Islam meant trying to preserve the special
adaptations that had been made to local culture. Fundamentalist Islam was
identified with opposition to popular religious customs and to Sufi pantheistic tendencies. In the twentieth century, fundamentalism and
Salafiyyah reformism were virtually synonymous. As the modern Indonesian experience evolved, the indigenous, syncretic tradition, especially in
the form of pride in the old court cultural traditions, came to be associated
first with the colonial administration and then with the most active of the
modern-educated classes. Thus, specifically Indonesian nationalism
avoided and sometimes opposed a fundamentalist or a reformist Islamic
tone. The nationalists who were favorably inclined toward the indigenous
culture became the most active spokesmen in the anti-imperialist struggle,
and more Islamically oriented groups frequently became their rivals. The
nationalists were not, however, the most radical group, since a communist
tradition soon developed, and it advocated social revolution. It was a
radical secularist tradition with close ties to Moscow, and it began its
transformation from a group of Europeans to an Indonesian party with the

creation of the Perserikatan Komunis di-India (the Communist Association of the Indies) in 1920.

Explicitly Islamic organizations were largely within the reformist tradition and often concentrated on the problems of purifying Islamic practices. They only gradually became more involved in politics, but because of the potential mass support, they were important political factors. By 1912, a number of small Islamic organizations had been created, and in that year, two organizations were established, the Muhammadiyyah and the Sarekat Islam, which were to develop into movements with nationwide followings.

The Muhammadiyyah was established as a primarily cultural and educational organization and attempted to remain aloof from political struggles as much as possible. Its organizers were inspired by the Salafiyyah ideas coming from the Arab East, and it worked to eliminate "superstitious beliefs" and to bring a full and accurate awareness of the meaning of Islam to Indonesians. It established a large number of schools, trained teachers, and had a wide range of publications and activities related to social welfare. Its schools helped to educate nationalist Indonesians, and its activities opposed the development of communism and radical secularism. The Muhammadiyyah continued as an active educational and cultural association throughout the era of the nationalist struggle for independence. Reformist Islam, in this case, did not provide so much a political organization as a religious dimension for the developing spirit of nationalism.

The Sarekat Islam was an expansion of a Javanese organization of Muslim merchants and businessmen. Part of the initial inspiration for the movement was to protect Muslims from the expanding economic power of the Chinese business community, but the movement grew rapidly into a mass movement for the expression of Indonesian opinion. It opposed the abuses by Dutch administrators and the local chieftains whom they supported, and it was drawn into advocating social as well as moral transformations. One element in the organization's rapid growth was the charismatic appeal of its early leader, H.O.S. Tjokroaminoto (1882–1934), who could appeal to the modern-educated people and at the same time benefit from the messianic expectations that his style aroused in the rural areas. The movement also attracted Marxist youth, and for a brief moment during and immediately following World War I, Sarekat Islam appeared to be laying the foundation for a mass, nationwide nationalist movement. However, the more religiously oriented leaders were forced to expel the communists, who attempted to take control, and the movement soon declined in importance because of internal divisions and loss of momentum.

The leader who had emphasized the religious dimension of the organization was Hajji Agus Salim (1884–1954), and after its decline, he worked to reorganize Sarekat Islam and then established other groups that could appeal more effectively to the modern-educated Muslims. That appeal was especially important because after the collapse of the Sarekat Islam, Indonesian political leadership began to pass into the hands of advocates of a more secularist, or at least less clearly Islamic, nationalism built on a more specifically Indonesian cultural identity. The leading figures in that trend were Sukarno and Muhammad Hatta.

The position of the modernist Islamic activists was that Islam provided the unifying link for Indonesian nationalism. Further, Islam was to lead the way in reforming society. Agus Salim, for example, called himself a socialist Muslim and claimed that the Quran presented socialist principles. Although he led the effort to expel communists from the Sarekat Islam, Salim was not a conservative, and he provided an active link between the early days of Islamic nationalism and the era after World War II.

The divisions among the Muslims made it difficult for a unified Islamic nationalist movement to emerge as an alternative to the more secular nationalism of Sukarno and Hatta, a fact that is illustrated by the experience and impact of the Nahdatul Ulama, an organization established in 1926. That group drew its major support from local ulama who were opposed to both secular nationalism and Islamic modernism. Nahdatul Ulama was opposed to Pan-Islamic ideas, believed that the Wahhabi movement in Saudi Arabia was heretical, and expressed vigorous opposition to both the Muhammadiyyah and the Sarekat Islam. Its activities helped to keep many local ulama out of the nationalist or Islamic activist movements for a relatively long time.

Conservatives and modernists formed a loosely organized alliance in 1937, the Majlisul A'laa Indonesia (MIAI), to combat certain government regulations, but the differences between the two positions were never really reconciled. During World War II, the Japanese created a more effective unification when they formed the Masjumi (Majlisul Sjuro Muslimin Indonesia) to replace the MIAI. Masjumi brought the Muhammadiyyah and the Nahdatul Ulama groups together as well as bringing previously unaffiliated religious leaders into a national association. After the war, Masjumi became organized into a political party and was active in the politics of the war for independence. Its party platform combined struggle in defense of the nation with struggle for the faith, and its social programs had wide appeal. Masjumi became, along with the Marxist party and the Partai Nasional Indonesia (PNI) of the secular nationalists, one of the basic poles of Indonesian political life.

During the time of conflict with the Dutch, which led to independence in the period 1945–1949, a variety of small parties and movements emerged. Some of them had a clearly Islamic tone and came to pose problems for the newly established Indonesian nationalist government. One of the most long-lived involved what have been called the Dar al-Islam revolts. In a number of areas, local movements worked vigorously to establish Islamic states. In some cases they were led by men who had cooperated with the nationalist struggle for a brief period but had soon ended up in conflict with the republican government as well as with the Dutch. The programs of those local movements were for the establishment of states based on Islamic law. The longevity of the Dar al-Islam revolts is demonstrated by the fact that the revolt in West Java lasted from 1948 until 1962, in the Celebes from 1950 until 1965, and in North Sumatra from 1953 until 1961. This more fundamentalist style of militance tended to be local in organization, and the national Islamic groups remained largely reformist (with fundamentalist aspects) or conservative.

In Indonesia, there was a wide diversity of activity. The Islamic experience did not resolve the two basic divisions within the country, although compromises seemed to be made. The real difference between conservative and reformist Islam was never fully resolved, although by the time of the struggle for independence, the two major organizations representing those two styles were cooperating in a single political group. The other division was between the more secular style of nationalism and the Islamic orientation. Again, the explicitly Islamic groups cooperated with nationalists after World War II, but the inherent tensions were not eliminated. Although compromises existed, no effective modern Islamic synthesis seemed to be emerging by the time of Indonesian independence. As a result, Indonesian politics would be characterized by instability until a strong leader created a new political regime for the independent country.

Islam in Independence

Pakistan: New Existence as a Majority. The creation of an independent Muslim state in India in 1947 was the culmination of the development of nationalism in South Asia. Although it was a goal whose definition seemed self-evident, the establishment of an Islamic state was clearly an important event that has had profound implications for the modern history of Islam. The Muslims of British India had consciously chosen the option of partition in order to have their own independent state. In other areas of the world, Muslims had achieved independence or were to do so later, but the establishment of Pakistan was the result of the nationalism of Muslims more than of an explicitly Islamic nationalist effort. With the creation of Pakistan, the ability of Muslims to create a clearly Islamic state was put to the test. The basic issue, in both religious and political terms, was, Can a distinctively Islamic state be created and succeed under the conditions of modern history?

The new state received major blows early in its history. Not only was the process of partition bloody and disruptive, leaving Pakistan with little effective governmental structure or personnel, but Pakistan was also deprived of its most effective unifying symbols and leaders with the deaths of the two major leaders of the Muslim League, Muhammad Ali Jinnah in 1948 and Liyaqat Ali Khan, Jinnah's quiet lieutenant in the nationalist struggle who was murdered in 1951. In the absence of a strong leadership that was capable of unifying the diverse elements within the new state, the profound political issue of the meaning of Pakistan became obscured by the personal struggles for political position and power among the remaining politicans.

In the Islamic experience of Pakistan in the two decades following independence, two major themes are important. The first, and most visible, is

the continuing failure to create a viable consensus on the meaning of an
Islamic state. The long-term evolution was in the direction of political
fragmentation rather than national and Islamic consolidation. The second
theme, which is too often ignored in view of the political difficulties, is the
continuing intellectual vitality of Pakistani Muslims in working to redefine
Islam in the modern context.

The new state of Pakistan had only its Islamic identity to unite its diverse
elements. The two parts of the country were geographically separated, and
there was little convenient access between them. East Pakistan was much
more densely populated, although less urbanized, than West Pakistan. The
country was composed of geographically compact linguistic units, speaking
languages not widely used outside of those areas. Bengali was the language
of the overwhelming majority in East Pakistan, and the West Pakistanis
were divided into a bare majority of Punjabi speakers and large minorities
speaking Pushtu, Sindhi, and Urdu. The language issue illustrates the major
difficulties of unification. Although Bengali was spoken by more than half
of all Pakistanis, the new government tended to be dominated by people
from West Pakistan, and they attempted to make Urdu the only official national language. That attempt failed, but neither section seemed eager to
find a compromise.

A significant characteristic of the role of Islam in the politics of Pakistan
was that it did not provide a commonly accepted, concrete program of action. Islam was, rather, a vaguely defined sentiment, which was, in different forms, common to virtually all Pakistanis. In British India, Islam,
however defined, had provided a distinctive identity in contrast to the
Hindu majority, but the process of becoming the dominant majority had
eliminated that condition. There was insufficient consensus on the specifics
of the meaning of an Islamic state to maintain Islam as the primary focus of
loyalty. As a result, other sociocultural identities began to emerge as the
basis for political action.

The process of political fragmentation was associated with the decline of
the original nationalist elite. As in many countries, the group that achieved
independence was displaced by a new generation of political leaders, and
the process was a two-step one in Pakistan. The old nationalist leaders were
removed first in East Pakistan, where an explicitly Bengali group of leaders
defeated the national elite in the 1954 elections. The major group in that
defeat was the Awami League, which had been established in 1949 as the
first primarily Muslim opposition party. It had soon gained wide support
by advocating significant autonomy for East Pakistan and official recognition for the Bengali language. In the period from 1954 until 1958, the
Awami League worked with the old national politicians of West Pakistan,
but neither group was able to create effective organizations beyond their
own regional spheres of influence. The Awami-West alliance did not succeed in providing stable leadership for Pakistan as a whole, and in 1958, the
military leadership took control of the government.

The effort to create an Islamic state was part of the problem of instability.

The leaders of the Muslim League and and the Pakistan movement were largely modern educated and relatively secularist in orientation, and their Muslim identity was more in their communal affiliation than in their intellectual position. Most of the conservative ulama and the fundamentalists had opposed the concept of Pakistan but took an active role in Pakistani politics after independence. They mobilized pressure groups to ensure that the more secularist elite would give real recognition to Islamic principles, but in the debates and struggles, a new synthesis did not emerge out of the interaction of the liberal nationalists, conservatives, and fundamentalists.

One of the major statements of the Islamic position was an official government report that examined some disturbances that occurred in 1953. They had been caused by fundamentalist and conservative agitation that had attempted to force an exclusionary definition of Islam upon the state. The focus had been opposition to the Ahmadiyyah movement and the demand for its suppression. The report, called the Munir Report, clearly identified the dilemmas in defining a modern Islamic state: If it were defined in the exclusive manner proposed by the ulama and the fundamentalists, the state could not be democratic; if the state were theocratic, it could not be a republic based on the will of the people. The conclusion of the report presents a clear expression of modern Islamic individualistic secularism. "The sublime faith called Islam will live even if our leaders are not there to enforce it. It lives in the individual, in his soul and outlook, in his relations with God and men, from the cradle to the grave, and our politicians should understand that if Divine commands cannot make or keep a man a Musalman, their statutes will not."[10]

In many ways, that spirit dominated the constitution that was approved in 1956, although many compromises had been made to accommodate the conservative and fundamentalist positions. It adhered to the principle of complete equality between Muslims and non-Muslims, and rather than imposing Islamic law, it said that the state would be a democracy based on Islamic principles. On the issue of theocracy, God's exclusive sovereignty over the whole universe was affirmed, but the people of Pakistan had a sacred trust to authority in their country. Although the constitution was seen as a successful compromise at the time, it did not make a stable political system possible. In 1958, following political anarchy, the constitution was suspended, martial law was proclaimed, and Muhammad Ayyub Khan took control of the government in a military coup.

The era of Ayyub Khan lasted from 1958 to 1969, and during that time Pakistan was given political stability not on the basis of an ideological consensus but through a strong executive backed by the armed forces. In contrast to other contemporary military regimes, the Ayyub government was relatively conservative in its approach to socioeconomic affairs. It was, however, committed to a relatively secularist concept of a democratic-Islamic Pakistan unified under a strong central government. The 1956 constitution was abrogated, and a new one was promulgated in 1962.

The Ayyub regime interfered very little with ulama affairs as long as they were not overtly political, an implicitly secularist approach. The government took effective steps to reform Muslim family law along liberal modernist lines and reaffirmed a liberal modernist educational policy in which, as the Commission of National Education reported, "Religion is not presented as a dogma, superstitution or ritual."[11] In the administration of law, the policy of maintaining an independent, modern-style judiciary that recognized the validity of Islamic principles but was not tied to traditional details was continued. The constitution of 1962 established, in general, a regime that was secularist in practice and Islamic modernist in interpretation, but open to compromise with conservatives and fundamentalists on details. It was a workable, pragmatic adaptation rather than a new ideological synthesis, and it was effective as long as the central leader had the power to enforce acquiescence. However, the old regional and ideological differences were not reduced; they were only temporarily submerged.

Pakistan, like many other states in the Muslim world, entered the 1960s under a regime that was moving in the direction of greater Westernization and modernization. In some ways more radical than the White Revolution in Iran and the policies of the Saudis, Ayyub's regime was less committed to a radical position than Nasser in Egypt or the Baʿth party in Syria. In the growing opposition to Ayyub during the decade, the forces that represented a more radical socialist program or a regional-linguistic nationalism appeared to be gaining power rather than the Islamic forces. The fundamentalists under Mawdudi were increasingly becoming another element in the conservative grouping rather than being radical or revolutionary critics of the existing system.

The future, in 1968–1970, appeared to belong to the Pakistani socialists and the regional nationalists, and by 1970, those two themes were being presented by the two major parties. The earliest of those parties was the Awami League, which had been weakened by internal divisions and the death of some of its major leaders. Its efforts to become an effective national party in the 1950s had not been successful and had undermined the party's mass support in East Pakistan. Then, under the leadership of Shaykh Mujib al-Rahman, it reestablished itself as the principle party by advocating East Pakistani autonomy with the promulgation of the Six Point movement in 1966. It is indicative of the problem of defining Islam's role that Islam was not mentioned in that six-point definition of the proposed federal state.

The ideological tradition of the Awami League was consistently more secularist than the thinking of much of the West Pakistani leadership. The Awami leader in 1956, H. S. Suhrawardi, for example, argued in the Pakistan National Assembly against Jinnah's two-nation idea: "The two-nation theory was advanced by the Muslims as justification for the partition of India and the creation of a state made up of geographically contiguous units where the Muslims were numerically in the majority. Once that state was created, the two-nation theory lost its force even for the Muslims."[12] According to that position, Islam was not a basis for the continuing identity of a state, and the new state should now become secular and democratic.

Ultimately, the repudiation of the two-nation theory, with its corollary that Pakistan is a single nation, became the basis for Bengali rather than Pakistani or Islamic nationalism in the Awami League. By the late 1960s, the conscious Bengali literary renaissance and increasing pressures for autonomy, if not independence, for East Pakistan produced a movement that was more secular nationalist than Islamic in the Awami League under Shaykh Mujib. Conservative and fundamentalist Islamic forces still had influence, and even Islamic modernist views maintained some popularity, so that Bengali nationalism did not divorce itself fully from its Islamic roots, but it was not an Islamic republic that emerged when East Pakistan became the independent state of Bangladesh after the elections, revolt, and war of 1970–1971.

The emergence of Bangladesh meant that Islam had been the basis for the creation of Pakistan but it could not provide a sufficient basis for long-term national unity. The style of Islam that emerged out of the conflict was a secularist one, associated with but not identical to the nationalist cause. After the experiment of the "Islamic state" in a unified Pakistan, the Muslim community in Bengal adopted a style that was closer to the experience of Islamic communities elsewhere.

The second major movement that had emerged in Pakistan by the end of the 1960s was a more explicitly socialist and democratic one led by Zulfikar Ali Bhutto. That movement took the form of the Pakistan People's party (PPP), which was established in 1967 with the slogan, "Islam is our faith, democracy is our polity, socialism is our economy, all power to the people."[13] In the PPP, a more typical radically oriented socialist party emerged, similar to the Ba'th in Syria or Nasser's Arab socialism. Just as the Pakistan idea had postponed the emergence of an effective secular nationalist movement in Bengal, it appears to have delayed the emergence of radical socialism in West Pakistan. However, by the end of the 1960s, the PPP was gaining strength by building on the unrest created by the relative autocracy of the Ayyub regime and the demand for more activist economic policies. Although the Awami League won the 1970 elections overwhelmingly in East Pakistan, the PPP won with less strength in the West. After the war and the breakup of the old state, Bhutto became the leader of the new Pakistan, now limited to the old western part.

Bhutto's platform in the 1970 election was socialistic to redress the economic problems of the people. It was called Islamic socialism, but Bhutto did say that his socialism would be of the Scandinavian rather than of the Marxist variety.[14] That statement indicates that the position was not militantly radical, but it certainly was secularist in its basic tone. In its platform of economic justice, the PPP was able to overcome conservative and fundamentalist opposition to win clear mass support. Like the Bengali nationalists, the PPP did not ignore or reject Islam, but Islam was put into a secularist framework that was quite different from the early expectations for an Islamic state.

Independent Pakistan thus passed through a long and difficult evolution.

The initial political instability led to a military regime of a more autocratic nature. Neither the early parliamentary government nor the Ayyub regime was able to create a new and satisfactory solution to the problem of creating a modern Islamic state. Instead, after more than two decades of independence, more common lines of political and social evolution developed, and they led to a successful secular nationalist movement in East Pakistan and a dominant radical socialist party in the west. Islam had emerged in a more common, adaptationist form by the end of the 1960s.

In Pakistan, the political evolution is of great importance and dominates the Islamic experience, but in addition to the political activities, Muslim intellectuals have opened new lines of thought. Fundamentalism has remained stable with the restatement of the positions of Mawdudi, and the conservatives have tended to adhere closely to the lines set by the earlier leaders. In these two styles of Islam, there have been no major new dynamic movements of reaffirmation as there were at the end of the nineteenth century, and the organizations and traditions established at that same time remain the dominant modes of conservative and fundamentalist expression.

It is in the area of intellectual adaptationism of the modernist style that the major new activities took place in the two decades following independence. In the area of socioeconomic thought, there were a number of scholars who began the process of defining a specifically Islamic socialism and democracy in terms that were not simply attaching Islamic names to Western concepts. As a result, the effort in the 1950s and 1960s began to shift from showing that all Western ideas are really Islamic, or that all Islamic ideas are really modern, to trying to define the modern Islamic tradition as distinctive. The shift can be seen, for example, in the works of Khalifa Abd al-Hakim, who saw Islamic socialism as the viable alternative to both communism and capitalism.

A similar and more dramatic shift can be seen in the scholarship of Islamic history itself. At the beginning of the century, there were Indian Muslim scholars, such as Amir Ali, who wrote about the history and nature of Islam. Those men were often respected for their sincere faith and vigorous hard work, but they never escaped from the position of being apologists or informed propagandists. However, following World War II, Pakistanis made significant contributions in the world of historical scholarship, and their work is accepted not simply as the product of a sincere faith but as the product of a vigorous scholarly tradition. The works on Islam by scholars such as Fazlur Rahman (b. 1919) and the products of the Islamic Research Institute under his direction are only some of the many scholarly works that combine the continuing modernist effort to define the meaning of the Islamic experience in the perspective of the modern experience.

Muslims in Independent India. It is a measure of the size of the Muslim community in British India that three of the four largest Muslim national groups in the world were originally within its borders. The Muslims that remained within India after independence are only a little more than 10 percent of the population, but they still represent the fourth-largest national community in the Islamic world, twice as large as the Muslim national communities in Egypt or Iran or Turkey and almost twice as large as all the Muslim communities in the Maghrib. Like the Muslims in Pakistan after 1947, the Indian Muslims were involved in an experiment that was unusual for the Islamic tradition, but the basic nature of that experiment was opposite from the Pakistani one. Rather than consciously seeking to create a viable state, the Indian Muslims faced the task of creating a viable Islamic experience voluntarily within a secular context. As one Indian Muslim expressed it: "Those Muslims who on the creation of Pakistan decided to stay on in India also made, through that decision, a choice that is unique in the history of Islam. Till then Muslims had lived as rulers, a persecuted or protected minority, or in unstable co-existence in a non-Muslim society. Never before had they shared power with others in a spirit of equality that transcended religious divisions."[15]

That summary paints an optimistic picture of the situation of the Indian Muslims. Many remained in India because they had no choice or were too poor to make the trip to Pakistan. The picture describes the goal rather than the reality, and the basic issue of the Indian Muslim experiment was whether or not it is possible to create an Islamic experience within a community that transcends religious divisons. The reality is that Indian Muslims have faced many grave problems and even the author who painted the glowing picture of Muslim Indian life felt that most educated Muslims at the time seemed "to be suffering from a feeling of despair and loneliness. They feel alienated from their own community."[16]

Throughout most of the postindependence era, Indian Muslims have been primarily conservative in outlook and have been unwilling to engage in reformist activities or to accept significant reforms for fear that their communal life might be weakened. Even the Indian branch of Mawdudi's fundamentalist organization acted in a primarily conservative manner, working with the traditionalist ulama to prevent changes in personal status law. The argument of the ulama was that although reform of Muslim personal law might be suitable in a country like Turkey, where the reforms were enacted by the Muslims themselves, such actions would not be appropriate for Indian Muslims.

Leadership in the Indian Muslim community went to those Muslims who had cooperated closely with the Indian National Congress, such as Abu al-Kalam Azad. That intellectual elite also contained a number of highly visible public figures who provided manifest proof of the functioning of composite Indian nationalism. Loyal Muslim allies of the Congress in the struggle for independence became the third and fifth presidents of the republic. Zakir Husain (1897–1969), who had been an associate of Mahatma Gandhi and active in the development of national education, was president in 1967–1969. Fakhr al-Din Ali Ahmad (1905–1977), the fifth president, was a British-trained lawyer who had been an active Congress politician in the state of Assam and had served in provincial and national cabinets after independence. However, a new leadership did not develop very rapidly to replace the old politico-intellectual elite that had formulated the ideals of composite nationalism. Although composing at least 10 percent of the population, Muslims held only about 4 percent of the seats in parliament and held an even smaller proportion of government administrative positions.

The ideal of composite nationalism requires a reduction of communal militance, and the Indian Muslims have faced problems in that regard. Although secularism seems to be a necessary corollary of composite nationalism, many of the Muslims have clung to a conservative style that opposes significant change. An even greater problem is that the Hindu majority has also been unable to eliminate communal militancy. Although the Hindu political elite is largely secularist and liberal in approach, the Hindu tradition has experienced a renaissance in the past century and a half that has produced vigorous Hindu activism. For example, Hindu fanatics murdered Gandhi in 1948 when he opposed the massacre of Muslims and the destruction of mosques, and since independence, the threat of communal violence has never been far below the surface of Indian affairs. During the 1960s, there was a resurgence of Hindu militance and communal violence, which increased the problems of the Indian Muslims.

The alternatives for the Muslims were to rebuild communal organization and activism or to reassert the validity of secularism. The followers of Mawdudi in India had begun to preach the first option with great vigor by the end of the 1960s, and the second alternative was stressed by a small minority of the intellectuals organized in the Indian Secular Forum. Their position was that "the basic cause of communal riots is communal politics. To fight this menace, we should make determined efforts to build up a strong united front of all those who have firm faith in secularism and who hate communal politics."[17] Those alternatives outline the two basic options open to Indian Muslims: maintain a conservative style, which perpetuates the community but keeps it essentially isolated, or accept Islam as an individual and personal faith and not the basis for a community (and hope that the Hindus can move in the same direction). At the end of the 1960s, the resurgence of communalism in India gave little hope for the ultimate success of the secularist experiment.

Communalism and Islam in Malaya. One of the basic elements of the Islamic experience in Malaya was also the problem of the relationship between Islam and communalism and its impact on politics. At independence, the basic spirit was nonreligious nationalism as exemplified by the policies of the Alliance party. The defeat of the Chinese-dominated communist revolutionaries by 1960 and the effective, if conservative, cooperation of the Malay, Chinese, and Indian organizations in the Alliance party gave added strength to the stability of the regime. However, the basis of the new Malay regime was not an elimination of communalism but a maintenance of communal identities with communal interests being carefully balanced. Such a regime requires continuing mutual trust and is always inherently unstable. The creation of the state of Malaysia as a federation of the Malay states, North Borneo, and Singapore in 1963 and the withdrawal of Singapore in 1965 did not change the basic nature of the regime.

In the context of an independent Malaya, and then Malaysia, the major roles of Islam were to be a crucial element in the identity of one of the large communal groups, the Malays, and to be the support for the conservative political elite based on the traditional Malay sultanates. The leading Malay political organization was the United Malays' National Organization (UMNO), which was led by Tungku Abd al-Rahman, and it maintained a moderate policy of cooperative communalism and provided the basis for the stable politics of the first years of independence.

Cooperative communalism required that the Malay Muslim leaders make at least some compromises with the Chinese and Indian groups, which provided the grounds for the emergence of a more militantly Islamic/Malay opposition after independence. In the northern state of Kelantan, the Pan-Malayan Islamic party, or Parti Islam Sa-Tanah Melayu (PMIP, sometimes referred to as the PAS), emerged as a militant Islamic party opposed to any compromise with other communal groups that would undermine the special rights of the Malay Muslims, and it advocated the creation of an Islamic state in which Islamic law would be fully implemented. The PMIP became an active fundamentalist group and gained significant electoral successes, winning control of state governments in the north and gaining a significant number of seats in the federal governments.

The Islamic pressures on the Malay leaders in the Alliance party increased during the 1960s, but the UMNO remained the dominant Malay party in national terms. However, the elections of 1969 posed a significant challenge to the policy of cooperative communalism. During those elections, the Malaysian Chinese Association (MCA) lost a number of seats to more radical groups that demanded greater equality and less communal privilege, and it appeared that the MCA was no longer able to ensure Chinese participation in cooperative communalism. In that situation, Malay/Islamic activism threatened to undermine the UMNO position, and efforts were made to associate the UMNO more visibly with the Malay/Islamic cause. In the process of this reorientation of the political scene, large-scale communal fighting broke out in Kuala Lumpur in May 1969, and the careful structure of balanced trust was broken. The government was placed in the hands of an eight-man National Operations Council under the leadership of Tun Razak. Order was restored, and a new regime was created on the same foundations as those of the Alliance party. Tungku Abd al-Rahman retired, and the new Alliance party leader was Tun Razak. The experiment in cooperative communalism did not totally fail, but it was replaced, after the 1969 riots, by a less optimistic, conservative alliance of communities, which was a fragile balancing of interests challenged by Malay/Islamic activism on the one hand and non-Malay radicalism on the other.

As in the case of India, by the end of the 1960s, it was clear that communalism is a strong force that can create violent confrontations. Neither the optimistic secularism of the Indian Muslims nor the cooperative communalism of the Malaysian Muslims has provided a way to avoid intercommunal conflict, although both outlooks have a significant degree of support. It would appear that the more comprehensive interpretation of the meaning and implications of the Islamic message—the vision of Islam as a community rather than as an individual's faith—remains a strong part of the modern Islamic experience in areas where Islam is a minority faith as well as in those areas where Muslims make up the dominant majority.

Radicalism and Islam in Indonesia. In the years after independence was achieved in Indonesia, four general themes and organizational types interacted. The most important initially was the old secular nationalist group that dominated the early independent governments. A second theme was social radicalism, which was represented most visibly in an active Communist party, the Partai Komunis Indonesia (PKI), and a third was reformist-fundamentalist Islam, which took a number of forms. The fourth element, which was of gradually growing importance, was the armed forces. The military emerged as a well-organized social force that was interested in the modernization and economic development of Indonesia, and it increasingly represented a specific interest group in Indonesian politics.

The interaction of those four elements provided the framework for the developing experience of Indonesian Islam. After the successful conclusion of the war with the Dutch, a parliamentary regime emerged that was dominated by parties representing the two general policy orientations of secular nationalism and the Islamic forces. The secular nationalists were better organized, and divisions were reduced as Sukarno became the dominant national leader by 1959. His prestige was based on his reputation as the leading nationalist and on his dramatic, popular, charismatic appeal.

The Islamic groups were strong more because of the widespread support for Islam than because of effective organization or unified leadership. At the end of World War II, politically active Muslims had been combined in Masjumi, but that unity soon crumbled. In 1947, the old Partai Sarekat Islam Indonesia (PSII), the small, relatively leftist heir of the Sarekat Islam, had already broken away from Masjumi, and, as parliamentary politics became more complex, the old Nahdatul Ulama (NU) group withdrew from Masjumi in 1952. In this way, Islamic political efforts were divided among a number of competing organizations.

After 1952, Masjumi represented the more urban elements and the tradition of the Indonesian modernist reformers, and it included both individuals and some cultural associations. Its main support came from the Muhammadiyyah. The NU, in contrast, continued to represent the more conservative ulama, was willing to accept many of the old syncretic practices, and was sympathetic to local, especially Javanese, cultural traditions. In its conservatism, the NU insisted on adherence to one of the four medieval schools of Islamic law, thus implicitly rejecting the Masjumi-Muhammadiyyah support for *ijtihad*. The PSII was more open to leftist ideas and remained a small minority party.

The platforms of all of those parties called for the creation of a formally

Islamic state, but the emphasis varied in terms of defining that goal. The stated goal of Masjumi was "the realization of the doctrine and law of Islam in the life of the individual, in society and in the Republic of Indonesia as a State, directed toward that which pleases God."[18] The NU goal was similar, but there was a more specific emphasis on the teachings of the traditional law schools, and it was less emphatic in its unwillingness to blend its Islamic goals with those of the secular nationalists. Its political practice was aimed at *sulh* ("peaceful reconciliation") as "the normal basis of contact with every kind of group as long as this is not detrimental to Islam and its struggle," and its goal was a state "based on Islam" but also a "state upholding the rule of law and based on the sovereignty of the people in the sense of mutual deliberation."[19]

The Islamic parties and groups did not present a unified front in the major political debate of the era: the definition of the ideological foundations of independent Indonesia. In general terms, the two alternatives were an Islamic state or a state based on the secular nationalists' ideological formulation, which came to be called the Pantjasila (Five Principles). These two positions were not mutually exclusive opposites, but they were different in style and tone. The Muslim parties wanted the state and legal system to recognize formally the dominant position of Islam, and the Pantjasila based the state on a belief in God but with specific religious practice being an individual matter. The latter was a recognition of a secularist position.

The elections of 1955 provided a test of the political strength of the various positions, and altogether, the Islamic parties won 43.5 percent of the votes in the parliamentary elections. That was a substantial achievement, but it came as a disappointment to the Muslim leaders, who had felt that the dominance of Muslims in Indonesia would be translated into an overwhelming majority for their parties. It was clear that the Islamic political scene was dominated by the Masjumi (20.9 percent) and the NU (18.4 percent) and that the other parties had little electoral significance.

On the other side of the Pantjasila-Islam debate, the largest vote was received by the nationalist PNI, which gained 22.3 percent of the votes. Significantly, however, the more radical secularism represented by the communists in the PKI received 16.4 percent. The major elections provided no single party or group of parties with sufficient support to form an effective government, and cabinets had to be compromise arrangements. As a result, the power of the charismatic president, Sukarno, gew rapidly, and in 1957, Sukarno began the creation of an authoritarian political regime, which he came to call guided democracy. Indonesia moved in the direction of an increasingly radical socialism and a growing cooperation between the president and the Communist party.

The new situation created major problems for the Islamic parties. Some of the Masjumi leaders joined with regional revolutionaries in 1958, and they attempted to establish an Indonesian republic in Sumatra. Islamic leaders were also suspected of giving support to the Dar al-Islam revolts, which were continuing. That suspicion brought the Masjumi leaders into direct conflict not only with the Sukarno regime but also with the military, which was beginning to emerge as a separate political force. Although the military was beginning to have doubts about the growing radicalism of Sukarno and his reliance on the PKI, it believed that the support given by the Masjumi leaders to separatist revolts was a threat to Indonesian independence.

The era of guided democracy lasted from around 1957 until 1965, when Sukarno was the dominant figure in Indonesian politics. He and other leaders, such as Nasser, Ben Bella, Kwame Nkrumah, Sékou Touré, and Modibo Keita, became the leading spokesmen for radical Third World socialism, and at the time, that seemed to be the style of rule that would dominate the developing world.

Islam was given a place in the guided democracy, but only the cooperative NU leaders had any visible role in politics. Sukarno frequently maintained that he was a Muslim strongly attached to his faith; he was, however, strongly opposed to the idea of an Islamic state whose actions would be subject to veto by the ulama. Islam's role in the state was to be the religious faith of the majority and, if they chose, the active faith of the majority in the nation's parliament. Sukarno believed that fundamentalists and conservatives were oriented toward the past and offered programs that would not aid Indonesia's progress. "Not back to the easy glory of Islam, not back to the time of the caliphs, but run forward, catching up with time, that is the only way to get glory again."[20] Islam in guided democracy was not to compete in glory with the leader and the basic principles of his regime. The socialism of Sukarno was willing to accept religious values as being important in the lives of the people, but it was thoroughly secularist in demanding that religious organizations and leaders refrain from political activities except in clearly subordinate roles.

The overthrow of the Sukarno regime came suddenly in 1965–1966 and was accompanied by a strong reaction against radical secularism. By 1965, the military had emerged as a significant force with sufficient unity to challenge even the great nationalist leader. When six generals were killed in a conspiracy apparently organized by the communists and with the assumed agreement of Sukarno, the army reacted by taking control of the government. Popular opposition to the radical secularism of the PKI was unleashed in a bloodbath in which thousands of communists were killed and the PKI was destroyed as an effective political force. Although the new regime, led by General Suharto, was militantly anticommunist, it was closely associated with the nationalist tradition and was relatively secularist in its approach. The military leaders remembered that Masjumi leaders had supported antigovernment revolts and therefore mistrusted them. The military leaders accepted the NU but were unwilling to open the door for an officially recognized revival of Masjumi. Finally, after long negotiations, a modernist-oriented Muslim party was allowed by the military regime. It could receive support from the old Masjumi people but was not to be identified as a new Masjumi in terms of leadership. The result was the creation in 1968 of the Partai Muslimin Indonesia (PMI) as a highly restricted Islamic party.

The "new order" created by Suharto did not represent a victory for Indonesian Islamic forces as it was a reassertion of the less radical nationalism of the early years of the republic after a detour into the realm of radical socialism under Sukarno. The issue of whether or not Indonesia would be a radical, secularist regime was resolved, but the older debate over the relative merits of a moderate secular nationalism as opposed to an Islamic state were not settled. The Suharto regime inherited the position of the moderate nationalists, although now Indonesia was led by the military rather than by the old parties. By the end of the 1960s, the role of Islam in Indonesia remained unclear.

Muslim Minorities and Nondominant Majorities in Africa

Virtually every country in Africa has at least a small Muslim community. In the parts of the continent south of the states of the Arab East and the Maghrib, these groups range in size and significance from a few thousand and less than one percent of the population in Zimbabwe to virtually the whole population of Somalia. One important feature of African Islam in the twentieth century is the expansion of the world of Islam as the conditions of colonial rule and independence provided opportunities for the conversion of individuals and groups. Non-Muslims found Islam to be an appealing identity in light of the rapid changes that were taking place, and their interest was aided by the modernization of communications and the expansion of the education systems.

Although small Muslim communities have grown in many areas during the twentieth century, the most important region for the development of Islam is the Sudanic area, which stretches from the Atlantic to the eastern shores of the continent through the areas just south of the Sahara. A wide variety of experiences has shaped the development of ideology and social structures in this region. It is not possible to describe the specific local conditions in the many different countries that have emerged during the twentieth century, but certain basic themes can be used to illustrate the main lines of this experience in both the colonial and the independence periods.

Adaptationism: Tranformation of Old Organizations

One of the major themes of the Sudanic Islamic experience in the twentieth century is the remarkable adaptation of a number of the older organizations to the changing conditions of modern times. That adaptation took a number of forms, depending on local conditions and the type of leadership within the movements. Although many of the institutions and structures that had existed in the nineteenth century simply lost effectiveness as a result of unimaginative conservative attitudes, some provide striking examples of the adaptability of the traditional Islamic institutions.

Some of them exhibit that characteristic in economic activities, and others became prominent in the political arena and played an important role in nationalism.

The Transformation of Sudanese Mahdism. One of the most remarkable transformations of an earlier Islamic movement is the experience of the Sudanese Mahdist movement, which changed from a nineteenth-century fundamentalist organization led by Muhammad Ahmad into an effectively organized nationalist movement and modern-style political party. The Mahdist state had been destroyed by the Anglo-Egyptian "reconquest" at the end of the nineteenth century, but the religious enthusiasm that had been aroused by the Mahdist era did not end with the defeat of the state. For the first two decades of British rule, there were a number of traditional-style religious revolts against the foreign, infidel rule, and it appeared that the Mahdist momentum would soon be dissipated in those fruitless conflicts. However, a son of the Mahdi, Sayyid Abd al-Rahman (1885–1959), gradually reorganized the followers of the Mahdi, called the Ansar, into an effective sociopolitical force.

Although most of the Ansar were rural tribal people who were still little affected by modern ideas, under Sayyid Abd al-Rahman's leadership, they were brought together with a significant number of the emerging modern-educated Sudanese. By his patronage and interest, Sayyid Abd al-Rahman won the friendship and support of many of those new Sudanese, and the alliance that he forged between the modern-educated Sudanese and the more traditional Ansar became the basis for a nationalist movement that called for the independence of the Sudan. Following World War II, that alliance was the basis for one of the major political groups, the Ummah party.

The gradual modernization of the Ansar can be seen in the vision of the sayyid's role in an independent Sudan. Initially he was the Ansar imam or religious leader, but in the political activity following World War I, it was thought that he could become the king of an independent Sudan. However, after the formation of the Ummah party, many suggested that Sayyid Abd al-Rahman could become Sudan's president.

Under the leadership of Sayyid Abd al-Rahman, the Mahdist movement was transformed from a fundamentalist revolutionary movement into an effective modern political interest group, and after Sudanese independence, Sayyid Abd al-Rahman and then his son became important leaders within the Sudanese parliamentary system. During the 1960s, a grandson of Abd al-Rahman, Sayyid Sadiq, became prime minister. Under Sadiq, an attempt was made to secularize the party, and that attempt caused a split within the Ansar, but Sadiq remained a key leader in the Sudan. After a 1969 revolution overthrew the parliamentary regime, Sadiq became a leading figure in the conservative modernist opposition to the socialist policies of the revolutionary regime.

Within the Sudan, a similar transformation took place among the heirs to the Khatmiyyah Neo-Sufi tradition. The Mirghani family worked through the nationwide organization of the Khatmiyyah Tariqah to become an effective political force and the largest rival to the revived Ansar, and the Khatmiyyah provided the focus and popular support for the nationalism that advocated unity with Egypt. Like the Ansar, the Khatmiyyah became the basis for a major political party that could operate effectively in the arena of modern-style politics.

In this way, the traditional Sudanese Islamic leadership shows that premodern styles of organization can be transformed into vehicles for modern political action. Nationalism in the Sudan rested firmly on the basis of mass Islamic support, and the political parties during the two eras of parliamentary regimes—1956–1958 and 1964–1969—revolved around existing religious loyalties. Even the major "secularist" party, the National Union party, was led by a modern-educated scion of one of the major old religious families, Ismail al-Azhari (1902–1969). Political parties have not been an official part of the government in the Sudan since the 1969 revolution and the development of the Sudanese Socialist Union as the major legal political organization. However, the Ansar and Khatmiyyah political organizations were replaced as the major forces in Sudanese politics not primarily because they were transformed religious organizations but because they shared the fate of other political parties and parliamentary systems with more modern foundations in many African countries.

The Heirs of Uthman Dan Fodio. When the British gained control of northern Nigeria, they adopted a policy of indirect rule that preserved the political structures that had been created during the time of the holy war of Uthman Dan Fodio. The royal courts of northern Nigeria had become established and conservative princedoms rather than maintaining the militant fundamentalist spirit of their founders, but they were still solid symbols of Islamic rule in the region. In this way, the British control preserved a clearly Islamic, if now relatively conservative, political regime.

During the first half of the twentieth century the northern areas of Nigeria remained relatively untouched by nationalist activism, and Nigerian nationalism, when it developed, was largely the creation of the modern-educated Nigerians in the southern cities. Following World War II, the situation began to change. The British began the process of creating institutions of Nigerian self-government, and political parties and interest groups were formed. Northern leaders soon realized that if they did not take action, an independent Nigeria would be created in which they would have little influence.

The leading figure in the northern Muslim political structure was the sardauna of Sokoto, al-Hajj Ahmadu Bello (d. 1966), who had been a district head and was quick to sense the changing nature of the political scene after World War II. In 1949, a small party, the Northern Elements Progressive Union, was organized by younger, modern-educated northerners, and it was soon allied with one of the southern nationalist parties. The sardauna quickly created the Northern People's Congress (NPC), which rapidly became the party of the northern princes and conservative leaders. The

NPC was able to mobilize large-scale support in the region, which was still relatively untouched by more modern political ideas.

During the 1950s, Nigeria moved toward self-rule and independence within the framework of a federal system containing three separate regions. The northern region was the largest, containing about half of the population and covering the northern two-thirds of the country. In this region, the NPC was the clearly dominant force. Each of the other two regions were similarly dominated by regionally based parties, the National Council of Nigeria and the Cameroons (NCNC) in the eastern region and the Action Group in the western region. Because of the size of the northern region, the NPC emerged as the largest party in the federal parliament after Nigeria became independent.

The NPC worked to preserve the more traditional structures of the northern areas and followed a relatively conservative policy in the legislature of that region. One of its early actions after independence was to revise the criminal code to bring it more in line with Islamic practices, and it reinforced the power of the Muslim law courts. The sardauna was an important figure in these developments and served as the prime minister of the northern region in the era of self-government from 1955 until he was murdered in 1966 after independence.

On the national scene, the sardauna was a powerful influence, but the NPC leader who served on the national level was al-Hajj Abu Bakr Tafawa Balewa (1912–1966), the first federal prime minister of Nigeria. Balewa was a modern-educated northerner who did not come from one of the ruling families but had become one of the leading men in the NPC. He recognized the need for significant modernization but hoped to accomplish this through gradual reform. He was able to act as a link between the more aristocratic and conservative northern leaders and the modern-educated southern politicians.

None of the three major political parties was able to break through the restrictions of regional interests, and the federal regime soon foundered on the provincial perspectives of the parties and the personal ambitions of many of the political leaders. The result was increasing political instability and regional rivalry. Early in 1966, eastern military officers revolted against the apparently northern-dominated federal regime, and they killed most of the high-ranking northern military officers and many of the major northern political leaders, including the sardauna and Balewa. During the following year, another coup occurred, and the possibility of northern secession was narrowly averted. Order was briefly restored by Lt. Col. Yakubu Gowon, a soldier of northern origin, but then the eastern region seceded and declared itself the independent state of Biafra. It was not until 1970 that unity was restored.

In this tumultuous context, the NPC presents a mixed example of Islamic adaptationism. It shows that traditional Islamic forces based on organizations created in the eighteenth and early nineteenth centuries could adapt to the changing political conditions involved in the emergence of Nigerian nationalism, but the adaptation was a structural adaptation made to preserve a conservative and traditional order. The NPC did not represent a modernization of the style or content of Islam in Nigeria as it tried to adopt the forms of modern politics in order to preserve traditional privileges. As a result, the NPC became identified as a parochial, conservative force that, in the end, failed to protect its patrons. Following the unrest of 1966, the old leadership and the traditional structures were significantly weakened as influential forces in Nigeria. The experience of the NPC illustrates that simply adapting forms and structures may not be sufficient as a means of providing continuity in the Islamic experience.

The Muridiyyah of Senegal. Some traditional Islamic organizations have effectively adapted themselves to modern economic conditions as well as changing their political roles. In Senegal, a branch of the Qadiriyyah emerged at the beginning of the twentieth century as a major economic force, and it was able to operate within the context of economic modernization. The leading figure in this transformation was Ahmad Bamba (d. 1927), who came from a family of religious teachers that had ties with the nineteenth-century militant, Ma Ba. Bamba had studied in Mauritania and had soon gained a reputation for both learning and piety. He had established the Muridiyyah branch of the Qadiriyyah in 1886, and for many years, the French suspected him of planning a holy war. However, under Ahmad Bamba, the old *tariqah* holy war tradition was transformed into a vigorous economic enterprise.

Followers of Bamba were encouraged to establish agricultural settlements, and those became the focal points for the *tariquah*'s activity. By hard work and the ability of the order to provide investment capital, the settlements became major peanut producers. Since that was Senegal's major cash crop export, the order was rapidly integrated, as an order, into the emerging modern sector of the Senegalese economy. In a context in which French rule reduced the major tribal leaders to subservient civil servants, the active order also was able to become an influential political force, although it took few major political initiatives.

The Muridiyyah is conservative in style, maintaining the old marabout structure of a "saint-dominated" *tariqah* and considerable tolerance in enforcing the rules of the faith. The emphasis in the *tariqah* is on hard work and obedience to the leader rather than on performing the five prayers or strict adherence to what fundamentalists would consider essential Islamic practices. In this way, the order maintains the old style of Islam while being active in modern life.

The transformation has been an effective one during most of the twentieth century, and it has only recently been challenged by the development of agricultural resources and industry along more modern lines and by the growing proportion of Senegalese workers who are inspired more by self-conscious economic interests than by a pious desire to serve an order. The order has also been challenged by the emergence of fundamentalist Islam among some of the modern-educated Senegalese. It is worth remembering, however, that the Muridiyyah was able by adaptation and transformation to survive the changes that were involved in the French imperial control, in the emergence of nationalism, in the modernization of the Senegalese economy, and in the change from colony to independent state. If the order was able to cope with all those changes, it may be that this type of adaptable traditional institution will be able to maintain its "tradition" of coping in the next stage of development.

That organization illustrates the vitality of some of the traditional Islamic organizations in the contexts of both colonial rule and independence. By reorganizing structures and assuming modern functions, older Muslim groups have effectively adapted to the changing conditions of the twentieth century. That adaptation was not a universal experience, and many such groups have played a decreasing role in the life of Islamic society in Africa. However, in most areas, there have been at least some groups that have made the transition relatively successfully.

Adaptationism: New Associations and Movements

A second type of adaptation has been the development of new organizations, sometimes building on past traditions and at other times creating new structures for the expression of the Islamic experience. When Islam can be identified with the emerging modern and national identities, it has a special appeal, and it has played an important role in the development of nationalist feelings. In spirit and style, many such groups have been reformist or fundamentalist, often mixing support for modern-oriented social reform with a fundamentalist reaffirmation of Islam. In Africa, as in other parts of the modern Islamic world, this adaptation has often taken the form of new associations.

Islam and Political Parties. One common type of modern association in Africa is the political party, and one interesting feature of the African Islamic experience is that few of the parties have been explicitly Islamic, in contrast to the experience in Indonesia or India. Muslims have been politically active, and Islam is seen as having relevance to political life. Islam has played a significant role in defining nationalist sentiments and shaping political programs, but parties have been influenced by Islam more than they have been created as the vehicles for implementing a specifically Islamic program.

That situation is at least partially the result of the political context in which the parties emerged in the twentieth century. In most of the Sudanic countries, Muslims are not a dominant majority. They are usually a bare majority or a strong minority, which means that explicitly Islamic parties would have real difficulty in achieving nationwide support. That fact is certainly illustrated by the experience of those political parties that were the product of a transformation of the older Islamic organizations. The NPC in Nigeria and the Ummah party in the Sudan could not gain significant support among the non-Muslim peoples in their country, which hindered their effective development as leading parties. The NPC was crushed by the factional and regional strife to which it had contributed, and the Ummah leadership was unable to create an operable solution to the civil war in the Sudan. In addition, those parties were not so much explicitly Islamic parties as they were parties formed by specific groups of Muslims to represent their particular interests.

When Muslim parties were formed, they often remained small and were viewed by many as being divisive. The nationalist leadership in Ghana, for example, strongly opposed the Muslim Association party because it introduced religion into politics, and such parties were banned in 1957 when Nkrumah came to power. It is only in an area like Mauritania, where Muslims are a dominant majority, that a party like the Union Socialiste des Musulmans Mauritaniens was possible. Even in Gambia, with a similar Muslim majority, the Muslim Congress party formed in 1952 was unable to succeed on the basis of appealing to common religious faith.

The common and most effective organizational participation of Muslims in politics was through cultural and religious associations that allied themselves with broader political parties rather than forming separate parties themselves. This type of structure provided a vehicle for presenting Muslim views and influencing political development. In the pluralist societies of Sudanic Africa, this mode of operation seems to have been the most effective means of representing and defending the political interests of the Muslim communities.

West African Wahhabis. One of the best examples of the interaction between a Muslim association and the general political scene is the experience of the West African "Wahhabis,"[21] a group of Islamic modernist reformers who were active in the area following World War II. For centuries, Muslim students from West Africa had studied in the Arab East, although never in very large numbers. The common pattern in the eighteenth and nineteenth centuries was for a scholar with a sound Islamic education gained in West Africa to go on pilgrimage and study in the holy cities and often at al-Azhar. This experience often had the effect of inspiring the scholar to work for Islamic reform when he returned to his homeland. This pattern has continued during the twentieth century.

West African Muslim students in Cairo during the first half of the twentieth century often had close contact with the Salafiyyah tradition and often learned much from members of the Muslim Brotherhood. A small group of such students returned to West Africa during World War II and settled in Bamako, where they felt there was a receptivity to ideas of Muslim reform among some of the population and the power of more conservative religious leaders was limited.

The young Azharis (former al-Azhar students) soon became active in organizing informal discussion groups and evening lectures. They advocated ideas and practicies similar to those of Salafiyyah groups elsewhere, and they opposed the popular local religious practices that seemed to recognize the *tariqah* leaders as special intermediaries to God. They upheld the right of *ijtihad* and opposed blind adherence to the traditional schools of law and thought. They strongly urged their listeners to study the Quran and the Sunnah and to base their lives on those sources and the examples of the *salaf.*

The young teachers gained a substantial following and soon requested permission from the French to establish a school. That request was denied for a time, although their popularity increased. In 1949, the teachers organized a formal association called the Subannu al-Muslimin, which was identified by its ideological position rather than by a particular ethnic group or social class. It rapidly expanded in French West Africa, and its schools were well attended and respected, although the French authorities were not helpful, and the association encountered the resistance of prominent conservative religious leaders. The Subannu revived interest in locally led education and interest in religious studies and the Arabic language outside of the traditional conservative schools.

This was an era of growing political activism in French West Africa and the emergence of elective political offices and parties. Members of the Subannu were involved in that activism as individuals. One of the major political issues of the 1950s was whether French West Africa would emerge as a single political unit or as a series of separate states. The Subannu, as a regional organization working to build a broader sense of Islamic community, supported the goal of the larger political entity and came to ally itself with a similar group within the largest party in the region, the Rassemblement Democratique Africain (RDA), which worked for the same goal. As the RDA began to utilize a more Islamic political vocabulary, this cooperation continued. The result, however, was not the creation of a Subannu political organization but, rather, the creation in 1957 of a large cultural association, which included the leaders of the Subannu, called the Union Culturelle Musulmane (UCM). The UCM attracted many well-known political leaders and influenced party platforms.

The goals of the UCM as stated in its statutes provide a good example of the mode of action of associations of its type.

> The association will not intervene in political affairs except for that which affects Islamic education and cult. It must not follow upon the heels or be under the dependence of any specific party, yet may accept assistance and the support of the elected representatives and of all those who hold authority. The association will have no link with any of the legal schools or sects within Islam. It will trace its patterns of behavior on the moderate judgment of the first companions of the Prophet. . . . The oral motto of the association will be "We worship but Allah" and the practical motto: "The obligation to conform to the Sunna."[22]

In this way, the history of the West African Wahhabis shows a reformist experience with a fundamentalist tone.

Hamallism. Another West African Islamic movement mixed the themes of social reformism and traditional organization. This movement, often called Hamallism, had its origins in a reform group within the Tijaniyyah

Tariquah. It began with the teaching of Shaykh Sidi Muhammad ibn Abd Allah (d. 1909), who attempted to restore Tijaniyyah devotional practice to a form that had been initially set by Ahmad al-Tijani. That restoration involved reciting a particular prayer eleven rather than twelve times and thus utilizing a prayer "rosary" with eleven instead of twelve beads. Although seemingly a minor matter, this reform attacked the authority of the leading Tijaniyyah teachers in the region, and it ultimately became a political matter since the Tijaniyyah establishment was recognized by the French authorities.

The movement did not gain wide support until after Sidi Muhammad's death, when it was led by his disciple, Hamah Allah ibn Muhammad Haydara (or Shaykh Hamallah, 1883–1943), from whose name the movement came to be called the Hamalliyyah or Hamallism. Under Hamallah, the movement became an advocate of social and religious reform. Although he had had a sound Islamic education, Hamallah soon became more respected for his mysticism and asceticism than for his scholarship. He lived a secluded life of meditation and taught only a selected few students, through whom his influence spread rapidly. Through his personal life he was a challenge to the more worldly and wealthy religious teachers, and the contrast in their life-styles gave added emphasis to his reformist teachings.

Athough no evidence was ever found to link Hamallah directly to anti-French action, the French administration mistrusted him and periodically deported him. However, that mistrust only spread his teachings to those places he was sent to, first in Mauritania and then in the Ivory Coast. Under this kind of pressure, Hamallah adopted a shortened version of the prescribed prayers, which is permissible in times of war or great personal danger. He gradually became a symbol for Muslims who opposed the rule of the French.

The Hamallists, as their numbers grew, came into increasing conflict with the followers of conservative teachers. This tension was strengthened by the social reform programs advocated by the Hamallist movement, which stressed the full equality of all people, supported the liberation of women, and opposed the materialism of the established religious leaders. Although Hamallah did not openly oppose the French, he condemned those Muslims who cooperated with them. The movement appealed to many in the lower classes and other people of more humble origins, and it can be considered as being a socioreligious protest movement in the prenationalist era.

Both Hamallah's aloof style and the French policy of sending him into exile meant that his followers were subject to little organizational discipline, and the movement tended to become a series of local, uncoordinated factions. Those factions had a tendency to become extremist, some adopting clearly heterodox practices such as facing west, toward the ocean across which Hamallah would return, rather than toward Mecca while praying and sometimes altering the profession of faith to state, "There is no god but God, and Hamallah is our shaykh." One of the most extreme of Hamallah's followers was Yaʿqub Sylla, who developed an even more extreme egalitarianism by rejecting all traditional authority of the tribal chiefs and marabouts and the authority of Islamic law. His followers established separate communities in which property and earnings were held in common under the local head of the group. Although Sylla's extremism was rejected by Hamallah, his faction continued to have influence in many areas, and after World War II, that influence was utilized by some in the RDA to help undermine the position of those chiefs who supported the French.

A more intellectual tradition of "orthodox" Hamallism also had a long-term impact. Hamallah had converted a major Tijaniyyah leader, Tierno Bokar Salif Tall (d. 1940), who "derived from the intellectual and mystical content of Hamallah's teaching the notion that Islam—or perhaps more precisely, reformed Tijanism—was a religion that an African could be proud of *qua* African."[23] That tradition represented an African Islam that opposed colonial rule and stressed equality and social reform. Through Tierno Bokar, Hamallism influenced a number of significant political leaders, like Modibo Keita, later president of Mali, and Diori Hamani, later president of Niger.

Hamallism was one of the factors that helped to prepare the way for African socialism in the region. It provided a justification in Islamic terms for egalitarianism and social reform, and it began the process of mobilizing people outside of the small group of educated elite in support of nationalist and socialist programs.

The Republicans of Mahmud Muhammad Taha. The most common Islamic associations in Sudanic Africa are not large movements or inter-regional organizations. Instead, the dynamism of regular religious activity and the expansion of Islam are usually centered in numerous smaller associations and clubs in the cities and towns of the region. These groups are often built around an individual intellectual whose special ideas form the basis for the organization's activities. In ideological content, the associations range from conservative Quranic study groups to radical secularists studying the latest liberation movement. Some of the groups have a formal organization, and others are little more than a group of people who regularly share a table in a coffeehouse. Groups of this type are not all religious in orientation, and those that are, are similar to informal groups that may meet regularly for playing musical instruments or dancing.

The smaller associations are the continuation of some more traditional Islamic groups that were similarly organized. They provide regular meeting places and are the center of informal social and intellectual life for many people. For the modern-educated Muslims, the regular weekly meeting of the local *tariqah* and the discussions and teachings of the local shaykh are no longer relevant or satisfying, and many such Muslims have formed their own club or found their own guide, whose activities and message relate more directly to the lives of people living in the conditions of modern change.

An excellent example of a well-organized small association is the Republican Brothers and Sisters in the Sudan, led by Mahmud Muhammad

Taha. It is primarily centered in Khartoum and Omdurman, although people from many parts of the Sudan who live in the capital are members. At the end of World War II, an informal discussion group centered around Mahmud favored Sudanese independence rather than unity with Egypt but was unsatisfied with the political parties that were emerging. As a result, its members formed the Republican party in 1945. The party did not become a significant element in Sudanese politics, but Mahmud's vigor and hard work succeeded in gathering a group of followers that survived the era of party politics.

The Republicans became a group dedicated to the revival of a reformed Islam. The heart of Mahmud's teaching was that Muslims should apply the basic principles of Islam rather than work to perpetuate forms and structures that developed as a result of specific historical circumstances. He distinguished within the Quran itself between the Meccan message, when universal principles were presented as the guide for religious faith, and the message after the establishment of the community in Medina. The second message prescribed rules that were designed specifically for the needs of that particular time and place, and as such, it is an important part of the message because it shows how the basic principles can be applied, but it is the example of that period, not its specific rules, that should be followed. Islam, properly understood, is the true basis for a society that is based on justice and equality and rejects all aspects of inequality. In this framework, the Republicans support full equality for women and oppose the special role of traditional religious leaders. Republicans are active in speaking at local cultural clubs, and they have won a small following among university students. Republican Sisters as well as Brothers take an active part in presenting the message of the group, often acting as street-corner preachers.

The Republicans were opposed by traditional Islamic groups as being heretical, and radicals and communists felt they were too tied to a fundamentalist style of thought. At times, the vigorous speeches of Mahmud and his followers resulted in public disturbances and created difficulties with the authorities, both before and after independence. But the organization managed to survive all the political changes and to bring a message of Islamic reform and revival in the Sudan. As such, it represents an important type of modern Islamic association: the small, dedicated association that, in functional terms, is the successor to the *tariqah*s in providing a vehicle for the expression of Islamic faith and for small-group social cohesion.

Islam and the Political Development of African States

Two important features of the political development of those African states in which Muslims form a significant proportion of the population are the general evolution of a state-supported ideology and the consolidation of national unity. In each of those areas, the states both were part of broader African trends and had distinctive characteristics influenced by Islam.

Development of National Ideology. It has been noted that in many areas of the Muslim world, Islam was a factor in providing popular support for the nationalist efforts to eliminate imperialist control and that support was often more in terms of providing a non-European identity than in specific doctrines or institutions. However, nationalism before independence was a general sentiment more than a concrete ideology. It is possible to unite most people in a country in the struggle for independence; it is after gaining independence that the real task of formulating a national ideology and program has to be faced.

In terms of the development of an ideology, it has been said that "Africa had to debate on Europe's terms before she could debate on her own."[24] That statement does not mean simply that Africans had to achieve political independence before they could develop their own perspectives; it means that on a more profound intellectual level, Africans first had to work through and out of perspectives that they had developed by receiving modern European educations and inheriting European-style political structures.

In independent Africa a common, though not universal, pattern is that the new states were first dominated by the politicians and structures that had been created by the imperialist-nationalist experience. The new political elite was Western educated and often more European than African in basic sentiments, and the new political systems were usually multiparty parliamentary systems. However, during the 1960s, in virtually every African state, that initial structure was significantly modified if not overthrown.

The second phase in the political evolution was also in many ways dominated by Western ideas. The parliamentary systems were liberal in ideology and often conservative in their socioeconomic views, and the first challenge came from the more radical, usually Marxist, European traditions. The result was that during the 1960s, many one-party regimes advocating various types of radical socialism replaced the earlier government structures. Often this change was accomplished by the actions of one of the early nationalist leaders, who turned his party into the dominant party and gained for himself an apparent monopoly of political power. That is what happened in Ghana under Kwame Nkrumah, Chad under Francois Tombalbaye, Mali under Modibo Keita, Guinea under Sékou Touré, and Tanzania under Julius Nyerere. As was the case in other parts of the Islamic world, the early 1960s was a time of the growing dominance of radical socialism in Africa. The major opposition groups in the states that did not come under this type of leadership were the representatives of this new force in African politics. It was only in a few, though sometimes major, states that the initial parliamentary period was not succeeded by a radical socialist phase—in Nigeria, the Sudan, and Upper Volta, it was the less radical military officers who gained control.

Radical socialism did not succeed in establishing permanent regimes in many areas. Its ideological vigor, and sometimes its doctrinaire inflexibility, roused considerable opposition. In addition, there was the vague feeling, sometimes more explicitly expressed than at other times, that radical socialism, like liberal parliamentarianism before it, was an "imported" dogma that was not directly suited to the African context. Many of its ideas were recognized as sound, but the total package was not considered appropriate for the sentiments and needs of the various countries. Radical socialism tended to create large-scale bureaucracies and dominating central political regimes that, however much the socialist leaders might talk about African socialism, did not fit the African traditions of tribal communalism and gentle decentralization.

As a result, in many areas, a third phase in the development of national ideologies had emerged by the end of the 1960s. The primary theme in this new phase was the effort to create a true synthesis of African and modern elements, not just a haphazard adoption of a few African symbols by basically European-oriented intellectuals and politicians. In addition, the new ideologies were to attempt to break down the long-standing division between the ruling elite and the general population. The bureaucracies of the era of independence had been fundamentally no closer to the masses than the imperial administration had been, and the new politicians had been no less jealous of their prerogatives than the old imperialists.

What was required was a convergent development of both the elite and the masses. As one sympathetic observer has explained:

> A new politics began to emerge. This proposed that the leaders in power would have to turn their backs on elitist self-promotion: would have to abandon, that is, the project of becoming a ruling class. . . . This politics looked for a comparable movement of cultural convergence from the direction of the masses. Just as the ruling few must break with the colonial heritage, so must the many begin to win clear of handicaps imposed by the precolonial heritage. No one need be asked to abandon the shrines of the ancestors; but the ancestors must learn to speak the language of modern reality, or else accept retirement into cultural decay.[25]

One of the pioneers in this new mood of African ideology was Julius Nyerere in Tanzania, a remarkably durable political leader who has survived and helped to shape the major transitions in his country. He was a major nationalist leader whose party emerged as the strongest in the multiparty stage of self-government. After independence, that party formed the one-party regime and was committed to a relatively radical socialist program, which began to create a large government bureaucracy. The new era was initiated in Tanzania by the Arusha Declaration in 1967, which set in motion movements of economic decentralization and popular participation that are characteristic of the emerging, more African ideological and political structures. In other areas, the rejection of radical socialism was less successful in its results and more violent in its implications. The Authenticity movement in Chad, initiated in 1973, and the national redemption and national renewal policies in Ghana and Upper Volta were attempts to create a new synthesis that were not as successful.

The role of Islam in this changing context is diverse and changing. In the days of parliamentary politics, Islam frequently provided at least one element of the identity of political action groups. On the whole, it was a conservative and more traditional Islam assuming a modern format, as was the case with the NPC in Nigeria and the Ansar and Khatmiyyah parties in the Sudan.

Islam also had a part in the emergence of radical socialism. In the early days of partisan politics, groups like the Hamallists had prepared the way for a popular acceptance of the more radical programs. During the second era, reformist styles of Islam came into prominence. Older leaders and traditional structures were rejected by the new radicals, and both reformist modernism and fundamentalism could provide popularly acceptable reasons for the radicals' attacks on traditional Islam. Although the radical socialists attacked the institutions of traditional Islamic society, they did not attack basic Islamic principles and often were careful to identify the new ideology as being in accord with the fundamentals of Islam. Although there was not as much effort to expound Islamic socialism in Africa as there was in the Arab East, some of the same sentiments existed.

In the emerging radical socialism, Islam was clearly a subordinate feature. As was the case of Touré's socialism in Guinea, "Islam was disciplined in the interests of a unified national development."[26] Although secularist in the sense of working to destroy the political relevance of the traditional Islamic institutions, there was less secularism than in the liberal ideology of the separation of religion and politics that had been frequently expressed in the parliamentary era. Radical socialism opened the way for a more radical modernist Islam and began the process of the reintegration of Islam into national ideologies.

In the emerging third phase, this new style of Islam was to play a role of growing importance. During the second phase, observers often spoke of the politicization of religion, a phrase that reflects both the subordination of Islam in a broader ideological framework and the secularist assumptions of the observer. By the end of the 1960s, a reverse process was beginning, but it went largely unnoticed. It is only since the rise of the Islamic revolutions of the 1970s that it is possible to recognize the beginnings of the "religionization" of politics in the preceding decade. Although the attempt to build a more authentically African ideology in the late 1960s was not confined to Muslim areas, in those areas, Islam was a part of the process.

In areas with strong Muslim populations, the transition took a number of forms. In Guinea, as in Tanzania, the transition was made by the ruling group itself under the leadership of Sékou Touré, and by 1967, doctrinaire radical socialism was being replaced. It had created a large bureaucracy rather than a successful socialist state, and the regime moved in the direction of what can be called African populism. In 1967 a "cultural revolution" was launched to bring the state closer to the people. The state was no less radical than before, but now it was more distinguishably Guinean. In an exchange quoted in 1968, some of the spirit of that transition can be seen. A young, educated Guinean complained that inflation had made it impossible for him to afford the price of a pair of trousers, and a revolutionary intellectual responded, "We did not take our independence just for trousers." At the same time, even one of the most fervent supporters of the government noted that "Guineans want to be as realistic as possible. We don't want to live on slogans."[27]

In the effort to stress the authentically local nature of the radicalism, there was a great celebration in Guinea in 1968 to accompany the return of the remains of Alfa Yaya, a religious leader in Futa Jallon who had been exiled by the French in 1911 and had died in Mauritania. The regime was seen as the true heir of the religious radicalism of Futa Jallon, which had been the source of holy wars in the eighteenth and nineteenth centuries. Although often viewed at the time as an example of the influence of Maoism, the transformation of Guinean radicalism, like the Arusha Declaration in Tanzania, was more the beginning of an authentically indigenous radical tradition that was more closely tied to local culture than the previous radical socialism had been.

In many areas, the debate was shifting, and Africa was beginning to debate "on its own terms" rather than on "Europe's terms." Revolutions in the Sudan and Somalia in 1969 and evolution elsewhere brought the end of both parliamentary "liberalism" and ideologically Western radical socialism. There was a revival of emphasis on religious values and the Islamic tradition, although that revival did not mean a restoration of old-style Islamic leadership and institutions.

Islam and Consolidation of National Unity. Achieving a sense of national unity within the boundaries created by the imperial experience has been a major problem for many African governments as sectional, tribal, and ethnic loyalties have provided the basis for sentiments that have undermined a broader sense of national integration. Islam's role in this area is varied and depends upon local conditions. At times, it represents an important vehicle for supratribal or sectional ideas, and at other times, it reinforces the identity of the divisive elements.

In areas where Muslims are a relatively dominant majority, the strength of the Islamic influence has varied. In some countries like Guinea, it has been combined with other nationwide sentiments to be a factor in national unification. However, in areas where internal social and ethnic divisions are strong, Islam has not been a sufficient unifying force for those divisions to be overcome. The experience of Pakistan has been repeated on a much smaller scale in Zanzibar, for example, where the appeal to the common Islamic faith of all Zanzibaris was not sufficient to overcome the divisions among the Arabs, Shirazis, and mainland Africans. The era of party politics leading up to independence was marked by a vigorous and sometimes violent conflict among groups of Muslims for whom ethnic identity was more important than the common faith.

The problem of the relation of Islam to national unity has been most frequently discussed in a number of states in the Sudanic area where a significant proportion of the population is not Muslim. In those states, Muslim and non-Muslim groups tend to be geographically concentrated, mixing only in some of the larger urban areas. Under these conditions, Islam has reinforced sectional and ethnic divisions by being identified with one particular group or section of a country, which has frequently resulted in tensions and, at times, major civil wars. The largest of these conflicts have been in the Sudan, Chad, and Ethiopia.

Those civil wars have been identified in a number of different ways. Some people have seen them as basically religious conflicts, and others have described them as essentially cultural-ethnic clashes. Another feature of the wars is that they can be seen as conflicts between central governments and regional or peripheral forces in countries with insufficiently integrated political systems. No single explanation of the conflicts is sufficient, but, to some extent, each of the dimensions of the conflicts must be considered if the wars are to be understood. Islam is not the sole cause, nor can it be ignored as it played a role in giving form to the conflicts as they developed.

In the Sudan, Ethiopia, and Chad, Islam provided a unifying feature for regions that were ethnically and tribally divided, and thus it helped to define the conflicts as interregional ones within the countries rather than being simply wars of tribal or ethnic separatism. In the Sudan, the Islamic groups were the dominant forces in the central government, and in Chad and Ethiopia, they were fighting against the established governments.

The Sudanese civil war had long-standing historical roots. An Arab-Islamic civilization was firmly established in the northern part of the country, and in the nineteenth century, various attempts were made by the governments in Khartoum, both the Turko-Egyptian regime and then the Mahdists, to extend their control into the non-Muslim southern areas. Those attempts were accompanied by exploitative commercial relations and the development of the slave trade. By the end of the century, the southern tribes had developed a tradition of mistrusting outsiders. The British in the twentieth century kept the southern provinces isolated from northern influence, and the process of modernization and economic development was much slower in the south. When nationalism developed, it was largely a northern phenomenon, and the independent state of the Sudan was dominated by northern politicans. The southern Sudanese feared northern domination, and the "Sudanization" of government services favored northerners to an extent that aroused suspicion in the southern region. A mutiny of southern soldiers in 1955 set the stage for a long conflict that rose and fell in intensity until 1972, when a new constitutional regime, which recognized southern autonomy within the Sudan, was created as a settlement for the war.

During the era of conflict, the early northern nationalists had difficulty in dealing with the problem. Political activity had developed within a framework of Muslim institutions and ideas, and Islam seemed to most Sudanese leaders to be a natural part of the concept of a unified Sudan. As a result, the leaders of both nationalist traditions—those advocating unity with Egypt and supported by the Khatmiyyah and those advocating an independent Sudan and supported by the Ansar—developed a national consciousness in which Islam was a key element. The idea of a fully secular state was not a part of their political vocabulary, which made compromise with the southern leaders difficult. Similarly, the southerners viewed every attempt at national unification as an attack upon the southern region, and they also had difficulty in accepting compromises. It was not until a new generation of leaders emerged in both regions that the 1972 settlement was possible. At that time, pragmatic military commanders and politicans were able to work out a special arrangement. The settlement occurred in the era of the third phase of the development of national ideology, in which the search for authenticity opened the way for an acceptance of the special traditions of the southern region, and the destruction of many of the institutions of traditional Sudanese society freed the ideology from dependence on Mahdist symbols as well as from the restrictions of the perspectives of the old parliamentary regimes.

Neither Chad nor Ethiopia has been as fortunate in resolving its conficts. In Chad, the Muslims are largely in the northern part, and they remained relatively aloof from modernizing developments during the colonial era. It was the southerners who had become the best educated and the most developed by the time of independence in 1960. Although the initial parliamentary regime provided a careful balance between Muslims and southerners, it was the latter, under Francois Tombalbaye, who were the clearly dominant force. The awareness of this domination was strengthened with the creation of Tombalbaye's one-party regime in 1962-1963. Increasing taxes and inefficient, sometimes corrupt, administrators soon led to some rural revolts, which were scattered and disorganized.

Muslim politicians opposed to the Tombalbaye regime created an organization and a basic ideology when they established the Front de Libération Nationale du Tchad (FROLINAT) in 1966. French military intervention on the side of the government did not succeed in crushing the militant opposition, and FROLINAT gained more support internationally because of that interference. The liberation group represented a variety of opponents of the regime, but most of them had a common Islamic identity. Along with the calls for social justice, FROLINAT also demanded the recognition of Arabic as an official language. The group received substantial support at various times from Libya and the Sudan. Primarily, FROLINAT was more of a liberation group composed of Muslims than an Islamic movement. Its programs were not distinctively Islamic in character and were aimed at giving the Muslim sections of the population appropriate influence in the government and its policymaking processes. That distinction means that the Chadian civil war was a sectional struggle for power with overtones of personal religious identity rather than a religious holy war. However, as a conflict between Muslims and non-Muslims, the war attracted the attention of the rest of the Islamic world, and the religious dimension of the conflict was a means by which FROLINAT could obtain international aid.

In Ethiopia, there is a substantial Muslim population and a long tradition of conflict between the Muslims and the independent Christian state. During the twentieth century, Ethiopian Muslims have faced non-Muslim control from two directions. In the latter part of the nineteenth century, Christian forces had consolidated control over a wide area to form the Ethiopian empire, which came to include many Muslim areas. In addition, Italian imperial control was established on the Red Sea coast in the colony of Eritrea. In that province, most of the coastal population was Muslim, and the highland population was primarily Christian. The Italians conquered all of Ethiopia in 1936 and then, in 1941–1942, lost control to the British. Following World War II, the future of the whole region was defined in a series of major diplomatic settlements, and the Ethiopian empire under Haile Selassie, who had come to power in 1916, once again became an independent state. However, there was difficulty in defining the status of Eritrea.

In Eritrea itself, Muslim leaders and tribal notables formed the Muslim League, which demanded independence. That demand was not the product of a long-standing nationalist movement but, rather, emerged out of the desire of Muslim Eritreans to avoid coming under Ethiopian imperial control. Although there were a number of significant tribal divisions and factions, Islam provided a basis for a regional unity of goals. Great power and UN negotiations did not, however, lead to Eritrean independence, the argument being that almost half of the population was Christian and desired some form of union with Ethiopia. A federal system was created in 1950–1952 that would guarantee Eritrean autonomy but place it within the Ethiopian state. Haile Selassie soon worked to reduce the separate arrangements for the province and, in 1962, abolished the federal system, making Eritrea an integral part of Ethiopia.

Opponents of the federation left the country and, during the 1950s, were active in trying to gain the support of Arab and Muslim states for their cause. The Eritrean Liberation Front (ELF) emerged out of this activity and by 1961 was an established group with offices in various Arab capitals. The 1962 annexation of Eritrea gave the ELF added impetus. It began to organize sporadic local resistance among Muslim tribes in the province, and in the early 1960s, the ELF continued along the lines of the earlier Muslim League as a primarily Muslim separatist movement led by conservative tribal and religious leaders. Its major theme was Muslim opposition to Christian control. Its primary goal was Muslim independence, and it did not advocate programs of social reform or significant modernization.

Because of its limited goals, the ELF made relatively slow progress during the 1960s. It was unable to appeal to the Christian half of the Eritrean population, and its younger, modern-educated members became increasingly dissatisfied with its conservative policies. However, through its diplomacy, the ELF gained increasing support within the Arab world, in terms of both diplomatic support and direct material aid for the war effort.

The repressive regime of Haile Selassie aroused growing opposition among the Christian Eritreans, and they gradually joined forces with the

ELF. That combination strengthened the more radical groups within the organization, and finally, in 1969, a separate, more radical group called the Eritrean People's Liberation Front (EPLF) was formed. With the creation of the EPLF, the Eritrean movement passed beyond the stage of Muslim separatism into a phase of working for a more unified, Eritrean national resistance. The cement for this broadening of the movement was a more radical ideology, which was acceptable to both Christians and Muslims. The movement for Eritrean liberation still retains a strong thread of Muslim separatism, but Islam by itself was not able to provide a basis for a unified national movement. Since the creation of the EPLF, a great deal of effort has been expended in trying to build effective cooperation between the two branches, with varying degrees of success. In that effort, conservative Islam represents an obstacle, but a more radical Islam may be emerging as a product of ELF—EPLF interaction.

Summary

Islam is a dynamic force in Africa, manifesting itself in many ways, and the twentieth-century Islamic experience shows a mixture of the basic styles in coping with the changing conditions of the modern world. In a sense, all Muslims have been adaptationists to a significant degree. Conservatives have continued, as best they can, to maintain existing structures and thought patterns, but often their effort has involved a degree of activism and adaptationism. Old-style organizations have been reshaped to meet new challenges, and even traditional religious figures like village holy men have been involved in a subtle transformation of life-style—as is illustrated by the village saint in the Sudan clinging to old customs but able to offer visitors Pepsi Cola cooled in his refrigerator.

Fundamentalism has been more a tone within movements than a foundation for distinct organizations. The West African Wahhabis, for example, were modernists in the Abduh tradition more than fundamentalists of the Saudi type. Individualism is also emerging as a modern style. The intellectual efforts to redefine the faith in a personally satisfying way, such as those by the Republicans in the Sudan, are a common part of the life of modern African Muslims. Islam can be said to be emerging as a religion as well as a way of life for many people of the continent. That idea does not involve a rigorous secularism so much as a redefinition of the meaning of faith in the context of modernizing societies.

Special Experiences of Islamic Minorities

More than one-fifth of the world's Muslims live as small minorities of less than 25 percent of the population of their countries. In some cases, they are the remnants of larger groups whose power has declined in the past century, and in other areas, they are new groups resulting from the expansion of Islam or the migration of Muslims. In either case, the experience of being a weak minority presents special problems not faced by Muslims elsewhere.

The real options for these minority communities are assimilation or a struggle to maintain a special, separate identity. Often, if the latter course is followed, Islam is part of an ethnic-communal identity that sets the Muslims off from the dominant majorities. Among the larger Muslim minorities, different groups follow different lines of adjustment, and intracommunal tensions arise. In this context of diversity, one can identify certain common programs that result. The first of those is the struggle for full independence, but although many Muslim minority groups have attempted to achieve independence, their position makes that goal unattainable unless there is a strong "outside" force willing to aid their struggle. A second program is to work for special recognition and autonomy within the home country. Formal arrangements of this type have often emerged, but there are always pressures on the autonomous groups as the dominant group or ideology continually works to reduce the special privileges of the Muslim minority, creating the conditions for both a more militant Muslim response and a gradual assimilation of Muslims. The third response to the minority situation is to maintain Islam as a personal faith, practiced in private, while conducting public life in conformity with the public life of the majority. This course of action is the one that is usually most strongly supported by the dominant majority leaders.

It is possible to discuss the experience of only a few of the many Muslim minority groups in a general survey of this type. However, by looking at some of those groups, the main lines of the minority Muslim experience can be seen.

Muslims in the Soviet Union

For Muslims in the old Russian Empire, the time of revolution and the overthrow of the imperial system came too soon. The tremendous vitality of the Muslim communities under the czar during the nineteenth and early twentieth centuries created a growing sense of Muslim identity and an increasingly effective synthesis of traditional and modern themes, but those activities had not crystallized into large-scale, effective Muslim movements or organizations by the time of the 1917 revolution.

In the process of revolution and counterrevolution that redefined the whole Russian Empire in the early days of the revolutionary regime, Muslims were actively involved in trying to shape their own future, and there were revolts against Russian control that succeeded in establishing independent Muslim states for short periods of time. Among the most important of those was the Basmachi movement. In 1917, Muslims sympathetic to the revolution had gathered in Khokand, in Central Asia, and announced the formation of an autonomous government, but that government soon clashed with a Russian Bolshevik republic that had been established in Tashkent and was better armed. The Khokand republic was crushed, and many of the Muslims of Turkestan moved into a position of more active and militant revolt against the new regime.

By 1919, Turkestani Muslim opposition had crystallized in the Basmachi movement, which was a nationalist movement built on the assumption that the new Bolshevik regime was as oppressive as the old imperial order. It was not, however, a traditionalist movement but a product of the emerging radical modernism that could be found in the Muslim intellectuals of the time. According to one of the leading intellectuals in the group, the struggle was waged for the defense of Islam and its task was "to strengthen in the East tendencies which conform to the structure of the East; working together with the Moslem people, to liberate them . . . and to give Eastern affairs into the hands of organizations possessing real vitality in the East."[28] The Basmachi attracted many of the active intellectuals of Russian Islam and also gained the support of Young Turk leaders like Enver Pasha, who fled to Central Asia after the defeat of his government in World War I and became active in supporting Muslim Turkish groups in a spirit of Pan-Turkish nationalism. Bolshevik forces were able to crush effective Basmachi resistance by 1923, but sporadic Basmachi fighting continued for more than a decade. Although the Basmachis had mounted a significant movement for Muslim independence and had gained popular support, the Muslim communities of Central Asia were ultimately unable to organize an effective opposition to the establishment of communist control.

For a period of time, it appeared possible to create an alliance between radical social reformers and Muslim nationalists as the emerging Muslim intellectual class, influenced by the ideas of Jadidism and other Muslim reformist movements, welcomed the goal of modernizing social transformation and became an active part of the communist movement. As the movements of open revolt were defeated and Moscow adopted a nationalities policy that resulted in the creation of various "autonomous" socialist republics in Central Asia, it was the young Muslim communist intellectuals who emerged as the leading spokesmen for the Islamic communities.

The leading figure of those spokesmen was Sultan Galiyev (d. 1930), who fully accepted the program of the Russian Communist party but developed a special interpretation of the application of communism in a Muslim context. He believed that it was necessary to establish revolutionary national governments before it would be possible to move into a stage of proletarian rule. He declared: "Since almost all classes in Muslim society have been oppressed formerly by the colonialists, all are entitled to be called proletarian. . . . It is therefore legitimate to affirm that the national movement in the Muslim countries is in character a socialist revolution."[29]

"Sultangaliyevism" became a rallying point for Muslim nationalist sentiments and soon was declared by the major communist leaders to be a "nationalist deviation." Its exponent was expelled from the party in 1923, and after imprisonment and exile, he disappeared and was probably executed. Nationalist deviation was a continuing part of the position of most Muslim communists, and they were all purged in the era leading up to World War II. Sometimes they had been part of movements of local resistance and, at other times, had simply continued the effort to revise communist dogma to adapt it to Islamic conditions. Their leaders were "double-adaptationists," attempting to create a synthesis by transforming both communism and Islam. By 1939, the old Muslim communist leadership had been effectively replaced by a new generation of intellectuals and administrators who were more fully in accord with the "orthodox" communist doctrine.

Following World War II, the primary styles of Islam were a conservative and a radical adaptationism. For the conservatives, the necessary adaptation was to create a personalized Islam that maintained the faith and participated in state-regulated religious activities. For the radicals, Islam was at most a part of a cultural heritage. The Islamic tradition continues to survive in the Soviet Union, but it does not have the visible dynamism of the late nineteenth century. Preserved in many ways by the conservative habits of personal life, it survives also as "a social bond of union which enables the Muslims to differentiate themselves from the Russians."[30]

Muslims in China

At the beginning of the twentieth century, the Muslims in China came into increasing contact with modernizing elements within and outside the country. They faced the choice of resistance or cooperation with the emerging political forces in China, particularly the republican and then later the communist movements. The basic issue was the survival of identifiable Muslim communities.

The Muslims in China have faced a variety of government policies. The nineteenth-century revolts brought direct suppression by the Manchu imperial forces, and the old imperial servants mistrusted Muslims. That situation meant, however, that the Muslims could be allies of the nationalist and republican movement that came to power early in the twentieth century. The new republican regime under Sun Yat-sen proclaimed that the republic was composed of five great peoples, one of whom was the Hui, or Chinese Muslims. Muslims participated actively in the nationalist cause, and some also joined the emerging communist movement. When the communists established the People's Republic in 1949, they continued to give recognition to the Muslim communities, but they emphasized that there were a large number of ethnic groups who were Muslim minorities, rather than a single people. The communist regime gave recognition to the various Muslim groups without emphasizing religion, since they hoped to reduce, if not eliminate, its influence.

The political history is reflected in the establishment of a large number of Muslim associations and groups. There were some that attempted to provide expression for an Islamic identity that was not tied to ethnic groups. In 1913, the Ahund Wang Hao-nan established the Muslim Progressive Society of China after he returned from a pilgrimage to the Middle East. He was impressed by the Islamic modernist movement and worked to strengthen Islamic education in China, emphasizing instruction in Arabic for children. The group became allied with the nationalist leader, Yuan Shih-kai. When he attempted to restore the monarchy with himself as emperor during

World War I, he was defeated, and the Muslim Progressive Society also disappeared.

Other pre–World War II groups that illustrate the adaptationist and reformist trends are the Muslim Literary Society, founded in 1926, and the Chinese Muslims Association, established in 1938. The Literary Society was an educational group that encouraged the study of the Quran and the *hadith*s and began a project of translating the Quran into Chinese. The Muslims Association was initiated by the government under a Muslim military commander to organize Muslim resistance to the Japanese.

In the civil war following World War II, the Muslims were not united in their participation, although most of the established leadership supported the Nationalist cause. With the establishment of the Nationalist government on Taiwan and the People's Republic on the mainland, the Muslim communities were divided. On Taiwan, the Chinese Islamic Association provides an organization for the Muslims who fled with the rest of the Nationalists. They maintain mosques and educational institutions and, for all practical purposes, have adopted an assimilationist style of religious life.

The People's Republic has maintained a dual line of policy, giving some recognition to special ethnic identities but following a vigorous line of limiting religious institutions and undermining traditional religious faith. The officially sponsored China Islamic Association maintains mosques and reading rooms and helps to organize pilgrimages to Mecca. It has provided a vehicle for passive assimilationism, which maintains a basis for Islamic identity while reforming or eliminating traditional Islamic structures. Land reform programs brought lands of religious endowments under government control, and independent Islamic schools were closed. Muslim education was placed in the hands of an Islamic institute, which is responsible for training Muslim leaders in the context of an appropriate communist ideology.

Many Muslims have accepted this transformation, but the option of direct resistance has also been chosen. In the perspective of the communists, these Muslim revolts were reactionary and antirevolutionary efforts to block the progress of the people, but according to the opponents of Chinese communism, the movements show the continuing opposition to the People's Republic. At no time since 1949 have Muslim revolts been a major challenge to the government although they, like the nineteenth-century revolts, have often had local significance. One anticommunist pamphlet lists communist-suppressed Muslim movements in 1946, 1950, 1952, 1957, and 1958 and refers to many more.[31] In nature, those movements were attempts to preserve a distinctive Muslim identity, often within the Chinese system, rather than movements for national independence. However, there were movements to establish an independent Islamic state in Honan in 1953, and another with the goal of establishing a Chinese Muslim republic with the slogan of "Glory to Islam."[32]

In China, the Muslim minorities have faced the same choices as elsewhere: assimilationism, cooperation, or militant separatism. Clearly, the militant option has failed, and cooperation, in China, is very one-sided. The Muslims cooperate in order to survive. The major form of Islam is increasingly a personalized assimilation with some government recognition of a special Islamic identity.

Muslim Minorities in the Middle East

Although Muslims are the dominant majority in most states in the Middle East, there are three areas in which that is not the case—Cyprus, Lebanon, and Palestine/Israel—and the situation of the Muslims in those countries is very different from that of the Muslim minorities in China or Russia. Although minorities or weak majorities in their own countries, these Muslims live in a region in which all the neighboring countries are strongly Muslim. As a result, it is possible for them to engage in Islamic affirmation with at least potential strong support from outside their own country.

In each of these three Middle Eastern cases, Islam is part of an ethnic or cultural identity that helps to characterize the Muslim groups. On Cyprus, the Muslims are Turks as well, and the interaction with the majority population is on the grounds of both Turkish-Greek and Muslim-Christian identities. Similarly, in Lebanon and Palestine/Israel, the Muslims are also clearly identifiable as Arabs.

In each of the countries, attempts have been made to create systems of balanced toleration and communal survival, with varying degrees of success. In the long run, no arrangement so far developed has eliminated potential conflict. On Cyprus, the Greek majority was inspired by the idea of unity with Greece, and the Turks feared it. When independence came, it was as an independent republic. The new regime had carefully outlined safeguards for the Turkish Muslim minority, but those did not work effectively. Increasingly, the two communities became geographically separated, with the Turks leaving most of the "mixed" areas under Greek pressure. The government itself was dominated by the Greek community, and the end result was a de facto communal partition of the island, which was solidified by the intervention of armed forces of the Turkish republic in 1974. Turkish military occupation of the northern third of the island continued throughout the decade. Communal autonomy is possible for the Turkish Muslim minority in Cyprus because outside assistance is available when the balanced federal system of the Cyprus republic fails to ensure Turkish communal survival.

The relationships among the religious (confessional) communities in Lebanon is more complex because of the large number of different communities within a single, small country. Because of historical conditions and the national development of Lebanon, when that country became independent at the end of World War II, it contained a number of clearly identifiable religious communities, with the largest being Maronite Christian, Greek Orthodox, and Shiᶜi and Sunni Muslim. A careful distribution of political power was worked out on the basis of those communal divisions, and until the 1970s, that distribution provided a basis for stability.

The Lebanese confessional political system depended on mutual confidence and trust among the various religious communities. It was based on the informal agreement that no group would attempt to disrupt the operation of the system and that none of them would call upon outside support to gain advantage within Lebanon. The agreement meant, in particular, that the Maronites and other Christians would not tie Lebanon too closely to the West and the Muslims would not attempt to integrate Lebanon into Pan-Arab unification schemes. The major crisis of the system before its breakdown came in 1958. At that time, a Maronite president attempted to gain an unconstitutional second term and was viewed as relying too much on Western support, and Lebanese Christians became fearful of the rising tide of Pan-Arab enthusiasm built up by the growing popularity of Nasser. However, after a brief civil war, the system was restored.

Although the confessional system was effective, it was inflexible, and it could not cope with the significant demographic and ideological changes that took place in Lebanon. The most important of those changes were the relative growth of the Muslim communities compared with the growth of the Christian ones; the emergence of a more secularist or leftist viewpoint, which was popular among younger Lebanese but could not be integrated into the confessional structure; and the growing importance of Palestinian revolutionary groups operating within Lebanon. By 1975, the pressures had built to the extent that a large number of religious and private groups organized small militias and began fighting in a multisided conflict, which destroyed the old Lebanese political system.

The Muslim communities reacted to the developments in a variety of ways. The Sunni community was most important in the major urban areas, and its leadership was associated with the compromise confessional structure. Although it was concerned about obtaining benefits for Muslims, it was largely conservative in terms of ideology and social programs. The Sunni conservative position was, however, conservative in that it was attempting to preserve the existing institutions, but those institutions themselves were the product of substantial modernization as the major Sunni associations in the late nineteenth and twentieth centuries had been influenced by the thinking of Abduh. The Sunni majority under this leadership adopted the option of maintaining a special religious communal identity within the confessional state.

There was a significant upsurge of effective communal organization among the Shiʿi Muslims during the 1960s. The Shiʿi community was largely rural and had little power within the confessional system, which was dominated on the Muslim side by the Sunni politicians. However, that situation changed when the Shiʿi leadership passed into the hands of Imam Musa al-Sadr (disappeared in 1978). Imam Musa was born in Iran, went to Lebanon in 1959 as a teacher, and soon became the center of an active organizing of Shiʿi communal life throughout the country. Through his charismatic personality, he was able to provide a link between the small Shiʿi upper class and the mass of poor peasants. With the new organization and leadership, the Shi'i community was able to assert itself as a political force. This revival did not involve the development of a new ideological position but was the product of communal reorganization for effective survival.

The second Lebanese communal leader who reoriented the role of his community was Kamal Jumblatt (killed 1977). Jumblatt came from a leading family in the Druze community, a Muslim group that had emerged out of the Shi'i tradition in medieval times and was prominent in the rural mountain areas in southern Lebanon. Jumblatt's basic political base was his traditional Druze following, but he emerged in the 1960s as one of the leading leftist politicians in Lebanon, and his Progressive Socialist party was one of the few groups to bridge the gap between confessional politics and the developing nonconfessional generation. This political activity did not, however, affect the nature of the religious community.

The Muslim communities in Lebanon were remarkably conservative in their adaptationism. Many Lebanese Muslims active in those communities were significantly modern in their orientations as individuals, but the communities themselves exhibited great continuity in their style and structure. Because of the virtually unique confessional structure, the Muslim communities adopted neither an assimilationist nor a separatist mode but remained basically communal in style, making alliances for pragmatic reasons. That position allowed them to survive but contributed to the inflexibility that led to the collapse of the system during the Lebanese civil war of 1975–1976.

The third major Muslim group in the Middle East that has faced the problem of being a minority is the Palestinian group. The complex history of the Arab-Israeli conflict has many dimensions and has been described in detail by many authors, but the Palestinians are not, strictly speaking, a Muslim minority. For the first half of the twentieth century, they represented the majority of the population in the territory of Palestine, but they came into conflict with the Zionist movement, which created the state of Israel in 1948. In a series of conflicts, the Palestinians became a minority in the Jewish state of Israel and established minority refugee communities in surrounding Arab states. Although the majority of the Palestinians are Muslim, a significant proportion of them are Christian. As a result of these factors, the experience of the Palestinians varies greatly from that of the more clearly Islamic minority groups.

There are two aspects of the Islamic dimension of the Palestine experience, and the first is internal. In the days before the establishment of the state of Israel, much of the leadership for the Palestinians came from Muslim notables, the best known of whom was al-Hajj Amin al-Husseini, the grand mufti of Jerusalem. The Palestinian leadership represented local power groups and often expressed itself in relatively cosmopolitan terms, appealing to Pan-Islamic and Pan-Arab support. As a result of repression and defeat, much of that leadership was eliminated as an effective force among the Palestinians.

During the 1960s, a new type of leadership emerged among the Palestinians, and it was drawn from the more modern-educated, younger generation. Some of the new leaders were Christian in background, and few had any significant religious training. The new leadership created the militant Palestinian organizations like Fatah under Yasir Arafat and the Arab National movement (later the Popular Front for the Liberation of Palestine) under George Habash. With these organizations, the Palestinians moved in the direction of a nationalist movement. They rejected thoroughly the idea of assimilation, either in Israel or in the various Arab states in which they found themselves. In establishing movements of national liberation, the Palestinians became secular in orientation, although many as individuals were firmly committed Muslims.

The second aspect of the Islamic dimension of the Palestine question is the impact of the issue upon Muslims elsewhere. Because of the central location of Palestine in the Islamic world and the special affection of Muslims for the shrines in the city of Jerusalem, the establishment of a non-Islamic state in Palestine roused great emotions, and opposition to Zionism became a rallying cry for many Muslim peoples. Ayatollah Kashani in Iran and the Muslim Brotherhood in Egypt organized volunteers in 1948 to fight the new state of Israel, and Muslim militants as far away as Indonesia and West Africa frequently included opposition to the establishment of a Jewish state in Palestine in their activist programs. The struggle with Israel became one way of measuring the success of the *ummah* in the modern world. As a result, many Muslim countries took a special interest in the Palestinian cause, and it became one aspect of modern Pan-Islamic ideas.

The experience of the Middle Eastern Muslim minorities presents aspects that are similar to such experiences elsewhere. However, because of their central position in the Islamic world, their experience has often varied significantly from that of minority Muslims elsewhere. The option of nationalist separatism is more viable in the Middle East, and assimilation not as easily imposed or accepted.

Muslim Minorities in the West

During the twentieth century, Islam has spread beyond the more traditional arena of Islamic activities in Africa and Asia, and in a variety of ways, Islam has been established in European and Western communities. Some Muslim communities, like those in the Balkan Peninsula, are the result of early Muslim expansions. In countries like Yugoslavia and Albania, they remain a significant part of the population and face the prospects of separatism or assimilation. However, as a result of the migration of peoples and ideas, Muslims have also created communities in other parts of the West. By the end of the 1960s, for example, Muslims were the second-largest religious group in France as a result of the Algerians who live in that country.

In most cases, these Muslim communities are basically immigrant ones and are identified with people who came from some Muslim land. How-one major Muslim movement is of a different origin, the Nation of Islam or the Black Muslim movement in the United States. Under the pressures of racial discrimination in the United States, some black leaders began to create separatist movements built on a variety of ideologies. One such movement came under the leadership of Elijah Muhammad (1897–1975) in 1934. Inspired by some contact with Islamic ideas, Elijah Muhammad developed an ideology of black separatism utilizing a particular interpretation of Islamic teachings. The organization insisted upon a strict moral code for its members and called for the creation of a separate black Islamic nation within the United States.

In its early history, the movement was limited to blacks and rejected white members, but changes were taking place within the movement by the 1960s. A leading figure in those changes was Malcolm X, who advocated a less racially exclusive organization. Malcolm and others in the movement had come into close contact with other Muslims and believed that Elijah Muhammad was in error in his doctrines on race. One leader in the organization described Malcolm's influence: "The primary influence in terms of changes was he foresaw the natural evolution of the movement. Malcolm saw the way Muslims were in the east. He came back with the description of what was supposed to be an Islamic community. He visualized the ultimate form of the organization was more like the Orthodox Islamic world."[33]

The inherent universalism of the Islamic revelation had its impact on the Nation of Islam movement, and it was being transformed from an ethnic separatist movement into a more cosmopolitan, nationalist liberation movement by the 1960s. Following Elijah Muhammad's death in 1975, his son Wallace Muhammad led the movement into the next step of a movement for cultural autonomy based on the special message of Islam. In this way, in the very different context of American society, the U.S. Muslim minority experiences many of the same problems and faces the same options as Muslim minorities elsewhere.

Conclusion

The first two-thirds of the twentieth century were years of great changes in the world of Islam. Utilizing conservative, fundamentalist, adaptationist, and individualist styles of Islamic experience, Muslims lived in the context of the vast transformations of modern history. Local conditions set limits to the options in many cases, but the great issues of the interaction of elements of continuity within the Islamic tradition with the ideas and structures presented by the West were a common theme.

At the beginning of the century, virtually all of the Islamic world was under European domination, and it was European power as well as European ideas that had to be faced. However, the diverse dynamism seen in the nineteenth century continued into the twentieth. Through movements of reform and nationalism, through redefinition and revival, Islamic societies not only survived, but most of them overcame foreign domination to emerge as independent states by the 1960s. By that time, intellectual adaptationism had created popular ideologies of a more radical style that were displacing the more conservative or religiously oriented ideologies. However, the more radical ideologies, too, were, in at least some ways, "imported" methods and concepts.

By the end of the 1960s, it was becoming clear that modernization was not simply adoption of Western ideologies and institutions, and indigenous forms of political organization and ideology were emerging. Those were clearly the product of the experience of modernization, but they were also, and just as clearly, tied in profound ways to the premodern heritage. It was this new development that dominated the Islamic experience of the 1970s.

7

The Resurgence of Islam:
The Spirit of the New Century

Introduction: Main Features of Change

The decade of the 1970s marked a time of major transformation and reorientation, and in the early years of its fifteenth century, beginning in 1979–1980, Islam was in the midst of a new surge of dynamism. In this vigorous reaffirmation, there are elements of both continuity and creativity. On the broadest level, this resurgence is the product of developments within modern society and the continuing appeal of the Islamic tradition.

The Transformation of the Modern

The impact of the "modern transformation" on the Islamic world is often noted, but during the 1970s, a less commonly observed but equally important aspect of the modern dimension of the Islamic experience was the impact on Muslim life of the "transformation of the modern," a key element in the resurgence of Islam. The nature of modernity itself has been transformed in the second half of the twentieth century, with profound implications for all of the people on earth. These changes have helped to shape the expression of the Islamic tradition at the beginning of its fifteenth century.

Transformation of Secularism. It has long been assumed that secularism is an inherent part of the process of modernization. Yet, by the 1970s, the real meaning of this assumption was subject to disagreement and its validity subject to question. If it simply means that traditional structures and concepts will be less important in a modernized society, it is valid. If, however, it means that religion will no longer be a vital force in the political and cultural life of modernized people, it is clearly not true. At least two observations support these conclusions. The first is that even the most clearly antireligious ideologies are increasingly recognized as assuming a religious form. They are not so much antireligious as attempting to replace one religion with another. A second observation is that religion, as traditionally

275

defined, exhibits signs of major vitality in modernized, secularized societies. "Born-again" Christians have assumed prominent political roles in the United States: A born-again Christian, Jimmy Carter, was elected president in 1976; all three major candidates for the presidency in 1980 presented themselves to the public as active, born-again believers; and by the 1980 election, evangelical Christians in general were assuming more active political roles. The old ideas of the separation of church and state in many countries clearly do not signify the separation of religion from politics. In the communist world, Polish workers have demanded religious services on state radio, and the pope of the Roman Catholic Church is a vigorous Christian leader who came from Poland, a country that has been formally communist for decades.

A renewed vitality of traditional religion is also visible in the Islamic world. Modern-educated Muslims are increasingly vigorous in the affirmation of their faith and of its relevance to all aspects of life. Modernization clearly does not mean the end of religion as a major force. On the contrary, during the 1970s, visible manifestations of Islam increased in even the most modernized areas.

This changing perception of the nature of secularism in modernizing societies is well illustrated by one study of religion and politics in Israel and Egypt. It began with the standard assumption that "secularization of the polity has been the most fundamental structural and ideological change in the process of development" and concluded that "secularization according to this definition is not taking place in either Israel or Egypt. Rather, the societies and politics of both are mixtures of the secular and the religious, and they are likely to remain so."[1] Increasingly, a strict definition of secularism is seen as applying specifically to the Western Christian experience but having less relevance to the process of modernization in societies with different religious traditions.

In the changing context of secularism in the modern world, the old modernist adaptationism of Muslim intellectuals has less impact on the development of Islamic thought and experience. There is less pressure to secularize and more pressure to redefine Islam in modern terms that recognize the comprehensive validity of the Islamic message in all aspects of life. Secularist modernism, in the context of the 1970s, remains influential in the Islamic world, but to many people it now seems simply a phase of intellectual development dominated by Western conceptualizations that came between the traditional and contemporary expressions of a more authentic Islamic thought.

"Postmodern" Redefinitions. The global experience of the modern style of life has not been totally satisfactory. By the end of the 1960s, people in modern societies were becoming convinced that the process of modernization had not solved the major problems of humanity and may have created new ones. In this context, there was a great effort throughout the world to redefine the modern and to restate the goals of modern life.

In the Islamic world, this redefinition started from a concrete base of experience. The first significant wave of modernization had produced liberal constitutional regimes that had become vehicles for corruption and oppression. The conviction that Western liberalism had failed was part of the incentive for Muslims to turn to more radical ideologies in the 1960s.

In area after area, however, a growing number of people had become convinced by the beginning of the 1970s that radical socialism had failed as dismally as its predecessor had. Many of the prominent figures in the era of radical socialism—such as Ahmad Ben Bella, Sukarno, and Nkrumah— were overthrown, and others—such as Nasser and Sékou Touré—began to alter the foundations of their radical experiments. Similarly, more conservative modernizing regimes, such as the Pahlavi state in Iran or Ayyub Khan's in Pakistan, were not significantly more successful. By the beginning of the 1970s, many people—modern educated as well as those with a traditional orientation—felt that the apparent possible options of modernity had all proved ineffective. Liberal, radical, and conservative modernizers had all been unable to fulfill even the minimum aspirations of the majority of their peoples.

The experience of the 1960s opened the way for experimentation with new options that were more authentically local and less foreign, and in many parts of the world, a search for viable postmodern concepts and institutions began. In the Islamic world, the search involved a reassessment of the Islamic tradition and an increasing willingness to use Islam, rather than an imported ideology, as the foundation for the future. Those factors do not imply an abandonment of the process of transformation or an attempt to revert to premodern society in an uncritical manner; they mean an attempt to build a postmodern society by utilizing traditions that are deeply rooted within society. This context gives a special character to the Islamic resurgence at the end of the fourteenth Islamic century.

Transformation of Radicalism. For much of the twentieth century, Marxism-Leninism has provided a substantial part of the ideological foundations of the radical perspective. That ideology was usually modified in some manner, and the result was the radical socialist programs of the 1960s. Socialists in the Islamic world were usually careful to distinguish their approach as emerging out of local conditions, and they often rejected the concepts of class conflict and affirmed the validity of religion while opposing "reactionary" religious institutions. In this form, the radical socialism of the 1960s made some compromises with local traditions, but it never became the ideology of the masses. When radical socialism was able to arouse the majority of a people, it was through charismatic leaders or emotional nationalist causes rather than because of its radical ideology.

The radical socialists and their more pure leftist critics agreed that radical socialism was not completely a Marxist-Leninist ideology as socialism in the Islamic world, like radicalism in other parts of the world, was beginning to represent new variations of older radical traditions. The earliest of those variations to emerge was the Maoist version of the Marxist-Leninist tradition. By the 1960s, the Soviet Union was no longer the most revolutionary society in the world, and communism had become an established system whose record could be examined. During the 1960s, the established communist parties in the Islamic world suffered from this examination and faced effective opposition from what was called the "new left."

Part of the criticism of the Soviet experience is reflected in the contemporary criticism of the radical socialist systems in the Islamic world once they were in power. Despite pronouncements supporting large-scale participation and decentralization of power, the radical socialist governments actually created larger bureaucracies and increasingly centralized control over the economy. Similarly, despite programs that proclaimed the democratic participation of the masses in politics, the radical socialist regimes remained dominated by small power elites, which sometimes justified their dominance on the basis of the necessary dictatorship of the vanguard of the revolution. A concrete product of the centralized power of the vanguard elite was the institution of centralized development planning, as seen in the proliferation of five-year plans. That centralization resulted in what one radical critic called the "dictatorship of the politbureaucracy."[2]

Another part of the radical socialist program was an informal effort at cultural centralization. Radical socialism theoretically recognized cultural pluralism and gave at least some support to the ideal of allowing people to maintain their own special cultural traditions. In practice, however, cultural and ethnic diversity within countries was opposed, and efforts were made to create homogeneous, centrally defined national cultures, as can be seen in the radical policies toward the Kurds in Iraq. Although the rationale was opposition to the reactionary forces, ethnic minorities often faced difficulties within the radical regimes unless they themselves were a prominent element in the ruling revolutionary vanguard.

By the end of the 1960s, the radicalism that was tied to large-scale bureaucratic structures, elite political domination, and centralized political structures was being widely rejected by both radicals and conservatives. That old approach became, in some ways, the conservative establishment, and the radical element in society was moving along new paths. The new radicalism emphasized the importance of effective mass participation in the political process. It looked to small-scale units for identity and often was willing to recognize ethnic and cultural pluralism. Although the new radicalism continued to reflect the structural ideas of socialism and often continued to utilize that label, it became more of a radical populism, stressing the great themes of national liberation rather than class struggle or supra-ethnic national unity, of decentralized structures, and of popular participation.

As radicalism became more oriented toward the masses, it incorporated the effective belief symbols of the masses, and in the Islamic world, that process meant the increasing importance of Muslim symbols and terms. By moving away from elite radical socialism, radicalism in the Muslim world became more Islamic in its foundation. This process has often been de-

. scribed by outside observers as reflecting an increasing influence of Maoism, but it may be more correct to identify it as the Islamic version of the same process that produced Maoism in China. It clearly is a product of internal developments as well as of external influences.

The new radical populism was strengthened by the process of modernization that had already taken place within Islamic societies. Until the mass media and the communications systems were effectively modernized, much of the population lived in relative isolation, and it was possible for a political elite to speak "in the name of the people" without any significant mass participation. However, as the masses began to be more informed through the network of modern communications, public opinion came to be a growing political force. As the revolution in Iran in 1978–1979 illustrates, even in a carefully controlled police state, antigovernment mass resistance can be generated through the use of modern means of communication. The potential for mass mobilization that has resulted from modernization has played a significant role in the transformation of radicalism in the Islamic world.

Revival of Traditional Themes

On a global scale, there was an important revival of traditional themes in the 1970s, especially in the realm of personal and group identity, which built on the changes that had taken place in the preceding decade and was related to the changing nature of modern society itself. Two basic areas in which this revival is most apparent are in the experience of ethnic groups and religious revivalism.

The context for the evolution was provided by the emergence of what has been called the postindustrial society or the beginning of the technotronic era. Although many of the events in this development took place in the so-called developed world, their impact and inspiration played a role in reinforcing developments elsewhere, including the Islamic world. Modernization created large-scale structures, with an emphasis on economies of scale and the virtues of mass production, and in social and cultural terms, those structures meant great pressures for global homogeneity. There was an expectation that modernization would produce similar, if not identical cultures and societies throughout the world. However, beginning in the 1960s, there began to be a reaction to that trend.

The giant structures of modern and modernizing societies, the great international corporations, the large bureaucracies, and the large political organizations were too large to provide a satisfying identity for individuals. The globalization of politics and economics opened up vistas of effectively universalized groups that could appeal to human hopes for unity, but the forms and structures for this vision were inadequate, and people became aware that more intimate communities were desirable to overcome the problems of large-scale organizations. The large structures created by modernism were neither universal enough nor intimate enough to meet the desires of many.

There was a revival of interest in and a growing attachment to ethnic and religious traditions, which could appeal to universal ideals while providing authentic intimacy in a community. Many people began to discover alternatives to modern political activism in communally oriented groups. The development of increasingly effective mass communications and popular coordination made it possible to conceive of a greater devolution of authority, leading to what one analyst calls "participatory pluralism."[3] In the Islamic world, the dynamics of the evolution of a modernized society combined with the strong continuity of traditional themes to create a resurgence of religion and ethnicity.

Ethnicity and Islam. One of the complex elements of the modern Islamic experience is the relationship between faith and ethnic loyalties. In the central parts of the Islamic world, the Middle Eastern countries, society has often been described as a mosaic of peoples and cultures, with the smaller units maintaining special identities while being integrated into a larger social framework. Because of the universal implications and aspirations of the Islamic message, Islam is often considered to be an opponent of ethnicity, and it is possible to see the recent revival of ethnic loyalties and the resurgence of Islam as competing forces. As one analyst said, "The coincidence of Islamic revival and ethnic consciousness in the context of the present crisis phase of the dialectical process pits Islam against ethnicity in virtually every Islamic country."[4]

The relationship is, however, more complex than that. For most major ethnic groups in the Islamic world, religion is one of the key features in the definition of a special ethnic identity. No Kurd, Malay, Azeri, Turk, or member of any of the many groups would envisage a definition of their special identity that would exclude Islam. When reformers like Ataturk, Reza Shah, or Muhammad Shah attempted such a definition, the majority of the population simply ignored their efforts. A revival of ethnic consciousness, such as that in Malaysia, thus involves a revival of religion rather than its negation. What is in conflict is not Islam and ethnic loyalty but, rather, differing identifications and interpretations of Islam. Kurds opposing the Khomeini regime in Iran may be opposing a particular form and interpretation of Islam, but they remain vigorously Islamic, and their faith plays an important role in the assertion of their special ethnic identity. In specific terms, the competing pattern is a univeralized Islam opposed to a pluralist Islam.

The Religious Revival. Commentators within the Islamic world itself often note that the Islamic revival in the 1970s was not a new or unique feature in the modern Islamic experience. An Egyptian journalist, for example, protested against the alarmist coverage of the Islamic revival as it appeared in the Western press: "They publish news, articles, and figures on the danger of the new Islamic movement as if there had never been, a century or so before, movements in the Islamic world much bigger than the present movement in Iran. The awakening of the Islamic world has not just begun. It began a long time ago."[5]

In a profound way, that objection is valid. The history of modern Islam is a record of dynamic activity, as the analysis of the past two centuries has shown. However, in the post–World War II era, there have been movements within the Muslim world that have tended to subordinate Islam to other causes. The early Westernizing and secularist reformers had this effect as did the emergence of nationalist and radical socialist ideologies, and the dramatic innovations of recent years have tended to obscure the underlying continuities of the Islamic experience. In a sense, the resurgence of the 1970s may be a fulfillment of the liberation process; first, direct foreign control is removed, and then ideological foundations are created on the basis of indigenous rather than borrowed fundamentals.

The era of Western domination, from the perspective of the Islamic revival of the 1970s, is but one episode in the long-term experience of Muslims, and the excitements of national liberation and secular reformism obscured but did not destroy the underlying continuities. The strength of these continuities does not, however, mean that old institutions and structures are being restored. Rather, in the global context of the transformation of the modern, Muslim societies are now undertaking the effort to modernize without Westernizing, to create social structures that are both modern and authentically Islamic.

The reservoir of strength for that effort has been the continuing faith of the masses in Muslim societies. A recent analysis of the contemporary Arab experience applies to the Muslim world in general. "Whether one wishes it or not, the Arab masses, while sometimes illiterate or, more generally, undereducated, are, to repeat, profoundly cultivated. This subconscious heritage in which village civilization and desert civilization, Koranic heritage and poetic heritage, are intermingled is not unimportant. From there, one day, the real renewals will rise."[6] At least some people identify the 1970s as being "that day."

In this context, the eighteenth-century Muslim experience assumes importance. During that century, too, Muslims were vigorously engaged in redefining what was authentically Islamic after obtaining relative independence from foreign control. The results of that effort were the creation of Neo-Sufism and the mood of socio-moral reconstruction. Specific structures created at that time have not been clearly perpetuated, but the spirit of the movements has remained a part of the "subconscious heritage" and provides a foundation for contemporary developments.

The eighteenth-century revival was fundamentalist and not conservative, which gives the legitimacy of preimperialist development to fundamentalism today. The fundamentalist style was firmly established long before it was called upon to oppose imperialism, and thus it did not die when the direct control of the imperialists passed away. Fundamentalism is thus not simply a "reactionary" style, reacting to immediate conditions, which gives contemporary fundamentalism a strength not found in the Westernizing modernist traditions, whose appeal is diluted by the disappearance of the need for the old type of apologetics and polemics.

Similarly, the eighteenth-century movements provided a relatively successful basis for combining the universalist Islamic message with an appeal to the noncosmopolitan masses. The Neo-Sufi orders took Sufism and Islamic universalism out of the hands of the cosmopolitan intellectual elite and created relatively effective mass movements. The new movements of the eighteenth century had an awareness of the larger *ummah* whole operating within the context of specific local conditions; in this way, the Neo-Sufi movements were an Islamic precursor to the present spirit of participatory pluralism. The *tariqahs* themselves are not the structures of the recent revival, but they helped to prepare the popular Islamic consciousness for the present resurgence.

The basic theme of the revived Islamic experience in the 1970s was well defined by Sadiq al-Mahdi, a leader of the Ansar in the Sudan and a descendant of the nineteenth-century Sudanese Mahdi. He stated: "I like to think that in the context of Sudanese and indeed Third World countries generally, there are two urgent quests: to satisfy the quest for identity and for modernisation. The communists and secularists want modernisation at the expense of identity. The Muslim Brothers are concerned with identity at the expense of modernisation. We satisfy the two quests."[7] Although the specific cases cited by Sadiq al-Mahdi show the particular politico-religious divisions in the Sudan, the issue is clearly presented: What Muslims want is a faith and programs that do not sacrifice their fundamental Islamic identity to a secularizing modernization nor adhere to old forms so that an authentic modernization is impossible. This search is the key to the Islamic experience of the 1970s.

Although many of the themes and developments in the Islamic world during the 1970s were transnational in character, the state and political boundaries remain one of the major, and perhaps the most important, frames of reference for religious developments. Within each state there are different styles of Islamic experience and organizations, and they interact within the framework defined by the political leaders. As a result, it is helpful to examine the experience of the 1970s in terms of the developments within the separate states, organizing the material on the basis of the Islamic style represented by the political leadership.

Traditional and Radical Fundamentalism

The fundamentalist style has the potential for leading in a variety of directions. Although it is often thought of as an effort of preservation, it is, in reality, more often profoundly revolutionary. Fundamentalists criticize existing institutions and ideas of society, judging them on the basis of an independent analysis of the Quran and the Sunnah, and the radical potential of this approach was illustrated in the nineteenth century by the speculative fundamentalism of Chiragh Ali in India. The fundamentalist spirit provides a means for rejecting the weight of tradition in a legitimate manner, which can appeal to the beliefs of the mass of the population.

During the 1970s, there were two general streams of Islamic fundamentalism. One was the more traditional in its tone and organization, with direct lines of continuity to the earlier, militant fundamentalist movements. The most visible of this type of fundamentalism is the Saudi monarchy, but many of the fundamentalist associations also have continued in established formats and maintained ideological positions that have long since been defined and upheld. The shift of emphasis back to more purely Islamic themes during the decade gave these groups greater visibility and prestige, and in many areas, the traditional fundamentalist groups became important sociopolitical forces.

In addition to that fundamentalist line of development, the 1970s was a period when the fundamentalist style also assumed a radical form. Expressing allegiance to the Quran and the Sunnah and rejecting existing institutions and medieval tradition, the radical fundamentalists engaged in a profound reorientation of the Islamic tradition. This radicalism was a synthesis of the transformed radicalism of the 1960s and the fundamentalist Islamic spirit. It emphasized mass participation, participatory control, small unit identity, and the elimination of old sociopolitical distinctions. To many observers, this movement was confusing because there seemed to be no appropriate terms in the modern political lexicon. Such radical fundamentalists were called Islamic Marxists or reactionary radicals, but use of those names was often followed by the comment that the two aspects of the movement were mutually exclusive and contradictory. However, the success of radical fundamentalism in the 1970s shows that semantic problems of analysts may not be a useful indicator of the viability of a movement.

Saudi Arabia: The Traditional Fundamentalist State

One of the remarkable changes that took place during the 1970s was the transformation of the position of Saudi Arabia in Middle Eastern and global politics. In the previous decade, the Saudi monarchy had been considered by the major radical socialist leaders as an unyielding opponent of socialism and progress, and Nasser had described the Saudis as wanting to destroy socialist revolution and had said that "Saud uses Islam to attack Socialism but he is fighting a losing battle."[8] However, after the Arab-Israeli War of 1967, it was Nasser who was in need of assistance, and Saudi Arabia provided financial support for Nasser's regime in Egypt. This aid marked the beginning of the emergence of Saudi Arabia as a major power in the Arab world as a whole rather than simply in the more conservative bloc. The pragmatic fundamentalism of Faysal opened the way for international prestige as well as for internal reform.

The influence of Saudi Arabia in the international scene was dramatically increased by the transformation of the world oil market in the period from 1970 to 1974, when producing countries assumed control of the oil prices and there were dramatic rises in oil profits. Although a relatively small kingdom, Saudi Arabia rapidly became an economic superpower. The vast revenues from its oil put the kingdom in a position to provide substantial support for its allies as well as to initiate ambitious development projects at home. The crucial element in this transformation was the leadership of King Faysal, who was able to maintain both a commitment to rapid development and the tradition of pragmatic fundamentalism. By the time he was murdered in 1975, he had become widely respected by a broad spectrum of world opinion. He had, for example, been named Man of the Year in January 1975 by *Time* magazine and had been described by Henry Kissinger as "a sort of moral conscience for many Arab leaders."[9] Among the mourners at his funeral were many Arab socialist leaders, including Houari Boumedienne of Algeria. The widespread respect for Faysal among radicals in the Arab world had been encouraged by his support of the Arab oil embargo in 1973–1974.

The basic program of the Saudi monarchy in the 1970s continued along the same lines it had followed previously in the spirit of Faysal's pragmatic fundamentalism. The aim was to blend modernization with fundamentalist Islam. On the Islamic side, the enforcement of Islamic rules regarding gambling and drinking, limitations on the public behavior and dress of women, and compliance with Islamic regulations regarding punishments prescribed in the Quran for such crimes as theft and adultery continued to be an important part of Saudi social policy. The constitution is the Quran, and the basic legal system is the Islamic court structure presided over by ulama of the Wahhabi tradition. The modernizing aspect of the Saudi program has seen vast investments in industrial development, education, and a modern military.

The process of blending the two elements is difficult, and the situation is unusual in that one of Saudi Arabia's problems has been having more money than can be used for development at the moment. However, during the 1970s, the program of pragmatic fundamentalism was remarkably successful. Increasingly, the government has come to rely on the modern-educated Saudis, a group that has grown rapidly. Although there has been little reorganization of the political structure to broaden the base of formal participation in politics, the informal structures of contact and consultation remain a vital part of what many Saudis defend as a unique style of democracy. One measure of the Saudi success in providing a place for the modern educated within the fundamentalist country is that Saudi Arabia has had virtually no brain-drain problem, as less than one-half of one percent of the Saudis who study abroad opt to stay abroad rather than return home after completing their studies.[10] That figure contrasts sharply with that for the other oil-rich states.

It might be said that Saudi Arabia's enormous wealth has made the pragmatic fundamentalist program a success. The wealth has clearly been an important element, but vast oil wealth did not preserve the Libyan or Iranian monarchies or a series of radical regimes in Iraq in the 1960s. The key element in Saudi Arabia has been the integrative value of the faith as defined by the Wahhabi tradition and applied within the flexible limits of pragmatic fundamentalism.

Some of the issues faced by the monarchy at the beginning of the 1980s illustrate both the strengths and the weaknesses of the policy. The ability to manage the problems of a transfer of power under crisis conditions shows the strength of the Saudi system, at least under the conditions of the 1960s and 1970s. The procedure is based on securing an informal consensus among the leading members of the royal family and the religious notables concerning succession to the throne. Even this relatively conservative group recognized the need for a more effective program of modernization in 1963–1964 and brought about the accession of King Faysal. Then, after the murder of Faysal in 1975 by a disgruntled member of the royal family, there was a stable transition of power to King Khalid. To some extent that transition involved a change in style of leadership, but the commitment to pragmatic fundamentalism has remained as strong, and effective, as before.

The Saudi monarchy is not without internal opposition, although the opposition is usually not visible. An event in November 1979 showed its existence. At that time, a group of militants gained control of the holy sanctuary in Mecca and were subdued only after some bitter fighting within the sanctuary itself. Interpretations of this incident and various conflicting claims provide an introduction to the various potential opposition elements within Saudi Arabia. In its pronouncements, the rebel group appears to have been a militant religious group demanding the purification of Islam in fundamentalist and messianic terms. One report[11] links the group to the extremist Wahhabi tradition of the old Ikhwan organization, which felt that Abd al-Aziz and his successors had not lived up to the true Wahhabi mission of purification of the Islamic world and full adherence to the Quran and the Sunnah. That objection reflects the fact that within Saudi Arabia, some people believe that the regime is not sufficiently fundamentalist. This is an important type of opposition, although it is not visibly widespread, because it disputes the basic legitimacy of the regime on the fundamentalist terms of the regime.

A different interpretation of the Meccan incident is that it was part of a "people's revolution" that represents the more radical elements of the opposition. This view was presented by a leader of the Arabian Peninsula People's Union, a group in the tradition of the radical socialism of the 1960s.[12] No connection between the two movements was established, but the report points up a type of potential opposition to the Saudi regime that was very weak during the 1970s. The charge that the Saudi monarchy was an ally of imperialism in the region brought little response, and that charge was contradicted for many people by the Saudis' active support of the Palestinian cause and their participation in the oil embargo in 1973–1974. The few radical opponents of the regime also faced problems posed by the fact that the Saudi government had greatly improved relations with the radical Arab regimes during the decade. Like the extreme fundamentalists, the radicals could mount little effective opposition to the Saudi regime during the 1970s.

A third portrayal of the Meccan group is that it was a Shiʿi revolutionary group that claimed its leader to be the hidden imam who had returned to establish his regime in the holy cities.[13] Although the claim was disproved, it was a reminder that there is a Shi'i minority group in Saudi Arabia that has expressed its dissatisfaction with the government. Although they make up only a small group, they are concentrated in the areas of the gulf coast oil fields and are an important part of the labor force there. There were Shi'i protest demonstrations in that region in 1979–1980 demanding a fairer distribution of the wealth and an end to anti-Shi'i discrimination in Saudi Arabia. The latter demand was encouraged by the Islamic regime in Iran, which charged that the Saudi monarchy was a "corrupt, mercenary agent of the United States" following a "satanic" foreign policy and oppressive domestic policies.[14] There was, however, little fear that an Iranian-style revolution would be possible in Saudi Arabia.

In the aftermath of the 1979 mosque incident, the Saudi government stepped up its efforts to maintain popular support. Crown Prince Fahd, one of the major leaders in the government, stated that "there is an Arabic proverb which says that good health may result from illnesses. The mosque events have shown us many things of which we had not been sufficiently aware."[15] As a result, the government began a campaign to reduce possible irritants within the political system. A crackdown on corruption was announced, and there was considerable discussion about initiating more formal structures of political participation through a consultative assembly. Clearly, the reaction was not simply a conservative retrenchment but one that was in the spirit of the pragmatic fundamentalism of the Saudi tradition. The 1979 incident did illustrate, however, the careful balancing of traditional and radical forces that the Saudi policy entails.

The experience of Saudi Arabia in the 1970s shows that Islamic fundamentalism in its more traditional form is a dynamic and viable Islamic style. The clear international influence of Saudi Arabia and its willingness to provide financial support for Islamic causes have given added prestige to fundamentalism in the Islamic world. By example and by its policies and actions, Saudi Arabia has helped to make the fundamentalist style an important part of the Islamic resurgence.

Libya: The Radical Fundamentalist Revolution

The emergence of radical fundamentalism as government policy is closely associated with the revolutionary regime in Libya. The Sanusi-Libyan monarchy was overthrown in 1969 by a group of young military officers led by Mu'ammar al-Qadhafi (spelled in a variety of ways in Western sources, including Gaddafi and Qaddafi). Although in some ways the Libyan revolutionaries seemed to be the heirs to the Nasserite tradition of Arab socialism, even their early pronouncements indicated that the fundamental tone of the new revolutions would be different. There was a much greater emphasis on the Islamic basis of the revolutionary program and a willingness to experiment in organizational format.

In more than a decade of development, the Libyan revolution has shown itself to be consistent in its fundamentalist style of Islam. In the Five Point

Declaration of 1 September 1969, the leaders stated: "The Revolutionary Command Council believes deeply in the sanctity of religions and in the value of the spiritual precepts emanating from the heart of our Sacred Book, the Noble Quran. It will continue to support religious precepts and to work for the destruction of false religious hypocrisy."[16] Building on those ideals, the leaders committed themselves to an Islamically based socialist program. "Our socialism is the socialism of Islam. It is the socialism of the true faith. It is the socialism which springs from the heritage and beliefs of this people." They noted that they desired "a socialism emanating from the true religion of Islam and its Noble Book. It is not the socialism of Lenin or Marx."[17]

Although many observers believed at the time that the program was a continuation of the old socialist themes of attempting to utilize Islam, there were indications of a more populist approach and a willingness to experiment in organization. Qadhafi, for example, stated: "Without the least doubt, we must ensure the control of the people over the basic means of production in the society. But there are a number of ways to achieve this. Nationalization is not the only means to that."[18] In other early speeches, there were indications that new popular organizations would be created that would give control of all aspects of life to the people. Although the Revolutionary Command Council and the military revolutionaries remained in visible control through much of the following decade, it is also true that significant efforts have been made to create a new populist system that avoids bureaucratic centralization and relies on people's committees for management and administration.

In developing the new ideology, Qadhafi advocated independent study of the Quran, and sterile intellectual formulations from the past were rejected in favor of an active adherence to the Quran as a source of liberation and progress in the modern world. He regularly lectured ulama on the need for this type of activity, and in supporting it, Qadhafi is soundly within the fundamentalist tradition of support for *ijtihad*.

A second element in the emerging ideology is an emphasis on Islamic unity. To a remarkable degree, Qadhafi has given a religious and radical, rather than a nationalist, orientation to the Libyan fundamentalist experiment, especially in relation to a "Libyan" identity. Although the Libyan people are often called a vanguard in the world revolution and are seen as having a special mission in presenting a new vision to the world, there was little sense in the evolution of Libyan society in the 1970s of an emerging Libyan nationalism.

The Libyan revolutionary identity reaches beyond itself. In its ideology, the state is ignored as much as possible as a basic operating unit; in fact, it appears from the rhetoric of the Third Universal Alternative that the state should be replaced by populist organizations and associations. It is only as a state that the original Libya had any significance since it was not a distinctive ethnic, linguistic, or religious entity. Qadhafi has worked to spread the Libyan revolutionary identity beyond the borders of the Libyan state, and he has formulated unity schemes with other states, including Tunisia, Egypt, the Sudan, and Syria. These schemes have often been expressed in terms of a vision of Arab unity, a more cosmopolitan nationalism, but there has been a significant element of a call to Islamic unity as well. These two dimensions were clear in the unity schemes developed in late 1980. In December 1980, Qadhafi and Assad, the president of Syria, announced arrangements for a unification of their two states. At the same time, the first effective unification was implemented as Libyan troops directly intervened in Chad and Libyan-Chadian unity was proclaimed. This action was seen as the foundation for a much larger Islamic unification in Africa, but the future of this policy became unclear following the announced withdrawal of Libyan troops from Chad in November 1981.

The Libyan regime has also provided support for revolutionary causes throughout the Islamic world, giving its strongest support to the Palestinians, in whom Islamic and Arab visions coincide. However, non-Arab Muslims, such as the Philippine Moros, were also included in the world circle of the Libyan revolutionary vision. The ultimate goal was an Islamic salvation for the world rather than simply a nationalist, and ultimately separatist, victory.

It is in the evolution of domestic social and political structures that the radicalism of Libyan fundamentalism is most evident. Initially, the organizational format seemed to follow more standard radical socialist lines. Political parties were banned; a single organization, the Arab Socialist Union, was created, with the Revolutionary Command Council remaining the final authority; and in the process, a bureaucratized socialist state seemed to be emerging. However, even at this stage of development, the unusual character of the Libyan revolution was visible. It was described as a "perverse revolution" in that "it claims a social revolution that will bring Libya into the company of the great twentieth-century revolutions for social liberation, yet it zealously pursues a revival of Islamic fundamentalism."[19] It was not yet clear to observers that a radical fundamentalism was a possibility.

The radical fundamentalist ideology and organization began to be more clearly defined in 1973. In April, Qadhafi announced a drastic revision of national policy, which amounted to a cultural revolution. In a five-point program for domestic affairs, all existing laws were abrogated, and Islamic law provided the basis for the new legal system. The revolutionary masses were to be armed, and all deviationists purged. A cultural revolution was proclaimed in which "all bourgeois and bureaucratic ideas shall be eliminated as they create an insular class which handicaps social progress,"[20] and books and writing that deviated from the Quran were to be eliminated from libraries and school curricula.

In administrative terms, the new national policy aimed at turning the government over to the masses. The vehicle for this transfer was the people's committees, which assumed control of government agencies, municipalities, schools, and large-scale private enterprises. By the end of

May 1973, more than four hundred such committees had been formed. In the offices of foreign companies, the new committees dismissed several Libyan executives and took control of company communication facilities. In the law school of Benghazi, the committee dismissed the dean and eliminated final examinations. The radio and television services were taken over by a committee, which held meetings to develop appropriate revolutionary programs.

The new revolution was guided by Qadhafi and the Revolutionary Command Council, but it began to assume a clearly populist character. The regime was fundamentalist in its insistence on Quranic rules—gambling, intoxicating beverages, night clubs, and other similar items were forbidden— and it was also presenting more clearly its positive program for development, which was radical in nature and based on Quranic principles. Qadhafi defined the new regime as a clear alternative to both communism and capitalism and called it the Third Universal Alternative.

In 1976, the first volume of *The Green Book* by Qadhafi was published, and in it, the political dimension of the Third Universal Alternative was more fully explained. The chief goal of the new revolution was the direct rule of the people through people's participatory committees. The spirit of this presentation is captured in the slogan No Representation in Lieu of the People, and parliamentary systems are rejected as denials of democracy. "Parliaments are the backbone of traditional democracy as it exists today. A parliament is a misrepresentation of the people. . . . A parliament is originally founded to represent the people, but this in itself, is undemocratic as democracy means the authority of the people not an authority acting on their behalf. The mere existence of a parliament means the absence of the people, but true democracy exists only through the participation of the people."[21] The solution posed by the Third Universal Alternative is rule by popular congresses and people's committees. Although news reports at the time emphasized the rather chaotic nature of the emergence of administration by people's committees, the system has in fact survived and expanded. For example, by the late 1970s, people's committees even took control of Libyan embassies overseas.

The second volume of *The Green Book* was issued in 1977, and it outlines the reorganization of economic life in accord with the Third Universal Theory. Under the new economic regime, popular participation was carried even further: Wages were abolished, workers became full partners in production, and workers' committees assumed full control of economic enterprises. Similarly, although private ownership was recognized, it was only for the satisfaction of an individual's needs and did not involve exploitation of others. Rent was seen as a form of exploitation, and it was abolished. A person could own only the home in which he lived, and rental properties passed out of the hands of the old owners. The guiding principle in this area was that "man's legitimate economic activity is solely the satisfaction of his needs. No person has the right to economic activity that provides him with more than is necessary to satisfy his needs, as any amount he acquires in excess of his needs is actually taken from the needs of others."[22] In this way, the radical transformation of the Libyan economy was initiated.

During 1979, the social basis of the Third Universal Theory was explained in the third volume of *The Green Book*, in which minorities and tribal groups are discussed in the context of popular unity, and the proper role of women is defined. Although there is emphasis on the proper roles for women in terms of maintaining households and raising children, women are seen as having the same rights as men in divorce and should not be forced to marry against their will. In addition, the rights of ownership for women are affirmed to the extent that the women are the owners of the residential homes because of their necessary and natural duties.

The Libyan regime, declared to be the Socialist People's Libyan Arab Jamahiriya by the General People's Congress in 1977, is thus a vigorous experiment in the total reconstruction of a society, and the conscious ideological foundation for this effort is the Quran. The spirit emphasizes the traditions of communalism, which is a significant part of both the Islamic and tribal heritages of Libya, and it reflects some of the tradition of the "unincorporated" society of medieval Islam. However, the form is a manifestation of radical populism. In Libya, a radical fundamentalism emerged during the 1970s as a significant venture in the modern Islamic experience.

Somalia: Radicalism and Nationalism

A military coup in 1969 brought an end to almost a decade of parliamentary politics in Somalia. The earlier regime had become divided by factionalism and appeared to most Somalis to be increasingly corrupt, so the new rulers were willingly accepted. During the following decade, Siad Barre, the leader of the revolutionary group, developed a program based on radicalism and nationalism. This program attempted to blend concepts of scientific socialism with Somali traditions and Islam to create a basis for rapid development. In this synthesis, there was less emphasis on Islam than in Libya, and the style was therefore less fundamentalist. However, it was a major effort to develop an authentically Somali radical tradition, balancing modern, Islamic, and Somali elements.

The role of Islam in this radicalism is often emphasized. President Barre stated: "Islam and socialism supplement each other because both advocate the advancement of the interest of the people, of mankind—justice, dignity, prosperity and equality. The Islamic tenets are the utterances of God and socialism is the sum of the constructive thoughts of mankind and one can say in essence socialism is a supplement to Islam."[23] However, the emphasis was upon Islam as a revolutionary ideology, and the more traditional Islamic leadership and practices often came into conflict with the emerging radical program of the Barre regime. Thus, when conservative ulama opposed measures providing legal equality for women, ten of them were executed in 1975.

The radical program of the Barre regime was of the new populist style. After a period of consolidation, a socialist charter was proclaimed, defining "scientific socialism" as a "term now introduced so as to insist that a marxist analysis had here acquired a local content and application."[24] An effort was made to create a system that avoided control by a bureaucracy and ensured popular participation. One of the early steps in this process was a language reform to strengthen literacy programs, and a specially adapted alphabet was written, which made it possible to proclaim Somali as the official language of the country. Then, in 1974–1975, large numbers of students and urban professionals went into the countryside in a massive national literacy effort. By 1975, significant participation in local self-government committees was being encouraged, and by 1976, the military regime felt that it was in a position to establish the Somali Revolutionary Socialist party (SRSP), through which popular participation could be formally organized.

An additional theme of the radical program was self-reliance, and Somalis were encouraged to establish rural collective and cooperative enterprises. The great drought in the Sudanic areas of Africa had a severe impact on Somalia, and that grave crisis gave added strength to the government in its efforts to reorganize rural economic life. Thousands of nomads were resettled in agricultural villages, and many more were settled along the seacoast in fishing cooperatives.

In a variety of ways, the Barre regime has succeeded in establishing a popular radical regime with reasonably effective programs. In the process of this mobilization, effective symbols of Somali national and religious traditions were used. In contrast to Libya, by 1977, it was nationalist rather than Islamic themes that had become most important. Somalia had long laid claim to the Ogaden Province of Ethiopia, where the majority of the population was Somali. In 1977, Barre led his country into war with Ethiopia on this issue, and the result was a reorientation of Somali foreign policy. Up to that time, the Barre government had been closely associated with the Soviet Union, and its radicalism was supported by the communist bloc nations. However, when the Soviets supported Ethiopia in the Ogaden War, Barre expelled them from Somalia and established more friendly ties with Saudi Arabia and other Islamic states. Soviet and Cuban aid made an Ethiopian victory possible in 1978, and since that time, there has been an increasingly Islamic tone to the policies and statements of the Barre regime. This dimension had been part of the program from the beginning but is now more visible.

Somalia provides another example of the creation and implementation of the new-style populist radicalism in an Islamic context. In this case, the tone has been more nationalist and socialist than fundamentalist. The example of Somalia represents an evolution beyond the bureaucratic radical socialism of the 1960s in the direction of a more distinctively Islamic and indigenous radicalism.

Conservative Adaptationism and Islamic Revival

The more conservative political regimes in the Islamic world had varying success in coping with the changes of the 1970s, ranging from the total collapse of the shah's regime in Iran to the continuing strength of the Jordanian monarchy. Virtually all of those governments had committed themselves to programs of adaptationist modernization in the preceding decade, and the "white revolutions" were seen as the major alternative to the radical socialism at that time. In that respect, these monarchical regimes had been successful as none of them were directly overthrown by the opposing radical socialism that made up the opposition of the 1960s. However, the new populist radicalism and revived Islam presented challenges that were more difficult to meet.

Monarchical regimes were in an awkward position in relation to the rising sentiments of militant Islam. By having committed themselves to a clearly modernizing adaptationist program, the monarchs had compromised their identity as preservers of the more traditional values, and monarchical survival came to depend upon the ability of the rulers to make further adaptations that recognized the growing force of radical fundamentalism and populism. The key to survival appears to be a careful reaffirmation of the Islamic tradition along with a renewed emphasis on nationalist causes. When this sentiment can be accompanied with a continuing, visible commitment to rapid modernization, the monarchies have survived, but in each of the states that began the decade of the 1970s as a monarchy, there has been a complex interaction of forces. In contrast to the relatively simple domination of one style, as in the traditional and radical fundamentalist states, a number of styles have been in competition in most of the monarchies. It is necessary to view them as a complex network of competing styles, and the struggle has seldom been clearly resolved in favor of one or another group.

Iran: From Monarchy to Islamic Revolution

At the beginning of the 1970s, the Iranian monarchy appeared to be in a virtually impregnable position. Its opposition was weak and divided, and the White Revolution seemed to be moving Iran rapidly along the path of modernization. Although the shah had vocal opponents, even many of them still spoke in terms of reforming and liberalizing the monarchy rather than eliminating it. Reflecting the ideas of the 1960s that assumed that the chief opposition to conservative adaptationism was radical socialism, observers critical of the shah tended to emphasize the liberal and radical socialist elements of the opposition. However, that emphasis ignored the development of significant links between the religious and secularist opposition groups that had begun to be built during the 1960s, such as in the Freedom Movement. The underlying continuity of the oppositional role of Islam in Iran remained strong, so it was possible for a perceptive and prophetic observer to write in 1969, "Despite all the inroads of the modern age, the Iranian national consciousness still remains wedded to Shiʿi Islam, and when the integrity of the nation is held to be threatened by internal autocracy and foreign hegemony, protest in religious terms will continue to be voiced, and the appeals of men such as Ayatullah Khumayni to be widely heeded."[25]

The traditional lines of opposition in Iran between the monarchy and other groups began to be re-formed in the early 1970s. As in the past, an oppositional alliance developed, and it brought together groups that had a variety of goals but a common interest in reducing monarchical power and eliminating foreign influence. In many ways, the old coalition of forces that had resulted in the constitutional movement of 1905–1906 was rebuilt, bringing together the religious leadership, the modern-educated groups, the traditional merchants, and representatives of the tribal and ethnic groups in Iran. As the monarchy grew increasingly autocratic, the incentives for more effective opposition grew until the revolution burst forth in 1977–1978. At that time, the leading element in the alliance was the religious leadership, which provided the symbols and terminology for the revolution.

The Adaptationist Monarchy and Islam. The basic power of the Iranian monarchy rested on the tradition of monarchical rule, which was accepted as necessary by the essentially conservative Iranian population. In the past, opposition had arisen to the extension of monarchical power and tyrannical rule rather than to the monarchy itself. However, during the 1970s, the power of the shah appeared to be increasing, and the monarchy attempted to eliminate rival sources of political influence, so opposition to the shah gradually became opposition to the monarchy itself.

In the expansion of his power, the shah relied on his control of the great wealth that came from the exploitation of Iranian oil resources and his manipulation and development of a modern army and secret police. These factors gave the shah the means to both co-opt and coerce potential rivals, and he used them with great ability in the first decades of his rule to balance the elements of opposition and divide them. However, by the middle of the 1970s, the shah had become so fully involved in the process of magnifying and glorifying the monarchy that he lost his ability to operate effectively in the Iranian political arena. One Iranian who was relatively sympathetic to the shah wrote that by this time, the shah "stopped paying attention to the susceptibilities of his audience or to the existence of public opinion. More and more he gave the impression of living in a world of his own imagining. . . . His own interests, which he readily confused with his country's, came first and foremost. In his boundless egoism, the Shah decided and the rest had only to obey."[26] This transformation of the monarchy was a crucial element in its ultimate collapse.

During the 1960s and 1970s, the effective means of repression and co-option undermined the organization and power of the nationalist and radical secularist opposition groups, and the dominance of the military and the growing penetration of all opposition groups by the secret police gave the monarchy the appearance of virtually absolute power. The one major opposition group whose influence and organization were not destroyed was the ulama, and the opponents of the shah increasingly joined forces with the religious leaders to re-create the traditional coalition of antimonarchical forces.

Mohammad Shah clearly recognized the power of Islam within Iran and attempted to mobilize it in support of the monarchy. In symbolic terms, he attempted to persuade the masses that he was the rightful guardian of Shiʿi Islam, and he tried to create an imperial cult that would replace the mass Islamic loyalties that were led by the ulama. The White Revolution was described as a major vehicle for the propagation of true Islam.

In organizational terms, the shah attempted to undermine the traditional religious institutions. He took firm control of religious endowments and reduced economic and political support for any social or educational organization that did not give him full support. He attempted to create an alternative "civil religion" under the control of the state, building or supporting state-sponsored mosques under the control of ulama who cooperated with the monarchy. He also tried to create educational institutions that would replace those under the control of the old religious elite. Religious courts were replaced by houses of justice or village councils that were under the supervision of the Ministry of Justice. "The Houses of Justice are one example of the legal expressions of civil religion, i.e., that the law of the Prophet is the law of the regime, and vice versa, in administering the affairs of the nation."[27]

Although Mohammad Shah was able to create an official religious establishment that was subservient to the monarchy, that establishment had little impact on the religious loyalties of most Iranians, partly because of the ineffective and insensitive way in which the policy was implemented. For example, the shah attempted to act as the patron of the great religious sanctuary in Meshed that is associated with the tomb of the Imam Rida. He controlled vast religious endowments for the shrine and made frequent pilgrimages there. In 1973, the endowments were used to build a large hotel in Meshed, and the royal family took an active part in the opening ceremonies. However the hotel was the Meshed Hyatt Hotel, a visibly foreign-style operation in a conservative sacred city, and its advertisements showed the hotel as serving the best foreign wines and liquors, despite the Islamic prohibition on alcoholic beverages.[28]

More significantly, the majority of Iranians saw the civil religion of the shah as a perversion of their Islamic tradition. Diminishing numbers of the faithful prayed in the "official" mosques, and few students chose to study in the government religious schools rather than with the more famous, independent *mujtahid*s. The religious policy of the shah failed to win him much support, and it increasingly alienated the ulama and, through them, the religious sensibilities of the masses.

Monarchical adaptationism in terms of religious policy proved to be a failure in Iran as its most significant result was to create the conditions for a religious revival that assumed antimonarchical tones. The coercive power of the state made the independent and often persecuted ulama into the heroes of the people and the only visible protectors of both the religious traditions of the society and the constitutional regime itself. In this way, the shah destroyed the basis for a conservative acceptance of the monarchical tradition in Iran.

Traditional Shiʿi Fundamentalism. The development of a repressive and autocratic monarchy made religious conservatism difficult in Iran during the 1970s. Although it is possible to speak of conservative Islam in terms of local village practices or rural attitudes, even those were affected in some ways by the modernization programs of the shah and the extension of state institutions into rural and village life. The establishment of a government-sponsored religious corps, which was sent into rural areas, heightened the growing lines of tension, and conservative leaders who accepted a role in the government religious establishment were departing from a truly conservative position. Thus, for most practical purposes, the conservative style of Islam was submerged during the 1970s, and in its place, the dominant styles were traditional and radical fundamentalism. By 1979, those styles had set the tone for even Iranian modernizing adaptationism.

The revival of ulama activism in 1963 was primarily a reaffirmation of Shiʿi fundamentals. The *mujtahids* were asserting the traditional position of the ulama as the chief religious guides in the country, and in many ways, theirs remained the most visible style of religious activism until the actual beginnings of the revolution in the following decade. Religious activism took many forms in the period leading up to the revolution. Although the group were all united in their opposition to the shah, they represented a variety of emphases within the broad framework of what could be called traditional fundamentalist revolutionary forces. Since the revolution, these groups have maintained a degree of separate identity and are representative of the variety of the nonradical groups in the Islamic republic. Reflecting the individualist tendencies of Shiʿism, many of these groups are associated with specific key individuals.

Ayatollah Ruhollah Khomeini is clearly the most prominent religious leader to emerge out of the revolutionary process, and his position in the revolution is complex because he performed a number of roles. Sent into exile after demonstrations and suppression in 1963, he was one of the most vocal opponents of the shah, and as other centers of opposition were crushed or co-opted, he emerged as the symbol of opposition for virtually every Iranian group. As such, one role that he performed was to be the symbol and focus of the revolutionary movement as a whole. In that capacity, he became the dominant political force in the Islamic republic created after the overthrow of the shah, and he was able to command the respect and obedience of even those groups that did not agree with his ideological positions.

Khomeini's second role was as the chief representative of militant but traditional Iranian fundamentalism. He had long advocated an active political role for the ulama. In his discussion of Islamic government, he stated, for example, that "the jurisprudents [scholars of Islamic law] must work separately or collectively to set up a legitimate government that establishes the strictures, protects the borders and establishes order. . . . The jurisprudents have been appointed by God to rule and the jurisprudent must act as much as possible in accordance with his assignment. . . . The temporary inability to form a strong and complete government does not at all mean that we should retreat."[29] Although in his early writings Khomeini had not opposed the monarchical system as such, by the 1970s, he was firmly and frequently stating that there were no kings in Islam. The manifest program of Khomeini became the destruction of the monarchy and its replacement by an Islamic, nonmonarchical regime. In carrying out the first part of his program, he led all elements of the revolution; in implementing the second, he operated as the leader of a particular group within the new regime.

The specific organizational following of Khomeini is made up of formerly conservative ulama who were mobilized by the revolutionary cause. Their goal is the establishment of a clearly Islamic regime, one that conforms to the Quran and the Shiᶜi traditions. Their ideology and program are fundamentalist in the traditional sense. They oppose gambling, alcohol, and the corruptions of luxury; they advocate the full implementation of Islamic law in terms of the Quranically defined punishment for crimes and other matters; and they oppose the modernization of the role of women in society. These are the standard themes of fundamentalism, and the ulama followers of Khomeini do not propose a radical social transformation.

Since the revolution, this group has manifested its power in a number of organizations, whose prominent leaders are former students and scholarly associates of Khomeini. When the revolution spread to the villages and towns, it did so through the mosque organizations and ulama who circulated cassettes of Khomeini's speeches and organized local revolutionary action groups. As the shah's regime collapsed, these groups obtained arms and became a popular militia. The emerging Revolutionary Council attempted to organize this force in the Pasdaran Inqilab (Revolutionary Guard). Following the establishment of the revolutionary regime, the Pasdaran remained active, armed forces able to enforce the policies of the fundamentalist ulama, although they were not always under the effective control of the central groups.

The political arm of the traditional fundamentalist group is the Islamic Republican party (IRP). The IRP emerged as an organized group presenting the program of the more broadly and loosely defined party of God, the general supporters of Khomeini who could be mobilized in the cities and towns. The IRP was organized by a former student of Khomeini, Ayatollah Muhammad Bihishti, who had been among the more reformist ulama but had become increasingly fundamentalist as the revolution progressed. His strong ties to Khomeini and his apparent control of the IRP made Bihishti one of the leading members of the ulama fundamentalist group. His party had an overwhelming majority in the parliament elected in 1980, and he was in the process of consolidating the role of the IRP when he was killed in an explosion during the summer of 1981. During that summer it was unclear who, if anyone, would assume leadership of the IRP as a successor to Bihishti.

Other former students of Khomeini are prominent figures in the general group that dominated the formal structures of Iranian politics by the summer of 1981. These include Hojat al-Islam Hashimi Rafsanjani, the speaker of the parliament, and the leading ayatollah in Tehran, Husayn Ali Muntaziri. Muntaziri had been active in the early ulama opposition to the shah and had been jailed and exiled. Following the revolution, he became active in organizing fundamentalist groups. When the senior ayatollah in Tehran, Mahmud Taliqani, died in September 1979, Muntaziri began to assume his position of leadership. Muntaziri has sometimes led the Friday prayers in Tehran, frequently holding a rifle, and is a highly visible spokesman for the militant traditional fundamentalists. He is often spoken of as the potential successor to Khomeini as the constitutionally mandated chief spiritual leader for the government.

The militant positions of the fundamentalists can be seen in statements by Muntaziri. He opposes secular leftists and liberals, saying that the "groups formed in the Shah's time, calling themselves supporters of the so-called masses, have been created and formed for American purposes. Most of these groups are tied to Washington and Moscow." He has called dissident Kurdish leaders "agents of Zionism and imperialism" and has advocated the spread of the Islamic revolution, saying, "All our brothers and sisters, like a bright torch and roaring waves, try to be determined to solve all our internal problems and make our best effort to export our revolution to the world."[30]

Liberal Fundamentalism. The liberal nationalist followers of Mosaddiq had become divided and disorganized in the decades following the collapse of the Mosaddiq government, and the most active segment of that tradition was represented by the Freedom movement, which had emerged in the 1960s. This group was a synthesis of the religious and liberal opposition to the shah, and the more secularist liberal nationalists diminished as an effective force. Within the remaining liberal group, there was a high level of commitment to the Islamic tradition, and the goals of the movement included a restoration of Islamic values in society. In this way, the group's members were fundamentalist in style, even though they were influenced by the liberal nationalist ideals. The political system envisaged by these liberal fundamentalists was a government operated by lay professionals under the spiritual guidance of the major religious leaders. However, the ayatollahs, in this system, would not be directly involved in the political process.

At least two senior ayatollahs in Iran were part of this group, and they provided a religious balance to the power of Khomeini and his more activist vision of the role of the ulama. Ayatollah Mahmud Taliqani cooperated directly with the Freedom movement, and he also had ties with the more radical opposition groups. For a number of years, he was the leading ayatollah in Tehran and was able to mobilize large-scale, urban support for the cause. He was often in jail during the time of the shah—he actually was first imprisoned by Reza Shah in 1939 for opposing the expanding power of the monarchy. Taliqani had advocated an active political role for the ulama in opposition to the tyrannical monarchy, but with the success of the revolution, he argued that it was time for the ulama to withdraw from direct political participation. This view brought him into conflict with the more traditional fundamentalists who dominated the new republic regime. When Taliqani died in September 1979, the liberal fundamentalists lost a powerful figure.

The second major religious leader within the liberal fundamentalist grouping is the Ayatollah Muhammad Kazim Shariat Madari. Born at the beginning of the century, Shariat Madari is an older ayatollah whose reputation as a religious scholar is higher than that of Khomeini, and he was already one of the three or four senior ayatollahs before Khomeini became a popular leader of the opposition. Although Shariat Madari was arrested for involvement in demonstrations in 1963, he adopted a relatively quietist political position in subsequent years. He did, however, become a leading spokesman for the religious opposition to the shah from within Iran during 1977–1978.

Shariat Madari's position is relatively liberal in its affirmation of the Islamic tradition. He believes that the ulama should act as the guides for government but not necessarily involve themselves directly in political affairs. In contrast to Khomeini's position, Shariat Madari believes that "in Islam there is no provision that the clergy must absolutely intervene in matters [of state]," and although he feels that there is no legal obstacle to one of the ulama assuming a political office, he does feel that it would be demeaning for a leading ayatollah to do so.[31]

In general terms, Shariat Madari does not see modernization as contradictory to Islam. He stated in 1978 that "despite what the Government [of the shah] says, our people do not demonstrate against modernization but against dictatorship." In social customs, he also presents a more liberal view, insisting that wearing the veil is a custom, not a requirement, of the faith. "We do not force women to wear the veil. But on the other hand, nobody has the right to order them not to."[32] Following the establishment of the revolutionary regime, Shariat Madari's views have often been in contrast to those of the more traditional fundamentalists led by Khomeini. However, Shariat Madari has refused to allow an open clash that would harm the unity of the new Islamic government, although he has continued to support a less clerical regime in which lay professionals would play an important role.

The major line of conflict between Shariat Madari and the traditional fundamentalists arose over the issue of the new constitution and the rights of minorities. Shariat Madari had a large number of followers among the Azeri-speaking population in western Iran, and many Azeris had participated in the revolution because of their opposition to the centralizing oppression of the shah's regime, which threatened the special cultural identity of the Azeris. The Azeris were not secularists and were also committed to the ideal of a reaffirmation of the Islamic nature of their society. They hoped that the new regime would give some recognition to their special traditions, but it soon appeared that the Khomeini regime was intent upon establishing a firmly centralized government, and separatist struggles broke out in 1979. Although Shariat Madari expressed reservations about the new constitution and tried to gain a relaxation of the centralizing tendencies of the new state, he did not encourage his followers to revolt. As a result, he has remained a spokesman for a more liberal Islamic regime but also has remained consistent in his belief that the great *mujtahids* should not involve themselves directly in political affairs.

The major political activists among the liberal fundamentalists are the lay professionals who are associated with ayatollahs such as Taliqani and Shariat Madari, and this group provides some of the most important personnel for the initial revolutionary government. Mehdi Bazargan, one of the founders of the Freedom movement, was the first prime minister after the fall of the shah's government and the brief transitional period. Bazargan, however, faced the growing power of the Islamic Republican party and the traditional fundamentalists and soon appeared to be managing a governmental structure without any real policymaking or political power. That that was the case became more apparent after the death of Ayatollah Taliqani. A major trial of strength occurred as a result of the occupation of the U.S. embassy by militants just a couple of months after Taliqani's death, and Bazargan resigned when he was unable to have any impact on government policy.

The next major event in the interaction between liberal and traditional fundamentalists came with the constitutionally defined presidental elections in 1980. The winner in that election, by a substantial margin, was Abu al-Hasan Bani Sadr, one of the key figures in the liberal fundamentalist group. He had been a supporter of the Mosaddiq movement as a student and had been wounded in the 1963 demonstrations. He came from a religious family but had received a Western education, studying economics in France. While in France, he had been active in the opposition movement and had become closely associated with Khomeini. At that time, Bani Sadr had clearly expressed the main themes of the opposition in a number of articles. In November 1978, he wrote: "The roots of the present impasse can be found in the extreme centralization of powers, personified by the King, and enforced by the Imperial Army and no less than five additional security forces. . . . Today the problem is not one of absorbing several colleagues of Mossadegh, as many in the West seem to think, but rather the participation in society of masses of young people." His solution was "the fall of the Shah's regime and the establishment of an Islamic republic founded on the popular support for Islamic precepts and the goal of national independence."[33]

He served as foreign minister in an early revolutionary cabinet but was forced out by the opposition of the traditional fundamentalists. However, he was able to win a clear majority in the popular voting for president. Early in 1980, as president, he faced the same opposition from the leaders of the IRP, and he could not translate his individual victory in the presidential elections into a victory for liberal fundamentalists in the subsequent parliamentary elections. The IRP gained a large majority of the seats and, after considerable political maneuvering, gained the appointment of one of the more religiously traditional politicians to the post of prime minister. The liberal fundamentalists were thus articulate but weak. For a period of time, it appeared that Bani Sadr was strengthening his position as a result of his leadership role in the war with Iraq, which started in 1980. However, by the end of 1981, he had been ousted from his position as president by the IRP-dominated parliament and had organized an opposition movement in exile in alliance with the "radical" fundamentalist group, the Mujahidin-i Khalq. The murder of Ayatollah Bihishti and other IRP leaders at the same time as Bani Sadr's flight from Iran created a confused political situation within the country. However, the supporters of Bani Sadr are clearly out of any formal positions of power and are now in a position of open opposition to both the IRP and Ayatollah Khomeini.

   Radical Fundamentalism. A remarkable feature of the Iranian Islamic experience in the 1970s was the emergence of a clearly radical type of fundamentalism. This general movement affirms the literal truth of the Quran and has developed a thoroughgoing ideology of social revolution on the basis of that affirmation. It developed as part of the reorientation of radicalism and the revival of religious activism. The movement has its roots in the Freedom movement of the early 1960s, but it soon moved beyond that group to create a new style of fundamentalism, which manifested itself intellectually in the thought and influence of Ali Shariati and organizationally in the Mujahidin-i Khalq or People's Mujahidin Organization of Iran (PMOI).

   Ali Shariati (1933–1977) came from a notable family of religious scholars. His father, Muhammad Taqi Shariati, was a well-known scholar of Quranic commentary, and he gave his son a firm grounding in religious studies. Father and son were both active supporters of the Mosaddiq movement and continued to work within that movement after 1953. Ali Shariati spent much of his life in jail or exile and died in England under suspicious circumstances. He studied in France and was familiar with a wide range of Western thought as well as being committed to the Shiʿi Islamic tradition. He lectured and taught in Iran at various times. His most famous lectures were given in the Husayniyyah Irshad, a private institution established in 1965 in Tehran as a religious studies center and an Islamic education center for the general population. Shariati's lectures in the late 1960s drew large audiences, and he attracted much attention for his wide-ranging and vigorous interpretation and for his reaffirmation of Islam.

   The foundation of Shariati's analysis was *tawhid,* the concept of the divine oneness, and in his interpretation of *tawhid,* he created the foundation for a thoroughly Islamic, radical ideology. He wrote: "My world-view consists of *tauhid. Tauhid* in the sense of oneness of God is of course accepted by all monotheists. But *tauhid* as a world-view in the sense I intend in my theory means regarding the whole universe as a unity."[34] The full implication of this theory for society is that accepting social contradictions or discrimination, accepting unnatural divisions among humans as valid, is a form of polytheism or *shirk* and should be opposed. Within the truly Tawhidi Islamic society, there is a full unity that is not just a legal construct.

> All men are not simply equal: they are brothers. The difference between equality and brotherhood is quite clear. Equality is a legal concept, while brotherhood proclaims the uniform nature and disposition of all men; all men originate from a single source, whatever their color. Secondly, men and women are equal. . . . Man and woman were created out of the same substance and material at the same time and by the same Creator."[35]

Expanding from this foundation, Shariati developed a broad range of ideas that defined a general Islamic philosophy of history and society. He was clearly committed to building a modern ideology on the basis of the Quran and the Shiʿi tradition, but he did not accept the current religious institutions and leadership as reflecting the basic needs of Islam at the time, and he was an advocate of new educational programs and social reform. His teachings clearly had important political implications as well during the time of the monarchy. One supporter wrote: "He fought on two fronts simultaneously. He opposed the extreme traditionalists who had spun a web around themselves, separated Islam from society, retreated into a corner of the mosque and the madrasa, and often reacted negatively to any kind of intellectual movement within society. . . . He also opposed the rootless and imitative intellectuals who had made the 'new scholasticism' their stronghold. Both groups had severed their relations with society and the masses of the people."[36]

Shariati came into contact with a wide range of people, especially while teaching at the Husayniyyah Irshad. He was on the board of directors with Seyyed Hossein Nasr, whose ideas of mystical unity were similar to Shariati's concept of *tawhid*, although Shariati went much further in drawing the social implications of that unity. Also on the board of the school at that time was Ayatollah Murtaza Mutahhari, a reformist religious teacher who was an active supporter of Khomeini. Mutahhari was a member of the ruling Revolutionary Council after the overthrow of the shah until he was murdered by an extremist group called Forqan. The ambiguity of Shariati's revolutionary heritage is illustrated by the explanations of the murder of Mutahhari, since some people claim that Forqan was inspired by Shariati's "anticlericalism" to oppose the emerging religious state, and others argue that Shariati and Mutahhari were working for the same goals and that Mutahhari's murder was a part of the imperialist counterrevolutionary activity.[37]

Although Shariati was persecuted by the shah's regime and his ideas clearly had revolutionary implications, Shariati was not himself the leader of a well-organized group. He did, however, help to provide the ideological foundations for a radical fundamentalism that assumed an active organizational form during these years. The most significant of the groups of this type was the Mujahidin (PMOI). The PMOI was established by young men who had been initially associated with the Freedom movement but who had become convinced, after the repression of 1963, that more militant and violent means were necessary if the shah's repressive regime were to be overthrown. Although they maintained ties with leading liberal fundamentalists, such as Ayatollah Taliqani, and continued to be influenced by their thought, they formed a separate, secret organization.

In their early discussions, the members of what was to become the PMOI worked to interpret Islam in light of a careful analysis of the Quran and the revolutionary needs of their society. In a summary of its history and ideology, the PMOI defined its position in 1979 in this way: "After years of extensive study into Islamic history and Shiʿi ideology, our organization has reached the firm conclusion that Islam, especially Shiʿism, will play a major role in inspiring the masses to join the revolution. It will do so because Shiʿism, particularly Hussein's historic act of resistance, has both a revolutionary message and a special place in our popular culture."[38] The concept of unity of society and order based on *tawhid* was explored by the early PMOI leaders, and they felt that an adequate and careful understanding of the Quran could provide the basis for a classless commonwealth. As the PMOI began to be more active, it helped to support the Husayniyyah Irshad and was closely associated with the ideas of Ali Shariati, whose writings and lecture cassettes have been widely distributed by the organization.

The growing militancy of the PMOI brought it into conflict with the shah's police, and in the early 1970s, virtually all of the early leaders were executed. However, the organization continued to be active, and it played a role in the revolution of 1978–1979. Following the establishment of the Islamic republic, the PMOI made a great effort to cooperate with the Khomeini regime, frequently expressing loyalty and adherence to Khomeini's leadership. However, the PMOI faced harassment and persecution at the hands of the more traditional fundamentalist organizations such as the Revolutionary Guard and the IRP, and by the fall of 1981, the Mujahidin leadership was in formal opposition to the Islamic republic. The Mujahidin had aided Bani Sadr in his escape from Iran and some of its leaders joined forces with him in creating an Islamic opposition-in-exile. Within Iran, the Mujahidin appeared to many observers to be the major focus of opposition to the IRP-dominated regime by the end of 1981.

Through its writings and activities, the PMOI has developed a broad basis for a radical Islamic fundamentalism. In its ideological work, the PMOI has "stressed the use of the fundamental works of Islam, particularly the Qoran and the Nahjol-balagheh [the major Shiʿi collection of traditions]. . . . However, the method involved is concerned not with that view of religion and the Qoran which ignores social factors but with the renewed attention to Islam as a social, even as a historical phenomenon."[39] The Quran is "a set of guidelines to praxis based on the ideological values which it presents in terms of the background of the Towhidi world outlook, from which the particular practical principles are inferred."[40] The goal of the implementation of this ideology is "leading the society to the complete obliteration of exploitation and the establishment of the Towhidi system,"[41] which means an emphasis on populist participation and a rejection of existing lines of social discrimination. The possibility of conflict with other Islamic groups is implicit in the slogan of the Mujahidin candidate for president in the 1980 elections: Islamic Republic: Yes! Reactionary Misuse of Islam: No![42]

Through the work of Ali Shariati, the PMOI, and a number of other groups, a vigorous radical fundamentalism has emerged in Iran. It represents a significant development in the fundamentalist style of Islam in the modern world, bridging the potential gap between secularist radicalism and traditional Islam.

Traditional and New Radicalism. The established organizations of secularist radicalism in Iran, like the Tudeh party, were greatly weakened by the repressive measures of the shah. Although they continued to operate, they had less impact upon the development of the revolution than did the emerging new style of radicalism represented by groups such as the Feda'-i Khalq-i Iran (Organization of Iranian People's Fedaii Guerrillas, commonly referred to as the Fedayan).

In the radical tradition, the emphasis is on the necessity for class struggle to overcome exploitation within society, and it is the working class and the poor masses who are to be mobilized in the creation of the new society. But for both the traditional and the new radicals, the role of Islam poses a problem. Islam has clearly been a bulwark of the traditional exploiting structures of society and is to be opposed, at least in that form, but given the clear Muslim identification of most of those who are to be mobilized, Islam cannot be openly attacked.

The overthrow of the monarchical regime was a point on which the religious groups and the secularist radicals could agree. The relationship was defined by the secretary general of the Tudeh party, Nureddin Kianuri, in 1979.

> The content of this revolution is anti-imperialist, popular and democratic. Of course it took place under Islam's umbrella, but this is precisely what Islam, or better, Shiᶜism is. It is anti-imperialist, anti-dictatorial and consequently democratic, popular and anti-capitalist. After all, the role Islam played in the pre-revolutionary period, not only politically and organizationally, through the mosques, was catalytic and principally indicative of its more profound content. It is precisely this content that our party recognized. . . . Shiᶜism is a revolutionary and progressive ideology which we will never encounter blocking our road to socialism which—let us make things clear—in our country cannot have a Muslim content but will be achieved through the cooperation of Muslim forces.[43]

In this way, old- and new-style secular radicals have recognized revolutionary Islam as an ally in the transformation of society. However, they have not made an effort to present their radicalism as a synthesis of Muslim and radical secularist ideas, which, in practical terms, has resulted in rather unsteady alliances of the revolutionary forces. Following the establishment of the Islamic republic, the more traditional radicals in the Tudeh cooperated more fully with the Khomeini regime, and the Fedayan were the target of traditional fundamentalist attacks. The future of the secularist radicals was unclear by the fall of 1980, although the groups like the Fedayan had a real influence among labor groups and among many of the college and university students. However, the existence of a radical Islamic alternative for those people provides a challenge to the secularist movements that they have not often faced in the past.

Summary. For many people, the Iranian revolution represents the major event of the Islamic revival of the 1970s. It clearly exhibited the continuing strength of traditional fundamentalism and marked the emergence of a radical style of fundamentalism. To many, it proved that modernization programs that ignore the profound Islamic base of society are insufficient, even when backed by the strongest coercive forces. These broader issues, rather than the headlines about the U.S. hostages, are the features of the 1970s experience with the greatest long-term significance. The experience of Iran presents a microcosm of the great issues that face Islamic communities and their governments in the last quarter of the twentieth century.

Afghanistan: Kings, Radicals, and Islamic Revolt

The conservative adaptationism of the Afghan monarchy also did not provide a basis for stable development during the 1970s. In contrast to the shah's regime, however, the Afghan monarchical system fell because it was too weak. The parliamentary system initiated in 1962–1963 failed to provide effective leadership for the country. King Muhammad Zahir moved very slowly and cautiously in implementing the new programs, and the many divisions within the country soon dominated the political scene. The desire for stronger leadership made it possible for Daoud Khan to lead the army in a coup, which established the republic of Afghanistan in 1973. Although the monarchy was formally overthrown, Daoud himself was from the old royal family, and the political elite was not significantly changed by the end of the monarchy.

From 1973 until the spring of 1978, Daoud Khan ruled the country as president. He continued a program of relatively gradual modernizing reforms, working to eliminate corruption in the bureaucracy and to modernize the criminal and civil law structures, including measures to give women equal rights. He also worked to establish a stronger centralized control over the various ethnic and tribal groups, which often were virtually autonomous. Because of the relative poverty of the Afghan economy, Daoud had to rely on foreign assistance, and most of it came from the Soviet Union. This situation helped to augment the strength of the leftist groups within the country, and they soon began to organize radical opposition to the republican regime. Daoud also faced conservative resistance by tribal and religious leaders who opposed parts of his centralizing reformist program, and that resistance resulted in a tribal-religious revolt in Panjsher in 1975. Although this revolt was soon crushed, the emergence of the conservative tribal resistance led by religious notables calling for the overthrow of the "godless, communist dominated regime" in Kabul was an indication of the future.

In the face of economic problems and growing opposition from both the left and the right, Daoud began to rely increasingly on the tribal leaders and old allies of the royal family. The cabinets of 1977-1978 were no longer balanced between the forces of the moderate left and the conservatives, and the organized communist groups united for more effective opposition in 1977. When the government began a campaign of repression against the major leftist leaders, those men were able to mobilize their civilian and military support, and they took over the government in April 1978.

The new regime, which proclaimed the formation of the Democratic Republic of Afghanistan, was led by a coalition of the activist leftists. The local communist party, the People's Democratic party of Afghanistan (PDPA), had split during the 1960s into the Khalq faction led by Nur Muhammad Taraki and the Parcham faction led by Babrak Karmal, and both groups had been active in the era of parliamentary politics. Parcham had originally supported the Daoud regime but had soon rejoined the Khalq faction in opposition. The new government in April 1978 included both Karmal and Taraki, along with another important Khalq figure, Hafizullah Amin.

The conservative adaptationism of the monarchy and the Daoud regime had failed, and a doctrinaire radical regime came into power. That regime provided the political background for what many observers called the resurgence of Islam in Afghanistan. However, the problems of the PDPA regime were not simply a conflict between secularist radicals and a resurgent Islam.

The struggles within Afghanistan after the April 1978 revolution represent a number of concurrent internal conflicts rather than a clearly defined civil war. The first conflict was within the new ruling group itself. The more conservative opposition did not become an important factor for some months, and the first "civil war" was a struggle for power within the PDPA. The Parcham faction was soon driven from the government, and Karmal ended up a political refugee in eastern Europe. Then Taraki and Hafizullah Amin engaged in a struggle for power, and during that conflict, the regime announced radical social reform programs and cut its ties with the more nationalist and tribal leaders. These actions aroused new lines of opposition in the countryside, but the mounting opposition did not prevent Taraki and Amin from fighting, and Taraki was killed in October 1979. Amin, facing mounting opposition on a variety of fronts, was himself overthrown and killed as a part of the Russian invasion of Afghanistan in December 1979. At that time, Babrak Karmal returned from exile to lead a new communist government backed by Soviet troops.

The second great conflict was more clearly opposition to the radical regime by the more conservative forces. The latter were not united, and at least sixty opposition groups of varying strength and composition had emerged by late 1979. The key feature of the emerging nonradical opposition was that it was primarily conservative in style. It was not a fundamentalist movement aiming at the establishment of a new Islamic regime; instead, the opposition worked to maintain conditions as they had been and opposed the radicals' social and economic programs. Tribal and ethnic groups revolted to preserve their special positions and traditions, and they opposed the attempts by the central government to establish control from the capital. This type of resistance has a long history in Afghanistan; it was strengthened by the radical nature of the new central government's programs, but it was not created by them.

In this conservative, ethnic opposition, Islam has a special role, but that role is different from Islam's role in Iran. Virtually all Afghanis are Muslim, although the country is divided into a number of distinctive and historically competitive ethnic groups. Islam is an important part of the special heritage and identity of each of these groups, so a movement to preserve a group's special heritage is also a movement to defend Islam. However, each movement defends the distinctive blend of Islam and local custom that characterizes a particular group. In this context, Islam reinforces particularist ethnic conservatism.

The largest of the groups is the Pashtun, which contains almost half of the population. Its members have dominated Afghan politics for a long time and were the major support group for the monarchy, so much of the ethnic opposition to the central government's control has, in the past, been opposition to Pashtun dominance. The northwestern regions of Pakistan are also primarily Pashtun, and the idea of creating an independent Pashtunistan or of expanding Afghan control into the Pashtun areas of Pakistan has been an important theme in Afghan politics.

Among the Pashtuns, Islam as an independent force inspiring revolution has been most important. The resistance groups that have emerged have clearly identified themselves as movements of Islamic revolution, and purely ethnic considerations are not as visible, although tribal and clan politics play a role. However, even with a common Pashtun heritage and a shared Sunni Muslim faith, the Pashtuns have not been able to create a unified opposition movement. At least six important organizations have been created, and each has presented a program based on Islamic themes. The leadership of these groups shows the emphasis on more cosmopolitan Islamic themes and the lesser role of explicitly Pashtun ideas.

One of the largest groups is the United Islamic Front led by Sayyid Ahmad Gaylani. Gaylani is a leading member of the Qadiriyyah Tariqah, is highly respected by his followers as a saint, and holds the traditional Afghanis together on the basis of that prestige. He was a close associate of the deposed king, Muhammad Zahir, and is sympathetic to a program of moderate modernization. He was a wealthy businessman before the revolution, owning the Peugeot dealership in Kabul, and has substantial experience outside of Afghanistan.

A more conservative group is the Afghan Liberation Front, led by Sibghat-ullah Mujaddidi. The Mujaddidi family had ties with the Basmachi revolutionaries in Central Asia following World War I and was an influential force in the opposition to King Amanallah's reform programs. Mujaddidi's positions remain conservative on social and political matters, and he benefits from the prestige of his family in gaining support for his group.

The Hizb-i Islam is the most clearly fundamentalist of the cluster of Pashtun opposition groups. It claims to be the oldest of the Islamic parties and is led by a former engineering student, Gulbuddin Hekmatyar. Hekmatyar believed that even the Daoud regime was dangerously radical, and he helped to organize the 1975 revolt in Panjsher. The program of the Hizb-i Islam is a traditional fundamentalist one, and its spirit is reflected in Hekmatyar's statement that "a pure Islamic system was established 14 centuries ago, and any regime that differs from that ideal is unacceptable."[44]

The fundamentalist-conservative-modernist spectrum of these groups is reflected in the many additional groups that emerged after the 1978 revolution. Even the threats of radical programs and then Soviet invasion have not been sufficient for the groups to merge, although by the first half of 1980, significant efforts were being made in that direction. Islam plays a crucial role among these groups as it provides the basis for what common ideology does exist, and it provides the common symbols of resistance, even if the style of Islam varies from group to group.

In addition to the groups which are based primarily in Pashtun areas, there are other antigovernment militant groups, and they represent specific tribal and ethnic interests and are clearly conservative in nature. They oppose government-imposed reforms, both because they want to preserve local customs and because they do not want the central government's control expanded. One of the earliest of these groups emerged in Nuristan under the leadership of a revered tribal leader, Muhammad Anwar Khan. The Nuristanis were converted to Islam only in the past century, and they bring a special Islamic zeal to the effort to protect and preserve their culture. They succeeded in establishing an area of Free Nuristan by early 1979. Other ethnic-religious groups resisting the regime are the Tajiks in the northeast; the Uzbeks and Turkomen groups along the Soviet border, where the old Basmachi tradition is remembered; and many other local opposition groups. In each, Islam is an important element in the identity that is being preserved, but the ethnic conservatism (as well as intergroup rivalry) is strong enough that Islam cannot provide unity for the resistance movements as a whole.

One special group is the Hazara. Its members, who are largely Shiʿi Muslims rather than Sunni, live in central and western Afghanistan, and they have been persecuted traditionally by the Sunni communities. They have been the best organized in terms of being able to unite the various factions within their community, and they have established a virtually independent area in central Afghanistan. Because of their Shiʿism they are often said to be receiving aid from the Islamic republic of Iran, but the

Hazara resistance movement has been largely self-sufficient and independent.

By the end of the 1970s, Afghanistan was the arena for a great deal of militant Islamic activism. However, in most cases, it was a militancy in the cause of a conservative style of Islam. The process of modernization and adaptation has been slow in Afghanistan, so the old ethnic-Islamic groupings have remained largely intact. As a result, when those groups were challenged by the extreme radicalism of the PDPA, a conservative rather than a fundamentalist militancy emerged, and the conservative adaptationism of the beginning of the 1970s had become, by the end of the decade, a conservative militancy.

Surviving Adaptationist Monarchies

During the 1970s, a number of adaptationist monarchies survived the tumult. In most cases, the key to survival was combining a rigorous opposition to secularist radicalism with an appeal to nationalist and religious themes, which was done in the context of a continued commitment to the economic modernization of a number of countries. This prescription has not eliminated political opposition, but at least until 1980, it has provided a means for preserving the monarchical traditions. The states in this group are the shaykhdoms of the Persian/Arab Gulf, Oman, Jordan, and Morocco.

The effectiveness of the appeal to nationalism is most apparent in Morocco, where the religious validity of the monarchical system was already firmly established. Hasan II faced a number of challenges, including attempts by the military to take control of the government, but those were defeated, and the radical political organizations remained strictly controlled by royalist security forces. Hasan was able to strengthen the appeal to the general population by, from the Moroccan perspective, a major nationalist victory. When the Spanish withdrew from their colony, Spanish Sahara, Hasan first secured a partition of the territory between Morocco and Mauritania. Then, when Mauritania withdrew, he took control of the whole area. He faced major opposition from the radical liberation front in former Spanish Sahara, Polisario, which demanded independence and received support from Algeria. In 1980, the conflict continued to be expensive for Morocco, but Moroccan expansion into areas traditionally claimed as a part of the nation was a popular cause in the country. Thus, although facing significant opposition, the adaptationist monarchy has survived in Morocco on the bases of its religious legitimacy and nationalist programs. In addition, increasing revenues from phosphate exports gave added impetus to economic development in the 1970s.

A remarkable record of monarchical survival is presented by the experience of Jordan during the 1970s. At the beginning of the decade, the kingdom had just undergone two catastrophic experiences. During the Arab-Israeli War of 1967, Israeli forces had taken control of all the territory west of the Jordan River, and the loss of the West Bank area was a crippling blow to the Jordanian economy. That area contained roughly 70 percent of the country's agricultural land and had accounted for almost three-quarters of the Jordanian gross national product. Continued economic survival depended upon foreign grants and subsidies. The second crisis had come with the rise of active Palestinian organizations, well-armed groups operating within Jordan with a high degree of autonomy. They continued the vigorous attack on the monarchy that had begun with the radical socialists in the early 1960s, and it became clear in 1970 that a major clash between the Palestinian groups and the monarchy was inevitable. This challenge was overcome late in that year when the Jordanian army crushed the armed forces of the Palestinian groups and defeated a brief Syrian intervention. King Husayn emerged from the conflict with the reputation of being an enemy of the Arab-Palestinian cause.

By the end of the 1970s, however, the position of Jordan had been transformed. By careful diplomacy and consistent adherence to principle, Husayn has become recognized as an Arab spokesman and as an ally of many of his former enemies. He submitted to the decision of the Arab Summit Conference of 1974 to recognize the Palestine Liberation Organization (PLO) as the sole representative of the Palestinian people, and in international diplomacy, he has worked with the leaders of the PLO, although he has not allowed Palestinian groups to operate openly in Jordan. He has worked closely with the socialist regime in Syria, and in the Iran-Iraq war that began in 1980, he became a major ally of the Iraqi socialist regime. In this way, he has reduced the sources of radical attacks upon his monarchy, and while doing so, Husayn has been able to reorganize the Jordanian economy successfully, and the standard of living has been improving at a sound rate.

The transformation of Jordan's position during the 1970s has not eliminated opposition to the monarchy, but it has significantly weakened it. Potential radical opposition has been reduced because of the international position of the state, and internally, improved living standards and active development policies have reduced the effectiveness of domestic radical opposition.

In the mid-1970s, after twenty-five years on the throne, the past precarious state of the monarchy and its present healthy condition were summed up in the phrase Peter Mansfield used to describe Jordan: "Jordan: the stubborn survivor." Mansfield went on to note that many "obituaries of the Hashemite kingdom of Jordan have been prepared for instant use. There have been many occasions in the past twenty-five years when the external and internal forces gathered against this last of the Anglo-Arab monarchies were so strong and numerous that its survival seemed impossible. But it still lives and the obituaries gather dust in the files."[45] In many ways, that passage catches the effective spirit of conservative adaptationism that characterized the Jordanian monarchy in the 1970s and allowed it to survive.

In a period of rising religious enthusiasm, King Husayn has followed a low-key religious policy. The monarchy continues to identify itself with the Islamic tradition, which reduces the effectiveness of the militant Islamic opposition. The monarchy also remains committed to a clearly modernizing development program. The religious prestige of the royal family is kept in the public eye by special events that emphasize the pious foundations of the family without committing the government to fundamentalist-type programs. As an example, in April 1977, King Husayn donated to the Jordanian people a letter written by the Prophet Muhammad to a Byzantine emperor. The letter had been a family heirloom, emphasizing the ties of the family with the Prophet, and would be shown in a mosque built specially for the purpose.

The essentially moderate nature of the official view of the relationship between government policy and Islam in Jordan is clearly illustrated by the government statement of policy presented by a new prime minister in December 1979.

> This nation, which was one of the first areas to be pervaded by the radiance of the early dawn of Islam, shall adhere to the spirit of enlightened Islam, far from intolerance and extremism. It shall continue to promote true and enlightened Islamic thought. The government shall continue to support solidarity in the Islamic world, to promote a comprehensive renaissance in the Islamic countries and to consolidate the bonds of close cooperation among Islamic states.[46]

In terms of the contemporary Islamic experience, the conservative adaptationism of the Jordanian monarchy continues to represent a careful blending of Islamic legitimacy and evolutionary modernization that attempts to avoid militant fundamentalism and secular radicalism. Although both remain threats, the monarchy was clearly successful in its balance as the fifteenth Islamic century began.

The small monarchical states on the Arabian Peninsula also faced a variety of challenges during the 1970s. Basically conservative in mood and attempting to preserve the monarchical systems, the greatest transformation was part of the monarchical policy of encouraging the development of the oil industry. The rapid growth of revenues from the export of oil created vastly new conditions in these small states, from Kuwait through the United Arab Emirates (UAE) and Oman. These states remained politically conservative in orientation while encouraging rapid economic development, which raised the inherent problem of a growing desire for increased political participation without major political structural change.

In general terms, the monarchies attempted, with substantial success, to reduce the demands for radical change in the political arena by programs of social welfare and rapid economic development. Islam has not played a particularly visible role in those attempts, although during the 1970s, most monarchies made an effort to be more manifestly Muslim through actions that ranged from the enforcement of the Islamic prohibition of alcohol in the UAE to a policy of basing the laws and constitution of Kuwait on Islamic law.

There has been little conservative opposition to the monarchical programs in these small states. By the 1970s, the challenge from the imamate in inner Oman had been defeated by the sultan, and Muslim conservatives elsewhere were a major part of the business and commercial groups that benefited from the development of the oil industry.

Through much of the 1970s, the most visible opposition to the monarchical regimes came from radical groups, who opposed the close ties of the rulers to the Western imperialist states and demanded a higher degree of economic and political democracy. One result of this opposition was that parliamentary regimes were suspended by the rulers of Kuwait (in 1976) and Bahrain (in 1975) and not implemented elsewhere. The leading parliamentary opposition group in Kuwait was Arab nationalist and socialist in orientation.

The most revolutionary movement emerged in the least developed country, Oman. In its southernmost province, a radical liberation movement was able to mobilize substantial popular opposition to the regime. The organization was initially called the Dhofar Liberation Front (DLF), and it received support from a variety of sources. It had emerged as a result of an alliance of forces ranging from supporters of the imam/antisultan tradition of inner Oman to Nasserites and regional separatists.

When the DLF was created in the 1960s, it had a clear focus for its opposition in the sultan, Said ibn Taymur, who was vigorously repressive and attempted to stop all modernization in the country. By 1970, the prospects for the DLF were rapidly changing as a result of both internal and external events. The decline of Nasserite socialism saw the radicalism becoming more populist in style, and it was influenced by the emergence of a radical independent regime in South Yemen. The major change, however, was the overthrow of Sultan Said by his son, Qabus, who quickly acted to develop a program of a visible, if conservative, modernization. Qabus was able to undermine the vigor of the opposition to the regime by his policies, and then, with the military support of Iran, he was able to defeat the liberation movement. In this struggle, the new sultan mobilized religious symbols as well as military force and development programs and worked to build a greater acceptance of the legitimacy of the existing political system in contrast to what he called atheistic radicalism.

By the end of the 1970s, the general political context had changed significantly, and Islamic themes were becoming increasingly important in the dynamics of domestic and regional politics. The potential of the major religious opposition was raised by the success of the Iranian revolution, and Shiʿi groups in the whole gulf region, but especially in Kuwait and Bahrain, were inspired by that successful Shiʿi revolution. However, the potential opposition was contained—at least through the spring of 1981—by careful surveillance and repression.

The emergence of fundamentalist Islam as a potentially significant political force is reflected in the Kuwait parliamentary elections held in February 1981. The ruler allowed a return to parliamentary government, and although conservative, progovernment candidates won a substantial majority of the seats, the old Arab nationalist-socialist opposition group was totally defeated. The new major opposition group that replaced it represents activist fundamentalist Muslim groups. Those groups, including the Social Reform Association (which is linked to the Muslim Brotherhood) and the Silfiyyin, have gained growing support among the younger, modern-educated Kuwaitis and are a clearly visible element in the student body of the national university.

The small monarchies of the gulf region survived the turmoil of the 1970s by a careful pragmatism. They are conservative in their basic goals but adaptationist in economic policy. When necessary, they were able to mobilize an appeal to Islamic tradition as a way of reinforcing the legitimacy of the political system that they were working to preserve. However, having survived the socialist challenges of the 1960s and 1970s they are facing more direct Islamic challenges in the form of revivalist and fundamentalist movements as the new Islamic century begins.

Islam in Radical and Secular Regimes

One feature of the Islamic resurgence during the 1970s was the increasing importance of Islamic themes in regimes that were more secularist or socialist in their identity. The gradual Islamization of symbols and policies within many of those states represents a significant change in emphasis. In some ways, this evolution is a natural product of an effort to create more authentically indigenous ideologies of modernization, and in other ways, it is a practical reorientation of policies in line with popular feeling.

In most of these states, this religionizing of politics provided greater recognition for fundamentalist ideas, but the general tone remained more modernist than clearly fundamentalist. It was not a context in which conservative Islam played a significant role other than providing ex post facto confirmation for the emerging mood. The basic goal of most of the regimes was to provide an ideological framework that was both manifestly modern and authentically Islamic.

The new ideological style placed a lower priority on secularism as an ideal or as a requirement for modernization, and the experiences of the radical and secularist regimes during the 1970s represent a significant departure from the earlier programs of modernization. Although all of these regimes continued to limit the political activity of traditional Islamic structures, many of them stopped the earlier advocacy of the separatism of religion and politics. The future of these programs will be of great interest to people who examine the relationship between secularization and modernization.

Egypt: Arab Socialism and the Revival of Islam

The death of Nasser in 1970 marked the beginning of a new era in Egyptian history. Although there had already been some movement away from the activist socialism of Nasserism following the Arab-Israeli War of 1967, it was under Nasser's successor, Anwar al-Sadat, that the major changes took place. For a variety of reasons, both domestic and international, Sadat created a major new policy orientation for Egypt. That new orientation included a withdrawal from socialist economic policies replacing them with policies that encouraged a mixed economy through utilizing local private enterprise and foreign investment. A second major policy reorientation took place in foreign affairs as there was a move away from close ties to the Soviet Union and eastern bloc countries and toward establishing friendly relations with the United States. A major policy transformation also occurred in Egypt's relations with Israel. At first, Sadat continued the militant policy of opposition to Israel and provided leadership in planning and executing the 1973 war against that country. However, in the postwar negotiations, Sadat worked vigorously for a negotiated settlement of the dispute, and his effort culminated with his trip to Jerusalem and the signing of an Egyptian-Israeli peace treaty in 1979. All of these major changes reflect what many observers call the de-Nasserization of the Egyptian regime.

The transformation of the old radical socialism provided the general policy context for Islam in Egypt during the 1970s. The traditions of Nasserism have not disappeared, and there are still many people who advocate the older policies. However, the dominant tone has been one in which Islamic themes have priority, and the socialist themes of the 1960s now represent an ideology of opposition. The new visibility of Islam in Egypt can be seen in many ways.

Official Policy. The official policies of Sadat's government gave greater recognition to Islamic themes. That recognition was the product of a general revival of Muslim consciousness, especially among the educated political elite, and the fact that the strongest political opposition in the 1970s came from the more fundamentalist groups in Egyptian society. Observers and Egyptians alike frequently point out the visible signs of a reaffirmation of Islam among educated Egyptians. Administrators are more regular in their prayers, the Friday prayers in the major mosques are much better attended, and growing numbers of female students in the high schools and universities have adopted Islamically suitable clothing. This reaffirmation has set the tone for government policies that are less secularist and more Islamic.

The general style of the official revival is modernist in content. Although influenced by fundamentalist ideas, the Sadat regime maintained the intellectual adaptationism of the tradition of Abduh's thought, and the growing emphasis on Islamic themes can be seen in the constitutional developments. As a part of the establishment of the new regime, a new constitution was promulgated in 1971, and in the development of that document, there was vigorous discussion of the role of Islam in the state. There was widespread acceptance of the principle that Islam should be declared the religion of the state; the major debate concerned the role of Islamic law in the legal system. The issue was whether the Shariʿah (the formal Islamic law code) should be recognized as *the* source or *a* source of legislation, and the result was a formula that affirmed the importance of the Shariʿah but did so in wording that was clearly modernist in style. The text that was approved in the popular referendum stated that "the principles of the Islamic shariᶜah are a principal source of legislation," which meant not only that the Shariᶜah was not the sole source of legislation but also that it was the basic "principles" of Islamic law rather than its medieval formulations that received constitutional recognition.[47] In 1980, the wording was amended, in line with government proposals and approved by popular referendum, to indicate a stronger role for Islamic law by referring to the Shariᶜah as *the* principal source of law.

Another aspect of the government's religious policy was its relaxation of control imposed by Nasser on the expression of fundamentalist ideas. In the days of Nasserite socialism, groups like the Muslim Brotherhood had been vigorously opposed. A report signed by Nasser in 1965, for example, stated, "As the Brotherhood hides behind the mask of religion, using it as a slogan to deceive our masses about the Brotherhood's own vassalage to imperialism and reaction, so the principles they espouse are far removed from Islam."[48] Although the Brotherhood remained formally illegal under Sadat, its members had great freedom of expression, such as in the publication of two widely read magazines, *al-Daᶜwah* and *al-Itisam*, which are popularly recognized as organs of the Muslim Brotherhood. In addition, other fundamentalist groups were active on university campuses and were allowed to participate in student union elections. Although the union itself was dissolved in 1979, after it became fully dominated by fundamentalist student groups, the government continued to allow such groups to engage in many activities.

President Sadat thus showed a much greater tolerance for fundamentalist groups than Nasser did, which reflects both the increasing power of those groups in Egypt and the stronger affirmation of Islam by the government. However, that tolerance did not mean that Sadat, or government policy, had become fundamentalist. Although Sadat encouraged governmental and religious cooperation within a framework of modernist Islam, he sharply attacked religious extremism. Following incidents of harassment of Coptic Christians and antigovernment demonstrations by fundamentalists, he emphasized, on a number of occasions, the importance of separating religion from politics and keeping religion free from fanaticism. In line with this attitude, he was sharply critical of the Islamic revolution in Iran and was willing to provide asylum for the deposed shah in 1980, despite strong local opposition. In September 1981, he initiated a more strict suppression of Islamic and other opposition groups within Egypt. Following his murder in October 1981, the long-term policies of his successor, Husni Mubarak, were not clear, but it was evident that Mubarak, initially, stressed discipline and control over potential opposition groups of all types.

Revived Fundamentalism. The tradition of fundamentalist associations in modern Egypt has deep roots. In the past, the dominant organization was the Muslim Brotherhood, and under Sadat, there was a tendency to speak of all fundamentalists as Muslim Brothers. However, during the 1970s, a large number of groups emerged that share a common spirit with the Brotherhood but are not organizationally tied to that association.

The differences among these groups are primarily in terms of method and degree of militance rather than ideology. Most programs advocate the creation of an Islamic state and the enforcement of Islamic law, and they are essentially similar to the programs of Hasan al-Banna. In this sense, the dominant style of Egyptian fundamentalism is more traditional than radical, and it does not represent a departure from the basic fundamentalist ideological positions of the past decades. Most groups took specific stands in opposition to the policies of the Sadat regime, opposing, in particular, the negotiations and treaty with Israel and the close ties with the United States.

The fundamentalist groups present a variety of formats. There are purely local groups, organized around private mosques, whose activities include establishing cooperative food stores or sewing rooms for poor women or aiding students in the schools. The most visible fundamentalist organizations are on the university campuses. Such campus groups were originally encouraged by the government to counter the influence of leftists among students, but they soon reflected the general religious revival and became actively independent. In 1977–1978, the largest of those groups, al-Jama'ah al-Islamiyyah (the Islamic Society), won the majority of the leadership posts in the student unions of virtually every Egyptian university. The Islamic Society is active in many areas of student life and helps provide inexpensive textbooks, tutorials, inexpensive and appropriately Islamic clothing for women, and a broad range of other social services. The Islamic Society follows the spirit of the Muslim Brotherhood, and some of its pamphlets and publications are distributed by Brotherhood groups.

In addition to the many public organizations like the Islamic Society, there are a number of fundamentalist groups that advocate direct revolutionary action. These are secret organizations that are quickly suppressed when their activities become visible to the public, and the most prominent of these during the 1970s was al-Takfir wa al-Hijrah. The group was accused of kidnapping and murdering a former minister of religious endowments, and many of its leaders were tried and convicted in 1977. The group's leader, Ahmad Shukri Mustafa, called for the overthrow of the regime and the establishment of an Islamic state, and it was reported that he made messianic claims. In 1974, another group, led by Salem Sariyah, attacked the military academy, and during the ensuing trial, the leader said that their goal was to "restore the glory of Islam, by bloodshed if necessary."[49] During the 1970s, other similar groups were reported, including the Soldiers of God and the Jihad. Following a series of bombings on Christmas Eve in 1979, seventy members of the Jihad were arrested, but reports during 1980 indicated that the Jihad continued to be active in Egypt and had support among expatriate Egyptians in places like Kuwait.[50] Militant groups of this type were directly involved in the murder of Sadat, and that event gave strong evidence of their strength.

Clearly, activist and militant fundamentalists are an important feature of the Islamic revival in Egypt. They set limits to the degree of secularism possible in government policy and encourage a more fundamentalist tone in the official modernist approach. Although represented by a number of new organizations, they have strong ties with the tradition of the Muslim Brotherhood and show the continuity of the present revival with earlier affirmations of Islam in Egypt.

Arab Socialism and Islam

The experience of Egypt illustrates that Arab socialism has been strongly affected by the development of Islam. Because of the changing position of radical socialism in the Arab world, socialist regimes have faced significant challenges. Arab socialism, which appeared to be the emerging dominant ideology in the middle of the 1960s, was in a weakened position in many areas by the beginning of the 1970s, and one result was that many regimes, like Sadat's in Egypt, become involved in major reorientations of policy.

A major theme in the reorientation of Arab socialism was the increased emphasis on Islam. Sometimes this was in reaction to the revival of the political power of traditional forces, at other times it was a product of growing fundamentalist pressures, and frequently, as was the case in Egypt, it reflected a growing religious consciousness among the modern-educated groups. These forces operated with varying degrees of strength in the states that had officially committed themselves to some form of Arab socialism in the 1960s.

During the 1970s, those regimes showed a remarkable degree of political stability in comparison to the 1960s. Changes of government as a result of coups or revolutions took place only in the Yemens, and although there was political unrest, the other Arab socialist regimes in 1980 were the political regimes that had existed in 1970. There were, however, significant challenges to the leadership in each of those countries. The basic dynamics of politics in all of them involved the ruling group adopting increasingly middle-of-the-road policies and facing opposition from both leftist and religiously oriented conservative or fundamentalist groups. The confirmation of the centrist position in each state meant a vivid departure from the more radical Arab socialist programs that had been initiated in the early and middle 1960s.

In Algeria, the overthrow of Ahmad Ben Bella in 1965 was accompanied by a greater emphasis on Islamic values and Arabic culture. Houari Boumedienne led the country from 1965 until his death in 1978, and he maintained that basic tone. There was still a commitment to a socialist program, but it was more closely tied to Islam and Arabism than to secularist radicalism, which is well illustrated by the Agrarian Revolution program initiated in 1971. One leftist critic of the reform described its basic ideological tone as being based on idealized peasant values: "Official propaganda now represents the peasantry as an example of austerity, diligence, Islamic orthodoxy and Arab cultural authenticity, opposed to a more easy-going, comfort-loving, religiously lax and westernized urban life-style."[51] In an oversimplified way, that statement describes much of the spirit of the socialist program in Algeria as it moved away from the radical socialism of the 1960s.

Although Boumedienne faced opposition from both more fundamentalist and more radical people, the opposition was not well organized, and it did not produce any significant turmoil or overt struggle for power when Boumedienne died. Instead, the transition of power went smoothly, in accord with constitutional procedures, and Chadli Benjedid (b. 1929) was elected president in 1979. The new government has continued the type of compromise that Boumedienne had formalized in the constitution of 1976, in which Algeria is described as a socialist state whose religion is Islam, and Benjedid has faced economic problems and some unrest from both leftists and fundamentalists. Early in 1980, demonstrations by fundamentalists in some indications of Islamic unrest among students. However, the general affirmation of Islam and the encouragement of Arabic culture have been important in Algeria but less dramatic than in many places in the Islamic world.

Similarly, an undramatic Islamic consciousness characterizes the experience of Tunisia in the 1970s. The major political concern in that country was the issue of the successor to Bourguiba, who, by the middle of 1980, appeared to have survived most of his political heirs and was working with new politicians. After the excursion into more radical socialism in the 1960s, Tunisia had returned to a more pragmatic socialist program. The Bourguiba regime had faced considerable leftist opposition, which had culminated in major labor unrest in 1978, but by 1980, the regime had come to terms with important union leaders. In general ideological terms, Bourguibism has stressed cultural modernity and Tunisia as a cultural bridge between Arab and Western civilizations. An essentially Franco-Tunisian ideological synthesis has strong appeal to the educated elite, although the general population is more closely tied to the Arab-Islamic tradition. "And even among many of the country's younger educated groups and nongoverning elites there is an increasing affinity to Islamic culture and tradition. More and more, this group appears to be seeking to reaffirm the universal qualities of Islam rather than to ignore, suppress, or amalgamate them within a European-oriented cultural matrix."[52]

In 1980, the long-term prime minister and presumed successor to Bourguiba, Hedi Nouira, was forced to retire because of illness. Mohamed Mzali became the new prime minister, and that popular politician began almost immediately to make the regime more flexible by compromising with labor union leaders and those who wanted a more liberal, possibly multiparty, political system. The change apparently reflected a willingness on the part of Bourguiba to shift emphasis. The current role of Islam is similar to what it was earlier, and it was outlined by Mzali in a statement of policy in May 1980. He

dealt with means of insuring intellectual and moral promotion to Tunisian citizens, pointing out that the government's aim was to "form mature Tunisians, deeply attached to their home country and aware of his [sic] belonging to a nation." . . . As regards Tunisia's foreign policy, Mr. Mzali reaffirmed Tunisia's attachment to its Arab-Muslim authenticity, to its belonging to the Maghreb community and Africa with a wide availability for Western modern technologies and also for the modern sorts of organization which make up today the strength of modern nations.[53]

The dominant style of Islam in Tunisia is clearly a modernizing adaptationism that is neither secularist nor fundamentalist, although it is under pressure from both of those styles.

In Syria, the pressures on the socialist secularism of the regime have been much stronger and better organized than in Tunisia. Leaders of the Ba'th party remained in political control, but a new pragmatic tone was set in 1970 when Hafiz al-Assad emerged as the dominant leader, and the "corrective movement," which was initiated at that time, moved away from the earlier dogmatic radicalism of the Ba'th Syrian regime. Assad emphasized a less vigorous socialization of the economy and worked to build a broader base of popular support through a national front.

Although Assad faced some opposition from the more radical forces, the most effective popular opposition came from groups that rallied support by appealing to a revived Sunni Muslim consciousness. One difficulty posed for Assad was that he comes from a Shi'i community in Syria, the Alawites, and he had relied heavily on Alawites to fill important government positions. It was thus possible for his opponents to arouse the Sunni majorities in major urban areas by describing his government as an attempt at an Alawi domination of Syria.

The first major crisis to assume a religious tone came with the presentation of a draft constitution in 1973. The proposed constitution emphasized the themes of Arab nationalism and liberation and the need for realizing a just socialist society. It did not, however, declare Islam to be the religion of the state, which aroused significant popular opposition. As a result, the draft was amended to include a provision that the president of the republic was to be of the Islamic faith. The constitution, as approved in March 1973, also stated that Muslim jurisprudence "is the principal source of legislation."[54] In the constitutional dispute, the Ba'th leadership maintained a secularist position of full equality for all religions, with the state guaranteeing "the free expression of religion as long as this does not jeopardize public order."[55] At the same time, it was clear that Assad had to soften this secularist position in order to accommodate the religious sensibilities of the Sunni majority.

In the latter part of the 1970s, it was clear that the compromise did not satisfy the more militant and fundamentalist opposition, and there were many demonstrations and acts of terrorism that were the product of the revived militancy of the Muslim Brotherhood in Syria. The opposition called for the overthrow of the Assad government and for the institution of an Islamic state. Through 1980, Assad had managed to control this Islamic opposition, but only with difficulty. Speeches by Assad discussing the Muslim Brotherhood illustrate the relationship between Islam and Ba'th policy at the end of the 1970s. The basic themes are the recognition of Islam as a key element in the Syrian-Arab identity, opposition to fundamentalist styles of Islam, and the maintenance of a political system that recognizes religious values but supports a secularist equality of religious believers within Syria. On 30 June 1979, for example, Assad stated:

> The meaning of the homeland loses its sense if its citizens are not equal. This equality is an integral part of Islam. We are leading the country in the name of the Arab Socialist Ba'th Party. I am leading it in my capacity as the party secretary general and the president of the republic, not in the name of a religion or a religious community, despite the fact that Islam is the religion of the majority. . . . Those who consider religion to be a matter of ritual and neglect its essence cause it to be an obstacle to progress. . . . We have always worked to strengthen religious values in the citizens' hearts. We have affirmed that Islam is a religion of life and progress. . . . [the Muslim Brotherhood members] want to monopolize Islam for themselves, despite the fact that no party has the right to monopolize Islam or any other religion. . . . The Arab Socialist Ba'th Party is a pan-Arab socialist party that does not differentiate between religions. As a faithful Muslim, I encourage everyone to have faith and to fight rigidity and fanaticism, because they contradict Islam.[56]

The same attempt to balance pragmatic socialism with nationalism and Islam was made in Iraq. After a decade of political turmoil, the Ba'th party came into control in Iraq in 1968. The branch of the party in Iraq emerged as a rival to the Syrian Ba'th, but the general tone of the Iraqi regime was remarkably similar. The Iraqi Ba'th regime of Ahmad Hasan al-Bakr also assumed an increasingly pragmatic and nondoctrinaire tone during the 1970s, and as a result, the regime continued into the 1980s.

In Iraq, the regime faced a variety of problems and types of opposition as the difficulties posed by the pluralistic nature of the Iraqi society continued into the 1970s. The Kurds of the north resisted centralized control measures and engaged in political and military opposition throughout the decade. In 1975, an agreement between Iran and Iraq undermined the effectiveness of the Kurdish resistance, and the willingness of the Bakr government to cooperate with the shah of Iran was a measure of the nondoctrinaire pragmatism of the regime. Appeals to Islam and national unity were insufficient grounds for the settlement of the Kurdish problem in Iraq, and the Kurdish resistance to the Khomeini regime in Iran after 1979 complicated matters for the Iraqi government.

A second problem was even more directly related to religious issues. The Sunni Arabs of Iraq dominated the political system centered in Baghdad, although they were a minority of the population, and the large Shi'i Arab population often felt subject to discrimination and periodic protests occurred. The Islamic revolution in Iran created the potential of Iranian support for Shiʿi opposition to the Baʿth regime, and as a result, relations between Iraq and Iran were strained and ultimately led to war in 1980. Attempts by Khomeini to dominate Shiʿi opinion in Iraq were, however, resisted by many Shiʿi leaders, as is illustrated by the refusal of Iraqi Shiʿi leaders to agree to Khomeini's proposal in 1980 to shift important Shiʿite colleges and their faculties to Iran.

In this complicated situation, the role of Islam is clearly complex. It is an important element in the Kurdish ethnic identity, so national integration struggles do not involve opposition to or support for religion. They involve, rather, the interaction of a more localized Islamic tradition with a more broadly interpreted Islam. The common Islamic faith of the Iraqis is part of the heritage of national unity to which the Baʿth leaders appeal. Relations of the government with the Shiʿi communities are equally complex, but in that case, the more general nature of a personalized Islam implied in a secularist program can be a vehicle for lessening intercommunal tension.

The key to Baʿth policy in terms of Islam is the attempt to present Islam as a basis for national unity rather than for division and as a support for Arab nationalism and a socialist program rather than as a part of the traditional social structure, which is being transformed. This basic tone survived the major change of leadership in 1979 when Ahmad Hasan al-Bakr retired and was succeeded by Saddam Husayn in a constitutionally regulated transfer of power. In outlining his positions upon becoming president, Saddam Husayn provided a statement of the general position of Islam in Iraqi policy, relating it to Iraq's history and its Arab nationalist role. He stated:

> the transfer of power from leader to leader in the moral and normal constitutional manner that took place in our country, party and revolution is unique among all the experiments in the ancient and contemporary worlds. It is unique but not strange because it emanates from the Arab nation's nobility, the greatness of the message of Islam and the principles of the Arab Socialist Baʿth Party. . . . In our life as Arabs and Iraqis and during our long history, moral and ethical values continue to be an important factor in achieving success and victory. . . . I will act inspired by the creed of the party and the Arab nation's heritage and the spirit of heavenly [divinely inspired] messages. . . . We are not an atheist state and our constitution establishes Islam as the state religion.[57]

The establishment of an Arab socialist regime had been most disputed and least successful in Yemen during the 1960s. Following the overthrow of the imam in 1962, a civil war had broken out between tribal-royalist forces and supporters of the socialist republican government, and each side had received significant support from non-Yemeni groups. Following the 1967 Arab-Israeli War, the Egyptian forces supporting the socialist regime were withdrawn, and Yemen began the process of reconstructing a national government. By 1970 a compromise was reached, with the conservative forces accepting the principle of a republican regime and the end of the imamate and the republican socialists agreeing to a more conservative orientation for the government. The results of the compromise were formalized in a constitution that went into effect in December 1970. In this constitution, the state was clearly defined as Arab and Islamic, with the tone being conservative rather than radical. The preamble to the 1970 constitution defines the moderate-conservative republican position clearly in regard to the identity of Yemen.

> We the Yemenis are an Arab and Muslim people. Our survival and that of our country is dependent upon adherence to our true Arab nationality. . . . We shall have no life among nations and we can claim no pride or character except through our true Islamic religion which has been the religion of our nation through the last fourteen centuries, and through following its divine guidance, achieving its precepts, abiding by its directions and strictures, and by remaining within its bounds."[58]

Yemen attempted to balance the forces of radicalism and conservatism in the 1970s with some success. The constitutional regime was replaced by a military government in 1974–1975, and that regime survived the murder of its leaders in 1977 and 1978 and moved toward a new constitutional regime. The governments during this time remained relatively balanced and continued efforts at modernization while maintaining a conservative social policy. The major opposition groups received outside support. The conservatives were aided by Saudi Arabia, and the radical groups were helped by the radical government that had gained control in Aden in the newly formed People's Republic of Yemen (South Yemen).

In the balancing of the political forces, Islam provided a variety of symbols. Its continuing strength can be seen in the fact that even the most radical opposition groups presented an Islamic justification for their actions. The Democratic National Front, for example, attacked the Saudi support for the government on a variety of grounds in the summer of 1980, including charging the Saudis with being imperialist agents attempting to undermine the religious faith of the Yemenis.

> Saudi reaction and the imperialist circles are using the agent Wahhabis as a (?smokescreen) for the deceptive ideological pretensions which are aimed at casting doubts on the religious beliefs of the Yemeni people in order to obliterate their heritage and role in (?championing) and defining the Islamic mentality. Saudi reaction and imperialist circles forget that the Yemeni people were the first to support the prophet, God bless him and grant him salvation, and were in the forefront during the Islamic conquests.[59]

The 1962 revolution and subsequent civil war destroyed the most visible traditional Islamic institution in Yemen, the Zaydi imamate. However, the emergence of an Arab socialist regime did not result in a socialist transformation of society. The most successful efforts of national integration were those that combined modernizing adaptationism with a recognition of the more conservative Islamic traditions of Yemen. Secularist radicalism was changed during the 1970s into a social radicalism that recognized Islamic principles.

The true strength of the conservative, moderate, and radical forces is obscured by the active intervention in Yemeni affairs of a variety of outside groups. It is clear, however, that Islamic themes and principles, whether stated in conservative, moderate, or radical terms, continued to be an important part of the ideological and social framework of Yemeni life.

The development of Arab socialism in the 1970s in those countries where it had become an official ideology illustrates the continuing strength of Islam. Secularist radicalism, from Algeria to the Yemen Arab Republic (North Yemen), has made increasing adjustments to Islamic sentiments. Although radicalism continues to be a crucial part of the ideological development of the Arab world, it became less secularist and more Islamic in tone during the 1970s. That trend is also an important dimension of the Islamic revival at the beginning of the fifteenth Islamic century.

Modernizing Adaptationism in Asian Muslim States

Islam became an increasingly important political factor in the major Asian Muslim states during the 1970s. In those countries in which Muslims were the dominant majority—such as Turkey, Pakistan, Bangladesh, and Indonesia—the dominant style continued to be modernizing adaptationism, but a greater emphasis was placed on Islamic symbols and issues of authenticity. In those states, an important political interaction took place between groups that supported a more clearly Islamic focus and those that were committed to a more socialist, and sometimes radical, orientation.

In general terms, the socialist-oriented groups gained control of the governments in the early part of the decade. Then, for a variety of reasons, which reflect special local conditions, political power passed to groups that gave less emphasis to socialist programs. This development was accompanied by a resurgence of more clearly religious themes in the political debates and policies. There remained a commitment to modernization and development, but the general ideological framework was shifting by 1980. As was the case in Arab socialist regimes, the interaction between the modernizing ideology and Islam was sometimes complementary and sometimes antagonistic.

Turkey

The least dramatic changes in government policy took place in Turkey. The major framework for government policy remained a commitment to the Kemalist reform ideals, but the gradual withdrawal from the extreme secularism of the policies of the early republic, which had begun after World War II, continued during the 1970s. A major factor was the activities of the politically organized minority parties, which advocated a more clearly Islamic state. Both of the major parties, the Republican People's party (RPP) and the Justice party (JP), had to compromise with the activist Islamic parties in order to form governments and to gain parliamentary majorities.

During the 1970s, there was a growing polarization of politics and gradually an increasing resort to terrorism on the part of the extreme elements of both the left and the right. Together, the RPP and the JP represented the vast majority of the population and were the heirs of pragmatic Kemalism, but this moderate center of the political spectrum was unable to unite effectively to control the extremist elements. Throughout the decade, both major parties preferred to form coalitions with groups like the National Salvation party in order to form governments. Thus, after the 1973 elections, in which neither party won a parliamentary majority, the RPP, under the leadership of Bulent Ecevit, formed a coalition government with the National Salvation party, which had won almost 12 percent of the votes. In this way, the RPP government, described at the time as "the most radical Turkey has ever had," included "the first Islamic party to share power since the Constitution was secularized in 1928."⁶⁰ When the JP, under Suleyman Demirel, formed governments in 1975 and 1977, they also included the National Salvation party. Thus, in the middle of the decade, the most vigorously Islamic and antisecularist party had substantial political influence.

By 1980, the most important impact of the politically extreme groups was because of their extragovernmental actions rather than because of their participation in the constitutional processes. Both radical leftist groups and groups like the National Action party led by Alparslan Turkes created militant groups that engaged in demonstrations and often came into conflict with each other and the authorities. Some groups from both extremes engaged in terrorism and murder campaigns in an effort to disrupt the existing political system.

The program of the militant left was both radical and secularist, and as many as an estimated sixty different groups were involved. The foundation of the ideology was varying forms of Marxism, and little attempt was made to integrate Islamic themes into the pronouncements or programs. In contrast to other parts of the Islamic world, an Islamic radicalism did not emerge as a significant force in Turkey during the 1970s, and radicalism remained militantly secularist.

The groups often called "rightist" in Turkey presented a range of conservative and fundamentalist viewpoints. The National Salvation party emphasized the importance of Islam, and the National Action party stressed nationalist themes and proposed a state-corporate economic system that has often been called fascist. The militant activism of youth groups sympathetic to and associated with the National Action party gave that party added strength in the context of political terrorism. At times, the two rightist parties have clashed, and their contrasting programs show that not all of the rightists in Turkey can be described as Islamic fundamentalists.

The growing disruption of the political scene by terrorism took a more directly religious form in the increasing religious communal strife, and ethnic and religious tensions sometimes reinforced the struggle between leftists and rightists. In a number of provincial towns, Shiʿi minority groups became identified with leftist forces, and right-wing militants received strong support from the Sunnis. As a result, local conflicts that were initially clashes between organized groups from the two extremes of the political spectrum turned into communal conflicts of a religious nature. Major Sunni-Shiʿi clashes occurred in Kahramanmaras (in 1978) and Corum (in 1980) when sectarian mobs went out of control, and many casualties resulted. Similarly, potential unrest among the Turkish Kurds was encouraged by Islamic revivalism and the Islamic revolution in Iran. In 1979, demonstrators in eastern Turkey supported the Islamic program of the National Salvation party, and demonstrators called Erbakan, the party leader, Turkey's Khomeini and displayed placards reading "toward an independent Islamic state" and "the events in Iran are just a start."[61] Extremist activitists in a number of areas began to establish separate areas of control, and religious communal feelings added to the turmoil of political extremism.

The inability of the major parties to cope with the terrorism and other national problems led the Turkish military leaders to take control of the government in September 1980. Following the pattern of the 1960 revolution, the officers acted in the name of preserving the Kemalist heritage, so, at the beginning of the new decade, the dominance of the modernizing adaptationist tradition was reasserted by the Turkish armed forces. In contrast to 1960, however, the forces of both radical secularism and fundamentalism were stronger and better organized, and a decade of political turmoil had created conditions in which the affirmation of Kemalism in 1980 was more defensive than in 1960. Moderate secularism was clearly challenged by both the reassertion of Islamic themes and the further development of radicalism.

Muslim South Asia

In Muslim South Asia, problems of political instability and national integration have led to official reassertions of the Islamic identity of the states. These reassertions came late in the decade of the 1970s, which had begun with a major crisis for Islam caused by the split in the original state of Pakistan. The failure of Islam to provide a sufficient basis for national unity had provided an opening for more secularist and radical leaders to assume control of the two states that emerged from the war of 1970–1971, Pakistan (the old West Pakistan) and Bangladesh.

The leadership in both states after the war was committed to programs that were radical socialist rather than Islamic in nature. Zulfikar Ali Bhutto led Pakistan in the effort to recover from the trauma of the defeat in 1971. His radicalism was relatively carefully balanced with Islamic themes, although there was little formal formulation of an Islamic socialism. In domestic policy, Bhutto initiated programs of agrarian reform and nationalization of industries, which led him into conflict with conservative religious forces, and he had little support from Islamic fundamentalist groups. Those groups provided one focus for opposition to his regime, but for a period of time, Bhutto's foreign policy helped to reduce the religious opposition. He moved Pakistan away from the formerly close alliance with Western powers and brought the country into a more intimate relationship with other Muslim states. The Islamic summit conference at Lahore in 1974, at which Bhutto was the host, helped to give an Islamic luster to his government. Thus, although the program of the Bhutto regime was not explicitly Islamic, it was able to balance Muslim and radical ideals during the time of Pakistan's greatest crisis. In the long run, however, this balancing did not succeed in eliminating opposition, which became more vigorous as Bhutto moved in an apparently autocratic direction.

The Bhutto regime attempted to legitimize itself on the basis of its reform programs and socialism rather than by an emphasis on Islam. It succeeded in re-creating an effective Pakistani state following the crisis at the beginning of the decade, but it could not avoid increasing charges of corruption and dictatorial rule. When Bhutto and his party won an overwhelming majority in the elections of 1977, charges of election fraud and illegal suppression of the opposition led to widespread unrest. Bhutto attempted to repress this opposition and also began to change the orientation of his programs in order to win the support of the more explicitly Muslim groups. In the weeks following the 1977 elections, Bhutto announced the prohibition of alcohol and gambling and declared that his government would take action to bring the laws of the country more directly into accord with the Quran. Those pronouncements did not prevent the leading military officers, led by Zia al-Haq, from taking control of the government in July 1977.

General Zia acted as the chief administrator of martial law and worked to create a modified political system. The initial justification for the regime was the need to overthrow the government of Bhutto, which was said to be dangerously dictatorial and corrupt. Accountability became the theme for the trials and punishments of the old regime politicians, which culminated in the conviction and execution of Bhutto in 1979. Although the accountability campaign was popular at first, the imprisonment and execution of Bhutto provided a focus for opposition to the Zia administration. Supporters of civilian political rule and the more radical politicians represented a core of opposition to Zia that, by the fall of 1980, was considered by some people to be a major challenge to Zia and by others to be too divided to be effective.

General Zia's major domestic policy initiatives have involved a vigorous effort to make the political and legal systems more clearly Islamic. The last-minute efforts of Bhutto to assume a more Islamic posture have been actively pursued by Zia. In 1978 and 1979, major efforts to revise the legal structure and to implement specific regulations of Islamic law were undertaken, and by 1980, government policy had become clearly Islamic in tone. This change was supported by the conservative religious elements and was distinctively fundamentalist in style. After periods of conservative adaptationism under Muhammad Ayyub Khan and more radical adaptationism under Bhutto, Pakistan took on a more fundamentalist orientation.

The early postindependence efforts to create an Islamic state on the basis of vaguely defined modernist ideas had failed, as had the conservative modernism of Ayyub Khan. The more socialist orientation of the Bhutto regime aided in Pakistan's recovery from the 1970–1971 crisis, but it seemed to be leading toward a secularist dictatorship. The new regime that came to power in 1977 affirmed the Islamic identity of Pakistan as being more explicitly fundamentalist, which was the result of a long evolution.

> More than three decades have passed since Pakistan was established as a Muslim homeland . . . her original purpose and aspiration have often been either overlooked or selectively used both by the political leadership and its opposition. The 1970s saw a re-emergence of emphasis on Islamic identity and ideology in the politics of Pakistan. . . . Whatever the fate of the Zia-ul-Haq's government . . . the re-emergence of Islam as a central theme in Pakistan's politics has resulted in a focusing on questions and issues of Islamic identity and ideology that will not easily disappear.[62]

The experience of Bangladesh runs parallel to that of Pakistan in that there has been a transition from a more radical regime to a military regime with a more Islamic tone. The leader of the new state in 1971 was Mujib al-Rahman, the head of the Awami League. Mujib renounced the idea of an Islamic state; declared the new nation to be secularist and socialist; nationalized many industries, banks, and insurance companies; and attempted to reduce the influence of the religious groups. In theory, the new socialist state was similar to the radical regimes of the 1960s as there was more bureaucratic centralism than populism. The programs of Mujib were unable to make progress in solving the country's many problems, and corruption and inefficiency, along with natural disasters, plagued the new regime. Early in 1975, Mujib assumed dictatorial powers, which increased opposition to him without enabling him to introduce more effective programs. In August of that year, he was overthrown and killed by a group of military officers. Despite Mujib's initial popularity, he had become sufficiently unpopular that his death aroused little response. Secular socialism had not solved the country's problems.

There were other radical alternatives in Bangladesh, but in 1975, they had neither the organization nor the support to replace Mujib. The secular radicals maintained that Mujib's socialism had been largely a middle-class program and was doomed to failure. This type of radicalism was represented by groups like the National Socialist party, led by Major Muhammad Abd al-Jalil, who had been a member of the Awami League and a guerrilla commander in the war against Pakistan.

In addition to the Marxist groups, there were Islamic radical groups that had substantial support. The best known of those groups was led by Mawlana Abd al-Hamid Bhashani, an old Awami League activist who had formed his own party as early as 1957, and he represented a continuation of the tradition of Bengali peasant radicalism that had produced the nineteenth-century revivalist movements. His program was a combination of an appeal to Islamic principles and programs of radical agrarian reform. He stated that "we are wretchedly poor, illiterate, backward. Our hope is socialism but socialism with belief in Allah, the Holy Prophet and the Koran."[63] Bhashani had opposed Mujib in the elections of 1970 and then continued his opposition to the secular socialism of the new government, which, in his view, was neither sufficiently radical nor sufficiently Islamic.

Following the overthrow of Mujib, there was a transition regime led by Khondakar Mushtaq Ahmad, a former associate of Mujib in the Awami League, with military officers in the background. After a few months of confusion, Major General Zia al-Rahman, the chief of army staff and martial law administrator, assumed real control. His official titles changed as he led an evolution toward a more civilian government: in 1977, he assumed the title of president, which was confirmed in a national referendum; then he was elected president in the direct elections of 1978; and then he became the civilian head of a civilian administration following his retirement from the army and the lifting of martial law in 1979. By 1979, he was supported by a political party called the Bangladesh Nationalist party (Bangladesh Jatiyabadi Dal, BJD), which was composed of his own supporters and a grouping of other parties. The BJD won a substantial majority in the 1979 parliamentary elections.

By the spring of 1981, Zia al-Rahman had restored a substantial degree of political stability to Bangladesh and had made real progress in solving many of the country's social and economic problems. Although he and his party were clearly the dominant political force, opposition groups had some freedom of operation. The era of Zia came to an abrupt end in May 1981, when Zia was killed in an attempted military coup. Although the rebels were quickly suppressed and power passed immediately to the vice president, the future of Zia's programs and the constitutional regime became unclear.

In the transition from Mujib to Zia, there was a clear transition from a self-consciously secularist regime to a regime with an Islamic orientation. One of the first actions of Mushtaq Ahmad's transition regime was to declare that Bangladesh is an Islamic republic, and the process of nationalizing the industries was reversed. A revival of Islam was encouraged, and the national rallying cry was based more on Islamic unity than on ethnic nationalism. Zia al-Rahman changed the constitution to reinstate Islam, and his regime emphasizes the importance of Islam in national life. Although the current regime's position is in clear contrast to the secularism of Mujib's pronouncements, it has not taken a vigorously fundamentalist position. Islamic law is respected, but, in contrast to Zia al-Haq's regime in Pakistan, it has not been adopted comprehensively as the law of the land. A special balance provides non-Muslims in Bangladesh protected rights, which means that even when the provisions of Islamic law are adopted, they do not necessarily apply to non-Muslims. Bangladesh has followed a policy of reaffirmation of Islam following a secularist interlude, but the style has been a modernist form of adaptationism. Its broad appeal is illustrated by the fact that, at least in 1979–1980, it was sufficiently radical for Mawlana Bhashani's group to join the BJD and yet sufficiently traditional in approach so that it did not arouse conservative opposition. Under Zia al-Rahman, Bangladesh has returned to a recognition of the importance of Islam in the country's national self-definition.

Indonesia

In Indonesia, the long dialogue between moderate secular nationalism and more explicitly Islamic perspectives continued during the 1970s. The government remained under the control of the modernizing adaptationists led by the major military leaders, and its chief opposition came from the Islamic forces. The more radical and secularist groups, such as the communists, remained organizationally weak under the continuing impact of the crushing of the Indonesian Communist party in 1965–1966.

During the 1970s, parliamentary elections and vigorous party activity were part of the evolution of the political system under the direction of President Suharto. Although the military was the strongest single interest group within the government, civilian politics played an important role. Suharto organized a political party, Golkar, which won majorities in the elections of 1971 and 1977, but those elections were not simply rubber-stamp referendums, and the opposition parties received a significant proportion of the vote. Golkar represented the leading elements in the military combined with the more secularist civilian modernizers.

In religious terms, the policy of the Suharto regime has been clear. It is modernizing adaptationist in style, and it recognizes the importance of religious and moral values but within the more generalized framework of the old Pantjasila program. Although Suharto has rejected radical secularism, he has attempted to avoid identifying government policy with specific Islamic regulations and has worked to limit the power of the more fundamentalist Muslims. For example, the government required the Islamic opposition groups to join together in a single political party, whose activities could be restricted by the government. The government-imposed name of this party, Partai Persatuan Pembangunan (United Development party, PPP), avoids mention of its Islamic identification. Another example of the government's attempt to limit the visibility of Islam was the Ministry of Education's order in 1979 that the long school vacation not be tied to the date of Ramadan. When schools of the Muhammadiyyah organization refused to comply, government financial aid to them was cut off.

The continuing adaptationism of the regime can also be seen in its support for specifically Indonesian, especially Javanese, cultural traditions. It is often said that Suharto himself is a Muslim whose faith strongly reflects the traditions of Javanese mysticism rather than the more fundamentalist traditions. In 1978, Suharto secured the passage of a declaration giving recognition to mystical beliefs and including them in school curricula. Although the more strict Muslim groups opposed the declaration, it was readily passed by the Golkar majority in the National People's Congress.

The general position of the government between communists and fundamentalists was summed up by a retired general, who noted: "We must keep the pendulum in the white middleground. . . . We cannot let it swing to red or the green [the color of Islam] extreme."[64] This compromise position, with its stress on avoiding Islamic extremes, was also emphasized by Adam Malik, who had been foreign minister for twelve years before he became vice president in 1977. In identifying what he saw as the principal task for Suharto during his third term as president at the end of the 1970s, Malik said it was to strengthen national unity against "very strong pressure on this society to get a more Islamic state. . . . Of course, we must prevent this. . . . It would mean the end of the republic."[65]

The more fundamentalist opposition has taken a number of forms. On the militant extreme, there has been a continuing revolutionary activism. The Dar al-Islam movement, which has advocated open revolt, was involved in a number of terrorist acts and rural opposition. In 1978, for example, there were trials of Komando Jihad figures. Originally, those militants had been active in the attacks on the communists in the 1960s and then had advocated the establishment of an Islamic state. A defendant in one of the trials explained his actions as a continuation of the Dar al-Islam struggle and accused the government of being "infidels, cruel and sinful in defending only their own interests." He also said that mosques built by such a government had "become places in which to campaign for the implementation of decisions which did not have Allah's blessing, such as family planning [and] the marriage law."[66] This continued militant opposition has meant that the country's leaders' general mistrust of the Islamic movements has been maintained.

Most of the major Muslim groups have been active in the political and cultural realms rather than involved in open revolts. The enforced creation of a single Muslim party, the PPP, initially obscured the rivalries among the Muslim groups, but by the 1977 elections, at least some of the internal divisions had been overcome. The general political program was the advocacy of a more strict adherence to the rules of Islam and the creation of an officially Islamic state. The government was charged with being secularist, and nonreligious and specific issues, such as the marriage laws, were raised. The PPP and the Muslim organizations won 29 percent of the vote in 1977 but showed substantial strength among the modern-educated groups and students. Charges of official corruption and civilian reservations about the continued political strength of the military also gave strength to the religious groups, as the major organized opposition to the Suharto government.

Islamic activism in Indonesia has remained traditionally fundamentalist in its programs. However, as growing numbers of students and modern-educated Indonesians are affected by religious enthusiasm, the beginnings of a more radical fundamentalism are emerging. In the long run, radical fundamentalism might become the heir to the radical secularist tradition as the major proponent of a revolutionary transformation of society. At the end of the 1970s, however, the dominant form of Islamic activism, whether in movements of revolt or political opposition, was more solidly within the tradition of the ulama reformers, like Abd al-Raʿuf al-Sinkili, who oppose adaptationism that appears to compromise the integrity of a strictly interpreted Islam.

Summary

In the four large Asian Muslim states of Turkey, Pakistan, Bangladesh, and Indonesia, the 1970s was a period of interaction between modernizing adaptationism and Islamic revivalism. In each of those states, the military played an important role in working to create relative political stability but did not provide the leadership for more radical socialist programs. Such programs were initiated by civilian leaders such as Sukarno, Bhutto, and Mujib, although radical socialism never became the major focus of the Turkish government's policy. In reaction to the ineffectiveness of the civilian leaders, the army intervened in each country. In Turkey, Bangladesh, and Indonesia, the military maintained the tradition of modernizing adaptationism, but in a modern rather than a more radical style, and this moderate military adaptationism placed varying degrees of emphasis on Islam. When the military faced militant fundamentalist organizations capable of organizing opposition, as was the case in Indonesia and Turkey, the military was less willing to compromise; in Bangladesh, greater stress was given to Islamic symbols as a part of the national unification program. In Pakistan, the forces of Islamic opinion were relatively strong, and the political position of the military was weak. In that situation, the military leaders adopted a policy of vigorous support for fundamentalist Islamic ideas. In those four states, the 1970s was clearly a decade of significant Islamic activity. Rather than being reduced to a minor role, Islam had become a major social and political force in each country by 1980.

Nondominant Majority Communities and the Islamic Revival

The Islamic experiences of those Muslim communities that are not dominant majorities present a wide spectrum of reactions to and participation in the Islamic revival of the 1970s. As was the case in the past, the key issue was the role of Islam in the process of national integration. In countries where Muslims made up less than 85 percent of the population, but still formed a significant group, the possibility of establishing an Islamic state was limited. It was frequently rejected, even by some Muslims, because of the challenge that an advocacy of an Islamic state posed to national unity. In this context, the growing strength of the transition from an emphasis on the community to an emphasis on the state that marked much of twentieth-century history played a significant role. Increasingly, Muslims in religiously pluralist societies accepted the importance of a state-defined national identity.

In the religiously pluralist states, Islam was important on two levels. As a world view that was part of local culture, it provided general support for the emergence of ideologies that were not manifestly "imported." It could be recognized as a source of law and ideals for the local cultural tradition, and in that way, it could provide at least part of the sentiment of national unity. However, on another level, in those states in which there was significant tension among the different ethnic groups, Islam could become an obstacle to national unity by reinforcing the special identity of a part of the society, and therefore encourage conflict or separatism. In those cases where groups were inspired by the Islamic revival to assert their special Islamic identity, Islam became an element of national disunity.

In the many countries in which Muslims are a significant but not a dominant part of the population, local conditions created special responses that varied from Islam as an integrative force to Islam as a divisive element. Although each was different, the experiences of Malaysia, Chad and Ethiopia, the Sudan, and Nigeria provide an introduction to the variety of experiences.

Malaysia: Islam and Ethnic Tensions

In Malaysia, Islam is the established religion of the state, but it is identified with the Malay ethnic groups that represent barely half of the population. In the years following independence, the government worked to create a balance among the major groups within the country, and the state has been led by a coalition of parties representing the major groups: the United Malays' National Organization (UMNO), the Malaysian Chinese Association (MCA), and the Malaysian Indian Congress. This alliance balanced group interests and maintained a modernizing adaptationist style. However, by the early 1970s, the alliance government had become an entrenched political establishment open to charges of corruption. It had failed to prevent the outbreak of communal violence in 1969, and it was also unable to prevent many of the ethnic Malays from believing that the programs of modernization were not benefiting them as much as they were other elements in the country.

In this context, a number of distinctive Islamic developments have taken place, and one is the development of an active assertion of the Islamic identity. During the 1970s, a vigorous spirit of missionary activity emerged as a powerful force among the Muslims, and it took the form of activities aimed at winning converts to Islam and at purifying the practices of those already Muslim. This *dakwah* spirit resulted in the creation of many religiously active groups and the development of government policies supporting its general goals.

During the decade, the more activist Muslims presented both traditional fundamentalist programs and ones with a more radical orientation. Movements like the Darul Arqam stressed a strict adherence to Quranic regulations and urged Muslims to eliminate manifestations of modern elements in their lives. Among the younger Muslims, a more radical fundamentalism began to be defined, and many groups that draw support from students have become a dynamic force in Malaysian Islam. The largest of the groups is the Angkatan Belia Islam Malaysia (Muslim Youth Movement of Malaysia, ABIM), led by Anwar Ibrahim.

The ABIM has been active in supporting peasants and a more radical social consciousness. Many of its modern-educated members have adopted a more clearly Islamic style of clothing and stress the relevance of Islam for modern conditions. Its leader states: "We don't deny the ritual aspects of Islam. We think that Islam should be viewed as a means of solving the evils of society—corruption, exploitation of the poor and so on . . . to be fundamentalist doesn't mean to be antagonistic. We integrate well, and present Islam in a rational manner."[67] Anwar Ibrahim also emphasizes that the Islamic resurgence is not essentially anti-Western but a part of the long historical process of bringing Islamic practice into line with the demands of the Quranic revelation and would be taking place whether or not the West had expanded. For him, the ideal of *tawhid* means that there must be a constant effort to improve human society.[68] The ABIM has contacts with similar youth movements in many parts of the Islamic world and represents a more cosmopolitan fundamentalism than the purely Malay-oriented traditional groups.

The government position has been to maintain an adaptationist style, with an increasing recognition of the importance of the *dakwah* spirit. It has tried to coordinate Muslim activities in officially sponsored programs; at the same time, it has attempted to blunt the effects of militant Islamic activism on intercommunal relations within the country. Prime Minister Datuk Hussein Onn, for example, proclaimed National Dakwah Month in December 1978 but opposed religious extremism. He stated: "We need missionaries, but not fanaticism. Islam can counter communism. If it fails, then don't talk about religion any more. Hinduism, Buddhism, Christianity, they will all be finished. But the extremists can also finish them off."[69] He described the basic political problem of the government's position on religions: "You may wonder why we spend so much money on Islam. . . . If we don't, we face two major problems. First, Party Islam will get at us. The party will, and does, claim we are not religious and the people will lose faith. Second we are to strengthen the faith of the people, which is another way to fight communist ideology."[70]

There is thus a broad spectrum of Islamic experience in Malaysia. The government has remained adaptationist but is under increasing pressure from the more activist Islamic organizations and the general resurgence of Islamic sentiment, which takes the form of political action through the Party Islam. In social terms, the more conservative Islamic sentiment has taken on a fundamentalist tone, and people who espouse it do not want to preserve the secularist compromises of the government. In addition, groups like the ABIM show the emergence of a nontraditional fundamentalism with more radical social programs. Because of the close relationship between the Malay ethnic consciousness and Islam, this growing Muslim mood is seen by some people as a challenge to stability and national unity. The Malay experience in the 1970s shows a resurgence of Islam complicated by an ethnic pluralism within the country. Neither modernization nor the adaptationism of the government since independence has reduced or changed the basically communal nature of the Malaysian political system. As long as Islam in Malaysia remains communal, it is a potentially divisive force.

Islam and National Disunity: Eritrea and Chad

The potential for Islam to play a supportive role in divisive conflicts is clearly visible in some African states in which Muslims are a significant part, but not a dominant majority, of society. During the 1960s, there were a number of countries in which open conflicts and civil wars took place. During the 1970s, some of those conflicts were successfully resolved, and others continued, often on increasing levels of violence. Such continuing conflicts were the civil strife in Chad and the war for Eritrean liberation, and in both of those cases, Islam was identified with one of the sides in the struggle. However, in both, the impact of the Islamic revival was related to the international context; internally, Muslim sentiments were unable to prevent disunity within the Islamically oriented groups.

In Ethiopia, the Eritrean liberation movement continued to fight the central government throughout the 1970s. In its origins, the Eritrean movement was largely Muslim separatist, but its support had broadened as a result of the repressive policies of the Ethiopian emperor Haile Selassie. By 1970, support for Eritrean independence came from virtually all elements in the province, both Muslim and Christian, and the situation had not changed when the revolution of 1974 overthrew the emperor and brought a radical military regime to power. This new government, led by the Dergue or the Provisional Military Administrative Council (PMAC), initiated many programs of radical reform within Ethiopia and was a major departure from the government of Haile Selassie. However, the new government was as firmly committed as the old one in its opposition to secessionist movements and in its emphasis on national unity. Since no compromise appeared possible between the demands of the central government and the aspirations of the Eritrean nationalists, the civil war continued.

During the 1970s, the Eritrean national movement was divided. The original organization behind the revolt had been the Eritrean Liberation Front (ELF), but by 1970, an organization with a radical ideological program had also existed. This was the Eritrean People's Liberation Front (EPLF), which represented a major departure from the socially conservative Muslim separatism of the ELF, and it benefited from the support of many younger Eritreans and many of the Christians who opposed the regime in Addis Ababa. The ELF and EPLF soon became active rivals and fought each other as well as the Ethiopian government until a truce was arranged in 1974. Between 1974 and 1977, the two groups were able to expand significantly the areas under their control, but the Ethiopian offensives in 1978–1979, with Russian and Cuban aid, reversed those successes. By 1980, the situation was still unstable, and the bloody conflict continued.

In Eritrea, Islam is an important element within the liberation movements, and it has helped to reinforce the identity that is being defined in Eritrean nationalism as one that is distinct from the central Ethiopian government. However, Islam is most clearly associated with the ELF and its socially conservative policies, and as a result, the more radical Eritreans fear that an emphasis upon Islam will lessen the possibilities of an effective social transformation. Islam also acts as an obstacle to the integration of the Christian Eritreans into the liberation movements, and one consequence of that problem is that the EPLF has been more clearly secularist in its radicalism. Islam has not been able to prevent, and may even be encouraging, disunity within the movement for Eritrean nationalism.

The general resurgence of Islam during the 1970s had an impact upon the development of Eritrean nationalism, but that impact was largely in terms of international support for the movement. Activist Islamic countries have been willing to support Islamically oriented liberation movements, which means that a number of Muslim states have provided financial and diplomatic aid to the Eritreans. Because of its more clearly Islamic orientation, this support has been primarily channeled through the ELF. Even more radical regimes, such as Baʿthist Iraq, have given most of their support to the ELF, even though in terms of social policies, the Baʿth might be expected to have sympathy for the EPLF. Saudi Arabia and the gulf states have also given aid to the ELF. Outside support for the EPLF has been limited. Some came for a time from the People's Democratic Republic of Yemen, but that country was supporting the Ethiopian revolutionary regime by the end of the decade.

In Chad, the civil war began in the 1960s and continued throughout the 1970s, although by the end of the 1970s, it had taken on a new form. Initially, the conflict was between northern Muslim groups and the southern-dominated government of Francois Tombalbaye, whose regime moved in the direction of increasing suppression of all political opposition, not just that of the northern Muslims. In 1973, the government announced a program of national renewal and authenticity, which was an effort to create an ideology based on Chadian customs that could provide a basis for national unity. The enforced abandonment of Christian personal names and the abolition of Western geographical names were two aspects of this program, and the policy of authenticity became a vehicle for disciplining the bureaucracy and punishing opponents of the regime. Customary rituals of initiation were required for all southerners, and a regime of fear and terror was established. Tombalbaye was overthrown and killed in a military coup in 1975, and a southern Christian general, Felix Malloum, became president. Malloum continued to fight the northern dissidents, but he also worked for a national reconciliation.

The leading Muslim organization continued to be FROLINAT, but its experience in the 1970s showed that a common Muslim faith was not sufficient to maintain unity among the northern forces in Chad. Within FROLINAT, Goukouni Oueddei became the leader, replacing Hissen Habre, who went into hiding for a time and emerged by 1978 as the leader of a separate force called the Forces Armées du Nord (FAN). That split illustrates the interaction of internal and external elements in the development of the Muslim opposition groups. By 1976, the international Islamic revival had had an impact on Chadian domestic affairs through the increasing aid given by Libya to FROLINAT in the name of Islamic unity. That aid played a role in the change of the FROLINAT leadership since Oueddei was willing to tie the organization more closely to Libya than Habre had been.

The fragmentation of FROLINAT also reflected internal elements. Habre was a French-educated soldier who had worked for a time with the Tombalbaye regime before joining FROLINAT. Although he had a northern tribal background, he was not particularly traditional or Islamic in his orientation. Oueddei, in contrast, was the son of a major tribal religious leader, and many of his relatives had been killed in the early years of the civil war. He had a reputation for piety and shared in the authority of his father, and it was his tribesmen who brought him to power in FROLINAT in 1976. The change in leadership did not, however, result in a significant redefinition of ideology. The civil war remained largely a sectional struggle for power within Chad that had religious overtones because one side in the struggle was largely Muslim by individual faith.

The inability of Islam to provide a basis for effective unity among the antigovernment forces was clearly shown when the north-south struggle reached the point of being resolved. In 1978, President Malloum succeeded in creating a "national government of reconciliation," in which he remained president, and Hissen Habre was prime minister—Oueddei's FROLINAT did not participate in this government. Habre did not disband the FAN, and it soon clashed with Malloum's government forces. Neither Habre nor Malloum was willing to control his forces, and by this time, at least eleven competing armed groups had become involved in the struggle. A series of truces were arranged by states such as Nigeria and the Sudan, and in mid-1979, negotiations resulted in the resignations of Habre and Malloum and the creation of a coalition provisional state council led by Oueddei.

In the new regime, Habre was the minister of defense and Oueddei was president, but it was not long before fighting again broke out, this time between the forces of Habre and Oueddei. The conflict this time was clearly a struggle for power between northern forces, and the southerners were not directly involved. The "victors" in the long civil war could not create a basis for unity. At the end of 1980, the Libyan army intervened directly in Chad on the side of Oueddei, and Habre was defeated. In January 1981, Qadhafi announced the unification of Libya and Chad, and Islamic themes played an important part in the rhetoric. Libyan military power was sufficient to enforce stability for a time, but local opposition and international protests combined to make the Libyan position difficult. In November 1981, the Organization for African Unity and the French government both offered assistance to the Chadian government, and Libya announced the withdrawal of its troops. At the end of 1981, the basic political situation in Chad was unclear.

For all practical purposes, the forces identified with Islam had won the

long war in Chad. However, it was clear that a common faith was not sufficient to provide a basis for unity, even among the victors. The Islamic
resurgence came, by 1980–1981, to play a direct role in Chadian affairs
through the Libyan intervention. However, the conflicts were resolved by
force rather than by ideological agreement.

National Unity and Islam: Nigeria and the Sudan

The great national conflicts within Nigeria and the Sudan were resolved
during the 1970s, and although tension and divisions remained, the civil
wars of the previous decades were brought to an end in settlements that emphasized national unity. In those settlements, communal and ethnic
rivalries were successfully subordinated to the needs for unity within each
country as a whole, and the evolution from community to state provided an
important aspect in this experience. Muslims tended to stress their identity
as Nigerian or Sudanese rather than to continue wars in which Islam acted
as a support for divisive ethnic and regional identities. This fact did not
mean that Muslims ceased to be concerned about issues of Islamic importance, but they were willing to advocate their views within the framework
of a religiously and ethnically pluralistic political system.

By the end of the 1960s, Nigeria had experienced violent coups and a major civil war. In 1966, a military regime had emerged under the leadership of
Yakubu Gowon, who had successfully maintained Nigerian national unity
through a civil war that resulted when the southeastern region had attempted to secede. At the beginning of the 1970s, Gowon began the process
of rebuilding Nigerian unity. With the help of growing oil revenues and a
general popular sentiment favoring an end to internal conflict, Gowon
made major strides in that direction. However, administrative inefficiency
and a growing belief that Gowon would not fulfill his often-repeated promise of restoring civilian rule led to growing discontent. He was overthrown
in a bloodless coup during the summer of 1975 and replaced by Brig. Mur-
tala Ramat Mohammed, a vigorous Hausa soldier from Kano in the north.
For a time in the 1960s, Mohammed had favored northern secession, but he
had worked closely with Gowon and had become a major advocate of
federal unity.

Mohammed initiated a rigorous anticorruption campaign and set in motion a phased program for a return to civilian rule. He was killed in an abor-
tive coup attempt in 1976, but Olusegun Obasanjo, the chief of staff of the
armed forces and de facto prime minister under Brig. Mohammed, quickly
assumed control and maintained Mohammed's policies. A new constitution
was drafted and approved by a constituent assembly, and national elections were held in 1979. A constitutional civilian regime assumed leadership
of the country as a result of those elections.

During the 1970s, a number of issues arose that showed that although the
general development was in the direction of a national, civilian regime,
there were still regional tensions in which Islam played a role. Islam tended
to be identified with the northern regional interests and, as a result, was

seen as a potentially divisive force. One key to a successful national solution to the problem of instability was to reduce the non-Muslims' fears of northern, Muslim domination while continuing to recognize the importance of Islam to many Nigerians.

One indication of the tensions involved appeared in 1974 with the announcement of the provisional census figures, which showed a substantial increase in the population of the north in relation to that of the south. The figures were vigorously opposed by many southern leaders because they were intended to be used as the basis for the civilian parliamentary representation and many southerners feared that if those figures were accepted, it would mean a northern and Muslim domination of any federal government. One of Brig. Mohammed's first actions was to abrogate the census. Fortunately, a nationally satisfactory distribution of parliamentary seats was devised as a part of the process of creating the constitutional regime.

One way in which regional rivalries were diffused was by restructuring the provincial divisions within the country. In 1976, Obasanjo redrew the provincial map and created nineteen states within the country. In this way, the broad regional identities were reoriented in the direction of recognizing the more specific local identities. Rather than emphasizing the broader Islamic identity of most of the northerners, the new arrangement stressed local ethnic groupings. As a result, the influence of Islam as a basis for regional political rivalries was reduced.

The continuing strength of Islamic sentiments can be seen in the discussions of the proposed constitution by the Constituent Assembly in 1978. Although there was little demand for the proclamation of an Islamic state, many members of the assembly sought to have some special recognition given to Islam. That idea took the form of proposals to have a special Federal Shariʿah (Muslim) Court of Appeals rather than having Shariʿa appeal cases handled by the general Federal Courts of Appeal. When the proposal was rejected, 88 of the 230 members of the assembly withdrew from the proceedings in protest. However, when Obasanjo made a special address to the assembly and warned strongly against a return to old-style politics, the boycotting members returned, and a compromise was arranged in which a three-member panel would advise the federal courts on cases involving Islamic law. Essentially, Islamic distinctiveness gave way to and was integrated into a national arrangement.

In the 1979 elections, all of the major participating parties were careful to avoid a direct appeal for religious or regional support. The constitution required that parties contending in the national elections have a national rather than a regional base for support, so, even though the major leaders of the new parties were men who had been prominent in civilian politics in earlier regimes, the context was significantly different. The winner in the national presidential election was Shehu Shagari of the National Party of Nigeria (NPN). He was a northern Muslim but had campaigned on a platform of national unity and integration and was committed to the continuation of a nonreligious federal arrangement as defined by the new constitution.

Islam remains an important part of the life of many Nigerians. However, the resolution of the crises of national unity created a growing awareness of the importance of the Nigerian identity as opposed to regional and religious identities. The events of the 1970s illustrate that there are still tensions within Nigeria, but, at least on the national level, the transition from a collection of communal identities to a broader identity defined by the state has gone relatively far.

The potential for Islamic activism still exists, however, but it is currently concentrated in local activities. An illustration of that potential is the emergence of the movement of Muhammad Marawa in Kano. By the latter part of 1980, this teacher had gathered a large number of followers into a movement that proclaimed the need for revitalizing Islam and announced the beginning of major messianic events. The new movement soon clashed wth local authorities and was finally crushed after the army was called in, but it had caused the largest-scale communal urban disorder in more than a decade. In such events, it can be seen that although Nigerian Muslims have made major adjustments to the religiously pluralist context, the possibility of more militant Islam remains strong.

In the Sudan, the negotiated settlement of the conflict in the southern region set the stage for a national political system that recognized the special autonomy of the south within the country. Under the leadership of Ja'far Numayri, a major effort was made to balance the wide range of interests in order to create and maintain a sense of Sudanese unity. The balance that emerged has always been delicate, but it was maintained into the 1980s.

An important requirement for a continuing sense of Sudanese unity and cooperation is that people in all regions must have the feeling that their particular identities are not threatened by national unity. The key to the 1972 settlement was that the southern leaders became persuaded that the central government was sincere in its recognition of southern interests and that southern autonomy would be validly recognized. In the same process, the northern leaders came to believe that recognizing southern autonomy would be the best way of preserving the Sudan and the special heritage of Sudanese nationalism.

Islam is a significant element within this balanced and pluralistic sense of national unity, and it is clearly a major part of the northern Sudanese sense of identity. Any political system that ignored or undermined Islamic sentiments would arouse the fears and opposition of many northern Sudanese; at the same time, because of its close association with the northern regional interests, any system that placed too much stress upon the Islamic element within the Sudanese society would create southern opposition and a suspicion that the special southern autonomy would be undermined. In the delicate equilibrium of post-1972 Sudan, there has been a major effort to recognize the importance of Islam within the country, but in ways that would not cause the southerners to feel challenged. The result has been a regime that is not secularist because it continues to recognize the political role of religion, but the leadership has resisted efforts to identify the government with one particular religious tradition.

The general position of the revolutionary leadership was to give strong emphasis to the importance of religious values, which was done by noting specifically the importance of Islam but shifting the emphasis in official pronouncements to an adherence to moral values in general. That tactic is illustrated by Numayri's comments in his speech on the third anniversary of the revolution. He said, "As long as the Revolution believes in the freedom and validity of religions and their moral value in developing society and their profound effect on the life of our people, its thought, feelings and conscience will not spare any effort to consolidate its immortal messages so as to deepen the spiritual aspect of life and to personify the concepts of sacrifice, self-denial, natural and intellectual harmony for our people."[71]

Throughout the 1970s, the Numayri government faced continuing challenges from people who opposed the nature of the balance in policy, but it also had a series of successes in maintaining the national unity created by the 1972 agreement. In the middle of the decade, there were a number of incidents of opposition in the southern region and major coup attempts by the more Islamically oriented northern groups. The latter combined elements of the Ansar (Mahdist) leadership, the most prominent of those leaders being the former prime minister, Sadiq al-Mahdi, with a variety of other groups. However, in 1977–1978, many of the major figures of the opposition were reconciled with the government. In particular, some of the remaining southern leaders, such as Aggrey Jaden and Philip Abbas Ghaboush, who had been implicated in earlier plots returned to the Sudan, and important Islamic leaders who also had been associated with earlier opposition efforts were reconciled. In March 1978, Sadiq al-Mahdi, who had been condemned to death in absentia a few years before, returned to the Sudan and became a member of the Political Bureau of the regime's mass organization, the Sudanese Socialist Union. He was joined in that group by Hasan al-Turabi, a former leader of the Muslim Brotherhood in the Sudan who had been imprisoned for opposition activities.

Sadiq al-Mahdi outlined some of the main points of his position while returning to a leadership role in the Sudan. In an interview with *Le Monde*, he said that in a developing country, "the army has a national role to play; that the multiparty system is no alternative to dictatorship; that Islam must become a force for progress; that economic development cannot be achieved outside the socialist model."[72] In his new viewpoint, he had moved away from his support for a multiparty parliamentary system in which Islamic groups like the Ansar would have been able to have a more direct political role.

The effort to make the Sudanese political system more clearly Islamic has not been abandoned, but it has tended to operate within the constraints of the national system. Islamic leaders like Hasan al-Turabi have not stopped working for a greater recognition of Islamic elements, but Hasan al-Turabi stresses the importance for Sudan of working through regular political channels and accepts the desirability of a gradual evolution, rather than an Islamic revolution, to achieve Muslim goals in the Sudan.[73]

The fragility of this political balance was shown in the late 1970s in the area of foreign policy. President Numayri gave support to President Sadat's efforts to achieve a negotiated settlement with Israel, and he did not fully join in the rejection of the Egyptian-Israeli peace treaty in 1979. In addition, Numayri has worked to advance some aspects of Egyptian-Sudanese co-operation with the long-term goal of some form of unity between the two countries. These policies have aroused opposition within the Sudan. Some southerners fear that any effective unity with Egypt would strengthen the Arab-Islamic elements in the Sudan, and the more activist Muslims object to the treaty and feel that Numayri should have given more active support to the militant Arab cause. In line with this opposition, Sadiq Al-Mahdi withdrew from the Political Bureau in protest. However, despite opposition, the balancing policies of Numayri have survived.

The emphasis on national unity in the Sudan during the 1970s thus produced a shift in emphasis. Islamic activism continues to be an important force, but its most effective proponents accept the need for national unity as being valid. Even the major fundamentalist leaders have operated within an adaptationist framework of adjusting to the special local conditions of the Sudan while maintaining their long-term goals.

Summary

In many areas in which Muslims are not the dominant majority, the decade of the 1970s was a time of vigorous activity. By that time, however, the state units had achieved sufficient importance to become the major framework within which the Muslims operated, so questions of national unity were of major significance. Islam acted sometimes as a divisive element by providing strength to regional and local identities and at other times helped to provide the basis for a spirit of compromise.

By the 1970s, the old issues of the relationship between Islam and nationalism had been replaced by the issues of Islam and national integration. As the experiences of the Sudan and Nigeria illustrate, it is possible for Islam to be an important factor without causing open conflict in a pluralist society. An equally important aspect, however, is that effective Islamic compromise within a pluralist context does not mean that Islam necessarily becomes simply a subordinate factor or one of clearly declining significance. The old assumptions about the inevitability of secularism in modernizing societies are challenged by the experience of those countries in which Muslims are an important but not a dominant proportion of the population.

Weak Muslim Minorities and Islamic Revival

Throughout the world, Muslim minority communities that make up less than 25 percent of the population of their countries had a variety of experiences during the 1970s. Clearly, the resurgent affirmation of Islam had an impact on their situation. Sometimes it helped to inspire and provide support for increasing militance, and in other cases, it encouraged the dominant groups to pay closer attention to Muslim sentiments than had been the case previously. In general, although most Muslims followed the line of assimilation and adaptation, there was a growing sense of pride in the Islamic heritage and a growing willingness to make Islamic affiliations more publicly apparent.

Major Minority Communities: Soviet Union, China, and India

The three largest Muslim minority communities—those in the Soviet Union, China, and India—expressed a growing willingness during the 1970s to publicly affirm their Islamic identities. However, in none of those three areas were there major mass movements of Islamic militancy; instead, the Islamic affirmation was made in the context of a continuing recognition of the importance of assimilation and integration. An important aspect of that recognition was the foreign policies of the national governments.

In the Soviet Union, the visible Muslim militancy of the early twentieth century was not revived. However, it became clear during the 1970s that Islam was not simply disappearing within the country as, in general terms, despite decades of efforts to eliminate the influence of traditional religions, Christianity, Judaism, and Islam all continued to have some visible impact upon life in Soviet Union.

A variety of elements are involved in the status of Muslims in the Soviet Union. Because of the process of political and economic development that has taken place under the communist leadership, their material standard of living has improved and is significantly better than in most neighboring Muslim areas. In addition, there has been a social transformation involving increasing literacy rates, a changing status for women, and a clear influence of Russian culture in its communist forms. However, these changes have not resulted in the destruction of distinctive local cultures in Muslim areas, and a wide range of traditional customs continue to be a part of the lives of most people, even if they are clearly communist in their education and general attitudes. Thus, development under Soviet control has not eliminated the special cultural characteristics of the various societies.

It seems clear that ethnic identities in Muslim areas of the Soviet Union have survived with some strength, but it is difficult to judge the strength of Islam in that survival. Islam is an important part of the cultural identity that has continued, but there was not a revival of Islamic militance in the 1970s. Following the Islamic revolution in Iran, many observers searched for evidence of such a revival among Soviet Muslims with little success.[74] What has been noted is that there is a growing informal Islamic activity, often centered in "underground" Sufi orders and around unofficial ulama, that might provide a focus for Islamic activism in the future.[75]

The long-term significance of the survival of Islamic ethnic identities rests in the demographic trends within the Soviet Union. It is often noted that if current trends continue, Soviet Muslims may represent at least 25 percent of the population of the Soviet Union by the end of the twentieth century.

Under conditions of being something more than a small minority, Islamic communities might affirm their identity in a more vigorous manner. In this context, although there was no militant resurgence of Islam during the 1970s in the Soviet Union, the decade was a time when the continued existence of Islam as an important factor within that country was reaffirmed.

In China, the decade of the 1970s was also a time of greater public visibility for Muslims. The Cultural Revolution of the 1960s had attacked all existing traditional religious institutions that had survived, and as a result, there was little public activity within any of the older religious groups. Buddhist temples, Christian churches, and Muslim mosques had been closed, and the religious leadership had been scattered and persecuted. In the late 1970s and after the death of Mao Tse-tung, the Chinese communist leaders began to reorganize the modernization effort within the country, and they gave greater public recognition to religious and ethnic groups as a part of a program to create a united front for mobilizing general popular support. As a part of this program, many of the strictest of the restrictions on religious expression were relaxed. Temples, churches, and mosques were allowed to be reopened, although they remained under tight control.

Although there is little visible evidence of a major Islamic resurgence or militant Muslim activism, Chinese Muslims, in remarkably large numbers, took advantage of the relaxation of controls to practice their faith publicly. Visitors to China in 1979–1980 reported that substantial numbers were attending mosques, and in western China, there were reports that those in attendance included young people as well as older Muslims. It was clear that the Islamic communities in China had survived the rigors of the Cultural Revolution. Thus, although integration and assimilation continued to be the dominant mode of life for Chinese Muslims, that quite clearly did not indicate the extinction of Islamic life in the country. Islam, along with other traditional religions in China, continued to provide a satisfying sense of identity and a moral basis for life.

Muslims in India faced the same options and problems in the 1970s that they had in previous years. Cautious conservatism could preserve a sense of communal identity but at the cost of relative stagnation and isolation within Indian society, and it also maintains the basis for communalism, which could erupt in violent riots from time to time. The other alternative is for Muslims to accept the official secularist mode as the basis for integration into Indian society, but that alternative requires a similar secularism on the part of the Hindu majority. During the 1970s, there continued to be a basic problem in choosing between the two alternatives because of the difficulty in separating religion from politics in India. As Professor Alam Khundamiri of Osmania University noted, "Ours may be a secular state, but it is a secular state in a nonsecular society."[76]

During the 1970s, little fundamental progress was made either in reducing the Muslim sense of isolation in India or in eliminating the threat of intercommunal violence. In 1969, Hindu-Muslim riots had been the worst since the days of independence, and they had marked an increasing level of tensions. During the following decade, a series of disturbances took place. In August 1980, the largest communal conflicts since 1969 took place, and although there were fewer casualties in 1980 than in 1969, the disturbances were more widespread.

Possible policies to integrate Muslims more fully raised problems that illustrate the complexity of the situation. Early in the 1970s, the Indian government attempted to integrate Aligarh Muslim University (the former Muhammadan Anglo-Oriental College) into the national educational system and sought to secularize the university. Many Muslims objected, and demonstrations in the school itself became so threatening that the school had to be temporarily closed. The Muslim dilemma is clearly presented in this clash. Separate cultural institutions continue to emphasize the isolation of the Indian Muslim community, but integration might undermine the special character of the Muslim experience and those institutions that support it.

In the face of these issues, Indian Muslims have remained basically conservative in their style. Islamic revolutions and resurgence have helped to make many people sensitive to the situation of the Indian Muslim communities, but the basic dynamics of the Indian Muslim experience have remained conservative and communal rather than significantly militant in a fundamentalist style.

Among the Muslims in the three largest minority communities, there had been a continuing awareness of the validity of the Islamic identity. During the 1970s, there were increasing opportunities to reaffirm the Islamic message publicly, but there was little militant activism, and the general mood was one of continuing the assimilationist style of minority life.

Minorities and Islamic Affirmation

In a wide variety of contexts, small Muslim minorities affirmed their Islamic identities more vigorously during the 1970s. Part of this affirmation was a reflection of the more general Islamic resurgence and received support from established Muslim states and communities; the affirmation was also part of longer evolutions of local conditions. The Muslim minority actions took many forms, ranging from open revolt against central governments to a peaceful increase in cultural and religious activities. A common feature in all of the areas, however, was a real sense of the continuing validity of the Islamic message in the context of the contemporary world.

The best-known Muslim minority militant movement is in the Philippines. There have long been strong Muslim communities in the southern islands, and they have resisted attempts by outsiders to control the region—having opposed the Spanish, the Americans, the Japanese, and finally the independent central government. This tradition of opposition was reinforced during the twentieth century by the immigration into the Muslim regions of significant numbers of non-Muslims. Conflicts over control of the land and, as the numbers of immigrants increased, Muslim fears about loss of control or identity created a foundation for tension, and by the end of the 1960s, sporadic Islamic resistance had increased in intensity.

In 1972, President Ferdinand Marcos declared martial law and ordered all people to turn in what guns they might possess. That action aroused both the indignation and the fears of many of the Philippine Muslims, and some revolted openly.

Although a major Muslim organization was leading the revolt, the Moro National Liberation Front (MNLF), Muslim opposition to the Marcos regime was not fully integrated or coordinated. Throughout the 1970s, fighting continued, and the goal of the Muslim insurgents was at least recognition of special Muslim autonomy within the Philippine republic —and some people demanded Muslim independence.

The MNLF reflected the separatist option chosen by many of the Muslim minority in the Philippines, and the group's continuing ability to resist central control despite its weak minority position rested to some extent on the international situation. In contrast to Muslim minorities in China and the Soviet Union, it was possible for Philippine Muslims to receive significant help from Muslims outside the country, and at times during the 1970s, they received substantial aid from Muslims in Malaysia and from Libya. In addition, the international situation set limits on the ability of the Marcos regime to suppress local Muslim groups. The Philippines relied heavily on petroleum imports from Islamic states, and Marcos attempted to handle the local revolt in a way that would not antagonize his major oil suppliers. Despite a series of cease-fires and suggested settlements, the conflict remained unresolved in 1980.

In Thailand, there has been a similar activist assertion of Islamic identity among the Muslim communities in the southern-peninsula region of the country. The nineteenth-century Patani sultanate had been under the loose control of the Thai monarchy, and in 1910, the region had been divided, with the southern parts of the sultanate coming under British control and becoming part of Malaya while the northern area remained under Thai control. Thai efforts to establish greater control in the region had usually met with Muslim resistance, and the ideal of Muslim separatism had remained a powerful force. Following World War II, there had been a major revolt in the Patani region. In the 1970s, Patani Muslim separatism was revived with some vigor, and it had the sympathy of neighboring Malays who lived in a region that also was experiencing an Islamic revival. The necessity for Thai-Malaysian cooperation in many areas has set limits to the ability of the Thai government to suppress the Patani separatism since too rigorous an anti-Islamic policy would be sure to arouse Malaysian opposition. Patani Muslim separatist groups have had only limited success in coordinating their actions, but they are still a force of some importance, especially as Islamic activism in Malaysia gains momentum.

In other areas of the world, the general sense of an Islamic revival combined with local conditions has led to a greater public reaffirmation of Islamic loyalties by many minorities, although with less militant consequences than in the Philippines and Thailand. In many of these other areas, the emphasis has been on cultural and religious elements rather than on more specifically political factors.

The largest established Muslim community in Europe is in Yugoslavia, where Muslims make up almost 20 percent of the population and are recognized as one of the major constituent nationalities in the Yugoslav federation. Many of the Muslims are concentrated in Bosnia and Herzegovina. In those regions, residents used to be required to be identified as either Serb or Croat, but in 1971, a national census offered citizens the chance to identify themselves as Muslim nationals. At the time, 39 percent of the people in Bosnia and Herzegovina declared themselves to be Muslims. Throughout the 1970s, the Yugoslav government gave increasing recognition to the Muslim nationality, which opened the way for a more public assertion of an Islamic identity. Although the increased recognition did not result in militant activism, in 1979–1980, some Yugoslav Muslim leaders, including the mufti of Belgrade, were inspired by the general Islamic resurgence and, in particular, by the Iranian revolution. In October 1979, for example, two prominent Muslim leaders were accused of spreading "Khomeini ideology."

In Western countries, Muslim immigrant and native communities were increasingly active in affirming their Islamic faith publicly during the 1970s. In West Germany, for example, German internal security officials noted that new Islamic centers, schools, and mosques were being organized all over the country, especially in areas where immigrant Turkish workers lived, and it was believed that much of this new activism was of a fundamentalist style.[77] The Muslim resurgence was clearly reflected among the Muslims in Germany.

In the United States, in addition to the activities of the Black Muslims, other Muslims have been increasingly active in organizing mosques and other cultural activities. Established U.S. Muslim associations are active in educational and cultural affairs, and new publishing ventures, like Creative Educational Concepts in Philadelphia, provide a whole range of religious educational materials for Muslims in the United States. Groups have also become active in community affairs—for example, the American Muslim Mission in Washington worked with Christian and Jewish leaders to defeat a proposal to legalize gambling.

In Western countries as elsewhere, Muslims during the 1970s were increasingly active in affirming the validity of their faith and in expressing their religious convictions publicly.

Summary

Among the many Muslim minority communities, there was an increasing sense of communal identity during the 1970s. That sense was sometimes recognized by and sometimes encouraged by a relaxation of earlier restrictions on Muslim activities. It also received support from resurgent Islamic sentiments in other parts of the world.

In the changing conditions of the 1970s, the basic options of separatist militance or assimilationism remained, but a new style of assimilationism developed that involved a willingness to accept existence in a religiously pluralistic society without forgoing public affirmation of Islam. In the global context of an increasing recognition of the validity of expressions of cultural pluralism, it became possible for Muslims to operate in a new style of minority life. This was essentially integration without full assimilation.

The Special Case of the Palestinians

Among the Muslim minority communities, the Palestinians continued to represent a special experience in the 1970s as their position was affected more clearly than any other minority group by the international dimension of their Islamic experience. The issue of the status of the Palestinians is something more than simply a matter of local conditions because the Palestinian cause itself was an important aspect of the more general Islamic resurgence.

In terms of the specific local conditions, there was a transformation during the 1970s. In the state of Israel itself, Muslims composed not quite 10 percent of the population at the end of the 1960s, and they had accepted their status as a minority and showed little sign of Islamic activism or any public assertion of the Islamic faith. However, the Arab-Israeli War of 1967 resulted in the Israeli occupation of the West Bank territories of Jordan and other areas with substantial Muslim populations, and that occupation brought Israeli Muslims into contact with larger Muslim communities and gave them a greater feeling of identity with Muslims elsewhere. In addition, following the 1967 war, activist Palestinian organizations became stronger and better organized within the Arab world, which provided Israeli Muslims with organizations which could express militant sentiments.

The Muslim minority in Israel became increasingly aware of and willing to work with Palestinians elsewhere, and protests within Israel could be tied to protests elsewhere more directly. Although many Israeli Muslims maintained the older, more passive acceptance of their minority position, increasing numbers began to see themselves as part of a broader community and to adopt a more activist style.

The broader Palestinian cause experienced a shift in tone during the 1970s. At the beginning of the decade, the expressions of Palestinian aspirations were dominated by more radical secularist and nationalist themes, but by 1980, there was a more clearly Islamic element in those expressions. An important factor in this change was the emergence of the Islamic revolution in Iran. Iranian Islamic revolutionary leaders gave strong support to the Palestinian groups, and Palestinian leaders, such as Yasir Arafat, allied themselves closely with Ayatollah Khomeini. In addition, the revival of Muslim sentiments elsewhere was accompanied by a more vigorously anti-Zionist position. Zionism was, for example, named in the resolutions and recommendations of the First Asian Islamic Conference in 1974 as one of the major enemies of Islam.[78]

This new emphasis was reflected in the activities of Palestinians under Israeli control. For example, in the student council elections at a major school in Nablus on the West Bank in 1979, an Islamic slate won, and an Islamic slate won one-third of the votes in elections at Bir Zeit University as

well. A number of militant Islamic groups had developed
by the end of the decade, and they were involved in
demonstrations in the Gaza Strip early in 1980. By 1980,
had become a more visible and dynamic part of the Pale
as a result of both local and international conditions, an
conflict had an Islamic dimension that was clearer and m
had been the case in previous decades.

Conclusion

Throughout the Islamic world, the 1970s was a period of dramatic
developments. Clearly, Islam was not a dying force, and its vitality was
shown in a variety of ways that ranged from major revolutions to the
reorientation of the dominant ideologies. That vitality was visible in all
three of the major dimensions of the contemporary experience.

On the local level, rapidly changing conditions provided the context for a
reaffirmation of Islam in a variety of ways. Because of the diversity of local
conditions, the form of this reaffirmation varied, and the Islamic response
to the changing conditions of the 1970s was not monolithic. However, in
country after country, the evolution of local conditions was strongly influenced by Islam.

In the broader dimension of modern global history, there were also major
transformations, and the failure of many modern approaches to the problems of contemporary society led to a resurgence of allegiance to nonmodern approaches. The standard modern ideology of secularism, ra-
tionalist science, and mass production had not proved adequate. As late as
the 1960s, it was possible to predict that traditional religions would gradually disappear as effective forces in the modern world and it would be possible to claim that the surviving religious traditions would have to come to
terms with the modern world. However, during the 1970s, it became clear
that the issue was not that simple. Even the modern world view was having
to change in order to cope with changing historical reality, and Islam could
reemerge as a competing world view—and did so with much success in the
1970s.

In the dimension of Islamic continuity and change, the 1970s was a time
when the dominant adaptationist style was significantly challenged by a
more fundamentalist style of Islam. In Islamic terms, one of the significant
developments of the decade was the emergence of a new, radical style of
fundamentalism during the process of interaction and conflict between
adaptationism and fundamentalism. The foundations of the Islamic experience that had been laid in the eighteenth century became more visible in
the 1970s. At the beginning of its fifteenth century, the Islamic world was
therefore in the midst of major transformations in all dimensions of its experience. In those transformations, elements of both continuity and
dramatic change are clearly apparent.

8

Perspectives and Prospects

Interpretations of the Resurgence

Unity and variety, consensus and conflict, continuity and change—the great themes of Islamic history are often described in these terms. They represent the aspects of the Islamic experience that must be understood and somehow, if possible, reconciled in any interpretation. The interaction of the elements of unity, consensus, and continuity with the factors of diversity, conflict, and change is the broad foundation of Muslim existence. It is also an important dimension in the perspectives of those people who try to interpret the Islamic experience.

The resurgence of Islamic activism in the 1970s and efforts to interpret that development raise the issues of the importance of continuity and change in a very clear way. Some interpretations emphasize the new elements in the situation, and others stress the importance of the underlying continuities within the Islamic tradition. One perspective notes the wide diversity of the experiences that have been grouped together under the common label of Islamic revival, and other perspectives identify common sources of inspiration within that diversity. It is clear that the modern history of Islam and Muslim communities, in general, and the Islamic experience of the 1970s, in particular, are complex subjects that can and must be approached from a variety of perspectives.

Discussions of the causes of the Islamic revival present a variety of factors that must be considered. One important perspective is that which views the resurgence in the context of crisis and crisis resolution. Muslim societies are in the midst of major transformations that create tensions and crises, which must be resolved. Different analysts identify a number of key issues as being the sources of the crises to which Muslims have reacted by a reaffirmation of Islam.

Within this framework, one broad perspective is provided by R. Hrair Dekmejian. He notes, "At the most general level of analysis, the recent quest for a return to the Islamic ethos appears to be a natural response to the successive pathological experiences which have buffeted Islamic societies in

contemporary times . . . the catalysts of the crisis environment which appear to have triggered a return to Islamic roots are multi-dimensional."[1] He
then describes these major catalysts as the crisis of political legitimacy and
ineffective leadership, the paucity of social justice, and the burden of continuing military defeats. The conclusion drawn is that "to an increasing
number of alienated Muslims, Islam does appear to provide a practical
political alternative as well as a secure spiritual niche and psychological anchor in a turbulent world."[2]

Other crisis-oriented perspectives sometimes stress the importance of
specific events or a different general framework as the catalyst for revival.
One frequently mentioned event is the Arab-Israeli War of 1967, in which
Muslim forces suffered a major defeat. At least part of the revival of the
1970s is traced to Muslim reactions to that catastrophe and the perceived
need for a rigorous transformation of Muslim society if such defeats are to
be avoided in the future.

A broader crisis perspective sees the revival within a religio-ideological
context and identifies the crisis as the grave problem of adjusting a traditional religion to the needs of the modern world. Geoffrey Godsell, for example, believes that since the sixteenth century, "Islam has been in chronic
crisis—a crisis which a non-Muslim might see as stemming from its inability
to come to terms with all that has been unleashed on the world (mainly
from the West) since the Renaissance. . . . today's assertiveness is in fact
defensive. . . . It is the plangent and defiant cry of the adherents of a great
religion which has yet to come to terms theologically and convincingly with
today's world."[3]

Those themes of crisis have been combined in the analysis of G. H.
Jansen. He notes that "precisely because of their setbacks, the Moslem people turned more than ever to Islam and Islam became more militant. . . . But
while defiant militancy was the public reaction, the private turning toward
Islam was done to find something enduring that would give strength and
comfort."[4] The crisis of adjustment to modern conditions is part of that experience. "The reformist Moslem has yet to come to terms with the problem
that, although certain elements in Koranic legislation may have been
suitable for seventh-century Arabia, and may even have represented advances on the customs of the time, they do not conform to the spirit of the
times in the last quarter of the 20th century."[5]

The crisis perspective emphasizes the underlying elements of continuity in
the contemporary Islamic experience, and Islam is seen as a kind of refuge
that maintains its appeal because it has remained constant. In the face of
rapid change, Islam presents an affirmation of traditional values that all can
understand and with which Muslims can identify. In some forms, this
perspective runs the risk of ignoring the many developments that have
taken place within Islam in modern times. However, Islam has a special appeal in the contemporary world in places where alternative world views, including the modern world view, have not succeeded in providing the basis
for just societies and a resolution of the great problems facing humanity.

A second perspective stresses the changes that have taken place within the Islamic world and sees them as an important factor in the Islamic resurgence of the 1970s. In contrast to the crisis perspective, this view notes the successes and strengths of Muslims in the contemporary world. By the 1970s, most countries in which Muslims are a majority had achieved political independence, Muslim leaders were becoming increasingly important in international affairs, and there was a sense among Muslims that they were at least beginning to assume a more prominent and appropriate role in the world.

This success perspective uses an important aspect of the Islamic tradition as its starting point. Within Islam, there has been an important interaction between the Islamic faith and the actual course of history. Throughout much of the Islamic experience, history has confirmed the Islamic faith as believers have been prosperous and powerful as a community. The great crisis of the modern Islamic experience was that the link between faith and worldly success appeared to have been broken.[6] During the time of this real crisis, there was less evidence of a general activist Islamic revival than in later times when conditions had changed. The most visible resurgence occurred in the 1970s, when Muslim states were independent and growing in importance, rather than in the earlier years of historical crisis.

The major new factor in this change of status for Muslims is seen by Daniel Pipes as being the impact of oil revenues. "In the 1970s came the oil boom, and suddenly Muslims could stand up to their Christian nemesis. The long slide downward was stopped, as some Muslims again enjoyed the wealth and power that was their due as God's community. The oil boom marked a turning point in Muslim consciousness: more than anything else, it prepared the way for widespread Islamic political activity."[7] In this way, although the success perspective identifies some elements of continuity with the past, the focus is on the new factors that effectively came into being in the 1970s.

The diversity of reactions to the changing conditions, whether in the context of crisis or success, is stressed by a third perspective. In this diversity perspective, local conditions are emphasized, and the common features tend to be tied to factors that are not specifically Islamic. For example, Aziz Azmeh notes the widespread phenomena that are called the Islamic revival and says: "Though these movements all fall loosely under the same Islamic rubric, they are utterly diverse. The anti-Communist witchhunt in Indonesia, undertaken in the name of Islam, has nothing in common with the constitution of a Muslim nationality in postwar Yugoslavia. . . . Islamic countries and Islamic movements are as diverse as the nature of the political movements carrying the Islamic banner."[8] He recognizes that the simultaneous occurrence of these movements gives rise to the impression of a general Islamic revival but feels that this universality is "a register of the fact that the postcolonial political and economic orders are giving way simultaneously in most countries with Islamic histories and under the impact of much the same forces which generated world recession."[9] For

Azmeh, the Islamic revival is better seen as part of a general Third World reorientation of social and political organization in the postcolonial era.

This emphasis on the diversity of the contemporary Islamic experience is also seen in Martin Kramer's analysis of the political role of Islam. After discussing Islamic ideals and then specific experiences in Muslim countries, Kramer concludes that "it is appropriate to end these country sketches by citing wide contrasts; they evidence the tremendous variety within political Islam. Each species within this broad genus has seen a unique evolution, bound to the special circumstances of widely separated locales. . . . The distinctive pattern that emerges is the lack of pattern."[10]

A fourth perspective is one that does identify a general pattern in the contemporary Islamic experience, and the key to this perspective is the identification of a broad evolution of Islamic society, which continues in special and often unique ways in the modern era. This approach sees the elements of continuity and change as interacting dimensions of the Islamic experience. Writers with the crisis, success, and diversity perspectives are also aware of this aspect of Islamic history but tend to stress other factors. In this evolutionary perspective, the approaches differ widely, depending on how the evolutionary dynamics are defined. However, there is a shared feeling that the Islamic past is a crucial factor in shaping the Islamic present and future.

The danger of the evolutionary perspective is that unique features of the present situation may be ignored if the approach is oversimplified. In such an approach, as Hamid Enayat has noted, the contemporary Islamic revival becomes "merely an optical illusion: Islam has always been there as a powerful force behind the periodic political upheavals in the Muslim world. . . . Only when some short-sighted regimes have chosen to suppress or offend the religious feelings of the subjects in the name of a secular ideal such as modernisation, development or nationalism, have the resultant eruptions appeared to an otherwise unwatchful external world as the awakening of a dormant force."[11] Enayat notes that this view ignores features of the current movement that make it different from earlier movements.

Enayat's discussion of these new features presents a general evolutionary picture rather than a description of particular events. The resurgence of the 1970s is seen in the context of the changing pattern of Muslims' responses to modernization in the past two centuries, and in this evolution, there are three basic stages. In the first, the desire for modernization was stimulated by European aggression and resulted in major reform efforts, with an emphasis on military development. In the second stage, beginning in the late nineteenth century, the inadequacy of the early reform efforts was recognized, and even more comprehensive reform efforts were made. In this phase, the elites in Muslim society accepted the West as the model, and "it was only natural that traditional values should either be relegated to a secondary place, or openly discarded."[12] However, that phase resulted in social disintegration without successful social reconstruction. In the wake of the failures of the second stage, there was a growing awareness among

Muslims of their own special heritage following World War II, and it is possible to conclude that "although some of the dramatic manifestations of the Islamic resurgence can . . . be attributed to coincidence or odd twists of destiny, its essential content is unquestionably derived from long historical processes."[13]

The power of the underlying continuity of Muslim feelings in this evolution is emphasized by Bernard Lewis in one of the earliest of the major discussions of the Islamic resurgence of the 1970s. Lewis identified the Islamic revival as a significant force before the Iranian revolution brought it to the attention of most people and noted that the Westernizing ideologies of radical socialism and nationalism were largely the product of the small group of educated elite. As movements worked to gain broader popular support, the continuing Islamic loyalties of the general population gained greater power. In discussing the Arab world, Lewis notes, "As the nationalist movement has become genuinely popular, so it has become less national and more religious—in other words, less Arab and more Islamic."[14] This new spirit is reflected in the basic political trends, even those in the more radical states. "Islam is still the most effective form of consensus in Muslim countries, the basic group identity among the masses. . . . One can already see the contrast between the present regimes and those of the small, alienated, Western-educated elite which governed until a few decades ago. As regimes come closer to the populace, even if their verbiage is left-wing and ideological, they become more Islamic."[15]

The Islamic resurgence of the 1970s is thus seen as being within an evolutionary framework with strong elements of continuity as well as unique factors created by the modern experience. Although the pattern of action and reaction described by Lewis and Enayat is defined primarily in terms of the modern experience, other evolutionary perspectives also note the continuity with premodern Islamic styles of coping with changing conditions.

Maxime Rodinson, for example, puts the current resurgence of Islamic fundamentalism or *intégrisme* in the context of the nature of Islam as defined by its early experience: "Islam has never ceased to be in some sense *intégriste*."[16] Detlev H. Khalid believes that a similar long-term pattern provides the context for the emergence of modern fundamentalism, and his view is summarized in the following way: "The history of Islam has been a continuous struggle between mysticism and formalism. Neither has managed to cope with the challenge of modernity. This has brought a new movement to the fore, usually called fundamentalism or integralist Islam."[17]

Many contemporary Muslims also describe the current Islamic experience in terms of an evolutionary perspective, and in many ways, those interpretations are an important part of the reaffirmation of Islam in the contemporary world. Muslims recognize that Muslim communities in the past and at present were and are not fully Islamic. Only the initial experience of the community under the leadership of the Prophet Muhammad and his companions is seen as fully conforming to the ideal, and that community has come to represent the ideal. The Muslim evolutionary perspective sees a general pattern of Islamic revival emerging as Muslim society developed, and often departed from the ideal. As one modern Muslim revivalist noted, "Islam needed in every age and still needs such strong men, groups of men and institutions which could change the course of the times and bring the world round to bow before the authority of the One, Almighty."[18] In this framework, Muslims believe that there has been a continual process of *taj-did* ("renewal") throughout Islamic history.

The evolutionary pattern seen in this tradition is one of a recognition of the community's departure from the ideal followed by an effort at renewal and revitalization. In this context, the Islamic resurgence of the 1970s is a part of a long tradition of self-renewal within the Islamic community. The unique aspects of the current resurgence are related to the particular departures from the Islamic ideal that have resulted from the modern Muslim experience. However, the process of renewal itself is an element of continuity, and as a result, many Muslims resist analyses that present the resurgence as being simply a reaction to the West or tied to specific events in recent years.

Conclusions

In this book, the perspective has been primarily evolutionary, and therefore, it runs the risks implied in that perspective. It may be that the significance of certain specific factors, like the oil boom of the 1970s, has been underestimated, but emphasizing single factors runs a parallel risk of underestimating the complexity of the issues involved or not giving due attention to the vitality of the elements of continuity within the Islamic experience. It is hoped that the emphasis given to the local dimensions of Islamic experiences in this study provides a sense of the diversity that is present and an awareness of the dramatic changes that have taken place, without losing a feeling for the continuities that also exist in the history of the Islamic peoples.

The general pattern identified in this book is the evolution of the Islamic communities through the interaction of the styles of Islamic experience. These styles are identified not so much by the content of ideas expressed as by modes of dealing with changing historical conditions and of interpreting the Islamic message. These styles take different forms in the various eras of Islamic history, and their special roles and programs are related to the local conditions of the societies in which they operate.

The great dynamic of this interaction of styles follows a pattern seen in the diversity of the Islamic experiences. As Islamic communities are created or expand, adaptation to local conditions is necessary, and such adaptations were the foundations for the great syntheses of Islamic history. New social and political structures were created, which provided the basis for expanding Islamic life, and intellectual adaptationism enabled Islamic thought to meet challenges such as those posed by the Hellenistic philosophical tradition.

With the great successes of Islamic adaptationism came a sense of the need to preserve the achievements, and a conservative style of Islamic action worked to preserve the gains that had been made and became a brake upon conscious changes adaptationists wished to make. However, at various times and in different places, the process of adaptation appeared to introduce such flexibility or so many compromises that the clearly Islamic nature of the community seemed to be threatened. In that situation, the process of renewal would take a fundamentalist form. The Quran and the Sunnah provide an absolute standard for judging the "Islamicness" of society, and those fundamentals have been used by activists throughout Islamic history as the basis for criticism of the status quo and for programs of Islamic renewal. This fundamentalism produced movements that sometimes were revolutionary and at other times were able to encourage a less militant affirmation of the Islamic fundamentals within the existing structures. Following this effort at "re-Islamization," which was often actually a further step in the initial Islamization of a society, the process of adaptation and conservative preservation could continue, with the basic Islamic nature of the community being reaffirmed.

The individualist style emphasized the more personal and individual aspects of Islam and interacted with the more communal orientation of the other three. In individual terms, this style often meant an emphasis on individual piety rather than on communal obligation, and in terms of the community as a whole, the style stressed the charismatic nature of leadership. In medieval Islamic civilization, the interaction of community and individual helped to provide the basis for the Islamic tradition of mysticism in contrast to the conservative and fundamentalist emphasis upon the law and communal obligation. In the modern Islamic experience, the tradition of the individualist style has opened the way for an acceptance of secularism in its nonradical forms. In all periods, the potential within the Islamic experience for the emergence of religiously oriented charismatic leadership provided a vehicle for a reaffirmation of Islam in the context of messianic expectations.

Since the eighteenth century, all of these styles have continued to be visible within Islamic life, and the interaction of these styles has provided the dominant modes of Islamic expression. The eighteenth-century experience helped to provide the definition of the fundamentalist style as it was to interact in the modern era. Modernizing adaptation and fundamentalist reaction provided the major vehicles for Islamic expression during the nineteenth century, and in the twentieth century, modernizing adaptation supported by a secularist individualism has become the dominant style under the influence of the special conditions of modernizing societies. However, as the compromises involved in these styles appeared to threaten the authentic Islamic nature of the community, fundamentalist pressures began to build, and because of factors like the oil boom of the 1970s, the reassertion of the fundamentalist style became an important force in the Islamic world.

Clearly, as discussed in Chapters 5, 6, and 7, a wide range of factors has been involved in the Islamic experience in the twentieth century. However, in addition to the local dimension and the dimension of the relationship of the Islamic movements to the basic elements of modern history, it is also helpful to note the continuing evolution of Islamic society in the framework of the Islamic dimension of styles and faith.

The rich diversity of the modern Islamic experience bears testimony to the continuing ability of the Islamic message to inspire a variety of people in many different ways. Although some of those people may simply be using Islam for other purposes, the experiences of Muslims since the eighteenth century make it impossible to speak of contemporary societies in the Islamic world as "post-Muslim" in the same way that people sometimes speak of Western society as "post-Christian." In this book, the diversity and conflict as well as the continuity and consensus of Islam have been explored as a way to understand the modern Islamic experience.

In a major review in 1976, Andrew C. Hess discussed the problems of interpreting the Islamic experience, and he noted that the elements of consensus and conflict are both important in Islamic history. In contemporary analyses by Westerners and Muslims alike, there is a new and necessary awareness of the role of conflict and diversity within Islam, and it is to be hoped that this book reflects that awareness. However, it is also true, as Hess notes, that "the cultural unity that Islamic civilization represented will continue to give the Middle East a cohesion Islamic historians can neglect at their peril."[19] The unity of the world of Islam, even beyond the Middle East, and its continuity with past experience have also been part of the perspective of this book.

Prospects

History is not a predictive science, and the social scientists have had little success in devising an accurate means of foretelling the future. However, it is possible to speculate about the future of the Islamic revival on the basis of its continuities with the past.

At the beginning of the fifteenth Islamic century, Islamic communities are engaged in a vigorous reaffirmation of the Islamic message, frequently utilizing a fundamentalist style. In the revival of the 1970s, a new type of fundamentalism was emerging, and it combined traditional themes with radical approaches. It has sometimes clashed with the more traditional fundamentalism in which much of the 1970s revival is expressed.

If the more traditional fundamentalism of the current revival proves inadequate, there are alternative ways for the continuing assertion of the validity of the Islamic message. Some Muslims have expressed the fear that if the current Islamic movement does not make rapid progress in solving the problems of Muslim societies, there will be many who will turn away from Islam. However, if past experience is any guide, the future will not include the demise of Islam even if the current experiments fail. What will happen is that there will be a shift in the dominant style.

If the current fundamentalism is discredited, it could be replaced in many different ways, depending on local and global conditions. If the failure leads to social collapse, the emerging dominant style might be a militant messianic Islam or the emerging radical fundamentalism. It could also mean a reversion to a more pragmatic adaptationism. Whatever happens, it is clear that with its unity and variety, its consensus and conflict, its continuity and change, Islam will continue in its fifteenth century to be a vital force in the world.

Notes

Chapter 1. Introduction

1. Donald Eugene Smith, *Religion, Politics, and Social Change in the Third World* (New York: Free Press, 1971), p. 3.
2. Tareq Y. Ismael, *The Middle East in World Politics* (Syracuse, N.Y.: Syracuse University Press, 1974), p. 204.

Chapter 2. The Islamic Dimension: Community and History

1. Mazheruddin Siddiqi, *The Qur'anic Concept of History* (Karachi: Central Institute of Islamic Research, 1965), p. 1.
2. Ismaʿil R. Al Faruqi, *Islam* (Niles, Ill.: Argus Communications, 1979), p. 13.
3. Fazlur Rahman, *Islam* (Garden City, N.Y.: Doubleday, Anchor Books, 1968), p. 19.
4. James A. Bill and Carl Leiden, *Politics in the Middle East* (Boston: Little, Brown and Company, 1979), p. 135.
5. N. A. Faris, "Development in Arab Historiography As Reflected in the Struggle Between ʿAlī and Muʿāwiya," in *Historians of the Middle East*, ed. Bernard Lewis and P. M. Holt (London: Oxford University Press, 1962), p. 435.
6. Richard W. Bulliet, *Conversion to Islam in the Medieval Period: An Essay in Quantitative History* (Cambridge, Mass.: Harvard University Press, 1979), p. 128.
7. Ira Marvin Lapidus, *Muslim Cities in the Later Middle Ages* (Cambridge, Mass.: Harvard University Press, 1967), p. 134.
8. Clement Henry Moore, "Authoritarian Politics in Unincorporated Society," *Comparative Politics* 6 (1974):216.
9. Arthur Goldschmidt, Jr., *A Concise History of the Middle East* (Boulder, Colo.: Westview Press, 1979), pp. 115–116.
10. William H. McNeill, *The Rise of the West* (Chicago: University of Chicago Press, 1963), p. 485.
11. Stanford J. Shaw, *History of the Ottoman Empire and Modern Turkey*, Vol. 1 (Cambridge, Eng.: Cambridge University Press, 1976), p. 59.
12. Halil Inalcik, *The Ottoman Empire: The Classical Age 1300–1600*, trans. Norman Itzkowitz and Colin Imber (London: Weidenfeld and Nicolson, 1973), p. 176.
13. Shaw, *History of the Ottoman Empire*, 1:87.

14. Marshall G. S. Hodgson, *The Venture of Islam*, 3 vols. (Chicago: University of Chicago Press, 1974), 3:14–15.

15. Quran, 17:88.

16. Ibid., 3:144.

17. Abdallah Laroui, *The Crisis of the Arab Intellectual*, trans. Diarmid Cammell (Berkeley: University of California Press, 1976), p. 16.

18. Seyyed Hossein Nasr, *Ideals and Realities of Islam* (London: George Allen and Unwin, 1966), p. 29.

19. Abul Aʿla Maududi (Abu al-Ala Mawdudi), *Towards Understanding Islam* (Gary, Ind.: International Islamic Federation of Student Organizations, 1970), p. 103.

20. Rahman, *Islam*, p. 43.

21. Ibn Khaldun, *The Muqaddimah: An Introduction to History*, trans. Franz Rosenthal, 3 vols. (New York: Pantheon Books, 1958), 2:163.

22. D. B. MacDonald, "Al-Mahdi," in *The Shorter Encyclopaedia of Islam*, ed. Hamilton A. R. Gibb and J. H. Kramers (Leiden: E. J. Brill, 1953), pp. 311, 313.

Chapter 3. The Foundations of the Modern Experience

1. Evelyn Baring, first earl of Cromer, *Modern Egypt*, 2 vols. (New York: Macmillan, 1909), 2:184.

2. H.A.R. Gibb, *Modern Trends in Islam* (Chicago: University of Chicago Press, 1947), p. 105.

3. Fazlur Rahman, "Revival and Reform in Islam," in *The Cambridge History of Islam*, ed. P. M. Holt, Ann K. S. Lambton, and Bernard Lewis, 2 vols. (Cambridge: Cambridge University Press, 1970), 2:640.

4. Fazlur Rahman, *Islam* (Garden City, N.Y.: Doubleday, Anchor Books, 1968), p. 239.

5. Stanford J. Shaw, *History of the Ottoman Empire and Modern Turkey*, Vol. 1 (Cambridge, Eng.: Cambridge University Press, 1976), p. 223.

6. Richard Repp, "Some Observations on the Development of the Ottoman Learned Hierarchy," in *Scholars, Saints, and Sufis*, ed. Nikki R. Keddie (Berkeley: University of California Press, 1972), p. 30.

7. Ibid., p. 32.

8. Norman Itzkowitz, "Men and Ideas in the Eighteenth Century Ottoman Empire," in *Studies in Eighteenth-Century Islamic History*, ed. Thomas Naff and Roger Owen (Carbondale, Ill.: Southern Illinois University Press, 1977), p. 16.

9. Ibid., pp. 19–20.

10. Niyazi Berkes, *The Development of Secularism in Turkey* (Montreal: McGill University Press, 1964), p. 52. See also Robert W. Olson, "The Esnaf and the Patrona Halil Rebellion of 1730: A Realignment in Ottoman Politics?" *Journal of the Economic and Social History of the Orient* 17(1974):329–332.

11. Stanford J. Shaw, *Between Old and New: The Ottoman Empire Under Sultan Selim III, 1789–1807* (Cambridge, Mass.: Harvard University Press, 1971), p. viii.

12. Joan E. Gilbert, "The Ulama of Medieval Damascus and the International World of Islamic Scholarship" (Ph.D. diss., University of California, Berkeley, 1977), Chapter 2.

13. See Albert Hourani, "Shaikh Khalid and the Naqshbandi Order," in *Islamic Philosophy and the Classical Tradition*, ed. S. M. Stern, Albert Hourani, and Vivian Brown (Columbia, S.C.: University of South Carolina Press, 1973), pp. 89–103.

14. Ibid., pp. 99–100.

15. Afaf Lutfi al-Sayyid Marsot, "The Political and Economic Functions of the ʿUlama in the 18th Century," *Journal of the Economic and Social History of the Orient* 16 (1973):132.

16. Peter Gran, *Islamic Roots of Capitalism: Egypt, 1760–1840* (Austin: University of Texas Press, 1979), p. 11.

17. Marsot, "Political and Economic Functions," p. 134.

18. Afaf Lutfi al-Sayyid Marsot, "The Ulama of Cairo in the Eighteenth and Nineteenth Centuries," in *Scholars, Saints, and Sufis*, ed. Nikki R. Keddie (Berkeley: University of California Press, 1972), pp. 161–162.

19. Ibid., p. 157.

20. Abd al-Rahman al-Jabarti, ʿAjaʾib al-ʾAthar fi al-Tarajim wa al-Akhbar, ed. Hasan Muhammad Jawhar et al., 7 vols. (Cairo: Lajnah al-Bayan al-ʿArabi, 1958–1967), 1:131–134.

21. Gran, *Islamic Roots*, pp. 48–49.

22. *Encyclopaedia of Islam*, 2d. ed., s.v. "Ibn Hadjar al-ʾAskalani."

23. Gran, *Islamic Roots*, Chapters 2 and 3.

24. J. Spencer Trimingham, *The Sufi Orders in Islam* (London: Oxford University Press, 1971), p. 85.

25. Rahman, *Islam*, p. 245.

26. Abdallah al-Salih al-ʿUthaymayn, *al-Shaykh Muhammad bin Abd al-Wahhab, Hayyatuhu wa Fikruhu* (Riyadh: Dar al-ʿUlum, n.d.), p. 125.

27. *Majmuʿah al-Rasaʾil wa al-Musaʾil al-Najdiyyah*, 4 vols. (Cairo: Matabaʿah al-Manar, 1928–1931), 1:3.

28. Quoted in Abul Aʿla Maududi, *A Short History of the Revivalist Movement in Islam*, trans. al-Ashʿari (Lahore: Islamic Publications, 1976), p. 93.

29. Aziz Ahmad, *Studies in Islamic Culture in the Indian Environment* (Oxford: Clarendon Press, 1964), pp. 202–203.

30. *Encyclopaedia of Islam*, 2d ed., s.v. "Hind, Growth of Muslim Religious Thought."

31. Salih ibn Muhammad al-Fulani, "Al-Kitab Qatf al-Thamar fi Rafʿ Asanid al-Musannafat fi al-Fanun wa al-ʾAthar," Dar al-Kutub (National Library), Cairo, Egypt, Talʿat 195.

32. J. C. van Leur, *Indonesian Trade and Society* (The Hague: W. van Hoeve, 1955), p. 289.

33. Clifford Geertz, *Islam Observed: Religious Development in Morocco and Indonesia* (Chicago: University of Chicago Press, 1968), p. 65.

34. G.W.J. Drewes, *Directions for Travellers on the Mystic Path* (The Hague: Martinus Nijhoff, 1977), p. 37.

35. Andrew C. Hess, "The Forgotten Frontier: The Ottoman North African Provinces During the Eighteenth Century," in *Studies in Eighteenth-Century Islamic History*, ed. Thomas Naff and Roger Owen (Carbondale, Ill.: Southern Illinois University Press, 1977), p. 86.

36. Charles-André Julien, *History of North Africa*, trans. John Petrie (New York: Praeger, 1970), p. 332.

37. Jamil M. Abun-Nasr, "Religion and Politics in Eighteenth-Century Tunisia," *Zeitschrift der Deutschen Morgenlandischen Gesellschaft,* Supp. 3:1 (1977), pp. 304–315.

38. Andre Raymond, "North Africa in the Pre-Colonial Period," in *The Cambridge History of Islam*, ed. P. M. Holt, Ann K. S. Lambton, and Bernard Lewis, 2

vols. (Cambridge, Eng.: Cambridge University Press, 1970), 2:280.

39. Ibid., 2:269.

40. *Encyclopaedia of Islam*, 2d ed., s.v. "Barakat."

41. Trimingham, Sufi Orders, p. 115.

42. John Voll, "Two Biographies of Ahmad Ibn Idris al-Fasi (1760–1837)," *International Journal of African Historical Studies* 6 (1973):637.

43. J. S. Trimingham, "The Phases of Islamic Expansion and Islamic Culture Zones in Africa," in *Islam in Tropical Africa*, ed. I. M. Lewis (London: Oxford University Press, 1966), p. 128.

44. Humphrey Fisher, "The Western and Central Sudan," in *The Cambridge History of Islam*, ed. P. M. Holt, Ann K. S. Lambton, and Bernard Lewis, 2 vols. (Cambridge, Eng.: Cambridge University Press, 1970), 2:364.

45. C. C. Stewart, *Islam and Social Order in Mauritania* (Oxford: Clarendon Press, 1973), p. 39.

46. Hamid Algar, "Shi'ism and Iran in the Eighteenth Century," in *Studies in Eighteenth-Century Islamic History*, ed. Thomas Naff and Roger Owen (Carbondale, Ill.: Southern Illinois University Press, 1977), p. 299.

47. Ibid., p. 301.

48. Nikki R. Keddie, "The Roots of the Ulama's Power in Modern Iran," in *Scholars, Saints, and Sufis*, ed. Nikki R. Keddie (Berkeley: University of California Press, 1972), p. 224.

49. Hamid Algar, "The Oppositional Role of the Ulama in Twentieth-Century Iran," in *Scholars, Saints, and Sufis*, ed. Nikki R. Keddie (Berkeley: University of California Press, 1972), p. 235.

Chapter 4. European Domination and Islamic Response

1. Wilfred Cantwell Smith, *Islam in Modern History* (Princeton: Princeton University Press, 1957), p. 41.

2. L. Carl Brown, *The Tunisia of Ahmad Bey, 1837–1855* (Princeton: Princeton University Press, 1974), p. 358.

3. Ibid., pp. 356–369.

4. Ibid., p. 366.

5. Richard L. Chambers, "The Ottoman Ulema and the Tanzimat," in *Scholars, Saints, and Sufis*, ed. Nikki R. Keddie (Berkeley: University of California Press, 1972), p. 46.

6. Norman Itzkowitz and Joel Shinder, "The Office of Seyh ul-Islām and the Tanzimat—A Prosopographic Enquiry," *Middle Eastern Studies* 8 (1972):93–101.

7. Richard L. Chambers, "The Education of a Nineteenth Century Ottoman *Alim*, Ahmed Cevdet Pasa," *International Journal of Middle East Studies* 4 (1973):463.

8. Quoted in Bernard Lewis, *The Emergence of Modern Turkey* (London: Oxford University Press, 1961), p. 166.

9. Ibid., p. 169.

10. Stanford J. Shaw and Ezel Kural Shaw, *History of the Ottoman Empire and Modern Turkey*, Vol. 2 (Cambridge, Eng.: Cambridge University Press, 1977), p. 212.

11. Afaf Lutfi al-Sayyid Marsot, "The Ulama of Cairo in the Eighteenth and Nineteenth Centuries," in *Scholars, Saints, and Sufis*, ed. Nikki R. Keddie (Berkeley: University of California Press, 1972), p. 163.

12. Quoted in Albert Hourani, *Arabic Thought in the Liberal Age, 1798-1939* (London: Oxford University Press, 1962), pp. 140-141.

13. Quoted in Nadav Safran, *Egypt in Search of Political Community* (Cambridge, Mass.: Harvard University Press, 1961), p. 90.

14. Leon Carl Brown, *The Surest Path, The Political Treatise of a Nineteenth-Century Muslim Statesman* (Cambridge, Mass.: Harvard University Press, 1967), pp. 74-75.

15. Jamil M. Abun-Nasr, *The Tijaniyya* (London: Oxford University Press, 1965), Chapters 2 and 3.

16. Hamid Algar, *Religion and State in Iran, 1785-1906* (Berkeley: University of California Press, 1969), p. 136.

17. Hamid Algar, "The Oppositional Role of the Ulama in Twentieth-Century Iran," in *Scholars, Saints, and Sufis,* ed. Nikki R. Keddie (Berkeley: University of California Press, 1972), pp. 238-240. This whole discussion of Iran relies heavily upon the works of Hamid Algar and Nikki Keddie. In addition to the works already cited, see Hamid Algar, *Mirza Malkum Khan* (Berkeley: University of California Press, 1973), and the following works by Nikki R. Keddie: *Religion and Rebellion in Iran: The Tobacco Protest of 1891-92* (London: Frank Cass, 1966); *Sayyid Jamal ad-Din al-Afghani: A Political Biography* (Berkeley: University of California Press, 1972); and *Iran: Religion, Politics, and Society, Collected Essays* (London: Frank Cass, 1980). For a statement of the more fundamentalist position in the crisis of constitutionalism, see Abdul-Hadi Hairi, "Shaykh Fazl Allah Nuri's Refutation of the Idea of Constitutionalism," *Middle Eastern Studies* 13 (1977):327-339.

18. Fazlur Rahman, *Islam* (Garden City, N.Y.: Doubleday, Anchor Books, 1968), p. 267.

19. Aziz Ahmad, *Islamic Modernism in India and Pakistan, 1857-1964* (London: Oxford University Press, 1967), p. 61.

20. Ibid., p. 62.

21. Peter von Sivers, "The Realm of Justice: Apocalyptic Revolts in Algeria (1849-1879)," *Humaniora Islamica* 1 (1973):53.

22. Ibid., p. 60.

23. C. Snouck Hurgronje, *Mekka in the Latter Part of the 19th Century,* trans. J. H. Monahan (Leiden: E. J. Brill, 1970), pp. 207-208.

24. R. Bayly Winder, *Saudi Arabia in the Nineteenth Century* (New York: St. Martins Press, 1965), p. 228.

25. Ibid., pp. 222-223.

26. B. G. Martin, *Muslim Brotherhoods in 19th-Century Africa* (Cambridge, Eng.: Cambridge University Press, 1976), p. 125.

Chapter 5. Twentieth-Century Islam: Dominant Majorities in the Middle East and Africa

1. The figures for Muslim populations and their proportions of the total populations used in this chapter are based on information appearing in Richard V. Weekes, ed., *Muslim Peoples: A World Ethnographic Survey* (Westport, Conn.: Greenwood Press, 1978).

2. Albert Hourani, *Arabic Thought in the Liberal Age, 1798-1939* (London: Oxford University Press, 1962), p. 343.

3. Majid Khadduri, *Political Trends in the Arab World* (Baltimore: Johns Hopkins Press, 1970), p. 69.

4. Hourani, *Arabic Thought*, p. 299.

5. Arnold J. Toynbee, *Survey of International Affairs 1925, Volume I: The Islamic World Since the Peace Settlement* (London: Oxford University Press, 1927), p. 426.

6. Sylvia G. Haim, ed., *Arab Nationalism: An Anthology* (Berkeley: University of California Press, 1962), p. 176.

7. Ibid., p. 56.

8. Hourani, *Arabic Thought*, p. 172.

9. Hisham Sharabi, *Arab Intellectuals and the West: The Formative Years, 1875-1914* (Baltimore, Md.: Johns Hopkins Press, 1970), p. 94.

10. Taha Hussein (Husayn), *The Future of Culture in Egypt*, trans. Sidney Glazer (Washington, D.C.: American Council of Learned Societies, 1954), p. 136.

11. Charles D. Smith, "The 'Crisis of Orientation': The Shift of Egyptian Intellectuals to Islamic Subjects in the 1930's," *International Journal of Middle East Studies* 4 (1973):406-407.

12. Nadav Safran, *Egypt in Search of Political Community* (Cambridge, Mass.: Harvard University Press, 1961), p. 142.

13. Khadduri, *Political Trends*, p. 231.

14. Hanna Batatu, *The Old Social Classes and the Revolutionary Movements of Iraq* (Princeton: Princeton University Press, 1978), p. 390.

15. Ibid., p. 397.

16. For these views see Haim, *Arab Nationalism*, p. 63, and Kamel S. Abu Jaber, *The Arab Baʿth Socialist Party: History, Ideology, and Organization* (Syracuse, N.Y.: Syracuse University Press, 1966), p. 129.

17. Tareq Y. Ismael, *The Arab Left* (Syracuse, N.Y.: Syracuse University Press, 1976), p. 91.

18. A full text of the program is reprinted in Gerald De Gaury, *Faisal, King of Saudi Arabia* (New York: Frederick A. Praeger, 1967), pp. 147-151.

19. See the speech quoted in De Gaury, *Faisal*, p. 167.

20. Muhammad Abdallah al-Samman, *Hasan al-Banna: al-Rajal wa al-Fikrah* (Cairo: Dar al-Iʿtisam, 1978/1398), p. 62.

21. Richard P. Mitchell, *The Society of the Muslim Brothers* (London: Oxford University Press, 1969), p. 30.

22. Kemal H. Karpat, ed., *Political and Social Thought in the Contemporary Middle East* (New York: Frederick A. Praeger, 1968), p. 125.

23. Ibid., p. 132.

24. Batatu, *Old Social Classes*, p. 25.

25. Richard D. Robinson, *The First Turkish Republic* (Cambridge, Mass.: Harvard University Press, 1963), p. 71.

26. Niyazi Berkes, *The Development of Secularism in Turkey* (Montreal: McGill University Press, 1964), p. 486.

27. Ibid., p. 482.

28. James Alban Bill, *The Politics of Iran: Groups, Classes, and Modernization* (Columbus, Ohio: Charles E. Merrill, 1972), p. 24.

29. Louis Dupree, *Afghanistan* (Princeton: Princeton University Press, 1980), p. 452.

30. George S. Harris, *The Origins of Communism in Turkey* (Stanford, Calif.: Hoover Institution, 1967), p. 70.

31. Sepehr Zabih, *The Communist Movement in Iran* (Berkeley: University of California Press, 1966), p. 259.

32. Seyyed Hossein Nasr, *Ideals and Realities of Islam* (London: George Allen and Unwin, 1966), p. 147.

33. *Turkish Daily News*, 4 June 1977.

34. Mohammad Hassa Faghfoory, "The Role of the Ulama in Twentieth Century Iran with Particular Reference to Ayatullah Haj Sayyid Abul Qasim Kashani" (Ph.D. diss., University of Wisconsin, Madison, 1978), p. 172.

35. Ibid., pp. 142–143.

36. Clement Henry Moore, *Tunisia Since Independence* (Berkeley: University of California Press, 1965), p. 33.

37. Ibid., p. 48.

38. Ronald Segal, *African Profiles* (Baltimore: Penguin, 1962), pp. 290–291.

39. Charles F. Gallagher, *The United States and North Africa* (Cambridge, Mass.: Harvard University Press, 1963), p. 95.

40. Segal, *African Profiles*, p. 295.

41. Robert Merle, *Ahmed Ben Bella*, trans. Camilla Sykes (New York: Walker, 1967), p. 43.

42. Frantz Fanon, *Studies in a Dying Colonialism*, trans. Haakon Chevalier (New York: Monthly Review Press, 1965), Chapter 1.

43. Merle, *Ahmed Ben Bella*, p. 133.

44. David C. Gordon, *The Passing of French Algeria* (London: Oxford University Press, 1966), p. 115.

45. Ibid., p. 117.

46. E.I.J. Rosenthal, *Islam in the Modern National State* (Cambridge, Eng.: Cambridge University Press, 1965), p. 320.

47. Leon Carl Brown, "The Role of Islam in Modern North Africa," in *State and Society in Independent North Africa*, ed. Leon Carl Brown (Washington, D.C.: Middle East Institute, 1966), p. 119.

48. Abdallah Laroui, *The Crisis of the Arab Intellectual*, trans. Diarmid Cammel (Berkeley: University of California Press, 1976), p. 37.

49. Gordon, *Passing of French Algeria*, p. 117.

Chapter 6. Twentieth-Century Islam: Eastern World, Nondominant Majorities, and Minorities

1. Aziz Ahmad, *Islamic Modernism in India and Pakistan, 1857–1964* (London: Oxford University Press, 1967), p. 166.

2. Ibid., pp. 152–153.

3. Allama Muhammad Iqbal, *The Reconstruction of Religious Thought in Islam* (Lahore: Muhammad Ashraf, 1968), p. 156.

4. Ibid., p. 173.

5. Ahmad, *Islamic Modernism*, p. 175.

6. Abul Aʿla Maududi, *The Process of Islamic Revolution* (Lahore: Islamic Publications, 1977), pp. 17–19.

7. Ahmad, *Islamic Modernism*, p. 214.

8. Abul Aʿla Maududi, *Towards Understanding Islam* (Gary, Ind.: International Islamic Federation of Student Organizations, 1970), pp. 14–15.

9. Ibid., p. 36.

10. Ahmad, *Islamic Modernism*, p. 242.

11. Ibid., p. 245.

12. G. P. Bhattacharjee, *Renaissance and Freedom Movement in Bangladesh* (Calcutta: Minerva Associates, 1973), p. 48.

13. Rounaq Jahan, *Pakistan: Failure in National Integration* (New York: Columbia University Press, 1972), p. 140.

14. Kalim Siddiqui, *Conflict, Crisis, and War in Pakistan* (New York: Praeger, 1972), p. 123.

15. A. B. Shah in the foreword to S. E. Hassnain, *Indian Muslims: Challenge and Opportunity* (Bombay: Lalvani Publishing House, 1968), p. 5.

16. Ibid., p. 9.

17. Ibid., in the text by Hassnain, p. 138.

18. B. J. Boland, *The Struggle of Islam in Modern Indonesia* (The Hague: Martinus Nijhoff, 1971), p. 49.

19. Ibid., p. 51.

20. Ibid., p. 126.

21. For the use of this name and a history of the movement, see Lansiné Kaba, *The Wahhabiyya: Islamic Reform and Politics in French West Africa* (Evanston, Ill.: Northwestern University Press, 1974).

22. Ibid., p. 237.

23. Pierre Alexandre, "A West African Islamic Movement: Hamallism in French West Africa," in *Protest and Power in Black Africa*, ed. Robert I. Rotberg and Ali A. Mazrui (New York: Oxford University Press, 1970), p. 508.

24. Peter Worsley, *The Third World*, 2d ed. (Chicago: University of Chicago Press, 1970), p. 120.

25. Basil Davidson, *Let Freedom Come: Africa in Modern History* (Boston: Little, Brown and Co., 1978), pp. 327–328.

26. Claude Rivière, *Guinea: The Mobilization of a People*, trans. Virginia Thompson and Richard Adloff (Ithaca, N.Y.: Cornell University Press, 1977), p. 235.

27. *New York Times*, 16 December 1968.

28. Alexander G. Park, *Bolshevism in Turkestan, 1917–1927* (New York: Columbia University Press, 1957), p. 41.

29. Alexandre Bennigsen and Chantal Lemercier-Quelquejay, *Islam in the Soviet Union*, trans. Geoffrey E. Wheeler and Hubert Evans (New York: Praeger, 1967), p. 112.

30. Ibid., p. 183.

31. Shen Ping-wen, *Chinese Communist Criminal Acts of Persecution of Religions* (Taipei: World Anti-Communist League, China Chapter, 1978), Chapter 4.

32. Raphael Israeli, "Muslim Minorities Under Non-Islamic Rule," *Current History* 78 (1980):161.

33. Clifton E. Marsh, "The World Community of Islam in the West: From Black Muslims to Muslims (1931–1977)" (Ph.D. diss., Syracuse University, 1977), p. 203.

Chapter 7. The Resurgence of Islam: The Spirit of the New Century

1. Bruce M. Borthwick, "Religion and Politics in Israel and Egypt," *Middle East Journal* 33 (1979):146.

2. This is the observation of the East German Marxist, Rudolf Bahro, cited in Fred Halliday, "The Arc of Revolutions: Iran, Afghanistan, South Yemen, Ethiopia," *Race and Class* 20 (1979):388.

3. Zbigniew Brzezinski, *Between Two Ages: America's Role in the Technetronic Era* (New York: Viking Press, 1970), p. 258.

4. R. Hrair Dekmejian, "The Anatomy of Islamic Revival: Legitimacy Crisis, Ethnic Conflict and the Search for Islamic Alternatives," *Middle East Journal* 34 (1980):11.

5. Abd al-Hamid Abd al-Ghani, "Al-harakah al-islamiyyah al-jadidah," *Akhbar al-Yawm*, 3 February 1979, p. 7.

6. Jacques Berque, *Cultural Expression in Arab Society Today*, trans. Robert W. Stookey (Austin: University of Texas Press, 1978), p. 62.

7. "Islamic Revival in Africa," *Africa Currents*, nos. 19/20 (Spring/Summer 1980):53.

8. "Speech by President Nasser at the Fifth Anniversary of the Union Between Syria and Egypt in Cairo, 21 February 1963," *Arab Political Documents 1963* (Beirut: American University of Beirut, n.d.), p. 38.

9. *Time*, 6 January 1975, p. 10.

10. *Christian Science Monitor*, 28 February 1980.

11. *New York Times*, 23 November 1979.

12. "Saudi Opposition Leader: 'The Mosque Incident Was Part of a People's Revolution," *MERIP Reports*, no. 85 (February 1980):17–18.

13. *Christian Science Monitor*, 23 November 1979.

14. Ibid., 20 February 1980.

15. *New York Times*, 17 February 1980.

16. "The Libyan Revolution in the Words of Its Leaders," *Middle East Journal* 24 (1970):210.

17. Ibid., p. 208.

18. Ibid., p. 209.

19. Ruth First, *Libya: The Elusive Revolution* (Baltimore, Md.: Penguin, 1974), p. 11.

20. "Gathafi's Important Speech," *Progressive Libya* 2:9 (May 1973):1.

21. Muammar Al Qadhafi, *The Green Book, Part One: The Solution of the Problem of Democracy* (n.p., n.d.), pp. 13–14.

22. Raymond N. Habiby, "Mu'amar Qadhafi's New Islamic Scientific Society," *Middle East Review* 11:4 (Summer 1979):37.

23. Anthony J. Hughes, "Somalia's Socialist Road," *Africa Report*, March–April 1977, p. 41.

24. Basil Davidson, *Let Freedom Come: Africa in Modern History* (Boston: Little Brown and Company, 1978), p. 334.

25. Hamid Algar, "The Oppositional Role of the Ulama in Twentieth-Century Iran," in *Scholars, Saints, and Sufis*, ed. Nikki R. Keddie (Berkeley: University of California Press, 1972), p. 255.

26. Fereydoun Hoveyda, *The Fall of the Shah*, trans. Roger Liddell (New York: Wyndham Books, 1980), pp. 150, 153.

27. George W. Braswell, Jr., "Civil Religion in Contemporary Iran," *Journal of Church and State* 21 (Spring 1979):243.

28. Ibid., p. 235.

29. Ayatollah Ruhollah Khomeini, *Islamic Government*, trans. Joint Publications Research Service (New York: Manor Books, 1979), p. 39.

30. *New York Times*, 23 March 1980.

31. Shahrough Akhavi, *Religion and Politics in Contemporary Iran* (Albany: State University of New York Press, 1980), p. 174.

32. *New York Times*, 4 June 1978.

33. Abol-Hassan Banisadr, "Breaking the Deadlock in Iran," in *Iran Erupts*, ed. Ali-Reza Nobari (Stanford, Calif.: Iran-American Documentation Group, 1978), pp. 1, 3, 6.

34. Ali Shariʿati, *On the Sociology of Islam*, trans. Hamid Algar (Berkeley, Calif.: Mizan Press, 1979), p. 82.

35. Ibid., p. 77.

36. Gholam Abbas Tavassoli, "Introduction," in Shariʿati, *On the Sociology of Islam*, pp. 20–21.

37. Hamid Algar, "Preface," in Ali Shariʿati, *Marxism and Other Western Fallacies*, trans. R. Campbell (Berkeley, Calif.: Mizan Press, 1980), p. 10; also Akhavi, *Religion and Politics*, p. 172.

38. Ervand Abrahamian, "The Guerrilla Movement in Iran, 1963–1977," *MERIP Reports*, no. 86 (March/April 1980):10.

39. "How to Study the Qoran," *Mojahed* 1:2 (25 February 1980):17.

40. "How to Study the Qoran," *Mojahed* 1:4 (April 1980):40.

41. "Getting to Know the PMOI," *Mojahed* 1:2 (25 February 1980):10.

42. "Rajavi Remarks at Mosaddeq Commemoration," *Mojahed* 1:3 (16 March 1980):12.

43. "Tudeh's Kianuri on Embassy Takeover, Relations with Khomeini," *MERIP Reports*, no. 86 (March/April 1980):24–25.

44. *Time*, 4 February 1980, p. 38.

45. Peter Mansfield, *The Arabs* (Harmondsworth, Eng.: Penguin, 1978), p. 433.

46. "The New Government's Policy Statement," *Al Urdun: A Jordan Newsletter* 5:1 (January 1980):3.

47. Joseph P. O'Kane, "Islam in the New Egyptian Constitution: Some Discussions in *al-Ahram*," *Middle East Journal* 26 (1972):137–148.

48. "Report by the Legislative Committee of the U.A.R. National Assembly, 20 December 1965," in *Arab Political Documents 1965* (Beirut: American University of Beirut, n.d.), p. 454.

49. *New York Times*, 17 November 1974.

50. *Christian Science Monitor*, 3 March 1980.

51. Nico Kielstra, "The Agrarian Revolution and Algerian Socialism," *MERIP Reports*, no. 67 (May 1978):11.

52. John P. Entelis, "Republic of Tunisia," in *The Government and Politics of the Middle East and North Africa*, ed. David E. Long and Bernard Reich (Boulder, Colo.: Westview, 1980), p. 448.

53. Foreign Broadcast Information Service, *Daily Report: Middle East and Africa* 5, no. 107 (2 June 1980).

54. Peter B. Heller, "The Permanent Syrian Constitution of March 13, 1973," *Middle East Journal* 28 (1974):55.

55. Ibid., p. 57.

56. Foreign Broadcast Information Service, *Daily Report: Middle East and Africa* 5, no. 128 (2 July 1979).

57. Ibid., no. 139 (18 July 1979).

58. "The Permanent Constitution of the Yemen Arab Republic," *Middle East Journal* 25 (1971):389.

59. Foreign Broadcast Information Service, *Daily Report: Middle East and Africa* 5, no. 163 (20 August 1980).

60. *New York Times*, 26 January 1977.

61. *Christian Science Monitor* (International Weekly Edition), 16 April 1979.

62. John L. Esposito, "Pakistan: Quest for Islamic Identity," in *Islam and Development*, ed. John L. Esposito (Syracuse, N.Y.: Syracuse University Press, 1980), p. 162.

63. Khushwant Singh, "Bangladesh, After the First Year: Will It Ever Be a Workable Country?" *New York Times Magazine*, 21 January 1973, p. 19.

64. *New York Times*, 30 April 1978.

65. United States Joint Publications Research Service, *Translations on South and East Asia*, no. 771, JPRS 71377 (28 June 1978).

66. Ibid., no. 769, JPRS 71311 (16 June 1978).

67. Rodney Tasker, "The Explosive Mix of Muhammad and Modernity," *Far Eastern Economic Review*, 9 February 1979, p. 24.

68. Based on comments and presentations by Anwar Ibrahim at the symposium, "Resurgent Islam: Prospects and Implications," sponsored by the College of the Holy Cross and held in Durham, New Hampshire, 2–5 October 1980.

69. Tasker, "The Explosive Mix," p. 23.

70. Ibid.

71. Democratic Republic of the Sudan, Ministry of Information and Culture, *Speech Delivered by President Nimeri on the 3rd Anniversary of the 25th of May Revolution at the Khalifa Square Rally* (Khartoum, 1972), p. 23.

72. *Arab Report and Record 1977*, no. 17 (1–15 September 1977).

73. Based on comments and presentations by Dr. Hasan al-Turabi at the symposium, "Resurgent Islam: Prospects and Implications," sponsored by the College of the Holy Cross, Durham, New Hampshire, 2–5 October 1980.

74. See, for example, reports in the *New York Times*, 12 April 1980; the *Christian Science Monitor*, 20 August 1979, 30 November 1979, 22 January 1980, and 25 January 1980; and *Newsweek*, 2 April 1979.

75. S. Enders Wimbush and Alex Alexiev, "Islam's Best Friend? Not Exactly," *Christian Science Monitor*, 24 April 1980; *New York Times*, 13 January 1980.

76. *New York Times*, 17 September 1974.

77. *New York Times*, 23 March 1980.

78. "The First Asian Islamic Conference: Resolutions and Recommendations," *The Journal: Rabetat al-Alam al-Islami* 5:9 (Shaban 1398/July 1978):18–21.

Chapter 8. Perspectives and Prospects

1. R. Hrair Dekmejian, "The Anatomy of Islamic Revival: Legitimacy Crisis, Ethnic Conflict, and the Search for Islamic Alternatives," *Middle East Journal* 34 (1980):3.

2. Ibid., p. 9.

3. *Christian Science Monitor* (International Edition), 18 December 1978.

4. G. H. Jansen, "Militant Islam: The Historic Whirlwind," *New York Times Magazine*, 6 January 1980, p. 43.

5. Ibid., p. 20.

6. For a general discussion presenting this analysis, see Wilfred Cantwell Smith, *Islam in Modern History* (Princeton: Princeton University Press, 1957).

7. Daniel Pipes, "'This World Is Political!!' The Islamic Revival of the Seventies," *Orbis* 24 (1980):20.

8. Aziz Azmeh, "Islam: The New Dawn," *Middle East*, November 1979, pp. 85–86.

9. Ibid., p. 90.

10. Martin Kramer, *Political Islam* (Beverly Hills, Calif.: Sage Publications, 1980), pp. 78–79.

11. Hamid Enayat, "The Resurgence of Islam, 1: The Background," *History Today*, February 1980, p. 16.

12. Ibid., p. 18.

13. Ibid., p. 20.

14. Bernard Lewis, "The Return of Islam," *Commentary*, January 1976, p. 44.

15. Ibid., p. 48.

16. Maxime Rodinson, "Islam Resurgent?" *Gazelle Review of Literature on the Middle East*, no. 6 (1979):2.

17. Detlev H. Khalid, "The Phenomenon of Re-Islamization," *Aussenpolitik* (English ed.) 29 (1978):433.

18. Abul Aʿla Maududi, *A Short History of the Revivalist Movement in Islam*, trans. al-Ashʿari (Lahore: Islamic Publications, 1976), p. 33.

19. Andrew C. Hess, "Consensus or Conflict: The Dilemma of Islamic Historians," *American Historical Review* 81 (1976):798.

Glossary of Non-English Terms

This glossary provides short definitions for some of the technical terms and names that appear in the text Names of people and groups and other proper names are not included.

ayatollah. Literally, this means a wonder or exemplar of God. It is a title for a high-ranking religious scholar in the Shiʿite tradition.

caliph. The Western form of the Arabic term *khalifah*, which means successor. In Islamic history, the caliphs were the successors of the Prophet as leaders of the Muslim community.

grand vizier. This title was commonly given to the highest administrative official in a premodern Islamic political system. The grand vizier of the Ottoman Empire was one of the most powerful figures in the state.

hadith. A statement or account of an action or saying of the Prophet Muhammad. These accounts were collected in medieval times and provide an authoritative basis for Islamic law, supplementing the text of the Quran.

ijtihad. The action of using informed, independent judgment in a legal or theological issue. A person who uses *ijtihad* is called a *mujtahid*.

imam. There are three significant meanings for this title: (1) the leader of a group of praying Muslims; (2) a general title for any Muslim leader with some religious authority; (3) in Shiʿite Islam, the title of the rightful, divinely guided ruler. In the Shiʿite tradition, there is a line of succession to the imamate from the Prophet Muhammad through his cousin and son-in-law, Ali.

jadid. Arabic word meaning "new." It is often used as a label for reforms and reformers. For example, Islamic modernism in Russia was called Jadidism, and the reforms of the Ottoman ruler, Selim III, were called the new order, or *nizam-i-jedid*.

khalifah. See *caliph*.

Kharijites. The name of one of the major traditions of Islam. It began in 657 when a group seceded from the army of the caliph, and later it developed an anarchic interpretation of the equality of all believers.

Koran. See *Quran*.

madhhab. This means an orientation or school of thought and refers to the schools of law, especially in Sunni Islam.

madrasah. An educational institution or school.

Mahdi. The title of the divinely guided figure who is expected to come in the last days and establish the rule of God on earth.

Mamluk. Literally meaning "owned," this term is applied to military slaves who were a ruling oligarchy in many parts of the Islamic world in premodern times.

millet. A religious community or social group. In the Ottoman Empire, the various *millet*s were granted semiautonomy under the guidance of their religious leaders.

mujaddid. Arabic word meaning "renewer." A widely accepted *hadith* reports that the Prophet Muhammad said that God would send a Mujaddid (Renewer) at the beginning of each century to strengthen the faith of the Muslims. Frequently, fundamentalist-style reformers were thought of as *mujaddid*s. The process of this type of renewal is called *tajdid.*

mujtahid. See *ijtihad.*

nizam-i-jedid. See *jadid.*

Quran. Record of the revelations Muslims believe were sent to mankind through the messenger of God, Muhammad. The Quran is thus the heart of the Islamic faith and the foundation for Islamic law and social order. In English usage, it is commonly called the Koran.

Rashidun. The period of the first four caliphs. Sunni Muslims believe that the community of Muslims at this time can provide a model for Muslim life.

salaf. The pious ancestors who lived at the time of Muhammad and the Rashidun caliphs are the *salaf.* They are believed by Sunni Muslims to have had special insight into the requirements of the faith because of their close association with the Prophet Muhammad. As a result, fundamentalist reformers and other renewers frequently call for a return to the attitude or the ways of the *salaf.* In the twentieth century, reformers in the tradition of Muhammad Abduh have been called the Salafiyyah because they called for a return to the principles followed by the *salaf.*

Shariʿah. The structure of Islamic law.

shaykh. This term can apply to a tribal leader, a religious teacher, or a ruler.

shaykh al-Islam. An honorific title for important Muslim scholars. In the Ottoman state, it was the title of the highest official in the government structure of Islamic schools and courts.

Shiʿism. A major tradition within Islam. It has its origins in the faction (*shiʿah*) within the community who believed that Ali was the rightful successor to the Prophet Muhammad.

Sufism. This dimension of Islam stresses the immanence of God. It manifests itself as the Islamic form of mysticism.

sultan. A ruler in later medieval Islamic states. Although the sultans had legitimate authority, they were primarily military commanders and therefore are not the same as caliphs, who led the early Muslim community as direct successors to the Prophet Muhammad.

sunnah. Accepted custom or practice. The Sunnah of the Prophet Muhammad is defined by the *hadith*s and is an authoritative model for Islamic behavior.

Sunni. Sunni Islam is the tradition that accepts the legitimacy of the caliphs who actually succeeded the Prophet, in contrast to Shiʿism. The majority of the Muslims in the world are Sunnis.

tajdid. See *mujaddid.*

Tanzimat. Literally, this means "reorganization." The term is applied to the program of modernizing reforms within the Ottoman Empire in the middle years of the nineteenth century.

taqlid. The action of imitation. The term is applied to the action of following precedents set by earlier thinkers and is the opposite of *ijtihad.*

tariqah. This means "path" and refers to the devotional path developed by Sufi teachers. It also refers to the social organization or Sufi brotherhood formed by followers of such Sufi teachers.

tawhid. Literally, "union or unity." In Islamic thought this is the term applied to the oneness of God and implies the absolute and single sovereignty of God in the universe. In modern Islamic thought, *tawhid* is stressed as the basis for unity of religion and politics and religion and economics.

ulama. Collective term for the learned men in the Islamic tradition.

ummah. This means "community" and refers to the total community of believing Muslims.

vizier. An administrative official, usually of high rank.

wali. A person who is believed to be close to God and has, as a result, special piety and spiritual power.

Bibliographical Comments and Suggestions for Further Reading

It is not possible to provide a comprehensive or a complete bibliography of the vast literature dealing with the modern Islamic experience. What is presented here is simply a series of suggestions for readers who wish to pursue some subject beyond the discussion in this book. This bibliographical essay does not mention all of the sources cited in this book, and many major studies are not discussed. However, the publications noted here do provide the foundation for further study of the issues of continuity and change in the modern Islamic experience. Although significant works have been written on this subject in many languages, this bibliography has been restricted to works in English that are relatively easily available. (Works in other languages are listed in the bibliographies discussed below.) As a convenience for the reader, the works have been grouped into special topic areas rather than simply being presented in alphabetical order.

INTERPRETING THE INTERPRETERS

The starting point for further reading on the subject may be studies that examine works similar to this book. It is of great importance to understand the strengths and weaknesses, the biases and the prejudices of people writing on the Islamic experience. Popular and scholarly Western attitudes toward Islam in the modern era have been carefully examined by Norman Daniel, *Islam, Europe, and Empire* (Edinburgh: Edinburgh University Press, 1966), and by Edward W. Said in his thought-provoking and sometimes controversial works, *Orientalism* (New York: Pantheon, 1978) and *Covering Islam: How the Media and the Experts Determine How We See the Rest of the World* (New York: Pantheon, 1981).

BIBLIOGRAPHIES

Two very helpful bibliographical sources are the essential *Index Islamicus, 1906-1955* (Cambridge, Eng.: Heffer, 1958), with supplementary volumes by J. D. Pearson, and the bibliographical section of each issue of *The Middle East Journal*. In addition, many of the books discussed in this essay have helpful bibliographies.

GENERAL SURVEYS

It is sometimes helpful to have access to a general interpretation of the whole sweep of Islamic history. Perhaps the most significant such study in recent years is

Marshall G. S. Hodgson, *The Venture of Islam*, 3 vols. (Chicago: University of Chicago Press, 1974). An older work, Carl Brockelmann, *History of the Islamic Peoples*, trans. Joel Carmichael and Moshe Perlmann (New York: G. P. Putnam, 1947), is useful for identifying many people and groups. Another very useful reference work is P. M. Holt, Ann K. S. Lambton, and Bernard Lewis, eds., *The Cambridge History of Islam*, 2 vols. (Cambridge, Eng.: Cambridge University Press, 1970). This work contains general surveys of Islamic history in the various regions of the Muslim world and includes special chapters on literature and social institutions.

For those who need a feeling for the general sweep of Islamic history but would like to have it in concise form, two brilliant articles may be of help: H.A.R. Gibb, "An Interpretation of Islamic History," in *Studies on the Civilization of Islam* by H.A.R. Gibb (Boston: Beacon Press, 1962), and Marshall G. S. Hodgson, "The Role of Islam in World History," *International Journal of Middle East Studies* 1 (1970):99–123.

INTRODUCTIONS TO ISLAM

The historical perspective needs to be supplemented by an understanding of the intellectual content of Islam. Many introductions to Islam have appeared in the past century. Frequently used introductions written by Western scholars are H.A.R. Gibb, *Mohammedanism: An Historical Survey*, 2d ed. (London: Oxford University Press, 1952), and the recently translated "classic," Ignaz Goldziher, *Introduction to Islamic Theology and Law*, trans. Andras and Ruth Hamori (Princeton: Princeton University Press, 1981).

It is, however, fortunate that in recent years, introductions to Islam written by Muslims have become increasingly available to the English-reading audience. Anyone who wishes to understand the meaning of the Islamic tradition for Muslims should utilize these important sources. The following are introductions to Islam written by important contemporary thinkers. Ismaᶜil R. Al Faruqi, *Islam* (Niles, Ill.: Argus Communications, 1979), is a very readable discussion written by a Sunni Muslim with substantial teaching experience in the West. There are many editions of Abul Aᶜla Maududi, *Towards Understanding Islam* (Gary, Ind.: International Islamic Federation of Student Organizations, 1970), a basic introduction written by the leading South Asian Muslim fundamentalist thinker of the twentieth century. Seyyed Hossein Nasr, *Ideals and Realities of Islam* (London: George Allen and Unwin, 1966), is written from the perspective of modern philosophical Sufism within the Shiᶜite tradition. An introduction by Sayyid Qutb, *This Religion of Islam* (Gary, Ind.: International Islamic Federation of Student Organizations, n.d.), written originally in Arabic, exists in many editions and is by one of the major scholars in the Muslim Brotherhood in Egypt. The author was executed during the Nasser era, but his works remain widely read in Egypt and throughout the Islamic world. Fazlur Rahman, *Islam*, 2d ed. (Chicago: University of Chicago Press, 1979), is the former director of the Islamic Research Institute in Pakistan, and his scholarly works have had a significant influence on the works of Western scholars. His perspective is that of a contemporary modernist within the Sunni tradition.

MAJOR WESTERN INTERPRETATIONS OF MODERN ISLAM

There is a long tradition in the modern West of describing the Muslim world and the modern Islamic experience. Much of this literature is ethnocentrically oriented polemic, which either sees Islam as a reactionary obstacle to progress or describes it as a major threat to the West. However, during the twentieth century, there have been a number of books that present significant insights into the modern Islamic experience, even though many have limitations because of the biases of the times.

An early work in this line is Lothrop Stoddard, *The New World of Islam* (New York: Scribner's, 1921). This work has a tendency to see Islam as a threatening force, but it provides a good picture of some aspects of Islamic dynamism during and immediately after World War I. About a decade later, a valuable collection of essays appeared: H.A.R. Gibb, ed., *Whither Islam? A Survey of Modern Movements in the Muslim World* (London: Victor Gollancz, 1932). Although the mood and tone of this work are clearly dated, valuable information is provided.

Two of the most influential works to examine and interpret the modern Islamic experience are H.A.R. Gibb, *Modern Trends in Islam* (Chicago: University of Chicago Press, 1947), and Wilfred Cantwell Smith, *Islam in Modern History* (Princeton: Princeton University Press, 1957). Gibb presents a critique of Islamic modernist thought that shaped both Muslim and non-Muslim views in the following years, and Smith discusses the relationship between the experience of the Islamic community in history and the Muslim sense of crisis in the modern world. Although now outdated, both of these studies continue to provide important frameworks for analysis and study.

The Islamic resurgence of the 1970s produced a large number of works. A great deal of significant and valuable research has been done, but it has appeared largely in academic journals or in a number of collections of papers on special subjects. Unfortunately, the most readily available material is the instant-history paperback and the journalistic potboiler. The best work of the journalistic variety is G. H. Jansen, *Militant Islam* (New York: Harper and Row, 1979). Paperbacks with clearly sensationalist titles are better avoided as propagandistic polemic is, unfortunately, relatively common.

Among the currently available collections, the following have been very helpful and are basically reliable: Michael Curtis, ed., *Religion and Politics in the Middle East* (Boulder, Colo.: Westview Press, 1981); John L. Esposito, ed., *Islam and Development: Religion and Sociopolitical Change* (Syracuse, N.Y.: Syracuse University Press, 1980); and Cyriac K. Pullapilly, ed., *Islam in the Contemporary World* (Notre Dame, Ind.: Cross Roads Press, 1980).

SPECIFIC AREAS AND ERAS

Each of the specific regions and periods discussed in this book are discussed in many articles and books. It is not possible to provide even a beginning bibliography for each area and period covered; what follows is a general list of the books that have been useful in the preparation of this volume. In most cases, these works have more extensive bibliographies that can be used as a basis for more intensive study.

Eighteenth Century

Despite its importance for Islamic history, the eighteenth century is only beginning to receive the attention it deserves. Perhaps the best collection of materials illustrating the main lines of contemporary scholarship is Thomas Naff and Roger Owen, eds., *Studies in Eighteenth-Century Islamic History* (Carbondale, Ill.: Southern Illinois University Press, 1977). The standard discussion of the Ottoman Empire in the eighteenth century is H.A.R. Gibb and Harold Bowen, *Islamic Society and the West*, vol. 1, pts. 1–2 (London: Oxford University Press, 1950–1957).

Although this book has been strongly criticized in recent years, it remains a valuable reference work. Coverage of the eighteenth century for special areas can be found in many of the books listed in other sections of this bibliography.

The Arab World

A good introduction to the great diversity of the Arab world can be found in William R. Polk, *The Arab World* (Cambridge, Mass.: Harvard University Press, 1980). A more general and historical survey can be found in Arthur Goldschmidt, Jr., *A Concise History of the Middle East* (Boulder, Colo.: Westview Press, 1979). Useful specialized studies, whose contents are indicated in the titles, are: Albert Hourani, *Arabic Thought in the Liberal Age, 1798–1939* (London: Oxford University Press, 1962); Nadav Safran, *Egypt in Search of Political Community: An Analysis of the Intellectual and Political Evolution of Egypt, 1804–1952* (Cambridge, Mass.: Harvard University Press, 1961); Hisham Sharabi, *Arab Intellectuals and the West: The Formative Years, 1875–1914* (Baltimore, Md.: Johns Hopkins Press, 1970).

One of the most impressive works published in recent years is the massive study by Hanna Batatu, *The Old Social Classes and the Revolutionary Movements of Iraq* (Princeton: Princeton University Press, 1978). Although the title may give the impression that this work deals with a limited subject, it in fact uses Iraq as a case study in exploring the relationship between ideology, social structure, and tradition in the Arab-Islamic context.

For the North African part of the Arab world, there are two very helpful historical introductions: Jamil M. Abun-Nasr, *A History of the Maghrib*, 2d ed. (Cambridge, Eng.: Cambridge University Press, 1975), and Charles-André Julien, *History of North Africa from the Arab Conquest to 1830*, trans. John Petrie (New York: Praeger, 1970). Useful and thought-provoking interpretations are presented by the North African scholar, Abdallah Laroui, in *The History of the Maghrib*, trans. Ralph Manheim (Princeton: Princeton University Press, 1977), and *The Crisis of the Arab Intellectual: Traditionalism or Historicism?* trans. Diarmid Cammell (Berkeley: University of California Press, 1976).

Brief surveys of the history and political development of each country in the Middle East and North Africa, along with special bibliographies for each country, can be found in David E. Long and Bernard Reich, eds., *The Government and Politics of the Middle East and North Africa* (Boulder, Colo.: Westview Press, 1980).

The Northern Tier

Because of the Islamic revolution in Iran during the 1970s and the intense interest in the development of that revolution around the world, a very large number of books and articles have been written. In preparing this book, the works of Nikki Keddie and Hamid Algar have been of special help. A good starting point are the chapters that each has written in *Scholars, Saints, and Sufis*, ed. N. Keddie (Berkeley: University of California Press, 1972). In addition, the following books by Algar are of real importance: *Mirza Malkum Khan* (Berkeley: University of California Press, 1973) and *Religion and State in Iran, 1785–1906* (Berkeley: University of California Press, 1969). Among the numerous works by Professor Keddie, the following are good starting points for additional reading about Islam and modern Iran: *An Islamic Response to Imperialism: Political and Religious Writings of Sayyid Jamal ad-Din al-Afghani* (Berkeley: University of California Press, 1968) and *Iran:*

Religion, Politics, and Society (London: Frank Cass, 1980). Among the many other books written on Iran recently, the following were especially helpful in writing this book: Shahrough Akhavi, *Religion and Politics in Contemporary Iran* (Albany: State University of New York Press, 1980), and Richard W. Cottam, *Nationalism in Iran* (Pittsburgh, Pa.: University of Pittsburgh Press, 1964). A new edition of the latter book is also available.

For Turkey, an excellent survey covering Ottoman and modern times is Stanford J. Shaw (and Ezel Kural Shaw for vol. 2), *History of the Ottoman Empire and Modern Turkey*, 2 vols. (Cambridge, Eng.: Cambridge University Press, 1976–1977). The process of modernization is carefully analyzed in Bernard Lewis, *The Emergence of Modern Turkey* (London: Oxford University Press, 1961), and basic issues of the modern Islamic experience are examined in Niyazi Berkes, *The Development of Secularism in Turkey* (Montreal: McGill University Press, 1964).

The standard introduction in English to the modern history of Afghanistan is Louis Dupree, *Afghanistan* (Princeton: Princeton University Press, 1980). There are also earlier editions of this work.

South Asia

The works of Aziz Ahmad provide a good starting point for further study on Islam in South Asia. Especially helpful are his *Studies in Islamic Culture in the Indian Environment* (Oxford: Clarendon Press, 1964) and *Islamic Modernism in India and Pakistan, 1857–1964* (London: Oxford University Press, 1967). Other helpful works are Freeland Abbott, *Islam and Pakistan* (Ithaca, N.Y.: Cornell University Press, 1968); G. P. Bhattacharjee, *Renaissance and Freedom Movement in Bangladesh* (Calcutta: Minerva Associates, 1973); Rounaq Jahan, *Pakistan: Failure in National Integration* (New York: Columbia University Press, 1972). A very interesting recent study is Nasir Islam, "Islam and National Identity: The Case of Pakistan and Bangla Desh," *International Journal of Middle East Studies* 13 (1981):55–72.

Southeast Asia

The three chapters in Volume 2 of *The Cambridge History of Islam*, ed. P. M. Holt, Ann K. S. Lambton, and Bernard Lewis (Cambridge, Eng.: Cambridge University Press, 1970), cover Islam in Southeast Asia and provide an excellent survey of Islamic history in that region. To go beyond this survey, there are a number of very good special studies that provide a basis for understanding the special character of the Islamic experience in that region. Some of those that have been most useful in the writing of this book are: B. J. Boland, *The Struggle of Islam in Modern Indonesia* (The Hague: Martinus Nijhoff, 1971); Deliar Noer, *The Modernist Muslim Movement in Indonesia, 1900–1942* (London: Oxford University Press, 1973); William R. Roff, *Kelantan: Religion, Society, and Politics in a Malay State* (London: Oxford University Press, 1974).

SAHARAN AND SUB-SAHARAN AFRICA

For the study of Islam in Africa, one of the best-known scholars is J. Spencer Trimingham. In a number of works, he has provided readers with introductions to Islamic history in many parts of Africa. A general summary of his work is presented in his *Influence of Islam Upon Africa* (New York: Praeger, 1968). Among his other works are *Islam in the Sudan* (London: Oxford University Press, 1949), *Islam in Ethiopia* (London: Oxford University Press, 1952), and *Islam in West Africa* (London: Oxford University Press, 1959).

One very useful volume that contains both specialized articles and a long general introduction is *Islam in Tropical Africa*, ed. I. M. Lewis (London: Oxford University Press, 1966). Special studies showing particular aspects and experiences of Islam in Africa are Mervyn Hiskett, *The Sword of Truth: The Life and Times of the Shehu Usuman Dan Fodio* (London: Oxford University Press, 1973); B. G. Martin, *Muslim Brotherhoods in 19th-Century Africa* (Cambridge, Eng.: Cambridge University Press, 1976); August H. Nimtz, Jr., *Islam and Politics in East Africa* (Minneapolis: University of Minnesota Press, 1980).

Major Muslim Minorities

The histories of the large Muslim communities that are minorities in their countries are complex. Some very helpful work has been done on the Islamic experience in Russia, and some of the most useful books are Alexandre Bennigsen and Chantal Lemercier-Quelquejay, *Islam in the Soviet Union*, trans. Geoffrey E. Wheeler and Hubert Evans (New York: Praeger, 1967), and Geoffrey Wheeler, *The Modern History of Soviet Central Asia* (New York: Praeger, 1964). A new book on the Muslim communities in China, Raphaeli Israeli, *Muslims in China, A Study in Cultural Confrontation* (London: Curzon Press, 1980), provides much information, but it does not fully supersede some of the older works such as Marshall Broomhall, *Islam in China: A Neglected Problem* (London: Morgan and Scott, 1910). Muslims in independent India have received remarkably little scholarly attention. One very helpful discussion appears in Chapter 6 of Wilfred Cantwell Smith's *Islam in Modern History* (Princeton: Princeton University Press, 1957), and significant issues of communal survival are discussed in S. E. Hassnain, *Indian Muslims: Challenge and Opportunity* (Bombay: Lalvani Publishing House, 1968).

Recent short but perceptive discussions of major minorities appear in Cyriac K. Pullapilly, ed., *Islam in the Contemporary World* (Notre Dame, Ind.: Cross Roads Press, 1980). One might note, in that book, Chapter 13: Alexandre Benningsen, "Religion and Atheism Among Soviet Muslims," pp. 222–237; Chapter 14: Ilhan Basgoz, "Religion and Ethnic Consciousness Among Turks in the Soviet Union," pp. 238–250; Chapter 18: Umar A. Hassan, "African-American Muslims and the Islamic Revival," pp. 284–295; Chapter 23: William L. Yam, "Islam in the Philippines," pp. 358–369.

Interpretations of Islamic Fundamentalism

One of the special issues raised in this book is the nature of Islamic fundamentalism. There are a number of very important studies that have helped to shape contemporary awareness of the style of Islam that this book calls fundamentalist. A work of critical significance is Richard P. Mitchell, *The Society of the Muslim Brothers* (London: Oxford University Press, 1969). This book is accepted even by many members of the Muslim Brotherhood as the standard authority on the history of the organization.

A second major work that has shaped many analyses of Islam in general and of Muslim fundamentalism in particular is Clifford Geertz, *Islam Observed: Religious Development in Morocco and Indonesia* (Chicago: University of Chicago Press,

1968). This comparison of two very different Islamic experiences has had a major impact on contemporary thinking about Islam.

A third significant contribution comes in the work of Ernest Gellner. His article, "A Pendulum Swing Theory of Islam," reprinted in *Sociology of Islam*, ed. Roland Robertson (Baltimore, Md.: Penguin, 1969), defines major styles of Islamic action. This analysis is applied to a specific case in his valuable study, *Saints of the Atlas* (Chicago: University of Chicago Press, 1969).

Keeping Informed

Day-to-day news tends to stress the sensational and violent, but major newspapers such as the *Christian Science Monitor* and the *New York Times* provide continuing coverage. For translations of speeches and articles appearing in the Muslim world itself, it is useful to gain access to the translations provided by the U.S. government through the Foreign Broadcast Information Service and the Joint Publications Research Service. The publications of these two organizations are available at any library that is a U.S. government repository.

Index

Guide to Alphabetization and Listings

In determining the order of names and terms in this index, some special practices have been followed:

(1) Names and terms beginning with the Arabic definite article (al-) are indexed under the letter following the article. When in the middle of the name or term, the article (al-) is treated as part of the word.

(2) Compound Islamic names are treated as a single name. Thus, names beginning with "Abd al-" are listed under that initial word rather than the second word in the compound. (Abd al-Qadir will be found under "Abd al-" rather than "Qadir.") Similarly, names ending in "al-din" will be listed under the first word of the compound name. (Hamid al-Din will be found under Hamid.)

(3) Special titles that normally precede personal names (like ayatollah, king, or sayyid) are not treated as part of the name and may appear in parentheses after the name.

(4) Individuals are listed under their family names or personal identification terms (like "Ibn" or a descriptive adjective like "al-Baghdadi") if these names are in common usage. Otherwise individuals are listed under their personal given names. Thus, it is "al-Mahdi, Sadiq," and "Ibn al-Arabi, Muhyi al-Din," but also "Qabus ibn Said."